Han Dynasty China

VOLUME I: HAN SOCIAL STRUCTURE

Institute for Comparative and Foreign Area Studies
University of Washington

HAN DYNASTY CHINA

Edited by JACK L. DULL *and* HELLMUT WILHELM

I. *Han Social Structure,* by T'ung-tsu Ch'ü

HAN SOCIAL
STRUCTURE

By T'ung-tsu Ch'ü

EDITED BY JACK L. DULL

Copyright © 1972 by the University of Washington Press
Library of Congress Catalog Card Number 65-11040
ISBN 0-295-95068-6

Printed in Japan by General Printing Co., Ltd., Yokohama

Library of Congress Cataloging in Publication Data

Ch'ü, T'ung-tsu.
  Han social structure.
  (Han Dynasty China, v. 1.)
  Translated of Han social structure.
  Includes bibliographical references.
  1. China—Social conditions.

ISBN 0-295-95068-6

UNIVERSITY OF WASHINGTON PRESS
SEATTLE AND LONDON

Library of Congress Cataloging in Publication Data
Ch'ü, T'ung-tsu.
    Han social structure.
    (Han Dynasty, China, 1)
    "Documents on Han social structure": p.
    Includes bibliographical references.
    1. China—Social conditions.   I. Title.
II. Series.
    DS748.H28   vol. 1   [HN673]   309.1'31   69-14206
    ISBN 0-295-95068-4

FOREWORD

The translation of the texts presented here and their initial analyses by Professor Ch'ü T'ung-tsu were made under my direction for the Chinese History Project of the University of Washington. Hence I welcome this opportunity to say a few words about the Project and the scholar who greatly advanced our work on the Ch'in and Han dynasties.

It was hoped that *The History of Chinese Society: Liao*, which appeared in 1949, would serve as a model for subsequent volumes. For various reasons this plan had to be abandoned. But while our Ch'in-Han material is being presented in a series of monographs, many features of the early volume have been retained.

Before Professor Ch'ü joined the Chinese History Project in 1945, Mr. Wang Yü-ch'üan had selected, translated, and annotated basic texts pertaining to major aspects of Ch'in and Han society. Not long after the end of the war he left the Project. Mrs. Lea Kisselgoff, who had studied under Professors Paul Pelliot and Marcel Granet in Paris, joined our staff in the early forties. She dealt painstakingly and competently with the many problems of meaning, interpretation, and bibliography presented by our primary and related sources. Mrs. Ruth S. Ricard saw the manuscript through its early phases. She combined an exceptional secretarial skill with great ingenuity in overcoming the endless technical difficulties involved in this task.

Professor Ch'ü, whose training and capacity eminently fitted him to become the Project's major Han specialist, added very substantially to the number of translated texts and annotation of the original Sections VII (Social Stratification, Kinship System, Customs and Traditions), VIII (Powerful Families), and IX (Temples and Monasteries). These three sections have been rearranged. Under Professor Ch'ü's hand, material was compiled that will make Section IX a highly illuminating monograph on Ch'in and Han religion, and the data on customs and

[v]

traditions will become an equally illuminating monograph on Ch'in and Han folklore. I trust that both these studies will soon find their way into print. The greater part of the data of Section VII and virtually the whole of Section VIII have been brought together in the present volume, for which Professor Ch'ü has written the analytic introduction.

All these studies were well advanced when Professor Ch'ü resigned from the Project to work at a special assignment at Harvard University, and later to teach at the University of British Columbia in Vancouver. Fortunately, he could still work on the Ch'in-Han material at the Far Eastern and Russian Institute of the University of Washington, to which the "dynastic" material of the Project had been transferred in the late fifties. Under Professor Hellmut Wilhelm's guidance and with Professor Jack L. Dull's editorship, Professor Ch'ü completed his task before joining (in 1965) his wife and children, who had returned earlier to the Chinese mainland.

Habent sua fata . . . This is not the place to tell the story of the Chinese History Project, on which the World War and the developments in China left their mark. Nor is this the place for a detailed discussion of Professor Ch'ü's methodological framework and conclusions. When he joined our staff, he viewed the history of Chinese society essentially as Max Weber did. And though I differed with him concerning Weber's idea of China's bureaucracy as an estate (*Stand*), I respected his freedom to develop his argument as befitted a free scholar in a free world.

For the record, I should like to restate a point on which Professor Ch'ü and I were at one: that the core of the social power structure in imperial China was a ruling bureaucracy. This stratum interlocked with and was supplemented by what we originally designated as "powerful families." Since then, the "notables" (or "gentry") in bureaucratic societies have been examined further. But the Ch'in-Han material on "powerful families" assembled in the present volume is among the richest of its kind. While here and elsewhere different interpretations can be expected, all serious students will agree that Professor Ch'ü's contribution has raised the investigation of Chinese society and history to a new level of factual inquiry and coordination.

KARL A. WITTFOGEL
Director
Chinese History Project

New York
March 1967

EDITOR'S PREFACE

T HIS volume, the first of a series of monographs dealing with various aspects of the history of the Ch'in-Han period, was originally conceived as one chapter in a much more modest undertaking: a one-volume history of the Ch'in-Han dynasties, which was to be a companion volume to the work on the Liao dynasty by Karl August Wittfogel and Feng Chia-sheng. Under Professor Wittfogel's earlier plan there was to be one volume for each of the major dynasties. When, in 1939, Wang Yü-ch'üan joined Professor Wittfogel on the Han Project, roughly the same categories were established as those used in the Liao volume, and Wang began translating and annotating texts for each of the sixteen sections into which the finished work was to be divided. Later, Ch'ü T'ung-tsu joined the Project, and although he continued some of the work begun by Wang, he concerned himself largely with the topic of social structure.

Over the years a greater appreciation of the wealth of materials available led to recasting the form that the finished work should take. It was decided that, instead of a section, a volume or monograph was justified for each major subdivision. This volume is the first product of that revised approach to the materials.

This volume and many, though not all, of the others in this series are organized much like the Liao volume: there is an interpretive introduction followed by documents translated from the Han histories, with annotations drawn from other contemporary, primary, and modern sources. The "introduction" is intended to stand as a monograph by itself and requires no further comment. The documents are grouped in three categories: (I) Kinship and Marriage, (II) Social Classes, and (III) Powerful Families. The documents are numbered consecutively within each category; thus a reference to I, 56, means document 56 in the first category. The translations adhere closely to the original text and are provided with extensive notes to clarify doubtful passages or to elaborate upon points raised in the passage. Chinese titles have been translated; the Chinese titles have been given on the first occurrence, and thereafter only the English translation is used. Generally, we have followed the translations of titles adopted by Homer H. Dubs, but have added many new ones.

Although Wang Yü-ch'üan translated some of the documents in this work while it was in its earlier stages, he is in no way responsible for the final product; that responsibility rests with Professor Ch'ü, who not only translated and annotated most of the documents in the first instance but also went over all the passages already translated. Since Professor Ch'ü returned to his homeland before the final copy was prepared, and since, at his request, we have ceased corresponding, I have been forced to make occasional stylistic changes that he has not seen. These changes are very minor and in no case has the meaning of the translation been altered.

The first half of this work, the "introduction," is entirely the work of Professor Ch'ü. Changes in this portion of the text, both stylistic and substantive, were made only with the full approval of Professor Ch'ü, and the basic argumentation is wholly his.

The author's views on Chinese society are well known from his earlier publications, and those views are reflected in this major contribution to our understanding of the Ch'in-Han period. Although I, as editor of this volume, did not feel that I could impose my own interpretations on the author, I personally feel that alternative interpretations of some of these materials on the Han are not only possible but also, in some cases, desirable. Furthermore, I would venture to suggest that there will be further discussions on the nature of Han society—discussions that will be engendered by the appearance of this work. In this way I hope that the volume will ultimately lead to a greater appreciation of the changing nature of early Chinese society and also to the asking (and answering) of larger questions concerning the "Confucianization" of Chinese society. The book provides us with an impressive amount of materials for understanding the nature of Han society; it also raises questions about Chinese society in the Han and particularly the post-Han periods. This characteristic of providing solutions to problems while simultaneously leading the reader on to new issues is precisely what we expect from a good book.

The creation and publication of this work were possible only because of the cooperation of many people and institutions; they all deserve a public expression of appreciation. First among them stands Professor Karl August Wittfogel, who conceived the work in the first place and who saw it through its earlier stages. After George E. Taylor, Director of the Far Eastern and Russian Institute, arranged to have the project transferred to the University of Washington, Professor Hellmut Wilhelm became its general director; he has given unselfishly of his time and effort in pushing this work to completion. On several occasions, I have sought advice from Professor Hsiao Kung-ch'üan and from Mr. Tu Ching-i,—advice for which I am very thankful. At various times during the preparation of this volume, research funds were provided by the Rockefeller Foundation and the Ford Foundation; without their generous assistance the work would have been impossible. Finally, publication has been made possible by a grant from the administration of the University of Washington. A special word of appreciation goes to Miss Arlene Cavanaugh for her careful typing of the manuscript.

JACK L. DULL, *Editor*
April 1967

CONTENTS

PART ONE

Analysis of Han Social Structure

PART TWO

Documents of Han Social Structure

Part One: Analysis of Han Social Structure

Chapter One

KINSHIP

THE patrilocal family, *chia* 家, was the basic social and economic unit in Ch'in and Han societies. It was a social group whose members lived together in the same household (*hu* 戶) and engaged in some form of economically productive cooperation. The size of a prefecture as a rule was determined by the number of households within it.[1] The nuclear family included the parents and their children, and the extended family consisted of two or more nuclear families.

The Chinese kinship system was patrilineal, that is, it reckoned descent only through the father. A man who assumed his father's family name affiliated only with the consanguineal kin group of his father and disregarded his mother's kin group. Thus the *Erh-ya* distinguishes four kinds of relatives: (1) the *tsung-tsu* 宗族, "the father's kin group or lineage," (2) the mother's relatives, which included the mother's grand-

---

[1] The prefect of a prefecture (*hsien* 縣) that had more than ten thousand households was known as a prefect (*ling* 令); whereas one for a prefecture with less than ten thousand households was a chief (*chang* 長), and his rank was lower (Pan Ku, *Han-shu*, Po-na ed., 19:16a, hereafter cited as *HS*; Ssu-ma Piao, *Hsü-Han-chih*, Po-na ed., 28:7b, hereafter cited as *HHC*). However, as Ying Shao pointed out, exceptions were found in the area of the northern frontiers and the Yangtze Valley (Ying Shao, *Han-kuan-i*, compiled by Sun Hsing-yen, *PCKTS*, A:32b, hereafter cited as *HKI*; *HHC* 28:7b, note; Yen Keng-wang, *Chung-kuo ti-fang hsing-cheng chih-tu shih* [2 vols.; Taipei, 1961], I, 44–47; Lao Kan, "Han-ch'ao ti hsien-chih," *Chung-yang yen-chiu-yüan yüan-k'an*, I [1954], 70).

parents, parents, brothers, sisters, paternal cousins, and children of the
mother's brothers and sisters, (3) the wife's relatives, which included
the wife's parents, brothers, and sisters, and (4) *ch'in-ch'i* 親戚, "relatives
by marriage," which included the husband's parents, brothers, sisters,
and so forth. Apparently an important distinction was made between
the father's lineage and all others; that is to say, only the father's lineage
was considered lineage, whereas all others who had a different surname
belonged to a different lineage. It was remarked that the mother's
parents were called "outside grandparents" because they had a different
surname and were therefore considered outside relatives.[2]

Tsung-tsu or *tsu,* a term extensively applied to the father's kin group,
may be defined as a patrilineage, or a kin group that included only
members who could trace actual descent in the male line from a common ancestor.[3] *Tsung-tsu,* a popular term in Han times, is mentioned
many times in our texts. A clear distinction was maintained between
the *chia,* a small residential unit, and the *tsung-tsu,* which usually included a number of families. Thus we find *tsung* and *chia* mentioned
together to mean separate groups.[4] And the members of a family were
called *chia-shu* 家屬, "the family members," whereas the members of a
tsung-tsu were given the name *tsung-jen* 宗人, or *tsu-jen,* "kinsmen." However, the term *tsung-tsu* denotes only the consanguineal relationship; it
does not tell whether the whole lineage lived together or not.

STRUCTURE AND SIZE OF THE FAMILY

In the fourth century B.C. a law, suggested by Shang Yang 商鞅,
was proclaimed in the state of Ch'in to the effect that persons who had
two or more adult sons living with them were required to pay a double
tax (see document I, 2). Another law prohibited fathers, sons, and
brothers from living in the same room (I, 4). Large households were

[2] *Erh-ya chu-su, SPPY* ed., 4:9b, hereafter cited as *EYCS.*

[3] Robert H. Lowie, *Social Organization* (New York, 1948), p. 9; George P. Murdock,
Social Structure (New York, 1949), p. 42.

[4] This distinction is clearly illustrated in the following example. Liu Pei 劉備 and
Liu Te-jan 劉德然 were members of the same *tsung.* The latter's father, Liu Yüan-
ch'i 劉元起, frequently gave financial assistance to Liu Pei, who was poor. Yüan-
ch'i's wife told him: "[We and Liu Pei] each belong to separate families. How can
we frequently do this to him?" Yüan-ch'i replied: "[It is lucky for] our *tsung* to have
a boy like him; he is not an ordinary person" (Ch'en Shou, *San-kuo-chih,* Po-na ed.,
Shu, 2:1b, hereafter cited as *SKC*). As is seen in some instances, a *tsung* usually consisted of a number of families (Fan Yeh, *Hou-Han-shu,* Po-na ed., 70:24b, hereafter
cited as *HHS; SKC,* Wei, 11:12b).

discouraged by the first law, for people had to bear the burden of extra taxes if they wanted to maintain an unseparated family. Few persons were willing to pay a double tax, and many could not afford to pay it. The aim of the second law is not clear, but the results were noticeable. Since many poor families did not have enough rooms for their members, it was not unusual for father and sons or brothers to live together in a single room. But when this condition was no longer permitted by law, some of the members had to move out of the household and earn a separate living.

The immediate effects of these laws on family structure and size, and on personal attitudes between family members, were pointed out by Chia I 賈誼 in the second century B.C. The law that aimed at reducing the size of the family had affected rich families as well as the poor ones who were unable to pay a double tax: both the wealthy and the poor tended to live apart from their adult sons. According to Chia I, a poor family often "pawned" a grown-up son to another family as a "bond servant." The rich, on the other hand, sent their adult sons away with a share of the family property (I, 3, and n. 8).

A greater emphasis on individualism accompanied the changing structure of the family at that time. According to Chia I, the daughter-in-law was often not on good terms with her husband's parents. The attitude of subordination and politeness advocated by the Confucian school was lacking. Instead she talked back to her parents-in-law and argued with them. The attitude toward property was also more individualistic. It was pointed out that he who lent a rake or a hoe to his father would assume the appearance of a benefactor and that when a mother took her child's dustpan and broom, the daughter would stand there and reprove her (I, 3). These instances not only indicate that separate property was owned by the children, but they also show the kind of individualistic attitude that emanates from the concept of personal ownership. Again this deviated from the ideal pattern set up by the Confucianists, who denied that a son or a daughter-in-law should possess any private property.[5] We do not know to what extent this ideal pattern was accepted by Chinese society as a whole, or to what extent the individualistic behavior was peculiar to Ch'in, which was considered less civilized in Chia I's time. Was the ideology of the Confucianists already established in Ch'in, and were the attitudes mentioned above a result of the new law, which directly challenged the Confucianists? Or were the Ch'in people little affected by the ideology? We lack the

[5] *Li-chi chu-su, SPPY* ed., 1:13b, hereafter cited as *LCCS.*

historical data to answer these questions. All we can do is accept what Chia I said and take the viewpoint that the changing family structure and changing attitudes were the outcome of the new law.

In 221 B.C. when the empire was unified, it was pointed out by the statesmen of the empire that all the territories had become command-eries and prefectures and that there was only one law within the empire.[6] If this was the case, the law suggested by Shang Yang would have been in effect for the whole empire. The code of the succeeding Han dynasty was mainly copied from the Ch'in code by Hsiao Ho 蕭何, and this special law was kept in the Han code for about four hundred years (*HS* 23:12a). According to the "Treatise on Punishment" in the *Chin-shu*, the Ch'in–Han law was still used in the early years of the Wei dynasty until a new code was promulgated. (The phrase "Ch'in–Han law" is very interesting. The term was used because Han law, which was still in force at that time, was copied from the Ch'in law.) It is of special interest to us that this law made by Shang Yang was also kept in Han law and was not abolished until the Wei dynasty. It is recorded in the *Chin-shu* that some old Han laws that were not in force in Wei times were abolished when a new body of law was formulated. The law that required father and son to live separately was abolished; thus father and son could own property together.[7] This statement clearly indicates that the law made by Shang Yang in the fourth century B.C. had been kept in the Ch'in and Han codes for more than five centuries.

A law that was maintained for such a long time must have had a great effect on the people, as can be seen from the actual conditions in the society. Lu Chia 陸賈, who had property worth two thousand catties of gold, gave each of his five sons two hundred catties of gold—telling them to make a living from it—and kept the rest for himself. He made an agreement with his sons that he would visit them in turn and that the son being visited would supply him and his attendants with food and wine; he also promised that each visit would be limited to ten days and that he would not pay more than two visits a year to any son (I, 13). This actual case in which the sons lived separately supports the remarks made by Chia I that rich families of Ch'in sent away their grown sons with a share of the family property. It should be noted that Lu Chia was a native of Ch'u who became an official and had his home in the modern province of Shensi and that the event occurred in the earlier years of Han. This suggests that places other than Shensi, which had

---

[6] Ssu-ma Ch'ien, *Shih-chi*, Po-na ed., 6:11a, 13b, hereafter cited as *SC*.

[7] Fang Ch'iao *et al., Chin-shu*, Po-na ed., 30:7a, hereafter cited as *CS*.

been the heartland of the Ch'in state, were also affected by the Ch'in law after the conquest and unification. It also suggests that the custom still prevailed in Han times. Such a practice could hardly be found in later dynasties. One who is interested in Chinese traditional law will find that for a son to live separately from his parents and to own private property was considered "unfilial" by the law, and from the T'ang through the Ch'ing dynasties such a person was subject to punishment. No such separation was allowed even if the parent approved such action; the parent who did approve was also subject to punishment.[8] A distinction was made by law between a parent who permitted his son to live separately and a parent who permitted his son to hold separate property. Toleration was given only to the latter.

The attitudes revealed in Lu Chia's case would also have been unthinkable in later dynasties. That each visit of the father was limited to only ten days and that he would not bother his sons too long or too frequently reveals that he was aware that a son would usually get tired of serving and supporting his parent if the visits were too long or frequent. Such individualistic attitudes obviously were closer to those of the Ch'in period, as described by Chia I, than to those of later times.

We are unable to tell how typical this case is, but evidence seems to indicate that it was not uncommon for children to live separately from their parents. In the biography of a grand administrator (*t'ai-shou* 太守) of the Ju-nan 汝南 commandery it is recorded that many persons who lived separately from their parents went back to them after they had been influenced by the grand administrator's integrity and encouragement (I, 59). Such a custom seems to have been widespread not only in this particular locality but also in other areas. In one instance the wife of one of six brothers who lived together with their mother suggested that she and her husband live separately (I, 62). Although her suggestion was not carried out and she was divorced by her husband, her situation should by no means be considered unique. It seems unlikely that she would have suggested living separately from her husband's brothers and parent if such a custom was not common in society.

Ch'en P'ing 陳平 lived with his elder brother, Po 伯, and Po's wife—a well-known example of siblings who lived together (I, 7). But it is not clear whether Ch'en still lived with his brother after his own marriage (I, 8). Evidence seems to suggest that it was rather common for brothers to live separately when they married. One man, in order to live apart

<hr>

[8] Ch'ü T'ung-tsu, *Law and Society in Traditional China* (Paris and The Hague: Mouton and Co., 1961), pp. 29-30.

from his brothers, divided the family property and took the things of
better quality for himself. He was criticized by the local people not
because of the separation but because of his greed (I, 55). In another
case, Miao Yung 繆肜 and his three younger brothers lived together and
held the family property in common. After they married, their wives
asked for a division of the property. Miao Yung blamed himself for his
failure to influence them, and struck his own cheek. The younger
brothers and their wives then confessed their fault and apologized (I,
61). Their original request, though not carried out, should not be looked
upon as abnormal or unusual. Miao Yung's negative way of dealing
with the matter shows that he had no means of stopping them but to
blame and punish himself. Such dogmatic measures were likely to be
taken only by the intelligentsia. Even among the intelligentsia probably
few would have cared enough about the division to take such an action;
and we cannot tell how often it would have had the desired effect.

Han documents on wood from Chü-yen 居延 provide some information concerning the family life of ordinary people. Since provisions were
given to the family members of the garrison troops and officers stationed
along the frontier, their names, relationship, and ages were usually
listed in the government records. Altogether there are sixteen such
documents; nine of them include only married couples and their unmarried children.[9] In five cases the married couples lived with unmarried siblings.[10] There are only three cases in which a person lived
with his parents. One family included a man, his mother, and his two
unmarried younger brothers. Another family included a man, his wife,
and his parents. A third family included a married couple, their elder
son and his wife, their younger son, and their daughter.[11] Thus all the
families consisted of only two generations. Most of them included only
three or four persons. There was only one family of six persons. The
largest family was the one consisting of a married couple, two sons, two
daughters, two brothers, and two sisters.[12]

Although there were families in which parents and married sons lived
together, the nuclear family was the common pattern in Ch'in and Han
times. The average size of a family was small, including only the couple
and their unmarried children. When the son married he often received
a part of the family property, moved away, and established a separate

---

[9] Lao Kan, *Chü-yen Han-chien* (Taipei, 1960), pp. 55 (2745), 65 (3281), 66 (3287),
66 (3289), 92 (4468), 102 (4963), 111 (5345), 113-14 (5462), 198 (9903).

[10] *Ibid.*, pp. 66 (3295), 82 (4069), 83 (4085), 108 (5242), 113 (5461).

[11] *Ibid.*, pp. 86 (4207), 65 (3282), 26 (1274).

[12] *Ibid.*, p. 83 (4085).

residence. The average family included only four or five persons. Thus people in pre-Ch'in and Han times often spoke of a peasant family of five persons who owned one hundred *mou* 畝 of land.[13] This represented the size of a typical farm family.

Larger families began to appear in the Later Han.[14] Some brothers lived together after they married and maintained an extended family, embracing such collateral relatives as uncles, nephews, and first cousins. In one instance, the brothers who lost their parents during their youth and lived together were admired by the village community (I, 58). Another report tells of a local community that was greatly influenced by a man who lived with his brothers for many decades (I, 58). Han Yüan-ch'ang 韓元長 and his brothers lived together until they were toothless.[15]

An extended family that included three generations was still un-common. Only two are mentioned in the *Hou-Han-shu*. A wealthy land-lord family held its property in common for three generations (I, 40). A scholar who lived with his uncles and first cousins and held common property for three generations was highly admired by his community (I, 69). Obviously these families would not attract the attention of the local community and would not be mentioned in the biographies if uncles, nephews, and first cousins usually lived together. Such admira-tion indicates that the custom was rare. It seems that as a rule collateral relatives did not live together in the same household. In one instance, a man's brother's son asked for a division of the property and a separate dwelling, and his uncle could not stop him (I, 63).

The size of the family in Han times was relatively small compared with later times.[16] At the most three generations lived together. Com-pared with later periods in Chinese history this is amazing, for a survey of the histories of later dynasties from Chin on shows that a family consisting of only three generations had little chance of being mentioned.

LINEAGE

A patrilineage—*tsung-tsu* or *tsung*—included all the male descendants of a common ancestor, and its members were bound together by con-

[13] *HS* 24A:6a, 11a; Lao Kan, "Han-tai ping-chih chi Han-chien chung ti ping-chih," *Li-shih yü-yen yen-chiu-so chi-k'an*, X (1948), 41.

[14] Moriya Mitsuo, *Kandai kazoku no keitai ni kansuru kōsatsu* (Tokyo, 1956), pp. 33-36, 44-46.

[15] T'ao Ch'ien, *T'ao Yüan-ming chi*, SPTK ed., 8:2a, hereafter cited as *TYMC*.

[16] Ch'ü, *Law and Society*, p. 19, n. 16.

sanguineal kinship ties. But since there were different degrees of relationship, the whole lineage was divided into subgroups. Each subgroup was a mourning unit in which various degrees of mourning were worn by members for each other. The lineage included members of the direct line from great-great-grandfather down to great-great-grandsons and the collateral relatives who were also descendants of the same great-great-grandfather, as follows: (1) brother, brother's sons, and brother's grandsons; (2) father's brothers, father's brother's sons and grandsons; (3) paternal grandfather's brothers, their sons and grandsons; and (4) paternal great-grandfather's brothers, their sons, grandsons, and great-grandsons. Since there were five degrees of mourning, this group was also called the group of five degrees of mourning, *wu-fu* 五服 (I, 74, n. 274). The various degrees of relationship between members within this group were all defined by the degree of mourning that was to be worn for a deceased member. One was closer to his brother's son (nephew) than to his father's brother's grandson: one year's mourning (*ch'i* 期) was worn for the former and five months' mourning (*hsiao-kung* 小功) for the latter. And the degree of relationship was the same between a man and his brother's grandson as between a man and his father's brother's grandson, because the degree of mourning was the same (*hsiao-kung*). For the same reason, the degree of relationship to the following persons was the same: great-grandfather's brother, great-grandfather's brother's son, great-grandfather's brother's grandson, and great-grandfather's brother's great-grandson.

No mourning was worn for kinsmen outside this group. Three months' mourning (*ssu-ma* 緦麻) marked the boundaries of the group; beyond this margin the bond of kinship came to an end (I, 74, n. 274). Thus a person's great-grandfather's brother's great-great-grandson was not included. Members outside the mourning group were considered kinsmen, but not mourning relatives.

Thus a lineage consisted of many subgroups by which the relationship of kinsmen was defined and systematized. There was some overlapping of subgroups, of course, because a man usually belonged to several mourning groups. For instance, A, who was B's great-grandfather's brother's great-grandson, was in the same mourning group as B. But A's brother's son, C, who was not a mourning relative of B, was in another mourning group with A. Since each mourning unit was neither exclusive nor permanent (membership changed with the addition of each generation), it was merely a loosely knit group with no formal organization.

The size of a lineage varied greatly in different cases. Several tens of Hsiao Ho's kinsmen joined the army of Emperor Kao (I, 11). If a lineage had scores of male adults qualified to join the army, it is quite probable that such a lineage would have a hundred members and would include more than three generations. But since this is the only reference in the history of the Early Han to the size of a lineage, we are unable to tell whether Hsiao's lineage was average in size or unusually large.

We have more information about lineages in the Later Han period. Sixty-four members of Li T'ung's 李通 lineage were executed by local authorities for his participation in a rebellion against Wang Mang (II, 51). The members of Lu K'ang's 陸康 lineage who were besieged in a city under the jurisdiction of Lu numbered more than a hundred (I, 78). Ma Ch'ao 馬超 said in a memorial that his whole lineage, with more than two hundred members, was killed by Ts'ao Ts'ao 曹操.[17] We also have data indicating the number of families within a lineage, although the number of members is not given. One lineage consisted of three hundred families.[18] In another instance the *Hou-Han-shu* mentions that Han Jung 韓融 led his lineage of more than one thousand families into refuge on a mountain during the rebellion of Tung Cho 董卓 in A.D. 189 (I, 76). This is the largest lineage mentioned in our texts. If an average family had four members, such a lineage would have four thousand men. It would not only be the largest in Han times but would outnumber any lineage known in the history of China.[19] It is more likely that the number included both Han's kinsmen and the other families that were attached to him. As we shall see in the chapter on powerful families, it was a common practice of these times, as well as at the end of the Later Han, for hundreds of families to be organized as a self-defense unit. The majority of them were either retainers or families voluntarily attached to a powerful family, whose kinsmen constituted only a small number.

There is no evidence that a whole lineage lived together as a unit. Instead of being encouraged by the government, as it was in later dynasties, such a practice was discouraged during the Han. When Emperor Wu was in power (140–87 B.C.), the government moved the strong and powerful families from various localities to the capital and adjacent areas; but it was also decreed that these lineages should not

[17] *SKC*, Shu, 6:9a.

[18] *SKC*, Wei, 11:12b.

[19] The largest lineage found in the history of China was a Ch'en family whose members numbered over three thousand in the Sung dynasty. For this and other large lineages see Ch'ü, *Law and Society*, p. 19, n. 16.

live together.[20] It is not clear whether this prohibition applied only to those powerful families whose names appeared on the list of families to be moved or whether it referred to all large kin groups. But since the purpose of the regulation was to reduce and weaken those large and powerful families, it seems likely that any kin group that was large and strong would be considered a potential threat to the government and would not be allowed to live together. The enforced moving of the powerful families was a consistent policy maintained throughout most of the Early Han period,[21] so it seems unlikely that the law prohibiting a large lineage from living together was formulated and enforced only in Emperor Wu's time.

It is of great interest to know how effective this law was. The case of Cheng Hung's 鄭弘 great-grandfather, who was moved with his two sons to Shan-yin,[22] provides an example of a large lineage that was forced to break up under the law. It is logical to assume that Cheng's was but one of a number of cases that occurred at that time.[23]

Was this prohibition still enforced in the Later Han? No detailed information is found in our texts. But it is certain that a lineage usually lived in the same locality (I, 41, 42, 76, 78). They often moved together during a time of disorder. For example, when Keng Ch'un 耿純 led all the kinsmen of his lineage to join the army of Kuang-wu, he burned all their houses to prevent them from going back. Later, Kuang-wu appointed one of the kinsmen prefect and ordered all the kinsmen to live in that prefecture (I, 41). It is not clear whether the lineage orig-inally lived together under the same roof or not, but it is certain that the living quarters of the kinsmen were close to each other. If they had lived separately and were distant from each other, it would have been a difficult job to burn down their houses. It is also not clear how they lived in the district in which one of the kinsmen was appointed prefect. But one point is important: Emperor Kuang-wu's action suggests that, unlike the Early Han emperors, he not only tolerated but encouraged a big family to live together. Kuang-wu himself came from a powerful family.

Other cases seem to suggest that though a lineage lived together in

[20] *HHS* 33:19b, commentary.

[21] Hsü T'ien-lin, *Hsi-Han hui-yao*, *TSCC* ed., 49:499–501, hereafter cited as *HHHY*.

[22] *HHS* 33:19b, commentary.

[23] The regulation made by Emperor Wu is not found in the *Han-shu*, but is inciden-tally mentioned in the biography of a man of the Later Han whose great-grandfather was on the list of those to be moved. This piece of valuable information would not have been known to us had it not been quoted by a commentator of the *Hou-Han-shu*.

one locality, each family remained a separate residential unit. The *chia* (family) is usually mentioned as the unit in our texts. The lineage of Han Jung, which took refuge on a mountain, is said to have consisted of one thousand families (I, 76). The *San-kuo-chih* mentions that T'ien Ch'ou 田疇 led his family members and kinsmen, numbering about three hundred families, to settle in Yeh 鄴.[24]

INHERITANCE

PRIMOGENITURE IN THE ROYAL FAMILY AND AMONG THE NOBLES

In Ch'in and Han times there were two main forms of inheritance. One was based on the property relationship, that is, the inheritance of the property of the dead. The inheritance might also include the succession to rights and privileges, such as to the throne or to a title. The first form was applicable to anyone who possessed property that could be bequeathed to someone else. The second form applied only to a special group of persons of political status. I shall discuss this type first.

The throne, the symbol of political entity and sovereignty, could be succeeded to by only one person. There could be only one emperor, and the empire could not be divided. Although a king in Han times was only a figurehead and had no actual political power, his throne could be succeeded to by one person only. Likewise, the titles of the various ranks of marquises could not be divided. Therefore only one son of an emperor, a king, or a marquis could have the privilege of possessing his father's throne or title, and the institution of primogeniture was followed.

Primogeniture had been in practice since Chou times, and the kind of primogeniture practiced by the Chinese was complicated. The right of inheritance did not always belong to the first-born son. A strict distinction was made between the children of the principal wife and those of the various concubines. The eldest son of the principal wife was entitled to be the successor; the sons of the concubines, even if older, were excluded from the succession. Anyone who put aside the sons of the principal wife and appointed the son of a concubine was severely criticized.[25]

In Han the eldest son of the empress was appointed heir apparent,

[24] *SKC*, Wei, 11:12b.
[25] For details of this practice in Chou times, see Ch'ü T'ung-tsu, *Chung-kuo feng-chien she-hui* (Shanghai: Commercial Press, 1937), pp. 145–54.

and all other sons, whether by the empress or the imperial concubines, were made kings.[26] Violations of this principle met with severe criticism. Thus when Emperor Kao intended to dismiss the heir apparent and appoint the son of his favorite concubine, many officials opposed him and remonstrated with him. One official declared before the emperor that he would not accept the edict if he removed the heir apparent. Another official asked the emperor to kill him before the appointment of a new heir apparent.[27] A similar action was taken by an official when he learned that Emperor Yüan wanted to dismiss the heir apparent, who was the son of the empress, and appoint the son of an imperial concubine.[28] As a result neither Emperor Kao nor Emperor Yüan succeeded in dismissing his heir apparent.

When an empress was dismissed and a new empress appointed, the son of the former was usually dismissed and replaced by the son of the new empress. In the Later Han a lady of the Kuo family was appointed empress to Emperor Kuang-wu, and her son was made heir apparent. Later, when Empress Kuo was deposed, a new empress was appointed; and her son was made heir apparent after the dismissal of the former heir apparent. The edict said that the son should be appointed in accordance with the superior status of his mother, and for this reason the son of the empress should be appointed heir apparent. It was reported that before the appointment of the new heir apparent, the son of the deposed empress had felt uneasy and had many times requested his own dismissal.[29]

As a rule the son of a concubine was appointed as the successor only when the son of the empress died or when the empress had no son.[30] If there were several sons by imperial concubines, usually the eldest was the successor. But it seems that seniority was not a determining factor; succession depended upon the personal relations between the emperor and the mother as well as between the emperor and the son. Emperor Wu had six sons, but only one of them was the son of the empress. When this son, the heir apparent, was killed, the king of Yen, the eldest among the brothers, expected to be appointed and therefore requested leave to stay in the imperial palace. Emperor Wu disliked this request

[26] *HS* 38:1a, 47:1a, 63:1a, 80:1a and 12a; *HHS* 2:1a, 10A:6a–b, 42:1b, 8:21b, 10B:16a.

[27] *SC* 96:2b-3a, 99:9a–b; *HS* 40:8a–10a, 42:2b, 43:17a–b.

[28] *HS* 82:6a–8a.

[29] *HHS* 2:1a, 10A:6a–b, 42:1b.

[30] *HS* 7:1a; *HHS* 3:1a, 4:1a, 6:1a and 22b, 9:1a, 10A:13a, 19b, 20b-21a, and 26b, 10B:1b and 6a.

and appointed a younger son heir apparent. Disappointed, the king of Yen rebelled.[31] In the Later Han, Emperor Chang was the fifth son of Emperor Ming, and Emperor Ho was the fourth son of Emperor Chang.[32] The emperor sometimes changed his mind about the heir apparent when there was a change in his affection for his son or for his son's mother. Thus an imperial concubine's son who had been appointed heir apparent might be dismissed and the son of another concubine made heir apparent.[33]

The same principle was observed among the kings and marquises. The eldest son of the queen was always appointed heir apparent. The son of a concubine was not qualified to succeed his father, even if he was his eldest son (*HS* 53:18a). All sons, other than the eldest son of the queen, had a chance to replace the heir apparent only when he was found guilty of some crime and dismissed. The king of Heng-shan had several sons, two by the queen. The eldest son of the queen was made heir apparent. After the death of the queen one of the king's concubines was raised to the position of queen. But when the king became angry with the heir apparent, he replaced him with the second son of the first queen (*HS* 44:14a–16b). The king of Chiao-tung disliked his eldest son, whose mother he did not love, and wanted to appoint a younger son of his favorite concubine. However, because he knew that this was not the correct order of succession, he did not make the appointment. After the king's death the oldest son was appointed by the emperor to be the successor (*HS* 53:17a–b). Such examples show that a king had to observe the prescribed order of succession very strictly. A kingdom was under the close supervision of the emperor, and the appointment of an heir had to be approved by the emperor. The heir apparent of a king who was found guilty of a crime was dismissed, and later when the king asked permission to reappoint him the request was refused by the emperor (*HS* 53:8b).

The idea that only the eldest son of the queen was entitled to the succession and that all other sons were excluded from this privilege was based on the principle that the title as well as the kingdom could not be divided. However, this was offset by another principle held by the emperor and his advisors: a kingdom should not become too large. If the territory of a large kingdom always remained the same, the kingdom might become strong enough to be a threat to the imperial court. A

[31] *HS* 53:7b–8a, 9a, 11a.
[32] *HHS* 3:1a, 4:1a.
[33] *HHS* 4:1a, 10A: 20b–21a.

measure to prevent this was suggested by an official of the central government and put into practice in 127 B.C. Under this new measure a king was permitted to give land to his sons and brothers, all of whom would then be ennobled as marquises by the emperor.[34] In this way the old principle of primogeniture was maintained as usual, yet the size and power of a kingdom was automatically reduced, for the oldest son who inherited the title of king received a much smaller kingdom.

It seems that the principle of primogeniture applied also to those officials and commoners who held an honorary rank, *chüeh* 爵, without a fief. In Ch'in and Han there were twenty ranks. Only the nineteenth and twentieth ranks were called marquises (*kuo* 國), and actually only the twentieth rank possessed a marquisate. The holders of other ranks were merely exempted from labor service.[35] In Han times the lowest ranks were granted to commoners (usually one rank to a person) on various occasions, such as accession to the throne, appointment of the heir apparent, capping of the heir apparent, appointment of princes to become kings, changes of the reign titles, sacrifices to Heaven, completion of the city wall of the capital, appearance of good omens, calamities, and so on.[36] As a rule only one person in a family was granted a grade in rank, usually the head of the household; but sometimes it was granted to the person who would be the successor to his father.[37] Under these specified conditions the principle of primogeniture certainly would be followed. In one instance it was clearly stated that the rank was granted to the eldest sons of all families (*HS* 6:3b).

THE PRINCIPLE OF EQUAL SHARES

Primogeniture, however, was not applicable to other forms of prop-

[34] *SC* 17:2a–b, 21:1a; *HS* 6:9a, 53:11b, 64A:19b.

[35] *HS* 1B:4b–5a, 19A:14a–b; *HHC* 28:14b, 15b; Nancy Lee Swann, *Food and Money in Ancient China* (Princeton, N.J.: Princeton University Press, 1950), pp. 30–34. Emperor Kao mentioned in an edict of 202 B.C. that those from the seventh rank and higher were treated as equals by the prefects in Ch'in times; he told his officials that they should respect the holders of these ranks. He also ordered that those from the seventh rank and above were entitled to collect taxes from their fiefs, and that those from the sixth rank down to the first rank were exempted from labor services. Obviously, as pointed out by the Han commentator, Tsan, the granting of fiefs to persons other than the nineteenth and twentieth ranks was a special favor of Emperor Kao when he first unified the empire (*HS* 1B:4b). There is no evidence that this privilege mentioned in the edict was in practice in later days.

[36] *HHHY* 35:362–65.

[37] In certain instances it is stated clearly that ranks were granted to the people, one grade to each family (*HS* 2:3a and 4b, 4:6a, 5:9b).

erty that were divisible. A king disliked his eldest son, whose mother was an unfavored concubine, and did not leave him any property when he died. An official urged the heir apparent and the queen to order the sons of the king to share their property with this unfortunate man. The suggestion was not adopted, which caused the eldest son to hate them.[38] This case implies that although the heir apparent was the successor to the kingdom, all other sons were given the privilege of sharing the property of the deceased king.

The principle of equal distribution of property was practiced by officials and commoners who had no hereditary titles to leave. Lu Chia's case affords a distinctive illustration. The retired official, who had five sons and two thousand catties of gold, gave two hundred to each of his five sons and made an agreement with his sons that the family in which he died during his brief biannual visits would inherit his personal property (I, 13). This case indicates two points: the equal right of inheritance among all sons and the disposition of property at will. We do not know how popular the practice of testacy was or whether there was a law governing it. But it is certain that the right to make a testament was fully recognized by custom, if not by law. Probably the principle of equal shares was enforced if men died intestate.

The popularity of equal sharing by all sons or brothers is also seen in another case. Hsü Wu 許武, who wanted to make his two younger brothers famous, divided the family property into three shares; but he took for himself the fertile land, big buildings, and strong slaves, and allotted the younger brothers inferior shares. Consequently he was looked down upon by the community because of his greed, whereas his two brothers were admired for being able to yield (I, 55).

WOMEN AND THE RIGHT OF INHERITANCE

Since the Chinese family system traces only through the male descendants of a common ancestor, a woman was excluded from the right of succession to a hereditary title as well as to the family property. The dowry was the only form in which she could obtain a part of the family property, and the amount she got certainly depended upon the will of her father or brother. Usually the dowry was a small portion of the family property and was not to be compared with what was inherited by her brothers. If her father was generous, a girl might get a dowry equal to the inheritance of her brother. Thus the wealthy merchant

[38] *SC* 59:8a–b; *HS* 53:18a–b.

Cho Wang-sun 卓王孫 gave one hundred slaves and a million cash to his daughter Wen-chün 文君, who had eloped with Ssu-ma Hsiang-ju 司馬相如; later when the husband was appointed to a high official post, Cho granted his daughter property that was equal to what he gave his son (I, 21, 24). Of course, he had been angry with his daughter because of her elopement when he gave her the first dowry. The second gift was given to her because he was impressed by the political status of his son-in-law. We cannot tell whether he would have given his daughter a more generous dowry, or even one comparable to what he gave his son, at the time she eloped if he had not been angry. Nor can we tell whether he would have given an equal share to her if he had not been impressed by the success of his son-in-law. The reaction of the son is not recorded, but the father's will to give an equal share to his daughter was apparently carried out without objection. It seems that the matter depended upon the will of the parent.

ADOPTION

To the ancient Chinese a male descendant was very important because he was the agent who carried on the function of ancestor worship and the continuation of the family. A female descendant left her family when she married and became a member of her husband's family; so she was not a permanent member of her father's family, and the continuation of the family did not depend upon her. The children she bore were descendants of her husband's family, and they worshipped his parents and his ancestors. Her children were considered outside relatives of her father's family.

A man who had only daughters was considered to have no descendants. Because there would be no one to worship his ancestors after his death, the family would come to an end. Concubinage was introduced to increase the possibility of having a son. But when this failed, adoption was the only means to prolong the family line, and thus to carry on all the necessary functions that had to be performed by a male descendant.

The first principle was that the adopted male must be a member of the same lineage. It was commonly believed that the spirit of a dead man would not accept any offerings from a man who had a different surname and who was not consanguineously related to him. There was a saying that "a ghost accepts no offerings from someone who is not of the same blood."[39] A story was told in Han times concerning an adopted son who

[39] *Ch'un-ch'iu Tso-chuan chu-su, SPPY* ed., 13:8b, hereafter cited as *TCCS*.

had a different surname. When he offered sacrifices it was his own ancestors who enjoyed the offering, not those of the family that had
adopted him. Finally, when this was discovered, the adopted son was
sent back to his own family and a son of a paternal cousin was
adopted.[40] A son adopted from a different kin group introduced alien
blood into the family.

Thus to adopt someone from a different kin group was considered
improper and, at times, unlawful. The *Shu-chih* of the *San-kuo-chih* reports that Wei Chi 魏繼 was adopted by Prefect Chang with the consent
of the former's father, but because the law of the time prohibited the
adoption of a man of a different surname, Wei resumed his own name.[41]
It is not clear whether it refers to the Han law or a law introduced in
Shu-Han. A similar prohibition is found in the law of the Chin 晉 (265–
420). The attitude toward adopting a man of a different surname is
illustrated in the case of Chia Ch'ung 賈充, a high official of the Chin
dynasty. Chia Ch'ung's son died during his childhood. When Ch'ung
died without a grandson, his wife adopted their daughter's son to be
the heir of Ch'ung's son. This was considered improper by a number of
officials, and efforts were made to correct the matter. Finally the case
was given special consideration and approved by the emperor. Yet it
was made clear in the edict that this special case should not be cited as
a precedent and imitated by others.[42]

Because our knowledge of Han law is based only on existing remnants, we do not know whether it prohibited the adoption of a man of
a different surname. But since such a prohibition is found in the laws of
Shu-Han and Chin, it seems unlikely that the adoption of a son of a
different surname would be tolerated by the law in Han times. In any
case, it is certain that such action was generally disapproved by society,
especially by the intellectuals who supported the doctrines of *li*. After
citing the story of the sacrifices by an adopted son mentioned above,
Ying Shao remarks: "It is clear that a ghost would not accept the
offerings [of a man of] different blood. Why should a man adopt the
son of others [who had no blood relationship]?"[43]

It is mentioned in the *I-li* that only a person of the same *tsung* was
eligible for adoption.[44] This doctrine was quoted by Ho Kuang 霍光
when Emperor Chao's grand-nephew was going to be appointed em-

---

[40] Ying Shao, *Feng-su t'ung-i*, in *CHHW*, 38:3a–b, hereafter cited as *FSTI* (A).
[41] *SKC*, Shu, 15:19a–b.
[42] *CS* 84:8a, 40:4a–b.
[43] *FSTI* (A), 38:3b.
[44] *I-li chu-su*, *SPPY* ed., 29:2a, hereafter cited as *ILCS*.

peror after the death of Emperor Chao (*HS* 8:3a). Emperor Ch'eng, who had no descendant, adopted his brother's son and made him heir apparent (*HS* 11:la-b). The regulations stated that a king or marquis who had no son could adopt either his grandson or his brother's son as his heir (*HS* 12:3a). Among the officials it was also a common practice to adopt a brother's son.[45]

However, deviations were found at all times, even when such action was held to be unlawful. Han was no exception. An essay written by Wu Shang 吳商 in the Later Han revealed that it was not uncommon for a man to adopt someone of a different surname when he had no son.[46] A male adopted from a different lineage might be someone who was no relation;[47] or a sister's son might be adopted. Two such cases are found in our texts.[48] And there are also examples in which a man was brought up in his mother's paternal family and took his maternal grandfather's surname.[49]

Sometimes it happened that a son was born to the wife or concubine after one had been adopted. The adopted son was often kept in the family.[50] On the other hand, adopted sons tended to resume their original surnames, usually after the death of the parents who had adopted them.[51] Chu Jan is an illustration of this. He asked Sun Ch'üan 孫權, the ruler of Wu, for permission to resume his own surname after the death of his adopted father; but the permission was not given. Years later Chu Jan's son again asked for permission to resume his surname, and permission was granted by Sun Ch'üan's successor.[52]

PATTERNS OF AUTHORITY IN FAMILY AND LINEAGE

AUTHORITY OF THE FATHER

A father was the head and the ruler of a family; all its members were under his command and control. The typical behavior pattern of a

[45] *SKC*, Shu, 5:19b.

[46] Tu Yu, *T'ung-tien* (Shanghai: Commercial Press, 1935), 69:382, hereafter cited as *TT*.

[47] For instance, Ts'ao Sung (*SKC*, Wei, 1:1b, note) and Wei Chi (*SKC*, Shu, 15:19a–b).

[48] Chu Jan 朱然 (*SKC*, Wu, 11:3b); Ch'en Chiao 陳矯 (*Wei-shih ch'un-ch'iu*, quoted in *SKC*, Wei, 22:16a, note).

[49] *SKC*, Shu, 10:1a, 13:6b and 8a.

[50] *SKC*, Shu, 10:1a ff.

[51] *TT* 69:382.

[52] *SKC*, Wu, 11:7b.

father was to be severe with his sons. This tended to produce dual patterns of behavior, as the actions of Teng Hsün 鄧訓 illustrate very well. Teng was humble and lenient with others but very severe with his family members. He never received his sons with a mild countenance and never gave them a seat. On the other hand, a son was expected to respect and fear his father. It was said that Teng was even respected and feared by his younger brothers, not to mention his sons (I, 57).

A child was under the complete control of his father. A son who intended to visit and console a fellow student who had lost his parent was beaten by his father and ordered to send some funeral gift instead of going to see his friend (I, 46). The marriage of children was also arranged by the father. Impressed by the physical features of Liu Pang, the father of the future Empress Lü promised to marry his daughter to him without asking the consent of his daughter or his wife. Although his wife was angry and objected to the betrothal because of Liu's poverty, Lü disregarded her opinion. The reaction of the daughter is not mentioned in the biography. That the mother was completely disregarded indicates the supremacy of the father over the mother in making the final decision. Before the betrothal the local prefect had asked for Lü's daughter for his son, but it was Lü who had rejected the proposal. It is apparent from his wife's complaints that she was willing to marry her daughter into the family of the prefect because of its status and wealth.[53]

Children were supposed to obey the orders of their parents. Chastisement was considered necessary when they were disobedient. It is said in the *Lü-shih ch'un-ch'iu*, a book written in the third century B.C., that "if there is no anger and chastisement in a family, faults in the small children will appear immediately." Thus anger and chastisement could not be neglected in a family "just as punishment is necessary for government in a state."[54] Apparently, according to the authors of this book, which certainly reflects the views of the time, the father's authority in punishing his children was recognized by society as well as by law, and a father was expected to be the ruler of a family much as the government ruled the country. It should also be pointed out that although the book mentions only children, chastisement was not limited to offspring who were still youngsters. An adult son was also under the control of his father and was subject to physical punishment. The age of the son who was beaten because he wanted to visit and console his fellow student is

---

[53] *SC* 8:3b–4a; *HS* 1A:3a.

[54] *Lü-shih ch'un-ch'iu*, in Pi Yuan (comp.), *Ching-hsün t'ang ts'ung-shu*, 7:3b, hereafter cited as *LSCC*.

not known, but he certainly was not a child (I, 46). One father intended to beat his eighteen-year-old son (I, 33); two sons who already held official posts were beaten by their fathers (I, 14, 75). It would seem that a man's status as a son in the family was not affected even if he had the responsibility and prestige of an official position. An adult heir apparent was also frequently beaten by a king (I, 25).

An analysis of the conditions under which a son was beaten in these cases would indicate more about the supremacy of the father in punishing his children than his justification. A son was given two hundred strokes by his father, an imperial chancellor (*ch'eng-hsiang* 丞相) who drank and paid no attention to government affairs, because the son attempted to remonstrate with him (I, 14). Another son was beaten because the father asked what the public opinion concerning him was and became angry at his son's reply (I, 75). The fact that the son was beaten because he planned to visit his friend indicates that a son would be punished if he took independent action that was disapproved by the father. In another instance a father wanted to beat his son because he fell asleep and paid little attention to his instruction (I, 33). It is clear that a father had the right to beat his son whenever he thought he deserved punishment; it made no difference if the son was not at fault. Only in one instance had a son who was beaten by his father committed a serious offense. First he intentionally injured his stepmother's brother, and then he wanted to have intercourse with his stepmother (I, 25).

Did a father have the right of life and death over his children? It seems that a father did have such authority in Ch'in times. When the First Emperor died, the younger brother of Prince Fu-su 扶蘇 concealed his death and issued a decree in the name of the deceased emperor ordering the prince to take his own life. After reading the decree Prince Fu-su said, "When a father orders his son to die, how dare [the son] ask again?" Thereupon he immediately committed suicide (*SC* 87:11b–12a). It may be argued that his father was the emperor, and an ordinary father would not have such power. But it should not be overlooked that the prince said "father" and not "emperor." This incident suggests that a son had to obey his father's order when the father wanted the son to end his life.

Han scholars, however, take a different view. The *Po-hu-t'ung* says: "Why should a father who kills his son be executed? . . . All human beings are given life by Heaven and come into existence merely through the medium of the parents. The king nourishes and educates them.

Therefore a father can have no claim on [the son] exclusively."[55] Apparently the power of life and death exercised by a father was not recognized in Han times. Moreover, evidence shows that a parent was held legally responsible for killing a son. Even infanticide was not exempt from punishment. A chancellor ruled that parents would be executed for infanticide; another official ruled that parents who killed their infants were to be punished as if they were guilty of homicide (*HHS* 77:16a, 67:34b). Once two murder cases were reported to a prefect: in the south of the city a man was killed by a robber and in the north of the city a man was killed by his mother. The prefect was so angry about the second case that he said it was not surprising for a robber to kill someone, but it was against Heaven and principle to kill a son. He then investigated this case first and punished the mother (*HHS* 67:34b–35a). We do not know how the mother was punished, but it is clear that killing a son was not to be tolerated and was subject to punishment according to law.

Among all other cases found in our texts in which the death of a son occurred, no son was killed directly by his father. Wang Mang is said to have killed three of his sons. One of them was ordered to commit suicide for having killed a slave (I, 37). Later, his eldest son was arrested on Wang Mang's orders and was sent to prison, where he took poison and died. Since Wang Mang was the top official in the government and the son was sent to prison, legally the son was killed by the government; therefore, we cannot consider this a case of a son being killed on the father's authority (I, 38). When Wang Mang wanted another of his sons to die, he gave him poison; but the son refused to drink it and committed suicide with a knife (*HS* 99C:13a). However, this incident took place after Wang Mang had ascended the throne, and it should be noted that an emperor had the power to force anyone to die by giving him poison or a sword.

The *Han-shu* reports that a father killed his son with poison (I, 29). But it is not clear whether he actually killed his son or ordered him to commit suicide by taking poison. The latter is more likely, since this was a more common method. In one instance in our texts it is clearly stated that the father ordered his son to take poison (I, 50). Obviously there must have been a great difference in legal responsibility between killing a son and ordering him to commit suicide. A king was angry at his son and scolded him, whereupon the son committed suicide. This

[55] Pan Ku, *Po-hu-t'ung*, in Lu Wen-ch'ao (comp.), *Pao-ching-t'ang ts'ung-shu*, 4:5b, hereafter cited as *PHT*.

event was reported to the emperor by the chancellor (*hsiang* 相). No action was taken by the government in this matter, so the father apparently was not held responsible for his son's suicide (I, 64). On the other hand, the report of the case to the court implies that the death of a son was a serious matter and called for investigation and that the outcome would have been different if it had been decided that the father was responsible.

AUTHORITY OF THE LINEAGE HEAD

The lineage head apparently did not exist in Ch'in and Han times. There is no mention of one in our texts or other supplementary works, so we cannot tell if there was the formal institution of a lineage head. Since the average family size at that time was rather small and the Han government discouraged the lineage from living together, it is safe to assume that the practice of having a lineage head was not common as it was in later times. The families of a lineage usually lived separately, and there is no evidence of lineage property or lineage temples, so apparently there was no need for a lineage head. However, there was a certain form of authority in a lineage. It is certain that any common action, such as the mobilization of the whole lineage, had to be organized under the command of a certain kinsman whose authority in the kin group was commonly accepted.

I have already mentioned that during the rebellion of Tung Cho in 189 a large lineage, Han, was moved to a mountain area under the leadership of one kinsman (I, 76). Another lineage in the same locality was led by a kinsman and moved from modern Honan to Chi-chou in modern Hopei. In another instance, the whole lineage of T'ien Ch'ou was moved to a mountain under his initiation and leadership. We do not know whether he was the head of the lineage, but one thing is certain: the plan would have been impossible if he had not had some kind of authority over his kinsmen. The *San-kuo-chih* reports that a large number of people followed him, and within a few years the number reached five thousand families. T'ien worked out a number of regulations and punishments, including the death penalty, for his followers. Afterward he led all his family members and kinsmen, numbering three hundred families, to Yeh and lived there.[56] Of course, his authority to make regulations and to impose severe punishments for all those attached to him was rather unusual and cannot be interpreted as the

[56] *SKC*, Wei, 11:10a–12b.

authority of a lineage head. He was the head of the whole group that lived in that community; but his particular authority over his kinsmen is clearly reflected in his leadership when he moved the whole lineage twice.

Authority over kinsmen is more clearly seen when military activities are involved. A lineage was often organized militarily under the command of one of its members. Thus Liu Chih 劉植 was able to organize his lineage and the retainers he led in occupying the principal city in their locality (I, 42). The entire Keng lineage was mobilized for war under the command of Keng Ch'un and his paternal cousins. Even the old and the sick were not exempted, and they carried coffins with them. Fearing that some of them might change their minds, Keng Ch'un ordered his cousins to burn their homes (I, 41). We do not know whether Keng Ch'un was the head, but his authority over his lineage was amazing. If the whole lineage was not under his complete control, the aged and the sick certainly would not have followed him, and he would not have dared to burn their homes.

LEGAL FUNCTION OF THE FAMILY

Since the head of the family was its ruler and his authority over its members was recognized by law and society, a family was functionally a unit of self-government. It was expected that order would be maintained within each family. Thus when Wang Mang's son, an official in the government, made an offensive remark to three other top officials, one of them complained to Wang Mang, who then punished his son.[57] The fact that the father was reprimanded instead of the son indicates that a father, whose patriarchal authority was supreme, was also responsible for his children's behavior.

The law also gave some legal responsibility to the family head. Persons engaged in trade or handicraft were allowed to assess their own taxes in Han times, but according to the law the head of a family in person was to assess the value of the family's goods. If his assessment was not accurate, or if he did not personally write it down, he was fined two catties of gold, and the goods that had not been assessed were confiscated.[58]

[57] I, 29. This is not the same Wang Mang who founded the Hsin dynasty.

[58] According to Ju Shun, who quoted the Han law, for all those who had to assess their own taxes, the head of a family was obliged personally to assess his goods (I, 30, and n. 130).

Collective responsibility of family members was another feature of Han life. The ancients usually considered that merely punishing the criminal himself in severe cases was not sufficient punishment to prevent a recurrence of crime. The arrest and punishment of the innocent family members of a criminal along with him was thought to increase the mental burden of the criminal so that he would hesitate to violate the law again. This philosophy is expressed in our texts in the statement of Han officials who favored the practice of collective responsibility (I, 17). At the same time, the practice was intended to make all family members watch each other's behavior.

Collective responsibility may have been exercised in two ways: either the family members received the same punishment as the criminal or they were punished less severely than the criminal. The punishment of the three *tsu* provides an example of the first category. It was first introduced by the state of Ch'in in 749 B.C. Under the law, the parents, siblings, wife, and children of a criminal were to be executed with him (I, 1, and n. 1). This punishment was adopted by Han when the code was formulated (I, 17; *HHS* 52:25a). Edicts to abolish this kind of punishment were issued in 187 and 179 B.C. (I, 16, 17); however, it came into practice again in 163 B.C. during the reign of the same emperor who had ordered it abolished. Actually the punishment of the three *tsu* for particularly heinous crimes was in practice throughout Early and Later Han.[59] In less severe cases the family members of the criminal were not subject to the death penalty, but were seized and made slaves. (See the section on Slaves in Chapter 4.)

ECONOMIC FUNCTION OF THE FAMILY

The family was a productive unit. The land and other forms of property, such as cattle, were owned in common, and the living of the family members was derived therefrom. They might also own some kind of property connected with their agricultural work: it was not uncommon for a family to build reservoirs and canals for irrigation (I, 40). They produced their own food and grew a variety of vegetables and fruit trees in the family garden.[60] Pigs and chickens were raised,[61] and

---

[59] I, 17; *HHS* 9:3a, 12a–b, 15a–b, 16b, and 17a, 19:14a and 18b, 72:28b.

[60] It is mentioned in a slave contract that the slave was assigned the work of planting ginger, scallions, garlic, melons, mulberry trees, and peach, plum, and pear trees in the garden; see the section on Slaves in Chapter 4.

[61] *HHS* 83:14b. Herding of pigs, sheep, and horses by family slaves is also mentioned in the slave contract.

some families even had fish ponds. Various implements and utensils were also made by the family. A slave contract reveals that brooms, bamboo rakes, well wheels, fishing nets, shoes, ropes, mats, charcoal, knives, and bows were made by the family slaves. One family head even went so far as to plant catalpa and lacquer trees so he would have his own wood and lacquer to make utensils (I, 40). Women in the household engaged in spinning and weaving, which provided the clothing for the family (I, 39, 43; *HHS* 83:12a–b).

The rules of the Jen family that stipulated that nothing that was not produced by their own fields and animals should be eaten or worn by the family members might not be typical (I, 10), but it is safe to say that self-support was the general pattern and that most of the food, clothing, and utensils used by the family they produced themselves.

Since the whole family was engaged in production, some system of division of labor had to be worked out, and there had to be some regulations on the supervision of team work, the control of production, and the distribution of the goods produced. The problem was more complicated when the family was large and owned a large piece of property.

All the family members, with the probable exception of the aged and the children, were required to participate in productive work, although a man might be exempted from physical labor in exceptional cases. A family of two brothers who owned a piece of land might work together on the same land or one of them might take care of the farming while the other engaged in study or other activities; for instance, Ch'en P'ing was supported by his elder brother so that he could engage in study (I, 7). Obviously this division of labor was based on the idea that study, which was a qualification for entering officialdom, led to more social mobility, and that if one member succeeded in attaining an official position the whole family would benefit. Strictly speaking, this kind of arrangement was also a form of division of labor. The willingness and effort to support one's brother in order to assist him in entering officialdom as a means for promoting the social mobility of the family is illustrated more clearly in a similar case. Two brothers lived together, and the younger brother purchased an official post with the family funds. For ten years he had no opportunity for promotion, and since his remaining in office resulted in the reduction of his elder brother's property, he intended to resign and return home (I, 18). The willingness of the elder brother to spend part of the family property to purchase a post for his brother and to support him when he became an official suggests that the sacrifice was for some rewarding goal. On the other hand, the attitude of the younger brother, who became impatient after having served in office for a long time, shows that he was considering seriously the loss of the family property, which had obviously not been expected.

There were also divisions of labor according to sex. Men engaged in farming, construction of irrigation works, domestication of animals, and the production of working tools and certain utensils; women were mainly concerned with spinning, weaving, sewing, the production of certain utensils, cooking, and other domestic services.

Slaves were also employed in family production, either for family consumption or for profit, and sometimes "guests" were also asked to engage in production. (See the sections on Slaves and Guests in Chapter 4.) The assignment of work to the various slaves and guests must have been a large and complicated job, especially when there were large numbers of them. In some wealthy families production was the duty of slaves and guests, while the members of the master's family were exempted from menial work. However, both slaves and guests and the master's family might work together. If this was the case, there had to be a division of labor between the two groups. Most likely the menial work would be assigned to the slaves and guests, while the master and his family members took up the more pleasant tasks. In the family of a wealthy marquis, the wife herself spun and wove, and all the family's seven hundred slaves were skilled in handicrafts (II, 36). Unfortunately we do not know what kind of work was assigned to other family members.

The assignment and supervision of the work probably was the responsibility of the family head. And to assure maximum productivity there had to be some regulations and the authority to enforce them. That no one should drink wine or eat meat if the domestic work had not been finished (I, 10) is but one example of family regulations observed by a family engaged in farming and the domestication of animals.

Economic cooperation was found among relatives who lived separately and owned individual property, and it was not uncommon for relatives to support each other. Many officials spent their salaries to support their kin, which frequently included all the members of the nine *tsu*. Sometimes the salary was distributed in such a manner that little money was left for the official's own use (I, 45, 48, 51, 56). The obligation to support relatives was stronger among close relatives. Thus a man who had divided the family property, giving half to his nephew, later often gave something to relieve his nephew when he lost his property (I, 63). There is a case in which a younger brother hired himself out as a farm laborer to support his elder brother and the brother's wife.[62]

A family or a lineage also had the function of providing charity and security to its members. Relief was given to kinsmen when they were in distress and need. The family provided security to those who were studying and not yet employed. Thus a man always turned to his kinsman instead of to an unrelated man for assistance. Failure to give relief to poor relatives usually led to disappointment and complaints. A man who had been engaged in traveling and study without success complained that no clothing or food was given to him by his brothers (I, 23).

EDUCATIONAL FUNCTION OF THE FAMILY

A family usually served the function of providing some form of education to its young members. The kind of education given to children was obviously conditioned by the intellectual as well as the socio-economic level of the family. A child of an illiterate father had little chance of receiving literary knowledge from him. Nor was a poor family able to send its children to the village school. Most likely the children would be sent to work in their early childhood, and the instruction they received from their elders was mostly training in connection with their professions. On the other hand, a child of a wealthy family was not bothered by work and could devote most of his time to getting the knowledge required to reach the upper class. A family of intellectuals would also do their best to give literary training to their children.

Above all, the family was the most important agent for the socialization of the children; that is, it was through the family that they learned to perform the social roles expected of them. Of course, the roles learned by children were predominantly kinship roles; but since the society put great emphasis on kinship roles, it is easy to see the importance of family education in ancient China. Such basic values as filial piety and brotherly love were all internalized during the early childhood. It may be assumed that the personality of a man was shaped and conditioned mainly within the family. The attitudes and behavior of adults and the

---

[62] II, 75. In an extreme case a younger brother even hired himself out as a wage laborer and offered all his earnings to his elder brother, a local official, in order to stop him from receiving gifts (I, 53).

approval or disapproval of the parents influenced the children greatly. Their early socialization thus took place within the kinship group, supplemented by other agencies—schools or private teachers.

The family was obviously aware of such a function. Various kinds of instruction were often given to children—instruction that the elders thought most important for moral integrity or social success. Pan Chao's 班昭 *Lessons for Women* was written primarily for her unmarried daughters.[63] Ma Jung 馬融, who appreciated her words, ordered his daughters—and his wife as well—to study them carefully (*HHS* 84:13a).

Whereas schools played only a limited role, the family continued the role of socialization indefinitely. Elders kept an eye on their children and continued to give them instructions and warnings even when they were of age. The father's permanent authority, together with his power of disciplinary action, made it possible for the family to prolong its educational role: such education was concerned not merely with the socialization of children but with the socialization of adults as well. Seniors seemed to take such a prolonged process rather seriously. Ma Yüan 馬援, who was far away in the army, worried about the ruthless behavior of his nephews and even sent warnings and instructions to them in a letter (*HHS* 24:18b–19a). Those who had an active interest in maintaining the good reputation of the family usually paid a great deal of attention to the behavior of its members, demanding that they abide by the *chia-fa* 家法, family instructions, handed down from generation to generation. The process of socialization, backed by sanctions, was indeed in operation almost endlessly in the kinship group.

RELIGIOUS FUNCTION OF THE FAMILY

It was commonly believed that when a man died his soul still needed food and drink, and that the only way it could enjoy these material things was to accept what was offered by its own living family members or kinsmen. For this reason, ancestor worship was an obligation of the children, and constituted a major function of the family. Sacrifices were usually offered in the family shrine or temple, but they could also be offered at the tombs or tombhouses, which were often built by officials and other well-to-do people.[64]

---

[63] *HHS* 84:7a–b; Nancy Lee Swann, *Pan Chao: Foremost Woman Scholar of China* (New York: The Century Co., 1932), pp. 82–90.

[64] III, 47; *FSTI* (A), 38:3a.

Usually an annual sacrifice was held on the *la* 臘 day in the winter.[65] That worshipping ancestors on the *la* day was a popular custom in Han is illustrated in the case of a slave who stole food and offered it to his deceased mother.[66] Every member of the family was expected to participate in the sacrifice, but men and women had different roles in religious services. It was a woman's duty to prepare wine and food to be offered to the ancestors (*HHS* 84:8a).

Moreover, other kinds of sacrifices were performed within the family. There was a sacrifice to the Kitchen God on the *la* day (*HHS* 32:16b–17a). Ssu-ming 司命[67] was a popular spirit worshipped by the people. Most of the families built a miniature house in which to put an image of Ssu-ming, and a sacrifice was also offered on the *la* day.[68] It seems that only the She God 社 was worshipped by the local community together,[69] whereas all other religious sacrifices were held by each family individually.

MILITARY FUNCTION OF THE FAMILY

Most families had no military function. However, some families and lineages did engage in military activities, and both their frequency and their consequences need special attention. Military functions in the family were all connected with periods of war and disorder. All our examples are found at the end of the Later Han and the era of the Three Kingdoms, when no protection was given to the people by the government, and when they were under constant threat of war and bandits. The poor and the helpless had no alternative but to run away; but the greater families organized their members to protect themselves and their family properties. The we-group sentiment was particularly strong during crises that involved the kinsmen; at such times they felt

[65] The meaning of *la* is given in the *Feng-su t'ung-i* as "to hunt animals and to offer them to the ancestors" (Ying Shao, *Feng-su t'ung-i, SPTK* ed., 8:8b–9a, hereafter cited as *FSTI*). Other cases also illustrate that the Han people usually worshipped their ancestors on this day (*FSTI* [A], 38:3a; Pan Ku *et al., Tung-kuan Han-chi,* in *WYT,* 21:4a, hereafter cited as *TKHC*).

[66] *TKHC* 21:4a.

[67] Ssu-ming was a god in charge of men's life and death. Thus when Chuang-tzu dreamed of a skull, he suggested that he would ask the Ssu-ming to give the skull some bone, flesh, and skin and to restore its life (*Chuang-tzu, SPPY* ed., 6:18a, hereafter cited as *CT*).

[68] *FSTI* 8:9b–10a.

[69] Lao Kan, *Chü-yen Han-chien k'ao-shih, K'ao-cheng chih pu (Kuo-li chung-yang yen-chiu yüan li-shih yü-yen yen-chiu so chuan-k'an 21,* 1943–44), pp. 49–60.

that they shared the same fate and that only blood relatives could lean on each other.

A family or a lineage that was strong enough to defend itself must have been large in size and wealthy enough to equip itself with arms and food. Those families and lineages that were able to defend themselves are described in the history as "big surnames."[70] Since a family was usually neither large enough nor strong enough to protect itself, the whole lineage was often the unit of self-defense. Furthermore, the family force usually included also the family's guests (retainers) and slaves. (See the section on the Growth of Powerful Families in Chapter 5.) The size of such a force as well as its fighting power was tremendous. Some cases reveal that a force organized by a lineage, including kinsmen and a number of guests, consisted of more than a thousand men. They built and held on to their fortifications against bandits and other forces attacking them. At times they were even strong enough offensively to overcome forces guarding a city and to gain possession of it (I, 42).

Although most of the families or lineages were merely interested in self-defense, there were kin groups whose members were politically ambitious and who engaged in military activities of a different nature. Taking advantage of social and political disturbances, they were inclined to take an active part in the struggle for power. As we shall see in the chapter on powerful families, many of them joined the uprisings or attached themselves to a powerful military leader.[71] In one instance all the kinsmen, including the aged and the women, were mobilized to join the army and stayed together with the group, whereas adult males of the lineage and their guests constituted the fighting force that was led by some of the kinsmen (I, 41). Such huge forces, sometimes numbering more than a thousand, were always considered of great value to military leaders who sought their affiliation.[72]

[70] III, 50; *HHS* 67:6b; see also Yü Ying-shih, "Tung-Han chen-ch'üan chih chien-li yü shih-tsu ta-hsing chih kuan-hsi," *Hsin-ya hsüeh-pao,* I, No. 2 (Feb., 1956), 228 ff.

[71] I, 11, 41, 42; III, 49; *SKC,* Wei, 11:10a–11a, 18:1a.

[72] I, 41; *SKC,* Wei, 11:11a, 18:1a–2a.

Chapter Two

MARRIAGE

AGE FOR MEN AND WOMEN TO MARRY

THE ideal age for a man to marry was said to be thirty and for a woman, twenty.[1] However, this was understood by some ancient scholars as the latest age for men and women to marry, and they held that a man could marry at the age of sixteen and a woman at fourteen.[2] The information we have indicates that very few people married at such a late age. The author of *Lessons for Women* married at fourteen (see document I, 54), and there are other examples showing that a girl was usually married at the age of fourteen or fifteen.[3] According to the Han system, the girls who were selected and taken into the inner palace were between the ages of thirteen and twenty (I, 52, n. 206). A family that requested that one of its daughters be selected for the heir apparent reported that the eldest was fifteen, the next fourteen, and the youngest thirteen. The youngest was finally selected (I, 52). Two other girls were also selected for the palace when they were thirteen, and two were sent into the palace at the age of sixteen.[4] It would seem safe to assume

---

[1] *Chou-li chu-su,* SPPY ed., 14:8a, hereafter cited as *CLCS; LCCS* 61:3a; *PHT* 9:1a.

[2] *TT* 59:340.

[3] *HS* 97A:24b, 27b; *SKC,* Wu, 12:10b, note.

[4] I, 66; *HHS* 10B:7a, 10A:20b–21a and 24a–b.

that most women married between the ages of thirteen and sixteen. A regulation issued in 189 B.C. that any unmarried woman between fifteen and thirty was to be taxed at five times the normal rate (*HS* 2:4b) is additional evidence that most women in Han times were expected to marry around the age of fifteen.

THE FAMILY AND MARRIAGE

The functions of a marriage, according to the *Li-chi*, were to unite the affections of the two families, to serve the ancestral temple, and to continue the family line.[5] Obviously, the family was the center of interest, and the individual interests of the marrying parties were not considered at all. Thus a marriage was always contracted by the parents. It was held that neither a man nor a woman should select his or her own mate and that a marriage must be arranged by the parents through a go-between.[6] The father's authority was always superior to the mother's in these matters. Mister Lü promised to marry his daughter to Liu Pang, the future Emperor Kao, without even consulting his wife, and later was able to carry out his intention even though she strongly objected.[7] There was a similar case in the Hsü family.[8] All the wedding ceremonies were conducted in the father's name. The go-between, who was received by the girl's father, was merely the representative of the boy's father.[9] It should also be pointed out that the grandfather had greater authority than the father (I, 8).

Ancestor worship in connection with marriage was very important: all of the six wedding rites were held in the temple of the girl's family; before the marriage was contracted, the matter was divined before the spirits of the ancestors in the temples of both families; before the bridegroom went to welcome his bride, instruction was given by his father with the words, "Go to welcome your helpmate in order to fulfill our affairs in the ancestral temple"; and visiting the family temple was an important activity to be observed by the bride after the wedding.[10] According to a quotation in the *Li-chi* attributed to Confucius, a bride's

---

[5] *LCCS* 61:3a.

[6] *Meng-tzu chu-su*, *SPPY* ed., 6A:4a, hereafter cited as *MTCS; PHT* 9:1a.

[7] *SC* 8:3a–4b; *HS* 1A:3a.

[8] Hsü Kuang-han 許廣漢 promised to give his daughter to the grandson of the dismissed heir apparent without consulting his wife. She was very angry when he told her the next day, but the marriage was contracted in spite of her opposition (*HS* 97A:10a).

[9] *LCCS* 6:5a–6b.

[10] *LCCS* 61:3a, 4:4b, 6:6b, 6:1a.

inability to visit the ancestral temple would lead to serious consequences: if the bride died before she could pay the visit to the temple,
she was not to be worshipped in the temple, her body was to be buried
with her father's family, and she was not to be considered as having
attained the status of daughter-in-law.[11] Obviously the status of daughter-in-law meant more to her and her husband's family than the status
of wife.

PROHIBITED AND APPROVED MARRIAGES

MARRIAGE BETWEEN PERSONS OF THE SAME SURNAME

A patrilineage was an exogamous group; its members were prohibited
from intermarrying. In fact, the rule of exogamy even applied to persons who bore the same surname but could not actually be traced back
unilaterally to a common ancestor. Thus according to Chou tradition
one was not allowed to marry someone from a family with the same
surname, no matter how remote the blood relationship.[12] It was held
by the ancients that such a marriage would not produce many children.[13] This taboo is also mentioned in the *Po-hu-t'ung*, a Han work, and
in an essay written by Yüan Chun 袁準, a Wei scholar.[14] It is not possible
to know whether the Ch'in and Han law prohibited this kind of marriage, as did the codes of T'ang, Sung, Ming, and Ch'ing. All we can
say is that since this taboo was already widely accepted in Chou and
Han times and was followed by all the succeeding dynasties, it seems
unlikely that T'ang was the first dynasty to make this taboo into law.
However, no matter how strong tradition and law were, there were
always deviations. We know of some in later dynasties, when marriage
between persons of the same surnames was unlawful and when violations were punished.[15] During Han times the younger sister of Empress
Lü married a Lü, and Wang Mang's wife was from another Wang
family.[16]

[11] *LCCS* 18:10a.

[12] *LCCS* 2:8a, 34:4b.

[13] *TCCS* 15:6a, 41:13a.

[14] *PHT* 9:12b; *TT* 60:346.

[15] Ch'ü T'ung-tsu, *Law and Society in Traditional China* (Paris and The Hague, 1961),
pp. 92–94.

[16] *TT* 60:345; *HS* 99B:1a.

CROSS-COUSIN MARRIAGE

Marriages between cross-cousins and maternal parallel cousins (mother's sister's children) were at times permitted and at times prohibited in China.[17] Were such marriages allowed in the Han? Yüan Chun argued in his essay that cross-cousins and maternal parallel cousins should not marry each other because of their close relationship. He mentions that the people of his time did not consider such marriages improper.[18] This must also have been true of Han times.

Emperor Wu married his father's sister's daughter (I, 22). This is the only instance of cross-cousin marriage found in our texts, but it would seem to show that marriage to one's father's sister's daughter was permissible. Yet it is not clear whether such a marriage was generally accepted in society, because Emperor Wu's marriage may have been contracted for political reasons. The princess who was so anxious to marry her daughter to the heir apparent (*HS* 97A:10a) was apparently interested in acquiring more political power. The political status and power enjoyed by a consort family was much superior to that of a princess's husband's family.

MARRIAGE BETWEEN RELATIVES OF DIFFERENT GENERATIONS

Sometimes a relative of an older generation married a relative of a younger one. Emperor Hui's empress was the daughter of his elder sister (I, 15). Fan Hung 樊宏, who was the maternal uncle of Liu Hsiu, married the latter's paternal cousin (*HHS* 32:1a, 2a). It seems that such marriages were permissible and that the problem of different generations was not taken into consideration. It may be mentioned in passing that relatives of different generations were not allowed to marry under the laws of the T'ang, Sung, Ming, and Ch'ing dynasties. According to those laws, marriage with one's sister's daughter was a serious offense.[19] However, Emperor Hui's marriage may have been contracted for political reasons. The ambitious, power-loving empress dowager, the mother of Emperor Hui and his sister, apparently intended to make her daughter's husband's family more closely associated with the imperial family (I, 15) and thereby assure her own control of political

[17] Ch'ü, *Law and Society*, pp. 95–96.
[18] *TT* 60:346.
[19] Ch'ü, *Law and Society*, pp. 94–95.

power. Similarly, a queen dowager made her father's brother's grand-daughter the empress of the new emperor, the queen dowager's grand-son (I, 36).

DIVORCE

According to the *Ta-Tai li-chi* and other sources,[20] there were seven conditions under which a man might divorce his wife: disobedience to parents-in-law, barrenness, adultery, jealousy, incurable disease, lo-quacity, and theft.

DISOBEDIENCE TO PARENTS-IN-LAW

A daughter-in-law was obliged to serve her husband's parents as carefully and dutifully as she served her husband. Detailed instructions are given in the *Li-chi* (*LCCS* 27:2a–5a). Final instructions and warnings were again given to a woman by her parents on her wedding day that she should always obey the words of her parents-in-law (6:6b–7a). Failure to observe these duties was a serious offense and called for divorce.[21] Pan Chao emphasized the importance of pleasing the parents-in-law in her famous *Lessons for Women*: a daughter-in-law who cared about her marriage should never displease or disobey a parent-in-law.[22] This warning was based on the commonly accepted assumption that the will of the parents-in-law in determining the daughter-in-law's married life was more important than the affection of her husband. It was held that a son should treat his wife nicely, even if he did not like her, if she served his parents well and was liked by them. But if she was disliked by them, she had to be divorced by her husband, even if he loved her.[23] Since the marriage was arranged entirely by the man's parents and had nothing to do with what the husband wanted, it follows that the will of the parents, not the husband, also counted for the dissolution of the marriage.

There is evidence that disobedience to parents-in-law was actually used as a reason to divorce a wife in Han times. A man blamed and

[20] Tai Te, *Ta-Tai li-chi*, in *WYT*, 13:6a, hereafter cited as *TTL*; *K'ung-tzu chia-yü*, *SPPY* ed., 6:13a, hereafter cited as *KTCY*; *Ch'un-ch'iu Kung-yang chuan chu-su*, *SPPY* ed., 8:10a, hereafter cited as *KYCS*.

[21] *LCCS* 27:5a–b; *KYCS* 8:10a; *TTL* 13:6a; *KTCY* 6:13a.

[22] *HHS* 84:11a–b; Nancy Lee Swann, *Pan Chao: Foremost Woman Scholar of China* (New York, 1932), p. 88.

[23] *LCCS* 27:6a; *HHS* 84:11b.

divorced his wife because she was late in getting water from the river when his mother was thirsty (I, 39). Another woman was sent away by her husband because she shouted at a dog in the presence of her mother-in-law (*HHS* 29:7b–8a). He apparently considered this rude and disrespectful. The husband took the initiative in both cases. The poem "The Peacock Flies to the Southeast" tells the story of a man who could not keep his beloved wife simply because she was disliked by his mother. Having failed to persuade his mother to let her stay with them, he and his wife committed suicide together.[24] It would seem that it did not matter much whether the daughter-in-law had actually disobeyed or failed to serve her parents-in-law; everything depended upon their attitude.

BARRENNESS

Male issue was considered the most important obligation of a family. Mencius once remarked that not to have offspring was one of the three most unfilial types of behavior.[25] Since the ultimate purpose of a marriage was the continuation of the family line, failure to fulfill this obligation brought serious consequences. The woman was commonly blamed for lack of offspring, so she was to be divorced if she bore no son for the family. Barrenness was a valid reason for divorcing one's wife in a society in which male descendants were considered most important to a family.[26] However, we do not know whether a man had to wait for a certain number of years before he could ask for a divorce on the grounds of barrenness.[27] It is also not clear whether concubinage was a modifying factor: was a wife still to be divorced if one of her husband's concubines had given birth to a son? There is only one known instance in which a wife was divorced because she had no son,[28] and there is no mention of her age or whether there were concubines in the family.

[24] *Ku shih yüan*, ed. Shen Te-ch'ien, *SPPY* ed., 4:1a–4a, hereafter cited as *KSY*.
[25] *MTCS* 7B:6b.
[26] *KYCS* 8:10a; *TTL* 13:6a; *KTCY* 6:13a.
[27] Under T'ang and Sung law a wife could not be divorced for barrenness if she was forty-nine or younger. Under Ming and Ch'ing law a wife over fifty without a son might appoint the son of a concubine to be the heir (Ch'ü, *Law and Society*, p. 119, n. 159).
[28] *TKHC* 19:7a.

ADULTERY

Adultery was another reason for divorcing a wife. Such behavior was intolerable, because the children borne by a woman who had had sexual relations with another man might be of different origin and thus mix the blood of the family.[29]

JEALOUSY

In a society that institutionalized polygamy a woman was not expected to be jealous. Jealousy would make concubinage impossible. It would also be impossible to maintain order in the family if a group of women were jealous of each other. Thus jealousy in a woman was considered an evil that brought disorder to the family and called for divorce.[30] One wife was divorced because she was so jealous that her husband was prevented from having a concubine (*HHS* 28B:20a–b). Another man who had a wife and a number of concubines divorced his wife because of her jealousy (I, 34).

INCURABLE DISEASE

Since ancestor worship was an important function of marriage and the wife had an important role in sacrificial activities, failure to perform such functions certainly affected her status. Thus, having an incurable disease[31] constituted another reason for divorcing a wife, because a woman who had one was not qualified to prepare sacrificial rice.[32]

LOQUACITY

A family was composed of blood relatives and their wives. Since the women came from different families and usually were strangers to each other, it was held that each should be concerned only with her husband's interests and show no affection for each other or for the husband's blood relatives. Otherwise there would be conflicts of interest, and gossip usually brought about more conflicts. Then discord might

---

[29] *KYCS* 8:10a; *TTL* 13:6a; *KTCY* 6:13a.
[30] *KYCS* 8:10a; *TTL* 13:6a; *KTCY* 6:13a.
[31] On incurable diseases, see Ch'ü, *Law and Society*, p. 120, n. 166.
[32] *KYCS* 8:10a; *TTL* 13:6a; *KTCY* 6:13a.

occur between brothers under the influence of their wives. So in order to maintain peace and harmony in a family, a woman was not to be allowed to talk improperly. It was explained that loquacity constituted a reason for divorcing a wife because such action sowed discord among relatives.[33] A wife was divorced because she complained that it was better not to have a brother-in-law like the one who was supported by her husband and who did not work (I, 28). Another woman was divorced because she suggested to her husband that they live separately from his brothers; he thought that such talk would lead to his estrangement from his mother and brothers (I, 62).

It is obvious that the husband's relatives were as important as the husband in determining a wife's status, and perhaps sometimes they were more important. It is mentioned in the *Li-chi* that a woman had to be obedient to parents-in-law and harmonious with her husband's sisters and sisters-in-law before she could please her husband (*LCCS* 61:5a). For this reason Pan Chao emphasized that a woman had to win the hearts of her husband's sisters and brothers (*HHS* 84:12a–13a).

Theft

Theft was the last of the seven reasons for divorce.[34] One man divorced his wife because she picked some jujubes from a neighbor's tree that overhung their yard (I, 28).

None of the seven conditions for divorcing a wife was primarily concerned with the interests of the husband or the wife, and theft was the only condition not closely connected with family interests. We do not know whether the seven conditions were put down in Han law as they were in T'ang and later laws. Some Chinese authors believe that they were included in Han law also, but there are no data to support this assumption.[35] Judging from the various cases found in our texts, it is certain that they were widely accepted and practiced in Han times.

Was it possible for a husband to divorce his wife for some reason other than these seven conditions? There is a record of one man who divorced his wife because he hoped that he could marry the niece of a high official (I, 71). We do not know whether he simply divorced her

[33] *KYCS* 8:10a; *TTL* 13:6a; *KTCY* 6:13a.

[34] *KYCS* 8:10a; *TTL* 13:6a; *KTCY* 6:13a.

[35] Ch'eng Shu-te, *Chiu-ch'ao lü-k'ao* (2 vols.; Shanghai: Commercial Press, 1927), p. 141, hereafter cited as *CCLK*.

or found some excuse to justify his action. But it seems that there was no law in Han times that provided punishment for a husband who divorced his wife on grounds not included in the seven conditions.[36]

A wife, however, was given some protection. Traditionally there were three conditions under which a wife could not be divorced,[37] even if she had one of the seven faults: (1) A wife who had worn three years' mourning for a parent-in-law could not be divorced. Here again the influence of the husband's parents shows that the relationship between parents-in-law and daughter-in-law was more important than the relationship between husband and wife. (2) A wife was not to be divorced if she had no relatives in her father's family to whom she might return. (3) A wife was not to be divorced if the husband's family had been poor when they married and had since become wealthy. The case of an officer who told the emperor that a wife who had shared the husks of grain with her husband in his poverty must not be sent away after he became successful (I, 49) suggests that this tradition prevailed in those days, although there is no evidence that the regulation was put down in law.[38]

Because the husband was considered the heaven of his wife, it was usually held that a woman had no right to leave her husband.[39] It is clear that no grounds were provided for a wife to divorce her husband. However, evidence suggests that some freedom was given to women in Han times; a wife might ask for a divorce if she was not satisfied with her marriage. According to one account, a princess divorced her sick husband and married again (I, 27, n. 119). A wife who was ashamed of her husband's poverty and humble occupation insisted upon having a divorce, left him, and remarried (I, 26). A woman who considered her husband ordinary and worthless deserted him; she asked for a divorce and then married again (I, 6). This kind of action was intolerable in later days. Desertion on the part of a wife, a very serious offense, was subject to punishment under T'ang and later laws, whether she merely left her husband or she married again.[40]

---

[36] Under T'ang and Sung law the husband was to be punished with a year and a half's penal servitude; under Ming and Ch'ing law the punishment was eighty strokes (Ch'ü, *Law and Society*, p. 123).

[37] *KYCS* 8:10a; *TTL* 13:6a; *KTCY* 6:13a.

[38] *CCLK*, p. 141.

[39] *PHT* 9:5a; *HHS* 84:10b. The *I-li* mentions that a wife should consider her husband as heaven and that a son should consider his father as heaven. This notion means that the husband or father, like heaven, occupied a supreme position (*ILCS* 30:9a).

[40] The punishment for desertion was two years' penal servitude in the T'ang and

REMARRIAGE

In the first century A.D. Pan Chao emphasized in her *Lessons for Women* that a woman should be devoted to her husband and should not remarry.[41] However, her attitude was not the usual one, and although her essay was admired by such distinguished scholars as Ma Jung (*HHS* 84:13a), it seems to have had very little influence on society. At least her theory against remarriage did not conform to the mores of her time. She wrote the essay after a disagreement with her husband's sister. We do not know the details of the disagreement, but judging from what she says in the essay about remarriage not being discouraged by earlier and contemporary persons, it was probably one of the points of their discussion.

In fact, there were no restrictions against remarriage; both divorcees and widows were free to remarry. Moreover, remarriage was considered proper, and a woman who remarried was not looked down upon by society. A man of superior social and political status would not hesitate to marry such a woman. This is in contrast with the phenomena of later days, when a remarried woman was an object of disgrace.

Remarriage on the part of women took place on all socio-economic levels. Again, this is in contrast with later days when most of those who remarried were women of poor and uneducated families. In Han we find evidence of remarriages among commoners—poor as well as wealthy. Ch'en P'ing married a woman, a daughter of a rich family, who had been married five times (I, 8). Remarriages were also not uncommon among the families of literati and officials. The mother of Empress Yüan first married a petty official; later she was divorced by him and remarried (I, 34). Ts'ai Yen 蔡琰, who was a well-educated woman and whose father, Ts'ai Yung 蔡邕, was an outstanding scholar and a high official, became a widow, was captured by the Hsiung-nu, and married a barbarian. Later, after returning to China, she married a high Chinese official (I, 77). That she was not looked down upon by society, including the literati, is seen in the fact that an account of her life is included in the "Lieh-nü-chuan" 烈女傳, "The Biographies of

---

Sung dynasties, and one hundred strokes under the Ming and Ch'ing. If she remarried, the offense was more serious and was subject to a heavier punishment—three years' penal servitude in the T'ang and Sung periods, and strangling in the Ming and Ch'ing (Ch'ü, *Law and Society*, p. 118).

[41] *HHS* 84:10b; Swann, *Pan Chao,* p. 87.

Women," in the *Hou-Han-shu* (84:22a ff.). Her biography is in a chapter with other prominent women, including a woman who refused to remarry, so it would seem that remarriage was irrelevant to a woman's integrity. Ts'ao Ts'ao's son Ts'ao P'i 曹丕 married the former wife of Yüan Hsi 袁熙 when Ts'ao Ts'ao was the most powerful man in the government; when Ts'ao P'i ascended the throne, she became the empress.[42]

Even women in the highest ranks of society remarried. The granddaughter of the king of Yen remarried after she became a widow. Her daughter, who was first married to a man of the Chin family, later left him and married the heir apparent; finally she became the empress when her husband became emperor (I, 20). Only in a society in which remarriage did not influence the status of a woman could a remarried woman have become empress. The attitude of Emperor Wu, the son of the empress in question, who went to welcome his half-sister, also indicates that he was not ashamed of his mother's remarriage and made no attempt to conceal the fact. Liu Pei, the ruler of Shu 蜀, also married a widow and later made her empress when he ascended the throne.[43] The ruler of Wu, Sun Ch'üan, also married a widow, and both of his two daughters married twice.[44] In Han times it was not uncommon for a princess to remarry when divorced or widowed (I, 27, 49).

These examples show clearly that remarriage on the part of women prevailed in the whole period of Early and Later Han and occurred at all socio-economic levels. But there were a few women who refused to remarry. One widow cut off her ear and vowed not to remarry (I, 73). Another widow committed suicide because her father was forcing her to remarry (I, 70). But cases such as these were very few when compared with instances of remarriage: they are the only two found in our texts. Such extreme measures as self-mutilation and suicide also suggest that remarriage was usually expected and would take place under normal conditions. The fact that the fathers of the two women were outstanding scholar-officials is most amazing. The Huan family, the family of the woman who cut off her ear, had included outstanding scholars and officials for generations. The woman's great-great-grandfather was appointed grand tutor of the heir apparent (*t'ai-tzu t'ai-fu* 太子太傅) because of his academic reputation. Her father was a prefect (I, 73, n. 270). The family of the woman who committed suicide had been prominent

[42] *SKC*, Wei, 5:5b–6a.
[43] *SKC*, Shu, 4:2a–b.
[44] *SKC*, Wu, 5:3a–4a.

for generations. The grandfather, Hsün Shu 荀淑, was a prefect who had been known as a famous scholar. All his eight sons were men of great repute, including Hsün Shuang 荀爽, the father of the woman who killed herself. He wrote many books and held a top rank in the government. Her cousins were also famous scholars (I, 70, n. 264). Apparently a scholar of such high repute did not consider the remarriage of his daughter a disgrace to the family. It is not clear whether the father of the woman who cut off her ear had urged remarriage, but the act of self-mutilation suggests that there had been such paternal pressure. The other woman's father had arranged the marriage for his daughter and even forced her to marry. In many cases the remarriage was initiated by the woman's family. A father who was angry at his son-in-law intended to obtain a divorce for his daughter and to marry her to someone else (I, 67); nor did the husband's family consider the remarriage a disgrace to the family. There is also record of a woman who urged her daughter-in-law to remarry when she became a widow (*HS* 72:5b).

One of the most famous love affairs of the Han involves a widow who eloped and married a scholar, Ssu-ma Hsiang-ju. Her father, a wealthy merchant, considered it a disgrace and refused to give any money to her (I, 21). His action, however, should not be seen as evidence of objection to remarriage. The father was angry because she eloped and because she disregarded his authority to arrange the marriages of his children. It was the elopement that was a disgrace to the family, not the remarriage itself.

CONCUBINAGE

Concubinage was approved and sanctioned by law and society in ancient China; that is, a man was allowed to have concubines besides his legal wife. However, the majority of the male population practiced monogamy. Polygyny requires a surplus of women; although we have no information on the sex ratio in Han times, there is no reason to assume that women greatly outnumbered men in ancient China. Furthermore, the practice of female infanticide must have kept down the female population to a certain extent. In any case, most men could not afford to have more than one wife. The Han documents on wood concerning garrison troops and officers stationed in Chü-yen show that all the men had only one wife; no concubines are listed.[45]

[45] Lao Kan, *Chü-yen Han-chien*, pp. 26 (1274), 55 (2745), 65 (3281) and (3282), 66 (3287), (3289) and (3295), 82 (4069), 83 (4085), 86 (4207), 92 (4468), 102 (4963), 108 (5242), 111 (5345), 113 (5461), 113–14 (5462), 198 (9903).

On the other hand, our texts show that only upper-class and wealthy men practiced polygyny. Since having more than one wife was an indication of a man's social success, it became a status symbol. The more superior one's social status the greater the number of concubines. The emperor, the heir apparent, or a king had numerous concubines. The number and rank of their concubines was prescribed.[46] However, the number of concubines an emperor or king actually had was usually greater than the number specified in the regulations. The imperial ladies of Emperor Wu and Emperor Huan numbered several thousand.[47] According to the regulations a king was not to have more than forty concubines, but it was reported that many kings and marquises had several hundred.[48] A moderate king memorialized that he had thirty-seven concubines (I, 60). The number of concubines kept by wealthy officials was also large, although the number was not officially prescribed. It was not uncommon for officials and wealthy commoners to keep numerous concubines and singing girls with whom they could have sexual relations; a high official is said to have had several score of concubines (*HS* 72:12b, 82:8b). One imperial chancellor had a hundred concubines, and he would not have intercourse again with those who had once been pregnant (I, 19). Even wealthy eunuchs kept a number of concubines (III, 64; *HHS* 61:14a).

Probably most of the women who became concubines came from poor families that could not support them. Many women were sold as concubines or slaves during a famine or time of disorder. Some were kidnapped and sold by others. An edict issued in A.D. 31 stated that those who had become slaves or concubines as a result of famines and disorders or because they had been kidnapped by bandits in Ch'ing-chou and Hsü-chou were to be allowed to leave; anyone who prevented them from returning home was to be dealt with according to the law for selling people (II, 58). A similar edict was issued in A.D. 38 to the effect that persons of I-chou who had become concubines in order to maintain themselves were to be allowed to leave, and that anyone who detained them was to be dealt with according to the law for kidnapping (II, 61).

Not all women became concubines under these miserable conditions. There are indications that some were daughters of wealthy and prominent families. The widowed sister of Empress Hsü of Emperor Ch'eng was a concubine of a high official (*HS* 93:8a). The sister of Tou Jung

[46] *HS* 97A:2a–3a, 21a; *HHS* 10A:3a–b.
[47] *HS* 72:12a–b; *HHS* 10B:11b.
[48] *HHC* 28:11a, note; *HS* 72:12b.

竇融, whose family had been distinguished for generations, was a concubine of a grand minister of works (*ta-ssu-k'ung* 大司空), Wang I 王邑 (*HHS* 23:1b).

Concubinage, though a form of polygyny, was based on the assumption that although a man could have a number of concubines, he could have only one legal wife. For a man to have more than one wife at a time constituted bigamy. Strictly speaking, concubinage was not considered marriage. The wedding ceremony was the basic criterion of marriage: it was said that when a girl was espoused by betrothal she was a wife; when a girl came to the man's family without a wedding ceremony she was a concubine.[49] Thus a strict distinction was made between a wife and a concubine. The status of a concubine was inferior to that of a wife, whom she had to serve and before whom she had to observe a humble attitude.[50] To treat a concubine as a wife, or vice versa, was traditionally held improper and strictly prohibited.[51] Such action usually brought about severe criticism and many objections.[52] A marquis in Han was dismissed and moved to another place because he interchanged the status of his wife and his concubine (*HS* 18:9b).

A son whose mother was a concubine also had a status inferior to the sons of the wife. There is a case in which a son of an unfavored concubine of a king was not well treated by his father and his half brother, the heir apparent (*HS* 53:18a). Kung-sun Tsan 公孫瓚, whose family had included high officials for generations, was nonetheless only a petty official in the commandery government because of his mother's inferior status (*HHS* 73:6b).

Because several women had to live together with one husband, there was always the problem of how to minimize jealousy and disagreement in order to maintain the necessary domestic peace. An ideology was worked out to justify the practice of having concubines and to condemn jealousy among the women. Girls were educated by their parents and society to be generous; jealousy was considered improper and was ridiculed. At the same time, supreme authority was given to the husband so he could control his wife and concubines and maintain family order. More important, he was given authority to divorce his wife if

---

[49] *LCCS* 28:7a.

[50] *PHT* 9:15a. A good example of serving the wife is seen in *HHS* 10A:24b–25a.

[51] When Duke Huan of Ch'i held a meeting with the feudal lords of the various states in 651 B.C., one of the regulations he announced, and to which the others assented, was that one should not make his concubine a wife (*MTCS* 12B:1a).

[52] *KYCS* 11:1a–b; *TCCS* 60:10a.

she was jealous. This certainly was the most effective means devised by man for dealing with a jealous woman.

Under the sanction of social pressure it is no wonder that many women acted according to the expected behavior pattern: they seemed not to be jealous. An imperial concubine, worrying over the small number of royal descendants, was so generous that she always recommended her attendants to the emperor and treated kindly those palace ladies who had been favored by the emperor (I, 52). Another generous honorable lady (*kuei jen* 貴人) who did not want to monopolize the favor of the emperor frequently refused to accept his attentions and asked him to have intercourse with other imperial concubines in a set order (I, 66). Among these generous women undoubtedly some of them, convinced that generosity was a woman's virtue, accepted the expected pattern; but just as surely some of them, jealous at the bottom of their hearts, under social pressure pretended not to be.

On the other hand, deviations were not uncommon. There were many women who did not care about social sanction and showed their jealousy openly. For example, a jealous wife was divorced by her husband, who kept many concubines (I, 34), and there must have been other cases that went unrecorded. There were possible deviations among both the husbands and the wives: a woman might deviate from the expected pattern and be jealous, and a man might deviate from the pattern and tolerate a jealous wife. The wife of Liang Chi 梁冀, the grand general (*ta-chiang-chün* 大將軍), was so jealous that he did not dare openly to keep a concubine (*HHS* 34:16b–17a).

Jealousy was more complicated in the family of the emperor or a king. Since the women kept in the inner palace were numerous, many of the imperial concubines did not have an opportunity to see the emperor or king very often. A woman might not have intercourse with the emperor for a year (*HS* 97A:6b); it was not even uncommon for a woman never to have a chance to see the emperor from the time she entered the palace (*HS* 10:13a). The chance was still less when one or a few beautiful women monopolized an emperor or a king. Since most of them were sitting idle, they must have been unhappy and jealous. Apparently the struggle for attention was very intense.

Furthermore, the problem of jealousy was complicated because of the desire for power. The empress usually possessed power over all other imperial ladies and also brought power to her father's family. Competition and jealousy always prevailed among the imperial concubines when an empress had not yet been appointed by the emperor.

Even when one of them was appointed, jealousy was still inevitable simply because the imperial concubines who were favorites of the emperor were always a threat to the empress, especially when she became older and less attractive. And favored concubines attempted to gain more favor, hoping to replace the empress.[53] Since the mother of the heir apparent was certain to become empress dowager and acquire the accompanying power when he became emperor, the jealousy of an empress was always intensified when she herself had no son but a son had been born to an imperial concubine.[54] The members of the consort family were sometimes so worried about the problem of a childless empress that they took an active part in solving it, either by human efforts or by magical means (*HS* 97A:7b, 20b). Jealousy was also intensified because of power politics when an empress had a son who was in danger of being replaced as heir apparent by the son of a favored concubine (I, 9; *HHS* 10A:6b). The hate and cruelty of Empress Dowager Lü, who murdered the prince and then mutilated his mother, can only be understood against the background of power politics (I, 9).

An emperor was in a position to exercise great control over his wives, for he possessed absolute power either to dismiss a jealous wife or to punish her by ordering her to commit suicide.[55] This sort of power not only overshadowed the husband-wife relationship but also conditioned the behavior of the palace women. Women in the imperial palace must have had to depend upon some kind of artifice to get rid of rivals they were jealous of. Thus jealousy was usually expressed in some tactful and subtle way: slander or a clever plot was common; sometimes the help of magic was called upon.[56] Many clever women were patient enough to conceal their jealousy and wait for a chance to take revenge after the emperor's death (I, 9; *HHS* 10B:12a). A woman dared to be jealous openly only when she could monopolize the affections of the emperor and control the situation, as in the case of Empress Chao, or when she was under the protection of her powerful family, as in the case of Empress Liang, who was the sister of the powerful grand general.[57]

---

[53] *HS* 97B:9a–11b; *HHS* 10A:6b, 22a, 25a–26a.
[54] *HS* 97A:12a, 97B:12b–16a; *HHS* 10B:1a, 10b, 11b.
[55] *HS* 97A:12a; *HHS* 10A:6b, 10b, and 22a–b, 10B:11b and 14b.
[56] *HS* 53:13b–16b, 97A:12a; *HHS* 10A:25a–b.
[57] *HS* 97B:14b–15a; *HHS* 10B:10b.

Chapter Three

POSITION OF WOMEN

WOMAN'S STATUS IN THE FAMILY

Humility and weakness were the patterns of behavior set for women in ancient Chinese society under the principle that women were inferior to men. Pan Chao[1] elaborated on this point in her famous *Lessons for Women:*

In ancient times, people put a baby girl on the ground on the third day after her birth. . . . To lay the baby on the ground signifies that she is inferior and weak, and that she should humble herself before others. . . . To be modest, yielding, and respectful; to put others first, and herself last; not to mention it when she does a good deed; not to deny it when she commits a wrong; to bear disgrace and humiliation; and always to have a feeling of fear—these may be said to be the ways in which she humbles herself before others. . . .

Yin and *yang* are not of the same nature; men and women behave differently. Rigidity is the virtue of the *yang;* yielding is the function of the *yin*. Strength is the glory of men; weakness is women's good quality. Thus in self-cultivation, nothing equals respect for others; in avoiding confrontation with strength, nothing equals compliance. Therefore it is said that the way

[1] For the life of Pan Chao and her "Nü-chieh" 女誡 *(Lessons for Women)*, see *HHS* 84:5a–13b; Nancy Lee Swann, *Pan Chao: Foremost Woman Scholar of China* (New York, 1932), pp. 25 ff.

of respect and compliance is woman's great *li* (proper rule of conduct).[2]

Women were always taught to be submissive to the authority of men. The *I-li* and the *Li-chi* mention three stages of subordination for a woman: to her father when she is a girl, to her husband when married, and to her son after the death of her husband.[3] Since every child was under the absolute control of the father, the first stage of subordination needs no special comment. The real subordination to a man began with marriage: the husband had full authority over his wife. By the time of the Han the recognition of such authority by society led to the development of the theory of *san-kang* 三綱, the three dominations. Under this theory the husband should dominate his wife in much the same way the ruler dominates his ministers and the father dominates his sons.[4] Thus a wife was expected to serve her husband respectfully and obediently.[5] Pan Chao instructed her daughters that a wife should never treat with contempt, quarrel with, or scold her husband. Such actions, as she saw it, would anger her husband and destroy the harmonious matrimonial relationship.[6]

The model of an obedient wife is the wealthy woman who returned to her father's family all the luxurious garments and ornaments she had received as dowry, and who wore short clothes made of hempen cloth when she learned that her husband was displeased with her and had complained about her way of living. She said to him, "Since I am at your service, I only follow your orders."[7] The case in which both the mother and the son came to apologize to the father and did not dare ascend to the main room until he accepted their apology illustrates the humble submission of the wife and the dignity and authority of the husband (see document I, 68). It also suggests that both the wife and

[2] *HHS* 84:7b–9a; cf. Swann, *Pan Chao,* pp. 83–84.

[3] *LCCS* 26:11a; *TTL* 13:6b; *KYCS* 6:3b; *PHT* 9:16a.

[4] *PHT* 7:15a; Tjan Tjoe Som, *Po Hu T'ung: The Comprehensive Discussions in the White Tiger Hall* (2 vols.; Leiden: E. J. Brill, 1949–52), II, 559; *Han-wen-chia,* quoted in *LCCS* 39:1b, note; *Lun-yü, SPPY* ed., 2:6a, Ma Jung's commentary; Tung Chung-shu, *Ch'un-ch'iu fan-lu, SPPY* ed., 10:5b, 1a: 6b, hereafter cited as *CCFL.*

[5] Giving their daughter final instructions on her wedding day, the parents usually said, "Be respectful and cautious, do not disobey your husband" (*MTCS* 6A:2b; James Legge, *The Chinese Classics* [5 vols. in 8; Hong Kong and London, 1861–72], II, 141). Pan Chao emphasized that controlling his wife was the role of the husband and serving her husband was the role of the wife (*HHS* 84:8b; Swann, *Pan Chao,* p. 84).

[6] *HHS* 84:9b–10a; Swann, *Pan Chao,* pp. 85–86.

[7] I, 35; see a similar case in *HHS* 83:12b.

the children were under the authority of the family head. Teng Chih 鄧騭, whose son had received a gift from a corrupt official, shaved the head of his wife and his son to acknowledge this fault to Empress Dowager Teng, his younger sister (I, 65). Since shaving the head, *k'un* 髡, was a regular punishment in Han times,[8] Teng's action implied that his wife was punished for her failure to fulfill the role of a mother.

But not all women acted passively and subordinately, for we also have records of women of strong personality and extraordinary ability. The daughter of Ma Jung, an outstanding scholar and official, was very eloquent and was able to overturn her husband's arguments when, on their wedding night, he attempted to ridicule her and her father (*HHS* 84:17a–b). A woman with a strong personality was usually able to influence her husband directly or indirectly. There are two recorded instances in which a husband's intention to dwell in seclusion was influenced by his wife's encouragement (I, 47; *HHS* 83:12b). Occasionally a wife was responsible for changing her husband's whole way of thinking. A young man who found and picked up a piece of gold was ashamed of himself, threw away the gold, and went to study with a teacher when his wife told him it was improper to possess things belonging to others. When he returned home to visit her one year later, she told him that returning before his study was completed was like cutting the unfinished cloth on a loom. Convinced, as well as depressed, by her words, he went back to study and did not return for seven years (I, 43). Apparently it is not an exaggeration to say that the man owed his education to his wife's efforts and that she greatly influenced his personality.

Usually a wife was allowed to be active only in domestic affairs; she was not supposed to be interested in social and political activities and was not allowed to interfere in such matters, which were considered exclusively men's affairs. However, a woman who had extraordinary determination might take an active part in men's business. An official's wife who was skilled in writing essays and calligraphy frequently wrote letters for her husband (*HHS* 84:19a). A woman of strong personality might even dominate her husband in his official affairs. When Grand General Ho Kuang sent a representative to tell Imperial Chancellor

[8] Shaving the head and wearing an iron collar, *k'un-ch'ien* 髡鉗, a five-year sentence, were punishments applicable to convicts sentenced to build the city wall at dawn, *ch'eng-tan* 城旦. See Shen Chia-pen, *Han-lü che-i*, in *Shen chi-i hsien-sheng i-shu chia-pen* (1929), 9:5a–6b, hereafter cited as *HLCI*; *CCLK*, pp. 51–52; A.F.P. Hulsewé, *Remnants of Han Law* (Leiden: E. J. Brill, 1955), I, 129.

Yang Ch'ang 楊敞 that they had decided to dethrone the emperor, Yang Ch'ang was so frightened he did not know what to say. Then his wife warned him: "This is an important affair of the empire. Now the Grand General has decided after deliberation and sent one of the Nine Ministers to report it to you. If you do not respond promptly, are not of the same mind as the Grand General, and hesitate without decision, you will be killed first." Then she and her husband talked together with the guest, and Yang Ch'ang promised to obey Ho Kuang's order (I, 31). Obviously, it was she who made the decision and dominated her husband. However, women of such dominating character and broad insight in politics were rare.

A wife who could manage and dominate her husband was usually respected and looked up to by him. It was said that Liang Chi's beautiful wife was very jealous and was able to manage and control him. She made him remove the Liangs from government positions and replace them with members of her family. He did not dare to keep his concubine openly, and had to hide her child. Finally she seized the concubine, cut off her hair, and beat her (*HHS* 34:16b–17a). In this unusual situation it seems that the expected "wife-subordinate-to-husband" pattern was reversed.

The status of the mother in the family needs special attention. Theoretically, children were under the authority of their parents, and no distinction was made between father and mother. The children were supposed to be filial to both and obey both.[9] However, the mother's status was conditioned by another basic principle: a wife was inferior to her husband. Thus the mother's status was also inferior to the father's. The point that there was only one supreme head in the family, and that the mother was not as superior as the father, was usually emphasized by ancient scholars.[10] A child wore a full three years' mourning for his father, but he only wore one year's mourning for his mother when the father was still alive.[11] It was explained that since three years' mourning was assigned for the father, the supreme head of the family, the mourning for the mother had to be reduced. Therefore, the mother was also under the control of the family head, the husband and father, and she was expected to obey him. There was no problem when father and mother agreed; but when disagreement and conflict arose, the father's

[9] In a chapter in the *Li-chi* giving instructions on how children should serve their parents, father and mother are mentioned together (*LCCS, chüan* 27 and 28).

[10] *Hsün-tzu*, 9:14a, hereafter cited as *HT; LCCS* 54:8b.

[11] *ILCS* 30:3b–4a.

authority took precedence. This point has already been discussed regarding the authority of the parents to arrange the marriages of their children. I have also indicated that both mother and children were under the authority of the same family head.

The problem of the mother's status was more complicated after the death of her husband. Theoretically, no one in the family was superior to a mother after the death of her husband; so she should have had the highest authority. But it was also held that a woman should obey her son after the death of her husband, which was in keeping with the belief that women were inferior to men. So the two theories were in conflict: If a son was to obey the will of his father and mother, how could a mother be expected to obey her son and be subordinate to him? Was there a change in the status of the mother and of the son after the father's death? Since a woman was unlikely to be a family head and it was usually the son who became the head if there were no other senior male members of the family, it seems that there was a change in the son's status when he became a family head. However, it does not follow that there was a change in the mother's status and that the mother was under the son's authority. On the contrary, there are indications that a son was still subject to his mother's authority after the death of his father. The mother's authority over a son is clearly illustrated in "The Peacock Flies to the Southeast." In this poem the mother becomes angry with her son, who wants to keep his wife in the family; finally, on the mother's orders, the wife is sent away.[12] Sometimes a mother even had a voice in her son's public life. Yen Yen-nien 嚴延年, a grand administrator who resorted to severe punishments to maintain law and order, was merciless in killing powerful and evil persons. Once his mother came from her native town to Lo-yang to visit him. She disapproved of his harsh policy and refused to go to his official residence. She allowed him to see her only after he had removed his hat and kowtowed; she then rebuked him and told him to be benevolent to the people, and he again kowtowed and apologized (*HS* 90:19a).

In short, there is no evidence to support the theory that a mother was subordinate to her son after the death of the father. I am inclined to think that it would be misleading to treat the so-called mother's subordination and the other two kinds of subordination on the same basis.

[12] *KSY* 4:1a–4a.

WOMEN'S STATUS IN SOCIETY

PROFESSIONAL AND ECONOMIC STATUS

Most women engaged in weaving and domestic work;[13] even the wife of an imperial chancellor did some weaving in her home (II, 36). But women in wealthy families were not usually expected to undertake productive tasks; only the women of poor families had to work. The family's profession generally conditioned the kind of work a woman was supposed to do; the women in farmers' families, for example, usually had to work on the farm (*SC* 8:4a). Weaving was the most common profession for women, either to provide clothing for the family or to supplement the family income. Usually women's work provided only a part of the family income, but occasionally a woman had the full responsibility of supporting her family when her husband was not engaged in productive work. For example, the wife of a gambler managed to support his mother (I, 67). And I have already mentioned the husband who left home and engaged in study for seven years. During his absence his wife wove to support her mother-in-law and sometimes even managed to send supplies to him (I, 43). It was not uncommon for a woman who had lost her husband to become the sole support of her family, often undergoing great hardship. One widow sold silk fabrics to support herself and her son (*HHS* 71:11a–b). Another widow with a twelve-year-old son made a living by making straw sandals in the capital. He was able to study for more than ten years and finally became an official; without his mother's support he would have remained an office boy in the commandery government and would not have had a chance for an official career (*HS* 84:1a–b). Liu Pei was also supported by his widow-mother who made shoes and straw mats.[14]

Some women of well-to-do families engaged in profitable businesses, and such trade sometimes provided opportunities for them to associate with customers of the upper class. A mother who sold pearls frequently went to the family of a princess; because of this connection her son became a paramour of the princess (*HS* 65:9a).

The most successful woman entrepreneur in ancient China was a

[13] I, 39, 43. Pan Chao mentions in her *Lessons for Women* that *fu-kung* 婦功, womanly work, was one of the four basic womanly qualities, and that a woman should devote herself to sewing, weaving, and preparing wine and food to serve to guests (*HHS* 84:10a–b; Swann, *Pan Chao*, p. 86).

[14] *SKC*, Shu, 2:1a.

widow whose husband's family owned cinnabar mines in Szechwan and who was able to keep and manage the business. Because of her great wealth she was well known all over the empire and was treated as his guest by the First Emperor of Ch'in, who built a terrace in her honor.[15] But such great success for a woman was unparalleled in Chinese history. It would have been impossible for a woman to accumulate so much wealth if her family had not left the well-developed enterprise to her. However, her managerial ability in operating such a big enterprise should not be overlooked.

Only a few occupations were open to women. Since magic was very popular in Ch'in and Han times, and since there was a division of labor based upon sex,[16] there was a considerable demand for sorceresses.[17] But because sorcery was a humble profession, the status of a sorceress and her family must have been inferior (II, 65).

The profession of a woman physician was a respected one. Sometimes opportunities for social mobility were given to her family members because of her professional connections with important families. A woman physician was an intimate friend of the wife of the grand general, and through his influence her husband was promoted to a higher post (*HS* 97A:25a–b). The brother of one woman physician, who was the personal physician of the empress dowager, was appointed prefect and was later promoted to the post of grand administrator.[18]

Perhaps singing and dancing were the most common professions for girls. Some cities were noted for providing singing and dancing girls, and there were specialists who brought up girls of poor families and trained them to dance and sing.[19] Beautiful girls with such skills were usually sought by the families of nobles, officials, and wealthy commoners.[20] They served as entertainers in the family as well as giving sexual satisfaction to their masters. Since the occupation of these girls

---

[15] *SC* 129:6b–7a; *HS* 91:5b.

[16] According to *CLCS* 26:5b–6b, sorcerers were concerned with certain sacrifices and the removal of diseases, and sorceresses were mainly concerned with purifying ceremonies (a ceremony, sacrifice, or bath to wipe out evil spirits, *fu-ch'u* 祓除 and *hsin-yü* 釁浴) and *yü* 雩, dances performed to pray for rain during a drought.

[17] *SC* 28:10b and *HS* 25A:14b–15a mention that Emperor Kao employed sorceresses from various places to worship various gods. Wang Fu 王符 complained that women in his time paid no attention to cooking and gave up weaving and taking care of silkworms; instead they learned sorcery and praying and engaged in music and dancing to worship the gods (*HHS* 49:6b–7a).

[18] *SC* 122:12a; *HS* 90:5b.

[19] *SC* 129:9a, 13b; *HS* 97A:22a–23a.

[20] *HS* 72:12b, 97A:23a, 97B:11a.

was not respected by society, their status was very inferior. However, a singing girl who was able to win the favor of her master sometimes ascended to a superior status and at times even brought social mobility to her father's family. The mother of the First Emperor of Ch'in was originally a dancing girl owned by a wealthy merchant (II, 3). Empress Wei was originally a singing girl of a princess. Her brother, Wei Ch'ing 衛青, became grand general, and her sister's son, Ho Ch'ü-ping 霍去病, was appointed general (*chiang-chün* 將軍), a post next only to Wei Ch'ing's (*HS* 97A:12b). Empress Chao was also a dancing girl in the family of a princess; because of her, her father was ennobled marquis (*HS* 97B:11a–b). Wang Weng-hsü 王翁須, who was the daughter of a poor family and who entered the family of the heir apparent as a singing girl, became the favorite of the son of the heir apparent. She gave birth to the future Emperor Hsüan. When he ascended the throne, Weng-hsü's mother, as well as her two brothers, were ennobled and became wealthy. Later, the son of the elder brother, Wang Chieh 王接, was appointed general of chariots and cavalry (*chü-ch'i chiang-chün* 車騎將軍), and the son of the younger one, Wang Shang 王商, became the imperial chancellor (*HS* 97A:21b–23b). Overnight, the status of the family changed entirely because of the singing girl.

Chinese women of Ch'in and Han times were not usually given as much education as men. Yet there were some outstanding women scholars.[21] Most of them were daughters of great scholars. When Fu Sheng 伏生, a Ch'in erudite (*po-shih* 博士) and a specialist in the *Shang-shu*, was too old to give lectures, Ch'ao Ts'o 鼂錯 was sent by the Han government to take lessons from Fu's daughter (*HS* 88:10b, note). It was Pan Chao, the daughter of Pan Piao 班彪, who completed the unfinished parts of the *Han-shu*, written by her brother, Pan Ku 班固, and from whom Ma Jung learned the meaning of the text.[22] Ts'ai Yung had a large collection of books and lost all of them during the war. After his death, his daughter, Ts'ai Yen, who could recite many of them, wrote them down at the request of Ts'ao Ts'ao (*HHS* 84:22b–23a). However, no woman was occupied as a teacher; probably there was no demand for women professional teachers.

Women were never appointed officials, although Pan Chao was summoned by Emperor Ho to continue the editing of the *Han-shu*, and she was frequently ordered to write essays when precious items of tribute were offered to the emperor. Furthermore, she was treated as a teacher

---

[21] I, 77; *HHS* 52:1b, 84:5a-b and 19b.
[22] *HHS* 84:5a–b; Swann, *Pan Chao*, pp. 61–69.

by the empress and some of the concubines. When Empress Dowager Teng personally attended the court, Pan Chao also participated in government affairs. Although she was given no official title, her son was ennobled as marquis and appointed chancellor of the state of Ch'i, apparently as a reward for her role and merit in the court (*HHS* 84:5a–b).

POLITICAL STATUS

Most women were not directly concerned with politics, nor were they given the chance to engage in government affairs. Women did not usually have a status in the political mechanism; however, some had influence in politics because of the political status of their husbands. The case of the wife of an imperial chancellor who urged her husband to accept the decision to dismiss the emperor, mentioned above, illustrates this point (I, 31).

Because a woman usually had no independent status of her own, her status depended on her family's—on her father's or brother's when she was unmarried and on her husband's or son's when she was married. However, the daughter of an emperor or a king, who held the title of princess and had a political status similar to a king or marquis,[23] usually conditioned the status of her husband and his family. Thus a man who married a princess not only shared the income of her fief but also had a superior status. Usually only a marquis could be the husband of a princess (*HS* 68:3b). In one instance even the paramour of a princess was able to make friends with the emperor and high officials (*HS* 65:9a–12a). Another paramour of a princess almost succeeded in getting the title of marquis and a high post (*HS* 68:3b). Certain political and legal privileges were given to the son of a princess. Since the daughter of an emperor always had a status comparable to a marquis, and her fief was classified as a marquisate, her eldest son inherited her fief and became a marquis.[24] The son of a princess had a special legal status: when he was accused of a crime, permission had to be obtained from the emperor before he could be tried and punished—a kind of legal privilege enjoyed by members of the imperial family, the heir of a marquis, and officials of certain ranks (*HS* 65:8a).

Because a princess was superior in status to her husband and his family members, there was a tendency to reverse the usual pattern of

[23] *HHS* 10B:23b–24a.
[24] *HHS* 10B:24a–b; *HHC* 28:7b.

wife-subordinate-to-husband. Hsün Shuang complained about this, saying in a memorial that the domination of a princess over her husband was contrary to the universal principle of *yin-yang* (*HHS* 62:5a–6a). In one instance a princess summoned her husband to come to her chamber and ordered him to lie under the bed while she was with her paramour. Finally the husband was unable to overcome his anger and killed the princess; he and his siblings were executed on the order of the emperor (*HHS* 47:19a–b).

A woman's status might also become independent of her father's or brother's status because of her connection with the imperial family; her new independent status would then condition the status of her father's family. Mobility and superior status were always given to the family of a woman who entered the inner palace by marriage. Usually a man was ennobled as a marquis when his daughter became empress. Also, the mother of an empress or empress dowager was sometimes ennobled.[25] The women so ennobled held the title of baronet (*chün* 君) and had a status similar to that of a princess.[26] Brothers and sometimes brothers' sons of an empress dowager were also ennobled as marquises. Furthermore, the father, brother, or some other member of a consort family often held such important official posts as imperial chancellor or grand general; this meant that great political power was concentrated in the hands of a member of the consort family. In short, the superior political and social status, as well as the political power, enjoyed by a consort family was made possible because of the woman's status. The change of family status was very striking; many families of poor and humble origin were immediately elevated into the highest social stratum when women of those families became empresses. (See the section on Consort Families in Chapter 4.)

Since the social mobility and the power of a consort family were based entirely on one of its female members, she had a new status in the family, influence which she had not previously enjoyed and which was certainly not enjoyed by a woman under ordinary conditions. She was respected by all her family members, including her seniors, for her new status gave her the power to control the male members of her family. Empress Dowager Ma was so strict with her family members that anyone who was at fault was reprehended, and one whose garments and carriages were not in accordance with the sumptuary laws was

---

[25] *HHHY* 34:35b; Hsü T'ien-lin, *Tung-Han hui-yao*, *TSCC* ed., 18:83–84, hereafter cited as *THHY*.

[26] *HHC* 29:9a, 30:18b.

sent back to his native village. When she complained that the tomb of her mother was slightly higher than that allowed by the law, her elder brother immediately made the adjustment and reduced the height of the tomb (*HHS* 10A:18a). In another case, the elder brother of an empress dowager, Teng Chih, who had discovered that his son was acting unlawfully and who feared his sister, punished his wife and son by shaving their heads in order to acknowledge their fault (I, 65). When Empress Dowager Tou was angry at her elder brother, Tou Hsien 竇憲, he was confined in the palace. Fearing that he might be punished by death, he asked to lead an expeditionary force to fight against the Hsiung-nu in order to redeem his guilt (*HHS* 23:20b). The actions illustrated in these three cases are certainly contradictory to the accepted principle that a younger brother or sister was subordinate to his or her elder siblings.

Even the "daughter-subordinate-to-father" pattern might be reversed. A man divorced his wife, and years later one of his daughters became empress. The empress ordered her father to take back her divorced mother, who had remarried and was now a widow (I, 34). Commanding a father was an action against the basic principle of the father's superior authority, and obviously it was her political status that gave her the power to do it. Her mother was divorced long before the daughter became empress. Apparently her disapproval of her father's action had been on her mind for a long time, but she would never have been able to change the marital life of her parents had she not become empress. Both Tou Wu 竇武, the father of Empress Dowager Tou, and Ho Chin 何進, the elder brother of Empress Dowager Ho, were unable to carry out their plans to dismiss all the eunuchs because the two empress dowagers disagreed with their suggestions.[27] Since the father or elder brother of an empress dowager was a minister of the state, he was obliged to treat her as his superior and accept her orders.

In the court the empress dowager enjoyed a superior status more or less comparable to the emperor's. It was often said that there existed only one ruler in the empire. For this reason even the father of Liu Pang had to give up his role of father and assume a humble role in the presence of his son who became the emperor; this action greatly pleased the latter (see p. 67). But it seems that an emperor's attitude toward his mother was different. The emperors showed affection and respect to their mothers, and often behaved humbly before them. When Empress Dowager Po learned that the heir apparent and the king of Liang had

[27] *HHS* 69:5a–b, 13b–14b.

been accused by the prefect of official carriages (*kung-chü ling* 公車令) of not dismounting before the palace gate, Emperor Wen took off his hat and apologized to her for not having brought up his sons strictly. She then sent a messenger to pardon the heir apparent and the king of Liang so that they could enter the palace.[28] Again, when the king of Liang died, Empress Dowager Tou wept and said that the emperor had killed his son. Emperor Ching was sad and tried to please her by ennobling all the children of the late king.[29]

When a dispute between two members of different consort families Tou Ying 竇嬰 and T'ien Fen 田蚡, led to a court debate, the empress dowager was greatly angered. Refusing to eat when the emperor came to dine with her, she complained: "Now I am still alive, and yet people oppress my younger [half-]brother. When I die they will all treat him as fish and meat. How can you, the emperor, act like a stone statue?" The emperor apologized and said: "Both [Tou and T'ien] are consort family members; therefore, a court debate was held. Otherwise this would be a case to be settled by a judicial official." Tou Ying was executed,[30] evidently under the pressure of the empress dowager.

The empress dowager often exerted great influence upon the emperor. Empress Dowager Tou was fond of Huang-Lao doctrines, and as a result Emperor Ching and all members of the Tou family had to read Lao-tzu and honor his methods.[31] Under the influence of Empress Dowager Wang, Emperor Wu, who was about to select an imperial chancellor and a grand commandant (*t'ai-wei* 太尉), gave the posts to Tou Ying and T'ien Fen respectively.[32] Several examples show that an empress dowager could influence the decision of the emperor and thus interfere with his administration. An official who was considered loyal by Emperor Ching was put to death under the pressure of Empress Dowager Tou.[33] She also caused the dismissal of three top officials during the reign of Emperor Wu. The emperor did not reappoint T'ien Fen, one of the three officials dismissed by the empress dowager, until after her death.[34] Emperor Ai had to dismiss Fu Hsi 傅喜 because Empress Dowager Fu disliked him.[35]

[28] *SC* 102:2b; *HS* 50:2a–b.
[29] *SC* 58:5a–b; *HS* 47:3b–4a.
[30] *SC* 107:11b–14a; *HS* 52:10b–12b.
[31] *SC* 49:7a; *HS* 97A:9a.
[32] *SC* 107:3b; *HS* 52:3a.
[33] *SC* 122:2b–3a; *HS* 70:2b–3a.
[34] *SC* 107:4a; *HS* 52:3a–4a.
[35] *HS* 82:9b, 10a–b.

At times the emperor even allowed the empress dowager to play a formal role in the court. Top officials serving under Emperor Wu were required to present copies of memorials to Empress Dowager Tou as well as to the throne.[36] The power of an empress dowager who attended the court in person was even greater. She was in a position to make important decisions and to issue orders, thus assuming the role of a ruler. In the Early Han two empress dowagers attended the court and practically controlled the government. In the Later Han nine emperors were under the domination of empress dowagers; there were altogether six empress dowagers who attended the court. Their success in manipulating power varied according to their ability and personality and also depended on the personality of the young emperor, the power of the consort family, the existence and the influence of rival forces, and so on; but there is one thing common to all cases—the empress dowagers all took advantage of the immaturity of the emperors. Thus Empress Dowager Wang attended court when the nine-year-old Emperor P'ing ascended the throne.[37] All the emperors of the Later Han who were under the domination of an empress dowager were very young.

Ordinarily an empress dowager was expected to relinquish power to the emperor when he reached maturity. Empress Dowager Liang attended the court when Emperor Huan was fifteen, but announced her retirement three years later.[38] However, Empress Dowager Teng, the most powerful woman ruler in Later Han, was able to remain in power even after the emperor was of age. At first she placed a hundred-day-old infant on the throne; after his death she put a ten-year-old boy on the throne. She ruled until her death, at which time Emperor An was twenty-seven years old; thus she held power continuously for about sixteen years. The *Hou-Han-shu* states that she exercised the power of an emperor, and that the emperor merely sat on the throne with folded hands.[39]

Since the empress dowager could not run the government by herself, she had to rely upon her father or brother, to whom she entrusted the actual administration of government affairs. Thus a member of the consort family always held the key government position when the empress dowager attended the court personally. Through the cooperation of the empress dowager and the consort family members, both the

[36] *SC* 107:4a; *HS* 52:3b.
[37] *HS* 12:1b, 98:14b.
[38] *HHS* 7:2b and 8a, 10B:6b.
[39] *HHS* 10A:23a–37b, 10B:2a.

inner palace and the outer court were under their control. This will be discussed in Chapter 5.

Chapter Four

SOCIAL CLASSES

Han society had a number of social classes, each constituting a group of persons of families of about equal prestige or—to use a term employed by Max Weber and other sociologists—status position.[1] The existence of social classes was manifested in the following ways: (1) The members of society were judged and ranked in a hierarchical order on the basis of commonly accepted values. In the eyes of contemporaries some were considered superior to others, some were inferior; moreover, a person was aware of his position in the prestige stratification. (2) There were indications of class consciousness: persons of similar status thought of each other as equals belonging to the same group. (3) Members of the same class had a similar style of life that was distinct from others. They were aware of such symbols of prestige and made an effort to cultivate and maintain them. (4) Members of the same class were considered equals or near-equals, and therefore were acceptable to each other for social interaction. A person usually married within his class. (5) Status groups enjoyed certain privileges. Sumptuary laws were formulated to guarantee these groups the monopoly of such things as style of houses,

[1] Max Weber, *From Max Weber: Essays in Sociology,* trans. H. H. Gerth and C. Wright Mills (New York: Oxford University Press, 1946), pp. 186–87, and *Max Weber: The Theory of Social and Economic Organization,* trans. A. M. Henderson and Talcott Parsons (New York: Oxford University Press, 1947), pp. 428–29.

clothing, carriages, and so forth. They were also given other legal privileges; for instance, officials could not be arrested or punished without the permission of the emperor.

On what basis were people ranked? What were the criteria of evaluation in the system of stratification?

First, people were evaluated according to their occupations. It was thought that some occupations made more of a contribution to society and were therefore more important than others.[2] To the ancient Chinese there was a basic division of labor between the mental and the physical. Mental labor, which required a great deal of learning, was indispensable to maintain the social and political order. Those who assumed such responsibility were considered superior and deserving of more esteem and better rewards than those who performed physical labor, which required little knowledge. This sort of evaluation was summed up by Mencius: "Some labor with their minds, and some labor with their strength. Those who labor with their minds govern others; those who labor with their strength are governed by others. Those who are governed by others support them; those who govern others are supported by them. This is a principle universally recognized."[3]

Mental labor became the symbol of superior status, and physical labor became a status disqualification. Mencius characterized those who performed mental labor as "great men" or *chün-tzu* 君子 in contrast to the "small men" or *hsiao-jen* 小人. This notion, which was a common belief in ancient ideology and had been widely accepted in Chinese society for centuries, provided a theoretical basis for the superior-inferior relationship between the two groups.

Second, since knowledge was a prerequisite for mental labor, education became an essential criterion of evaluation. The literati were highly respected by the society at large.

Third, wealth, which determined a person's life chances, also conditioned to a considerable degree his status position. Among other things, wealth provided the means for an education. Wealth was particularly important in Han times, because it was a preliminary qualification for

[2] Ch'ü T'ung-tsu, "Chinese Class Structure and Its Ideology," in *Chinese Thought and Institutions,* ed. John K. Fairbank (Chicago: University of Chicago Press, 1957), pp. 235–36.

[3] *MTCS* 5B:1b–2a; Legge, *Chinese Classics,* II, 125–26. For similar statements made by other scholar-officials in Chou times, see Ch'ü T'ung-tsu, *Law and Society in Traditional China* (Paris and The Hague, 1961), pp. 226–30.

the appointment to the rank of "gentleman."[4] Wealth was also necessary to maintain the style of life appropriate to a given status position.
However, wealth in many cases was a consequence of rather than an
effective means to high status position, and a person's position in the
economic order did not always correspond to his status position in the
social order. Wealthy merchants were still inferior to high officials. And
scholars, though propertyless, were generally highly respected. Thus
wealth or property per se was not always recognized as a status qualification; nor was the lack of it a status disqualification.[5]

Fourth, political power is a criterion deserving special attention.
Mencius's statement indicates clearly that the social hierarchy was
politically oriented and that there was a clear-cut demarcation between

[4] This preliminary qualification, known as *tzu-hsüan* 貲選 (selection by virtue of
property), should not be confused with the purchasing of an official post. One of the
qualifications of the candidate for official appointment, according to a Han regulation, was the possession of a certain amount of wealth. In the early days one hundred
thousand cash, ten *suan* 算, was set up as the minimum. Since this standard was too
high and many scholars who did not have enough property were blocked from entering officialdom, Emperor Ching reduced the minimum to forty thousand cash, four
suan, in 142 B.C. (*HS* 5:9a).

It is not clear whether this qualification was required of all officials or only those of
a particular group. Yao Nai, a Ch'ing scholar, argues that it applied only to the
candidates for the post of "gentleman," who were close to the emperor and needed
money for their carriages and clothing (Wang Hsien-ch'ien, *Han-shu pu-chu* [Ch'ang-sha:
Wang-shih chiao-k'an ed., 1916], hereafter cited as *HSPC*). Yen Keng-wang, who does
not agree with Yao, thinks that the qualification was applicable to all officials (Yen
Keng-wang, "Ch'in Han lang-li chih-tu k'ao," *Li-shih yü-yen yen-chiu-so chi-k'an*,
XXIII [1951], 117–18). Judging from the complaint of Tung Chung-shu to Emperor
Wu that the selection of gentlemen and *li* (the petty officials of the various bureaus in
the central government and subordinate officials of the local government) was based
upon their wealth (*HS* 56:13b), it seems that wealth was a qualification for both the
gentlemen and the *li* (Ch'ien Mu, *Kuo-shih ta-kang* [2 vols.; Taipei, 1956], I, 96–97).

In any case, it is certain that only a man possessing a certain amount of wealth was
qualified for the post of gentleman. Both Chang Shih-chih 張釋之 and Ssu-ma
Hsiang-ju were given this post by virtue of property (I, 18, and 21, n. 92). According
to Ju Shun, who quotes *Han-i-chu*, five hundred thousand cash was required for the
post of gentleman in regular attendance, *ch'ang-shih lang* 常侍郎 (I, 18, n. 73).

Finally, a word should be said about the historical developments in connection
with official appointment. The preliminary qualification for the post of gentleman
was a regulation that was in practice in the Early Han. Yen Keng-wang points out that
candidates for the post of gentleman came mainly from two channels: *jen-tzu* 任子
(those who received appointment by virtue of being the son or relative of a high official) and *tzu-hsüan*. But after Emperor Wu introduced the system of recommendation
of men as "filially pious and incorrupt," this became a new channel. *Tzu-hsüan* was
no longer in practice in the Later Han (Yen, *op. cit.*, pp. 89–90, 113–27).

[5] On the correlation between wealth and status, see *From Max Weber: Essays in
Sociology*, pp. 186–87; *Max Weber: The Theory of Social and Economic Organization*,
p. 425.

the ruler and the ruled. A close correlation existed between the distribution of power and the distribution of prestige and wealth. Official position gave its holder both power and prestige as well as the opportunity to become wealthy or to enhance his class position. A poor and propertyless man would have a superior status once he became a noble or an official; at the same time his political position could rapidly bring him wealth and property. It is no exaggeration to say that stratification in China was primarily based on political power, and wealth played only a secondary role. The higher a person's position in the political hierarchy, the higher was his status.

The distribution of prestige, wealth, and power were the three dimensions of social stratification. Each constituted a separate hierarchical order with respect to a specific value distributed among the members of society. But they were interrelated with each other, and together they represented the distribution of values in society and determined position in the stratified order. Therefore, all three must be taken into account in a study of social stratification.

Finally, a word should be said about the unit of stratification. Sociologists have convincingly emphasized that prestige or other rewards given to one member of a family have to be shared with the other members.[6] This was particularly so in ancient China, where kinship ties were strong and intimate. Certainly the children, who were taught to learn and maintain the style of life appropriate to their status group, shared the prestige of their father. But this prestige was also shared by all the members of the extended family—uncle, nephew, or paternal cousin. As shown in Chapter 5, it was not uncommon for more than one member of the family to be office holders. In such instances the social position of the family was determined by the combined status of all its members who held official ranks. Not only did family members tend to identify with each other, but also all the family members of an official were identified with him by the members of the community. For these reasons we must regard the family, rather than the individual, as the basic unit of each social class.

THE EMPEROR AND THE IMPERIAL FAMILY

At the apex of the social pyramid was the emperor, whose status and

[6] Thus Talcott Parsons sees social class as an aggregate of kinship units of approximately equal status in the system of stratification (*The Social System* [Glencoe, 1951], p. 172). See also J. A. Schumpeter, *Imperialism and Social Classes* (New York, 1951), p. 148; Bernard Barber, *Social Stratification* (New York, 1957), pp. 73–76.

power were unique and without parallel. Strictly speaking, the emperor
was not a class, for there was no other person of equal prestige and
power. He was the source of all power, and all others merely acquired
a share of power through him.

The term *huang-ti* 皇帝 (emperor), which was initiated by the First
Emperor of Ch'in, was "the title for the most venerable" 至尊之稱.[7] The
title Son of Heaven, which continued to be used in Ch'in and Han times,
had been the conventional designation for the emperor in Chou and
earlier times. But the power of the Son of Heaven in feudal times was
in no way comparable to that of the emperor of the Ch'in and Han
dynasties. In the earlier period feudal lords enjoyed a great amount of
freedom, and the Son of Heaven was unable to interfere with the in-
ternal administration of the feudal states. It was the First Emperor of
Ch'in who unified the whole empire and introduced centralized government. Before his conquests no ruler had ever been so powerful and no
sovereignty so extensive. For this reason the First Emperor of Ch'in
initiated the title *huang-ti* to show his superiority over the Son of Heaven
of earlier days. Han rulers used the same title.[8]

The emperor's title as Son of Heaven has two important implica-
tions. Theoretically the emperor was appointed by the decree of Heaven
and was therefore responsible only to Heaven and subject to no human
authority. Heaven alone had the right and the power to dismiss him
from the throne. The ideology that the emperor was the Son of Heaven
but the parent of the people (*HS* 72:26a) indicates that he had a unique
status under the sun. He was inferior to and subject only to the will of
Heaven, while all human beings were inferior to him and under his
command. This even included his own parents. The mother of the king
of Ch'in, who later became the First Emperor of Ch'in, was ordered by
him to leave the palace (*SC* 85:6b). When Emperor Kao ascended the
throne, he paid a visit to his father every five days and observed the
manner of an ordinary son. The household steward (*chia-ling* 家令) said
to the father, "Heaven has not two suns and the land has not two rulers.
Although the emperor is [your] son, he is the lord of men. Although
you, Venerable Sire (*t'ai-kung* 太公), are [his father], you are his subject.
Why should you make the lord of men pay respect to his subject?"
Taking the advice, the father held a broom, welcomed the emperor at
the door, and walked backwards. Emperor Kao, greatly startled, descended and supported his father. But his father said: "The emperor is

---

[7] Ts'ai Yung, *Tu tuan*, *SPTK* ed., A:1b, hereafter cited as *TYTT*.
[8] *SC* 6:10b–11b; *TYTT* A:1a–b.

the lord of men. Why should you disturb the rules of the empire on my account?"⁹ The king of Huai-nan once called Emperor Wen "elder brother," and his action was described in the *Shih-chi* as arrogant.¹⁰

The term *chen* 朕, for the first person singular, was reserved exclusively for the emperor.¹¹ Furthermore, his name could never be spoken or written;¹² those who forgot to observe the name taboo were subject to punishment (*HS* 8:13b). Neither ministers nor subjects dared to address the throne directly; whenever they addressed the emperor the term *pi-hsia* 陛下, "under the steps to the throne," was used. In indirect references the term used to designate the emperor was usually his carriage, *ch'eng-yü* 乘輿, or he was simply called *shang* 上 meaning "above" or "the superior one."¹³

The emperor enjoyed a unique style of life, which no one else was allowed to imitate. Special kinds of hats, garments, carriages, and flags¹⁴ were designed exclusively for him. A king might be given special permission to use the flags of an emperor, but one who imitated the emperor's yellow carriage top and flags without special permission acted unlawfully.¹⁵ Anyone who stole garments or other articles used by an emperor was subject to severe punishment.¹⁶ When an emperor left the palace and was on a tour, his guards cleared the roads, and no one was

⁹ *SC* 8:30b–31a; *HS* 1B:9a–b.

¹⁰ *SC* 118:1b; *HS* 44:1b.

¹¹ According to Ts'ai Yung, the word *chen*, which meant "I," was used by the superior as well as the inferior in the earlier days. During and after Ch'in times only an emperor could call himself *chen;* the practice was followed by Han (*TYTT* A:1b–2a). The *Shih-chi* says that the step was taken in 221 B.C. when the First Emperor of Ch'in united the empire and ordered his ministers to deliberate on the matter of imperial titles. He proposed and adopted the term *chen* (*SC* 6:10b–11b). The action was obviously the result of an attempt to dignify the emperor.

¹² For example, marquises had been called *ch'e-hou* 徹侯, but since Emperor Wu's name was *Ch'e* when he ascended the throne, they began to be called *lieh-hou* 列侯 or *t'ing-hou* (*HS* 19A:14b).

¹³ Ts'ai Yung explains that ministers did not dare address the emperor directly in the court. They reported to the imperial attendants who held arms and stood under the steps of the hall; this was called "reaching the superior through the inferiors" (*TYTT* A:2a–b).

¹⁴ For details see *HS* 1A:26a, note, 57A:19b, 87A:7b and 14b.

¹⁵ A few kings were granted the flags of an emperor (*SC* 58:3a; *HS* 47:2a, 53:4a). This was extraordinary, and as a rule it was illegal to use them. The king of Huai-nan was accused of imitating the yellow carriage top of the emperor's carriage (*SC* 118:1b; *HS* 44:5a). The king of Chiang-tu was charged with the same offense and also with using the emperor's flags (*HS* 53:6a–b).

¹⁶ There was an article in Han law dealing with the matter. But the sentence is incomplete and does not specify the penalty. It read: "Those who dare to steal the things worn and used by the emperor . . ." (*SC* 9:15a, note; *TYTT* A:2b).

allowed to pass except his attendants; violators were to be punished.[17] Those who intruded into the outer gate of the palace were sentenced to labor on city wall construction; those who intruded into the palace were to be executed. This law applied to officials and nobles as well as to commoners.[18]

Those who were not humble enough before the emperor and did not show respect to the emperor were punishable under the law of impiety (*pu-tao* 不道) and great disrespect (*ta-pu-ching* 大不敬).[19] Because a marquis did not dismount from his horse in front of the palace gate, he was accused of "disrespect" and was demoted in rank (*HS* 18:6b). Another marquis lost his rank because he wore a one-piece casual garment into the palace (*HS* 18:4a). A marquis who got drunk and sang in the Imperial Temple during a sacrifice was accused of "great disrespect" and committed suicide (*HS* 17:7a). An imperial guard was put in prison because he left the emperor's bow on the ground.[20] One official was executed because he disapproved of an imperial edict and criticized a deceased emperor (*HS* 75:3b–4a). An official and a commoner were accused of slandering the court and were executed.[21] To curse the emperor was great perversion (*ta-ni* 大逆) or great perversion and impiety (*ta-ni pu-tao* 大逆不道).[22] Thirteen marquises were cut in two at the waist because of such action.[23]

The power of an emperor was supreme and his word was law. All laws had to be approved and promulgated by him; only he could abolish the existing law.[24] As a rule, criminals were punished according

---

[17] Cf. *SC* 102:3b–4a; *HS* 47:2a, 50:3b, 52:13a.

[18] *HS* 16:4a, 18:4a, 97A:19b.

[19] *HS* 17:7a, 18:6b, 60:17a, 72:29a–b, 75:3b–4a, 78:14a, 80:4b–5a, 90:19a. On *pu-tao, ta-pu-ching*, and *pu-ching* 不敬, see Tu Kuei-ch'ih, *Han-lü chi-cheng*, 3:8a–9a, hereafter cited as *HLCC; HLCI* 3:10a–13a and 14b–16a; *CCLK*, pp. 114–17; A. F. P. Hulsewé, *Remnants of Han Law* (Leiden, 1955), I, 156 ff.

[20] Li Fang *et al., T'ai-p'ing yü-lan, SPTK* ed., 347:5a, hereafter cited as *TPYL*.

[21] *HS* 80:3b–6a, 90:19a.

[22] *HS* 16:20b, 66:5b. On *ta-ni* or *ta-ni pu-tao* see *HLCI* 3:2a–2b; *CCLK*, pp. 124–25; Hulsewé, *Remnants of Han Law*, I, 158 ff.

[23] *HS* 15A:13a and 13b, 16:7b, 14b–20b, and 25a, 17:3a, 5b, 6a, and 7a. Among the various cases of "cursing," two were definitely connected with black magic. Sorcerers were employed to perform the curse, and sacrifices were invoked for the purpose (*HS* 63:14b–15a, 66:5b). It is not clear whether all other persons who suffered the death penalty had employed sorcery in cursing or had been guilty of cursing in the ordinary sense. Probably most of the curses were magical.

[24] For instance, the law of collective responsibility for family members was abolished by Emperor Wen in 179 B.C. He also abolished the mutilating punishments, *jou-hsing* 肉刑, in 167 B.C. (*SC* 10:5b–6a, 13a–14a; *HS* 4:5a and 13a, 23:12b–14b). On collective responsibility and mutilating punishments see *HLCI* 9:7a–13b and 17a; *CCLK*, pp. 44–51, 58–59; Hulsewé, *Remnants of Han Law*, I, 112 ff., 124–28.

to the law, and the administration of justice was in the hands of the commandant of justice (*t'ing-wei* 廷尉). However, if the emperor insisted on his point, his will was final, and his authority superseded that of the commandant of justice.[25] He could also kill a person on his own volition; for example, Emperor Wu, for supernatural reasons, once ordered that all prisoners in the capital, regardless of the degree of their crimes, be executed (*HS* 8:1b). That the emperor was the highest judicial authority can also be shown by the fact that in certain cases final judgment was left to him. According to the system of justice all cases that could not be settled by the 2,000-picul local officials should be reported to the commandant of justice; if he was unable to make a decision, the case was to be reported to the emperor for final decision (*HS* 23:19a–b). Han law also required that permission be obtained from the emperor before nobles and certain officials could be arrested, tried, and punished.[26] Certain other special cases also had to be reported to the emperor by the commandant of justice.[27] On the other hand, a criminal might be pardoned by order of the emperor, and general amnesties were occasionally issued by the emperor for various reasons.[28]

With the exception of petty officials, all officials, central as well as local, were appointed by the emperor, and he also determined whether they should be promoted, demoted, or dismissed. Members of the imperial family, as well as certain high officials, were ennobled by the emperor.

The supremacy of the emperor may also be seen in the system of the court conference (*t'ing-i* 廷議). When there were difficult problems to settle, usually the imperial chancellor, the grandee secretary (*yü-shih ta-fu* 御史大夫), marquises, erudites, and other high officials (e.g., of the 2,000-picul rank) were ordered to hold a conference in the court. Their decision was reported to the emperor, but he might not approve it.[29] Sometimes the conclusion reached by the officials was rejected and they

[25] *SC* 102:3b–4b; *HS* 50:3a–4a.

[26] *HS* 1B:10b, 8:24a, 12:3a, 65:8a, 66:4b. For specific examples see *HS* 44:6a–b and 10b, 47:5a–b and 6b.

[27] *HS* 8:10b, 23:20a.

[28] *HS* 4:11a, 5:3b and 4a, 6:2a and 6b, 7:6b–7a; *HHHY* 63:623–31.

[29] For instance, a court conference was held in 133 B.C. to discuss peace or war with the Hsiung-nu (*HS* 52:15b–19a). The most famous debate on the policy of government control of salt and iron was held in 81 B.C. (*HS* 7:4a; Esson M. Gale, *Discourses on Salt and Iron: A Debate on State Control of Commerce and Industry in Ancient China* [Leiden: E. J. Brill, 1931], pp. 1 ff.). For a discussion of court conferences see Wang Yü-ch'üan, "An Outline of the Central Government of the Former Han Dynasty," *Harvard Journal of Asiatic Studies*, XII (1949), 173–78.

were ordered to reconsider and report again. No action could be taken until the emperor approved the suggestion.[30]

The emperor was also the highest priest in the empire. Since he was the Son of Heaven, only he was qualified to worship Heaven. He also offered sacrifices and prayers to the supreme gods, big mountains, and large rivers.[31] Furthermore, the *feng-shan* 封禪 sacrifices, which included worshipping at a sacred mountain and erecting there a stone tablet on which the merit of the emperor was engraved, were to be performed by the emperor.[32]

Next to the emperor were his imperial relatives. Among them the empress dowager occupied the highest position and was the most powerful. This was so not only because she was the wife of the late emperor, but also because she was the mother or grandmother of the reigning emperor. The last factor seems to be the more significant. Empress Dowager Wang was the empress of Emperor Yüan and the mother of Emperor Ch'eng. A lady of the Fu family, the grandmother of the future Emperor Ai, had only been an imperial concubine of Emperor Yüan. However, when her grandson ascended the throne upon the death of Emperor Ch'eng, she also became empress dowager, enjoying a status more or less comparable to that of Empress Dowager Wang, who had been very powerful during the reign of Emperor Ch'eng and who now had to restrain her activities considerably. Empress Dowager Wang was not active again until Emperor Ai died, at which time she appointed another king to be the new emperor.[33] Emperor Ai's mother, Ting, had only been a queen, but when her son became emperor, she then became the empress dowager; and Empress Chao of Emperor Ch'eng, although she also became empress dowager, obviously was less powerful than the former (*HS* 97B:12b–18a). An empress dowager of an older generation was always superior in status to one of a younger generation. Thus Empress Dowager Wang, the empress of Emperor Yüan, was more powerful than her son's wife, Empress Dowager Chao (*HS* 97B:18a–b). In Emperor Ai's time the power was in the hands of his grandmother, Empress Dowager Fu, but not of his mother, Empress Dowager Ting.

The status of an emperor's mother or grandmother was dependent upon possession of the title of empress dowager. Thus the ladies Fu and

[30] II, 17; *HS* 35:3b, 44:6a–b and 13b–14a, 53:6b and 16a–b.

[31] *SC* 28:12b–14b, 16a–b, 17a, 20a–b, 22a, and 26a–b; *HS* 25A:11a–12b, 13a–b, 14a, 16a–b, and 22a.

[32] *SC* 28:1a, 5a–6a, 9b, 21b–22a, 33b–34a, and 35a–b; *HS* 25A:5b–6a, 8b–9a, 17b, 30a–b, and 31b–32a; *HHC* 7:6a ff.; Édouard Chavannes, *Le T'ai Chan* (Paris, 1910).

[33] *HS* 82:9b and 10a, 97B:21a–b, 98:13a–14b.

Ting, the grandmother and mother of Emperor Ai, were very anxious to have conferred upon them the title of empress dowager (*HS* 82:10a, 97B:20b–21b). The mother of Emperor Ling, a lady of the Tung family, was merely the wife of a marquis and could not compete with Empress Dowager Tou, the empress of Emperor Huan. She participated in politics only after the death of Empress Dowager Tou. Moreover, when Emperor Ling died and Emperor Hsien ascended the throne, it was Empress Dowager Ho, the empress of Emperor Ling and the mother of the new emperor, who attended the court. Empress Dowager Ho refused to allow Empress (the title was honorary) Tung to interfere in politics even though she was the grandmother of the new emperor and the mother-in-law of Empress Dowager Ho, simply because she did not have the status of empress dowager (*HHS* 10B:13a–14a).

I have already pointed out that great emphasis was placed on mother-son relations in Han times and that the emperors showed great affection and respect to their mothers. The predominance of the empress dowager usually led to political dominance. It was not infrequent that an emperor sought the approval of the empress dowager in political affairs. Emperor Wen wanted to exterminate the whole family of a criminal who had stolen from the imperial ancestral temple. The commandant of justice attempted to convince him that according to the law only the criminal himself should be executed. Emperor Wen reported this to the empress dowager and only with her consent was the punishment carried out as the commandant had suggested.[34] Top officials had to present memorials to Empress Dowager Tou, who played a predominant part in government affairs. She was able to influence the decision of the emperor and interfere with the administration. Once Emperor Ching ordered his son, the king of Lin-chiang, who had occupied the land of the ancestral temple, to appear in the office of the commandant of the capital (*chung-wei* 中尉). The king requested the facilities to write to the emperor, and when Chih Tu 郅都, the commandant, refused to grant them, the king committed suicide. The empress dowager was angry and manipulated the law in order to charge Chih Tu with a certain offense. He was thus dismissed. Finally she caused his death against the wish of the emperor who wanted to exempt him from punishment. The emperor said to the empress dowager, "Chih Tu is a loyal official." She retorted, "Was not the king of Lin-chiang a loyal official?"[35] The empress dowager continued to play a domineering role

[34] *SC* 102:4a–b; *HS* 50:3b–4a.
[35] *SC* 122:2b–3a; *HS* 90:2b–3a.

over Emperor Wu, her grandson. Tou Ying, the imperial chancellor, T'ien Fen, the grand commandant, and Chao Kuan 趙綰, the grandee secretary, were followers of Confucius and condemned Taoist teachings. This attitude greatly displeased the empress dowager. When Chao Kuan requested that officials should no longer present their memorials to the empress dowager, she was so angry that all three of these top officials were dismissed. Emperor Wu, an admirer of Confucianism, was able to appoint T'ien Fen as the imperial chancellor only after the death of the empress dowager in 135 B.C.[36]

An empress dowager played a more active role in government if the new emperor was a youth and she was his regent. She attended the court with the young emperor and issued edicts.[37] In theory she ruled jointly with the emperor; in fact she was the real ruler who exercised political power and made important decisions. The emperor, who was usually young, was merely a figurehead under her control. Empress Dowager Lü, who was the first woman in Chinese history to introduce the system of an empress dowager attending the court, is a case in point. Nominally, her son, Emperor Hui, was on the throne for seven years; he actually ruled for only about one year and then left all affairs to his mother. Thus Emperor Hui was completely ignored by the great historian, Ssu-ma Ch'ien, and the annals of Empress Lü come immediately after those of Emperor Kao (*SC, chüan* 8 and 9). Apparently he gave up his role because the empress dowager was too domineering and cruel to the members of the imperial family; although he did not approve, he was too weak to keep her from doing it. After his death a young emperor was put on the throne, but it was actually the empress dowager who issued all the edicts and ruled the empire. Later the young emperor was dismissed and killed by the empress dowager, and another king was made emperor. However, the empress dowager was still the ruler. It was explained by Ssu-ma Ch'ien that the new emperor did not start a new reign because all edicts were issued in the name of the empress dowager (*SC* 9:7a). Pan Ku, who disagreed with Ssu-ma Ch'ien and recognized Emperor Hui as emperor, still had to include Empress Lü in the annals; according to Pan Ku, Empress Lü's reign began in the first year after the death of Emperor Hui (*HS, chüan* 3).

Empress Dowager Lü's pattern was followed by several other empress dowagers who were also interested in exercising power. Empress Dowager Wang was the second to attend court in the Early Han,

---

[36] *SC* 107:3b–4b; *HS* 52:3a–4a.
[37] *TYTT* B:3a–b.

remaining on the throne from 1 B.C. until A.D. 6, when her nephew Wang Mang became the acting emperor (*HS* 12:1b, 98:14b). In the Later Han there were six empress dowagers who attended the court. Empress Dowager Tou attended court for three years until a coup d'état in 92 brought the downfall of her family. Empress Dowager Teng ruled from 106 until her death in 121. Empress Dowager Liang was on the throne from 144 until 150, when she announced her retirement. The short-lived regencies of the other three empress dowagers (Yen, Tou, and Ho) were interrupted by coups in 125, 168, and 189 (*HHS* 10A:21a and 27a ff., 10B:6a–b, 2b–4a, 12a–b, and 17a).

The power of an empress dowager who attended the court was imposing. Ministers presenting memorials were required to submit one copy to the empress dowager and another to the emperor.[38] In fact all edicts were issued by her, and she was in a position to appoint and dismiss officials.[39] An empress dowager even personally investigated judicial cases and issued pardons to prisoners during a time of famine.[40]

If the emperor died without an heir, it was usually the empress dowager who selected and appointed the new emperor.[41] In extreme cases she could even dismiss the emperor and appoint another. Although the dismissal of the king of Ch'ang-i, who ascended the throne after the death of Emperor Chao, and the appointment of Emperor Hsüan were initiated by Ho Kuang and other top officials, the proposal was approved by the empress dowager and carried out under her authority (*HS* 68:5b and 6b–12a).

Under the empress dowager were the empress and the various imperial concubines. The empress, who assisted the emperor in serving in the ancestral temple, and who was considered the "mother of the empire,"[42] was supreme among the wives of the emperor. All these ladies were selected from the good families in the capital. Those whose age was between thirteen and twenty and who had been judged satisfactory by physiognomists were selected by imperial messengers (*HHS* 10A:4a). Families of nobles and high officials could also ask for permission to present their daughters to the inner palace (10A:12a–13a).

[38] *TYTT* B:3b.
[39] *SC* 3:4b, 9:5b, 7a, and 9b; *HS* 12:1a–b, 82:10a–b, 98:14b–15a; *HHS* 4:1b–3a and 27a–28a, 5:1b–2b and 30b, 6:22b, 7:7a–8b, 10A:15b–16b, 28a ff., and 35b, 10B:2b and 6a.
[40] *HHS* 10A:29b–30a and 31a.
[41] *HS* 98:14b; *HHS* 10A:26b–27a and 29a, 10B:3a, 6a–b, and 12a.
[42] *HHS* 10A:10b–11a, 16a, and 26a–b.

The empress was usually selected from among the imperial concubines; a woman was seldom appointed empress before the wedding.[43] In most cases the empress was appointed by the emperor, but sometimes the decision was made by the empress dowager.[44] As a rule the imperial concubine who had given birth to a son who was chosen as heir apparent was appointed empress.[45]

An empress, though considered the "mother of the empire," was subordinate to the emperor, and her status was not secure. She could be dismissed by order of the emperor,[46] or sometimes she was given poison and ordered to commit suicide (*HS* 97B:8a).

The status of the imperial concubines varied according to their titles. In the Ch'in dynasty there were seven ranks.[47] In Early Han there were altogether fourteen ranks, each corresponding to a certain post or rank in the bureaucracy. Thus a concubine of the first rank, brilliant companion (*chao-i* 昭儀), was equivalent in position to an imperial chancellor and in rank to a king, while a concubine of the fourteenth rank was equal to an official of 100 piculs. Girls of good family (*chia-jen-tzu* 家人子), who were not included in the fourteen ranks, were considered equivalent to petty officials below 100 piculs (*HS* 97A:2a–3a). In the Later Han there were only four ranks (*HHS* 10A:3b).

All the imperial concubines were subordinate to the empress. The Honorable Lady Teng, an imperial concubine of Emperor Ho, never dared to sit or stand with Empress Yin. She also tried not to answer any questions raised by the emperor when the empress did not answer (*HHS* 10A:25a). Many empresses were so jealous that concubines who had had sons were murdered (10B:1b). Similarly, an imperial concubine who was pregnant took drugs to induce an abortion because she was afraid of the empress (10B:16b).

NOBLES

The nobles comprised three major groups: the imperial relatives, the consort families, and the meritorious officials.

---

[43] *HS* 97B:28a–b; *HHS* 10B:9b–10a.

[44] I, 15; *HS* 97B:11a–b; *HHS* 10A:13b and 26a–b.

[45] *HS* 97A:8a, 10b, and 13a, 98:3b; *HHS* 10A:6a–b.

[46] *HS* 97A:9b, 12a, 13b, and 27a, 97B:7b; *HHS* 10A:6b and 22b; 10B:11b, 14b–15a, and 21a–b.

[47] *HHS* 10A:3a. The text includes the empress and the number is eight.

IMPERIAL RELATIVES

With the partial establishment of feudalism (*feng-chien* 封建) in the Han, a number of kingdoms and marquisates were set up. All sons of Emperor Kao, and brothers, paternal cousins, and brothers' sons, as well as some men who were not members of the imperial family, were ennobled as kings. They were sent to nine different kingdoms, where they were expected to protect the emperor.[48] After the kings of different surnames were gradually disposed of, a fundamental policy was set up by the emperor that only the members of the imperial family could be made kings,[49] so this highest rank came to be occupied exclusively by imperial relatives. All the sons of an emperor except the heir apparent were made kings, and other relatives were made marquises.

At first a king governed almost independently; little control was imposed by the central government. Later, after a policy had been adopted by the Han government to weaken the kings, they lost their power to rule their kingdoms (see pp. 165–67). But a king still enjoyed the superior status next only to that of the emperor. He also collected taxes from his kingdom (*HS* 14:4a).

Under the principle of primogeniture, only the eldest son by the legal wife of a king was entitled to be his heir; other sons received no land at all in the early days of the dynasty.[50] Nobility was extended to other sons of a king after Emperor Wu established a new system to weaken and reduce the size of a kingdom: all kings were allowed to distribute fiefs to their other sons and their brothers, who would then be ennobled as marquises by the emperor (see Chapter 5, note 13). A marquis received a definite amount of tax from his marquisate, depending upon the number of households assigned to him by the emperor.[51]

Princes and other imperial relatives were similarly ennobled as kings and marquises in the Later Han. Altogether 137 imperial relatives were made marquises in A.D. 37, a year after the empire had been unified.[52]

---

[48] *SC* 17:1b–2a; *HS* 14:2a–3a.

[49] *SC* 9:4a, 57:10b; *HS* 18:1b–2a, 40:18b and 29a.

[50] *SC* 112:12a; *HS* 64A:19b.

[51] *HS* 1B:19a; *HHC* 28:14a–15a.

[52] *HHS* 1B:12a; see also Ch'ien Ta-chao, "Hou-Han-shu pu-piao," in *Erh-shih-wu shih pu-pien* (Shanghai: K'ai-ming shu-tien, 1936–37), *chüan* 3 and 4, hereafter cited as *HHSPP*.

CONSORT FAMILIES

The family members of an empress or empress dowager invariably enjoyed a very high social and political status in Han times. Since the emperor, whose status was without parallel, always married someone of lower status, we may say that the consort family always married "up"; such a marriage automatically raised the family's status. Indeed, the system of the consort family provided the fastest channel of social mobility, enabling persons to move up to the top in the socio-political stratification order. The contrast between original family status and the newly acquired status in many cases was strikingly obvious.

Among the consort families of the Early Han, only five were prominent before one of their women became the imperial consort;[53] generally the wives of the early rulers did not come from prominent families. The empress of the founder of the dynasty, Empress Lü, was a commoner. The Tou, Wei, and Wang were all families of humble origin. The Chao and Hsü were families of petty officers who had suffered castration (hence they were considered humble by their contemporaries).[54] Empress Tou's family was poor, and one of her two brothers became a slave who made charcoal for his owner.[55] Emperor Hsüan's mother, Wang Weng-hsü, was the daughter of a poor family. She left her home and was raised by a Liu family because her parents were unable to support her. Later she was given by the Liu family to another person who sought to keep and train some girls to sing and dance. Weng-hsü's parents were unable to follow her because they did not have enough money for traveling. Finally she became a concubine of the son of the heir apparent, the father of Emperor Hsüan. When Emperor Hsüan ascended the throne, his maternal grandmother and her two sons (Weng-hsü's brothers) came to the court riding in an ox-drawn carriage (*HS* 97A:21b–23a). Empress Wei, Emperor Wu's wife, whose family was described as humble by the historian, was a singing

[53] Empress Chang of Emperor Hui was the daughter of a king, Chang Ao 張敖, and her mother was a princess, Empress Lü's daughter. Empress Po of Emperor Ching was related to an earlier consort family, Emperor Wen's mother's family (Empress Dowager Po). Empress Ch'en of Emperor Wu was the daughter of a princess. Empress Shang-kuan of Emperor Chao was the granddaughter of a general, Shang-kuan Chieh 上官傑. Her mother was the daughter of Ho Kuang, the grand general. Empress Ho of Emperor Hsüan was the daughter of Ho Kuang. See I, 15, 20, 22; *HS* 97A:18b–19a and 26b.

[54] *HS* 97A:3a, 7b–8a, 17a, 21b–23a, and 23b.

[55] *SC* 49:5a–6a; *HS* 97A:7b–8a.

girl kept by a princess. She was the illegitimate child of a former slave of the princess who had had an affair with a petty officer serving in the household of the princess. Her younger brother, Wei Ch'ing, was a servant of the princess and frequently served as her attendant escort.[56]

Beginning with Emperor Hsüan, however, there was a tendency for the emperor to marry the daughter of a prominent family. The emperor first married the daughter of an official who had been castrated; he later married Ho Kuang's daughter; and his third empress was the descendant of a marquis (*HS* 97A:23a, 26b, 27b). With the exception of Empress Chao, who was a palace maid who had been taught to sing and dance (*HS* 97B:11a), all other consort families after Emperor Hsüan were more or less prominent—either families of high officials or members of a previous consort family.[57]

Whether the consort family had been prominent or not, it immediately became prominent through ennoblement, which brought with it prestige and wealth. Although a regulation had been established by Emperor Kao that only meritorious officials could be made marquises, this regulation gradually became a formality, and as a rule one or more members of the consort family were ennobled as marquises. Among the consort members listed in *Han-shu, chüan* 18, as marquises, only seven were ennobled because of merit.[58] The father of an empress or an empress dowager was always ennobled; if he had died he was ennobled posthumously.[59] Brothers of an empress might not be ennobled, but they were always ennobled by the next emperor when the empress became empress dowager.[60] Even though the mother of an emperor was not an empress in her lifetime (an imperial concubine, a queen, or a concubine of an heir apparent), her brothers or her brother's children would be ennobled by her son when he became emperor.[61] That the maternal uncles of an emperor were ennobled without exception was

[56] *SC* 49:9b–10a, 111:1a–b; *HS* 55:1a–b, 97A:12b.

[57] Empress Hsü of Emperor Ch'eng was from an earlier consort family (Empress Hsü of Emperor Hsüan). Both Hsü Yen-shou 許延壽 and Hsü Chia 許嘉, Empress Hsü's grandfather and father, had been the grand minister of war and general of chariots and cavalry under Emperor Hsüan and Emperor Yüan respectively (*HS* 97A:26a–b, 97B:1a–b). Empress Fu of Emperor Ai was the niece of Emperor Ai's grandmother (I, 36). Empress Wang of Emperor P'ing was the daughter of Wang Mang (*HS* 97B:28a).

[58] *HS* 18:1b–2a. The seven consort members who were ennobled because of merit were: Lü Tse 呂澤, Lü Shih-chih 呂釋之, Tou Ying, Wei Ch'ing, Ho Ch'ü-ping, Ho Kuang, Shang-kuan Chieh, and Shih Kao (*HS* 18:2b, 3a, 4a–b, 5a, and 7a).

[59] *HS* 97A:7a and 8a, 97B:20b; *HHS* 10A:20b, 10B:16a–b.

[60] *HS* 97A:9a, 11a, 26b, and 28a, 97B:12b; *HHS* 10A:15a–18b, 16:16b.

[61] *HS* 97A:7a, 21a–b, and 23a, 97B:21a–b and 22a; *HHS* 10B:19a, 34:11a.

clearly explained in a statement by Emperor Chang. When Empress Dowager Ma did not want her brother to be ennobled, the emperor said to her, "Since the rise of Han maternal uncles [of an emperor] have been ennobled as marquises just as imperial princes have been made kings" (*HHS* 10A:16b). Emperor Ho also said, "According to tradition all the maternal uncles are granted ranks and fiefs" (*HHS* 23:25a). It was also said that an empress's mother's family was highly respected in Han times and that members of the consort family were honored and favored.[62]

At the same time that the consort families were given prestige through ennoblement, they also gained political power through official appointment. With a few exceptions[63] the members of a consort family, particularly the father and brothers of an empress or empress dowager, were given official appointment.[64] Other family members, such as her paternal uncles, cousins, and nephews, were often appointed to various offices.[65] Even the children of an empress's sister were given appointments.[66] Members of consort families frequently became high or even top officials. Four consort family members held the post of imperial chancellor: Lü Ch'an 呂產, Tou Ying, T'ien Fen, and Wang Shang.[67] But the customary practice was to make them generals; they held such titles as grand general, general of chariots and cavalry, or general of flash cavalry (*p'iao-ch'i chiang-chün* 驃騎將軍).[68] From Emperor Wu's time on, all consort family members who were given the top post and the authority to assist the emperor in the government (*fu-cheng* 輔政) were appointed grand minister of war (*ta-ssu-ma* 大司馬), either as an additional title to the office of general or as an independent title.[69]

[62] *HHS* 10B:7b; see also 10B:15b, 34:8b.

[63] Tou Kuang-kuo 竇廣國, Empress Dowager Tou's younger brother, and Tou P'eng-tsu 竇彭祖, her elder brother's son, were ennobled but not appointed officials (*HS* 97A:9a). Wang Hsin 王信 and T'ien Sheng 田勝, Empress Dowager Wang's brother and half-brother, respectively, also received only noble titles (*HS* 97A:11a). Emperor Hsüan's mother's two brothers, Wang Wu-ku 王無故 and Wang Wu 王武, were merely made marquises (*HS* 97A:23a). Empress Wang's father, Wang Feng-kuang 王奉光, and her two brothers, Wang Shun 王舜 and Wang Chün 王駿, were merely ennobled without official appointment (*HS* 97A:28a).

[64] *HS* 97A:13a and 19a, 98:3b; *HHS* 10A:6b–7a and 26b, 16:16a, 23:18b–19a, 24:27a, 34:11b and 15a–b; III, 66, 71.

[65] *HS* 97A:9a, 21a–b, 23b, 26b, and 28a; *HHS* 10A:34b, 23:18b–19a, 24b–25a, and 26b; III, 66.

[66] *HS* 55:6a, 68:1a–b.

[67] *HS* 97A:5a, 9a–b, 11a, and 23b.

[68] Po Chao 薄昭 (*HS* 19B:2b), Tou Ying (*HS* 97A:9a), Wei Ch'ing (*HS* 97A:13a), Ho Ch'ü-ping *(ibid.)*, and Shang-kuan An 上官安 (*HS* 97A:19a).

[69] Ho Kuang, who was made grand minister of war and grand general by Emperor

An emperor usually treated a maternal uncle with great honor and trusted him with the key post in the government. It was said that the father of the empress was superior to the emperor's maternal uncle (*HS* 97B:1b), but it seems that he was not as influential. Hsü Chia, Emperor Yüan's mother's paternal cousin, was appointed grand minister of war and general of chariots and cavalry to assist the emperor in the government. He continued to hold this post in the time of Emperor Ch'eng, whose empress was his daughter. But Emperor Ch'eng also appointed his mother's elder brother, Wang Feng 王鳳, grand minister of war and grand general. The two consort family members were treated with the same honor. Tu Ch'in 杜欽 told Wang Feng to pay special respect to Hsü Chia because traditionally the father of the empress was superior to the emperor's maternal uncle. Three years later, however, the emperor, who wanted to entrust government affairs to his maternal uncle, dismissed his father-in-law (*HS* 97B:1b–2a). During the entire reign of Emperor Ch'eng the post of grand minister of war was in the hands of one consort family. Five of its members held the post continuously, one succeeding the other. The emperor even recollected that one of his paternal uncles had died before he could receive the appointment. In fact, only one of his paternal uncles was passed over, and that was because he was guilty of certain offenses (*HS* 98:4a–12b).

Ennoblement and the holding of the key official post certainly gave the members of the consort family wealth, prestige, and power. The change of power was very sudden and striking for a family that had been poor and humble. The family could be elevated from a low level to the highest stratum overnight. When Tou Chang-chün 竇長君 and Tou Kuang-kuo's 廣國 elder sister became empress, two top officials remarked: "Our lives are in the hands of these two persons. These two come from a humble origin and we should select teachers for them" (*HS* 97A:8b). The case of Wei Ch'ing is most illuminating in showing that no matter how humble one's origin the new status gave all the social honor and power a consort family could have. Wei had been the servant of a princess and frequently served as her attendant escort. When he was told by a physiognomist that he would become a marquis, he laughed and said, "A slave will be content if he can avoid beatings and scoldings." When his sister became empress, he was appointed general and later promoted to grand general and ennobled

Wu in 97 B.C., was the first consort member entrusted with the task of *fu-cheng* (*HS* 7:1a, 68:2a). See also Chapter 5, p. 170 and n. 25.

marquis. When the princess wanted to select a husband from among the various marquises, all her attendants recommended Wei Ch'ing. At first she was reluctant because he had been her attendant, but finally she was convinced of his unique status and took him as her husband (see document I, 27).

Unlike the consort families of the Early Han, nearly all the empresses in the Later Han came from wealthy and prominent families. Both wives of Liu Hsiu, the founder of the dynasty, were daughters of wealthy families. Empress Kuo's father, a member of a prominent family, married the daughter of a king. He once gave to his half-brother landed property and houses worth several million cash (*HHS* 1A:6a). Empress Yin's family, which had suddenly become very rich in Emperor Hsüan's time (73 to 49 B.C.), owned 70,000 *mou* of land and a large number of carriages, horses, and slaves (*HHS* 32:12a–b, 16b–17a).

The consort families Ma, Tou, and Liang were all powerful families that had been prominent since the Early Han. The ancestors of the Ma family were moved from Han-t'an to Mou-ling at the time of Emperor Wu because they fell into the category of 2,000-picul officials. One of the ancestors had been a marquis. All three of Ma Yüan's brothers and his nephew were 2,000-picul officials in the time of Wang Mang. Ma Yüan, the father of the empress, possessed several thousand cattle and horses and many thousand *hu* of grain, and kept a large number of guests. Later he became a general and was ennobled (*HHS* 24:1a ff.). The Tous were the descendants of the consort family of Emperor Wen. The family was moved to P'ing-ling during the reign of Emperor Hsüan because it included a 2,000-picul official. For generations the members of the family had been either grand administrators or colonels (*hsiao-wei* 校尉) in the Ho-hsi area (Kansu). Tou Jung, the empress's great grandfather, was the chief commandant of the dependent state (*shu-kuo tu-wei* 屬國都尉) of Chang-yeh under the Keng-shih emperor, and a general under Wei Ao 隗囂. Later he joined Liu Hsiu, and because of his participation in a campaign against Wei he was ennobled and appointed grand minister of works (*HHS* 23:1a ff.). The Liang family, which had possessed wealth of ten million cash, was moved to Mou-ling in Emperor Wu's time. Liang T'ung 梁統, the great-great-grandfather of the empress, was a grand administrator and a marquis. His son married Emperor Kuang-wu's daughter. His two granddaughters were imperial concubines, and one of them was the mother of Emperor Ho. Both Empress Liang and her aunt married Emperor Shun. The empress later arranged the marriage of her younger sister who became the empress of Emperor Huan (*HHS* 34:1a ff.).

Other families, although unknown in the Early Han, were prominent in the new dynasty. The Teng, Yin, Wang, Fu, and Ts'ao were all families of high officials, and Teng was the most prominent among them. Empress Teng's grandfather, Teng Yü 鄧禹, was a follower of Kuang-wu who by virtue of his military merit was ennobled and given top posts in the government: minister of the masses (*ssu-t'u* 司徒) and grand tutor. Four of his sons were made marquises, and his sixth son, Teng Hsün, the empress's father, was a colonel and a grand administrator. The Teng family was related to another consort family, Yin (Empress Teng's mother was Empress Yin's niece). Three of its members also married princesses (*HHS* 16:1a ff.). The Fu family also had been prominent for generations. The empress was the eighth generation descendant of Fu Huan 伏湛, a minister of the masses. Her father, who inherited a marquisate, married the daughter of Emperor Huan (*HHS* 10B:19b).

There was a tendency for the imperial family to maintain conjugal relations with the previous consort families. Male members often became husbands of the princesses, and girls were often selected to become concubines or empresses. Altogether five empresses came from previous consort families (Yin, Tou, Teng, Liang, and Sung); four of the families produced two empresses.[70]

Only one Later Han consort family was of commoner origin. Empress Ho's father had been a butcher (II, 85). This is the only record in the Later Han of a poor and humble family who became a consort family and thus became prominent overnight.

Following the practice of the Early Han, the father or brother of an empress or empress dowager was usually ennobled as a marquis. Emperor Ming was the only emperor who neither ennobled members of his empress's family, Ma, nor gave high posts to its members. However, when Emperor Chang ascended the throne, he made all three brothers of Empress Dowager Ma marquises. He said to her, "Since the rise of Han, maternal uncles [of an emperor] have been ennobled as marquises just as imperial princes have been made kings."[71]

The father or brother of an empress or empress dowager was usually given a high post in the government. Beginning with Emperor Chang the consort members began to occupy such top posts as general of chariots and cavalry and grand general. Thus they were promoted to a

[70] *HHS* 10A:22a, 10B:9b, 10b, 12a, and 14a–b.
[71] *HHS* 10A:15a–16b and 18b–19a.

rank equal to (and at times even superior to) that of the Three Lords (*san-ssu* 三司).[72] At the same time, the consort family began to rise to power with the holding of such a post. This will be discussed in Chapter 5.

MERITORIOUS OFFICIALS

A third group, called meritorious officials, consisted of those nobles who won their ranks by virtue of their merit, especially military accomplishments. Seven loyal followers of the founder of the Han were thus ennobled as kings because of their extraordinary military merits in overthrowing the Ch'in dynasty and defeating Hsiang Yü 項羽, the principal rival of Liu Pang.[73] In addition, 137 men of less merit were made marquises.[74]

However, the emperor considered these nonrelatives untrustworthy and unsafe; so within a few years these kings of different surnames were disposed of one after another by the emperor and his wife.[75] With the exception of the king of one kingdom (*SC* 17:1b), all of them were replaced by members of the Liu family. Emperor Kao then laid down the rule that only the members of the imperial family could be made kings. He and a group of his officials took an oath that they would destroy anyone not a member of the Liu family who proclaimed himself king.[76] From this time on, kingship, the highest noble rank, was exclusively reserved for the imperial relatives. The rank of marquis,[77]

[72] The rank of grand general, general of flash cavalry, general of chariots and cavalry, or general of the guard *(wei chiang-chün* 衛將軍) was next to that of the Three Lords. (The Three Lords were the same as the Three Ducal Ministers, namely the grand ministers of war, works, and masses.) When Tou Hsien was made general of chariots and cavalry, his rank was inferior to that of the Three Lords; but when he was promoted to grand general, his rank was superior. Teng Chih, who was made general of chariots and cavalry, was given the same treatment enjoyed by the Three Lords, *i-t'ung san-ssu* 儀同三司. Liang Chi, who enjoyed a unique status in the court and was treated differently from all other officials, even sat separately from the Three Lords. See *HHS* 10B:2b–3a, 16:16a, 23:24b, 34:20a; *HHC* 24:8b–9b.

[73] *SC* 8:29a, 17:3a; *HS* 13:5b–6b.

[74] *SC* 18:1b; cf. *HS* 16:1a and 22b, where slightly higher figures, based on a longer period, are given.

[75] *SC* 8:31a ff.; *HS* 1B:7a ff.

[76] *SC* 9:4a, 57:10b; *HS* 18:1b–2a, 40:18b and 29a.

[77] In the Early Han there was only one rank among the marquises, namely, *lieh-hou* (Ch'ien Ta-hsin, *Nien-erh shih k'ao-i*, TSCC ed., 9:193, hereafter cited as *NESKI*). There were five ranks in the Later Han, namely, *hsien-hou* 縣侯 (prefectural marquis), *tu-hsiang hou* 都鄉侯 (marquis of a district near a local, e.g., prefectural or commandery, seat), *hsiang-hou* 鄉侯 (marquis of a district), *tu-t'ing hou* 都亭侯 (marquis of a *t'ing* 亭 near a local—e.g., prefectural or commandery—seat), *t'ing-hou*

with marquisates varying from several hundred to over ten thousand households,[78] became the highest rank a meritorious official could obtain.

OFFICIALS

STATUS OF OFFICIALS

Next to the nobles in status were the officials. Although some high officials were ennobled, most officials were non-nobles. I have already mentioned that mental labor, which was associated with governing, was highly valued in Han society. The ruling class was superior, and they ruled the inferiors. Officials thus enjoyed an extremely superior status.

The status of an official depended on his rank in the bureaucracy. Included among the top officials in the Early Han were the three grand tutors (*t'ai-shih* 太師, *t'ai-fu*, and *t'ai-pao* 太保), the imperial chancellor, the grand commandant, the grandee secretary, and the generals. They were officials of the 10,000-picul rank. The grand tutors, whose rank was classified as Supreme Lords (*shang-kung* 上公), held the highest rank in the government. The imperial chancellor, the grand commandant, and the grandee secretary were classified as the Three Ducal Ministers (*san-kung* 三公, literally: Three Dukes) (*HS* 19A:3a–4b). The Supreme Lords and the Three Ducal Ministers remained the top posts in the Later Han dynasty. But there was only one Supreme Lord, the grand tutor. The grand commandant, the minister of the masses, and the minister of works were the Three Ducal Ministers. The rank of the grand general was comparable to that of these three ministers.[79] Below the Three Ducal Ministers were the 2,000-picul officials, including the Nine Ministers (*chiu-ch'ing* 九卿), the grand administrators, the chancellors of kingdoms, and so forth.[80] They were all high officials who were treated with great respect.

(marquis of a *t'ing*). See Ku Yen-wu, *Jih-chih-lu, chi-shih* by Huang Ju-ch'eng, *SPPY* ed., 22:15a–b, hereafter cited as *JCLCS;* Yen Keng-wang, *Chung-kuo ti-fang hsing-cheng chih-tu shih* (2 vols.; Taipei, 1961), I, 49–50. Besides these ranks, there was both in Early and Later Han a rank known as *kuan-nei hou* 關內侯 (marquis within the passes), which was inferior to the rank of the regular marquis mentioned above *(HS* 19A:14b; *HHC* 28:15b).

[78] *SC* 18:1b; *HS* 16:1a–b.

[79] *HHC* 24:2a–9b.

[80] *HS* 19A:4b ff.; *HHC, chüan* 25, 26, 27, 28; Wang Yü-ch'üan, "An Outline of the Central Government of the Former Han Dynasty," *Harvard Journal of Asiatic Studies,* XII (1949), 150 ff.

The status of the imperial chancellor in the Early Han was almost without a parallel. When he paid a visit to the emperor, the emperor had to stand up for him; if the emperor was driving he got down from his carriage to greet the imperial chancellor. The emperor usually paid him a visit when he was ill and offered sacrifices for him when he died.[81] It was very unusual for an emperor to visit other officials when they were ill (*HS* 59:3b).

Since the imperial chancellor was the superior of all officials, his prestige was almost unique in the bureaucracy. Even the grandee secretary assumed a humble position in his presence. In the court the grandee secretary always stood behind the imperial chancellor (*HS* 78:8b). Once a grandee secretary was accused of failing to visit the imperial chancellor when he was ill and of not standing behind him in court. An edict was issued blaming him for treating the imperial chancellor impolitely, and for these (and other) reasons the grandee secretary was demoted (*HS* 78:8b–9b). The humility of inferior officials in the presence of an imperial chancellor is clearly shown in a case in which a medium-ranking official, who was a favorite of the emperor, was charged with neglecting court etiquette and was summoned to the office of the imperial chancellor. The official, in his bare feet, took off his hat, apologized, and kowtowed to the imperial chancellor. The imperial chancellor did not rise from his seat and did not return the salute.[82]

The superior status of an imperial chancellor dominated even family relationships. One imperial chancellor placed his elder brother, also a marquis, in a seat less honorable than his own,[83] which deviated from the principle under which a younger brother always respected his elder brother. The fact that political status superseded family status implies that political status dominated even family relationships, not to mention other forms of social relationships. This confirms our point of view that prestige was mainly derived from political power.

After Emperor Ch'eng had established the practice of acknowledging the existence of three imperial chancellors instead of one,[84] all of the

---

[81] *HS* 84:11a; 86:15b; *HHS* 46:24a; Wei Hung, *Han-chiu-i*, in *PCKTS*, A:5a, hereafter cited as *HCI*.

[82] *SC* 96:7b–8a; *HS* 42:6b–7a.

[83] *SC* 107:5a–b; *HS* 52:4b.

[84] At the suggestion of Ho Wu 何武 in connection with the establishment of the offices of the Three Ducal Ministers, Emperor Ch'eng in 8 B.C. changed the title of grandee secretary *(yü-shih ta-fu)* to grand minister of works *(ta-ssu-k'ung)* and increased the salary of the grand minister of war *(ta-ssu-ma)* and grand minister of

Three Dukes were treated with the great respect that in earlier days had been reserved for the imperial chancellor. Thus the emperor rose from his seat and descended from his carriage when he met one of the Three Ducal Ministers. All officials had to salute them (*HHS* 46:24a).

As a rule, only officials of similar ranks who treated each other as equals or near-equals associated with each other, and families of such officials tended to intermarry. Children of a high official, particularly a marquis, often married a princess, prince, or king or became a consort of an emperor (an imperial concubine or an empress).

Superior-inferior relationships naturally existed between officials of different grades. Official posts determined the status of the two and the way of dealing with each other. Furthermore, a promotion or demotion meant also a change in social status and a change in behavior patterns. When Tou Ying held the post of grand general, T'ien Fen was only a gentleman. T'ien behaved as if he were a son when he visited Tou and served him wine. But when he became imperial chancellor and Tou lost his post, T'ien was less polite and began to dispute with him.[85] This implies that political status was a determining factor in social prestige and that prestige changed with corresponding changes in the official post held. Another example will illustrate this point clearly. When Chang T'ang 張湯 was a petty official he always ran after Chu Mai-ch'en 朱買臣 obsequiously. But when Chang became grandee secretary and acting imperial chancellor, Chu was demoted and became the subordinate of the imperial chancellor. Chang then treated Chu impolitely; when Chu visited him, he did not rise from his seat and did not return the salute.[86]

Although the status of officials varied according to their rank in the bureaucratic hierarchy, the officialdom as a whole had a social status much superior to that of nonofficials. The difference was manifested in the style of life enjoyed by officials—a style of life distinctly marked off from the rest of the population. Differences in the consumption of material goods as well as differences in ceremonials were regulated in

---

works to that of the imperial chancellor *(ch'eng-hsiang)*. The three were treated alike. About three years later, when Chu Po 朱博 was holding the post of grand minister of works, he suggested reinstating the old system, and said that he was willing to assume the office of grandee secretary. His request was approved by Emperor Ai. But in 1 B.C. Emperor Ai again introduced the system of the Three Ducal Ministers, and the title of imperial chancellor was changed to grand minister of the masses. See *HS* 10:15b, 11:4b and 8a, 83:15b–16b.

[85] *SC* 107:2b–3a and 8a ff.; *HS* 52:2b and 7a ff.

[86] *HS* 59:5b–6a, 64A: 13a–b.

sumptuary laws. Carriages of various special designs were assigned to officials of different ranks (*HS* 5:7a–b). The function of such sumptuary laws obviously was to maintain the prestige of the ruling class—to make the great men feel and look great. This was always a matter of concern to the government in the early days of the dynasty.

In the early days of the Early Han, since most of the newly appointed officials were military men who cared very little about their carriages or garments, the emperor complained of their wearing ordinary dress that did not differ from the people's. For this reason a regulation was put into effect that those whose dress, carriage, horses, and attendants were not in accordance with their official posts and those who went to the villages without observing the proper decorum would be subject to punishment (*HS* 5:7a–b).

Officials were highly respected in society, and the people were conscious of their own inferior position. On the other hand, a superiority complex dominated the officials' way of life and attitudes toward the people. Prestige depended mainly on the possession of an official title and post, and the change in attitude toward a man after he became an official is quite illuminating. Usually a commoner was treated lightly by others, but as soon as he became an official he was treated much differently, even by relatives. This is clearly illustrated in the well-known case of Su Ch'in 蘇秦 of the fourth century B.C. When Su Ch'in did not succeed in getting an appointment, his brothers and their wives, and his sisters, wife, and concubines all ridiculed him. Later when he became chancellor of the Six Kingdoms and returned home, his brothers and their wives and his own wife waited upon him at dinner, prostrating themselves and not daring to raise their faces to look at him. He asked his brother's wife, "Why were you so haughty before and so humble now?" She crawled on hands and knees with her face touching the ground and apologetically said, "Because you have a high post and plenty of gold." Then Su Ch'in sighed and said, "Although the same person, when one is rich and honorable he is feared by his relatives, but when he is poor and humble he is treated lightly. How much more so with other people!" (*SC* 69:16b–17a). Ssu-ma Hsiang-ju, the famous Han scholar, was hated by his father-in-law in the early days of his marriage. When he became general of the palace gentlemen (*chung-lang-chiang* 中郎將) and was sent on a mission to the Southwest Barbarians, he was welcomed by the local officials. Cho Wang-sun, his father-in-law, and other prominent persons of the community had to present an ox and wine to him through the medium of his attendants.

Cho regretted that he had not given his daughter to Ssu-ma earlier (I, 21, 24).

A great distance was always maintained between officials and commoners. When an official's carriage reached the village gate, all the people, including the elders, always ran and hid themselves (*HS* 46:2b–3a). There was very little social communication between the two classes. Probably wealthy merchants were the only ones able to associate with the officials. In any case, association with officials always meant honor and prestige. Wang Chi 王吉, the prefect of Lin-ch'iung, succeeded in promoting the prestige of Ssu-ma Hsiang-ju when he was poor by showing others that Ssu-ma was his respected friend. As a consequence Ssu-ma was invited to a banquet by a local wealthy iron manufacturer, Cho Wang-sun. Cho later became angry with Ssu-ma when he ran away with his daughter. Cho's brothers and others, pleading on behalf of Ssu-ma, said to him: "Besides, [Ssu-ma] was the guest of the prefect· Why should you insult him like that?" Cho finally gave money and slaves to his daughter and her husband (I, 21). It is obvious that from the beginning Ssu-ma's association with the prefect was always in the minds of these persons, and it is also clear that the ultimate purpose in pleasing the friend of the prefect was to please the prefect. The prefect, who according to the history had devised the plot, certainly knew the significance of his friend's association with him.

Chances for social communication between officials and commoners were very few. If there were any, the humility of the commoner was always observed. Thus when two melon-cultivators went to visit a retired official and presented melons to him, they were ordered to sit outside the window and were given only vegetables to eat, whereas the host enjoyed a number of delicious dishes in his room.[87]

Subordination in one form or another was usually expected when there was an open conflict between an official and a commoner. Some means of saving the face and prestige of the official at the expense of the commoner was usually worked out. Yüan She 原涉 was the most powerful man in his community, but when the prefect was angry with him because one of his slaves had injured someone and escaped, Yüan had to come to apologize to the prefect, baring his shoulder, binding his arms, and piercing his ear with an arrow. These were tokens of submission and a means of preserving the awe of the prefect (III, 47). Yüan She was the son of a grand administrator who had died when he

[87] *SKC,* Wu, 7:18a–b.

was young. He had himself been a prefect, but had resigned and had never been reappointed.

WEALTH OF OFFICIALS

Officials, whose functions contributed the most to society, were rewarded with high salaries and better living conditions. Theoretically, the higher a person's virtue and ability, the higher the rank he would occupy, and consequently the larger his salary would be. Obviously this kind of theory assumed that in a society in good order the virtuous and intelligent persons would be appointed to the government. Thus to be poor and humble in such a society was considered shameful by Confucius.[88] An inferior position and poor income meant that one was not virtuous and not intelligent.

The ranks of officials in the Han were indicated by piculs, varying from 10,000 piculs down to 100; the salaries actually received varied from 4,200 to 192 piculs a year. The petty officials, the so-called picul-consuming officials (*tou-shih li* 斗食吏), received only 1.2 piculs per day.[89]

According to Li K'uei, a farmer owning 100 *mou* of land had an annual income of 150 piculs.[90] Therefore, a 2,000-picul official's income was about ten times that much. Even the official of the lowest rank (100 piculs) had an income that was slightly more than the farmer's, for 150 piculs was an optimistic estimate; furthermore, the farmer did not always have a good harvest, and he was subject to all kinds of government taxes (*HS* 24A:6a–b, 11a–b). Officials were far better off than a small landowner. In fact, the salary received by most of the officials was sufficient to maintain a good standard of living and a style of life appropriate to the status group. Let us take the example of Kung Yü 貢禹: he received 110,000 cash a year when holding an 800-picul rank, and he later received 144,000 cash a year when promoted to the rank of 2,000 piculs (*HS* 72:13b–14a). Since ten catties of gold (one hundred thousand cash) was considered the value of the property of an average middle-class family (*HS* 4:19a), this means that the yearly salary of such an official was the equivalent of the total property of a middle-class family.

High officials who enjoyed a large salary invariably brought wealth

---

[88] *Lun-yü chu-su, SPPY* ed., 8:3a; Legge, *Chinese Classics*, I, 76.

[89] *HS* 19A:1a and 16a; *HHC* 28:16b–17b.

[90] *HS* 24A:6a. According to Ch'ao Ts'o, 100 *mou* produced only 100 piculs (*HS* 24A:11a).

to the family. Kung Yü's own statement may be cited as an example.
Before he was appointed to office his family had only 130 *mou* of land
and less than ten thousand cash, and he could hardly support his wife
and children. When he was summoned to the capital, he sold 100 *mou*
of land for travel expenses. He was then appointed to an office with the
rank of 800 piculs, which brought a monthly income of 9,200 cash. His
food was provided by the government, and in addition he received
various gifts from the emperor, including silks, cotton, clothes, wine,
meat, and fruit. Later he was promoted to the rank of 2,000 piculs,
which provided him with a monthly salary of twelve thousand cash.
(According to *HS* 19A the post he held was "equivalent to 2,000 piculs"
with a monthly salary of 100 piculs.) Kung Yü said happily, "The more
the salary and the gifts, the richer my family is getting every day and
the more honorable I myself am becoming every day" (*HS* 72:13b–
14a). Grandee Secretary Chang T'ang, who was very virtuous and
whose property consisted only of his regular salary and gifts from the
emperor, left five hundred catties of gold (five million cash) to his
family (*HS* 59:6b). This is in accord with the statement of Chi An 汲黯,
who remarked that the salary of the Three Ducal Ministers was very
substantial (*HS* 58:5b).

Other extra income of officials, whether lawful or not, should also be
taken into account: the higher the rank the more extra income one
could usually get. Many officials got magnificent incomes from their
fiefs, and both consort members and meritorious officials were ennobled
as marquises with households varying from several hundred to more
than ten thousand. An imperial chancellor was invariably a marquis.
When Kung-sun Hung 公孫弘, a non-noble, was appointed imperial
chancellor, he was made a marquis and ennobled with five hundred
households; this became a precedent for ennobling subsequent imperial
chancellors.[91] And in some cases one or two thousand households were
granted to such an official.[92]

An estimate of the average income enjoyed by a marquis was offered
by Ssu-ma Ch'ien. Assuming that on the average two hundred cash was
collected from each household, the historian figured out that a marquis
given one thousand households would have an annual income of two
hundred thousand cash (*SC* 129:14b). However, the tax in question was

[91] II, 22. The table in *HS* 18:4b gives 373 households instead of 500.

[92] For instance, when Chu Po was appointed imperial chancellor, he was ennobled
with two thousand households. Since this was not in accordance with the tradition,
Chu requested accepting only half of the households (*HS* 83:18a).

not a sort of household tax; it was the poll tax and land tax that a marquis was entitled to collect from the various households specified in the ennoblement. The poll tax (*suan fu* 算賦) per capita was 120 cash, from which the marquis paid 63 to the emperor as tribute (*hsien-fu* 獻賦) and retained 57. On the basis of this, Lao Kan offers an interesting account of the often-quoted estimate of Ssu-ma Ch'ien. If the family members of a household averaged four adults, the marquis would receive 228 cash per household in his fief; it would be very close to 200 if the average was three and a half adults.[93] The problem is further complicated because the income of a marquis in the Early Han was determined not only by the number of households but also by the size of the territory that was assigned as his marquisate. The number of households from which a marquis collected the tax might exceed the number specified at the time he was ennobled.[94] K'uang Heng 匡衡 was ennobled with 647 households when he was made the marquis of Lo-an district. There were supposed to be 310,000 *mou* of land within the district of Lo-an, but owing to a mistake on the map concerning the boundary, he actually collected taxes from 350,000 *mou* of land. The mistake was discovered later by the commandery government, and an adjustment was made accordingly. But because a subordinate official of the imperial chancellor intervened, the commandery followed the original map and gave back 40,000 *mou* of land to K'uang. As a result he was able to collect land tax on this additional acreage, which provided 1,000 piculs of grain. Later, K'uang Heng was charged with stealing land from the government for personal profit, and was dismissed. From this example it becomes clear that although a marquis was ennobled with a specific number of households, his actual income was related to the size of his marquisate.[95]

[93] Lao Kan, "Han-tai ping-chih chi Han-chien chung ti ping-chih," *LSYY*, X (1948), 41.

[94] According to *SC* 18:1b and *HS* 16:1a–b, when the meritorious officials were first made marquises by Emperor Kao, numerous people had fled away during the turmoil, and only 20 to 30 per cent of the population remained. For this reason, a big marquisate had only ten thousand households, and a smaller one had five hundred or six hundred. A few generations later the people returned to their native places and the population also increased; consequently a big marquisate included as many as thirty thousand to forty thousand households, and the households of a smaller marquisate also doubled. Quoting the example of Ts'ao Shen 曹參, Yen Shih-ku pointed out that Ts'ao was ennobled with only ten thousand households but that many years later his descendants possessed twenty-three thousand households (*HS* 16:1b).

[95] *HS* 81:11a–12a. The number of households, 647, is based on the table in *HS* 18:8b. *HS* 81 gives only six hundred, apparently a round number. K'uang Heng was ennobled in 36 B.C. The error in the map was discovered by the local government in

It is also clear that a marquis was entitled to collect land tax in kind (*t'ien-tsu* 田租), which was one-thirtieth of the crops. But it is not clear whether a marquis had to hand over part of the land tax to the central government. In any case, it seems that such an income was quite substantial. We do have an example of a high official who received an annual income from his marquisate (with 13,640 households) of more than ten million cash. This amounted to about 734 cash per household. It is impossible that such an enormous income could have been derived entirely from the poll tax, for the average household in Han times comprised only four to six persons, some of whom were children exempted from the poll tax. When the official's son inherited the marquisate, he thought that he did not deserve such an enormous income and requested to have his marquisate reduced. Permission was granted by the emperor, who ordered that the son be assigned a new marquisate in a different area. The number of households remained the same, but the income was reduced by one half (*HS* 59:12a). This amount, though substantially reduced, was still twice as much as the estimate given by Ssu-ma Ch'ien. This case also substantiates the assumption that the income from a marquisate was not always determined by the number of households. The practice was different in the Later Han; as a rule a marquisate was determined by the number of households, not by the size of its territory.[96]

Officials frequently received gifts from the emperor. They consisted of gold, houses, farms, or slaves.[97] The gifts received by one imperial chancellor totaled tens of millions of cash (*HS* 81:13b). It was not unusual to give several hundred or a thousand *mou* of land to an official. In an extraordinary case the emperor gave 100,000 *mou* of land to a single person (*HS* 86:12a). Some officials increased their wealth enormously through corruption and other unlawful means. For these reasons,

---

32 B.C. K'uang was dismissed in 27 B.C. Ch'ien Ta-hsin thus held that the 1,000 piculs of grain collected by K'uang covered a period of three years. Commenting on K'uang's case, Ch'ien reached the conclusion that although a marquis was ennobled with a specified number of households, the income derived from a marquisate was not always determined by the households awarded to him, but by the actual size of the marquisate (*NESKI* 8:182). It seems that after a marquisate had been set up, the size was then determined by its territory (Ch'ien Mu, *Ch'in Han shih* [Hong Kong, 1957], pp. 237–38; Yen Keng-wang, *Chung-kuo ti-fang hsing-cheng chih-tu shih*, I, 51–52).

[96] *HHS* 61:26a. The only exception to this rule was the large marquisate of such meritorious officials as Teng Yü and a few others who were ennobled with four prefectures (*HHS* 1A:23b). Liang Chi also received the same treatment (*HHS* 61:26b).

[97] *HHHY* 42:434.

entering officialdom always brought great fortune. A man would change from poor to rich overnight. Many poor people who could hardly support themselves and their families became rich after their appointments.[98] A man who started his official career as a subordinate possessing only a horse accumulated a wealth of a hundred million cash when he reached the status of a high official (*HS* 60:2a).

A grandee secretary who had property worth five hundred catties of gold (five million cash) was considered a man of very modest means by the emperor (*HS* 59:6b). The average must have been higher than this amount. Yang Ch'ang 楊敞, who had been grand minister of agriculture (*ta-ssu-nung* 大司農) and imperial chancellor, left five million cash to his younger son, Yang Yün 楊惲, and several million to his second wife (*HS* 66:10b). Another imperial chancellor, Chang Yü 張禹, had property worth eighty thousand catties of gold (eight hundred million cash). His biography states that he had 40,000 *mou* of fertile land in the irrigated area within the passes and other kinds of property of the same value (*HS* 81:13b–14a). Tu Chou 杜周, a grandee secretary who had been in office for a long time, and whose two sons were grand administrators, accumulated a wealth of one hundred million cash. One of his sons, Tu Yen-nien 杜延年, who had held the post of grand keeper of equipages (*t'ai-p'u* 太僕) for more than ten years and received gifts from the emperor and others, accumulated property worth several tens of millions (*HS* 60:2a, 5a). Che Kuo 折國, a great grandson of a marquis and himself a grand administrator, had property worth two hundred thousand cash and owned eight hundred slaves (II, 72). A prefect in the Later Han accumulated a wealth of thirty million (*HHS* 56:13b).

Corrupt and unlawful officials, needless to say, accumulated more wealth. The family of a eunuch accumulated a fortune of a thousand catties of gold (*HHS* 26:9a). A former grand administrator, who was accused of being overbearing, accumulated property worth tens of millions (III, 16).

Nearly all officials invested their money in land. One general bought much land, with houses and slaves, for his father (*HS* 68:1b); and the wife of a general who was on the battlefield bought land at home (*HHS* 18:11b–12a). It was generally considered that landed property was the most secure investment and that family wealth could best be handed down to future generations if it was in the form of land. Hsiao Ho, the chancellor of the state of Han, always bought land in secluded places,

[98] For instance, Ch'en P'ing (I, 7 and 8), Kung-sun Hung (II, 22), Chu Mai-ch'en (*HS* 64A:11a ff.), K'uang Heng (II, 37).

hoping that it would not be taken away by force from his descendants by powerful families.[99] But officials usually bought the most fertile land. The land Chang Yü purchased was in the area along the Ching and Wei rivers; it was the most expensive land in the country because of its fertility, owing to local irrigation facilities (*HS* 81:13b–14a). Tung-fang Shuo remarked that the land in this area between Feng and Hao was called "earth fat" and that one *mou* cost a cattie of gold (ten thousand cash) (*HS* 65:6b). Prices of ordinary land in other areas were lower.

Some officials invested their money in businesses and handicrafts for more profit. Chang An-shih 張安世 accumulated his wealth because his wife wove and the family slaves were engaged in various kinds of handicrafts (II, 36).

Because of their wealth, officials usually enjoyed a luxurious life. Many officials built large houses that they filled with precious articles.[100] Emperor Ch'eng complained that many nobles and officials were expanding their residences, ponds, and gardens, keeping a great number of slaves, wearing luxurious garments, possessing musical instruments, and keeping singing and dancing girls that went beyond the sumptuary regulations (*HS* 10:13b).

PRIVILEGES OF OFFICIALS

Officials were the privileged class. They enjoyed a monopoly of certain material goods, which was accorded to them in the sumptuary laws. Under the privilege of *jen-tzu*, children and junior relatives of high officials were automatically entitled to enter officialdom.[101] And the system of recommendation usually worked to their benefit. Although recommendation was open to all, most of those recommended by local authorities were family members of officials. This was particularly noticeable in the Later Han.[102] By this means they more or less monopolized preferential opportunities for obtaining office. This will be discussed more fully in Chapter 5.

Officials also had many regular privileges. First of all, their arrest had to be approved by the emperor prior to any action, a privilege known as *hsien-ch'ing* 先請 (previous request). In some cases a court discussion

[99] *SC* 53:5a; *HS* 39:5b.
[100] III, 17; *HS* 68:14a, 81:14a, 98:9b; III, 63.
[101] *HS* 11:3b, note; *HHHY* 45:463–65; *THHY* 26:289–90.
[102] See Chapter 5, pp. 204–05; see also Ch'ien Mu, *Kuo-shih ta-kang,* I, 133-34.

was held before the emperor, but the final decision was in his hands.[103]

In the Early Han the privilege of previous request was granted to all officials from the rank of 600 piculs up; it was even granted to the gentlemen of the palace (*lang-chung* 郎中), who only held a rank of "equivalent to 300 piculs," when their crimes deserved a punishment of more than *nai* 耐 (or *erh* 耏), a punishment which left the criminal's head unshaved.[104] Cases recorded in *Han-shu* 74 and 78 indicate definitely that no action could be taken if the request was disapproved by the emperor.[105]

However, Ch'ao Ts'o's case seems to have been different. He had a new entrance to his office made, and its path intruded upon the land outside the wall of the imperial temple. When he knew that the imperial chancellor, Shen-t'u Chia 申屠嘉, was going to impeach him, he confessed to the emperor. As a result the emperor rejected the request of the imperial chancellor, telling him that Ch'ao Ts'o was not guilty. Shen-t'u Chia became extremely angry and said that he regretted that he had not executed Ch'ao Ts'o instead of making the request;[106] his words seem to imply that prior approval was not always required. This discrepancy may be explained in two ways: either the imperial chancellor's statement was merely an emotional one that should not be considered evidence that prior request was not always required (that he actually did make the request of the emperor indicates that such action was usually expected), or an imperial chancellor was the only one who had the power to arrest and punish an official without the consent of the emperor.

The second assumption is supported by other cases. On one occasion an imperial chancellor asked permission to investigate the illegal activities of a retired official. The emperor replied, "This is the business of an imperial chancellor. Why should you ask permission for it?"[107] In another case an imperial chancellor summoned an official, Teng T'ung 鄧通, charged him with lack of respect while waiting upon the emperor in the court, and ordered him beheaded; but Teng was released when a messenger came from the emperor to summon him.[108] However, the imperial chancellor, who was aware that Teng was a male favorite of

[103] *HS* 83:19a–b, 86:15a–16a. On *hsien-ch'ing,* see *HLCI* 10:1a–b; *CCLK,* pp. 118–19; Hulsewé, *Remnants of Han Law,* I, 286 ff.
[104] *HS* 1B:10b, 4:11b, 8:24a; *HHHY* 62:613–15.
[105] *HS* 74:14a–b, 78:9a–b, 13a–b, and 14a–b.
[106] *SC* 101:8b–9a; *HS* 49:23a–b.
[107] *SC* 107:9a; *HS* 52:8a.
[108] *SC* 96:7b–8a; *HS* 42:6b–7a.

the emperor, was merely trying to terrify Teng. The assumption that the imperial chancellor had the right to punish an official without the consent of the emperor is contradicted in the instance of a director of justice (*ssu-chih* 司直) of the imperial chancellor who guarded the city gates but failed to prevent the "rebellious" heir apparent from escaping. The imperial chancellor intended to execute him; but he was released when the grandee secretary warned the imperial chancellor that before a 2,000-picul official could be punished a request had to be made to the emperor and that the chancellor was not at liberty to execute such a person. His words and the subsequent action of the imperial chancellor suggest that an imperial chancellor was not exempt from the regulation mentioned above. But this case is complicated by the reaction of Emperor Wu and its consequences. The emperor, who was furious, interrogated the grandee secretary: "The director of justice was guilty of allowing the rebels to go. The imperial chancellor's intention to behead him is in accordance with the law. Why did you, the grandee secretary, stop the imperial chancellor without authority?" The frightened grandee secretary committed suicide (*HS* 66:4b). Although it may be argued that the emperor's words imply that the imperial chancellor was authorized to punish an official without previous request, the extraordinary situation at the time—a rebellion that cost the life of the heir apparent and many others—should not be overlooked. In fact the emperor had issued an edict ordering his officials to arrest and kill the rebels and to close the city gates to prevent the heir apparent from escaping. It seems reasonable to assume that the statement made by the grandee secretary was in accordance with normal procedure, whereas the furious statement of the emperor was exceptional under the exceedingly unusual circumstances.

In the Later Han similar legal privileges were extended even to officials holding ranks lower than 600 piculs; for example, the chiefs of small prefectures and the chancellors of marquisates (*hou-kuo* 侯國), whose ranks were only 300 or 400 piculs,[109] enjoyed this privilege.

Officials, when arrested, were imprisoned and fettered in the same way as commoners.[110] An edict was issued in 195 B.C. by Emperor Hui that any official who held the title of *wu ta-fu* 五大夫, whose rank was more than 600 piculs, or who had served the emperor and was known by him was not to be fettered (*HS* 2:2a). When trials were in progress, officials were not exempted from torture (for example, *HS* 32:9a).

---

[109] *HHS* 1A:30b; *HHC* 28:7a.
[110] *SC* 53:5b, 57:6a; *HS* 39:5b, 40:25a and 30a, 86:16b.

Officials could not be sentenced and punished by the legal authorities without the approval of the emperor.[111] During the Han many high-ranking officials were executed. Many others escaped execution by committing suicide, either voluntarily or because they were told to. Some officials committed suicide before arrest to avoid punishment.[112] Such action was usually encouraged by their subordinates and students, who were more interested in decorum than in the lives of the top officials to whom they were attached. It was traditionally held that an imperial chancellor or a general should not appear before the judicial authorities to defend himself (*HS* 78:14b, 86:16a). At the same time, induced suicide was also institutionalized as a formal action in lieu of execution. In 174 B.C. Chia I complained in a memorial to Emperor Wen that high officials were executed in the same manner as commoners, and suggested that a high official should be ordered to commit suicide rather than be publicly executed (*HS* 48:22a, 23a–b). His suggestion, according to Ssu-ma Ch'ien, was accepted by Emperor Wen, and as a result all high officials were allowed to commit suicide instead of being executed. Even though this practice was no longer observed in Emperor Wu's time and officials were again imprisoned pending punishment (*HS* 48:25b–26a; III, 15), top officials, such as imperial chancellors, were frequently given the opportunity to commit suicide. Wang Chia 王嘉, an imperial chancellor, did not take the poison presented to him by a subordinate when he was summoned to the office of the commandant of justice, and the emperor was very angry because he submitted to imprisonment instead of committing suicide (*HS* 86:16a–b). This implies that under certain conditions top officials were expected to commit suicide. But it seems that this depended on the will of the emperor. If he intended to have an imperial chancellor executed, there was little chance of his escaping punishment (*HS* 66:5b).

EUNUCHS

The status of eunuchs was a very complicated one. On the one hand, they were commonly humiliated because of their castration. This can be seen in the subjective evaluation of the eunuchs themselves. The statement of Ssu-ma Ch'ien contained in a letter he wrote to one of his friends explicitly reveals an attitude of self-humiliation after he had been punished by castration. It reads:

[111] *SC* 101:8b–9a; *HS* 49:23a–b and 25a, 64B:19b–20a, 76:5b–6a.
[112] *HS* 40:30a, 59:6b, 78:14b, 79:12a, 83:19b, 86:6a; II, 34.

Considering that my body has been mutilated and I am in a humiliated position, that I am blamed whenever I make a movement, and that I am at fault when I am seeking perfection, therefore I feel much depressed and find no one to speak to. . . . Even though my talent is [as brilliant as] though I were carrying with me the Sui pearl and the Ho jade and though my behavior is comparable to that of Hsü Yu and Po I, yet [since my body is not in perfect form] there is nothing [for me] to be proud of; on the contrary, this is something merely to be ridiculed and which defiles myself. . . . Nothing is more shameful than castration. A man who has suffered such a punishment cannot be treated by others as an equal. This has been so for a long time, not merely for one generation. . . . [Eunuchs] have been humiliated since ancient times. Even a man of average talent would be discouraged in matters connected with eunuchs; how much more would a high-spirited scholar be? . . . At the highest [level is the man who] does not disgrace his ancestors, then comes [the one who] does not disgrace himself; then comes [the one who] does not disgrace his principle and countenance, then comes [the one who] does not disgrace his words; [and among the various punishments, in the order of humiliation, first] comes [the one who] brings disgrace by being imprisoned, then comes [the one who] brings disgrace by wearing a cloth [which is a symbol of punishment], then comes [the one who] brings disgrace by being fettered and beaten, then comes [the one who] brings disgrace by having his head shaved and wearing an iron collar, then comes [the one who] brings disgrace by having his skin mutilated [i.e., tattooing] and his body and limbs cut [i.e., cutting off the nose or feet], and at the lowest [level] castration is the extreme [disgrace]. . . .

Because of the words uttered by my mouth, I received this misfortune. I have been attacked and ridiculed by the people of my local village and my relatives, and I have defiled my ancestors. How can I have the face to visit the grave of my parents again? Even after a hundred generations my blame will be still greater. . . . Every time I think of this shame, my back sweats and my clothes thus become wet. I am merely a minister in the women's compartment. How can I withdraw and hide myself in a mountain cave?[113]

The letter speaks for itself. That castration was considered more shameful than any other kind of mutilation seems to have its root in the traditional attitude of the supremacy of the male. Castration, which made family continuation impossible and thus hampered ancestor worship, certainly took away the main role of a male descendant in a family. At the same time castration deprived a man of his masculinity and forced him to take up a semi-feminine role in society. This meant great frustration in a society in which male superiority was widely accepted. When Ssu-ma Ch'ien wrote the foregoing letter he was holding an

---

[113] *HS* 62:14b–19a. The meaning of many phrases adopted in this translation is based upon Li's commentary in the *Wen-hsüan*, 41:9b–26b, in the *Liu-ch'en chu Wen-hsüan* edition, *SPTK* ed., hereafter cited as *WH*.

honorable post, prefect of the palace writers (*chung-shu-ling* 中書令), and he had the favor of the emperor (*HS* 62:14a). His frustration obviously illustrates that he was ashamed of being a eunuch and felt inferior and that holding a high eunuch post did not compensate for the loss of his masculinity.

The inferior status of eunuchs can also be seen in the subjective evaluations of others toward this group. Yüan Ang 爰盎, an official, protested to the emperor that his majesty should not ride in the same carriage with a eunuch: "I hear that the Son of Heaven shares the six-foot carriage only with the outstanding persons of the empire. Now although the Han court is lacking in [outstanding] persons, why should Your Majesty ride in the same carriage with a [man who has suffered castration with] knife and saw?" The emperor agreed with him and thereupon the eunuch was ordered out of the carriage (*HS* 49:3a).

However, both Ssu-ma Ch'ien and Yüan Ang represent the attitude of a scholar-official. It is understandable that a man who had become a regular member of the bureaucracy, the most honorable channel of social mobility, would look down upon a eunuch. And it is also understandable that a man would be depressed if he were forced to change his status from that of an official to that of a eunuch. But the situation and attitude might be different for a poor family that could hardly support its children. Having their sons castrated so that they could become eunuchs was an easy solution to an economic problem. They did not have to borrow money for capital, which was required for almost any business. The job also required no long-term professional training. Furthermore, this job also provided a channel for social mobility that might lead to wealth and power. This certainly was an attraction for those who lacked reading ability and other qualifications required for entering officialdom, but who sought ways of social mobility. This kind of attitude must have existed at a time when people began to realize that eunuch-status brought the same kind of fortune and power that officials enjoyed, while painstaking preparations were required only for the latter.

Here we must make a distinction between ordinary eunuchs and those who held superior posts and were entrusted with power. Their status and prestige must have been very different. There were those petty eunuchs who rendered all kinds of domestic services within the palace. There were also eunuchs who supervised other eunuchs who were in charge of matters concerning the imperial concubines, various imperial parks and gardens, various sacrifices within the palace, and so forth. Above all of them were those who attended the emperor and whose duties were more or less associated with the administration of court affairs—providing information to the emperor, receiving memorials from officials, announcing imperial edicts, serving as ushers in the court when a king paid a visit to the emperor, and also serving as ushers in the inner palace and accompanying the emperor there. The bureaucratic hierarchy among the eunuchs was officially recognized and institutionalized. The ranks held by the eunuchs varied from 100 piculs up to "equivalent to 2,000 piculs." Eunuchs were thus given both superior bureaucratic status and a high official salary comparable to that of the officials. The status of eunuchs in the Later Han was even higher because the rank of the regular palace attendant (*chung-ch'ang-shih* 中常侍) was raised from 1,000 piculs to "equivalent to 2,000 piculs," and some of them were even ennobled as marquises.[114] Their success in political affairs certainly had a great effect on their status: it offset the general attitude of humiliation of the eunuchs by society.

There is abundant evidence in support of this contention. Shih Hsien, whose favor from Emperor Yüan surpassed all others at court, was treated respectfully by the other officials (III, 32). The eunuchs in the Later Han who exercised great power in the government enjoyed a superior status in society. Association with them was often a status symbol. This is clearly illustrated in the following case. A rich man, Meng T'o 孟佗, associated with the slaves of a powerful eunuch, Chang Jang 張讓, and treated them nicely and generously. All of them were grateful to him and asked what they could do for him. The rich man said, "All I want is a salute from you." At that time the carriages of the guests who came to visit Chang numbered several hundreds and sometimes even a thousand. When Meng arrived, the eunuch superintendent of slaves led many other slaves in saluting and welcoming him on the road. Thereupon they took his carriage through the gate. All the guests were frightened. They thought that Meng must be on good terms with the eunuch, so they presented gifts to Meng (III, 69).

Many people sought to be the adopted sons of eunuchs. Apparently this was because the adopted heir of an ennobled eunuch—whether of the same family or of a different surname—was allowed to inherit his noble title (*HHS* 78:12a–b; III, 64). Obviously this provided one of the easiest ways of social mobility—a way which was impossible under the usual rule, according to which a son or a close relative of a noneunuch was allowed to inherit a noble title. Ts'ao Ts'ao's father, Ts'ao Sung, was

[114] *HHC* 26:5a ff.; III, 58, 59, 69.

the adopted son of a powerful eunuch. Because of this connection Ts'ao Sung not only inherited the marquisate but also was able to become a top official, grand commandant.[115]

The wealth, status, and power of eunuchs in the Later Han was so impressive that many persons castrated themselves and their sons in order to become eunuchs (*HHS* 78:5a). Obviously this would not have happened if such a career had remained an inferior one and if it did not offer a fair chance for social mobility and political power.

COMMONERS

Commoners were traditionally classified in the following order: scholars, farmers, artisans, and merchants. The classification was not an arbitrary one, but implied the evaluation of the four main occupations and represented a ranking of occupational groups. Although sometimes merchants were mentioned before artisans, scholars and farmers were always the first to be mentioned, and scholars always headed the list. This suggests that artisans and merchants had a more or less similar position, but scholars and farmers were always superior to them, in the order mentioned.

SCHOLARS

The term *shih* 士, in its broad sense, included both scholars who had already entered officialdom and the commoner-scholars. Since the vast majority of the civil officials had been students and many of them still were scholars, the distinction between scholars and officials was not clear-cut, and the two usually overlapped. The term in its narrow sense, however, referred only to those who were engaged in study or teaching and who had not yet entered officialdom. The group included those who sought to enter officialdom as well as those who refused to enter. Once they were appointed they were considered not scholars but officials.

Scholars had the highest status among the commoners, for they were the only group engaged in mental labor, which was traditionally considered superior to physical labor. Knowledge in the classics, which was a prerequisite for official appointment, was highly valued in Chinese society. The scholars, possessing such qualifications, were thus potential candidates for officialdom, the most honored position in society. In

[115] *HHS* 78:14a; *SKC*, Wei, 1:1a–b.

fact civil officials were mainly recruited from the scholars. Entrance to officialdom was open to them in many ways. One way was to become a student in the Imperial Academy (*pi-yung* 辟雍), studying under the erudites. In the Early Han, after a year of study in the Academy, the students were given a test and those who had mastered one subject or more were appointed men of letters (*wen-hsüeh* 文學) or masters of precedents (*chang-ku* 掌故); those whose achievements were rated excellent were eligible to be gentlemen of the palace (*HS* 88:4b–6a). In Wang Mang's time and during the Later Han, students were appointed gentlemen of the palace, members of the retinue of the heir apparent (*t'ai-tzu she-jen* 太子舍人), men of letters, or masters of precedents, according to the results of the tests.[116] They could then be promoted to erudites and other higher posts.[117]

Scholars were also frequently recommended by the various officials of the central and local governments as "men of wisdom and virtue" when an edict was issued asking for such recommendations. After arrival in the capital the candidate wrote an essay in answer to questions put by the emperor and was then appointed to a post according to his success in answering the questions; usually the man whose essay pleased the emperor was given a high post.[118] One man who was recommended and made an erudite later became the imperial chancellor (II, 22).

Outstanding scholars with unusual reputations and academic accomplishments, such as famous teachers, were usually summoned with great honor to the imperial court and appointed erudites or were named to higher posts such as grand administrator or minister.[119] Ssu-ma Hsiang-ju, whose *fu*-poem 賦 was greatly admired by Emperor Wu, won an audience and was given an official post (*HS* 57A:3a–b, 25b). Scholars were often appointed by grand administrators and other high officials as their subordinates. This practice was particularly popular in the Later Han. Many outstanding scholars were appointed by the Three Ducal Ministers and grand generals.[120]

Scholars could present memorials directly to the emperor to recommend themselves. It was said that about one thousand scholars attempted to show off their talents by this means in Emperor Wu's time.[121]

[116] *HS* 88:6a; *HHS* 79A:3b.
[117] *HS* 88:11a–b and 17b–18a; *HHS* 67:31a and 33a, 79A:14b and 15a, 79B:2b–3b and 17b.
[118] *HHHY* 44:451–53; *THHY* 26:279–81; *HS* 56:1a ff., 64A:1a ff.
[119] *HS* 71:3b, 72:19a and 22a–b, 88:7a, 14b, 16a, and 22a–b; *HHS* 35:21a, 53:7b–8a, 79A:12b and 13b, 79B:11a, 12b, 13b–14a, 18a, and 22a, 80A:15b–16a.
[120] *HHHY* 45:468–69; *THHY* 27:293–94.
[121] *SC* 126:7b–8a; *HS* 65:1a.

One of them, Tung-fang Shuo, presented a large bundle of memorials consisting of three thousand tablets; the emperor, who spent two months in reading them, appointed him a gentleman (*SC* 16:7b–8a). Chu-fu Yen 主父偃, Hsü Lo 徐樂, and Yen An 嚴安 all entered officialdom by this means (*HS* 64A:17a–19a).

The socio-economic status of scholars varied: some were rich, some were poor; some were descendants of officials' families, and some were commoners. There were also different kinds of scholars. They were either (1) professional teachers, (2) students enrolled in the Imperial Academy, (3) students studying in the schools sponsored by commandery governments, (4) students of the professional teachers, or (5) self-taught students. It was not uncommon for a scholar to open a school in a village or town, and sometimes a moderate house was built especially for this purpose (*HHS* 57:9b, 33b). A single teacher might have from several hundred to more than a thousand students.[122] Since tuition was expected from every student—one student who was too poor to pay picked up firewood and performed various services for his fellow students (II, 66)—a teacher with hundreds of students must have had a considerable income. The teaching profession seems to have been a decent one and one sought by many people (*HHS* 79B:6a, 7a, 14b). A teacher in a village was usually respected by the villagers and assumed leadership in the community; for example, he was usually sought as an arbitrator in disputes (*HHS* 67:27b). Many teachers became erudites and some became officials of high rank—grand administrators and ministers. One was even appointed imperial chancellor.[123]

Among the students, the status of those who studied at the Imperial Academy was superior. Students who studied under the erudites were selected from persons above the age of eighteen by the grand minister of ceremonies (*t'ai-ch'ang* 太常). Also, those who were interested in literature and who behaved well could be recommended by the local authorities to study at the Academy (*HS* 88:4b). When the institution was first set up in Emperor Wu's time, the number of students was limited to fifty only; in Emperor Chao's time it was increased to one hundred; and later, in Emperor Hsüan's time, to two hundred. The number increased to one thousand under Emperor Yüan; this number was maintained by Emperor Ch'eng except for a short time when the number

---

[122] II, 81, 83; *HS* 88:15b, 22a, and 26b; *HHS* 27:18a, 35:14b, 67:9b and 33b–34a, 68:2b, 79A:6a, 12b, 13b, 14a, and 21b, 79B:6a, 11a, 11b, 13b, 14a–b, 18a, and 22a–b, 80A:13a and 25a.

[123] II, 66; *HS* 71:3b; *HHS* 67:27b, 79A:6b, 7b, 8b–9b, 11a–b, 13b, and 14a, 79B:6a–b, 7a–b, 11a, 11b–12a, 13b, 14b–15a, 18a–b, and 22a.

reached a maximum of three thousand. The number was increased by Wang Mang to more than ten thousand men (*HS* 88:5b–6a). In the Later Han the Imperial Academy, after suffering a decline under Emperor An, was enlarged; the number of students increased to as many as thirty thousand and more in Emperor Huan's time (*HHS* 79A:3b–4a). To be recommended and accepted as a student in the Academy meant social success and esteem. This is fully illustrated in the biography of Kuo T'ai 郭泰(太). He was poor and of humble origin and never entered officialdom. But his repute and prestige were unparalleled in his time; for example, he became a friend of the governor of Honan, Li Ying 李膺. When he left the capital for home he was seen off by many officials and scholars, the carriages amounting to several thousand. He later became a teacher and had more than one thousand students. He was so admired by his contemporaries that once when one of the stretched corners of his cap drooped because of the rain, many persons imitated the style. When he died, more than a thousand attended his funeral (*HHS* 68:1a–2b). Another student of the Imperial Academy was admired by a prominent official, Yüan Shao 袁紹, and became his close friend (*HHS* 67:35b–36a). Prominent officials often sought to associate with famous scholars. In one instance two renowned scholars purposely declined to receive high officials who had come to visit them in order to impress others (*HHS* 68:8a–b).

The influence of the students of the Imperial Academy was also manifested in their role in shaping the popular opinion of the scholar-officials, that is, in their expression of approval or disapproval of the behavior of others. Their criticism affected both a person's reputation and his political career. Appointments made by high officials were often based on their evaluation (*HHS* 68:8b–9a).

The influence of the students of the Imperial Academy is fully illustrated in the political movement against the powerful eunuchs in the second century. They were really the backbone of support for the group of officials and members of the consort family who fought against the eunuchs. The association of the officials and the students and the fact that the leaders of the students, Kuo T'ai and Chia Piao 賈彪, were also leaders of the movement and that their names were listed by their followers together with those officials of high integrity as eminent leaders are indications of their superior prestige (*HHS* 67:5a–6a).

It is obvious that only those scholars whose families were rich enough or who were lucky enough to be supported by their family members could be free to be full-time scholars; all others had to support themselves by some kind of work. With the exception of a bookseller (II, 82) and a drug seller (II, 81) none of them engaged in a trade. It seems that scholars avoided becoming merchants, whose status was an unfavorable one and a hindrance to an official career. Bookselling was the exception, probably because it was connected with study and was therefore not looked down upon by society as were the ordinary trades. Farming was one of the most favored occupations for the scholar, probably because it was an honorable one and was considered more acceptable than other kinds of labor. Many scholars, including Cheng Hsüan 鄭玄, engaged in farming (II, 83, 84). Poor students often supported themselves in other humble occupations. A poor scholar maintained a humble living by gathering and selling firewood (I, 26). A number of students supported themselves by being wage laborers.[124] Among them, three hired themselves out to work on a farm, studying while they rested.[125] Some were asked to husk rice, and some were pig breeders.[126] Although a humble occupation was generally a status disqualification, it seems that a scholar who engaged in such an occupation would not be looked down upon by society. Thus Sun Ch'i 孫期, a scholar whose family was poor and who supported himself and his mother by pig breeding, was followed by a number of students (II, 87). Another pig breeder also became a teacher (II, 66). The only case that indicates that such a humble occupation was shameful is found in the statement of a friend of an official; however, emphasis was put on the fact that the young man in question was the son of a high official (II, 76). It seems that the matter would have been different if the young man had merely been an ordinary scholar or a student with a nonofficial background.

A similar attitude is found also in cases where scholars engaged in other kinds of humble occupations. The student who hired himself out to husk rice for others did not lose his status as a student of the Imperial Academy; on the contrary, he won the friendship of a prefect (*HHS* 64:2b). Another poor student of the Imperial Academy was a painter and was respected by Kuo T'ai and Ts'ai Yung, the leading scholars of his time (*HHS* 53:12a).

Most important of all, poverty and humble occupations were not a hindrance to the social mobility of the scholars concerned. For example, Chu Mai-ch'en, the firewood seller who was divorced by his wife because of his poverty, finally succeeded in having an audience with the

---

[124] II, 25, 37, 55, 71, 75; *HHS* 37:1a, 53:12a, 64:2b, 67:21a, 68:5a, 76:18b.
[125] II, 25, 75; *HHS* 76:18b.
[126] II, 22, 66, 76; *HHS* 64:2b, 83:11b.

emperor and became a grand administrator (I, 26). Several pig breeders were recommended and appointed officials, including the one who was reproved by his deceased father's friend for engaging in such an occupation (II, 22, 66, 76). One of the pig breeders, Kung-sun Hung, was appointed an erudite, through recommendation, and became the first commoner-scholar to become an imperial chancellor in the Han. Until then the post had always been held by marquises, most of whom were military men (II, 22). A number of poor students who had been hired laborers were recommended and appointed officials.[127] Ni K'uan 兒寬, a student of the Imperial Academy who cooked for his fellow students and hired himself out from time to time, became a grandee secretary (II, 25). K'uang Heng, the son of a farmer and a poor student who supported himself by being a hired laborer, attained the position of imperial chancellor (II, 37). The scholar-painter mentioned above was offered appointments by the grand commandant and by the grand general, but accepted neither position. He was also appointed an erudite by the imperial court and again declined to take the post (*HHS* 53:12a–15a).

One student of the Imperial Academy changed his name and took the job of government runner. Apparently such an occupation was considered shameful, but he was later summoned to the capital and given an appointment (II, 52). Sorcery and trading were the only humble occupations that were detrimental to a scholar's official career. In order to avoid an appointment, Wang Lieh 王烈 "debased himself by becoming a merchant" (II, 79). However, he was later appointed to an official post by Ts'ao Ts'ao. Another scholar avoided official appointment by announcing that his family had practiced sorcery.[128]

Scholars who had been summoned and appointed by the imperial court or high officials obviously had more prestige than those who had never been summoned. It seems that the more a man was summoned the more prestige he had, and scholars in general were pleased at the public recognition that such summonses brought them. However, it was not absolutely necessary for a scholar to become an official in order to maintain his prestige. In fact there was a tendency in the Later Han for scholars to decline the summonses and the appointments. Declining meant purity and loftiness of character; hence declining brought even more prestige. It seems that the scholar's status was determined mainly by his academic accomplishments and personal integrity rather than

---

[127] II, 25, 55, 71, 75. See also II, 37; *HHS* 37:1a ff.
[128] *THHY* 27:294–98.

by such factors as official rank. This is fully illustrated in the case of Cheng Hsüan, whose scholarship and status could not be surpassed by other contemporary scholars.

Although one of Cheng's remote forefathers (his eighth generation ancestor) had been a high official, his family was poor. Cheng had been a village official in his youth, but he disliked the job and went to study at the Imperial Academy. Returning home, he taught several hundred students and devoted his spare time to farming. The general of the rear (*hou chiang-chün* 後將軍), Yüan Wei 袁隗, memorialized that Cheng should be appointed an attendant within the palace (*shih-chung* 侍中), a post he did not accept because of the death of his father. Later he was summoned by the grand general, Ho Chin, who received him with great politeness. He stayed only one night and fled. K'ung Jung 孔融, the chancellor of a kingdom, who highly respected him, instructed a prefect to name a rural district in Cheng's honor. T'ao Ch'ien 陶謙, an inspector (*tz'u-shih* 刺史), treated him as a teacher and a friend. The grand general, Yüan Shao, once brought together a large number of guests and invited Cheng, who was asked to take the seat of honor. Ying Shao, a renowned scholar who had been a grand administrator, requested that he be allowed to be Cheng's student. Yüan, in a memorial, urged the appointment of Cheng as general of the palace gentlemen on the left (*tso chung-lang chiang* 左中郎將), but he did not accept the position. Later, when Cheng was summoned by the court and given the position of minister of agriculture, he was welcomed and seen off by the local authorities all along his route. Upon his arrival Cheng dismissed himself on the grounds of illness and returned home. When he died, more than one thousand persons who had been his students came to attend his funeral (II, 83; *HHS* 35:21b).

Cheng's case illustrates the kind of prestige a commoner-scholar possessed in the Later Han. It was a period in which scholars were highly respected and were given opportunities to move up in the class structure by official appointment. It was also a period in which the commoner-scholars could have a status comparable to that of the officials, and in exceptional cases a commoner-scholar with outstanding accomplishments could even have more prestige than officials.

FARMERS

The abolition of the feudal land system and the introduction of the private ownership of land, a policy of Lord Shang adopted by the state of Ch'in in the fourth century B.C. (*HS* 24A:7a–b, 14b), produced a drastic change in the socio-economic life of the farmer. In feudal times only the feudal lords owned landed property, which was in the form of a seigniory or manor, and those who cultivated the land for their lords were serfs. They were not free and were obliged to pay dues and render corvée, including military service.[129] After the new law was introduced, people were free to buy and sell land. But not all owners were cultivators: those wealthy people, such as merchants, who were able to buy a large amount of land were either unable or unwilling to cultivate it themselves; on the other hand, most of those who cultivated the land were too poor to buy any, so it was unequally distributed among the population. In the words of Tung Chung-shu 董仲舒, a Han political thinker who was concerned with the problem of the unequal distribution of land and traced its origin back to Shang Yang's policy, "the rich owned land piece after piece, while the poor did not own enough on which to stand an awl" (*HS* 24A:14b). These landless people naturally became the tenants of the wealthy owners and paid them a fixed amount of rent, usually 50 per cent of their produce.[130] Or they became wage laborers and worked on the farms of others. Ch'en She 陳涉, the first leader of the rebellion that overthrew the Ch'in government, was a hired laborer.[131]

Large landowners were usually wealthy people who were not primarily farmers. In previous sections I have mentioned that almost every noble and official owned some landed property. Wealthy merchants, to be discussed later, also owned land. Ordinary landowners, other than officials and merchants, usually were small landowners. Since officials and merchants were large landowners and also possessed other forms of wealth, it would be misleading to include them with the ordinary small proprietors in a discussion of the economic position of landowners. The same principle holds true in the discussion of social status. Those landed proprietors who were nobles, officials, or merchants had a status determined by their membership in those groups, not by any qualification as landowners. For these reasons I discuss the socio-economic status of nobles, officials, and merchants who were also landowners under their own classifications, and concern myself here only

[129] Ch'ü T'ung-tsu, *Chung-kuo feng-chien she-hui* (Shanghai, 1937), pp. 230–48; O. Franke, "Feudalism: Chinese," *Encyclopaedia of Social Sciences*, VI, 213-14; Derk Bodde, "Feudalism in China," in *Feudalism in History*, ed. Rushton Coulborn (Princeton: Princeton University Press, 1956), pp. 62–65.

[130] *HS* 24A:15a, 19b; Hsün Yüeh, *Han-chi, SPTK* ed., 8:2a, hereafter cited as *HC*.
[131] *SC* 48:1a; *HS* 31:1a.

with those landowners who invested their money mainly in agriculture and did not engage in political and commercial activities. In other words, under the category of "farmer" I include only those who either cultivated the land themselves or supervised or managed a farm. Those absentee landlords who lived in the city and collected rent from their tenants and performed no managerial or supervisory activities but instead engaged in professions other than farming are not considered farmers.

Even within the group here designated as farmers there was a great variation between those who were landowners and those who were tenants or wage laborers; similarly a distinction must be made between large and small landowners. The average holding of a cultivator-owner in pre-Ch'in and Han times seems to have been about 100 *mou* (*HS* 24A:6a, 11a). The economic condition of such a farmer was described by Li K'uei in the fourth century B.C. as follows:

The total crops produced from 100 *mou* of land is 150 piculs, from which he [the farmer] has to pay 10 per cent tax to the government; the net income is 135 piculs. Suppose he has a family of five members. The food consumed by the whole family will be 90 piculs. The balance left for other necessary expenditures is only 45 piculs. As the price of a picul is 30 coins, the total amount of cash the family owns is 1,350 coins. They spend 300 for religious sacrifices. Every person has to spend 300 for clothing; therefore the total amount spent by five members is 1,500. Hence there is a regular deficit of 450. And besides they have to meet urgent expenses, such as those for illnesses, funerals, and irregular taxes.

Therefore, Li K'uei concluded that the farmers were always in distress and did not find farming encouraging (*HS* 24A:6a–b). Although this description was written in the fourth century B.C., it seems that the same description held true for Ch'in as well as for Han.

The living conditions of a family of five members with a property of 100 *mou* of land was discussed by Ch'ao Ts'o in 178 B.C. along the same lines. Besides tilling the soil, they had to cut wood for fuel, work in the government buildings, and render labor services. According to him, no less than two persons in the family were obliged to render such services. The annual income derived from 100 *mou* of land, which was not more than 100 piculs of grain, could not meet the family's expenses. All expenditures, such as treating guests, attending funerals, visiting the sick, caring for orphans, and bringing up children had to be defrayed from that income. The situation was still worse when there was a calamity or exceptional taxation. Those who had something to sell sold it at half its value, and those who had nothing had to borrow at 100 per cent interest. Consequently they had to sell their land, their houses, and even their wives and children in order to pay their debts. Numerous farmers lost their land and became fugitives (*HS* 24A:11a–b).

Even men who possessed 130 *mou* of land could hardly support their families. Kung Yü's wife and children only had such food as husks and beans to eat, and they had to wear clothing made of coarse material (*HS* 72:13b). His statement, "My wife and children did not have enough husks and beans to eat and their coarse clothing was not in good condition," probably should not be taken literally, but since it was mentioned in a memorial, it could not be far from the truth. It seems unlikely that a family with 130 *mou* of land could enjoy an existence better than such rough food and coarse clothing.

The economic condition of those whose land was less than 100 *mou* was still worse. Ch'en P'ing's family, which owned 30 *mou* of land, was considered poor by society; no one was willing to marry his daughter to such a poor man. They lived in a poor area against the city wall and used a piece of an old straw mat as a door. Although he was living with his elder brother, who did the farming, and the brother's wife, still he had to support himself by rendering services at funerals. This indicates that a farmer with such a small piece of land could not maintain a family of more than two members (I, 7, 8). Unfortunately we have no more data on the lives of these small landowners, but the few cases mentioned are sufficient to show that they were "poor and humble," as pointed out by Ch'ao Ts'o (*HS* 24A:12a).

Those who had no land at all usually became tenants of wealthy landowners, to whom they paid 50 per cent of their harvest (*HS* 24A: 15a, 19b). The livelihood of such tenants, according to Tung Chung-shu's description, was miserable: they usually "wore the coverings of oxen and horses and ate the food of dogs and pigs." Furthermore, under the pressure of greedy and cruel officials many of them ran away and became bandits (*HS* 24A:15a). A similar statement concerning their lot was made by Wang Mang (*HS* 24A:19b).

The wage laborers who worked for others on a short-term basis were insecure because of the irregularity of their jobs; they could not always find work. Ch'en She, who was a wage laborer, once told his co-workers that if one among them became rich and honorable, he should not forget the rest. One of them ridiculed him: "You are a hired laborer. How can you become rich and honorable?"[132] Although Ch'en later did become a king, his good fortune came about only because of a revolution and was certainly atypical. The statement of the co-laborer reflects the general attitude and holds true under normal conditions.

The status of the farmer seems to have varied according to the possession or lack of property, the size of the property held, the manner of managing and cultivating the land, and the like. Landowners were superior to landless tenants and wage earners. Large landowners had more prestige than small landowners. It was not that Ch'en P'ing was a farmer but that he was a poor farmer that made him the object of humiliation and unacceptable for marriage (I, 8).

The farmer's work was considered productive and fundamental, for it supplied food for society. The work of merchants and artisans, on the other hand, was nonproductive and secondary.[133] It follows that farmers contributed more to society and deserved more rewards; theoretically they had a social and legal status superior to merchants and artisans. There were no special sumptuary laws against the farmers as there were against the merchants. On the contrary, the title "diligent farmer" (*li-t'ien* 力田) was specifically created to encourage farmers; those who received this title were exempted from corvée for life and sometimes were given land or silk as rewards.[134] Moreover, farmers could enter an official career by recommendation.

But social reality did not correspond to the ideal. Merchants possessed wealth and controlled the life chances of farmers, and they enjoyed material comforts and were respected by society. Farmers were looked down upon by society because of their poverty. The discrepancy between the legal status and the social esteem of farmers and merchants was noticed by Ch'ao Ts'o: "Now the law despises merchants, but the merchants have become rich and noble; it esteems farmers, but the farmers have become poor and humble. What is esteemed by the people is despised by the ruler; what is scorned by the officials is honored by the law" (*HS* 24A:11a–12a).

Although legally farmers were permitted to enter officialdom, because of poverty and lack of leisure time to study most farmers were illiterate, and rarely did a farmer have a chance of being recommended for officialdom. In one instance a farmer who personally cultivated his

---

[132] *SC* 48:1a; *HS* 31:1a.

[133] *SC* 68:4a; *HS* 24A:8b.

[134] *HHHY* 48:493–94. On *li-t'ien* see Chao I, *Nien-erh shih cha-chi, SPPY* ed., 2:19a, hereafter cited as *NESCC*.

land was appointed to office by a grand administrator; later he was
offered the position of grand administrator (II, 84). The famous scholar
Cheng Hsüan, who did some farming and was followed by a thousand
students, was recommended and appointed to official posts several
times and was even assigned to such a high post as minister of agriculture.[135] An agricultural laborer in the Later Han who studied in his
leisure time was recommended as "filially pious and incorrupt," appointed prefect, and later promoted to the post of grand administrator
(II, 75). But cases like these were rare.

ARTISANS

Our knowledge about the lives of artisans is limited because very
little information is available. The only valuable information provided
by a Han historian is that the economic position of the artisans was
somewhere between that of merchants and farmers. In other words,
artisans made more money than farmers but less than merchants (*SC*
129:15b). A craftsman who made knives and swords is mentioned in
the biography of merchants, where it says that he became wealthy and
was able to eat the food usually enjoyed by nobles and officials (*HS*
91:11a).

Artisans had a more favorable legal position than merchants, who
were not allowed to wear silks or ride on horses and in carriages. There
were no such sumptuary laws regarding artisans. Nor were artisans
legally prohibited from entering officialdom.[136] Apparently these laws
gave artisans a legal status superior to merchants and assured them of
more social mobility, particularly through the channel of officialdom.
For example, a painter who attended the Imperial Academy was highly
respected and admired by the student-leader of the academy, Kuo
T'ai, and by an outstanding scholar-official, Ts'ai Yung. He was recommended and offered positions by both central and local governments, but declined all appointments (*HHS* 53:12a–15a). Of course the
man's reputation was based on his status as a student in the Imperial
Academy, but still it is important that a painter was eligible for the

[135] II, 83. Similarly, Yang Chen 楊震 had been a student of the grand minister of
ceremonies, Huan Yü 桓郁, and then became a tenant farmer with his students helping him in his agricultural work. Yang finally became a grand commandant (*Hsü-
Han-chih*, quoted in *HHS* 54:1b, note and 54:5b).

[136] We do not know when artisans began to be treated the same as merchants. The
earliest evidence is found in the Sui dynasty in a law prohibiting artisans and merchants from entering officialdom (Wei Cheng, *Sui-shu*, Po-na, ed., 2:10b).

Academy and that this occupation did not affect his prestige. Obviously this contrasts with the general attitude toward merchants: an official who appointed a merchant was impeached, and in another case a man avoided an appointment by saying that he was a merchant. (See the section in this chapter on Merchants.)

There is no information on the social status of artisans. Since merchants were inferior to farmers, yet the social statuses of the two groups were actually reversed because merchants were wealthier than farmers, it is quite possible that the social status of artisans might not have corresponded to their legal status. Artisans were generally wealthier than farmers but not as wealthy as merchants, so it is reasonable to assume that artisans might have had a social status superior to farmers yet inferior to the wealthy merchants who enjoyed superior prestige and who associated with high officials. But in general it seems that artisans and merchants enjoyed a more or less similar status. Sometimes merchants were mentioned before artisans,[137] which deviates from the conventional order of the four main occupations: scholars, farmers, artisans, and merchants. This seems to suggest that merchants and artisans were treated as a group in society.

MERCHANTS

The term "merchant" in Ch'in and Han times referred not only to various traders and shopkeepers but also included persons engaged in mining (particularly iron and cinnabar), salt manufacturing, cattle and pig breeding, raising fish, manufacturing, and money-lending.[138] Frequently a person had more than one occupation, such as a combination of farming, animal breeding, and trade.

It was not uncommon for animal breeders and merchants to invest their money in land. The Jen family engaged in both farming and animal breeding (I, 10). Pu Shih 卜式, who was a farmer and sheep breeder, gave all his land to his younger brother and kept only the sheep, numbering about one hundred. Ten years later the sheep had increased to more than a thousand, and he bought land again (*HS* 58:8b–9a).

A regulation prohibiting merchants from owning land was introduced in 119 B.C. (*HS* 24B:12a), but it is doubtful that it was effective. Fan Chung, who is described as a descendant of forefathers who "had been skilled in farming for generations and who were fond of business,"

---

[137] For instance, see *Han-fei-tzu, SPTK* ed., 19:8a–b, hereafter cited as *HFT*.
[138] *SC, chüan* 129; *HS, chüan* 91.

was also engaged in raising fish and breeding cattle and owned more than three hundred *ch'ing* of land (I, 40). That merchants often owned landed property is clearly indicated in Chung-ch'ang T'ung's statement: "The powerful men are engaged in trade. . . . Their landed property extends to all directions" (*HHS* 49:25b).

Among the commoners, merchants had an economic position much superior to those in other professions. It was generally held at that time that artisans made more money than farmers but less than merchants (*SC* 129:15b). In comparing the livelihood of farmers and merchants, Ch'ao Ts'o remarked that great merchants wore silk, ate only good grain and meat, rode in well-built carriages, and drove fat horses (II, 18).

Of course there were peddlers and merchants with only a small amount of capital who lived on their small profits. Unfortunately their lives were overlooked by ancient historians, so our knowledge concerning them is very limited. We only know of those who made fortunes in various businesses. A seller of dry tripe is said to have traveled with a long chain of outriders. A retailer of suet and a dealer in sauces each accumulated a wealth of ten million cash (*HS* 91:10b–11a). These seem rather exceptional. A trader who had property worth one thousand catties of gold (ten million cash) was classified as a big merchant (II, 3, 30). This amount is a hundredfold more than that possessed by an average middle-class family, and because of the size of this fortune, such a merchant and his family were among those moved by the government to the mausoleum towns. (Usually a family with a fortune of one to three millions was ordered to move to a certain place designated by the government.)[139] A dismissed official once said: "If an official fails to attain [a position of] 2,000 piculs, or if a merchant fails to acquire [a fortune of] ten million cash, how can he equal others?" (III, 15). This indicates that such an amount was quite a high standard for a merchant. Ssu-ma Ch'ien shows, in his "Biographies of the Moneymakers," that a man (farmer, merchant, or artisan) who had a capital investment of one million cash on which he earned a profit of 20 per cent would have an annual income of two hundred thousand cash, an income the same as that of a noble who was enfeoffed with a thousand households.[140] Such an income would naturally enable the merchant to enjoy good

[139] In Emperor Wu's time wealthy persons with property worth three hundred million cash were to be moved by the government (III, 19). Later, in Emperor Hsüan's time, the criterion was lowered to one hundred million (III, 33, 35).

[140] *SC* 129:14a–15a; *HS* 91:5b–6b.

food and nice clothing.[141] A man with a fortune of ten million cash was considerably more prosperous (*SC* 129:18a). The same historian points out that such men would have wealth comparable to that of the lord of a big city, and that a man with one hundred million cash would have the pleasures of a king (*SC* 129:21a).

The merchants who made such fortunes, accounts of which are found mainly in the "Biographies of Moneymakers" in the *Shih-chi* and *Han-shu*, were involved in several different activities. I Tun 猗頓 and Tung-kuo Hsien-yang 東郭咸陽 made fortunes by manufacturing salt. The latter had a wealth of one thousand catties of gold (ten million cash).[142] There were also five renowned iron smelters: Kuo Tsung 郭縱, whose wealth is said to have been equal to that of a king; a Cho family who owned one thousand slaves and enjoyed the possession of lands and ponds and the pleasure of hunting like a ruler; Ch'eng Cheng 程鄭, whose wealth equaled that of the Cho family; a K'ung family with a fortune of several thousand catties of gold; and a Ping family of Shan-tung, who even accumulated as much as one hundred million cash.[143] A widow from Pa, in modern Szechwan, made a fortune in cinnabar mining.[144] There were two cattle and horse breeders, Wu-chih Lo 烏氏倮 and Ch'iao Yao 橋姚, who became very wealthy.[145] A sheep breeder, Pu Shih, once voluntarily contributed two hundred thousand cash to the government (II, 29). Tiao Chien 刀間, a man who engaged in fishing, salt production, and trade, accumulated a wealth of several tens of millions (II, 1).

Aside from manufacturing and similar endeavors we also have records—some of which are vague—of a few men who became wealthy in other lines of business. A moneylender increased his capital tenfold during the rebellion of 154 B.C.[146] Among the merchants who engaged in general trading, Lü Pu-wei 呂不韋 accumulated a wealth of one thousand catties of gold (II, 3). Two other men accumulated fortunes of fifty million cash.[147] Lo P'ou 羅裒 of Ch'eng-tu, who made a fortune of ten million cash within several years, finally possessed one hundred million cash.[148] In addition, there were fourteen merchants who could

[141] *SC* 129:14b; *HS* 91:6a, 24B:10a.
[142] II, 30; *SC* 129:6a; *HS* 91:5a.
[143] *SC* 129:6a, 17a–18a; *HS* 91:5a, 7b–8b.
[144] *SC* 129:7a; *HS* 91:5b.
[145] II, 6; *SC* 129:19b; *HS* 91:10a.
[146] *SC* 129:19b–20a; *HS* 91:10b.
[147] *HS* 91:9a, 11a.
[148] II, 41; *HS* 91:8a.

match this amount.[149] These facts support the statement of Ssu-ma Ch'ien that some of the big, wealthy merchants, who engaged in trade, smelting iron, or making salt, accumulated a wealth of ten thousand catties of gold (one hundred million cash).[150]

Since there are no biographies of moneymakers in the *Hou-Han-shu*, information concerning the activities and wealth of merchants in the Later Han is generally lacking. But we know that the Fan family, which was engaged in trade, farming, fish raising, and animal breeding, owned 300 *ch'ing* of land and accumulated a wealth of one hundred million cash (I, 40). Shih-sun Fen 士孫奮, a rich man well known in the capital, had property worth at least one hundred seventy million cash; at one time he lent thirty million cash to Liang Chi (III, 63). According to the *San-fu chüeh-lu*, quoted in the commentary to the *Hou-Han-shu*, he served as a subordinate official in his youth. We do not know how he made such a fortune, but it is quite obvious that it was not derived from the income of such a minor post. He must have come from a very wealthy family, most likely a family engaged in business. There were two big horse sellers who each accumulated property worth one thousand catties of gold. It was their contribution that enabled Liu Pei to gather a group of followers and participate in the fight against the Yellow Turban rebels.[151] In his struggle for political power, Liu also relied on the wealth of a rich man, Mi Chu 麋竺, whose family had been engaged in business for generations. Mi owned ten thousand slaves and guests, and wealth worth one hundred million cash. When his sister was married to Liu Pei, Mi presented to Liu two thousand slaves and guests, plus gold, silver, and cash to finance his troops. The *San-kuo-chih* mentions that Liu, who had been defeated by Lü Pu 呂布 and was in great distress, was able to strengthen his position because of Mi's financial help.[152]

The wealth of big merchants who made a fortune of from ten to one hundred million certainly was comparable to that of the high officials, whose wealth fell within this category. This figure corresponds to the estimate of Shih Tan 師丹, who said that the powerful and wealthy officials and commoners possessed property worth a hundred million cash (*HS* 24A:19b). The person who had the greatest fortune in Han times apparently was Liang Chi, a powerful and corrupt official who

[149] *HS* 91:9b, 10b–11a.
[150] *SC* 30:7a–b; *HS* 24B:9a.
[151] *SKC*, Shu, 2:1b.
[152] *SKC*, Shu, 8:6b–7a.

accumulated as much as three billion cash (*HHS* 34:25a). His great wealth was quite exceptional; it seems that under ordinary conditions neither an official nor a merchant was able to accumulate such a fortune.

In pre-Ch'in times we do not find any historical evidence to indicate that there was discrimination against merchants. On the contrary, it seems that their social and political status was rather high. Both Pao Shu-ya 鮑叔牙 and Kuan Chung 管仲, famous ministers of the state of Ch'i, engaged in business together before they entered officialdom (*SC* 62:1b). Tzu-kung 子貢, who was one of the disciples of Confucius and an official in the states of Lu and Wei, was a very successful businessman and because of his wealth was able to ride in carriages and associate with the feudal lords. It was said that they treated him as an equal and that he was the man who made Confucius more and more famous (*SC* 129:5a). Fan Li 范蠡, who had been the highest official of the state of Yüeh, became a businessman after he resigned (*SC* 129:4a–5a).

Merchants in Ch'in times also enjoyed a superior social status. An iron manufacturer is said to have enjoyed a luxurious and pleasant life, comparable to that of a ruler (II, 5). Another iron manufacturer was able to ride in a carriage and associate with the feudal lords.[153] A wealthy cattle breeder was permitted to come to the imperial court to visit the First Emperor of Ch'in and was treated as a feudal lord (II, 6). A widow who was the owner of a cinnabar mine was honored by the same emperor and treated as his guest. Ssu-ma Ch'ien remarked that it was their wealth that made them famous and caused them to be treated politely by the emperor (*SC* 129:6b–7a).

Furthermore, merchants were not barred from political activities. Lü Pu-wei, a very wealthy merchant who invested his capital in a political gamble (II, 3), became the imperial chancellor of Ch'in and was ennobled as a marquis. He was so honored that the First Emperor addressed him as "uncle" (II, 3, 4). This merchant was certainly not merely interested in making a profit; his political ambition must have been based on the acceptability of his having a political career, otherwise he would not have risked his property in this way. It might be argued that he was appointed and ennobled because of his unusual merit, but the fact that a great number of scholars came and stayed with him as his guests and that when he was dismissed from office the rulers of all the feudal states sent messengers to visit him (*SC* 85:5a–b, 7a) indicates that his social status was superior and that his formal occupa-

[153] *SC* 129:18a; *HS* 91:8b.

tion did not have any unfavorable effect. Furthermore, the appointment of merchants was rather widely practiced in Ch'in times. Lü's case was not unique. A Ch'in general in 207 B.C., who was considered a merchant, was the son of a butcher (II, 10).

A similar tendency prevailed in the early days of Han before restrictive measures were introduced. In 197 B.C. many generals under the command of Ch'en Hsi 陳豨, the rebellious chancellor of the kingdom of Tai, were originally merchants; on this account, great rewards were offered to them to disorganize the rebellious force (II, 16).

The earliest law showing merchants in an unfavorable position is found in 214 B.C. Merchants, together with those who had been fugitives and sons-in-law who lived with the families of their wives, were sent to conquer parts of modern Kwangtung and Kwangsi and remained there in garrisons (II, 7). It should be pointed out that only a man of a poor family was willing to live with his wife's family, and consequently he had an inferior status in society.[154] That merchants were treated the same as these undesirable persons and fugitives indicates that merchants were treated unfavorably by the government. It was a regular practice of the Ch'in government to send the "convicted ones" to guard the frontiers, a practice known as *che shu* 謫戍. According to Ch'ao Ts'o, this category included not only convicts but also those whose names had been on the registries in the market and those whose fathers or grandfathers had been on such registries (II, 7, n. 21).

More discriminatory regulations were set up against merchants in Han, and the class as a whole had a more unfavorable legal status than in Ch'in. The old practice of sending active and former merchants as well as the sons and grandsons of merchants, together with other unfavored groups, to be garrison troops and frontier guards was still followed by Emperor Wu (II, 7, n. 21, and 32). Furthermore, various measures were taken to restrict their social and political activities as soon as the empire was pacified and unified. Emperor Kao, who obviously intended "to hamper and humiliate" the merchants, issued an edict prohibiting them from wearing brocades, embroideries, silks, and certain other kinds of fine cloth, from carrying weapons, and from riding on horses (*HS* 24B:3a). Under Emperor Wu heavy taxes were also levied on the property of the merchants as well as on their small carts

---

[154] I, 31 Kung Yü 貢禹 mentions that both merchants and sons-in-law who lived in the family (adopted sons-in-law) were prohibited from becoming officials in Emperor Wen's time (*HS* 72:16b).

and boats.[155] For failing to make reports of their economic worth or making false assessments, merchants had their properties confiscated, causing many of them to become bankrupt.[156] In addition, a regulation was decreed that prohibited merchants from owning landed property; the land as well as the slaves of violators was to be confiscated.[157] The prohibition was restated in an edict issued in 7 B.C. (*HS* 11:3b).

Opportunities for social mobility were further blocked by not allowing merchants to enter officialdom. This meant that merchants had to remain in the lower stratum of society. This seems to have been a consistent policy pursued by the Han government with but few exceptions. Although the sumptuary laws concerning merchants set up by Emperor Kao were repealed by Emperor Hsiao-hui and Empress Lü, still no merchants were allowed to become officials (II, 15). The same practice was maintained in the reigns of Emperors Wen and Ching (*HS* 5:9a, 72:16b). The situation did not change until Emperor Wu's reign, when the national resources were exhausted by the continuous wars against the Hsiung-nu and other barbarians (*HS* 24B:5b ff.). In order to meet those financial difficulties the help of the merchants was sought in the hope that with their personal experience in making money they might increase the national income by various means. Tung-kuo Hsien-yang, a highly successful salt manufacturer, and K'ung Chin 孔僅, a wealthy iron manufacturer, were appointed assistants to the grand minister of agriculture (*ta-nung ch'eng* 大農丞) in charge of the salt and iron industries. Their proposal to put the salt and iron industries under state monopoly was accepted, and many rich salt and iron manufacturers were made government functionaries. As a result, as observed by Ssu-ma Ch'ien, there were more and more merchants among government officials.[158] Within three years K'ung Chin was promoted to the post of minister of agriculture.[159] Sang Hung-yang 桑弘羊, the son of a merchant, because of his mental ability in calculation, was appointed an official in charge of accounting in the same ministry. Later he was promoted to the post of chief commandant for grain (*chih-su tu-wei* 治粟都尉) and acting minister of agriculture in place of K'ung Chin. Finally he became the grandee secretary (II, 30).

[155] *SC* 30:10b–11a; *HS* 6:6a and 13b, 24B:3a, 11b, and 12a; Nancy Lee Swann, *Food and Money in Ancient China* (Princeton, 1950), pp. 231, 280–82.

[156] *SC* 30:10b–11a, 14b–15a; *HS* 24B:12a, 13b–14a; Swann, *Food and Money*, pp. 282, 294–96.

[157] *SC* 30:11a; *HS* 24B:12a.

[158] II, 30; see also *SC* 30:10a–b; *HS* 24b:11a.

[159] *SC* 30:12b–13a; *HS* 24B:12a.

This extreme contradiction of the original restrictions set up by the earlier emperors certainly had a great effect on promoting the social status of the merchants. It appears that once one or two members of this social group—long depressed and disprivileged—had the chance to enter officialdom, they used the unusual occasion to introduce more merchants into this more honorable but less gainful profession. In other words, the appointment of one or two merchants to important posts not only promoted the social mobility of those individuals but also enhanced the social mobility of the group as a whole. But this kind of mobility was checked by traditional forces after the death of Emperor Wu. Although Sang Hung-yang remained in his post until he rebelled under the next emperor, no other merchant was ever appointed to an important post. In an edict issued in 7 B.C. Emperor Ai again enacted the law that merchants were not permitted to be officials and that violators would be punished according to the law (II, 44). This edict suggests that the old law had never been abolished, but that it was not strictly observed by the government officials. Probably Emperor Wu's practice had contributed somewhat to the laxity of the law.

In Wang Mang's time many merchants were again appointed, but none of them held an official post higher than that of 600 piculs. They were assigned to posts in the ministry of agriculture, and many of them were sent out to the various commanderies to supervise the government monopolies (II, 46). All such jobs were performed by wealthy merchants. A wealthy merchant was appointed as supervisor of markets of the capital (*ching-shih ssu-shih* 京師司市) (II, 38); and two wealthy merchants were appointed by Wang Mang as communicators (*na-yen shih* 納言士) (II, 42).

The situation in the Later Han underwent little change. We do not know how many of the earlier restrictions were still in practice, but we do know that some of them were kept and that merchants were still in an unfavorable position. They were still not allowed to ride on horses or in carriages.[160] The fact that white garments were worn by merchants[161] shows that there were sumptuary laws for them. There is no evidence of their obligation to render service in the garrison forces, but merchants could be recruited. The number of merchants who joined the army must have been considerable, for Sun Chien 孫堅 was able to raise an army of more than one thousand, composed mainly of

---

[160] *HHC* 29:10b.
[161] *SKC*, Wu, 9:21b.

merchants and skilled soldiers.[162] Under what conditions these merchants were recruited we are unable to tell, but it seems unlikely that they joined the army on an entirely voluntary basis.

Li Ku 李固 was once accused of appointing merchants as officials (II, 80), and Wang Lieh debased himself by becoming a merchant in order to avoid official appointment (II, 79). This would indicate that businessmen were legally not qualified to be officials; however, as had happened in the Early Han, such rules were not always observed. Many merchants were appointed and ennobled by the Keng-shih emperor (*HHS* 11:6b). A prominent merchant and his father were officials under Wang Mang's regime; later he followed Emperor Kuang-wu and became a high official in the court. He became grand minister of works, was ennobled as marquis, and married a princess (II, 51). The son of a deceased chancellor who engaged in peddling because of poverty was summoned by the government many times and was finally appointed grand administrator (*HHS* 52:20b, 25b–26b). Mi Chu, a wealthy merchant's grandson, was first appointed to office by T'ao Chien then by Ts'ao Ts'ao, and finally became a general under the regime of Liu Pei, who married his sister.[163] Wang Lieh's case shows that sometimes top officials who had the power to appoint officials ignored the regulations that prohibited merchants from becoming officials; Ts'ao Ts'ao still intended to appoint Wang Lieh after he had debased himself by becoming a merchant (II, 79).

Because of the total complex of political and legal measures that were unfavorable to the merchants as a whole, the social status of this group in Han times was somewhat inferior. This was reflected in the general attitude of Han society toward merchants. Yang Yün, a dismissed official whose father had been an imperial chancellor, once wrote in a letter to a friend: "Fortunately I have [some] savings from my official salary and am buying at low prices and selling at high prices, thereby pursuing the way of one-tenth profit. These are the activities of worthless merchants and a vile and humiliating position, but I personally practice it. One who is a man of low standing, where all defamations will flow in upon him, is trembling without being cold. Even those who know me well are, however, following the popular tendency. How can

---

[162] *Ibid.*, 1:1b–2a.

[163] Mi Chu was made a subordinate official by T'ao Chien; Ts'ao Ts'ao appointed Mi an acting grand administrator. Mi became general of the left *(tso chiang-chün* 左將軍), under Liu Pei, and later was promoted to the post of "general who pacifies Han" *(an-Han chiang-chün* 安漢將軍), a rank superior to the other generals *(SKC*, Shu, 8:7a–b).

there be any praise?" (*HS* 66:14b–15a). The generally unfavorable attitude toward the class as a whole and his own regret for descending from a superior status to an inferior one is clearly reflected in this quotation and in other parts of Yang's letter. Ts'ui Shih 崔實, the son of a high official who sold all his family property for his father's funeral and then supported himself by selling wine, was ridiculed by his contemporaries (*HHS* 52:26a–b).

The social status of merchants was not entirely determined by such legal restrictions and the unfavorable attitude of society. Their tremendous wealth and economic power, their association with nobles and officials, and the fact that many members of their group did succeed in entering officialdom did offset some of the negative attitudes and regulations and increased their prestige to a considerable extent. The importance of wealth in determining social status should not be overlooked in Han society, where the wealthy generally looked down upon those with less wealth, and those whose wealth was a hundredfold or sometimes even a thousandfold more than the average were respected and feared by their economic inferiors (*SC* 129:15b). The discrepancy between the law that was unfavorable to merchants and their actual social prestige was remarked upon by Ch'ao Ts'o, who said that merchants who became rich were despised by the ruler but were esteemed by the people and officials (II, 18). Because of their wealth merchants were also able to associate with nobles and officials and were received by them with great respect and honor (II, 18, 28). Nobles and officials were most honored by society; associating with them had to bring great honor to merchants.

OTHER OCCUPATIONS

Different occupations were accorded different kinds of prestige. Some were considered humble and were looked down upon in society, and the men who engaged in such an occupation had an inferior status. Such subjective evaluation was manifested both in the attitudes and verbal expressions—explicit or implicit—of others toward men of certain occupations, as well as in the attitude of the man himself. These data, though fragmentary and limited, will give us some idea of the relative prestige of different occupational groups, and the occupations that were looked down upon.

Physicians

Physicians could make a good living from their specialized profession. Judging from the case of Hua T'o 華佗, who was recommended as "filially pious and incorrupt" by the chancellor of the kingdom of P'ei and summoned by the grand commandant, it seems that the profession of physician was not a humble one and that there was no discrimination that prevented a physician from entering an official career (*HHS* 82B:9b). One physician was appointed grand palace grandee and prefect of the gentlemen of the palace (*t'ai-chung ta-fu* and *lang-chung-ling* 太中大夫 and 郎中令), and many of his offspring became high officials (*HS* 46:7b). Also the brother of a woman physician who was closely associated with an empress dowager was appointed chief commandant (*tu-wei* 都尉) (*SC* 122:12a).

The social status of a physician was not a very superior one when compared with that of officials and scholars. Hua T'o, although very famous and successful, nevertheless was ashamed of his profession. His attitude toward Ts'ao Ts'ao was certainly a manifestation of his own feelings about his profession. As a physician he felt inferior, but among physicians he was keenly aware of his own success and importance. The combination of the two may have led him to flout Ts'ao Ts'ao's commands, which no one dared do, for his own psychological satisfaction. Unfortunately, his actions led to his fatal punishment (*HHS* 82B:12a).

Another example also shows that the status of a physician was humble. A man whose father was a veterinarian for cows was described as coming from a family that had been "poor and humble for generations." A veterinarian's status would probably have been inferior to an ordinary physician's; however, it did not preclude his entrance to officialdom. The veterinarian's son was recommended by the local authorities as "filially pious and incorrupt" and later was summoned by the central government (*HHS* 53:5b–6b).

Occultists

The occult arts were very popular in Ch'in and Han times. There emerged a group of persons known as *fang-shih* 方士, occultists, who were concerned with alchemy and communication with immortals.[164] Some of them were employed by the government, performing various sacri-

---

[164] On *fang-shih* in ancient China see Ch'en P'an, "Chan-kuo Ch'in Han chien fang-shih k'ao-lun," *LSYY*, XVII (1948), 7-57.

ficial and magical services. A few of them who convinced the emperors of their supernatural powers were given official titles and enormous amounts of wealth.

One occultist was designated grandee (*ta-fu* 大夫) and treated as a guest by Emperor Wen.[165] Two were given the title of general by Emperor Wu, and one of them was even ennobled as marquis with a fief of two thousand households and a residence complete with one thousand slaves and various kinds of furnishings formerly used by the emperor. He even married a princess, and nobles and high officials visited him and drank in his house.[166] Such cases, however, were rare; these three were the only ones among a great many occultists mentioned in the texts (*HS* 25B:16a). Furthermore, Emperors Wen and Wu, particularly the latter, were extraordinarily interested in magical practices and had great confidence in them. Emperor Ch'eng's fondness for performing sacrifices in his old age also brought forth occultists. All those who presented memorials concerning sacrifices and magic were allowed to come to the court and await the emperor's decision regarding an audience or an appointment. However, they were merely asked to perform sacrifices, and none of them was appointed to office (*HS* 25B:15a). Emperor Ai, because of illness, also summoned occultists, but they too were only ordered to participate in sacrifices (*HS* 25B:17b).

Occultists were still very active in the Later Han, although they failed to achieve prominence in the imperial court. Three well-known occultists were summoned and kept by Ts'ao Ts'ao, who appointed them military officials.[167]

There were also diviners and physiognomists. Chia I and another official who visited a famous professional diviner were very much impressed by him (*SC* 127:1a–5b). Divination was particularly popular in the Later Han when the *ch'an-wei* 讖緯,[168] writings on the occult arts of prognostics, flourished. Many scholars were interested in such works and arts, particularly astrology and other means of divination. The combination of scholarship and practical knowledge in divination gave

---

[165] *SC* 28:20b; *HS* 25A:16b.

[166] *SC* 28:25a, 27b–28a; *HS* 25A:20b, 23b–24a.

[167] Ts'ao P'i, *Tien-lun*, quoted in *HHS* 82b:22a, note; also in *SKC*, Wei, 29:7a, note; Ts'ao Chih 曹植, *Pien-tao lun*, quoted in *SKC*, Wei, 29:7a–b, note.

[168] Though the *ch'an-wei* may be traced to the Warring States period, they did not become influential until the end of the Early Han. They flourished in the Later Han. See *HHS* 59:14b–15b; Ch'en P'an, "Ch'an-wei shih ming," *LSYY*, XI (1947), 297–316, and "Ch'an-wei so-yüan," *LSYY*, XI (1947), 317–35.

these scholars prestige in society. Many entered officialdom:[169] Hsieh I-wu 謝夷吾 was recommended to the court by the minister of the masses who asked Pan Ku to write a memorial of recommendation for him; Fan Ying 樊英 was even treated like a teacher by the emperor (*HHS* 82:11a ff., 19b ff.).

The status of a professional diviner, however, was not comparable to that of the nonprofessional scholar-official diviners. There are indications that divination was a humble occupation. Yen Chün-p'ing 嚴君平, a famous professional diviner who considered divination a humble occupation and yet one that could benefit others, received only a few customers a day, earning one hundred cash each day to support himself. He spent the rest of his time teaching *Lao-tzu;* Yang Hsiung 楊雄 was one of his students. Li Ch'iang 李彊, the inspector of I-chou, who wanted to appoint Yen as his subordinate, treated him with great politeness but dared not mention his offer. Yen was described by Yang as a man of lofty spirit who refused to enter officialdom (*HS* 72:2a–b).

Very little is known about professional physiognomists. A famous woman physiognomist is mentioned in the biography of Chou Ya-fu 周亞夫, an outstanding official of the Early Han; and a professional physiognomist was appointed a gentleman by Ts'ao Ts'ao.[170]

There also existed an occupational group known as *wu* 巫, sorcerers or sorceresses,[171] whose function was different from that of the *fang-shih.* Their function was to pray,[172] to dance[173] during a sacrifice, and to conjure a spirit by invocation or incantation. A sorcerer or sorceress thus served as the medium whose body a spirit entered.[174] With the assistance of incantation, sorcerers were also active in curing the diseases of others.[175] Some sorcerers or sorceresses engaged in black magic,

[169] As shown in *HHS* 28A and 28B, most of the men served as subordinate officials in the local government; others were officials in the central government. A few of them held such high posts as grand administrators and palace attendants. One even reached the posts of minister of works and minister of the masses (*HHS* 82A:11a–b and 16a–b, 82B:5b–6b).

[170] *SC* 57:7a; *HS* 40:26a; *SKC*, Wei, 29:10a–b.

[171] There were both sorcerers and sorceresses, generally referred to as *nan-wu* 男巫 and *nü-wu* 女巫 respectively (*CLCS* 17:8b, 26:5b–6b). However, sometimes the term *wu* was specifically reserved for sorceresses, whereas a sorcerer was called *hsi* 覡 (Tuan Yü-ts'ai, *Shuo-wen chieh-tzu chu,* in the series *Kuo-hsüeh chi-pen ts'ung-shu chien-pien* [Shanghai, 1936], 5A:52–53, hereafter cited as *SWCTC; HS* 25A:1a).

[172] *HS* 25A:14b–15a, 24b.

[173] Thus, a sorceress usually performed the dance during a sacrifice for rain, *yü* 雩 (*CLCS* 26:6a–b). *Shuo-wen* defines *wu* as a person who summoned a spirit by dance (*SWCTC* 5A:52).

[174] *HHS* 59:15a, note. For a concrete case see *HS* 25A:21a–b.

[175] *HS* 25A:21a; *HHS* 82B:15a.

such as cursing by means of a spell or an image that was usually buried in secret.[176] Sorcery was an unfavored occupation in Han times, and sorcerers were normally not qualified to enter officialdom. Kao Feng 高鳳 was a scholar who escaped from official appointment by announcing that his was a sorcerer's family (II, 65).

Butchers

The occupation of a butcher was a humble one. Nieh Cheng 聶政, who had committed murder, escaped, and become a butcher, once said that he lowered his determination and humiliated himself by becoming a butcher in the market. Both he and Chu Hai 朱亥, another butcher, were so deeply impressed by two nobles who paid polite visits to them that they died for the nobles.[177] Mi Heng 彌衡 once used the epithets "butcher and wine-seller" to humiliate two officials he did not respect (*HHS* 80B:24b).

Butchers were not prohibited from entering officialdom. A butcher's son was a general in the Ch'in army in 207 B.C. (II, 10). Another butcher, Fan K'uai 樊噲, became a top official, was ennobled as marquis, and married Empress Lü's sister.[178] However, he was one of the early followers of Emperor Kao in the rebellion against Ch'in; so his case was rather exceptional and cannot be used as a basis for generalization. At the end of the Later Han a daughter of a family of butchers was selected for the inner palace and became empress in A.D. 179. When her son ascended the throne and she became empress dowager, her father and mother were ennobled and her brother became the grand general (II, 85). We do not know how long her family had been butchers, but the humble past of the family was forgotten and had no immediate effect on the social position of its members. Since only girls of good families could be selected for the inner palace, the inclusion of this girl in the list implies that the family of a butcher, even though his occupation was a humble one, was still considered to be a good family. Ho Chin, her brother who became grand general, also was the political

---

[176] Black magic, particularly the use of a human image and the casting of spells, was referred to as *wu-ku* 巫蠱 in Han times. Emperor Wu put to death an imperial chancellor, Kung-sun Ho 公孫賀, who was accused of engaging in witchcraft and burying an image in an attempt to bring harm to the emperor (III, 23). A similar accusation led to the death in 91 B.C. of Emperor Wu's heir apparent and thousands of others involved (*HS* 45:15a–b, 63:1b ff.).

[177] *SC* 77:4b–5a, 86:7a–b.

[178] *SC* 95:1a; *HS* 41:1a, 4b.

leader in the fight against the powerful eunuchs, in which he was supported by many eminent families (III, 70). This would seem to indicate that butchers were not categorized with those who were prohibited from an official career.

Runners

The occupation of government runner was considered a humble one. The fact that a former student of the Imperial Academy changed his name when he served as a street runner implies that engaging in such an occupation made him feel ashamed. An inspector of a regional division who had studied in the Imperial Academy with him regretted that his former colleague had become a runner and ordered the prefect to replace him (II, 52); however, it seems that there was no discrimination against a runner that prohibited him from entering officialdom, for this runner later became a grand administrator.

GUESTS

Pin-k'o 賓客 or *k'o* 客, which may be translated as "guests," was a special group from pre-Ch'in through Han times. The term means either of two groups: the first included those who still had their own occupation and family but visited the host and were received and entertained by him; the other group stayed at the house of the host and were supported by him. This group was sometimes referred to as *shih-k'o* 食客, meaning a guest supported by someone.[179] The men referred to as *shih-k'o* were adherents rather than guests in the ordinary sense. But the term *pin-k'o* or *k'o* was more common, and we can tell only by the context whether a *k'o* was merely a visitor or a person supported by a host. We will deal only with the second group, whose status and role deserve our special attention. Ordinary guests, who were not attached to the host and who had no obligations to render services, are of interest to us only in terms of association, that is, "who associated with whom?" They should not be treated as a separate social group.

The practice of keeping guests can be traced back to the Warring States period. Prince T'ien Wen 田文 of Ch'i, Prince Chao Sheng 趙勝 of Chao, Prince Wei Wu-chi 魏無忌 of Wei, and Chancellor Huang Hsieh of Ch'u, all tried to have more and more guests.[180] They, and

---

[179] *SC* 75:11b, 76:2a, 77:1a, 107:7a; *HS* 52:6a–b.
[180] *SC* 76:1b, 78:7a, 85:5a.

others, kept a maximum of about three thousand guests.[181] Lü Pu-wei, the imperial chancellor of Ch'in, also kept three thousand guests.[182] The number of guests one was able to keep seems to have been a status symbol, and keeping guests also served as a means to augment political power.[183] A prince with such an enormous number of guests under his command usually was powerful enough to control the state. Sometimes a state did not even dare to fight with a neighboring state because the ruler had thousands of guests (*SC* 77:1a).

The host was expected to provide lodging, food, clothing, and even carriages for his guests and to treat them generously. Some of the most honored guests were even given luxurious articles; for example, a guest proudly wore a scabbard decorated with pearls and jade, and many of the guests of Huang Hsieh wore shoes decorated with pearls (*SC* 78:7b). Probably this served the function of conspicuous consumption, for it showed how wealthy the master was and how generously he treated his guests.

Obviously only the wealthy nobles and officials could afford to support a large number of guests. Prince T'ien Wen was unable to support his three thousand guests with the income from his fief of ten thousand households and had to increase his income by lending money for interest. When the interest was not paid on time, he was unable to support his guests (*SC* 75:8b–9a).

Since the number of guests kept by a master was enormous, it is obvious that they must have varied greatly in personality and qualifications; and of course their selection depended heavily on the attitudes and disposition of the master. Some masters received all kinds of people who came to them, and the home of such a person became a haven for fugitives and criminals. Even thieves were included (*SC* 75:8b–9a). Some, however, were more careful in selecting their guests (*SC* 77:6b). The guests of Lü Pu-wei, for example, were scholars who compiled the work *Lü-shih ch'un-ch'iu,* which is still extant (*SC* 85:5a–b).

The guest seldom had definite obligations, and usually no routine work was assigned to him. He was expected to render occasional service according to his abilities when there was such a demand. When Prince T'ien Wen wanted to send someone to collect his debts, he inquired of his guests whether one of them was versed in accounting and competent for the job (*SC* 75:8b–9a). Sometimes the mission was difficult or even

---

[181] *SC* 75:3a, 8b, and 11b, 76:1a, 77:1a, 78:7b.
[182] *SC* 85:5a.
[183] *SC* 75:3a, 77:7a, 78:7a.

dangerous. A guest was expected to do what the master asked of him and even risk his life for him. Hundreds of guests were ready to give up their lives to follow Prince Wei Wu-chi, who, though he had no army, decided to fight on the side of his besieged relatives. One of the guests who was too old to go along cut his throat to express his loyalty (*SC* 87:3b–5a).

The social status of guests was not an inferior one. A master, though much superior in political and social status as well as in wealth, had to treat his guests politely. The guests of Prince T'ien Wen received the same food as he; once a guest became very angry and left because he thought his rice was inferior to the master's (*SC* 75:3a–b). When Prince Wei Wu-chi went to welcome a guest personally, he asked him to take the seat on the left and he himself held the reins and drove the carriage (*SC* 77:2a–b). As a rule, the superior always took the seat on the left of the driver, and it was always the inferior who drove. In this case the prince took this humble position to show his respect.

But guests did not all have the same status, nor were they all treated the same. Three grades of lodging were provided for the guests of T'ien Wen. Better food and carriages were given to those who lived in the first-grade residence (*SC* 75:8a–b). Only the most honored guests wore such luxury articles as shoes decorated with pearls (*SC* 78:7b). It is hardly necessary to mention that some guests were respected more than others (*SC* 76:4a, 77:2a–b). Those who were less respected always occupied seats of less honor and were looked down upon by the other guests (*SC* 75:4b–5a, 76:2b). As a rule, those who engaged in humble occupations and were looked down upon by society were also held in less respect by this particular group. Thus all the guests of T'ien Wen were ashamed of being associated with a thief and a man who could imitate the sound of crowing cocks (*SC* 75:4b–5a). A man without special ability was also considered inferior by the master and by his fellow guests (*SC* 76:2b).

A guest was not permanently attached to a master, but was free to come and go. He could leave when he was not treated politely or when he disapproved of the behavior of his host (*SC* 75:3b, 76:1b, 77:7a). It was quite common for a guest to leave and to attach himself to a new host whom he admired. Frequently guests left their host when he lost his political status and power, and it was not uncommon for them to seek an opportunity to return when he regained his power (*SC* 75:10a, 11a–b).

This pre-Ch'in practice of keeping guests was continued in Ch'in

times. Li Ssu 李斯, the imperial chancellor, and Chao Kao 趙高, the
powerful eunuch, each kept a number of guests (*SC* 87:21b). Both
T'ien Heng 田横 and Chang Erh 張耳 had reputations for their ability
to keep outstanding and loyal persons as their guests. All the guests of
T'ien Heng, numbering five hundred men, are reported to have taken
their own lives when their master refused to submit to Emperor Kao
and committed suicide.[184] Chang Erh, who had been a guest of Wei
Wu-chi in his youth, was fond of keeping guests when he rose to prominence. About a dozen of his guests, highly admired by Emperor Kao,
were made administrators or chancellors.[185]

Keeping guests was still very popular in Han times; however, not a
single host kept a number of guests comparable to those mentioned
above. The maximum number was one thousand; two kings and a
general each had one thousand guests (*HS* 34:24a; II, 11). Usually a
master had several tens or hundreds of them. It is interesting to note
that the number of guests kept by a master again increased in the era
of the Three Kingdoms. There were two instances of men who kept
more than a thousand guests.[186] This sudden increase is understandable: during the wars and disturbed periods in the Later Han and
thereafter, every powerful person was ambitious to use his strength to
acquire political power and tended to keep a large number of guests or
retainers who actually were his personal troops.

As in pre-Ch'in times, many nobles and high officials kept guests.[187]
It was also not uncommon for a petty official to have guests.[188] Even
commoners had them. This was a new development that had no precedent in earlier days: the keeping of guests became popularized. A
redresser-of-wrongs or a violent wrong-doer often kept guests or assassins:[189] those who engaged in violent action were usually involved in
unlawful activities—such as revenge or redress of grievances—and the
assistance of a group of bold and brave men was necessary.[190]

In Han times, as in the earlier days, guests were supported by the
host.[191] But there were also many other advantages that could be obtained. Under the protection of a powerful master a guest usually was

[184] *SC* 93:5a–6a; *HS* 33:6a–b.
[185] *SC* 89:1a–b, 11b–13b; *HS* 32:1a, 8a–10a.
[186] *SKC*, Wei, 12:20b, 18:1a.
[187] *HS* 58:6b, 74:1a; *HHS* 1B:27a, 28A:24a, 29:23b.
[188] *HHS* 18:19b, 20:4b.
[189] III, 20, 38, 47; *HHS* 77:18b–19a.
[190] *HS* 92:4b, 6a; III, 38, 47.
[191] *HS* 58:6b, 66:2b, 72:25b.

able to avoid the payment of taxes.[192] Furthermore, the government had difficulty in levying labor and military service upon the guests of powerful persons.[193] Under the protection of a master some guests engaged in robbery, murder, and other unlawful activities.[194] As a rule guests gave only occasional service in return, and the kind of service varied according to the particular situation and the requests of the master. But as time went on guests began to render services more or less regularly, and gradually they assumed the role of a client or retainer. It seems that there developed a sort of patron-client relationship. The master became more demanding and arrogant, while the guests became more subservient.

Guests served in various capacities. There were intelligent men who served as personal advisors to high officials.[195] Others were engaged in physical and menial work. Some guests served as bodyguards.[196] It was not uncommon to ask a guest to assassinate an enemy.[197] Under unusual conditions guests were even asked to engage in robbery and other unlawful activities.[198] As a rule guests were expected to share the suffering of their master and offer help in times of emergency or danger. One man who was arrested by one of Wang Mang's officials was rescued forcibly by his guests.[199] Guests also had obligations to defend the family of their master when it was attacked by bandits or enemies.[200] It was a common practice for guests to follow their master to war: both the king of Wu and the rebellious heir apparent appointed guests to lead troops against the imperial army.[201] Ch'en P'eng 岑彭, a prefect whose city was under the attack of rebels, led his guests in fierce fighting at the time.[202] Retainers or guests became the core of the organized forces of the powerful families that took an active part in the rebellion against Wang Mang and in the power struggle during the transitional period at the end of Wang Mang's reign. (See Chapter 5.) Emperor Kuang-wu's military force was greatly strengthened by those persons

[192] *SKC,* Wei, 15:14a.
[193] *Ibid.,* 12:20b.
[194] III, 30, 31, 37, 41, 45, 63; *HS* 86:2a; *HHS* 23:26a, 33:17b; *SKC,* Wei, 11:14b, 12:21b–22a.
[195] *HS* 52:2b–3a, 58:6b.
[196] *SKC,* Wei, 11:9a–b, 18:5a.
[197] III, 29, 47; *HS* 84:2b, 92:7b; *HHS* 31:8a.
[198] III, 31, 37, 41; *HS* 47:5a, 86:2a.
[199] *HHS* 15:3b. For similar cases see *SKC,* Wei, 18:5a; *SKC,* Wu, 11:8a.
[200] *HHS* 33:12a–b.
[201] *HS* 35:12a, 63:2b–3a, 66:3b and 5a.
[202] *HHS* 17:16a.

who led a large number of guests and kinsmen and became his followers (I, 41, 42). The military services of guests obviously were a help in seeking military and political power. This was even more true at the end of the Later Han and in the era of the Three Kingdoms, when there were frequent wars and great disturbances and all powerful persons sought to organize forces strong enough to protect their families and properties or to seek political power to enable them to rule some territory.

It was not uncommon for guests to become voluntary followers of a military man, serving as his personal troops. When Pao Yung 鮑永, the grand general of the Keng-shih emperor, heard about the emperor's death, he dismissed his troops and went to Liu Hsiu, the future Emperor Kuang-wu, with his generals and loyal guests, numbering about a hundred men (*HHS* 29:9a). The *San-kuo-chih* reports that several hundred guests were willing to follow Sun Ts'e 孫策 when he became a colonel.²⁰³ In other cases, it is not clear whether the guests under the command of a military man were on a voluntary basis. In any event, the master was able to lead and command his guests more or less at will. By the end of the second century, this sort of personal attachment had gradually led to the development of personal troops, known as *pu-ch'ü* 部曲. The *San-kuo-chih* states that all the big families had *pu-ch'ü* under their command.²⁰⁴

The evidence seems to indicate that guests constituted an essential part of the *pu-ch'ü*. The biography of Li Tien 李典 in the *San-kuo-chih* reads, "[Li Tien's uncle, Li Ch'ien 李乾] grouped together several thousand families of guests at Ch'eng-shih," and "[Li] Tien's lineage and *pu-ch'ü*, numbering more than three thousand families, resided at Ch'eng-shih."²⁰⁵ That "guests" and "*pu-ch'ü*" are used interchangeably shows clearly the correlation between the two. But it should be pointed out that personal troops (*pu-ch'ü*) were by no means made up entirely of guests. In fact those who were willing to become someone's personal troops, the so-called *i-tsung* 義從 (i.e., voluntary followers), might be recruited.²⁰⁶

²⁰³ *SKC*, Wu, 1:10a.

²⁰⁴ *SKC*, Wei, 28:20a. On *pu-ch'ü* see III, 71, n. 458.

²⁰⁵ *SKC*, Wu, 18:1a, 2a.

²⁰⁶ For instance, Kan Ning 甘寧 originally had eight hundred slaves and guests under his command, but Huang Tsu 黃祖 induced some of Kan's guests to leave. Later, when Huang permitted Kan to get back his guests and *i-tsung*, voluntary followers, several hundred men returned to Kan's camp (*Wu-shu*, quoted in *SKC*, Wu, 10:11a).

The size of a body of *pu-ch'ü* under the control of a person or a family was sometimes quite large, numbering from a hundred to several thousand.[207] As the struggle for power intensified and only the strongest could survive, the big families began to attach themselves and their *pu-ch'ü* to the strong military leaders. In a single instance, one member of a powerful family attached his kinsmen, guests, and *pu-ch'ü*, numbering three thousand families, to Ts'ao Ts'ao.[208] The system of *pu-ch'ü* was closely connected with the growth of warlordism in this period.

With the development of *pu-ch'ü* there were certain significant changes in the role and status of guests. It is obvious that when guests became personal troops under the command of a private person, they became more dependent and lost their freedom of mobility.[209] Since they were under more complete control, their status must have been inferior to what it had been in the earlier days. And in the earlier days guests had been kept as individuals, whereas now the family was the unit of the *pu-ch'ü*.[210] The attachment of the whole family of a guest to a master indicates that the master had more responsibility in the support of guests, but on the other hand the master extended his control over a whole family. Also the attachment was more permanent and required more loyalty.

Guests were usually not asked to perform domestic or productive work in the pre-Ch'in through Early Han periods; however, there is evidence of a new trend in the first century A.D. Ma Yüan, who raised animals and cultivated land on the frontier, commanded the service of several hundred families who were attached to him as guests. Because of this he was able to raise several thousand livestock and accumulate several thousand piculs of grain. Later when he moved to the capital, he also asked his guests to encamp and to cultivate land in the imperial park (*HHS* 24:2a, 5a). In the first instance he became wealthy by exploiting his guests. In the second, the guests supported themselves by their own labor. T'ao Hsi-sheng is right in pointing out that most of the guests in the Early Han did not engage in productive work but that from the end of the Early Han the guests participated in production, particularly in the cultivation of land.[211]

This tendency was more dominant at the end of the Later Han and

[207] *SKC,* Wei, 28:30b; *SKC,* Shu, 2:8b, 11:1a; *SKC,* Wu, 6:5b, 10:4b, 11:14a.
[208] *SKC,* Wei, 18:1a–3a.
[209] Thus the *pu-ch'ü* were usually taken over by the son or other relative of the deceased master (*SKC,* Wei, 18:1a; *SKC,* Wu, 10:4b).
[210] *HHS* 24:2a; *SKC,* Wei, 18:la and 2a, 28:30b.
[211] T'ao Hsi-sheng, "Hsi Han shih-tai ti k'o," *Shih-huo,* V, No. 1 (1937), 1–6.

in the era of the Three Kingdoms. For example, a grand administrator sent ten of his guests to build a house and plant orange trees. The family derived a profit worth several thousand rolls of silk from the produce yearly and became wealthy.[212] Obviously, the guests instead of being a burden to the master were exploited by him. They actually became tenants.

Sometimes guests were treated as slaves and servants. Guests and slaves are frequently mentioned together, and we find such terms as *t'ung-k'o* 僮客 and *nu-k'o* 奴客 in our texts (see II, 24, n. 80). Since there are indications that these guests were transferred in the same manner as slaves, and that slaves and guests were expected to perform the same kind of menial work, we believe that though they were two distinct classes of persons, their status was more or less the same.[213] This is further supported by evidence that in the Later Han a guest sometimes meant a hired servant who received definite wages. It was said that when a prefect was unable to own a slave he would have such a guest.[214] Thus the evidence suggests that the fundamental difference between the two was that one was not free and the other was merely a hired laborer. The status and role of such a guest was not much different from that of a slave.

Since there was a change in the nature and the treatment of guests, it is reasonable to assume that the social status of this group also underwent important changes. As a whole, guests in the Early Han had a status superior to those of later times. As in pre-Ch'in times, guests during most of the Early Han were treated generously and politely by their masters. The status of guests in the Later Han, and especially in the era of the Three Kingdoms, was markedly inferior; guests were asked to engage in productive and menial labor and were treated more like slaves or servants. When guests became the personal troops of a man their status also diminished. Then they were more closely attached to the master and became less free. At the end of the second century, a guest might even be beaten by the master.[215]

But a guest was not a person who had lost his personal freedom. During the Early Han period guests were free to come and go as in the pre-Ch'in era (*HS* 52:6a). In spite of the change in status, in the Later Han they were still free to leave their masters.[216]

[212] *Hsiang-yang chi,* quoted in *SKC,* Wu, 3:7a, note.
[213] *SKC,* Shu, 8:6b–7a; *SKC,* Wei, 5:11b.
[214] Wei Cheng *et al., Ch'ün-shu chih-yao, SPTK* ed., 45:10a.
[215] *SKC,* Wei, 23:4b.
[216] *HHS* 20:4b; *Wu-shu,* quoted in *SKC,* Wu, 10:11a, note.

Before this section is concluded, the government policy toward guests should be discussed. A policy of noninterference was usually adopted by the government concerning the keeping of guests as long as the guests did not violate the law. Since they frequently engaged in unlawful activities, many of them were arrested and punished.[217] The government also realized that keeping a number of guests meant power for the master, which constituted a potential threat; drastic measures were sometimes taken to reduce the power of such masters. Guests were sometimes even arrested with their master when he was found guilty and subject to punishment (III, 4). The most radical and extensive measure was taken by Emperor Kuang-wu, who ordered the arrest and execution of several thousand guests attached to kings and marquises (*HHS* 1B:27a, 28A:24a). Later when Tou Wu's force was defeated, all his relatives as well as his guests were exterminated (III, 65).

SLAVES

At the bottom of the social strata were the slaves, whose social and legal status was most inferior. Special dress and decoration were designed particularly for this group to give them social dishonor. They had the most humble way of life, which clearly marked them off from the rest of the population. The social distance between slaves and free men was great: there was no social communication between them. Normally intermarriage between the two groups was prohibited. Social mobility among the slaves was very slight. In fact, they formed a caste rather than a class.

ENSLAVEMENT

Many Han scholars, including Cheng Hsüan, Hsü Shen 許慎, Ying Shao, and Li Ch'i 李奇, held that in ancient times law violation was the only source of enslavement and that all male and female slaves were criminals. Basing themselves upon these statements, modern Chinese scholars, Liang Ch'i-ch'ao and others, concluded that convicts in Han times were actually slaves.[218] However, as pointed out by Wu Ching-ch'ao, convicts who were subjected to servitude, which varied from one

---

[217] III, 37, 64; *HHS* 10A:29a–b, 33:15b.

[218] Liang Ch'i-ch'ao, "Chung-kuo nu-li chih-tu," *Tsing-hua hsüeh-pao*, II (1925), 532.

to five years, were not slaves.[219] Wilbur shows that although *t'u* 徒, "convicts," and *nu* 奴, "slaves," are frequently mentioned together, there was a distinction between the two and that convicts should not be confused with slaves.[220] There is also clear evidence showing that the term *t'u* is always used alone when it means convict (see II, 8, n. 28).

It is obvious that no matter how much alike *t'u* and *nu* were treated,[221] there was a fundamental difference between the two: *t'u* were sentenced to servitude for a definite period of time, whereas government slaves were in servitude for an indefinite period.

In fact, as pointed out by Wu Ching-ch'ao and Wang Shih-chieh, it was the family members of the criminals who were made government slaves.[222] It is clearly stated in Han law that a person might be submerged into slavery because of the crimes of his father or elder brothers.[223] It is also clear that a criminal's wife and children who were enslaved had their faces tattooed.[224] Probably they belonged to the families of those who had committed serious crimes—such as rebellion and other major offenses—that called for the death penalty. Thus the wives and children of the leaders of the Rebellion of the Seven Kingdoms were enslaved in 154 B.C., an event that we know of only because they were pardoned fourteen years later.[225] On the other hand, it seems unlikely that family members of those who had committed minor offenses were enslaved while the criminals themselves were subjected only to a short period of servitude, say five years. The law of collective responsibility and the enslavement of family members, though once abolished by Emperor Wen, was restored after only a short period and remained in effect throughout the history of Han.[226]

The only law that ordered the enslavement of the criminals themselves as well as their family members is found during Wang Mang's reign. In order to stop the casting of illegal coins, an edict was issued in

[219] Wu Ching-ch'ao, "Hsi-Han she-hui chieh-chi chih-tu," *THHP*, X (1935), 246.

[220] Martin Wilbur, *Slavery in China During the Former Han Dynasty* (Chicago, 1943), pp. 81–82.

[221] Both five-year convicts and slaves had their heads shaven and wore the iron collar (II, 8, 13; *SC* 104:1b). Besides, both slaves and convicts were sent to fight in wars or to engage in the same kind of service (II, 8; *SC* 6:14a, 92:18b; *HS* 24B:25a, 34:13a, 99C:5a; Wei Hung, *Han-chiu-i pu-i*, *PCKTS*, A:4a, hereafter cited as *HCIPI*).

[222] Wang Shih-chieh, "Chung-kuo nu-pei chih-tu," *She-hui k'e-hsüeh chi-k'an*, III (1925), 306–7; Wu Ching-ch'ao, *op. cit.*, p. 18.

[223] *LSCC* 21:154, Kao Hsiu's commentary; *CLCS* 1:7a, Cheng's commentary.

[224] *SKC*, Wei, 12:9a.

[225] *HS* 6:1b, especially commentary by Ying Shao.

[226] Liang Ch'i-ch'ao, *op. cit.*, pp. 532–33.

A.D. 10 that when one family cast coins, five families were held responsible and would be seized and made male and female slaves (II, 47). In A.D. 14, although the punishment was reduced somewhat, those who cast coins illegally were seized with their wives and children and made slaves (II, 49). It was reported that the total number of persons enslaved amounted to over a hundred thousand.

Private slaves frequently became government slaves through donation or confiscation. Ch'ao Ts'o once suggested to Emperor Wen that he allow the people either to redeem their crimes or to acquire rank by presenting their private slaves to the government (*HS* 49:14a). Emperor Wu also encouraged people to donate their private slaves so as to be free from labor service for life, to be appointed to the position of gentleman, or, if already in office, to be raised in rank (II, 26). Private slaves were frequently confiscated by the government as a punishment to the owners who in one way or another had violated the law. In Emperor Wu's time ten million male and female slaves owned by merchants were confiscated because the owners had failed to assess their property according to the law.[227]

The Han state was constantly at war with the Hsiung-nu and the barbarians of the Western Regions. Since warfare has frequently been the main source of slaves in human history, we are confronted with the question whether or not the Han government did the same thing as the Romans. In the *Shih-chi* and the *Han-shu* the total number of Hsiung-nu killed and captured in each campaign is given. The number varies from several thousand to seventy thousand.[228] Unfortunately, with a few exceptions, the number of persons killed and the number captured are not mentioned separately. The number of captives is given in three instances: 3,017 persons were captured in the campaign of 127 B.C.; 15,000 men and women were taken in 124 B.C.; and in the campaign of 121 B.C. 4,730 were taken by a general, and another 1,768 by a colonel.[229] No detailed information is available concerning the fate of the captured.

When thousands of Hsiung-nu followed their king, Hun-yeh 渾邪, in surrendering to the Chinese, the Han government treated them generously and supported them. From this, T'ao Hsi-sheng argues that captives were not enslaved.[230] The fallacy of his argument, as pointed

[227] *SC* 30:15a; *HS* 24B:14a.
[228] *SC* 111:13a and 14a; *HS* 6:9a–b, 10b, and 12a–13b, 55:18b–22a.
[229] *SC* 110:23b, 111:3b, 4b, and 9b; *HS* 55:3a–b and 8b, 94A:19b.
[230] T'ao Hsi-sheng, *Hsi Han ching-chi shih* (Shanghai, 1935), p. 56. The same view

out by Wilbur, is that he fails to distinguish between captives taken on the battlefield and those who voluntarily surrendered.[231]

Some other Chinese writers, such as Lao Kan and Wu Po-lun, hold the opposite view and assert that captives taken in war were all enslaved.[232] Wu, who misunderstands the meaning of a passage, even goes to the extreme of saying that one of the reasons for waging wars with the Hsiung-nu was to capture slaves.[233] The expeditions against the Hsiung-nu, as Chien Po-tsan points out, obviously were launched for reasons other than capturing slaves.[234]

That captives were not treated in the same way as those who surrendered is supported by the following example. Chin Mi-ti's 金日磾 father, who was a king of the Hsiung-nu, was killed for not surrendering; Chin Mi-ti himself was seized and enslaved together with his mother and younger brother (*HS* 68:21a). Another king and his followers, who surrendered voluntarily, were all given rewards (*HS* 24B:8a). These facts indicate that captives were enslaved, whereas those who surrendered were not.

However, there is no evidence that all the captives of war were enslaved. It seems likely that evidence of some kind would appear in the histories if large numbers of captured foreigners were made slaves. Basing himself on the assumption that several thousand or more private slaves could be absorbed by the government only with considerable difficulty during the years 119–113 B.C., Wilbur doubts that as many Hsiung-nu could have been enslaved without creating a similar problem. He also points out that non-Chinese slaves comprised only a small element in the total slave population.[235] His conclusion, which agrees with that of Wu Ching-ch'ao, that a number of captured Hsiung-nu were enslaved but did not constitute an important part of the slave population in Han times is quite plausible.[236]

The case of Chin Mi-ti, who was a captured Hsiung-nu, does not give us much data concerning the captured slaves, but it does afford an

---

was held by Ma Ch'eng-feng, *Chung-kuo ching-chi shih* (2nd ed., 2 vols.; Ch'ang-sha: Commercial Press, 1939), I, 237–44.

[231] Wilbur, *Slavery in China*, p. 98.

[232] Lao Kan, "Han-tai nu-li chih-tu chi-lüeh," *LSYY*, V (1935), 9.

[233] Wu Po-lun, "Hsi Han nu-li k'ao," *Shih-huo*, I (1935), 281. For criticism see Wu Ching-ch'ao, *op. cit.*, p. 265.

[234] Chien Po-tsan, "Kuan-yü liang-Han ti kuan-ssu nu-pei wen-t'i," *LSYC*, No. 4, 1954, pp. 8–9.

[235] Wilbur, *Slavery in China*, pp. 114–16.

[236] Wu Ching-ch'ao, *op. cit.*, p. 265; Wilbur, *Slavery in China*, p. 116.

illuminating illustration of the treatment and social status of a captured foreign slave. Chin was first made a slave and assigned to the work of caring for horses. When he was freed by Emperor Wu, he was appointed to office immediately. He was promoted to the post of general, ennobled as a marquis, and appointed as second regent, which shows that a foreign slave who was manumitted could rise to the top position in the government. Ho Kuang, the grand general, who was the key man in the government, at first declined the appointment of regent and recommended Chin for the position instead. Ho married his daughter to Chin's son (*HS* 68:20b–23a), which also indicates that a prominent Chinese family did not hesitate to marry its daughter to a manumitted foreign slave when he became an important figure in the government.

The sudden rise of Chin Mi-ti was very unusual, but once he had become an official other members of his family easily followed him. Both of his sons became high officials (*HS* 68:23a–b). Chin Mi-ti's younger brother, Lun 倫, who had been made a government slave at the same time as Chin Mi-ti, was also freed and appointed a gentleman at the Yellow Gate (*huang-men lang* 黃門郎). Chin Lun's son An-shang 安上 was ennobled as a marquis because of his merit. All four sons of An-shang were 2,000-picul officials. So also were his six grandsons and two great grandsons. Altogether there were seventeen high officials in the family of the two brothers, Mi-ti and Lun (*HS* 68:23b ff.). Pan Ku was impressed by the prosperity of the Chin family, in which seven held the post of attendant within the palace, a 2,000-picul official who was a close attendant of the emperor (*HS* 68:27a).

Foreign slaves were also presented to the Han government by their own tribes in the form of tribute. In A.D. 49, 922 chieftains of the Wu-huan 烏桓 submitted and came to the Han court with their men to present tribute, among which male and female slaves were included, together with cattle, horses, arrows, and various kinds of furs (*HHS* 90:5a). Although this is the only record in our texts, we doubt that this was the first time slaves were presented as tribute. Probably this one was noticed because of the size of the submitting group. Tribute on a small scale would have been overlooked by the historian.

Foreign slaves of various tribes were also presented as gifts and bribes to the Han officials in charge of supervising these tribes. The *Hou-Han-shu* notes that when Li Hsün 李恂 was appointed lieutenant-colonel of the western frontier (*hsi-yü fu hsiao-wei* 西域副校尉), male and female slaves, horses, gold, silver, incense, and rugs were presented to him on several occasions by the hostage princes, delegates, and the merchants of the various foreign regions (II, 69). The slaves presented must also have been of the Western Regions.

Furthermore, non-Chinese slaves were also imported from the aboriginal tribes on the southern coast and the southwestern regions. Yüeh, the ancient name for the territory of modern Chekiang, Fukien, Kwangtung, and Kwangsi, was one of the centers from which aboriginal slaves were imported to China proper. Such a term as *yüeh-pei* 越婢, the female slave from Yüeh, is found in our text (*HS* 53:5b). In 113 B.C. the dowager queen of Nan-Yüeh, who was a Chinese, was accused by the chancellor of Yüeh of scheming to surrender the kingdom to Han and to take a large number of attendants in order to sell them in Ch'ang-an as slaves (*HS* 95:15a). This accusation may have been unfounded, but it suggests the possibility that Yüeh slaves were sold in China, where we know there were slave merchants.[237]

Pa and Shu, present-day Szechwan and Yunnan, were also centers for the supply of aboriginal slaves. The merchants of these places were mainly engaged in trading horses and yaks from Ch'iung-tu 邛都 and Tse-tu 莋都 and slaves from Po 僰 and Tien 滇. Both the *Shih-chi* and the *Han-shu* mention slaves from Po, but the geographical treatise of the *Han-shu* notes slaves from Tien as well as from Po; it is clearly stated that the people of Pa and Shu went to the south to buy the slaves of Po and Tien.[238] All these names referred to aboriginal tribes in what is now southern Szechwan and Yunnan; these tribes were known to the Han people as the Southwest Barbarians. Since the people of Pa and Shu, as pointed out in the texts, became prosperous and wealthy because of this trade, the demand for aboriginal slaves must have been very great at that time. It is of interest to note that a commentator of the Later Han remarked that there were female slaves from Po in the former capital, Ch'ang-an (*SC* 116:2b). Obviously he would not mention it if there were only a few Po slaves in the capital.

It may be concluded from the foregoing material that foreign slaves, especially the aborigines of present-day Szechwan and Yunnan and the south coast, were quite popular in Han times.[239] However, this should not be exaggerated. Many writers, impressed by the history of other societies in which foreign tribes were a major source of slaves, such as the slaves brought to the Mediterranean countries by the Turks in the Middle Ages, tend to hold the view that foreign slaves also played a major

---

[237] Wilbur, *Slavery in China*, p. 94.
[238] *SC* 129:7b–8a; *HS* 28b:20a, 95:2a.
[239] Cf. Wilbur, *Slavery in China*, p. 116.

role in Han times. This is not warranted by the evidence. There is nothing to indicate that large numbers of foreign slaves, either captured in wars or purchased through slave traders, were employed by the Han government or by private persons. On the contrary, evidence seems to suggest that non-Chinese slaves comprised only a small element in the slave population of Han times.[240]

Some very poor people had no means to support themselves or their family except by selling themselves or their children into slavery. This was recognized by law and sometimes even encouraged by the government, and was particularly true when there was famine or war. In 205 B.C. because of the misery caused by war and the great famine, Emperor Kao-tsu decreed that people might sell their children and go to Shu and Han for food (II, 12). And in 202 B.C. when the empire was pacified, an edict was issued to free those persons who had sold themselves into slavery because of famine (II, 14).

Because of the popularity of buying and selling slaves, there were slave merchants in Han times (II, 2, 11, 19). Slaves were usually sold with cattle and horses from the same pens (II, 2). It was not uncommon for female slaves dressed in embroidered clothes and silk shoes to be kept in pens (II, 19). Transactions involving slaves also took place directly between the owner and the buyer (II, 13).

Government slaves could become private slaves in several ways. Slaves were usually granted to nobles and high officials; for example, a gift of three hundred male and female slaves, together with landed property and cash, was presented by Emperor Wu to his half sister (I, 20). Slaves were also frequently bestowed as rewards for merit. Grand General Ho Kuang was given one hundred and seventy male and female slaves because of his loyalty and services (*HS* 68:12a). The largest reward of this kind recorded in our texts is one thousand slaves; they were given to a magician when he was ennobled by the emperor (*HS* 25A:24a).

As discussed above, a free man legally lost his freedom only when it was decided, either by the man himself or by his parents, that he was to be sold, and a contract was then made. However, not infrequently a free man was seized by a powerful person and made a slave; the powerful Liang Chi, for example, seized several thousand free people, men as well as women, and made them his slaves (II, 78). Sometimes free people were kidnapped and sold as slaves (II, 2).

[240] *Ibid.*, p. 116; Chien Po-tsan, *op. cit.*, pp. 8–10.

GOVERNMENT SLAVES

The total number of male and female slaves owned by the Han government was given by Kung Yü in 44 B.C. as more than one hundred thousand (II, 39). Kung Yü was an able official and the grandee secretary at the time, and his estimate must have had some factual basis. Most likely such figures were kept by the government.[241] Unfortunately his figure is the only one concerning the total number of government slaves in the entire Early and Later Han periods; thus, no comparable figures from other periods are available. Granted that his figure is reliable, another problem is whether this figure is representative only of his time or whether it represents the general situation throughout Han times.

The keeping of such a large number of slaves certainly was a great burden on the government. It was estimated in Emperor Wu's reign, when a large number of private slaves were confiscated from private owners and distributed among the various bureaus, that four million piculs of grain had to be transported via the Yellow River to support these government slaves and convicts. Furthermore, additional grain was bought by the bureaus for the same purpose (II, 31). A minister was dismissed from office because sufficient food and clothing were not provided for the government slaves (*HS* 60:5b).

What kind of work was done by these one hundred thousand government slaves? Did they engage in productive labor and contribute to the income of the state?

One very large group of government slaves was engaged in looking after government-owned animals. Thirty thousand male and female slaves were assigned to take care of three hundred thousand horses in the various horse pastures along the borders (II, 31, n. 107, and 39, n. 127). When a thousand or more private male and female slaves were confiscated from the wealthy merchants in Emperor Wu's time, the slaves were assigned such tasks as rearing dogs, horses, birds, and other animals in the various parks (II, 31).

Many male and female slaves served in the palace as well as in the various government bureaus. Female slaves who served in the inner palace were obviously attendants and domestic servants in the women's quarters.[242] According to the *Han-chiu-i*, palace maids (*kung-jen* 宮人)

[241] II, 39, n. 127; Wilbur, *Slavery in China*, pp. 398–400.
[242] *HS* 74:9b, 97B:11a, and Yen's note to 12a ff.

were selected from among the female slaves to serve the empress and the imperial concubines. Wet nurses were also selected from the female slaves of the palace. The same source mentions that those who served in the inner apartment of the palace were all selected from female slaves from the age of eight and older, and were dressed in green garments. They were under the instruction of the aged female slaves.[243] There were three thousand male and female slaves each in the office of the grand provisioner (*t'ai-kuan* 太官)—that is, the imperial kitchen in charge of food preparation—and the office of the provisioner of wines and fruits (*t'ang-kuan* 湯官). They all wore aprons and served wines and foods (II, 31, and n. 108).

All the official bureaus within the palace had the service of a number of male and female slaves who wore red kerchiefs and served as messengers in announcing the names of officials to be summoned; government slaves were employed in the office of the imperial chancellor and acted as time announcers and ushers, and clever male slaves were selected to do clerical and accounting work.[244] Male slaves and convicts were also found serving under the colonel-director of retainers (*ssu-li hsiao-wei* 司隸校尉) with twelve hundred men as a unit.[245]

Were slaves employed in government industry? The only instance found in the texts is that of skilled and clever male slaves who were kept by the minister of agriculture to manufacture implements (*HS* 24A:16a). However, no slaves were employed in iron mining and manufacturing, one of the main government industries. According to Kung Yü, convicts were employed in the bureau of iron to dig copper and iron ore from the mountains, and more than a hundred thousand labor units were required yearly.[246] It is also reported in the *Yen-t'ieh lun* that convicts were employed in casting iron implements and produced a large supply of them.[247] In 22 B.C. 180 convicts who worked in the bureau of iron at Ying-ch'uan rebelled (*HS* 10:7b), and again in 14 B.C. 228 convicts under the supervision of the Bureau of Iron at Shan-yang rebelled, freeing all the convicts and forcing them to join their group, which numbered several hundred persons (*HS* 10:12b–13a). Only convicts— no slaves—are mentioned in these cases, which suggests that slaves were not employed in manufacturing iron. The last case is more obvious on this point. The rebellious convicts attempted to raise a strong army to

[243] *HCI* B:2a, 3a.
[244] *HCI* B:3a, A:7a, B:2b.
[245] *HCIPI* A:4a.
[246] *HS* 72:15a; cf. *HS* 24B:18b.
[247] Huan K'uan, *Yen-t'ieh lun* (Shanghai, 1934), 6:55, hereafter cited as *YTL*.

revolt against the government. It seems unlikely that there were slaves in the bureau of iron if they were not included in the rebellious force. It is also interesting to note in the statement made by Kung Yü that a labor force of a hundred thousand convicts was needed in iron mining, this being equal to the number of slaves owned by the government, an estimate also given by that same statesman.

Now let us turn to other kinds of government enterprises to see if slaves were employed in them. Vast areas of public land, including farms, wasteland, forests, and so forth, were owned by the government. A large labor force must have been needed for farming, forestation, and the like, but there is no indication that slaves were assigned to cultivate the public land. Instead, convicts, garrison soldiers, and commoner-volunteers were stationed along the frontier as military colonists.[248] Thousands of laborers were employed to transport grain from modern Shantung and Honan to the capital via the Yellow River. According to one text, however, corvée laborers, *tsu* 卒, numbering sixty thousand men, were employed instead of slaves (*HS* 24A:17a).

Most of the labor force was drawn from corvée laborers and convicts. More than seven hundred thousand convicts were used to build a palace and the imperial tomb for the First Emperor of Ch'in (*SC* 6:24b, 31a). The same practice is also found in Han times (*HS* 5:6b, 8:18b, 10:8b). In the spring of 192 B.C. one hundred forty-six thousand commoners, men as well as women, were conscripted for thirty days to work at building the city wall of the capital; in the autumn twenty thousand convicts were assigned work at the same task (*HS* 2:3b). The employment of commoners and convicts, but not slaves, in the construction of city walls is surprising. Obviously the labor service of commoners was limited to a definite and brief period under the corvée regulations, and the incomplete work had to be finished by the convicts.

Other kinds of public works, such as the construction of dams and dikes, required a large number of workers, but slaves did not constitute a part of the work force. For example, in several instances corvée laborers were mobilized to stop the flooding of the Yellow River (*HS* 29:3a, 5b, 10b, 11b). Corvée laborers were also used to dig canals and build roads, and 2,690 convicts were used in A.D. 63 to open up the Pao-Hsieh road in modern Shensi.[249]

We may conclude that government slaves were mainly employed in

[248] *HHHY* 56:563, 59:585 ff.

[249] *HS* 29:4a, 5a; *YTL* 6:55; Wang Ch'ang, *Chin-shih ts'ui-pien* (Ching-hsün t'ang ed., 1805), 5:12b–13b, hereafter cited as *CSTP*.

palace service, office work, tending of animals, and the manufacture of agricultural implements. Except for the last category, most of the work was nonproductive. Complaints to this effect were rather common among men of the Han dynasty. There was a court debate held before the emperor in 81 B.C., during which the "men of virtue and letters" complained that the government male and female slaves, who sat around but who required clothing and food, did not work to their full capacity, so that the government enjoyed no advantage in possessing slaves. This aspect of the contrast between a commoner and a slave was described as follows: "The common people are not free from work from morning to evening, whereas [government] male and female slaves idle about with folded hands."[250] Kung Yü also complained that more than one hundred thousand government male and female slaves idled about without work and that the government had to tax the commoners to support them at an annual expense of five to six hundred million cash (II, 39). Personal prejudices are undoubtedly involved in these two statements and the expressions "idle about with folded hands" and "idle about without work" cannot be taken too literally. Serving in the palace or in a government bureau, taking care of horses, or manufacturing agricultural implements certainly involved some kind of labor and would not be merely sitting idle. However, the statements confirm our conclusion that government slaves were not employed in such strenuous work as mining, public works, and the like. Obviously, two points are reflected in these statements: (1) the work in which government slaves were engaged was less strenuous than the hard labor done by convicts and corvée laborers; (2) the work done by the slaves was generally considered nonproductive and therefore was a burden on the government as well as on the commoners.

Although convicts and corvée laborers were employed in more strenuous work, it does not mean that slaves were more generously treated. The different kinds of work they did is accounted for by the qualifications of the two groups in relation to their jobs. Wilbur points out that while plebeians and convicts served only brief periods, slaves were most useful in work for which long experience was valuable. Thus they were used chiefly in service capacities and skilled work.[251] Government bureaus that required large numbers of clerks and attendants certainly would not want a continuous flow of newcomers who were not experienced in the routine. Furthermore, convicts who were guilty

[250] *YTL* 6:49.
[251] Wilbur, *Slavery in China*, p. 227.

of crimes must be considered more dangerous than slaves and were simply not the right kind of persons to employ in palace and government bureaus.

It is clear, therefore, that the Han government kept and maintained an enormous number of slaves whose service, though nonproductive, was considered necessary. It seems that the government was not concerned about the burden of maintaining such nonproductive slaves, a burden about which Kung Yü and others complained. Obviously, slaves presented no financial problem to the government in ordinary times. But it is difficult to understand why it was willing to maintain a large number of slaves in a time of financial deficiency. The *Shih-chi* and the *Han-shu* report that when the imperial treasury and the government treasury were empty, a measure was taken by Emperor Wu in 127 B.C. to encourage people to contribute male and female slaves, rewarding them with the privilege of exemption from labor service for life, or of appointment as gentlemen (II, 26). This clearly implies that the government was anxious to get more male and female slaves. Since it was a policy worked out in a time of financial difficulty, it seems to suggest that owning slaves benefited the government economically in some way. Another example also supports this assumption. During the reign of Emperor Wu government slaves of the Shang-lin park, together with poor people whose property was worth less than five thousand cash, were ordered to take care of the deer in this imperial park; for the privilege of collecting deer manure, which they presumably sold, they paid the government five cash per day. By Emperor Yüan's time, the total income from this source, according to *Han-chiu-i*, had reached seventy billion cash and was used for a military campaign against the Western Regions.[252]

But there is no evidence that slaves were used in other lucrative government work. Nor is there evidence that the government, which already possessed about one hundred thousand slaves, needed the services of extra slaves. Since detailed information is not available, we are unable to say how the slaves were used by the government to cope with the financial problem, or how effective this measure was.

PRIVATE SLAVES

The owners of private slaves, were, first of all, the nobles and officials

---

[252] *HCI* B:8a. We agree with Wilbur (*Slavery in China,* p. 330, n. 4) that something is wrong with this figure, but the case still shows that these government slaves contributed to the treasury.

who got their slaves either by purchase or as grants from the government, and, second, the commoners, including merchants, who also owned slaves.

Nobles and officials usually had a large number of slaves. A chancellor of Ch'in, Lü Pu-wei, owned ten thousand slaves; according to extant records this is the largest number of slaves owned by an individual in the Ch'in–Han period (II, 4). The paramour of the empress dowager of the First Emperor of Ch'in also owned several thousand slaves (II, 4). Chang Liang 張良, a prince of the state of Han, had three hundred slaves (*HS* 40:1a). In Han times a magician who was appointed general received one thousand slaves from Emperor Wu (*HS* 25A:24a). Seven hundred slaves were owned by a minister marquis (II, 36). The family of Wang Shang, an imperial chancellor, owned slaves numbered by the thousands (*HS* 82:4a). This figure was given by Chang K'uang 張匡 in a memorial in which he brought charges against Wang Shang, so some exaggeration may be expected. However, in the biography of Empress Dowager Wang it is recorded that the number of slaves of the five marquises (her five brothers) ranged from several hundred to several thousand (*HS* 98:9b). A grand administrator's family in the Later Han had eight hundred slaves (II, 72). Each of the Ma brothers, who were members of a consort family, owned more than one thousand male and female slaves (II, 67). Several thousand slaves were owned by Grand General Liang Chi (II, 78).

The number of slaves owned by merchants was sometimes quite large. A wealthy merchant of Lin-ch'iung had several hundred slaves. An iron manufacturer owned eight hundred slaves and gave one hundred of them to his daughter as a marriage gift (II, 24). A wealthy merchant at the end of the Later Han owned ten thousand slaves and guests and donated two thousand slaves and guests to Liu Pei, who married his sister.[253] Since slaves and guests are mentioned together in the text, we do not know how many of the ten thousand men were slaves, but it is probable that the number was great.

Although these are only fragmentary data, and some cases are rather unusual, readers will get a general impression that nobles, high officials, and wealthy merchants or manufacturers usually owned a large number of slaves. This was also reflected in a proposal made by Imperial Chancellor K'ung Kuang and Grand Minister of Works Ho Wu in 7 B.C. suggesting the limiting of the number of slaves that might be owned by men of various status positions. A king was to be limited to two hundred

[253] *SKC*, Shu, 8:7a.

slaves, a marquis or princess to one hundred, and an official or a commoner to thirty slaves (*HS* 24A:18b–19a). This measure was, of course, disadvantageous to the powerful families and action on it was deferred, which implies that the nobles and high officials usually owned more slaves than would have been allowed in the proposed regulation.

Private slaves served in various capacities. Their functions may be discussed under the following categories.

Industry and Business

That a large number of slaves were owned by wealthy businessmen and manufacturers indicates the extensive employment of slaves in these fields. The exploitation of slaves in business and industry had a long history. Po Kuei 白圭, a merchant in the fifth and fourth centuries B.C., is said to have shared the pleasures and sufferings of his slaves who were engaged in business (*SC* 91:5a). Tiao Chien was one of the many who successfully employed slaves in fishing, the salt industry, and business, and because of their efforts he was able to accumulate a large fortune (II, 1). Both of the famous iron miners and manufacturers in the area that is present-day Szechwan owned several hundred to a thousand slaves (II, 5, 24). It is not specifically stated that the slaves were employed in mining, but since male slaves were used in manufacturing charcoal (*HS* 97A:8a), it seems unlikely that an iron miner who owned about a thousand slaves would not employ them in his enterprise.

Agriculture

Wu Ching-ch'ao points out that slaves were not used in farming and says that because agricultural techniques were not highly developed in Han times, it would have been uneconomical to employ slaves in farming.[254] But his assumption does not correspond with evidence that agriculture in the Han was rather advanced. The argument that a farmer with one hundred *mou* of land could hardly support his family does not mean that a large landowner would not profit by employing slaves in his fields. The texts mention a male slave who was assigned to field work by his master (II, 13). The saying, "You should consult about farming with your male slaves, and you should consult about weaving with your female slaves," suggests that it was not uncommon to use male slaves in agriculture. Wang Pao's 王褒 "slave contract" also mentions that male

[254] Wu Ching-ch'ao, *op. cit.*, pp. 266–67.

slaves planted ginger, melons, scallions, and mulberry, peach, plum, and pear trees. Slaves also took part in harvesting and gathering beans.[255] A wealthy landlord who engaged in farming, fish raising, and animal breeding was able to double his profit yearly because both his family members and his slaves diligently worked together (I, 40).

We are unable to solve the problem of how much slaves were used on farms. Were tenants and hired laborers used more frequently than slaves? There is just not sufficient data to warrant estimates of the relative roles of tenancy and hired labor in Han agriculture. Students of Han history know too little about the management of land in those days, and it is dangerous to make a generalization based on a few pieces of fragmentary data. Farm laborers and slaves used in farming are mentioned only incidentally by the authors of our texts in the course of describing some event that was considered important; so the frequency of mention does not necessarily indicate the importance or nonimportance of hired labor or slaves in farming. But because tenancy is frequently mentioned in the discussions of the unequal distribution of land between wealthy landlords and poor, landless peasants (*HS* 24:15a, 19b), it seems more likely that tenancy was prevalent. Pointing out that there was a large supply of landless free labor and that slaves constituted only a small part of the total population and were mostly employed in nonproductive activities, Wilbur reaches the conclusion that slaves were probably unimportant in agriculture.[256]

Handicrafts

When a household was a self-sufficient unit, it was expected that the everyday utensils and tools would be made by the family itself or, if the family owned slaves, by the slaves. This was the situation in Wang Pao's slave contract. The slave was asked to make brooms, bamboo rakes, well wheels, fishing nets, shoes, ropes, mats, charcoal, knives, bows, and so forth. Except for a few items, these utensils and tools were made for household consumption only.[257]

Commodities were sometimes produced for sale outside the family to supplement the family income. The wife of a marquis who had a fief of ten thousand households engaged in spinning and weaving, and all of

---

[255] Yen K'o-chün (comp.), *Ch'üan shang-ku san-tai Ch'in Han san-kuo liu-ch'ao wen* (Huang-kang Wang-shih, 1894), 42:11b–12a, hereafter cited as *SKCHW*.

[256] Wilbur, *Slavery in China*, pp. 215–16.

[257] *SKCHW* 42:12a–b.

the seven hundred slaves were trained and skilled in handicrafts. This way the marquis was able to increase his wealth and make a great fortune (II, 36).

Domestic Service

Domestic service was one of the common duties expected of male and female slaves. Those families who used slaves in their businesses, crafts, and productive work must have also kept a number of slaves for domestic service. The services listed in Wang Pao's slave contract include house cleaning, washing dishes and clothes, pounding rice, cooking, serving food and wines, shopping, feeding animals, and guarding the house at night. In short, a slave was expected to do all kinds of domestic tasks under the command of his master.[258]

Bodyguards and Military Service

Some male slaves were chosen as bodyguards and mounted retainers. Wei Ch'ing, a slave, was a horseman who escorted the princess of P'ing-yang (I, 27). One case shows clearly that the so-called *ch'i-nu* 騎奴, "mounted slaves," not only rode horseback as escorts but usually carried weapons (*HS* 77:17b).

Slaves were sometimes ordered to engage in unlawful activities. In one instance, slaves were ordered to shoot the officers who came to arrest a criminal hiding in the residence of a princess (III, 29). A "mounted slave" was once ordered to destroy the drum of an official bureau (*HS* 77:17b). Male slaves were even assigned tasks that included murder and robbery (*HS* 47:5a).

Slavery in the military service is best illustrated in the following example. A military officer was killed in battle; his son, who was also in the army, rushed to attack the enemy force with a group of followers. At first several tens of his friends volunteered to follow him, but when they reached the front only two of them had the courage to advance. More than ten male slaves, on horseback, followed the son. Only the officer's son and one of his friends got back. All the slaves were lost (II, 23). Several interesting points are illustrated by this: (1) attendant male slaves joined the army with their master; (2) personal slaves had to defend their master under any conditions whatsoever; (3) the volunteers withdrew from a critical situation, but the slaves could do nothing but

[258] *SKCHW* 42:12a.

risk their lives. In another example, in A.D. 19 large numbers of Hsiung-nu invaded the Han border. Wang Mang attempted to raise troops by enlisting the criminals under the death penalty and the male slaves owned by officials and commoners (*HS* 24B:25a, 99C:5a).

Entertaining

Wealthy families usually kept a number of male and female slaves as entertainers—musicians, singers, and dancers.[259] Female slaves of beauty and talent usually performed dancing and singing (I, 25; *HS* 97B:11a). Since dancing and singing abilities require years of training, it seems likely that some girls were trained in their youth for this purpose and sold as singing girls (*HS* 97A:22a–b).

Masters also had sexual privileges with their young female slaves. Wang Mang once bought a female slave and presented her to a general, saying that he did this because the general had no son and this slave was fertile (*HS* 99A:2a). A master often had sexual relations with his more intimate female slaves, called *fu-pei* 傅婢 or *yü-pei* 御婢. The former term is understood by Yen Shih-ku to mean a "close favorite who attends to her master's clothes and bed" (II, 19, n. 63). The term *yü* means "to wait on." Many persons were accused of having illicit intercourse with a father's *fu-pei* or *yü-pei* (I, 25; *HS* 41:9b, 97A:19b).

STATUS OF SLAVES

Slaves were legally unfree and were owned as property either by the government or by private persons. A privately owned slave was under the complete control of his master. Slaves could be sold or given to others as gifts (II, 17, 24). A slave had to obey and render any kind of service wanted, and the master had the right to chastise a disobedient slave. Wei Ch'ing once said when he was a slave that a slave would be satisfied if he could be exempt from scolding and beating.[260] It was entered in Wang Pao's slave contract that the slave was to be subject to a hundred strokes when he disobeyed his master.[261] The law also recognized the inferior status of a slave, who was not treated as the equal of a commoner before the law. A slave who had shot and injured a com-

---

[259] There is a record of a king who was about to die and made a will that his male and female slaves who could perform music should follow him in death (*HS* 53:9a).
[260] *SC* 111:1b; *HS* 55:1b.
[261] *SKCHW* 42:12b.

moner was subject to the death penalty. (This law was only abrogated in A.D. 35 by the order of Emperor Kuang-wu; see II, 60.) Han law did not permit a master to kill a slave of his own free will. Two kings lost their kingdoms because of murdering their slaves.[262] Another kingdom was abolished because a king ordered the death of several slaves who were to be buried with him (*HS* 53:9a–b). The investigation of the wife of an imperial chancellor who was suspected of murdering a female slave shows that even a chancellor's wife was not free from legal responsibility (II, 35). Wang Mang ordered his son to commit suicide when he learned that he had murdered a slave (I, 37), and his granddaughter and her husband also committed suicide when he scolded them because she had murdered a female slave (*HS* 99C:4a). This provides more evidence that killing a slave was a serious illegal matter that might involve the family in trouble. It seems unlikely that Wang Mang would have shown such a severe attitude if there had been a law that tolerated such action.

But it does not follow that the punishment for murdering a slave was the same as for ordinary homicide. Emperor Kuang-wu's edict of A.D. 35 (II, 59) proves that before that date a lesser punishment was applied to those who killed their slaves. Furthermore, a master was given the privilege of asking the local government to authorize the killing of a slave. It is not clear whether the master asked for permission from the government so that he himself could kill the slave or whether he only presented the guilty slave to the government and asked to have him put to death (II, 9). A similar law existed under the Chin dynasty: when a slave resisted his master, the master could petition the government to have the slave killed (*CS* 30:10a). No matter who actually put the slave to death, it is certain that a slave was pretty much at the mercy of his master; the government merely acted as an agent to authorize the action in which the master took the initiative. Tung Chung-shu must have had this in mind when he suggested the abolition of the slavery system in order to eliminate the killing of slaves on the authority of the masters (*HS* 24A:15b). The same is also implied in Wang Mang's statement that masters had arbitrary authority over the lives of their slaves (II, 2).

More legal protection was given to slaves in the Later Han. It was Emperor Kuang-wu's edict of A.D. 35 that abolished the law demanding the death penalty for a slave who had shot and injured a commoner (II, 60). At the same time heavier punishment was imposed upon those

262 *HS* 15A:7b; *TKHC* 21:7b.

who injured or killed a slave. An edict of the same emperor indicates that cruelty was frequently involved in punishment of slaves by their masters. It was decreed that anyone who burned a slave should be punished according to the law and that those who were burned should be freed and permitted to become commoners (II, 59). Moreover, another edict, also issued in A.D. 35, ordered that anyone who killed a slave should not receive a reduction in punishment (II, 59). The *Tung-kuan Han-chi* reports that a prefect arrested and killed a eunuch's wife who had murdered a female slave and then disposed of the corpse in a well.[263]

As we would expect, most slaves were engaged in manual labor and lived in a humble way; however, not all slaves lived under miserable conditions. Some of them had better conditions than the ordinary poor commoner. The contrast was noted by Pao Hsüan 鮑宣, who said that whereas the commoners were half starved and wearing ragged clothes, the slaves of the powerful families were enjoying wine and meat, and such slaves as the Dark-green Heads and the Hut Dwellers even accumulated wealth and became rich (*HS* 72:26a).

It should be stressed that slaves were not all treated the same way, nor did they have the same status. Probably status was conditioned by the way a person became a slave, by the kind of work assigned to him, by his manner of dress, by the way he was treated, and the like. A slave who had his head shaved and wore an iron collar (II, 13) certainly had a status much inferior to those who were dressed in silk and embroidered clothes (II, 19; see also *HS* 10:13b). The slaves who were assigned to do menial labor, such as making charcoal, farming, and so on, must have been inferior to those whose duty it was merely to do domestic work. The "big slave" or the "superintendent slave," who acted as a steward and who had the authority to supervise the work of other slaves, certainly was the one who had the most superior status among the various household slaves. He must have been exempt from menial labor and had many other privileges that ordinary slaves could not have. He was the person entrusted with the general management of the household and was consulted by the master or mistress. That superintendent slaves were favorites of their masters and had illicit relations with their mistresses—in one instance the event happened after she was a widow and in another while the master was still alive—is an indication of their intimacy and the trust placed in them (II, 33, 77). The so-called Dark-green Heads also had a superior status compared with other slaves. A

[263] *TKHC* 20:4a.

male slave of this kind was sent to the court by his official-master to pay a visit on his behalf (*HS* 68:14b).[264] Among the female slaves, those whose job it was to sing and dance and those who had intimate personal relations with their masters must have enjoyed a comfortable and luxurious life and had a status superior to other female slaves in the household.

The superior status of certain slaves was evident both within the household and outside of it. The king of Ch'ang-i was so friendly with his male slaves that he allowed them to wear caps that were not to be worn by humble persons and he drank and played with them (*HS* 27B1:10b, 68:8b–9a).

Although the general formal status of slaves as a whole was inferior to commoners, some slaves in exceptional cases enjoyed a status superior to that of the commoners; their own status was of course determined to a great extent by the status of their masters. Slaves of influential persons usually were able to have social contact with officials. Some of Tiao Chien's slaves rode in carriages and associated with grand administrators and chancellors (II, 1). When Ho Kuang held the key position in the government and all official promotions depended on his recommendations, all officials served his chief slaves, Feng Tzu-tu 馮子都 and Wang Tzu-fang 王子方, and paid no attention to the imperial chancellor (*HS* 68:16b). Liang Chi's superintendent slave, Ch'in Kung, was so important that his dignity and power shocked the public. All the inspectors and 2,000-picul officials paid visits to him and came to bid him farewell when they left (II, 77).

Relying on the influence of their masters, the slaves of powerful families usually were arrogant, overbearing, and violent (II, 63; III, 26, 34, 43). A slave of a redresser-of-wrongs, who was a retired official, had an argument with a butcher and injured him (III, 47). The slaves of Ho Kuang's family frequently carried weapons to the market, fighting and quarreling, and the officials were unable to stop them (III, 26). A male slave of a princess once killed a commoner in the marketplace (II, 63).

Occasionally these influential slaves were even overbearing and rude to officials. Once the slaves of Ho Kuang's family argued over the right-of-way with the slaves of the grandee secretary; they entered the grounds of the grandee secretary's office and wanted to break down the gate. They did not leave until the secretary kowtowed and apologized (III, 34). On another occasion, forty armed slaves were sent by a powerful

[264] On the Dark-green Heads, see II, 53, n. 160.

official to attack the bureau of music; the officials of the bureau were forced to make a very humble apology (III, 43). Similar cases were also found in the Later Han. Pan Ku's male slave once stopped the carriage and outriders of the prefect of the capital and cursed the prefect. The prefect was afraid of Tou Hsien 竇憲, the grand general, with whom Pan Ku was closely associated, and did not dare to do anything (*HHS* 40B: 26b–27a).

The mobility of slaves was slight. A slave, whether owned by the government or a private person, became a commoner when emancipated; this is clearly stated in the edicts of manumission of government slaves, as well as of private slaves (II, 45, 58, 59, 61).

The chance of a slave entering officialdom was rare and exceptional, although there were no such restrictions—as in Ch'ing times—that a slave could not be an official even if manumitted or that only after four generations could the descendant of an emancipated slave participate in the examinations and become an official.[265] In Han times a slave who was freed and made a commoner could immediately be appointed to office. Luan Pu 欒布, who had been a private slave, was first appointed a general by the king of Yen, a rival of Liu Pang, and then became a Han official and a marquis (II, 11). Chin Mi-ti, who was an enslaved barbarian, was freed by Emperor Wu and immediately appointed to an official post; he later became a high-ranking official (*HS* 68:21a–23a). Wei Ch'ing, whose mother was a slave maid of a princess, and who himself had been a mounted courier of the princess, later became grand general, was ennobled as a marquis, and married the princess whom he had served (I, 27, and n. 121). Ch'in Kung was made the chief of the grand granary (*t'ai-ts'ang chang* 太倉長) while he was still the superintendent slave of Liang Chi (II, 77). The most illuminating case is that of a male slave who saved the life of his infant master and brought him up under extreme difficulties; he was appointed to office at the same time as his young master and both held the same title. Later the slave was promoted to the position of grand administrator (II, 53). This suggests that no discrimination was made between the master and the slave and that the idea, which was popular in later dynasties, that a slave should not be permitted to mix with members of his master's family did not exist in Han times. Three male slaves because of their merit in murdering their master, who had rebelled against Emperor Kuang-wu, were ennobled as marquises with the unusual title "unrighteous marquis" (II, 57).

[265] Ch'ü, *Law and Society,* p. 132, n. 6.

The mobility of female slaves depended largely upon their beauty, charm, and the opportunity of being married to a free man or a man of superior status. When a slave girl became a favorite of her master she had already advanced her status, and if she became a concubine she was no longer a slave. If a slave became an imperial concubine, she had an even greater chance to climb up the social ladder. Wei Tzu-fu 衛子夫, who was the daughter of a slave maid in the family of a princess, was favored by Emperor Wu, became a concubine in the palace, and later became empress (*HS* 55:1a).

MANUMISSION AND GOVERNMENT POLICY

A person once enslaved lost his personal freedom forever. His descendants, male or female, became "born slaves" (II, 8, and n. 29) of the government or of a private household, depending on the status of their parents. Obviously children of slave parents were slaves at birth. But what of the child of a slave and a free man? It was said that when a free man married a female slave, a child of this marriage was called a *huo* 獲; when a male slave married a free woman, the child born of the union was called a *tsang* 臧 (*HS* 62:20b). As *tsang* and *huo* were humiliating terms for male and female slaves,[266] their use suggests that the child of such a union was still considered a slave.

A slave could be free only when he was manumitted. Manumissions were granted to government slaves under various conditions. Sometimes such a privilege was limited to a special group. For instance, in 140 B.C. the family members of the leaders of the Rebellion of the Seven Kingdoms, who had been made government slaves, were pardoned by Emperor Wu. The rebellion took place in 154 B.C.; so the persons who were freed had been slaves for fourteen years. Such a favor, however, must be considered unusual. Ying Shao commented that "Emperor Wu pitied them, pardoned them, and sent them away" (*HS* 6:2a).

Government slaves who became too old to render routine services to the government were at times manumitted in their old age. In 7 B.C., when Emperor Ai ascended the throne, an edict was issued that all government slaves, male and female, who were over fifty were to be dismissed and made commoners (II, 45).

---

[266] The exact meaning of each term, according to Yang Hsiung's *Fang-yen*, a work on dialects of various localities in Han times, varied according to localities. However, the term *tsang* generally referred to male slaves and *huo* to female slaves; quoted in *HS* 62:20b.

General manumission, which applied to all government slaves with-out special qualification, was rare. If such a manumission had been put into effect, the government would have been left with few slaves. There were only two general manumissions in Early and Later Han: one oc-curred in 160 B.C. (II, 2) and the other in A.D. 110 (II, 74). Individual manumission could be granted to any particular government slave. Since this kind of action did not involve the problem of dismissing a large number of government slaves whose services were demanded by the government, it seems that individual manumission was more fre-quent than a general one or one on a large scale. Any slave whose physical appearance, personality, diligent service, or meritorious be-havior impressed the emperor might be freed by him. However, such individual cases are mentioned only accidentally when other more im-portant events are involved. We are therefore unable to determine how frequently individual manumissions were granted. In one instance, a male slave was freed by Emperor Wu, who was impressed by his dig-nified manner and his excellent service in taking care of the horses (*HS* 68:21a). In another, a palace female slave was freed by Emperor Hsüan because of her merit in taking care of him during his childhood (*HS* 74:10a).

According to the *Han-chiu-i*, government slaves could buy their free-dom by paying ten million cash.[267] It is unlikely that a government slave could become rich enough to pay this amount of money. As was discussed earlier in this chapter, only a few wealthy merchants and high officials had accumulated a wealth of ten million. The *Yen-t'ieh lun* states that certain government male slaves accumulated a wealth of a hundred catties of gold (one million cash).[268] Since this was probably as much as any slave had ever accumulated, it would have been impossible for such a person to pay the required amount to buy his freedom.

The manumission of private slaves depended on the owner. The usual way for a private slave to be freed was to buy himself from his master, that is, buy his freedom. A marquis was deposed because he seized and re-enslaved a former slave who had purchased his freedom (*HS* 17:7b). A slave might also be freed by his master on his own volition.[269] Thus everything depended upon the master, and very little could be done by

---

[267] *HCI* B:4a. Suspecting that a thousand myriad is too large an amount to be paid by a slave, Lao Kan suggests that "thousand" is a clerical error for "ten"; that is, the price for buying one's freedom would be a hundred thousand cash (Lao Kan, "Han-tai nu-li chih-tu chi-lüeh," *LSYY*, V [1935], 5).

[268] *YTL* 6:4a.

[269] *TKHC* 21:4a.

the government. However, at times the government did interfere, usually when the empire was just at peace again after a period of war and disturbance. In 205 B.C., when there was a great famine, Emperor Kao ordered that people might sell their children (II, 12), and three years later an edict was issued to the effect that all commoners who had sold themselves to other people because of the famine were to be manumitted and become commoners (II, 14).

A similar policy was inaugurated by Emperor Kuang-wu. It was decreed in A.D. 26 that the wives who had been remarried to others by their husbands and the children who had been sold by their parents were allowed to return to their homes if they wished to; anyone daring to hold them would be punished according to the law (II, 54). An edict was also issued in A.D. 31 to free those who had become slaves because of famine and poverty (II, 58). Other edicts to free slaves were issued by Emperor Kuang-wu in A.D. 31, 36, 38, and 39. But, differing from the general manumission mentioned above, these were applicable to people of a particular locality only—the people who had been enslaved by the Red Eyebrows, and the natives of modern Szechwan and Kansu who had been seized and enslaved when Kung-sun Shu 公孫述 and Wei Ao were the rulers of these areas. It was mentioned in the edicts that those who had sold themselves did not have to pay back the money and also that those who dared to detain the slaves would be sentenced according to the law of kidnapping people (II, 58, 61).

The government interfered with the manumission of private slaves only during the first several years of the Early Han and again for several years at the beginning of the Later Han (in this period only the first of the five measures was of a general nature, the others applied only in a specific territory where war and disorder had occurred). This would indicate that in times of peace the buying of slaves was legally permitted and that manumission would not be decreed by the government.

Was the government concerned with the number of slaves a person owned? Yes, occasionally. Tung Chung-shu once urged Emperor Wu to abolish the system of slavery, but his suggestion was not accepted (*HS* 24A:15b). In 13 B.C. an edict was issued by Emperor Ch'eng, who complained that most of the nobles and the ministers were living extravagantly and, among other things, kept a large number of male and female slaves; for this reason he ordered the high officials to restrain such practices (*HS* 10:13b–14a). This order was apparently not carried out. No concrete step was taken until 7 B.C., when Emperor Ai ordered his officials to work out a measure to limit the number of slaves as well as the size of farms that could be owned by persons of various statuses. Thus the maximum number of slaves, excluding those whose age was over sixty and below ten, owned by a king was to be limited to two hundred persons; by a princess or a marquis, one hundred; by a marquis within the passes, an official, or a commoner, thirty. The excess slaves were to be confiscated by the government. However, this measure was inconvenient to those consort families and powerful officials whose lands and slaves far exceeded the suggested number, and they were so influential that the policy was never put into effect (*HS* 24A:18b–19a).

In A.D. 3 a measure that limited the number of slaves owned by various officials and commoners was worked out and presented to Emperor P'ing. However, no details are given in the text (*HS* 12:6a), nor is there any information regarding the effectiveness of the measure. A more radical change was made by Wang Mang in A.D. 9 when he decreed that slaves were to be called "personal adherents" and could not be bought and sold. This measure, which made the selling of human beings unlawful, obviously was an attempt to abolish slavery. But opposition was so strong that three years later Wang Mang was forced to cancel it. An edict was issued saying that those who had recently bought and sold slaves were not to be punished (*HS* 24A:19b–20a).

Chapter Five

POWERFUL FAMILIES

A NUMBER of powerful families, known as *hao-tsu* 豪族, *hao-tsung* 豪宗, *hao-yu* 豪右, *ta-tsu* 大族, *ta-hsing* 大姓, and the like,[1] dominated Han government and society and exercised control over the rest of the population. They included (1) old families: the descendants of the ruling houses of the six kingdoms overthrown by the Ch'in, (2) imperial relatives of the ruling family of the Han who were made kings and marquises, (3) consort families, (4) officials, (5) wealthy merchants, and (6) redressers-of-wrong *(yu-hsia)*.

With the exception of the last group, all these families had one power in common—economic power. They all possessed wealth and landed property, thus influencing the life chances of the rest of the population. The power of the first four groups, which constituted the ruling class, was mainly political. The old families had been members of the ruling

---

[1] Powerful families were given such names as *hao-tsu (HHS* 56:6b); *hao-tsung (HHS* 31:12a); *hao-chia* 豪家 *(HHS* 64A:22a); *ta-tsu (HHS* 1B:12a, 76:2a); *ch'iang-tsung* 強宗 *(HS* 76:2a; *HHS* 31:1b; Hsia Ch'eng, *Hou-Han-shu,* quoted in *HHS* 33:19b, note); *hao-yu (HHS* 3:4a, 46:12a, 56:10b, 77:6b, 82A:8a), since the right side was considered superior to the left, *yu* means the big families, i.e., *hao-yu* has the same meaning as *yu-hsing* 右姓 or *ta-hsing; hao-hsing* 豪姓 *(HHS* 67:20b and 33a); *ta-hsing (HS* 72:25a, 76:2a, 83:13b, 90:16b, 100A:2a; *HHS* 21:5b, 26:21a, 67:11a, 77:6b–7a, 82A:8a; Hsia Ch'eng, *Hou-Han-shu,* quoted in *HHS* 33:19b, note); and *yu-hsing (HHS* 31:1b).

class in the past, but the imperial relatives, consort families, and officials came to power for the first time during the Han. The possession of political power made them the most powerful groups in society, for no other power was able to check or challenge it.

There was, of course, a close connection between political and economic power. Many consort families and officials came from wealthy families; on the other hand, political power automatically brought wealth to the holder of a noble rank or an official post. A poor man whose family became a consort family or one who was made an official became rich overnight.

The power of the wealthy merchants derived, of course, from economic power. But here, too, there was a connection between economic and political power, for such merchants often attempted to convert economic power into political power, and some of them succeeded.

The power of the *yu-hsia* 遊俠, the redressers-of-wrong, was primarily based on sheer physical force, which enabled them to control behavior or even to have life-or-death control over others. As a rule, they had neither political nor economic power; but there was a close connection between such nongovernmental coercive power and political power. The *yu-hsia*, who often associated with the nobles and officials, were backed by political power. On the other hand, the nobles and officials who were associated with the *yu-hsia* were supported by them and commanded their services. There were also nobles and officials who were engaged in *yu-hsia* activities.

EARLY HAN

OLD FAMILIES

The old families were the descendants of the ruling families and nobles of the various feudal states that had monopolized land and political power for generations in Chou times—for example, the three families of the state of Lu (Meng-sun 孟孫, Chi-sun 季孫, and Shu-sun 叔孫), the T'ien family of Ch'i, and the Chao, Ch'ü, and Ching families of Ch'u.

With the formation of a unified empire and the collapse of the various feudal states, the ruling families and the nobles of these states also collapsed and lost the privileges they had enjoyed for centuries. One important change is obvious: their political power was gone with the collapse of feudalism. However, they still kept their family property and were wealthy. For instance, Chang Liang, who was the son of the chancellor of the state of Han, had three hundred slaves when Han was overthrown by Ch'in, and thereafter spent all his family property in seeking revenge.[2] Moreover, such families still had a superior status in society simply because their traditional status could not be wiped out of the minds of their contemporaries overnight. This psychological factor obviously played an important role in maintaining their power. Formally they were deprived of political power; but they had been in power for centuries, and status and power were closely interrelated, so it is understandable that because of their superior status they had a potential power that enabled them to have others under their command. This potential power sometimes led to the realization of actual power, such as when the control of the central government became weak in a period of crisis. This is clearly seen in the rebellion against Ch'in after the death of the First Emperor.

With a few exceptions most of the rebellious forces were organized under the leadership of the old families of the various states. One of the most powerful rebelling forces was organized under the command of the Hsiang family, whose forefathers had been generals in Ch'u for generations and who had been ennobled in Hsiang (see document III, 6). When the prefect of Tung-yang was killed by a group of rebellious young men, they wanted to make Ch'en Ying 陳嬰, a subordinate of the prefect, their leader and king. Ch'en refused, saying: "The Hsiang family has for generations been a family of generals; it is famous in Ch'u. Now if we wish to launch an important undertaking, there is no man but [one of the Hsiang family] who can be the general. If we rely on this famous lineage, it is certain that we can overthrow Ch'in." Following his advice, the group placed the army under Hsiang Liang's command.

The potential power of the old ruling families is best illustrated by the T'ien family, the descendants of the family of the king of Ch'i. As a matter of fact, Ch'i was under the complete control of the family from 209 to 202 B.C., engaging in successive campaigns against the Ch'in empire, the force of Hsiang Chi, and finally against the Han. T'ien Tan 田儋 first made himself king of Ch'i and rebelled against Ch'in. When he was killed in action, T'ien Chia 田假, the younger brother of a former king, was made king, with T'ien Chiao 田角 as chancellor and T'ien Chien 田間 as general. T'ien Jung 田榮, T'ien Tan's cousin, was angry, and attacked and drove out the king. He

[2] *SC* 55:1a; *HS* 40:1a.

thereupon made T'ien Tan's son, Shih 市, the king; he himself became the chancellor; and his brother, Heng 横, was made general. After Hsiang Yü had overthrown Ch'in, he made T'ien Shih the king of Chiao-tung. T'ien Tu 田都 and T'ien An 田安 were also made kings. T'ien Jung killed all three and made himself king. After T'ien Jung was defeated by Hsiang Yü and was killed, T'ien Heng made T'ien Jung's son, Kuang 廣, the king, and he himself became the chancellor. Later Ch'i was attacked by the Han army and the king was captured. Thereupon T'ien Heng made himself king. After he was defeated by Han and the king of Han had united the empire, he took refuge on an island with five hundred of his followers. Emperor Kao-tsu, aware of the power of the T'ien family and their potential threat to Han, summoned T'ien Heng to the capital, but he committed suicide on the way.[3] This illustrates how powerful an old ruling family could be years after it had been deprived of political power. Not only were the kings members of the T'ien family, but the important posts, such as chancellor and general, were also all monopolized by this family.

Although other old ruling families were not as powerful as the T'ien family, their potential power should not be overlooked. Even where the old ruling families were not the actual leaders of rebellion, they were often used as figureheads in order to establish authority and to assure commandership. Thus when Ch'in Chia 秦嘉 rebelled he made Ching Chü 景駒, a descendant of a lineage belonging to the ruling family of Ch'u, the king of Ch'u (*SC* 7:4a). When Chang Erh and Ch'en Yü 陳餘 led a troop of several ten thousands to fight against Ch'in, they were convinced that it would be difficult for strangers to establish independence in the area of Chao but that success would be assured if a descendant of the old ruling family of Chao were made king.[4] Both must have understood this tactic thoroughly. As a matter of fact, they had urged Ch'en She, the first to start the rebellion against Ch'in, not to make himself king but to appoint descendants of the ruling families of the six states as kings. Ch'en rejected the suggestion. Fan Tseng[5] 范增 considered this the reason for the lack of influence and the failure of Ch'en, and warned Hsiang Liang not to repeat the same mistake. His advice was accepted by Hsiang, and thereupon a grandson of the former king of Ch'u was made the king in order to accord with the will of the people (*SC* 7:5a–b). Members of the Hsiang family, as noted

---

[3] *SC* 94:1a ff.; *HS* 33:2a ff.; III, 5.

[4] *SC* 89:7b; *HS* 32:5b.

[5] *SC* 89:2a–b; *HS* 32:1b–2a.

above, had been generals of Ch'u for generations and had a strong army under their command, yet the influence of a descendant of an old ruling family, who at that time was merely a powerless shepherd (*SC* 7:5b), was still to be relied upon. This shows clearly the potential power of these old ruling families and confirms the statement of Lou (Liu) Ching 婁(劉)敬, who said to Emperor Kao that during the revolution no one except the T'ien of Ch'i and the Chao, Ch'ü, and Ching of Ch'u was able to start a revolt.[6]

The Ch'in, when it was about to unify the empire, certainly was aware of the power and the potential threat of these old families, and took measures to reduce their power. A branch of the ruling family of Wei was removed to Hu-yang by the Ch'in when Ch'in had overthrown the Wei (III, 48). Fragmentary information indicates that similar actions took place in some other states overthrown by Ch'in.[7]

The Han house, which had become aware of the power of these old families during the revolution, took similar measures in a more systematic and extensive way. In 198 B.C. Lou Ching reminded the emperor of the power the old families had shown by their revolts against Ch'in and warned the emperor that the Han government was subject to threats from two directions: the Hsiung-nu in the north and the strong lineages of the six states in the east. He proposed moving various families, such as the T'ien of Ch'i, the Chao, Ch'ü, and Ching of Ch'u, the former ruling families of the old states of Yen, Chao, Han, and Wei, and other famous families of powerful persons to the area within the pass (Kuan-chung), so that they would be under close and direct supervision and control. His proposal was accepted, and these powerful families were moved to the area within the pass (III, 8, 9). The policy of moving the old families from various places to the capital clearly

---

[6] III, 8. Because of his advice on where the capital should be located, Kao-tsu conferred on him the imperial surname Liu (*SC* 99:3a).

[7] Pan Ku mentions that the Pan family, descendants of Tzu-wen 子文, a top official of the state of Ch'u, was moved to the area between Chin and Tai, modern Shensi (*HS* 100A:1a). Certainly the Pans were not the only family removed from this state. According to *Hsin T'ang-shu*, 75:8a., the Ch'üan family was moved to modern Kansu when the Ch'in conquered Ch'u and moved its big families to Lung-hsi. A noble family of the state of Chao, descendants of Chao She 趙奢, was moved to Hsien-yang when Chao was overthrown by the Ch'in (*Hsin T'ang-shu*, 72B:23a). The Ch'in policy was best summed up in *Hua-yang kuo-chih*. Kings Hui 惠王 and Wen 文王 and the First Emperor, who conquered the six states, always moved the powerful persons and those engaged in *hsia* activities to Shu, Szechwan (Ch'ang Ch'ü, *Hua-yang kuo-chih, SPTK* ed., 3:8a, hereafter cited as *HYKC*). The largest transfer took place in 221 B.C. when the Ch'in moved the powerful and wealthy families of the empire to its capital, altogether one hundred twenty thousand households (III, 2).

indicates that they were the most powerful families in the early days of the Han and that they were considered the greatest threat to the security of the newly established dynasty.

Because of this measure the power of these old families was apparently greatly reduced. Besides, they were gradually forgotten by the people, and since their status and power were mainly based on their past history, they lost their prominence and influence as time went on. They were much less powerful by the middle of the Han than they had been in the earlier days. However, this point should not be exaggerated, for we know that these families still had some influence and power. In one instance, the descendants of a general of the state of Chao were considered a powerful family; they were moved from their native place to Tu-ling by the Han government in the first century B.C. However, for generations members of the family were able to hold the post of grand administrator of border provinces (III, 10). The Feng family, which was a branch of the ruling family of Wei and had been moved to Hu-yang by Ch'in, remained the distinguished family of the commandery. Its influence and power were fully expressed when various persons raised a revolt against Wang Mang in the latter part of his reign. The family gathered their guests, called on the powerful persons, and established barracks and ditches for self-defense, waiting for the person to whom they wished to submit (III, 48).

IMPERIAL RELATIVES

The close imperial relatives were made kings by Emperor Kao, and the size of the early kingdoms was large. The kings, with the assistance of their chancellors and other officials, exercised direct control in their territories.[8] The central government, conscious of their power and fearful of the potential threat to its own position, tended to reduce their strength and put them under more control. On the other hand, the kings always attempted to increase their power and remain as strong and independent as possible. The antagonism, when intensified, usually led to open conflict.

Some statesmen of the central government were well aware of the size and potential power of these large kingdoms and pointed out that they were threats to the sovereignty of the emperor, even though the kings were his blood relatives.[9] Emperor Wen was advised by Chia I

[8] *HS* 19A:14b–15a; *HHC* 28:10b–11a.
[9] *HS* 48:7b ff., 49:22b–23a, 64A:19a–b.

to enforce a strong policy of reducing the size of the large kingdoms and rearranging the territory of certain kingdoms in such a way that the remote ones were isolated and put in disadvantageous strategic positions.[10] Further measures to reduce their size were suggested by Ch'ao Ts'o and adopted by Emperor Ching in 154 B.C.[11] These actions that tended to weaken the power of the kingdoms forced them to choose either to submit and be weakened or to resist in order to maintain their power. They chose the second course, and participated in the famous rebellion that drew upon the joint force of seven kingdoms. This organized force was so strong that no one was sure of the outcome; the Han generals at first did not dare engage in battle with the army of Wu, which alone had a force of five hundred thousand men (*HS* 35:6a ff.).

After the rebellion had been put down, the central government was even more conscious of the power of the kingdoms, and further measures were taken to weaken them. A king was not allowed to govern his own country or to appoint his officials—except the petty officials. Thus a kingdom was put under more strict control and supervision by the central government.[12] In Emperor Wu's time, the system of appoint-

[10] *HS* 14:3a–b, 48:11a–b, 27a–28a, and 28b–29a.

[11] *HS* 14:3b, 35:5b–6a, 49:23b.

[12] It was decreed in 145 B.C. that kings were not allowed to govern their kingdoms, that all high officials were to be appointed by the emperor, and that the number of officials serving in a kingdom was to be reduced. A king was only authorized to appoint officials below the rank of 400 piculs (*HS* 19A:15a; *HCI* B:5a; *HHC* 28:11a ff.).

The chancellor and the commandant of the capital of the kingdoms were responsible directly to the central government and were not under the control of the kings. A king could not mobilize the army under the command of the chancellor and the commandant of the capital (*HS* 38:5a–b, 44:12b–13a). Neither could he interfere in the administration of other civil officials. Administrative and judicial power was in the hands of the clerk of the capital of the kingdom (*nei-shih* 內史); after the abolishment of the clerk of the capital in 8 B.C., this power was transferred to the chancellor (*HS* 19A:14b–15a; *HHC* 28:10b–11b). In fact, a chancellor was the agent through whom a king could communicate with the emperor. This official was given the power and had the responsibility of reporting to the emperor on the misbehavior of a king and of making accusations against him. See *HS* 47:7a, 53:16a; *HHS* 14:12a–b, 42:4a, 12a, 24a, and 30b, 50:3a, 5a, 6b, 7a, 10a, and 13a. A chancellor was punished by the central government if he failed to report the illegal activities of a king or if he cooperated with him (*HS* 53:7b).

Furthermore, a king was also under the supervision of an inspector, who could report on and make accusations against a king whose kingdom was included in the region (*chou* 州) under his supervision (*HS* 38:12a, 53:2b; *HHS* 42:4a, 50:7a and 10a). The role of the inspector and chancellor in supervising the kings was clearly stated by Emperor Ch'eng, who said that "the feudal lords are restricted and under the pressure of the Han law because they are in the hands of the inspectors and chancellors" (*HS* 97B:4b).

ing all the sons of a king to be marquises (the marquisates were created by dividing the father's kingdom among the sons) was a milder and more tactical measure to reduce the size and strength of the various kingdoms so greatly that no kingdom could be a threat to the central government.[13] Pan Ku remarked that since a king only received taxes and had no hand in politics, his influence was not much different from that of a wealthy family (*HS* 14:4a).

More restrictions were imposed on the kings and marquises in the Later Han. When it was disclosed that a king had sent his guests to murder someone, a large number of guests of kings and marquises were arrested and executed on orders from Emperor Kuang-wu (*HHS* 1B:27a). And kings and marquises were under closer and stricter supervision than in the Early Han.[14] Many kings were accused of plotting rebellions and were punished, even when the only evidence was that they had been reading magical books and offering sacrifices (*HHS* 42:10a–b and 25a, 50:3a). Even minor infractions were reported by the inspector or chancellor, and punishments were usually invoked. A chancellor accused a king and asked for his dismissal because he did not wear a king's garment when he was on a tour and because he had taken the belongings of his subordinates without payment (*HHS* 42:24a). Another king was accused and punished because he took a concubine during the mourning period for his father and left the palace in a plain garment (*HHS* 14:12a–b). Another king was accused and demoted because he had married the wife of another, had beaten his subordinates and others, and had been cruel and full of faults (*HHS* 50:7a). As a result of these various measures, kings and marquises became even less powerful in the Later Han period.

---

[13] This device was suggested by Chu-fu Yen. He pointed out that the feudal states were too big and too strong, and that since only the eldest son by the legal wife of a king was entitled to be his heir, the other sons received no land at all and the size of a state was never reduced. He proposed that all kings be permitted to distribute fiefs to their sons and brothers and that they be ennobled by the emperor as marquises. By this means these brothers and sons would be glad to be ennobled and the kingdoms would be automatically reduced and weakened. Chu-fu's proposal was put into practice by Emperor Wu (*SC* 17:2a–b, 21:1a, 112:12a–b; *HS* 6:9a, 14:3b, 15:1a, 53:11b, 64A:19b).

[14] A king sometimes was under special supervision. Once a king was accused, and the chancellor and the commandant of the capital of that kingdom were ordered by the emperor to live in the king's palace to guard him (*HHS* 42:29b). In another case, an internuncio (*yeh-che* 謁者) was sent from the imperial court to supervise a king who was not allowed to communicate with any of his officials (*HHS* 42:26a).

CONSORT FAMILIES

We have already mentioned that members of the consort families were usually appointed high officials, and that many of them held top posts in the government. Here an interesting contrast may be drawn between members of the imperial family and the consort families. Princes, who were usually ennobled as kings, enjoyed a higher noble rank than the members of consort families, who were made marquises. However, princes, with only rare exceptions, were excluded from official posts; so they were kept from political power, while nearly all of the close relatives of the consort family were made officials.

Nine consort families rose to power in the Early Han. The first powerful consort family was the Lü family, which rose to power under the protection of Empress Dowager Lü, the most ambitious and the most powerful figure in the court after the death of her husband. After she had put to death several kings—Emperor Kao's sons by his concubines—she defied her husband's oath[15] by making her two nephews and one grandnephew kings. Members of her family were assigned to various important posts in the government, although the post of imperial chancellor remained in the hands of a nonrelative, Ch'en P'ing. She did everything possible to strengthen the power of her family while she attended the court personally and made decisions on all important affairs. Finally, before her death, in an attempt to consolidate the power of the Lüs, she appointed her nephew Lü Ch'an chancellor of state (*hsiang-kuo* 相國; Ch'en P'ing was still the imperial chancellor), and put the southern and northern armies under the command of Lü Ch'an and another nephew, Lü Lu (*SC* 9:5b–9b).

The Lü family, which had not yet consolidated its power, was unable to maintain it after the death of the empress dowager. The imperial relatives, the Lius, and the officials loyal to them began to challenge the Lüs. But the Lü family, with military power at hand, was so strong that rivals were afraid to take any decisive action immediately. They were able to wipe out the Lüs only after they had tricked Lü Lu into giving up his post of supreme general and transferring the command of the northern army to Chou P'o 周勃.[16]

---

[15] Emperor Kao and his ministers declared in their oath that they would attack anyone who was not one of the Lius who made himself a king (*SC* 9:4b and 9b, 17:1b; *HS* 40:18b).

[16] *SC* 9:10a–13b; *HS* 3:4a–6b.

Emperor Wen, who had witnessed the violent struggle between the Lü family and the imperial family, apparently tried to curb the power of the consort family. He put to death his maternal uncle, Po Chao, whom he had made the general of chariots and cavalry.[17] The consort families gradually rose to power again under Emperors Ching and Wu, who deliberately took measures to reduce the size and power of the kingdoms held by the imperial relatives. During this period we see the rise of the Tous, the Wangs, the Weis, and the Hos. Tou Ying was appointed grand general by Emperor Ching in 154 B.C. to put down the rebellion of the seven kings.[18] The power of the consort family was enhanced by Emperor Wu, who for the first time made consort members, Tou Ying and T'ien Fen, imperial chancellors. With the highest post in the government, the consort family was able to exercise power in the central government. T'ien Fen, the emperor's maternal uncle, usually initiated the appointment of high officials. Once Emperor Wu was so impatient that he said to him, "Are you through with the list of officials you are going to appoint? I also want to make some appointments." The historian remarked that power had shifted from the emperor to T'ien.[19]

Next we see the rise of two closely related families, the Weis and the Hos. Both Wei Ch'ing, Empress Wei's younger brother, and Ho Ch'ü-ping, her sister's son, were ennobled and appointed generals with the additional title of grand minister of war—a title that was said to have been created especially for them by Emperor Wu because of their success in military expeditions against the Hsiung-nu.[20] The dismissal and suicide of the empress, who was involved in the alleged rebellion of the heir apparent, led to the downfall of the Weis. However, Ho Ch'ü-ping's half brother, Ho Kuang, continued to serve the emperor and remained his confidant. Shortly before the emperor's death, Ho Kuang was given the title that had been held by Wei Ch'ing, and was empowered to assist the young emperor in the administration of the government. It should be pointed out that consort members had been appointed generals before,[21] and they were often sent out on military expeditions. Wei Ch'ing and Ho Ch'ü-ping had also been generals with the title of grand minister of war, but Ho Kuang was the first consort

[17] *HS* 4:12a. According to *HS* 18:3b, Po Chao was put to death because of killing an official.

[18] *SC* 107:1b; *HS* 52:1b.

[19] *SC* 107:3b–5a; *HS* 52:3a–4b.

[20] *SC* 111:4b, 8a, and 14b–15a; *HS* 55:4a, 7a, and 13a, 97:13a; *HHC* 24:8b.

[21] Po Chao (*HS* 4:12a); Tou Ying (*SC* 107:1b; *HS* 52:1b).

family member who was empowered to participate in the administration of the government in the capacity of a grand minister of war and grand general;[22] this established a precedent. Wang Shang was the last consort member who held the post of imperial chancellor (29–25 B.C.).[23] All others were given the title of grand minister of war.[24] Thus both government administration and military power were in the hands of consort families.

There was a close connection between the rise to power of the consort families and the military position they held. Although the position of grand minister of war was not exclusively occupied by consort members, they had it most of the time. From the time that Ho Kuang was appointed by Emperor Wu until the end of the Early Han, only five[25] of the thirteen holders of this title were not consort members. Thus except for sporadic and brief interruptions this key post was in the hands of the consort families for about three-quarters of a century. The combined years of the five nonconsort members holding this post was less than eleven years. Ch'ien Mu correctly points out that from the time of Emperor Wu and thereafter, with the appointment of a member of the consort family as the grand minister of war and grand general to assist the emperor in government administration, the consort families began to occupy an important position in government.[26]

Ch'ien also observes the division between the inner and outer court: the outer court was represented by the imperial chancellor, whereas the inner court was represented by the consort family, which was closer to the emperor.[27] The control of memorials was the main function of

[22] *HS* 7:1b, 68:2a.

[23] *HS* 82:2a. See also the section on Consort Families in the Early Han in Chapter 4.

[24] Ho Kuang (*HS* 68:2a); Ho Yü 霍禹 (68:15b); Hsü Yen-shou 許延壽 (97A: 26a–b); Shih Kao (82:6a); Wang Chieh (97A:23b); Hsü Chia 許嘉 (97A:26b); Wang Feng (98:4a); Wang Yin (98:10a); Wang Shang (98:12a); Wang Keng 王根 (98:12a); Wang Mang (98:12b and 14b); Fu Hsi 傅喜 (97B:21a); Ting Ming 丁明 (97B:22a); and Fu Yen (97B:21a). See also *HS* 19B:9b ff.

[25] Chang An-shih, Han Tseng 韓增, Shih Tan, Wang Shang, and Tung Hsien 董賢 (*HS* 19B:11b, 12a, and 17a).

[26] Ch'ien Mu, *Kuo-shih ta-kang*, I, 114–15.

[27] *Ibid*. A definition of the inner court (*chung-ch'ao* 中朝 or *nei-ch'ao* 內朝) and the outer court (*wai-ch'ao* 外朝) is given by Meng K'ang as follows: the former included the grand minister of war, general of the left, general of the right, general of the van (*ch'ien-chiang-chün* 前將軍), general of the rear, attendant within the palace, regular attendant, mounted attendants without specified appointments (*san-ch'i* 散騎), and masters of officials (*chu-li* 主吏). The outer court included the imperial chancellor and the officials down to the 600-picul rank (*HS* 77:8a). Meng's definition of the inner court, though authoritative, is not comprehensive. Ch'ien Ta-hsin suggested that

the inner court; and the fact that Ho Kuang was the acting master of writing should not be overlooked. Thus when Emperor Hsüan wanted to take away power from the Ho family after Ho Kuang's death, he ordered that officials could bypass Ho Shan 霍山, the acting master of writing, and present their memorials directly to him (*HS* 7:1b, 68:17a).

The shift of the locus of power from the outer to the inner court was significant in the political history of Han, and is the key to understanding the changes in the power structure of the central government. The creation of the inner court was a device to concentrate power in the hands of the emperor, thereby reducing the power of the imperial chancellor. At the same time, the choice of the consort family, which was close to the emperor, to help the emperor run the inner court resulted in the transfer of power from the imperial chancellor to the consort families.

On the surface there was a division of power between the inner court and the outer court. Ho Kuang once said to the imperial chancellor, "I govern the inner [court] and you, Lord, govern the outer [court]" (*HS* 66:7b). In fact, with the control of the inner court Ho Kuang controlled all government affairs. The government officials listened to him and disregarded the imperial chancellor, even though he was formally superior. Chü Ch'ien-ch'iu, the imperial chancellor, once called a court conference to discuss the case of an official who was charged with the unauthorized release of a prisoner. Ho Kuang, who was greatly displeased, charged the imperial chancellor with summoning high officials to a conference without authority and of expressing opinions different from those of the inner court. This charge led to the execution of the commandant of justice and the privy treasurer (*shao-fu* 少府), the imperial chancellor's son-in-law, on the grounds that they had manipulated the law (*HS* 60:3a–4a). These charges clearly indicate that the outer court was dominated by the inner court.

Ho Kuang's power reached its climax after the death of Emperor Chao. The emperor died without an heir, and a court conference was

---

"officials who concurrently serve in the palace" (*chi-shih-chung* 給事中) were also included (Ch'ien Ta-hsin, *San shih shih-i*, in *Ch'ien-yen-t'ang ch'üan-shu* [1808], 2:9a–10b, hereafter cited as *SSSI*). Besides, Lao Kan added the head of the Left Bureau (*tso- ts'ao* 左曹) and head of the Bureau of the Right (*yu-ts'ao* 右曹), and masters of writing (*shang-shu* 尚書). For a discussion of the inner court and the outer court, see Lao Kan, "Lun Han-tai ti nei-ch'ao yü wai-ch'ao," *LSYY*, XIII (1948), 227–67, especially pp. 231–32, for the preceding remarks; Wang Yü-ch'üan, "An Outline of the Central Government of the Former Han Dynasty," *Harvard Journal of Asiatic Studies*, XII (1949), 166 ff.

held to appoint a new emperor. Although many high officials participated, including the imperial chancellor, Ho Kuang's voice was dominant. All the other officials held that the son of Emperor Wu should
succeed to the throne, but Ho Kuang disagreed. An official, whose
memorial pleased Ho Kuang, mentioned that it was not necessary to
appoint according to seniority. Ho Kuang showed the memorial to the
imperial chancellor and others and then appointed the king of Ch'ang-i,
the great-grandson of Emperor Wu. The imperial chancellor was not
given a chance to oppose the suggestion; the empress dowager was
merely told to issue the edict (*HS* 68:5a–b). She was the granddaughter
of Ho Kuang and only fourteen or fifteen years old. Later, the imperial
chancellor, the grandee secretary, and other officials were summoned by
Ho Kuang to participate at a court conference. All of them were
firightened by Ho Kuang's suggestion to dismiss the newly appointed
emperor, but none of them dared say anything. Finally all of them
kowtowed and said, "All the lives of the people are in your hands,
Grand General. We follow what you, General, command." Then he,
together with other officials, went to report to the empress dowager.
Although the name of the imperial chancellor appeared first in the
memorial and Ho's name next, it is obvious from the foregoing story
that Ho dominated the proceedings. It is reported that someone was
sent in advance by Ho Kuang to inform the imperial chancellor that
he had decided to dismiss the emperor. Thus the imperial chancellor
could only follow what the grand general suggested. And when the
king of Ch'ang-i was dismissed from the throne, Emperor Hsüan was
appointed under the leadership of Ho Kuang (*HS* 66:9a–b, 68:5b–11b,
97A:20b).

Ho Kuang controlled the government for about two decades until
his death. Emperor Hsuan was so humble that all affairs had to be
reported to Ho Kuang before they were presented to him, and he always
treated Ho Kuang with great respect. He even felt fearful and uneasy
when Ho rode in the same carriage with him (*HS* 68:20a–b). In fact,
Emperor Hsüan only began to take charge of the administration after
Ho Kuang's death (*HS* 68:14b).

Here we see not only the emergence of a powerful person but also
of a powerful family. The total number of members of a consort family
to be appointed officials was frequently amazing. During the reign of
Emperor Chao, Ho Kuang's son, grandnephew (Ho Ch'ü-ping's grandson), sons-in-law, and other relatives all occupied important positions
in the government (*HS* 68:17a, 22a–b).

A family in power for such a long time certainly would not be tolerated by an emperor who wanted to exercise his own power. Hence, after the death of Ho Kuang, measures were taken to reduce the power of the Ho family. Ho Yü, the son of Ho Kuang, lost his position of general of the right (*yu chiang-chün* 右將軍) while remaining in the office of grand minister of war; but since he no longer controlled the seal of the grand minister of war, he possessed only an empty title. Memorials could now be sealed and presented directly to the emperor instead of going through Ho Shan, the acting master of writing. Moreover, the various relatives of the Ho family were removed from important posts or transferred to ones of less importance. Their posts were then given to members of the new consort families, Hsü and Shih, the emperor's grandmother's family, and the family of the empress (*HS* 68:14b–17a). Realizing that their power was being taken away from them, the Ho family was greatly displeased and felt uneasy. They also feared that the crime of murdering Empress Hsü would be disclosed. Finally, they plotted to kill the imperial chancellor and rebel. This plot led to the execution of Ho Kuang's wife, son, and other relatives of the family. It was reported that several thousand families were involved and exterminated (*HS* 68:17a–19a).

The downfall of the Ho family did not mean that subsequent consort families were to be powerless. On the contrary, consort families continued to dominate the Han government. It has already been noted that although the position of grand minister of war was not the exclusive property of the consort families, it was in their hands most of the time.

The most powerful consort family was the Wangs, in which there were altogether ten marquises, five grand ministers of war, and a large number of others holding important posts in the government (*HS* 98:19b). Above all, from 33 to 7 B.C. the key post of grand minister of war was monopolized by its members successively. Wang Feng, maternal uncle of Emperor Ch'eng, occupied this post for eleven years. Practically all important government appointments were made by him. Once when the emperor was going to appoint an official, his attendants warned him that it had not been reported to the grand general. The emperor said, "This is a small affair. Why is it necessary to inform the grand general?" His attendants kowtowed and insisted upon the matter. Then the emperor told Wang Feng, but the appointment was not made because Wang Feng did not approve it.[28] After Wang Feng's

---

[28] *HHS* 98:5b. The following information on the Wang family is from *HS* 98:16b–17a, 99A:33a–b and 44a–b.

death, four other members of the family were appointed to the post,
one succeeding the other. And finally, it was taken over by Wang
Mang, the most powerful consort family member of all.

The Wang family was in power two decades under the protection of
Empress Dowager Wang. She held the title of empress dowager during
the reigns of four emperors and attended court personally in the reigns
of the last two emperors for a period of eight years. Also Wang Mang's
daughter became empress in A.D. 4. A family that monopolized political
power for such a long time, without parallel in the history of Han,
certainly was able to command absolute and complete control of the
power mechanism; this situation finally led to usurpation in A.D. 5.
After Wang Mang had put a two-year-old boy on the throne, he became
the regent, held the title of regent emperor, wore the emperor,'s hat and
garments, issued edicts as the emperor, and was treated by the officials
as emperor. Finally, he made himself the emperor and established the
New (新 *hsin*) dynasty.

OFFICIALS

High Officials

We have already mentioned that high officials enjoyed substantial
salaries and other incomes. Some of them who were ennobled as marquises derived magnificent incomes from their marquisates. They were
entitled to collect the poll tax and land tax from a specified number of
households, varying from several hundred to more than ten thousand
households. (See the section of the Wealth of Officials in Chapter 4.)
According to the estimate of Ssu-ma Ch'ien, a marquis with one thousand households had an annual income of two hundred thousand cash.[29]
Of course, this is only a rough estimate, and perhaps a conservative
one. One high official who was ennobled with 13,640 households received an annual income of more than ten million cash. Even when an
adjustment was made to reduce his marquisate, he still received an
income of about five million cash (*HS* 59:12a).

Nearly all officials invested their income in landed property. A high
official, Chang Yü, bought 40,000 *mou* of expensive and fertile land
located in the irrigated area along the Ching and Wei rivers (*HS*
81:13b-14a). A dismissed official, whose name was Ning Ch'eng 寧成,
possessed more than 100,000 *mou* of land near a reservoir; he rented it

[29] *SC* 129:14b; *HS* 91:5b–6a.

to the poor people and commanded the service of several thousand families. Within a few years he accumulated a fortune of several thousand catties of gold.[30] Many officials also received land from the emperor as gifts; for instance, Pu Shih was given 1,000 *mou* of land by Emperor Wu (*HS* 58:10b).

Possessing the major means of production in society, the officials were in a position to control the life chances of others and to command their services. Moreover, their economic power was backed by political power. They usually exploited the people unmercifully and were overbearing in the commuinty where their property was located. Kuan Fu 灌夫, once a powerful official, had accumulated several tens of millions in cash and owned ponds, farms, and gardens. His family members and guests who were seeking privileges and profit were so overbearing in his native place, Ying-ch'uan, that the family was hated by the people. The children of the area sang a song, "While the Ying River is clear the Kuan family will be secure; when the Ying River is muddy the Kuang family will be exterminated."[31]

Officials were able to increase their wealth by using their political power. One of the common practices was to occupy public land; and many officials also seized land from others. Because the land came to be centralized more and more in the hands of the officials and other wealthy families, the poor were forced to become the tenants of landlords or to run away.[32] This problem became so serious that a proposal to limit the amount of land that could be owned by an individual was made by Tung Chung-shu in the second century B.C. (*HS* 24A:14b–15b). His proposal was not adopted, and the situation became worse and worse as time went on. A similar proposal was made by Shih Tan at the end of the first century B.C. A conference was held and a measure that stated that no one, whether a noble, an official, or a commoner, could own more than 3,000 *mou* of land, was adopted by the imperial chancellor and the grand minister of works. But because this regulation was disadvantageous to the powerful landowning officials, it was not put into practice. In fact, no action was taken. Wang Man'g reform in A.D. 9, which decreed that land could not be sold or owned by individ-

[30] *SC* 122:4a; *HS* 90:4a.

[31] *SC* 107:7a; *HS* 52:6a–b.

[32] See the memorials of Ch'ao Ts'o, Kung Yü, and Pao Hsüan (II, 18; *HS* 72:16a and 25a). Pao Hsüan told Emperor Ai that one of the seven reasons why the farmers ran away was that the powerful families gnawed as a silkworm, without satisfaction (*HS* 72:25a).

uals, was an attempt to launch a frontal assault on the basic economic problem of his day (*HS* 24A:18b–19b).

A government post usually brought with it power that was not directly connected with government administration or was outside the sphere of routine administration. The one who held the post might use his power to consolidate his position in the government, or, especially if he had military power, he might use it to challenge the authority and threaten the power of the central government. He might also abuse his power for personal and family advantages. For instance, he could appoint family members, guests, or other persons closely associated with him to official positions or remove all those officials from the government who were not in agreement with him. He might also use his power to monopolize a government project (III, 40); or he could use his official and personal connections to influence government officials. For example, a public reservoir was abolished because the act was to the personal advantage of an imperial chancellor (*HS* 84:22a).

An official not only had personal power, but his whole family was powerful and influential as well. The family members must be considered as a unit, not merely as a group of individuals, for usually more than one member of a family held official positions. This was possible because of the system of *jen-tzu,* under which a family member of a 2,000-picul official who had been in office for three years was given the privilege of entering officialdom.[33] All nine sons of Shih Tan thus became attendants within the palace by virtue of this system (*HS* 82:9a). Furthermore, high officials in the central government and local officials were empowered to recommend a scholar to the court for official appointment. And they were also able to select and appoint their subordinates. Through personal connections between officials, family members of officials could easily be recommended or appointed. All five brothers of Ho Wu, a prefect, were subordinate officials of the commandery. When Ho Wu served as an inspector of Yang-chou 揚州, a subordinate official serving in one of the commanderies under Ho's jurisdiction was the nephew of the minister of agriculture. The minister introduced his nephew to Ho Wu's younger brother, who then talked to Ho Wu and persuaded him to see this subordinate. Shortly after the visit the man was recommended by the grand administrator to the central government (*HS* 86:2b–3a).

Family members of high officials found it easier to reach the higher posts. Thus, Tung Chung-shu once complained to the emperor that

[33] *HHHY* 4:63–64.

most of the chief officials—that is, grand administrations and prefects—came from among the gentlemen of the palace, the palace gentlemen (*chang-lang* 中郎), and the children of the 2,000-picul officials (*HS* 56:13a–b). In fact, there is evidence that frequently more than one member of a family held high official posts and that some families continued to be prominent for generations.

The *Shih-chi* says that six or seven younger brothers and children of Cheng Tang-shih 鄭當時 reached 2,000-picul positions "because of [him]."[34] Similarly, all four sons of Shih Fen 石奮, grand tutor to the heir apparent, were 2,000-picul officials. Hence he was known as the "lord of 10,000 piculs." His youngest son, Shih Ch'ing 石慶, became imperial chancellor, and thirteen of Shih Ch'ing's children became 2,000-picul officials (*HS* 46:1b, 3b, 5b). Of course, a family was more powerful the more members it had holding official posts; and a family that had a long history in officialdom certainly was more powerful and influential than one with a shorter history, not to mention an "upstart" family. Thus the Chang family, whose members had continuously occupied official posts for eight generations, was exceptionally powerful. Chang T'ang was appointed grandee secretary. His son, Chang An-shih, reached the post of grand minister of war and general of chariots and cavalry. All three sons of Chang An-shih (Ch'ien-ch'iu 千秋, Yen-shou 延壽, and P'eng-tsu 彭祖), as well as Yen-shou's son and grandson, Fang 放, were attendants within the palace and general of the palace gentlemen. According to the *Han-shu,* during and after the time of Emperor Hsüan more than ten offspring of Chang An-shih held the posts of attendant within the palace, regular palace attendant, heads of key bureaus (*chu ts'ao* 諸曹), mounted attendants, and colonel, one after another. It says that among the meritorious officials only the Chang family and the Chin family could match the consort families in imperial favor, honor, and closeness (*HS* 59:14b). In fact, the Chang family was in power for more than a century. Not only was it powerful in the Early Han (since 126 B.C. when Chang T'ang was appointed commandant of justice), but it was also prominent in the Later Han for two generations. Chang T'ang's great-great-great-grandson, Ch'un 純, served as minister of works under Emperor Kuang-wu (*HHS* 35:3b, 7a). Chang Ch'un's son also occupied the post. It was the only family that was able to hold a marquisate in both Early and Later Han—for a period of nearly two hundred years (*HHS* 35:9b). In another case,

---

[34] *SC* 120:8b; *HS* 50:13b. The *Han-shu* says "brothers" instead of "brothers and children."

Tu Chou was the grandee secretary. Two of his sons were grand administrators. His yougest son, Yen-nien, was one of the nine highest ministers for more than ten years and later was promoted to the post of
grandee secretary. Yen-nien's son, Huan, was a grand administrator
and later grand minister of ceremonies. Five of Huan's six younger
brothers became high officials. His youngest brother had been grand
administrator of five commanderies and a regional inspector. According to the *Han-shu,* among the brothers and other relatives there were
altogether ten persons who became 2,000-picul officials (*HS* 60:2a,
5a–6a, 14b).

Theoretically, officials were powerful only when they were in office.
Once they retired or were dismissed they were not in control of any
part of the power mechansim, and therefore possessed no political
power. But this does not mean that because they had no direct control
over the power mechanism they were without influence. Officials who
retired or were dismissed still had a close association with the active
officials. Besides, when one family member was removed from office,
there were usually other members still in power. Only in very serious
cases were all the family members dismissed from their offices. So in one
way or another a retired or dismissed official might influence the power
mechanism through his personal contacts with his close friends or relatives who were still in power. He could also rely on their power to
engage in personal activities that would otherwise be impossible. He
might ask their favor and usually was under their protection. Kuan Fu
was a dismissed official who associated with powerful and cunning
persons. His family and guests were violent and overbearing in the
community. But the imperial chancellor reported the case to the emperor and requested an investigation only after he and Kuan had had
a dispute. In fact, the case was dropped by the imperial chancellor
after a reconciliation was effected through the medium of guests.
Kuan's arrogance and unlawful activities were also known to the grandee secretary and other government officials, but they said nothing
about it until they were asked by the emperor during a court dispute
(III, 16).

Officials, whether active of retired, usually had interests in common
and cooperated with and protected one another. The reasons are obvious. Because of the diversity of functions and the authority of the
bureaucratic mechanism, no one was powerful enough that all parts
of the bureaucracy were under his control; thus he had to ask for the
cooperation and favor of others when attempting to seek personal ad-

vantages or to avoid accusations and punishments. Only when a top
official was so powerful that the entire political mechanism was under
his control did he disregard such cooperation. Also, the system of dividing up the whole empire into many administrative areas. called for
cooperation between central and local officials and between officials
of different localities, such as when an official in one locality had his
native home in a different locality under the jurisdiction of another
official and wanted his relatives and guests to be under the protection
of the other official. And another official might seek the same kind of
protection from someone else, particularly if his family and guests
were arrogant and engaged in unlawful activities in the local community. There are cases in our texts of a top official in the central government asking a favor of a prefect of a prefecture in which a number
of his guests stayed (*HHS* 34:20a–b).

Subordinate Officials

To be sure, only ranking officials exercised control over government
bureaus and decision making; their subordinate officials lacked such
authority and power. However, since they were the ones who executed
the orders of the superior officials, they were in a position to influence,
directly or indirectly, the decisions of their superiors, to delay deliberately the implementation of policies, to take advantage of a government
order for their own interest, or to abuse their power. There was a Ho
family in which five brothers were subordinate officials of a commandery. Both the commandery and prefectural government personnel
were afraid of them. Ho Hsien 何顯, one of the five brothers, whose
family was officially registered as a merchant, refused to hand in his
tax to the government. The officer in charge of the market arrested
and humiliated a member of Ho Hsien's family, which so angered
Ho Hsien that he wanted to retaliate by manipulating the administrative law to punish the officer (*HS* 86:1b).

Of course what is most important is that since subordinate officials
had direct contact with the people, and control of the situation for
dealing with them, they had a direct impact on their fate.

The subordinate officials often associated with high officials and
kept a number of guests in their homes. For example, Tu Chien 杜建,
whose guests pursued illicit profit, was a subordinate official serving
in the office of the governor of Ching-chao. He was described as a
powerful redresser-of-wrongs. When he was arrested by the governor,

numerous high officials, powerful and influential men, pleaded with the governor on his behalf. The governor refused to give in, and Tu's kinsmen and guests attempted to rescue him by force (III, 30). In another instance, a subordinate official, also under the governor of the capital, was described as a powerful redresser-of-wrongs and a close friend of the powerful eunuch, Shih Hsien (III, 38).

In the Han the position of a subordinate official was respectable, and occupants of such positions possessed the potential for a promising political career. Subordinate officials in a commandery of a prefecture were frequently promoted to higher posts through the system of recommendation. I have already mentioned that most of the persons recommended as "filially pious and incorrupt" had been subordinate officials of the local government and that they were often promoted to such posts as prefect or palace gentleman in the central government. Indeed, many high officials in the Han, as pointed out by Hsü T'ien-lin, had been subordinate officials.[35]

Powerful families were, of course, interested in such posts. Here it should be noted that in the Han the grand administrators and the prefects generally were non-natives, whereas the subordinate officials serving in the local government were usually recruited from among the natives.[36] Since the outsiders—that is, the non-natives—were excluded from the recruitment, it was easy for the local powerful families to control the jobs. Scholars of ordinary families simply could not compete with them. Because of personal connections, a prefect or an administrator also had a tendency to appoint members of prominent and powerful families to be their subordinate officials. The prominent and powerful families thus more or less monopolized these posts. Many subordinate officials are described in the histories as coming from *ta-hsing* (big families) or *chu-hsing* 著姓 (prominent families).[37] In one instance five younger brothers of a prefect became subordinate officials of the commandery government (*HS* 86:1b). Kuo Ch'ang 郭昌, a subordinate official of a commandery, was a member of a prominent family of the commandery. We know that his family was very wealthy because he yielded his father's landed property and house, valued at several million cash, to his half-brother. Kuo Ch'ang married the daughter of a king; his own daughter married Liu Hsiu during the uprising that led to the

[35] *THHY* 2:94; see also Yen Keng-wang, *Chung-kuo ti-fang hsing-cheng chih-tu shih* (2 vols.; Taipei, 1961), II, 333.

[36] *Ibid.*, I, 345–53.

[37] *HHS* 10A:6a, 16:24a, 62:16b, 77:2b; *SKC*, Wei, 15:15b, note.

re-establishment of the Han house, and she later became an empress (*HHS* 10A:6a). Chao Ch'i 趙岐, who was a subordinate official of a commandery, was the grandson of a censor and a son-in-law of the powerful consort family of Ma Jung (*HHS* 64:22a–b). Chung Hao 鍾皓, a subordinate official of a commandery, was a member of a prominent family of the commandery; his nephew married someone in one of the most distinguished families, that of Li Ying (*HHS* 62:16b). Hsü Shao 許劭, a subordinate official of a commandery, came from a distinguished family in which three members had been lords for three successive generations (*HHS* 68:10b). That the position of subordinate officials was monopolized by the local powerful families in Early and Later Han is summed up in the *Sung-shu*, which says: "The subordinate officials of the commanderies and the prefectures all came from the powerful families."[38] Such monopoly of power was very significant. It gave the powerful families more protection, and it also helped them to manipulate and control the local government and to consolidate and strengthen their power. In short, it greatly contributed to the perpetuation of the powerful families in their localities.

WEALTHY MERCHANTS

Wealthy merchants, industrialists, and big landlords must be treated as a power group because of their great economic power. Of course, landlords engaged in other occupations as well, so the term "landlord" could also include breeders and farmers. I have already pointed out that officials, merchants, and landlords cannot be separated from each other. The official-landlord, however, because his status and sources of income were different from those of other groups, should be treated as a separate entity in order to avoid confusion with the ordinary landlords who were not officials. In this discussion the term "landlord" refers only to the commoner-landlord. It should also be made clear in this connection that merchants and landlords cannot be separated from each other, because most of the merchants owned landed property and the big landowners invariably invested their money in trade, cattle breeding, or moneylending. A landlord without some investment in business was rare. One family suddenly became very wealthy and owned 700 *ch'ing* of land (*HHS* 32:16b-17a); although it is not clear how this family became rich, it seems very unlikely that a commoner-farmer could acquire such a fortune without investing in business. A small

[38] Shen Yüeh, *Sung-shu*, Po-na ed., 94:1b, hereafter cited as *SS*.

landowner, who owned only about 100 *mou* of land, could hardly hold onto his property let alone become wealthy. In any event, such a small landowner was economically too insignificant to be treated as a powerful family. As far as powerful families are concerned we include only the merchant-landlords.

This class possessed wealth and controlled market prices and the circulation of capital. Since they possessed and had control over the major means of production, the land, they were able to exercise control over the life chances of most of the population engaged in farming. This was clearly indicated by Ch'ao Ts'o in his memorial saying that because of the poor income of the farmer, which was insufficient to meet his expenses and to support his family, particularly when there was a calamity or an urgent tax, he had to sell his property at half price or borrow at 100 per cent interest; thus many of them were forced to sell their land or their children in order to pay their debts (*HS* 24A:11a–b). In this way the merchants were able to exploit the farmers and to buy land from them at a low price—a process referred to by contemporaries as *chien-ping* 兼并. (Literally, *chien-ping* means "to swallow up, to engulf," thus to grab the property of others.) This term often refers to the process by which the wealthy swallowed up the landed property of others.[39] That the power of the wealthy merchants was formidable in the eyes of the government is clearly reflected in the fact that wealthy families, families of powerful persons, and those who engaged in *chien-ping* were included among the families to be moved to the various mausoleum towns by the Han government.[40]

The industrialists who monopolized the manufacture of iron and salt similarly exercised control over the life chances of others and usually commanded the services of a large number of people. K'ung Chin 孔僅 and Tung-kuo Hsien-yang said that those who monopolized the products of the mountains and seas became wealthy, "gained profits from the small people and commanded their services."[41] According to Ts'ui Shih, they usually commanded the services of more than a thousand people.[42] To have such a large number of people under one's command certainly was sheer power in itself, constituting a threat to the government as well as to the community. The wealthy merchants were described by Ssu-ma Ch'ien as a class "commanding the services of the

[39] *SC* 30:3a; *HS* 24A:11b, 14a, 15b, and 18b; *HHS* 28A:4b.
[40] *SC* 112:12b; *HS* 28B:18b, 64A:19b.
[41] *SC* 30:10a; *HS* 24B:11a.
[42] *Cheng-lun,* quoted in *TT* 1:72.

poor."[43] He explained that among the people, if a man's wealth was ten times their own, they would behave humbly toward him; if a man's wealth was a hundred times their own, they would fear him; if his wealth was a thousand times their own, they would render services to him; and if his wealth was ten thousand times their own, they would act as his servants (*SC* 129:15b). According to Huang T'an 桓譚, a statesman of the first century, even people of the middle class were willing to render service to wealthy merchants: on behalf of the merchants they would engage in moneylending, act as their trustees, receive accounts, present memorials, and work as diligently as if they were servants (*HHS* 28A:4b–5a).

Because of their enormous wealth, big merchants were even able to exercise control over the ruling class. Ssu-ma Ch'ien notes that even the nobles had to bow their heads and depend upon the merchants for financial assistance.[44] When there was an urgent need the nobles usually requested a loan from the wealthy merchants. When the rebellion broke out in 154 B.C. and the feudal lords who joined the imperial army sought loans to provide for their expenses, they were turned down by many moneylenders on the grounds that the outcome of the revolt was uncertain; finally they had to accept an offer at 100 per cent interest.[45] This shows that the nobles were not powerful enough to control the wealthy merchants, who were themselves strong enough to exploit the nobles under favorable circumstances. During times of calamity even the government sought loans from the big merchants, but without much success.[46]

Ssu-ma Ch'ien pointed out that the wealthy merchants, relying upon their wealth and influence, were also in a position to settle arbitrarily matters in dispute in the village communities.[47] His statement, though brief, clearly shows the power exercised by the wealthy merchants who controlled the behavior of others and commanded their obedience. The connection between economic power and the ability to exercise power over others obviously was very close.

Merchants usually were lacking in political power, but their economic power often enabled them to associate with those who had political power. In a society in which economic power was under constant threat from political power, the combination of the two, either directly or

[43] *SC* 30:7a–b; *HS* 24B:9a.
[44] *SC* 30:7a–b; *HS* 24B:9a.
[45] *SC* 129:19b–20a; *HS* 91:10b.
[46] *SC* 30:7a, 12b, and 14a; *HS* 24B:8b, 12a, and 13a.
[47] *SC* 30:3a; *HS* 24A:14a.

indirectly, was the only way that economic power could be secured. Thus the merchants usually attempted to associate with the powerful nobles and officials in order to seek their protection. Both a certain K'ung family and Tiao Chien were known to have associated with nobles or officials.[48] As remarked by Ch'ao Ts'o, merchants who associated with kings and marquises were more powerful than officials (II, 18). Sometimes a special arrangement was made so that both parties derived advantages from the relationship. A wealthy merchant who bribed two marquises and relied upon their power in money-lending is but one of many recorded examples. His power was such that no one dared to fail his obligation to pay interest and capital when it was due (II, 41). The nobles and officials who were powerful politically were relatively weak in economic power and usually had little access to the various means of investment and speculation; therefore, their association with wealthy merchants was also a benefit to them. Petty officials who were not content with their small salaries usually carried on speculative trading and had to depend upon the help of their merchant friends. A high official was accused of giving information to merchants on some action the government was going to take so that the merchants could hoard goods that they would later sell at a great profit, which was to be shared with the official (II, 28). Although the accusation was proved to be only partially true, the story reveals a common pattern by which officials and merchants served each other in making money.

The relationship between merchants and nobles or officials, however, was not always friendly and cooperative. Sharp competition for wealth sometimes led to open conflict. Since the legal status of merchants was unfavorable, and the nobles and officials had political power, the merchants were always in a less favorable position. Thus the goods hoarded by wealthy merchants were confiscated by the government when an accusation was made against them by the grand minister of agriculture (II, 34, n. 114). However, the political power of influential officials was sometimes offset by the economic power of wealthy merchants; this kind of strategy, if used wisely and properly, could lead to the victory of the merchants. They know that most of the officials were corrupt, and that was a weak point that they attacked. In one instance some angry merchants offered money to uncover a crime committed by a minister who had confiscated their hoarded goods and whom they hated deeply. The minister lost the battle as well as his life (II, 34).

[48] *SC* 129:18a–b; *HS* 91:8b–9a.

In some rare instances wealthy merchants were able to manipulate political power or even to possess it; in effect, economic power was tranformed into political power. Lü Pu-wei, by means of his enormous wealth, succeeded not only in manipulating the appointment of the future ruler of the state of Ch'in, with whom he associated, but also in actually controlling the power mechanism of the state (II, 3). A merchant with such ambition and talent was exceedingly rare, but this example fully illustrates the political influence of economic power and the possibility of using wealth in political investment. There are several examples of wealthy merchants who succeeded in entering officialdom and thereby acquired political power. (See the section of Merchants in Chapter 4.)

The government was well aware of the economic power of the big merchants, and various measures were taken to check and to control their activities. We have already pointed out the various discriminatory laws against merchants and the effect of these laws on their social status and social mobility, especially the chances of gaining political power. We should also mention another kind of control that was applied: the transfer of wealthy merchants from the various commanderies to the mausoleum prefectures near the capital. Merchants were not indicated as a special category. Only "wealthy persons" in general or those who had property worth more than one million or three millions were mentioned as the ones to be moved, but it is obvious that merchants with wealth in this category were to be transferred (III, 2, 19, 28, 33, 35). It was a measure designed to put all powerful persons and families under more direct control; and apparently the government thought that wealthy persons, including merchants, had the kind of potential power that made them a possible threat.

From the foregoing discussion it is clear that power was distributed among various groups and that political power was the basic source of all power. The more access a group had to the control of the political mechanism the more powerful they could become. Economic power, although not dominant in a politically centered society, was a secondary source of power; and there was a close connection between economic and political power.

YU-HSIA

A power group whose power was derived from neither political nor economic power but from physical coercive power was the redressers-of-wrong, known as *yu-hsia (shieh)*, *ch'ing-hsia* 輕俠, or *jen-hsia* 任俠. *Yu-hsia* has customarily been rendered as "wandering knights" or "knights-errant." Since the term "knight" has a special meaning in European history designating a formal rank in society, it is misleading.[49] *Ch'ing* means "light and fast." *Yu* could mean "to wander" or "to be associated with others" (*chiao-yu* 交遊). It seems more likely that in this context it implies associating, which was a characteristic of *yu-hsia*. Thus Han Fei defines *hsia* as a person who gave up his official post and was fond of association.[50] Ju Shun defines *jen* as "to trust each other," and *hsia* as "to hold the same opinion on what is right and wrong." But according to Yen Shih-ku, *jen* means "to resort to one's physical strength," and *hsia* means "to assist others by means of force" (*HS* 37:1a). While the two commentators differ in their definitions, their statements describe some aspects of the behavior of these people. A more comprehensive description was given by Ssu-ma Ch'ien, the author of the "Biographies of *Yu-hsia*," as follows: "Although their actions may deviate from proper righteousness, they always keep their word; resolute in action, they are faithful in carrying out a promise; caring not about their own lives, they go to the assistance of those in distress; and when they have preserved others from perishing they do not brag of their ability and will feel ashamed in boasting of their kindness to others."[51] This authoritative statement gives a vivid description of the activities of *yu-shia*. We may say that *hsia* designates a kind of personality and behavior char-

---

[49] See P. T. Ho's comment on Burton Watson's translation of the "Biographies of *yu-hsia*"; Ho Ping-ti, "Records of China's Grand Historian: Some Problems of Translation," *Pacific Affairs*, XXXVI (1963), 176.

[50] *HFT* 18:5b.

[51] *SC* 124:1b. Burton Watson translates the phrase *"chi i tsun wang ssu sheng i"* 既已存亡死生矣 as "whether it means survival or destruction, life or death" *(Records of the Grand Historian of China* [2 vols.; New York: Columbia University Press, 1961], I, 453). In the first place, the order of the fifth and sixth words should be reversed to read *"sheng-ssu"*; see the comment by Li Li to Takikawa Kametarō, *Shiki kaichū kōshō* (Tokyo: Tōhō bunka gakuin Tōkyō Kenkyujō, 1932–34), 124:3. Next, it is impossible to treat *"tsun, wang, sheng, ssu"* as four nouns in this context; instead *"tsun"* and *"sheng"* are used as verbs, i.e., "to preserve the person who is going to perish and to keep alive the person who is going to die." Actually both mean the same thing; to preserve others from perishing. Moreover, *"chi i,"* meaning "since already," cannot be translated as "whether." Grammatically speaking, there must be a verb after *"chi i."* It is also obvious that the phrase mentioned above and the subsequent phrase *"erh pu chin ch'i neng"* 而不矜其能 should be treated as one sentence; it is impossible to start a sentence with the particle *"erh."* Erroneously breaking the sentence into two independent sentences, Watson's translation reads: ". . . whether it means survival or destruction, life or death. Yet they never boast of their accomplishments. . . ."

acterized by heroism, especially heroism connected with the redressing
of wrongs. "Redresser-of-wrongs" thus seems to be the closest to the
original meaning, but since the Chinese term has no exact equivalent
in English, we prefer the romanization.

The statement of Ssu-ma Ch'ien, who greatly admired *yu-hsia*, represents the ideal type, the good *yu-hsia*. Not all the persons called *yu-hsia*
conformed to this high standard. On the contrary, they might just as
well be wrongdoers and bring distress to others. In fact it was also
Ssu-ma Ch'ien who said that there were those who associated with
powerful persons, used wealth to command the services of the poor,
were violent and overbearing to the weak and helpless, and were unrestrained in their desire for self-satisfaction. Although he added that
these persons were disowned by the genuine *yu-hsia* (*SC* 124:3a), his
remarks suggest that this kind of person was not uncommon and that
they also considered themselves *yu-hsia*.

The flourishing of *yu-hsia* can be traced back to the time of the
Warring States. What we might call the *yu-hsia* spirit was apparently
aroused by those nobles of the various states who kept a large number
of guests, such as Prince Meng-ch'ang 孟嘗君 of Ch'i, Prince Ch'un-
shen 春申君 of Ch'u, Prince P'ing-yüan 平原君 of Chao, Prince Hsin-
ling 信陵君 of Wei, and the Heir Apparent Tan of Yen. The mention of
the names of these guest-loving princes in the biographies of *yu-hsia* in
the *Shih-chi* and *Han-shu* is a clear indication that a great number of
yu-hsia were kept among the guests and that actions of the guests were
also considered typical of the behavior of *yu-hsia*.[52] There were all
kinds of guests, diversified in character, ability, and activities. (See the
section on Guests in Chapter 4.) But they may be classified into two
main categories, as suggested by T'ao Hsi-sheng, the *yu-hsia* and the
pien-shih 辯士 (debaters); the latter were those who were talented in
debate and devising plans and devoted to scholarly activities.[53] The
number and percentage of *yu-hsia* in comparison with the other group,
which might be called literati, apparently varied and depended largely
upon the attitudes of those who kept guests.[54]

According to Ssu-ma Ch'ien, Prince Meng-ch'ang was one of the four
who kept more *yu-hsia* than anyone else. The historian remarks that in
his time there were many violent young men in Hsieh, the place where
the prince's fief had been located, and goes on to explain that the

[52] *SC* 124:2b; *HS* 92:1b.

[53] T'ao Hsi-sheng, *Pien-shih yü yu-hsia* (Shanghai, 1931).

[54] *Ibid.*, pp. 68 ff.

prince had introduced into Hsieh more than sixty thousand families who were persons engaged in *hsia*-type and illicit activities (*SC* 75:12a–b).

The activities of the *yu-hsia* in the time of the Warring States are probably best illustrated by the assassins, the *tz'u-k'e* 刺客. They were not professional assassins, and their missions were not carried out on a payment basis. Instead, they risked their lives to recompense those who had treated them with respect and good will. Sometimes they avenged a personal grievance for others; at times the motive was political (*SC* 86:6b–8b and 3b, 14b ff.). The political motive in particular must account for the popularity of assassins in the era of the Warring States. Since each state was struggling for power, and some were too weak to oppose the others in an open war, they usually sought to solve the problem by assassination. For example, Ching K'o 荊軻 was sent by the heir apparent of Yen to assassinate the king of Ch'in (*SC* 86:14a ff.).

With the rise of Han the law was loose, and according to Pan Ku the *yu-hsia* were still popular. Keeping guests was prevalent among the nobles and officials; the king of Wu and the king of Huai-nan each kept thousands of guests. Consort families, such as the Tou, T'ien, and Wang, as well as some officials, such as Ch'en Hsi, Kuan Fu, and Cheng Tang-shih, also kept a large number of guests.[55] Apparently *yu-hsia* still constituted a part of the guests, and those who associated with them were also considered men of *hsia* behavior (*HS* 50:12a–b, 52:6a).

Besides, there were a few high officials (some were retired officials) who are described in the *Shih-chi* and *Han-shu* as persons engaged in the activities of the *yu-hsia* or *jen-hsia*: Chang Liang, Chi Pu 季布, Chi Hsin 季心, Kuan Fu, Chi An, Cheng Tang-shih, and Ning Ch'eng.[56] Among the persons included in the collective biography of *yu-hsia* there were three ranking officials: Lou Hu 樓護 was a grand administrator; Ch'en Tsun 陳遵, whose grandfather was the commandant of justice, was a grand administrator and later a chief commandant; Yüan She, the son of a grand administrator, was a prefect.[57] Some of the *yu-hsia* were the subordinate officials in local government, for instance, Chü Chang 萬章 and Tu Chien (III, 38, 30). An analysis of their behavior indicates that any of the following activities could characterize men as *hsia*: keeping promises, relieving others in distress, harboring fugitives, associating with guests, or spending wealth generously in receiving them.

[55] III, 11; see also *HS* 34:24a, 35:12a, 44:8b, 50:12b, 52:1b, 2b, 4b, and 6a–b.
[56] *SC* 55:3a; II, 13; *SC* 100:3b; *HS* 37:3b; III, 16; *SC* 120:2a; *HS* 50:7b; *SC* 120:7a; *HS* 50:12a; III, 15.
[57] *HS* 92:7b–8a, 9a–11b, 13a–b.

But most of the *yu-hsia* were people of humble origin; that is, they were commoners, hence the terms *lü-hsiang chih hsia* 閭巷之俠 (*yu-hsia* of lanes and alleys) and *pu-i chih hsia* 布衣之俠 (commoner *hsia*).[58] One was an arrow maker; two lived in the wine market (III, 38). Another was a gambler (III, 12). But in most cases the occupation is unknown.[59] And of course the income of these people varied according to their occupation. A high official such as Kuan Fu had property worth several tens of millions of cash (III, 16); but this was rather exceptional among the *yu-hsia*. In most cases they were poor and lived humbly. Chü Meng 劇孟 left property worth only ten catties of gold when he died (III, 12). Chu Chia 朱家 is said to have had no surplus money in his family and to have lived humbly (III, 1).

But in spite of their humble economic position the *yu-hsia* were able to meet their personal expenses. Many of them were supported by those nobles and officials who spent generously to keep a number of guests. It seems that many *yu-hsia* were able to support themselves and help others because of gifts received from friends, sometimes large sums of money. Kuo Hsieh 郭解, who was poor, received gifts amounting to more than ten million cash when he was moved by the government to another district (III, 20). In another instance, a powerful eunuch offered his furniture and other property, valued at several millions, to a *yu-hsia* who was his friend (*HS* 92:7a). It was said that Cheng Tang-shih could travel a distance of a thousand *li* without carrying any food (*SC* 120:7b; *HS* 50:13a). By appealing to his associates a *yu-hsia* was also able to raise funds on behalf of others. In this way Yüan She collected money for a coffin and other funeral articles for his friend who had no means to bury his deceased parent (III, 47).

One of the basic codes of honor observed by the *yu-hsia* was to offer financial help to others in need. Chu Chia is said to have given money to others generously, but he himself lived frugally and without savings (III, 1). While Yüan She offered money to the poor, his wife and children had financial difficulty at home (III, 47).

The basic activity that characterized the *yu-hsia* as a group was the redressing of wrongs. As indicated in the statement of Ssu-ma Ch'ien quoted above, the *yu-hsia* felt they had to go to the aid of those who were in trouble. They were thus described as the men upon whom one in distress could depend. They considered it an obligation to receive

---

[58] *SC* 120:2b; *HS* 92:7b.

[59] Probably many had no regular occupation, and merely engaged in such activities as casting coins illegally, violating graves, and robbing (III, 20).

any fugitive who went to them for refuge. It was said that Chu Chia, a famous *yu-hsia,* had harbored and served about one hundred distinguished men and that the ordinary men saved by him were countless. Chi Pu was one of the heroes saved by him, in spite of an order issued by Emperor Kao to the effect that anyone who harbored this man would have his three *tsu* exterminated (II, 13; III, 1). Such daring action was often taken by a *yu-hsia* to save others or to take revenge for himself or on behalf of others. They never appealed to law in order to redress a wrong; instead, they resorted to physical force or violence, or the threat of violence. By this means they were in a position to exercise the power of coercive force over others, either to force them to do something or to restrain them from doing something. In short, coercion was the basis of their power, enabling them to have control over the activities and even the lives of others.

The government was the only authority with legal power to exercise coercion. The *yu-hsia* represented the illegitimate use of coercive power and violence. Whether a *yu-hsia* was a redresser-of-wrongs or a wrongdoer himself, he invariably broke the law. As pointed out by Han Fei, "The *hsia,* relying on physical force, violated the prohibitions."[60] This use of force, although illegitimate, was justified in the eyes of the *yu-hsia,* for it was not always possible to correct a wrong by legal means (otherwise there would have been no need for the services of a *yu-hsia*). Often the wrong had been committed by an official, either intentionally or unintentionally. In such instances the official became the target of the redressing, and many officials were murdered by the *yu-hsia* (III, 42).

Apparently the *yu-hsia* had a set of values not compatible with the general moral code of society as a whole, or of the intellectuals in particular. Ssu-ma Ch'ien points out that the *yu-hsia* were rejected by the Confucianists and the Moists. Although the historian was an admirer of *yu-hsia,* he remarked that their activities were not in line with proper righteousness (*SC* 124:1a–b). The Legalist Han Fei also condemned the *yu-hsia* for violating the law by means of violence.[61] A more offensive attitude was taken by Pan Ku, who accused them of "usurping the power of life and death" from the government and said that they themselves were deserving of the death penalty (*HS* 92:2a–b).

The illegitimate use of force was certainly not tolerated by the government. The *yu-hsia* were considered lawbreakers, destructive of

---

[60] *HFT* 19:4b.
[61] *HFT* 19:4b.

social and legal order. Those who violently engaged in robbery, murder, and other illegal activities fell into the category of criminals. In one way or another they interfered with the government administration, challenged the government authority, and violated the law in an open and explicit manner. For this reason many officials dealt harshly with this group, an action that was usually encouraged and supported by the emperor. (See page 195 and the section in this chapter on the Control of the Powerful Families.) In fact, it represented the government policy.

Since the values and means adopted by the *yu-hsia* were fundamentally different from those of society, it is not surprising that those who shared these values and advocated the use of the same means cooperated in one way or another in order to protect each other from outside attacks and develop strength and power to carry out violent activities. This is revealed in the statement of Ssu-ma Ch'ien referred to above. Hsün Yüeh also points out that "there were those who inflicted rewards and punishments at will and associated with others to establish force if necessary."[62] A similar point is emphasized by Ju Shun, who said that they were a group of persons who trusted each other and held common opinions on what was wrong and right, and that they were able to exercise their power in their local communities and were strong enough to exert pressure on the dukes and the marquises (*HS* 37:1a).

As a rule a *yu-hsia* who could command awe and respect had many followers. It was said that Chi Hsin was admired by others to the extent that men within an area of several thousand *li* were willing to die for him (*SC* 100:3b; *HS* 37:3b). The followers and guests of Kuo Hsieh not only offered their services to him but also assassinated his foes without his knowledge. A number of persons arrived at his home with carriages every night and asked to take some of the fugitives staying with Kuo into their own homes (III, 20).

It was quite a common practice for the *yu-hsia* to keep a number of followers and adherents whose services they commanded. Many of these followers were fugitives and criminals. And *yu-hsia* often kept a number of assassins whose services were always available (III, 38). Organized group action was common, and was particularly noticeable among those engaged in such unlawful activities as counterfeiting coins, robbing graves, and banditry. Gangs were organized by young men of the various local communities in the capital. They robbed passengers,

[62] *HC* 10:3a.

murdered officials, and avenged others in return for a reward. Pellets of different colors were used to assign jobs to members: those who drew red pellets were to kill a military officer, those who got black ones were to kill a civil official, and those who got white ones were to take care of the funerals of the members who lost their lives in carrying out their missions (III, 42).

Although the men who were engaged in such activities were not considered genuine *yu-hsia,* and Chu Chia would have considered such activity shameful, it seems that many *yu-hsia* belonged to this category that deviated from the ideal pattern described by Ssu-ma Ch'ien. Even Kuo Hsieh, a *yu-hsia* of good reputation, engaged in plundering, making coins illegally, and robbing graves, not to mention others who were described by Ssu-ma Ch'ien as no more than robbers (III, 20; *SC* 124:7b).

In short, the *yu-hsia* often constituted an organized destructive force. According to Pan Ku they formed bands whose members acted against popular interests but were willing to die for the group (*HS* 92:1b).

Yu-hsia usually had wide connections. In two instances more than one thousand carriages arrived with people attending the funeral of a *yu-hsia*'s mother (III, 12; *HS* 92:8a). People who came to meet Yüan She on a certain occasion arrived in several tens of carriages (III, 47).

Some *yu-hsia* were able to associate with nobles and high officials who were fond of guests. Yüan Ang, a chancellor, made friends with two famous *yu-hsia,* Chü Meng and Chi Hsin. Chi Hsin, who was a murderer, was harbored by Yüan, and was also the friend of such officials as Kuan Fu and Chi Pu. Both were treated by Chi as his younger brothers.[63] Lou Hu, another *yu-hsia,* was the guest of a powerful consort family, the Wangs. The Wang brothers were fond of associating with *yu-hsia* and harboring fugitives.[64] A certain *yu-hsia* was a close friend of the powerful eunuch, Shih Hsien; another *yu-hsia* was a good friend of a general, Sun Chien (*HS* 92:7a, 17a). The association with nobles and high officials not only promoted the prestige and influence of the *yu-hsia,* but also gave them protection. When Kuo Hsieh's name was on the list of those powerful and wealthy families to be removed from their native places to a mausoleum town, Grand General Wei Ch'ing spoke to the emperor about him saying that Kuo's family was poor and did not belong with those who should be moved. The emperor said, "This commoner is so powerful that he can make you, General, speak for him.

[63] *SC* 100:3b, 101:7a; *HS* 37:3a–b, 49:6a–b.
[64] *HS* 92:7b–9a, see also 90:20a.

This shows that he is not of a poor family." Kuo's family was moved (III, 20). Very likely the emperor was conscious of the power of the *yu-hsia* and his connection with the powerful officials, and for this reason turned down the proposal of the general. Tu Chih-chi 杜稺季, a great *yu-hsia,* was a good friend of two high officials. One of them spoke to the newly appointed governor of the capital, asking a favor of him on behalf of Tu. Later a subordinate official of the governor requested the impeachment of Tu, but the governor refused to take any action against him (*HS* 77:12b–13a).

The power and influence of *yu-hsia* depended largely on their associations. Usually their activities and influence were limited to a local community, such as a village or a district. But in a large city like the capital a number of *yu-hsia* were found in different zones, with each man designated according to the neighborhood under his control. The activity center was a street, lane, or neighborhood instead of the entire city. Thus in the capital there were *yu-hsia* in many streets and lanes: Chia Wan was the leader in the eastern market; Chü Chang, in the west of the city market; and Chao Fang 趙放, in the wine market (III, 38). In most cases a *yu-hsia* was powerful only within a prefecture; but some were able to exert their power over a wider area. Kuo Hsieh's influence and power extended to neighboring prefectures. For example, two families living in the capital had been involved in a dispute that powerful local residents were unable to settle, but Kuo Hsieh, though not a native of the locality, was able to intercede and arbitrate it successfully. He frequently went to other prefectures and commanderies, offering his good offices and settling things for others. Furthermore, the powerful persons of neighboring prefectures often came to call on him and offer their services (III, 20). And as was true of Chi Hsin, the young men within a distance of one thousand *li* were willing to die for him (*SC* 100:3b; *HS* 37:3a).

Wherever the center of activity might be the *yu-hsia* had one thing in common: they assumed a kind of leadership and were powerful in the local community. They were usually respected and feared by the people. A sign of impoliteness could be considered an insult, and violent action might result. Whenever Kuo Hsieh entered or left the village all of the people got out of his way. One time a man who remained squatting and staring at him would have been killed by Kuo's guests if Kuo had not stopped them (III, 20). Kuo was so ill-tempered in his youth that he killed many people who dared to show anger toward him or who gave him a cross look. Yüan She behaved similarly (III, 47).

The influence of a *yu-hsia* in the community is manifested in still another way in Kuo's biography. A man was repeatedly released from corvée service because Kuo told a subordinate official in charge of the matter: "I think highly of this man. Whenever his term comes for corvée service see that he is exempted." In this way Kuo won the support of the young man, who had previously been hostile to him (III, 20). We can see from this that a *yu-hsia* was often close to the local officials, and he could manipulate his personal connections with them to assume leadership in the community.

Some *yu-hsia* were famous and influential. Chü Meng was a *yu-hsia* of Lo-yang, but his name was known to all the powerful leaders and high officials in the capital. When Wu and Ch'u rebelled in 154 B.C., Chou Ya-fu, the grand commandant, led the Han troops to put down the rebels. He thought that Chü Meng might be on the side of the rebels and feared that he might keep him from reaching Honan safely. Apparently Honan was the area under Chü Meng's control, and Chou felt he might be assassinated by Chü's men at any time. When he met Chü Meng and learned that the powerful *yu-hsia* was not cooperating with the rebels, he was pleased and said, "Wu and Ch'u have started a big affair, but since they did not try to get Meng, I am sure they will not be able to accomplish anything." The historian remarked that during a time of turmoil having Chü Meng on the general's side was as good as conquering an enemy state (III, 12). The words speak for themselves. The importance of this commoner *yu-hsia* apparently lies in his tremendous number of followers, who were widely distributed over an extensive area. Thus the Han army could have been in a dangerous strategic position, exposed to attack from both the front and the rear, which would have shaken the whole defense line. But the grand commandant decided to hold Ying-yang as his base and disregard the defense of the area to the east, knowing that Chü Meng would not attack in the rear (*SC* 57:9a; *HS* 40:27a–b). A *yu-hsia* as powerful as Chü Meng was very exceptional.

Since *yu-hsia* were so powerful, often violated the law, and constituted a threat to the peace and order of the empire, especially during periods of disorder, the government was certainly aware of their threat and often took drastic measures to deal with them. That was why *yu-hsia* were included among those powerful and wealthy families to be moved by the government from various places to the mausoleum towns. One of the groups to be moved, the *hao-chieh* (powerful persons) apparently included *yu-hsia*. Pan Ku mentioned that the customs were not the same in the various mausoleum towns, because people were moved to and from different places. And he went on to say that the *hao-chieh* were engaged in *yu-hsia* and unlawful activities (*HS* 28B:18b–19a; see also the section in this chapter on Control of the Powerful Families). As a matter of fact, *yu-hsia* might have been moved because they were categorized either as "*hao-chieh*" or "wealthy." Thus the famous *yu-hsia*, Kuo Hsieh, was classified as "wealthy" and moved by the government (III, 20).

Drastic measures were taken by the government, especially under Emperor Wen, Emperor Ching, and Emperor Wu. *Yu-hsia* were usually severely dealt with by law, and many were killed. Kuo Hsieh's father, who was also a *yu-hsia*, was executed in Emperor Wen's time (III, 20). Emperor Ching was even more rigid in dealing with the law-breaking *yu-hsia*. In pursuit of his severe policy of wiping out these dangerous persons, he purposely appointed the so-called harsh officials, the *k'u-li* 酷吏, as grand administrators of those commanderies where *yu-hsia* were violent and powerful. The Hsien family of Chi-nan and Chou Yung 周庸 of Ch'en were thus executed by officials dispatched by him (III, 14). Later, Emperor Wu appointed several harsh officials as grand administrators who wiped out powerful persons with imperial approval. He also approved the execution of Kuo Hsieh.[65] In Emperor Ch'eng's time several *yu-hsia* in the capital were put to death by Governor Wang Tsun 王尊.[66] Wang Mang was also determined to exterminate the powerful *yu-hsia* (*HS* 92:17a).

---

[65] Kuo Hsieh's family was exterminated upon the suggestion of the grandee secretary, Kung-sun Hung, who held that it was unpardonable for a commoner redresser-of-wrongs to exercise the power of life and death. Actually, the guilty person was a guest of Kuo who murdered a scholar without Kuo's knowledge. Legally, in the opinion of the officials concerned with this case, Kuo was not guilty, but apparently Emperor Wu and the central government were more concerned with wiping out powerful persons than with justice. See III, 20.

[66] *HS* 76:27a merely mentions that the governor of the capital, Wang Tsun, executed several powerful and cunning persons of Ch'ang-an: Chia Wan, Chü Chang, arrow maker Chang Chin 張禁, a man of the wine market, Chao Fang, Yang Chang 楊章 of Tu-ling, and others. *HS* 92:7a–b mentions that Wang Tsun arrested powerful *hsia* and killed Chü Chang, arrow maker Chang Hui 張囘, and Chao Chün-tu 趙君都 and Chia Tzu-kuang 賈子光 of the wine market. All of them were famous powerful persons of Ch'ang-an who avenged grievances and kept assassins. Probably Chang Chin and Chang Hui were the same person, and Chao Chün-tu was the style name of Chao Fang. See III, 38, for translations of these passages.

CONTROL OF THE POWERFUL FAMILIES

The presence of many powerful families in society certainly constituted a great threat to the security of the government, and the Han
government obviously was aware of it. Various measures were taken to
curb their power and put them under surveillance.

Moving Powerful Families to the Capital and the Mausoleum Towns

Old Families. I have already mentioned that after the Ch'in had conquered the various states it moved some of the old families of these
states to the capital, and Emperor Kao continued this practice. The old
families were among the most powerful groups in society and therefore
became the main concern of the government. At the suggestion of Lou
(Liu) Ching they were moved to the mausoleum towns "to strengthen
the trunk and to weaken the branches" (III, 8). Under this policy the
old families gradually waned and a new group of powerful families
emerged. By the time of Emperor Wu the government was moving
other powerful groups from various places to the mausoleum towns in
order to weaken them and keep them under surveillance. In the words
of Chu-fu Yen, who advised Emperor Wu to move the various powerful
families to Mou-ling, this measure, "within, . . . will strengthen the
capital region, and, without, . . . will eliminate the treacherous and
cunning persons. This is called getting rid of the harmful without using
punishments" (III, 18). Pan Ku also mentions in his treatise on geography that the powerful families were moved "to strengthen the trunk
and to weaken the branches; it was not merely for the sake of establishing the mausoleum" (*HS* 28B:18b).

The powerful families moved by Emperor Wu included high officials,
wealthy families, and families described as *hao-chieh ping-chien.*

High Officials. All high officials of the 2,000-picul rank were moved
from various places to the mausoleum towns from time to time (III, 18,
n. 119). It was recorded that in 65 B.C. the families of the imperial
chancellor, generals, marquises, and 2,000-picul officials were moved
to Tu-ling (III, 35). The families of both Chang Ch'ang and Tu Yeh
had been moved to Mou-ling because their grandfathers had been
grand administrators (*HS* 76:13a–b, 85:20b).

Wealthy Families. Under Emperor Wu a family with property worth
three million cash was obliged to move (III, 19). Later, in Emperor

Hsüan's time, the standard was lowered to one million (III, 33, 35). P'ing Tang's 平當 grandfather, whose wealth amounted to one million, was thus moved to P'ing-ling (*HS* 71:10a).

Families Described as hao-chieh ping-chien.[67] Pan Ku, in his famous *fu* poem, *Liang-tu-fu*, mentions high officials, wealthy persons, and *hao-chieh ping-chien* 豪桀并兼 as "three groups selected" to be moved by the government (*HHS* 40A:16a, and note). Obviously the third group was treated as one category. But since the term *hao-chieh* is not defined and its meaning is vague, the usage and meaning of this term must be explored in order to know who these persons were.

The term *hao-chieh* originally meant a person of outstanding talent and ability.[68] Such a person was admired by Mencius, who said, "*Hao-chieh* scholars rise up even without a King Wen [as a leader]."[69] Gradually the term was used to mean a person who was awe inspiring and able to command obedience from others. It implies that he could assume a certain kind of leadership. Thus T'ien Jung and T'ien Heng of the powerful old families of the state of Ch'i were described as *hao-chieh*.[70] During the time of the rebellion against Wang Mang many rebel leaders who raised troops to occupy a city were described as *hao-chieh*. The *Hou-Han-shu* mentions that Liu Po-sheng 劉伯升 and Tou Jung held discussions with the *hao-chieh* before they decided to join the uprising.[71]

It is most interesting to note that *yu-hsia*, redressers-of-wrong, were referred to as *hao-chieh* in the biography of *yu-hsia* in the *Shih-chi* and *Han-shu*.[72] Sometimes they were simply referred to as *hao*[73] (powerful), *hao-shih* 豪士[74] (powerful men), *hsien-hao* 縣豪[75] (a *hao* of a prefecture), *hsien-hao* 賢豪[76] (worthy *hao*), or *ming-hao* 名豪[77] (famous *hao*).

These examples seem to indicate that the usage in Han times was somewhat different from the original meaning of the term *hao-chieh*.

[67] *SC* 112:12b; *HS* 6:9a and 28a, 28B:18b, 64A:19b.
[68] *MTCS* 5B:2b, 13A:4b; *The Works of Mencius,* in James Legge, *The Chinese Classics,* II, 254 and 454.
[69] *MTCS* 13A:4b; Legge, *Mencius,* p. 454.
[70] *HS* 33:2a. *SC* 94:1a reads *hao tsung ch'iang* 豪宗彊 instead of *hao-chieh tsung ch'iang* 豪桀宗彊·
[71] *HHS* 12:4b and 15b, 13:21a, 14:1a–b, 18:1a and 18a, 23:4a; III, 48.
[72] *HS* 92:2b, 10b, 13b, and 17a.
[73] *SC* 124:6a; *HS* 92:1b–2a, 3b, 5a, and 15b.
[74] *SC* 124:3b; *HS* 92:3a.
[75] *HS* 92:5b.
[76] *SC* 124:3b and 6a–b; *HS* 92:5b.
[77] *HS* 92:7b and 15b.

In the Han dynasty the term emphasized particularly the possession of awe-inspiring power. For this reason I suggest translating *hao-chieh* as "awe-inspiring powerful persons" or "powerful persons." The term itself is a neutral one, without moral judgment. In short, it seems that any person, whether a *yu-hsia* or not, who was powerful enough to command obedience of a group of men, exercise control over others, or interfere with the government administration could be called *hao-chieh*. Such persons by virtue of their power were often referred to as *hao* (powerful persons) or *hao-ch'iang* 豪強 (powerful and strong persons) in the histories.[78]

The term *ping-chien* or *chien-ping* means "to swallow up the property of others." Obviously this activity was not limited only to the wealthy merchants who were often accused of such activities.[79] There is evidence that other powerful persons, *hao-chieh* or *yu-hsia,* were also engaged in *ping-chien* activities. Hence there was such an expression as *jen-hsia ping-chien* 任俠并兼 (persons engaged in *hsia*-type activities and encroachment) (*SC* 129:13b). A petition presented by the elders of a prefecture near the capital reported that "Chü Chang and several other *yu-hsia* [whose names also appear in the biography of *yu-hsia* in the *Han-shu*] swallow up [the property of others], command the services of others, and encroach upon the small people" (*HS* 76:27a). All of these statements indicate that many persons known as *hao-chieh* or *yu-hsia* were engaged in the activities of *ping-chien*. Hence the *Han-shu* states that there were *hao-chieh* who encroached upon the small people (*HS* 28B:22a; III, 37).

Because many of the powerful persons were overbearing, treacherous, and engaged in unlawful activities, the word *hao* was often used together with the word *hua* 猾, meaning treacherous or cunning; thus the term *hao-hua* had a bad connotation.[80] Kuan Fu was described as a person who associated with the *hao-chieh ta-hua,* powerful persons and greatly cunning persons (III, 16).

Members of an ordinary big family or *tsu* would not have been called *hao-chieh*. But because of its power in society, a big family or *tsu* must be included among the powerful families. Local officials often found it difficult to control such a family or *tsu*. A certain Hsien family, comprising more than three hundred households, was described as "power-

[78] *SC* 122:4b and 12b; *HS* 90:4b, 6a, and 14a; III, 37.

[79] II, 18; *HS* 24A:14a and 15b. On the meaning of the term *ping-chien* or *chien-ping,* see the section on Wealthy Merchants in the Early Han in this chapter.

[80] *SC* 122: 2a; *HS* 90: 2a–b. For other examples, see *SC* 122: 14b; *HS* 76: 27a, 90: 7b ff.

ful and cunning"; the local officials were unable to control them
(III, 13). In another case, local officials did not dare arrest guests who
were engaged in robbery; the guests were associated with a Kao
family that was referred to as a *hao ta-chia* 豪大家, a powerful and great
family (III, 37). The *Han-shu* mentions that the *hao-chieh ta-hsing* (powerful persons and big families) in a locality intermarried with each other.
The Grand Administrator Chao Kuang-han 趙廣漢, whenever he received a report that led to the arrest and prosecution of these persons,
always pretended that the report was made by the junior relatives of
the *hao-chieh* and the big families. Thus the powerful and big *tsu* were
turned against each other and became enemies (III, 31). This clearly
indicates that a big family or *tsu*, by virtue of its size, was powerful in
the community; it also shows that there was a close connection between
the big families and the *hao-chieh*.

The government certainly was aware of the power and the potential
threat of the big families or *tsu*. That was why Emperor Wu, who
moved the various powerful families, also moved the powerful and big
tsu (ch'iang-tsung ta-tsu 強宗大族*)* and did not allow the whole *tsu* to live
together. Cheng Hung's great grandfather was moved to Shan-yin
with his three sons because of this regulation.[81]

The policy of compulsory moving continued until 40 B.C., when
Emperor Yüan issued an edict ordering that no mausoleum town was
to be established for him (*HS* 9:10a–b). Both Emperor Ch'eng and
Emperor Ai also issued orders to stop moving the people to the vicinity
of the mausoleums (*HS* 10:10b–11a, 11:5b–6a). The reason for discontinuing the moving apparently was not because Emperor Yüan
wanted to avoid disturbing the people, as mentioned in the edict, but
because by this time the powerful families had become increasingly
powerful while the government had become increasingly ineffective,
and was no longer able to move them. The regulation was un-
enforceable.[82]

---

[81] Hsia Ch'eng, *Hou-Han-shu*, quoted in *HHS* 33:19b.

[82] Yang Lien-sheng, "Tung-Han ti hao-tsu," *THHP*, XI, No. 4 (1936), 1009. That
the government was unable to move the powerful families is clearly indicated in a
memorial presented to Emperor Ch'eng by an official, Ch'en T'ang 陳湯, who said
that the people in the empire had not been moved to the mausoleums for more than
thirty years, that the wealthy men had become very numerous east of the pass, and
that many of them occupied fertile land and commanded the services of the poor.
Thus Ch'en advised the emperor to move them in order to strengthen the capital and
weaken the feudal lords. Ch'en expressed his willingness to be the first to move to
Ch'u-ling so that others would follow his example (III, 39).

Punishing Powerful Families

A more drastic measure taken by the Han government was to punish the powerful persons by law. Many grand administrators were famous for their determination and ability to wipe out the "powerful and cunning persons." Since they were extremely cruel and unrestrained in killing, they were known as the *k'u-li*, the harsh officials, and a collective biography was reserved for them in the *Shih-chi* and the *Han-shu*. A grand administrator once executed two hundred prisoners together with two hundred others who had gone secretly into the jail to visit the prisoners (*HS* 90:6b). Another administrator, Wang Wen-shu 王温舒, arrested a large number of "powerful and cunning persons." More than a thousand families were involved; many were executed, and in some cases the whole *tsu* was exterminated (III, 22). Several hundred young men were arrested by a prefect and thrown into a big cave in the jail, where they all died (*HS* 90:20b–21a). Another grand administrator, whose aim it was to wipe out the powerful, supported the weak and poor and always attempted to protect them from punishment, even if they had violated the law; "the powerful and awe-inspiring persons who encroached upon the small people" were always found guilty by manipulating the wording of the laws (III, 37). The power of local authorities to suppress powerful families could be so great that even the family of a high official, Ning Ch'eng, was exterminated by an official who was appointed the grand administrator of Nan-yang where the Ning family lived (*SC* 122:3a; *HS* 90:6a).

These cruel officials should not be considered isolated cases of persons who were fond of killing. Their activities were connected with the government policy of suppressing the powerful families. In other words, they were not only encouraged by the emperor, they were carrying out the government policy. The *Han-shu* points out that Wang Meng 王孟 was well known for his *hsia* activities in the area of the Yangtze and Huai rivers and that the Hsien family of Chi-nan and Chou Yung of Ch'en were well known as *hao;* when Emperor Ching heard about them he sent his officials to kill them all.[83] The actions of Wang Wen-shu, one of the well-known harsh officials, clearly were approved by Emperor

[83] III, 14. In what is apparently another version of this case it is said that the local authorities were unable to control the Hsien family of Chi-nan, and therefore Emperor Ching selected Chih Tu to be the grand administrator of that commandery; Chih Tu then executed the most evil members of the Hsien family. See III, 13.

Wu, who was determined to curb the power of the powerful persons. Wang arrested a large number of "powerful and cunning persons"—more than a thousand families were involved. He presented a memorial requesting the extermination of the whole *tsu* of the great "powerful and cunning persons"; in the case of lesser figures only the person concerned was to be put to death. Because of Wang's specially established relay system, the permission was granted within two days. Wang was fond of killing without mercy, and yet Emperor Wu considered him capable and promoted him to the post of commandant of the capital.[84] The *Shih-chi* states that all grand administrators, chief commandants, and 2,000-picul officials imitated the administration of Wang Wen-shu (*SC* 122:17a). It is not merely a coincidence that among the thirteen harsh officials mentioned in the biography of harsh officials in the *Han-shu,* nine were officials under Emperor Wu.[85]

Emperor Hsüan was more moderate than Emperor Wu. His policy was traditionally described as a "mixture of the government of a sage king [*wang* 王] and a military lord [*pa* 霸]"—that is, he governed through both moral influence and force and compulsion. But he was equally determined to curb the powerful families. Thus when he was unsatisfied with the ineffectiveness of a grand administrator, Tu Yen-nien, he issued an edict to reprimand him. Thereafter, Tu selected capable officials to arrest the powerful and the strong persons within his commandery. The emperor, now very pleased, sent a messenger to deliver an edict to him, rewarded him with twenty catties of gold, and appointed him the grand administrator of another commandery (*HS* 60:5b). The emperor rewarded with gold and promotion another administrator, Yen Yen-nien, who had wiped out the powerful Kao family and put scores of men to death; however, because of Yen's cruelty the emperor declined to make him the governor of Feng-i, one of the metropolitan commanderies (*HS* 90:18b).

In addition to moving powerful families and appointing harsh officials to deal with them, special authority was given to certain officials so that they, too, participated in the government policy of suppressing such families. In 106 B.C. regional inspectors, *pu-tz'u-shih* 部刺史, were first established to oversee the local administration. One of the six duties of these inspectors concerned the control of powerful families. They were authorized to investigate whether the strong *tsu* and the powerful persons (*ch'iang-tsung hao-yu* 強宗豪右) owned landed property

---

[84] *SC* 122:14b–15a; *HS* 90:8a–b.
[85] Yen Keng-wang, *Chung-kuo ti-fang hsing-cheng chih-tu shih,* II, 410.

beyond limit, whether the strong oppressed the weak, and whether the majority was violent to the minority. They were also empowered to investigate whether the highest local authorities (2,000-picul officials) under their jurisdiction were partial to and affiliated with the powerful and strong persons.[86]

LATER HAN

The Growth of Powerful Families

As time went on, the power of some of the powerful families—the old families of the feudal states and the feudal lords of the Han—gradually waned, while the power of others increased. By the end of the Early Han the power of the powerful families had reached its peak. They began to dominate the government and society. It was the powerful families who alienated and destroyed Wang Mang's government. During the course of the power struggle, several of the leaders of the most powerful families, Wei Ao, Kung-sun Shu, and Liu Hsiu, supported by a number of the lesser powerful families, commanded a large number of troops, occupied and controlled an area, and established independent centers of political and military power. Each sought the alliance of lesser large families and strove for power. With a few exceptions, most of the supporters of Liu Hsiu were powerful families—families of prominent officials, wealthy landlords, and merchants.[87] It was these powerful families who helped Liu Hsiu conquer his rivals and unify the empire. With the establishment of the Later Han dynasty they gained political power, which allowed them to consolidate and strengthen their positions, and they remained powerful throughout the dynasty. They dominated the government to such an extent that the history of the Later Han may be seen as the history of powerful families. They became omnipotent because of their (1) increasing economic power, (2) increasing political power, and (3) increasing size. We shall analyze these reasons one by one.

[86] Ts'ai Chih, *Han-kuan tien-chih i-shih hsüan-yung*, compiled by Sun Hsing-yen, *PCKTS*, p. 7b, hereafter cited as *HKTI; HS* 19A:15a–b, note; *HHC* 28:1b, note.

[87] For details see Yang Lien-sheng, "Tung-Han ti hao-tsu," pp. 1017–18; Utsunomiya Seikichi, *Kandai shakai keizai shi kenkyū* (Tokyo, 1954), pp. 393–96; Yü Ying-shih, "Tung-Han cheng-ch'üan chih chien-li yü shih-tsu ta-hsing chih kuan-hsi," *Hsin-ya hsüeh-pao*, I, No. 2 (Feb., 1956), 226–44; Hans Bielenstein, "The Restoration of the Han Dynasty," *Bulletin of the Museum of Far Eastern Antiquities* (Stockholm), No. 26 (1954), pp. 94–96.

Economic Power

I have already mentioned the growing importance of landlords. The process of land concentration, which had begun in the time of Emperors Wen and Ching, became more and more intense in the second half of the first century. The large landlords were mainly nobles, officials, and merchants. A commoner-landlord holding a large estate was rather rare, for it was difficult, if not impossible, for a farmer to accumulate a large amount of land. As Ch'ao Ts'o pointed out, most of the farmers who owned only about 100 *mou* of land found it very difficult to hold onto their land and property. Under financial pressure they would eventually lose their land and become tenants of the wealthy landlords (*HS* 24A:11a–b).

This serious situation called for a land reform. Thus a measure to limit the size of landholdings was suggested by Shih Tan in 7 B.C. This policy, however, was killed by the powerful officials who considered it disadvantageous to them (*HS* 24A:18a–b). Next came Wang Mang's land reform, which made it illegal for people to buy and sell land. This reform also failed because of the opposition of the powerful families. He was forced to abolish it within four years.[88]

Since Wang Mang's policies in general were against the vested interests of the wealthy, powerful families, they became his strongest opponents. First they joined the peasant rebellion of the Red Eyebrows; but they gradually became an independent force striving for power and eventually overthrew Wang Mang's dynasty and established their own government.

Liu Hsiu himself was a member of the imperial clan and a great landlord who was able to sell surplus grain in A.D. 22 when there was a famine in Nan-yang and many of the retainers of the powerful families were engaged in robbery.[89] Most of his ardent supporters were also wealthy landlords—for instance, the Yin family (which owned 700 *ch'ing* of land) and the Fan family (which owned 300 *ch'ing* of land).[90]

When the new dynasty was established, this group now possessed political power and was able to consolidate its economic position, increase its wealth, and acquire more land. The new dynasty certainly

[88] *HS* 24A: 19b–20a; Nancy Lee Swann, *Food and Money in Ancient China* (Princeton, 1950), pp. 210–12.

[89] *HHS* 1A:2a; Utsunomiya, *Kandai shakai keizai shi kenkyū*, pp. 379–92; Bielenstein, "Restoration of the Han Dynasty," pp. 96 ff.

[90] I, 40; *HHS* 32:16b–17a.

could not adopt a land reform policy that opposed the interests of these wealthy landlords. The land, often in very extensive holdings, usually was not registered or it was falsely registered with the cooperation of the local officials. Liu Hsiu made an attempt in A.D. 39 to survey and record the amount of cultivated land in the empire, but he failed. The local authorities who conducted the survey tended to be lenient with the powerful families and dealt harshly and unfairly with others. The situation was even worse in Honan, where the capital was located and there were many officials who were close to the emperor, and in Nan-yang, the emperor's native place, where many of his relatives lived. These influential persons usually had huge landholdings, and it was beyond the power of the local government to make a true survey.[91] Although the emperor put to death more than ten grand administrators who had made false reports on cultivated landholdings, the effect was doubtful. In fact land became much more concentrated in the hands of the powerful families than in the Early Han. The nobles, consort families, officials, eunuchs, and merchants all acquired large landholdings through exploitation or encroachment.[92] In the Later Han there were no echoes of the proposals of Shih Tan and Wang Mang; no attempt was ever made by the government to regulate or limit the amount of landed property a family might possess.

The wealth and commercial activities of the powerful families are summed up vividly by Chung-ch'ang T'ung (*HHS* 49:22a–b):

As to the families of the powerful persons, houses are connected one after another, numbering several hundred; fertile land spreads all over in the countryside. The slaves form groups by the thousands, and those who are attached to them are counted by the myriad; carriages and ships are sent out to buy and sell [commodities], and they reach in all directions—everywhere. They dispose of [some things] and lay up [other things], and these fill the capital and the cities. The precious jades and the valuable goods are so numerous that even a big house is not able to store them. Horses, cattle, sheep, and pigs are so numerous that even a valley is not able to hold them.

Political Power

Powerful families gradually began to monopolize political power in the Later Han. The system of *jen-tzu* (that is, the system under which a relative of a 2,000-picul official was given the privilege of being ap-

[91] *HHS* 1B:15b–16a; 22:12b–13a.
[92] For examples, see III, 56; II, 67; *HHS* 32:10b, 34:19a.

pointed automatically a gentleman in the court)[93] and the system of recommendation were both already in practice in the Early Han. The first was a privilege enjoyed by the members of high official families. The system of recommendation in theory was open to all. Although the system of *jen-tzu* provided a channel for the privileged class to enter officialdom, it was actually the system of recommendation that greatly contributed to the monopoly of political power by the powerful families.

This was a system under which a local official was authorized to recommend to the central government worthy men under various categories, such as "virtuous and wise," "upright," and "filially pious and incorrupt."[94] In Early Han the system of recommendation was instituted only occasionally. Vacancies for men of the "filially pious and incorrupt" category were often not filled. As is indicated in edicts of Emperor Wen and Emperor Wu, the local officials were reluctant to make such recommendations. An edict of 168 B.C. said that the emperor thought highly of the "filially pious" and the "fraternally respectful" and the "incorrupt" officials, and yet now in a prefecture of ten thousand households it was maintained that nobody could meet these qualifications. How, the emperor asked, could this be the actual situation? (*HS* 4:12b–13a). An edict of 128 B.C. said that orders had been issued instructing the local authorities to recommend the "incorrupt" and the "filially pious" and "now there are instances in which not a single person has been recommended in a whole commandery."[95]

The situation was different in the Later Han. While the "virtuous and wise" were still recommended only occasionally—that is, when an edict was issued that specifically ordered it—the recommendation of the "filially pious and incorrupt" became a regular practice and increasingly important.[96] Officials were told to make annual recommendations.[97] An edict of A.D. 76 mentioned that as many as one hundred

[93] *HS* 11:3b, note; *HHHY* 45:463–65; *THHY* 26:289–90.

[94] *Hsiao lien*, "filially pious and incorrupt" was actually two categories: *hsiao-ti* 孝悌, those of filial and brotherly love, and *lien-li* 廉吏, the incorrupt officials. However, as Hsü T'ien-lin points out, they became one category by the time of the Later Han. *HHHY* 45:461–63; *THHY* 26:282–85; Yen Keng-wang, *Chung-kuo ti-fang hsing-cheng chih-tu shih*, I, 83–84.

[95] The emperor therefore ordered his government to impose punishments on officials who failed to make recommendations (*HS* 6:7a).

[96] See Yen Keng-wang, "Ch'in Han lang-li chih-tu k'ao," *LSYY*, XXIII (1951), 118–23.

[97] It should be pointed out that when an edict was issued by Emperor Wu in 134 B.C., it merely ordered that the commanderies and the kingdoms recommend one

persons were recommended as "filially pious and incorrupt" or as "abundantly talented" each year by the inspectors, grand administrators, and chancellors (*HHS* 3:5b). Gradually, by the time of Emperor Ho, a quota varying from one to six persons was set up in proportion to the population in a locality.[98]

In theory, the basic qualification for office was talent or virtue; but in fact personal factors often were influential. The judgment of a local official was usually based on the prevailing opinion of the locality, which was the opinion of the prominent scholar-officials. They knew only the members of the powerful families with whom they associated. Members of nonprominent families who had no association with the local elite had little chance of coming to their attention. Local officials also tended to select members of the prominent families, for there was a close connection between the two groups. Wang Fu pointed out that in making recommendations family history was the first thing to be considered.[99] This was particularly true of the recommendation of the "filially pious and incorrupt." Most of the persons recommended in this category were selected from among the subordinate officials serving in a commandery or prefectural government.[100] Since most of the subordinate officials came from prominent families in the locality, this meant that most of the "filially pious and incorrupt" were selected from the prominent families.[101] Also, a subordinate official so recommended was often promoted to higher posts, such as gentleman of the palace or prefect.[102] Recommendation provided one of the best channels for moving up in the bureaucratic hierarchy.

Since recommendation was so important to success in a political career, prominent families often sought the favor of the local officials so that their relatives might be recommended (*HHS* 61:33b). T'ien Hsin 田歆, the governor of Honan, received many letters from the consort families asking for favor when he was about to recommend six "filially pious and incorrupt" (*HHS* 2:4b). He found it difficult to disobey them, and yet he was somewhat conscientious. Finally, he independently

---

person in each of the categories "filially pious" and "incorrupt" (*HS* 6:3b); it does not say that a recommendation was to be made yearly. The term *sui-ch'a* 歲察 or *sui-chü* 歲舉, yearly recommendation, first appeared in an edict of A.D. 36 (*Han-kuan mu-lu,* quoted in *HHC* 24:5b, note).

[98] For details see *HHS* 37:20a–b; *HHC* 28:3b.

[99] Wang Fu, *Chien-fu lun, SPTK* ed., 8:6a–b, hereafter cited as *CFL.*

[100] Yen Keng-wang, *Chung-kuo ti-fang hsing-cheng chih-tu shih,* I, 83.

[101] For instances, Kai Hsün 蓋勳 (*HHS* 58:16b); Wang Kung 王龔 (*HHS* 56:6b); Yin Hsün 尹勳 (*HHS* 57:27a).

[102] See Yen Keng-wang, *Chung-kuo ti-fang hsing-cheng chih-tu shih,* II, 333–34.

recommended as one of the six a local scholar of good reputation (*HHS* 56:13b–14a). All in all, members of nonprominent families, who often had no association with the local elite or the local officials, were virtually excluded from recommendation.

At the same time, personal loyalty developed among the scholar-officials. The person who was recommended as "filially pious and incorrupt" by a local official was obliged to be loyal to him and return his kindness whenever possible (*HHS* 32:5b). Gratitude was also expected from a previous subordinate by the official who had employed him and from a student (*men-sheng* 門生) by his teacher.[103] To acknowledge his loyalty he was obliged to observe mourning for his former teacher or superior and to offer help in time of distress or danger. For instance, when Ti-wu Chung 第五種 impeached a eunuch and was exiled to the frontier where the eunuch's grandson was a grand administrator, one of Ti-wu's subordinate officials killed the escort officers and ran away with him (*HHS* 41:11b–12a). It should be noted that a teacher did not necessarily mean a person who actually taught someone. One often acknowledged someone as his teacher in order to establish a personal tie.[104] This sort of personal loyalty between a subordinate and a superior greatly strengthened the political position of the powerful families. They were backed by a group of persons loyal to them.

Size

The size of powerful families was formidable. Unlike an ordinary family, which was composed of two or three generations (with an average of five or six persons in each nuclear family), a powerful family often had a large number of family members living together in the same place (not necessarily under one roof). This was possible because of their great estates. Apparently they also realized that living together as one unit meant more power and more protection. Such families were already in existence in the Early Han. For instance, there was a Hsien family in which there were more than three hundred households (III, 13). The government, which was aware of their power, took measures to reduce their size. Thus Emperor Wu prohibited the powerful and big lineages from living together and ordered them to be moved and split up (*HHS* 33:19b, note). When the government stopped moving

---

[103] Yang Lien-sheng, "Tung-Han ti hao-tsu," pp. 1034–37.

[104] *JCLCS* 17:24a–b; Yang Lien-sheng, "Tung-Han ti hao-tsu," pp. 1030–37; Kamada Shigeo, *Shin Kan seiji seido no kenkyū* (Tokyo, 1963), pp. 450 ff.

the powerful families after 40 B.C., the growth of big families went unchallenged. Such families became more and more common at the end
of the Early Han. For instance, the Fan family had three generations
living together (I, 40); and more than sixty members of a family were
executed by a high official (I, 72). Sun Sung 孫嵩 told Chao Ch'i, whose
family members were killed by a grand administrator, "my family
members number one hundred, and we are strong enough to help
you." Chao then took refuge in Sun's family (*HHS* 64:23b). Because
of sheer size these big families were able to dominate and control the
small families, referred to as *tan-men* 單門, *tan-chia* 單家, *hsi-tsu* 細族,
ku-men 孤門, *tan-wei* 單微, or *ku-wei* 孤微. A member of one *tan-chia* who
was not submissive to the four big families in T'ien-shui was so disliked
by them that they wanted to punish him.[105]

A large, powerful family included not only its own members but
also many slaves, retainers, and other kinds of people who attached
themselves to the family. It was not uncommon for a wealthy family
to own several hundred or even a thousand slaves (II, 67, 68, 78). Besides,
such powerful families usually kept a large number of guests or retainers in their households. The guests or retainers (discussed in Chapter 4) were persons supported, maintained, and usually well treated by
a wealthy and powerful family (III, 23; *HS* 84:4b); their status was
more or less superior to that of the slaves. As a rule they were not engaged in domestic service, but they were expected to offer their help
in times of emergency or danger. When a family was attacked by
bandits or enemies, its retainers had an obligation to defend it (*HHS*
33:12a–b). They often served as the personal troops of a military man,
and in time of war the retainers fought together with their master
(*HHS* 29:9a, 17:16a). They became the core of the organized forces
of powerful families that took an active part in power struggles during
the transitional period in the first century. Liu Po-sheng, the elder
brother of Liu Hsiu, organized his retainers and the youths of Ch'ung-
ling 春陵 when he started his rebellion (*HHS* 14:1b). Both Teng Ch'en
鄧晨 and Ts'ang Kung 臧宮 joined the rebellion with a group of retainers (*HHS* 15:11a–b, 18:19b).

There are three instances in which all kinsmen and retainers of a
family were mobilized, and they numbered more than a thousand men:
the Yin family had over a thousand men, the Keng family had more
than two thousand, and the family of Liu Chih had "several thousand"
(III, 49; I, 41, 42). In these three cases there is no differentiation be-

[105] Hsieh Hsia's 薛夏 case, quoted in *SKC*, Wei, 13:31b, note.

tween kinsmen and retainers, but since a person's kinsmen would not be very numerous, probably not more than a hundred, it is reasonable to assume that the majority of them were retainers.[106] In any case, a family having such an organized force under its command certainly was formidable. No wonder Liu Chih and his followers were able to occupy the city of Ch'ang-ch'eng, the gates of which they later opened to welcome Liu Hsiu (I, 42).

Though not all the powerful families were ambitious and aggressive enough to play an active role in the power struggles, all of them were engaged in self-defense in order to protect their families and their property. This became a common pattern during the rebellion in Wang Mang's time, when the government was unable to maintain order and the populace was confronted with the threat of war and bandits. The powerful families organized themselves into self-defense units and built strong fortresses.[107] Small and relatively weak families attached themselves to the powerful families for protection. In one instance more than a thousand families attached themselves to a powerful family (*HHS* 32:2b). This sort of attachment certainly strengthened the powerful families. Some of them in the metropolitan area were so strong that even Teng Yü, a general of Emperor Kuang-wu, was unable to disorganize them (*HHS* 17:7b). The Red Eyebrows and the Copper Horses also were unable to take the fortification of Ti-wu Lun's powerful family (*HHS* 41:1a–b). As late as A.D. 40 many large families in various places still held strongholds and sometimes even killed the local officials (*HHS* 1B:16a–b).

The same pattern was repeated in the late part of the second century and the early years of the third century when the government of the Later Han collapsed. For instance, Hsü Chu 許褚 led his kinsmen and other people, altogether several thousand families, in defending his fortification. Li Tien's kinsmen and personal troops numbered about three thousand families (about thirteen thousand persons). Small families, as before, usually attached themselves to such powerful families for protection. In one case over five thousand families took refuge on a hill where a powerful family had its stronghold.[108]

[106] This assumption is supported in the case of Li Tien. *SKC*, Wei, 18:1a mentions that Li assembled several thousand families of guests in Ch'eng-shih, and page 2a adds that *tsung-tsu* and *pu-ch'ü* numbering more than three thousand families lived in Ch'eng-shih.

[107] III, 48, 50; *HHS* 11:17b and 22a, 32:2b, 33:12a–b and 15b, 41:1a–b.

[108] *SKC*, Wei, 18:10b and 2a, 11:10a.

CONSORT FAMILIES

The Rise to Power

I have already mentioned that the consort families of the Early Han had great power and that nearly all consort families in the Later Han were families that were already prominent and wealthy. Those in the Later Han, therefore, were able to become even more powerful than their counterparts in the earlier period. Empress Kuo's family was not only wealthy and prominent but was also extremely powerful. Her mother was the daughter of a king. Another king, the future Empress Kuo's maternal uncle, had a hundred thousand men under his command. He joined Wang Lang 王郎, one of the rebel leaders, but Liu Hsiu first persuaded the king to join him, and then married his niece in order to win his support. With the king's assistance, Liu Hsiu was then able to occupy Han-tan and to consolidate his power in Hopei (*HHS* 21:11a). The family of Emperor Kuang-wu's second empress was also wealthy, powerful, and large. When Liu Po-sheng rebelled, Yin Shih 陰識, the brother of the future Empress Yin, led his junior relatives, kinsmen, and guests, numbering more than a thousand, to join Liu's group (*HHS* 32:11a). Marital connections with these two families undoubtedly contributed to the political and military success of Liu Hsiu.

The consort families Ma, Tou, Teng, and Liang were all powerful families. Ma Yüan, Empress Ma's father, whose forefathers, brothers, and nephew had been 2,000-picul officials, was a cattle breeder in Kansu. He was so powerful that he kept a large number of retainers and commanded the services of several hundred families in that area (*HHS* 24:1a–2a).

Both the Tou and the Liang were also powerful families in what is now Kansu. For generations the Tous had been grand administrators or colonels in this area. Tou Jung himself was the chief commandant of the subordinate state of Chang-yeh. Since members of his family had been high officials in Ho-hsi, he was chosen to be the leader of five commanderies in Kansu, with the task of carrying out the duties of the grand general of the five commanderies, a position specially created by Tou and his followers because of the circumstances of the time. Two grand administrators who had no connection with the group were forced to resign. An alliance with Tou Jung was eagerly sought by Liu Hsiu in an attempt to wipe out his two rivals in Kansu and Szechwan, Wei Ao and Kung-sun Shu, respectively. Tou's power was clearly indicated in Liu Hsiu's letter to him in the following words: "During the fight between the Shu and Han, the power rests on you, General. There will be a shift of weight depending on whether you put your feet on the left side or on the right side." The five governors and their guests had differing views on the alliance, and finally it was Tou Jung who made the decision to join Liu Hsiu to help him defeat Wei Ao. As a reward, both Tou Jung and his younger brother were ennobled and appointed high officials. Three members of the family married princesses. The *Hou-Han-shu* says that four members were simultaneously holding 2,000-picul positions, that each had his residence in the capital, that they possessed over one thousand slaves, and that none of the imperial relatives or meritorious officials could match them in power and wealth (*HHS* 23:1a ff., 14b).

The Liang family was both prominent and wealthy. It was "moved" to Mou-ling in the time of Emperor Wu because the family property was worth more than ten million cash. Liang T'ung, the great-great-grandfather of two empresses (Empress Liang of Emperor Shun and Empress Liang of Emperor Huan), was a grand administrator in Kansu, and was a powerful associate of Tou Jung's clique, which kept Kansu under their control (*HHS* 34:1a–2a).

The family of Teng Yü, although unknown in Early Han, rose to prominence and power through his military accomplishments at the time Liu Hsiu began his military campaigns. He served as a general, and after the conquest held several of the top official positions in the court, including minister of the masses and grand tutor. Three members of his family had high military posts and his granddaughter became the empress of Emperor Ho (*HHS* 10A:23a, 16:1a ff.).

All of these examples clearly indicate that the empresses were selected from powerful families, which could expect to be even more powerful once they were consort families. That was why powerful families were anxious to have their daughters admitted to the palace as honorable ladies (*kuei-jen*, the highest ranking imperial concubine) in the hope that one of them eventually would become an empress. Then they would be able to increase and consolidate their power. I shall explain these two points in reverse order.

Although the powerful families had both economic and political power, they were by no means invulnerable. On the contrary, a powerful family could lose its power and even find itself in serious danger.

This was because the emperor in such a highly centralized government was the source of political and military power. He not only could remove a family from the power hierarchy, but he also could take disciplinary and punitive actions against it—such as sending it back to its home town and putting its members under the surveillance of the local officials (and, strange as it may seem, a powerful family, in spite of its awe-inspiring influence in the past, would immediately be subject to all kinds of humiliations once its members were placed under the surveillance of local officials).

In extreme cases the members of a powerful family might be put to death. Even the whole family might be exterminated. Of course, it was not always the emperor himself who initiated such action: another family, whose members were holding the key posts in the government or who were in a position to influence the emperor, might take the initiative. This may be seen as a struggle for power between two powerful families. In any case, it might lead to the downfall of a powerful family. The family of General Ma Yüan had been very powerful. Yet immediately after the general's death, Emperor Kuang-wu, who was influenced by slander and angry at Ma Yüan, cut off his marquisates. Further slanders by other officials made the emperor even angrier. The Ma family was so frightened that they did not dare to bury the general in the family graveyard; both his wife and his children tied themselves up with straw ropes to apologize to the emperor.[109] It was precisely because this family was losing its power and was being oppressed by other powerful families that Ma Yen 馬嚴, the late general's nephew, being upset and worried about the situation, made a request to present Ma Yüan's daughters to the heir apparent (*HHS* 10A:12a–13a). His plan worked out well, and it was surely the turning point that not only prevented the downfall of the family but also allowed it to rise to power again for about a quarter of a century.

The family of Tou Jung, whose alliance was eagerly sought by Liu Hsiu, was one of the most powerful families. Yet he could not prevent his family from downfall. Right after his nephew was executed, Emperor Ming cited the case of Tou Ying[110] as a warning to him. Years

---

[109] Taking advantage of Ma Yüan's failure in conducting a military campaign against a barbarian tribe, the Wu-hsi-man 五溪蠻, Liang Sung 梁松 and Tou Ku 竇固, members of two powerful families, slandered him. Since the Ma family was already in trouble, other officials brought additional charges concerning supposed valuables (it was really *i-ssu* 薏苡, a kind of plant) that Ma had procured for himself earlier (*HHS* 10A:12a, 24:18a–21a).

[110] Tou Ying 竇嬰, a consort family member, was executed by Emperor Wu. See the section on Jealousy and Politics in this chapter.

later, when his elder son, Tou Mu 竇穆, was accused by someone, all
the members of the Tou family were dismissed from office. An official
was stationed at the household of Tou Mu to keep him under surveillance. This official reported to the emperor that the Tous were com-
plaining, so they were ordered to return to their home town. Shortly
thereafter Tou Mu was accused by the local authorities of offering a
bribe; he and his son were put in jail, where both of them died. Another
son, Tou Hsün 竇勳, the husband of a princess, also died in prison
in the capital. Tou Ku 竇固, Tou Jung's nephew who had been dismissed together with other relatives, held no official post for more than
ten years. He re-entered government service and became prominent
after he had defeated the Hsiung-nu in A.D. 73. However, the person
who contributed most to the prominence and power of the family was
Tou Hsün's daughter, who became the empress in A.D. 78.[111] Because
of her position the power of the family then reached its climax, far
surpassing what it had been in the time of Tou Jung. The Tou family
dominated the government for about fourteen years, until the death of
Tou Hsien in A.D. 92.

The family of Liang T'ung, another of the powerful military leaders
who had assisted Emperor Kuang-wu in seizing control of the empire,
also suffered great distress soon after his death; his elder son, Liang
Sung 梁松, was dismissed, put into prison, and died there. The younger
son, Liang Sung 梁竦, whose daughter gave birth to Emperor Ho, also
died in prison; at the time he was being investigated by a grand administrator on charges of perversion—false charges fabricated by members
of the Tou family. His family members were exiled to Chiu-chen. The
family was allowed to return to its hometown only after the death of
the empress dowager, for it was only then that Emperor Ho learned
that the Honorable Lady Liang was his real mother. The members
of the Liang family, now acknowledged as a consort family, rose to
prominence again. And finally the family became all-powerful when
one of its daughters became the empress of Emperor Shun.[112]

All these cases indicate clearly that although these families had
been powerful for generations they were unable to protect themselves.
Only when they had become consort families were they saved from
destruction and in a position to regain or enhance their power. Since
consort family status was the basis of their newly gained power, it is

[111] *HHS* 23:14b–15b, 16b, and 18b, 10A:19b–20b.
[112] *HHS* 34:6a and 8a–11b. The elder son's name is Sung 松, first tone; the other
son is Sung 竦, third tone.

essential to know how powerful the consort families actually became.

The *Tung-kuan Han-chi* mentions that Emperor Kuang-wu, aware that previous consort families had grown too powerful, did not give too much power to members of his consort families. The members of the families of his two empresses were, at most, given the rank of the Nine Ministers, and the number of high posts occupied by them was far less than were usually occupied by consort families—such as the Hsüs, the Shihs, and the Wangs—in the Early Han.[113] The *Hou-Han-shu* states that Emperor Ming neither ennobled the members of his consort family nor allowed them to play an important role in the government.[114] It is true that the Ma brothers were only given such medium posts as general of the palace gentlemen as rapid as tigers (*hu-pen chung-lang-chiang* 虎賁中郎將) or attendant gentlemen of the Yellow Gate (*huang-men shih-lang* 黃門侍郎) (*HHS* 24:27a, 29b). However, the emperor treated his mother's family with more honor; for example, Yin Hsing 陰興 was appointed privy treasurer (*HHS* 32:16b).

The consort families began to rise to full power under Emperor Chang. He ennobled all three brothers of Empress Dowager Ma and appointed them commandant of the guard (*wei-wei* 衛尉), colonel of the guards of the city gates (*ch'eng-men hsiao-wei* 城門校尉), and colonel of the elite cavalry (*yüeh-ch'i hsiao-wei* 越騎校尉). One of the brothers, Ma Fang 馬防, who led an expedition against the Hsiung-nu, was given the title of acting general of chariots and cavalry (*HHS* 24:27a ff.). At the same time Emperor Chang also made all four brothers of his empress court officials close to the emperor (*HHS* 23:18b–19a). It is said that the Tou family became so influential that even the princesses and the other consort families, the Yins and the Mas, were afraid of them; for example, a princess was forced to sell her land to Tou Hsien at a price much below its real value (*HHS* 23:19a–b). The family's power reached its peak under Emperor Ho, when Empress Dowager Tou attended the court in person. In A.D. 89, Hsien, her elder brother, was appointed general of chariots and cavalry to lead an expedition against the Hsiung-nu. After the victory he was promoted to the rank of grand general, a rank inferior only to that of the grand tutor, the top-ranking post in the government and above that of the Three Ducal Ministers. He and his three brothers were ennobled. All the brothers and their three uncles were promoted to the rank of 2,000-picul of-

---

[113] *TKHC* 2:3b–4a.

[114] *HHS* 2:27a–b. *HHS* 10A:15b also mentions that the emperor guarded against the brothers of the empress, not allowing them to occupy key posts.

ficials. Besides, there were more than ten men in the family holding such posts as attendant within the palace, general-grandee (*chiang ta-fu* 將大夫), and gentlemen clerk (*lang-li* 郎吏) (*HHS* 23:19b, 20b, 24b–25a, 26a–b). All officials obeyed them. Even the retainers and the slaves of one of the Tou brothers relied upon their influence to oppress the people and seize their property. The officials dared not report such cases (*HHS* 23:26a).

After the downfall of the Tous, five more consort families rose to power one after another—Teng, Yen, Liang, Tou, and Ho. Indeed, from 89 to 189 only two consort families, the Yin and the Sung, failed to rise to power. For about half the time in the century beginning with Emperor Ho's accession in 89, the Han court was controlled by the consort families, the most powerful of all powerful families, as we may see in this table:

FAMILY IN POWER	A.D.
Tou	89–92
Teng	105–121
Yen	125
Liang	135–159
Tou	167–168
Ho	189

The Yens, Tous, and the Hos were only in power for very short periods. The Tengs and the Liangs, who were each able to wield power for more than a decade, were the most powerful consort families in Later Han. An analysis of the six powerful consort families reveals a general pattern in their rise to power.

First, all these families gained power under an empress dowager who personally attended the court. Although the members of the Tou family had already gained the favor of the emperor after a lady of the Tou family became empress in 78, they did not reach their peak until 89, when the empress dowager attended the court after the death of Emperor Chang. The Liang family was the one in which the empress's father, Liang Shang 梁商, was appointed grand general, and after his death the post was given to his son, Liang Chi (*HHS* 34:11b, 15b). The family continued to wield power under the empress dowager who attended the court in person for six years.

The role of the empress dowager was very significant in connection with the power of the consort families. Since the emperor was young (Emperor Ho was ten years old when he ascended the throne; Emperor

An, thirteen; Emperor Shun, eleven; Emperor Ch'ung, two; Emperor Chih, eight; Emperor Huan, fifteen; Emperor Ling, twelve; Emperor Hsien, nine), the empress dowager was in a position to control him and the government. The emperor was merely a figurehead. Of course, the empress dowager could control only the inner palace; she had to rely on her father or brother and trust him with the government and administration. Working together, they had both the inner and outer court under their control. Tou Hsien usually reported to the empress dowager and secured her consent before a memorial was formally submitted by the grand commandant to her. In this way all requests were approved without difficulty (*HHS* 23:20a).

Second, military power was usually in the hands of the consort family; indeed, it was the backbone of the consort family. Since the days of Emperor Kuang-wu, it was a customary practice to appoint a consort member commandant of the guard or colonel to command the imperial guards or to guard the city gates of the capital.[115] From the time of Emperor Chang on, beginning with the appointment of Ma Fang, the father or brother of an empress or an empress dowager was often given the highest military post—general of chariots and cavalry or grand general.[116] Such a post was invariably given to a consort member when the empress dowager attended the court in person. For about a century, especially from 89 to 189, the Han court was dominated by a member of a consort family who occupied such a post. With military power in the hands of the consort families, the highest civil officers apparently had no means to challenge the grand general. Not only were those who had the rank of the Three Lords unable to challenge him—for example, Liang Chi (*HHS* 34:20a)—but even the grand tutor, who was classified as the *shang-kung*, the superior minister, and therefore superior to the grand general in rank, was also powerless before him. For example, Ch'en Fan 陳蕃 was dominated by Tou Wu, the grand general (*HHS* 69:6a).

We have already mentioned that power was divided between the outer court and the inner court in Emperor Wu's time and that grad-

---

[115] *HHS* 10A:6b, 10B:2a and 3b, 16:16a, 23:24b and 26b, 24:27a, 29b, and 31a, 69:1a and 4a.

[116] Ma Fang was appointed general of chariots and cavalry; Tou Hsien, general of chariots and cavalry, promoted to grand general; Teng Chih, general of chariots and cavalry, promoted to grand general; Keng Pao 耿寶, grand general; Yen Hsien 閻顯, general of chariots and cavalry; Liang Shang, grand general; Liang Chi, grand general; Tou Wu, grand general; Ho Chin, grand general; Ho Miao 何苗, general of chariots and cavalry.

ually the inner court, which was closer to the emperor, began to play a more important role in government administration. This was even more true under Kuang-wu, who deliberately shifted power from the outer court to the masters of writing in order to govern the empire directly through them. As a result, the offices of the Three Lords became honorific posts without real power, unless the occupants were at the same time assigned to take charge of the duties of the masters of writing.[117] They were much less powerful than the imperial chancellor in the Early Han. This explains why the Three Lords, representing the outer court, were powerless to challenge the grand general, who represented the inner court.

The grand general, though holding a military post, might also be assigned the duties of the masters of writing. Thus a consort member could have both military and administrative power. This was the case with Liang Chi, Tou Wu, and Ho Chin, who together with the grand tutor were empowered to assist in running the government (*HHS* 34:15b, 69:4a and 11b–12a).

Third, when a consort family was in power, as indicated above in the case of the Tou family, usually many members were appointed to official positions in addition to the person who held such a key post as grand general. This means that the various government posts were distributed among the family members so that a more complete control and manipulation of the power mechanism would be possible. In the Teng family, Teng Chih was appointed general of chariots and cavalry, and all his brothers and cousins had important government posts (*HHS* 16:16a–21a). According to the *Hou-Han-shu,* in the Teng family, which had been prominent for generations—in fact, since the restoration of the Han—there were twenty-nine marquises, two lords, thirteen persons holding high military posts including that of grand general, fourteen full 2,000-picul officials, twenty-two colonels, forty-eight inspectors and grand administrators, and numerous persons holding the posts of attendant within the palace, general, grandee, gentleman, and internuncio (*HHS* 16:23a).

The Liang family, which was in power for about a quarter of a century, was the most powerful consort family in the Later Han. The post of grand general was held successively by Liang Shang and his son, Liang Chi, the brother of the empress. His younger brother was the governor of Honan; later this post was given to Liang Chi's son, Yin 胤. Several members of the family were made marquises, and seven

[117] *HHS* 49:32b; *HHHY* 19:207–8.

women of the family were given the title "baronet." Altogether there
were fifty-seven members who held such posts as minister, general,
governor, and colonel (*HHS* 34:11b, 15b–16a, and 21b–23a).

Liang Chi, who was the acting master of writing, had complete
control of government affairs under the two-year-old Emperor Ch'ung.
None of the officials dared to disobey his orders, and they had to pay
him a visit when they were appointed or promoted. Numerous persons
offered gifts in order to get official appointments or to be exempted
from punishments when guilty (III, 63). The visitors were so numerous
that his doorman was able to accumulate a thousand catties of gold
by asking gifts from them (*HHS* 34:19a). Even his superintendent-
slave was in such a powerful position that the regional inspectors and
2,000-picul officials came to pay him visits (II, 77).

Many officials lost their lives because they disobeyed Liang's orders.
The cases of Li and Tu illustrate the fate of high officials who did not
hesitate to challenge the powerful consort family. Li Ku, who was the
grand commandant, entered into controversies with Liang Chi about
many issues and especially about the appointment of a new emperor.
His opposition angered the grand general, who then told the empress
dowager to dismiss Li. He was falsely accused and executed (*HHS.*
63:15a–17a). Tu Ch'iao 杜喬, another top official who memorialized
that the members of the Liang family did not deserve to be ennobled
and who refused to appoint officials recommended by Liang, was also
arrested and died in prison (*HHS* 63:22a–24a). A lesser official was in
a much weaker position: one who held the post of gentleman of the
palace presented a memorial accusing Liang Chi. Fearing the worst,
he subsequently circulated a false report of his own death, even going
so far as to put a straw image in his coffin. In spite of the subterfuge,
Liang Chi was able to cause his death (III, 63).

Liang Chi was so domineering that eight-year-old Emperor Chih
once complained that he was an overbearing general. The emperor
was poisoned by Liang, who disliked his comment (*HHS* 34:15b).
After the death of Emperor Chih, a court conference was held to discuss the appointment of a new emperor; among the participants in the
conference were the Three Lords, officials ranked at fully 2,000 piculs,
and various marquises. The grand commandant, Li Ku, and some
other high officials nominated the king of Ch'ing-ho. This was in
conflict with the grand general, Liang Chi, who wanted to appoint the
marquis of Lü-wu. A conference was again held the next day, and
because they were frightened of Liang Chi, the minister of the masses,

the minister of works, and other officials who were on the side of Li Ku gave up and said, "We follow what you, Grand General, command." Only Li Ku and another official, Tu Ch'iao, insisted. Liang Chi ordered the conference adjourned. Li Ku, who held a top rank in the government, simply was not powerful enough to oppose the dictatorship of Liang Chi. As we have seen, Liang Chi was able to bring about the dismissal and death of both Li Ku and Tu Ch'iao (*HHS* 63:15a ff.). One of the obvious advantages a consort family had over other high officials was that the officials could always be removed from the government through the empress dowager.

Liang Chi continued to dominate the newly appointed emperor, Emperor Huan. All the palace guards and the personal attendants of the emperor were Liang's men, so that everything done by the emperor was reported to Liang (*HHS* 34:20a). It is reported by the historian that all important government affairs were decided by him and that even the emperor had to listen to him and could not interfere. This made the fifteen-year-old emperor very unhappy (III, 63, n. 339, and 64).

The Liang family, like many other powerful families, also engaged in various unlawful activities. It took several thousand free men and made them slaves (II, 78). Liang Chi once offered a gift of four horses to a stingy wealthy man from whom he asked the loan of fifty million cash. When the man gave him only thirty million, Liang became angry and informed the local officials that the man's mother was his escaped slave who had stolen ten bushels of white pearls and a thousand catties of gold from his family. The man was then arrested and subsequently died in prison; all his property, which was appraised at one hundred seventy million, was confiscated (III, 63).

Liang's retainers, who were sent to various foreign countries to look for unusual commodities, demanded all kinds of services from the local officials and oppressed and exploited the people. Many of them were engaged in extortion and other unlawful practices (III, 63). The family also harbored criminals and fugitives (*HHS* 34:19b), and the local authorities dared neither to investigate nor to arrest them.

The Decline of the Consort Families

Although two more consort families rose to power after the downfall of the Liangs, their power was not comparable. In fact, the power of the consort families began to decline toward the end of the Later Han, when control of the government passed increasingly into the hands of

the eunuchs under Emperors Huan and Ling. The eunuchs, who occupied various important posts in the government and exerted great
influence over the emperors, upset the established pattern of power
and constituted a grave threat to the consort families. They attempted
to keep the eunuchs out of government, but the eunuchs were already
too powerful to be curbed. The intensified struggle between the consort
families, supported by the bureaucrats and the students of the Imperial
Academy, and the eunuchs finally led to bloody conflicts and coups
d'état, which caused the downfall of two consort families, the Tou and
the Ho. In the first coup, of 168, the eunuchs killed the empress dowager's father, Tou Wu, and moved the empress dowager to a building
in the Southern Palace, where she later died (*HHS* 10B:12b–13a,
69:6b–8a). In the second coup, of 189, the eunuchs killed the empress
dowager's brother, Ho Chin (*HHS* 10B:17a, 69:16a–b). The power
struggle between the consort families and the eunuchs will be discussed
more fully in a subsequent section on the eunuchs. It will suffice here
merely to mention the decline and downfall of the consort families at
the hands of the eunuchs.

The second coup, which resulted in the downfall of both power
groups, also contributed to the disintegration of the imperial dynasty,
which led to a long period of disorder and disunion. After the coup the
government was in the hands of war lords. General Tung Cho, who
was summoned by Ho Chin to wipe out the eunuchs, dismissed the
young emperor and poisoned Empress Dowager Ho and, later, also
the dismissed emperor. Emperor Hsien, put on the throne by Tung
and entirely at the mercy of Tung and his generals, was forced to move
back and forth between Ch'ang-an and Lo-yang. After the emperor
was moved to Hsü by Ts'ao Ts'ao, he became a puppet of Ts'ao, who
controlled the government and whose associates and relatives commanded the imperial guards. The emperor, unhappy and helpless,
once told Ts'ao, "If you can assist me in government, it is very generous
of you; if not, please be kind enough to leave me alone" (*HHS* 10B:17a–
18a and 20a–b).

As even the emperor himself was at the mercy of Ts'ao Ts'ao, it is
not difficult to understand the position of the consort families. Thus
when Ts'ao wanted to kill a pregnant imperial concubine, whose father, Tung Ch'eng 董承, he had already killed, the emperor was unable
to plead successfully for her (*HHS* 10B:20b). Empress Fu's father, who
was the son-in-law of Emperor Huan, was appointed "general who
supports the state" (*fu-kuo chiang-chün* 輔國將軍) by Emperor Hsien.

But because he realized that he was not in a position to compete with Ts'ao Ts'ao, the man who controlled the government, he declined to accept the post and instead occupied a lesser position. This unprecedented action certainly reflects a decline in the power of the consort families. A later development indicates even more clearly their unfavorable position. Empress Fu, terrified by Ts'ao's killing of the Honorable Lady Tung, wrote to her father about it and urged him to consider the possibility of taking some action. He did not dare to do anything. When her action was disclosed several years later, it greatly angered Ts'ao Ts'ao, who prepared an edict on behalf of the emperor forcing him to dismiss her. He sent his men and troops to the palace to arrest her, and as she was being taken away she walked in bare feet in front of the emperor and said to him, "Can't you save me?" The emperor replied, "I myself do not know when I am going to die." The empress was put in the palace prison, where she died. Her two sons were poisoned, and more than one hundred relatives were put to death (*HHS* 10B:19b–22a).

Ts'ao Ts'ao's own daughter was made empress the following year. This last consort family in the Later Han was rather atypical, for Ts'ao was already the most powerful man in the court and his power was not derived from new consort status.

Jealousy and Politics

Conflicts were found both within the palace and outside. Jealousy prevailed among the ladies in the palace, each seeking the favor of the emperor. But the matter of power also entered the picture and aggravated the conflict, not infrequently leading to violence. Empress Lü mercilessly mutilated Lady Chi, Emperor Kao's favorite concubine whose son almost replaced Empress Lü's son as the heir apparent, and she killed Lady Ch'i's son and three other sons of the emperor (I, 9). Chao Fei-yen 趙飛燕, the favorite concubine and later empress of Emperor Ch'eng, with the consent of the emperor, put to death two babies born to two palace ladies (*HS* 97B:12b ff.).

Jealousy and conflicts led to numerous intrigues, black magic, and accusations within the palace. The consort family members, because of their common interests, were often involved. Obviously they wanted their daughters or sisters to monopolize the favor of the emperor. Thus Ho Kuang, whose granddaughter was the empress, attempted to prevent other imperial concubines from seeing the emperor (*HS*

97A:20b). And his wife murdered Empress Hsü in the hope that her own daughter could be made empress (*HS* 97A:25a–26a). Empress Hsü's sister engaged in black magic, attempting to bring harm to the imperial concubines who were pregnant (*HS* 97B:7b).

Several empresses in the Later Han had no sons. The mother of a prince thus became a potential threat to the empress and her family, and attempts were made to prevent other families from rising to power. Emperor Chang's Empress Tou had no son; she slandered Honorable Lady Sung, the mother of the heir apparent, Ch'ing 慶, and Honorable Lady Liang, the mother of Prince Chao 肇. The first accusation led to the dismissal of the heir apparent and the suicide of his mother. Realizing that the Liangs would come to power sooner or later when Honorable Lady Liang's son became emperor, the Tous then falsely accused Liang Sung, the father of Honorable Lady Liang, of perversion. He died in prison and his family was banished to Chiu-chen (*HHS* 10A:20b–21a, 34:8a–9b).

Empress Yen, of Emperor An who had no son by her, murdered Palace Maid Li who had given birth to the heir apparent, Pao 保, and then urged the emperor to dismiss the heir apparent. When the emperor died Empress Yen and her brother, Yen Hsien, put a king's son on the throne. They also caused the downfall and the death of Crand General Keng Pao, Emperor An's maternal uncle. Several others who were closely associated with him were also involved and suffered punishment. In this way, the Yen family was able to consolidate its power (*HHS* 10B:1b–3b).

Empress Liang had no son. Because of the Liang family neither the mother of Emperor Ch'ung, a woman of a Yü family, nor the mother of Emperor Chih, with the surname Ch'en, received the title of empress dowager (*HHS* 10B:7b).

When an emperor died his consort family usually gave way to a new consort family and power shifted from the one to the other. The top post in the government was then taken over by a member of the new family. The family out of power was naturally not happy about the transfer, and conflicts were inevitable. This was the case between Tou Ying, the nephew of Empress Dowager Tou, the mother of Emperor Ching and grandmother of Emperor Wu, and T'ien Fen, the brother of Empress Dowager Wang, the mother of Emperor Wu. The struggle for power between the two families was intense, including mutual accusations by these two men. It ended only with the defeat and death of Tou Ying in 131 B.C. (III, 16).

The situation became very complicated when there were two or more consort families both related to the same emperor—that is, the consort family of the empress dowager and the consort family of the empress. Furthermore, sometimes there was more than one empress dowager.

Such a complex situation would arise when a prince who was not a blood relation of the empress dowager became emperor; he would then bring onto the political scene his own grandmother and mother and consort families related to each of them. This was the case in the conflict between the Wang family and the Ting and Fu families. Empress Dowager Wang was the mother of Emperor Ch'eng; since Emperor Ch'eng had no son, the future Emperor Ai, who was a prince, was appointed heir apparent. When Emperor Ai ascended the throne in 7 B.C., his grandmother of the Fu family and his mother of the Ting family were both made empress dowagers. Empress Dowager Wang thereupon ordered her nephew, Wang Mang, who was holding the post of grand minister of war to resign and give way to the new consort families (*HS* 98:13a). Several other members of the Wang family were also removed from active political life at the capital: Wang Ken 王根 was ordered by the emperor to return to his fief; Wang K'uang 王況 was not only dismissed from office but was also reduced to commoner status. Furthermore, two members of the family of Emperor Ch'eng's empress—that is, members of Empress Dowager Chao's family—were also deprived of their marquisates and made commoners (*HS* 11:4a). Members of the Fu and Ting families were thereupon ennobled and appointed to official positions. Six members of the Fu family were ennobled as marquises and two members became grand ministers of war. Two members of the Ting family also became marquises, and one member was appointed to the position of grand minister of war (*HS* 19B:17b–18a, 97B:21a–22a). However, the two new consort families collapsed at the death of Emperor Ai, who died without a son. The old consort family, under the protection of Empress Dowager Wang, again came into power. Wang Mang resumed the post of grand minister of war, and all the members of the Fu and Ting families were dismissed from government offices (*HS* 97B:22b). Empress Dowager Chao (Emperor Ch'eng's empress) and Empress Fu of Emperor Ai were both deprived of their empress status and made commoners (*HS* 97B:18a–b, 24a). Another prince was appointed emperor. Fearing that his power might be taken away again by the new consort family, Wang Mang this time manipulated the situation so that the young emperor's mother, of the Wei family, and her brother were not allowed to come to the capital. The struggle for power was so acute that Wang Mang even killed his own son, who had considered Wang Mang's action improper and had attempted to make it possible for the Wei family to come to the capital. Members of the Wei family were also executed because of the plot (I, 38; see also *HS* 99A:20b).

The conflict between Empress Ho and Empress Tung, Emperor Ling's mother, was intense and open. Empress Tung began to have an interest in government affairs after the death of Empress Dowager Tou in A.D. 172. Tung Chung 董忠, her elder brother, was appointed general of chariots and cavalry. When she urged the emperor to appoint Prince Hsieh as the heir apparent, conflict arose between her and Empress Ho, the mother of Prince Pien, who had murdered the mother of Prince Hsieh. When Emperor Ling died and Empress Dowager Ho attended the court in person, her brother, Ho Chin, became the grand general; there was then a struggle for power between the two generals (Ho Chin and Tung Chung) as well as between the empress dowager and Empress Tung. Eventually Empress Tung was ordered by the emperor, at the request of the Ho family, to leave the capital, and Tung Chung committed suicide when troops led by Ho Chin surrounded his residence (*HHS* 10B:13a–14a).

Conflict Between the Emperor and the Consort Families

As indicated in our survey, the consort families were the most powerful group in the Early Han (under Empress Dowager Lü and again toward the end of the period under Empress Dowager Wang); in the Later Han (and especially much of the time from 89 to 189) it was this group that controlled the Han government and dominated the officials. At times they even dominated the emperors, especially when they were young. But it would be an exaggeration to suggest that their power was invulnerable and went unchallenged. On the contrary, they were often challenged by the emperor himself and, in the Later Han, by another power group, the eunuchs. This conflict and struggle for power between the eunuchs and the consort families will be discussed in a later section. Here we discuss only the conflict between the emperor and the consort families.

The struggle for power between the emperor and the consort families was sometimes unavoidable. Emperor Hsüan, who was put on the throne by Grand General Ho Kuang, left all government affairs to the grand general and treated him with extreme politeness. However, he actually felt deeply uneasy, and was not happy that the Ho family had been solidly entrenched for a long time (*HS* 68:12b, 14b, 20b). As soon as Ho Kuang died the emperor himself began to exercise the powers of government and took various measures to reduce the power of the Ho family. Ho family members were removed from key positions, they were deprived of their military power, and incoming memorials were routed directly to the emperor, without going through the regular channel of the master of writing, a post held by Ho Shan (*HS* 68:15b–18a).

A similar relationship existed between Liang Chi and the emperor. The *Hou-Han-shu* notes that the emperor had to listen to Liang and was not able to have a voice in government affairs and that he was also very dissatisfied with the situation (*HHS* 34:23a).

A consort family, no matter how powerful, was not invulnerable. In the last analysis, the emperor, the highest political power, was the source of power. It was he who gave political power to the consort families. As long as the empress and her family won the favor of the emperor, they would remain in power; but there was no assurance that such a relationship could be preserved. If an empress lost favor and was dismissed, the fate of the entire consort family was changed. Because of such developments the Wei family was exterminated (*HS* 97A:13b). In another instance the relatives of Empress Hsü were all sent back to their native place (*HS* 97B:7b). Again, when Empress Yen was dismissed by Emperor Ho because of alleged black magic, one of her brothers, her maternal grandmother, and her grandmother's two sons were all beaten to death in prison; her father committed suicide; her other two brothers and other relatives were exiled to Jih-nan; and all male relatives were dismissed and sent back to their native homes. Those who were exiled were not allowed to return to their native commandery until A.D. 110, when Empress Dowager Teng issued an edict pardoning the Yen family. About five hundred million cash of the family property, which had been confiscated, was given back (*HHS* 10A:22b). When Empress Teng was dismissed by Emperor Huan, her uncle and her cousin died in prison, other relatives were dismissed and sent back to their native commandery, and the family property was confiscated (*HHS* 10B:11b–12a). The father and the brothers of Empress Sung were executed when she was dismissed by Emperor Ling (*HHS* 10B:15a).

The dismissal of an empress was rather exceptional, of course, and some kind of accusation or intrigue was usually involved. A consort family could ordinarily expect to have the protection of an empress, and particularly that of an empress dowager. But, it must be stressed, this largely depended upon the emperor. The Wang brothers, the maternal uncles of Emperor Ch'eng, were powerful because of this kind of relationship. However, when the emperor found out that a terrace in their garden was built like the White Tiger Hall of the palace and scolded them, they wanted to mutilate themselves in order to apologize to the empress dowager. This greatly angered the emperor, who ordered the master of writing to report to him the precedent in which Po Chao, a consort family member, was executed by Emperor Wen. The Wang brothers apologized to the emperor by each carrying an ax on his back. Wang Yin 王音, the general of chariots and cavalry, though not involved, also indicated his guilt by sitting on straws.[118] In the Later Han dynasty Emperor Ho, angry at Tou Hsien because he had forced a princess to sell him a piece of land at a very low price, scolded him and said, "Now even the land of a princess has been taken away unjustly. How much worse it must be with the small people! For the government to get rid of you would be as easy as getting rid of a baby chicken or a rotten rat." Tou Hsien was greatly frightened. The empress, his sister, apologized to the emperor for him (*HHS* 23:19a–b).

These warnings were not merely empty words. In fact, the emperor could cause the downfall of a consort family by any one or more of the following measures: (1) dismiss them, frequently the whole family, (2) send them back to their native commandery, (3) banish them to the frontier, (4) put them in prison, (5) impose the death penalty, and (6) in serious cases, exterminate the whole *tsu*. Several consort families were wiped out by the last method. Officials, who were dominated by members of the consort family when they were in power, would immediately take the opportunity to humiliate them or treat them harshly once they were dismissed, imprisoned, or sent back to their native place by the emperor. Not infrequently many members of consort families were put to death or forced to take their own lives by the local officials.

Emperor Wen put to death his maternal uncle, Po Chao,[119] and Emperor Wu executed Tou Ying, his grandmother's nephew (III, 16). The Shang-kuan family and the Ho family were exterminated by Em-

---

[118] *HS* 98:10b–11b. "Carrying an ax on one's back" suggests execution. "Sitting on straws," according to Yen, suggests that a criminal is going to be executed (*HS* 98:11b).

[119] *HS* 16:3b states that Po Chao was charged with killing a Han official and committed suicide. However, *HS* 98:11a–b says that Emperor Wen executed Po Chao.

peror Chao and Emperor Hsüan respectively. Ho Yün 霍雲, Ho Shan, and Fan Ming-yu 范明友, all relatives of Ho Kuang, upon being accused of plotting a rebellion, committed suicide. Ho Kuang's wife, his son Ho Yü, his daughters, and Teng Kuang-han 鄧廣漢 (another son-in-law) were all executed. Several thousand families that were involved were exterminated (*HS* 68:18b–19a, 97A:20a–b).

Although powerful families became increasingly powerful in the Later Han and most of the consort families had already been powerful before their daughters became empresses, none of them was able to avoid a downfall. I have already mentioned that the Mas, the Tous, and the Liangs—the most powerful families in the days of Liu Hsiu—were unable to protect themselves against the government. They rose to power again only after they had become consort families. Nevertheless, they still could not avoid a precipitous decline in family position. After the death of Empress Dowager Ma in A.D. 79, the Ma brothers were dismissed and sent back to their marquisates. Later Ma Kuang 馬光, one of the brothers, was falsely accused by a slave and committed suicide. His family was then moved to its native commandery, where his son, K'ang 康, was killed by the local authorities. The children of the family were not allowed to return to the capital until a pardon was granted in 113 by Empress Dowager Teng (*HHS* 10A:28a, 24:29a–33a).

A man as powerful as Tou Hsien, who led an expedition that defeated the northern Hsiung-nu, was dismissed by Emperor Ho in 92, and he and his two younger brothers were sent back to their marquisates. Although the empress dowager, Tou Hsien's sister, was still alive, the three brothers were forced to commit suicide by the harsh chancellors appointed by the emperor to supervise them. Apparently the chancellors were encouraged, if not instructed, by the emperor to force the Tou brothers to take their own lives. Their relatives, who were dismissed and sent back to their native commandery, were not allowed to return to the capital until permission was granted by Empress Dowager Teng in 109 (*HHS* 10A:28a, 23:27a–b).

The Teng family also suffered a downfall right after the death of Empress Dowager Teng. Falsely slandered by the emperor's wet nurse, the empress dowager's elder brother, Teng Chih, was dismissed by Emperor An and sent back to his marquisate. His land and property were confiscated. Teng Chih, his son, and his cousins committed suicide. All the family members were dismissed and sent back to their native commandery. Two of his nephews were forced by the local authorities to commit suicide (*HHS* 16:20b–21a). The Yen brothers and their partisans, all of whom were involved in a political intrigue concerning the dismissal of the heir apparent, were executed by Emperor Shun (the dismissed heir apparent). The family members were banished to Pi-ching and the empress dowager was placed in a travel-palace (*HHS* 10B:4a).

Empress Dowager Liang's brother, Liang Chi, who murdered Emperor Chih and put Emperor Huan on the throne, remained in power years after the death of the empress dowager. He had complete control of the government. Even the new emperor was under his domination. As he approached his majority the emperor became less and less tolerant of the situation. The struggle for power between the two eventually led to the downfall of the all-powerful Liang family in 159, after the emperor had been on the throne for twelve years. Although the emperor and five eunuchs planned together to get rid of Liang Chi, the action was initiated and taken by the emperor himself by resorting to the legitimate, supreme power that he possessed. The emperor, formally presiding in the main hall of the palace, summoned the masters of writing, made the necessary announcements, and collected the tallies from the various officials so that they could not be used by the Liangs. Finally, the emperor ordered a eunuch, leading the imperial guards who numbered more than one thousand men, and the colonel-director of retainers to surround Liang's residence. The emperor also ordered his superintendent of the imperial court (*kuang-lu-hsün* 光禄勳), bearing a tally, to take back the seal of the grand general from Liang Chi. Liang Chi's marquisate was drastically reduced, and both he and his wife committed suicide.

Their son, and all relatives of the Liang family and the Sun family, Liang Chi's wife's family, were put in the imperial jail and executed. The family property was confiscated. Several score of high officials who had been close associates of the Liangs were also put to death, and more than three hundred officials who were Liang's former subordinates or guests were dismissed. It was said that the court became empty (*HHS* 34:23a–25a).

An emperor who was of age was usually able to exercise his power to remove a consort family from power and cause its downfall. Only when the government had degenerated to such an extent that the emperor had become a mere figurehead was the emperor unable to challenge the consort families. This was the case with Wang Mang, whose family was in power, under the empress dowager, from 33 B.C. until the end of the Early Han (with the exception of a short interruption between 7 and

1 B.C.). Emperor P'ing, a nine-year-old boy, was completely under the control of Wang Mang, whose daughter became the empress. Wang Mang first became regent, then assumed the title of acting emperor under the two-year-old Ju-tzu Ying, and finally he usurped the throne.[120]

OFFICIALS

High Officials

High officials in the Later Han dynasty were more powerful than their counterparts in the Early Han, for they began to monopolize political power. Family members of high officials often remained in officialdom generation after generation. This period saw the emergence of the *shih-chia* 世家, aristocratic families, who exercised control over the government. In the Early Han there were a few instances in which members of a family held high posts for several generations, but such cases were rare. Beginning with the first century, however, it was much more common. It is frequently mentioned in the *Hou-Han-shu* that the members of families were "2,000-picul officials for generations"; for example, Teng Ch'en (*HHS* 15:10b, and note), Tou Jung (23:6b), Lu Kung 魯恭 (25:5b), Yang Hsü 羊續,[121] Kai Hsün (58:16b, and note), Kung-sun Tsan (73:6b), and Li Chang 李章.[122] Also we find such terms as *chia-shih i-kuan* 家世衣冠, "wearing official garments for generations," being applied to certain people, for example, Chu Hui 朱暉 (43:1a), Kuo Kung 郭躬 (46:1a), Yang She 羊涉 (67:28a), Yin Hsün,[123] Yang Ch'iu 陽球 (77:12a), and Wang Yün 王允 (66:16a). I have already mentioned that the families of both Ma Yüan and Tou Jung had been high officials for generations before they became consort families. The family of Chang T'ang had been prominent since Emperor Wu's time. His great-great-grandson, Chang Ch'un, who served as a high official under Emperor Ai, Emperor P'ing, and Wang Mang, became grand minister

[120] *HS* 99A:5a ff.; Homer H. Dubs, *The History of the Former Han Dynasty*, III (Baltimore: Waverly Press, 1955), 136 ff., hereafter cited as *HFHD*.

[121] *HHS* 31:21a states that his ancestors had been 2,000-picul officials, ministers, and colonels for seven generations. His grandfather was colonel-director of retainers, and his father was grand minister of ceremonies.

[122] *HHS* 77:6a mentions that his ancestors had been 2,000-picul officials for five generations.

[123] *HHS* 67:27a. His uncle, Yin Mu 尹睦, was a minister of the masses, and his brother, Sung 頌, a grand commandant. The source says that many of his kinsmen held superior posts.

of works and thus spoke of himself in a memorial as *lei-shih t'ai-fu*, "assistant to the emperor for generations" (*HHS* 35:1a, 3b, 7b, 8a). In the family of Kuo Kung, a commandant of justice, there were altogether seven commandants of justice, one grand commandant, more than twenty persons who were regional inspectors, officials at the 2,000-picul rank, palace attendants or generals of the gentlemen of the palace, and many others holding the position of attendant secretary (*shih-yü-shih* 侍御史), as well as other lesser posts (*HHS* 46:1a–4b). From K'ung Pa 孔霸 (one of the Nine Ministers during the reign of Emperor Ch'eng) to K'ung Yü 孔昱, members of the family held high positions for seven generations. There were altogether seven marquises and fifty-three persons who occupied the positions of ministers, chancellors, inspectors, and grand administrators (*HHS* 67:32b). In the Ts'ui family, Ts'ui Ch'ao 崔朝 served as attendant secretary under Emperor Chao. His son, Shu 舒, was a grand administrator. The latter had two sons. The eldest, Fa 發, occupied the post of grand minister of works in Wang Mang's time; the younger son, Chuan 篆, during the same period was a grand governor (*ta-yin* 大尹). Chuan's grandson, Yin 駰, was a prefect; Yin's son, Yüan 瑗, a chancellor; Yüan's son, Shih, a grand administrator and master of documents; and Shih's cousin, Lieh 烈, occupied the posts of minister of the masses and grand commandant. Lieh's son, Chün 鈞, was an administrator and was later promoted to colonel of the guards of the city gates. The family was prominent for a period of about three hundred years (*HHS* 52:1a ff.).

Two of the most prominent families in the Later Han were the Yang family and the Yüan family. Both had occupied top posts in the government for generations. In the Yang family, Yang Ch'ang had served as the imperial chancellor under Emperor Chao. Although the family suffered a downfall after the execution of his son, Yang Yün, it rose to prominence again a few generations later when Yang Chen 楊震 (Yang Ch'ang's great-great-grandson) became a minister of the masses and then a grand commandant. His eldest son, Mu 牧, became a chancellor; his younger son, Fu 敷, a palace attendant; and his second son, Ping 秉, reached the post of grand commandant. Ping's son Tz'u 賜 and grandson Piao 彪 both occupied the posts of minister of works, minister of the masses, and grand commandant; thus the family had produced four grand commandants, the highest position, in four successive generations (*HHS* 54:1a ff.).

In the renowned Yüan family, Yüan An 袁安 served as minister of the masses and minister of works. In the second generation, one of his sons,

Ch'ang 敞, became a minister of works; another son, Ching 京, a grand administrator. In the third generation, Yüan T'ang 袁湯 became minister of works, minister of the masses, and grand commandant, and two other family members became superintendents of the imperial court. In the fourth generation, Yüan T'ang's eldest son, Ch'eng 成, who died while still a young man, reached only the post of general of the gentlemen of the palace of the left. But his other two sons reached top positions—Feng 逢 became minister of works and Wei, grand tutor. Yüan Ch'eng's son Shao became a grand commandant and grand general. Yüan Chi 袁基 and Yüan Shu 袁術, sons of Yüan Feng, were grand keeper of equipages and grand administrator, respectively (*HHS* 45:1a ff., 74A:1a ff., 75:8a ff.). It was because of this prominent family background that Yüan Shao and Yüan Shu were able to command the services of a large group of capable men and thereby strive for power with Ts'ao Ts'ao and other ambitious leaders.

Subordinate Officials

I have already mentioned that the posts of subordinate officials of the local government were more or less monopolized by the local powerful families. They remained important in the Later Han. Their power is clearly indicated during the time of the rebellion against Wang Mang. A jail officer (and later a student) led several score of retainers to join Liu Hsiu and became one of his meritorious generals (*HHS* 20:4a–b). Another subordinate official of a local government, Wang Tan 王丹, whose family had accumulated a wealth of one thousand catties of gold, led his retainers to present one thousand piculs of grain to Liu Hsiu's general, Teng Yü, who did not have enough rations for his troops (*HHS* 27:5a). Among the various rebels a subordinate official of a prefectural government, Ch'in Feng 秦豐, raised enough troops to conquer several cities and had several myriad of soldiers under his command (*HHS* 17:19a–b, note). P'eng Ch'ung 彭寵, who was appointed by the Keng-shih emperor as the general of the flank (*p'ien-chiang-chün* 偏將軍) and the acting grand administrator of Yü-yang, had been a subordinate official in a commandery office. He was loyal to Liu Hsiu at first, but later rebelled and made himself the king of Yen (*HHS* 12:12b ff.).

As a power group, subordinate officials were in a position to abuse their power, interfere with the government administration, or even engage in unlawful activities. Liu Chieh 劉節, a subordinate official of a commandery, had under his control a thousand families of retainers, and many of them were engaged in robbery. The Liu family never rendered any labor or military service to the government. Once when the prefect wanted to enlist some of Liu's retainers, a subordinate official advised the prefect not to attempt it because the Liu family had never rendered such service. Not accepting the advice, the prefect told Liu to comply with his order. Liu hid the retainers and told the investigator of transgressions (*tu-yu* 督郵) to charge the prefectural government with recruiting troops. In great distress, a subordinate official of the prefecture requested permission to render the service on behalf of Liu's retainers. Finally the prefect reported the case to the grand administrator, and because of his intervention Liu was forced to join the troops on behalf of his retainers.[124] In another instance, a prefect wanted to punish one of his subordinate officials, Ssu Ts'ung 斯從, who was engaged in *yu-hsia* and unlawful activities. Another subordinate official advised him not to take such action, saying that Ssu was a member of a big family, that he had many followers in the locality, and that they would rebel if Ssu were punished. The prefect, who was extremely angry, executed Ssu. Consequently, Ssu's kinsmen and followers gathered a force of more than a thousand men and attacked the prefectural city.[125]

EUNUCHS

The Emergence of Powerful Eunuchs in Ch'in and Han

Eunuchs have had a long history in China. The first powerful eunuch, Chao Kao, came to power after the death of the First Emperor, who died during a tour on which he was accompanied by his youngest son and the imperial chancellor, Li Ssu. Taking advantage of this unusual opportunity, Chao Kao succeeded in convincing the imperial chancellor to enthrone not the oldest prince but a younger son, with whom Chao was closely associated. By this means he was able to build up his own power. At first there was cooperation between Chao and the imperial chancellor, but after the younger prince ascended the throne, Chao took steps to enhance his own position at the expense of the imperial chancellor. The imperial chancellor was kept from seeing the emperor and finally was slandered, imprisoned, and executed. Thereafter the eunuch was appointed imperial chancellor with powers unparalleled

[124] *SKC*, Wei, 12:20b–21a.
[125] *SKC*, Wei, 11:14b.

in subsequent Chinese history. Actually he enjoyed a combination of two kinds of power: that of an imperial chancellor, who by occupying the highest bureaucratic power position was able to control all officials; and that of a chief eunuch, who because of his close association with the emperor was able to control the emperor's person. He finally murdered the young emperor and appointed another prince in his place. It was reported by the historian that Chao even intended to make himself emperor (III, 7, n. 54).

The power of the eunuchs in the Early Han was not very striking. Although Emperor Wu employed eunuchs as prefects of the palace writers to handle documents, they were not entrusted with power and therefore were not politically influential. Eunuchs did not become powerful until the time of Emperor Yüan (48 to 33 B.C.), when the emperor, who did not enjoy good health, entrusted Hung Kung 弘恭 and Shih Hsien with government affairs. Thereafter all matters had to be reported to these powerful eunuchs, and decisions were then made by the emperor through them.[126]

Since Hung and Shih were the first powerful eunuchs in the history of Early Han—no eunuchs had held such power in the previous one hundred and sixty years—this inevitably led to a struggle for power between this group, which included some officials, and other officials. Thus the general of the van, Hsiao Wang-chih 蕭望之, who had been the emperor's tutor when he was heir apparent, requested that the eunuchs be removed from their posts as palace writers. But his suggestion was not accepted by the emperor. Instead, Hsiao was accused by the eunuchs, dismissed, and finally committed suicide when his arrest was ordered (*HS* 78:11a–14b). Many other officials who made accusations against Hung or Shih found themselves facing countercharges brought by the eunuchs; these officials were either punished, executed, or forced to commit suicide (*HS* 73:5a, 75:8a and 11a). Thus all officials became fearful of Shih (Hung died within a few years after Emperor Yüan came to the throne) and did not dare to show disrespect (*HS* 73:4b–5b). Even the imperial chancellor and the grandee secretary complied with his requests and did not dare to mention his faults (*HS* 76:24a–b). On the other hand, officials who were attached to him received high official posts (*HS* 73:5b). One who had lost his post because he had criticized Shih was finally convinced by a friend that he

---

[126] III, 32. On the duties of the prefect of palace writers or prefect of the internuncios of the palace writers *(chung-shu yeh-che ling* 中書謁者令), see *HHC* 26:8a; *HKI* A:20b; *HCI* 1:3a; *HCIPI* A:4b; see also III, 38, n. 215.

must flatter and cooperate with Shih if he wished a successful official career (*HS* 64B:18b–19a). As a matter of fact, the appointment of officials was completely manipulated by Shih, who by various arguments was able to control the emperor. One official was sent out of the capital as a grand administrator because Shih considered the man's close contact with the emperor to be a threat to his own position (*HS* 75:8b). The brother of an imperial concubine, who was recommended by certain officials as a candidate for the post of grandee secretary, did not receive the appointment because Shih convinced the emperor that a member of a consort family should not be appointed to such a high-ranking post (III, 32).

When Emperor Ch'eng ascended the throne he dismissed Shih and abolished the office that Shih had occupied—an office that had given eunuchs control of documents. Reverting to the system in effect prior to Emperor Wu's time, he assigned the duty of handling government documents to ordinary officials instead of the eunuchs.[127] Thereafter, in the remaining years of Early Han, no other eunuch was ever as powerful as Shih Hsien had been.

Eunuchs became very powerful in the Later Han when Emperor Kuang-wu began to replace the ordinary officials with eunuchs in all posts within the palace. Positions, such as regular palace attendant, that had been given to officials other than eunuchs in Early Han were now exclusively held by the eunuchs.[128] This institutional change was very significant in the development of the power of the eunuchs. The regular palace attendant was an important official whose duty it was to serve as an attendant to the emperor; he was to answer any question the emperor might ask, and thus served more or less in the capacity of an adviser.[129] According to Chu Mu 朱穆, who urged the emperor to use ordinary officials to replace the eunuchs for this position, the occupant was entrusted with the power of overseeing the affairs of the masters of writing (*HHS* 43:17b). The lesser attendant of the Yellow Gate (*hsiao huang-men* 小黃門), though inferior to the regular palace attendant, also was an important official. It was his duty to wait on the emperor, receive documents from the masters of writing, and maintain communication between the palace and the outer court when the emperor was

[127] III, 32. The post of prefect of the internuncios of the palace writers was abolished by Emperor Ch'eng in 29 B.C., and in its place there was established a prefect of the palace internuncios (*chung yeh-che ling* 中謁者令); see *HS* 10:4b–5a, 19A:9a; *HHC* 26:8a; and *HCI* A:3a.

[128] *HHS* 43:17a–18a, 78:3a; *HKI* A:18b.

[129] *HHC* 26:5a.

in the inner court. He also maintained very close contact between the palaces of the empress and of the emperor.[130]

The post of regular palace attendant, which was the highest post held by a eunuch, was raised from the rank of 1,000 piculs to the equivalent of 2,000 piculs, and the number of such posts was also increased from four to ten. These changes signify the importance of eunuchs in the Later Han government. At the same time, the number of positions of lesser attendant of the Yellow Gate was increased from ten to twenty (*HHS* 78:3a–b).

There was a close connection between the rise to power of the eunuchs and the empress dowager's participation in affairs of state. According to Chu Mu, when Empress Dowager Teng participated in government affairs, she did not personally receive the officials; hence she relied upon the eunuchs, as regular palace attendants and lesser attendants of the Yellow Gate, to serve as a medium between herself and the emperor. From this time on, as Chu informed the emperor, the eunuchs were able to grab power from their ruler (*HHS* 43:18a).

A eunuch was ennobled as marquis for the first time when Cheng Chung 鄭眾 helped Emperor Ho remove Tou Hsien from his position of power in 92. Until then this noble rank had been enjoyed only by imperial relatives, members of consort families, imperial chancellors, and other meritorious officials. Thereafter, the emperor usually called upon Cheng for advice, and, the historian remarked, from this time on the eunuchs began grasping for power (III, 58; *HHS* 23:26b–27a, 78:3a–b).

The eunuchs were somewhat overshadowed by the all-powerful consort families, the Teng and the Liang, in the first half of the second century. But they became extremely powerful, and began to monopolize the power, after they had wiped out the Liang family in 159. Thereafter, in the reigns of both Emperor Huan and Emperor Ling, power was in the hands of the eunuchs until the rebellion of Tung Cho in 189. Court affairs were dominated by the powerful eunuchs. The appointment and dismissal of officials was under their control. A rich man who offered a bribe to a powerful eunuch was appointed inspector (III, 69). Another official was promoted to the post of grand commandant because of bribery of the eunuchs (*HHS* 78:14a). Many officials who sought their favor were obedient and submissive to them (*HHS* 65:15b). Those who disobeyed their orders were either dismissed or punished. In 172 Liu Meng 劉猛, the colonel-director of retainers, was

[130] *HHC* 26:5b–6a.

ordered to find and arrest the men who had written on the gate of the palace the charge that Empress Dowager Tou was murdered by the eunuchs, Ts'ao Chieh 曹節 and Wang Fu. Liu Meng sympathized with the offenders and intentionally delayed his action; this displeased the eunuchs and he was demoted. Tuan Ying 段熲 who was then appointed colonel-director of retainers, dealt with the matter in accordance with the will of the eunuchs and arrested more than a thousand persons. Under the instructions of the two eunuchs and in cooperation with them, he also brought an accusation against Liu Meng, who was then punished (III, 68). Many other officials were also punished and some even lost their lives because of their accusations of the powerful eunuchs (III, 64, 65; *HHS* 54:9a–b, 78:31a–b).

The eunuchs were given even more power by Emperor Ling, who appointed a eunuch to one of the eight newly created positions of colonel. The military power entrusted to the eunuch was so great that he actually was the marshal (*yüan-shuai* 元帥) who not only controlled the colonel-director of retainers but also had the grand general under his command (III, 71). The position of grand general, a post usually held by a member of the consort family in Later Han, was no longer that of the supreme commander-in-chief; the highest military power was shifted from the consort family to the eunuchs, although the former still held the title of grand general. This situation led to a more acute conflict between the two groups. Another one of the eunuchs was appointed general of chariots and cavalry, a post second only to grand general (*HHS* 78:34a).

Although eunuchs normally were not married and had no children, they should not be thought of merely as powerful individuals; they must be considered members of powerful families. From A.D. 135 on, eunuchs were allowed to adopt a son so that he could inherit their noble titles. Moreover, brothers, uncles, nephews, and adopted sons of many powerful eunuchs were grand administrators and prefects and held other government positions in the times of Emperors Shun, Huan, and Ling.[131] This created a power network with the eunuchs as the nucleus and their family members as the local agents. Thus power in the hands of the eunuchs meant that there were powerful families, not merely powerful individuals, attached to the palace. This made their control of the power mechanism more extensive and therefore more complete.

Those relatives of eunuchs who were appointed grand administrators

[131] *HHS* 6:15b, 57:19a, 54:15a, 16b–17a, 18b, 21a–22b, and 31a.

and prefects were much more powerful than ordinary local officials. Relying upon their personal connections with the eunuchs, they were violent and abusive; some of them even engaged in various kinds of illegal activities (III, 64, 65, 68, 69). Since such officials were supported and protected by their powerful eunuch relatives, very few other officials—even those holding superior posts—dared to interfere with their activities. A few conscientious officials who accused or punished them were usually falsely charged by the eunuchs before the emperor, and as a result were either dismissed or punished (III, 64, 68).

Conflicts Between Eunuchs and Consort Families

The growth of eunuch power inexorably led to conflicts between the eunuchs and the consort families who had long monopolized political power. The first broke out in 92 when Emperor Ho sought the help of a eunuch, Cheng Chung, in a plot against the Tou family. As we have seen, Tou Hsien was dismissed and forced to commit suicide (*HHS* 23:26b–27a, 78:3a and 6a). The eunuchs won again in a conflict with the consort family in 121; this clash led to the downfall of the powerful Teng family (*HHS* 16:20a–21a). Such conflicts continued throughout the history of the Later Han and were intensified as the eunuchs became increasingly powerful.

But these struggles for power were not always simply a matter of the eunuchs fighting a particular consort family. Sometimes they opposed a group composed of consort family members and other eunuchs. While Emperor Shun was still heir apparent, he was slandered by two eunuchs, Chiang Ching and Fan Feng 樊豐, and dismissed. When Emperor An died, Empress Dowager Yen and her brother Yen Hsien placed an infant on the throne. This young emperor died within a year, and Yen, in cooperation with Chiang, decided to appoint another prince as emperor. Before this prince arrived Sun Ch'eng 孫程 and eighteen other eunuchs plotted a coup d'état, killed Chiang and two other eunuchs of his group, and welcomed the dismissed heir apparent and made him emperor. General Yen and his brothers were arrested and executed, and the empress dowager was removed from the palace to a travel-palace where she died a year later. Sun Ch'eng and the other eighteen eunuchs were all ennobled as marquises. Furthermore, Sun and two other eunuchs were appointed chief commandants of cavalry (*ch'i tu-wei* 騎都尉) (*HHS* 6:1a–3a, 78:7b–12a). Appointments to this position placed eunuchs in command of a part of the imperial army in the capital, apparently giving them military power that made them more powerful than before.

The Liang family and the eunuchs maintained friendly relations with each other for their mutual advantage. Thus Liang Chi ordered his two sons to become friends of an important eunuch (*HHS* 34:12a–b). When Liang Chi became grand general, he was closely associated with Ts'ao T'eng 曹騰, a powerful eunuch; the appointment of Emperor Huan was initiated by these two men (*HHS* 63:16a–b). Liang Chi also cooperated with eunuchs in the killing of Tu Ch'iao, a top official (*HHS* 63:23b–24a). But eventually it was a small group of eunuchs, working with Emperor Huan, who in 159 managed to bring about the downfall of the Liang family, which had been in power for more than twenty years. The five eunuchs Emperor Huan had consulted who were instrumental in the coup were all ennobled for their meritorious service (III, 64; see also *HHS* 34:23b–24a).

After the downfall of this most powerful consort family, the power of the eunuchs went almost unchallenged. The government was practically under their control. Since the eunuchs constituted a great threat to the consort families, the struggle between the two became intensified. The consort families, realizing that they were too weak to challenge the eunuchs alone, began to cooperate with the officials, who were also threatened by the eunuchs, in a desperate fight against them. An open conflict broke out in 168 when Empress Dowager Tou personally attended the court and her father, Tou Wu, the grand general, backed by other high officials, attempted to remove all the eunuchs from power. One of the regular palace attendants was killed, but before the others could be arrested the eunuchs—through the twelve-year-old emperor, whom they controlled—issued an edict ordering the arrest of the grand general. With several thousand soldiers under his command, he attempted to use his forces to overcome them. But the eunuchs were able to mobilize the imperial guards and other troops to challenge him. He was defeated and committed suicide because the majority of his troops feared the eunuchs and had surrendered. The empress dowager was then removed from the palace, and the grand tutor, who had been cooperating with the grand general, was arrested and killed. The victorious eunuchs, Ts'ao Chieh, Wang Fu, and others, were all ennobled (III, 66; see also III, 68).

The final conflict between the two broke out in 189 when Emperor Ling died. The eunuch who held the post of colonel and the grand general each attempted to destroy the other. The grand general, Ho

Chin, won the first victory by killing the eunuch colonel and taking command of his troops. But because of what had happened to Tou Wu (his troops had surrendered to the eunuchs), Ho Chin did not trust these troops so he summoned General Tung Cho and his army to the capital. The empress dowager was forced to dismiss all those eunuchs who held the posts of regular palace attendants and lesser attendants of the Yellow Gate. But Ho himself was killed by the eunuchs when he went to visit the empress dowager at the palace. In retaliation all the eunuchs were killed by the troops under the command of Ho's subordinates and other generals, who attacked and burned the palace. The eunuchs were completely destroyed, but the incident also led to years of disorder that ultimately caused the overthrow of the Han dynasty (III, 71).

An analysis of the activities of the eunuchs reveals that their intimacy with both the emperor and the empress dowager certainly was one of the crucial reasons for their almost unchallengeable power. They were usually trusted by the emperor, who thought that they had no connections outside the palace and were, therefore, trustworthy and reliable (III, 32). Because of their intimacy they were in a better position than others to influence the emperor. The officials, including members of the consort family, who were unable to see the emperor very often, were definitely in a disadvantageous position. This strategy was used by Chao Kao to limit the imperial chancellor's access to the emperor, thus weakening the power of the imperial chancellor (III, 4; *SC* 87:13b–14a). The intimacy between the emperor and the eunuchs also provided opportunities for the eunuchs to slander officials and members of consort families, many of whom lost their positions and lives because they had no chance to explain or appeal charges brought against them (III, 4, 65; *HS* 78:7b–8a; *HHS* 54:9a–b, 63:6a). Frequently their memorials were held by eunuchs and never presented to the emperor. In this way the crimes of some eunuchs that were reported in memorials could not be made known to the emperor, and the officials who made the reports were frequently falsely accused by the eunuchs and were punished. Even an heir apparent was slandered by the eunuchs and was subsequently dismissed, and a prince was slandered and executed (*HHS* 15:20a; III, 68). These instances indicate that since the eunuchs were closer to the emperor than the heir apparent, the heir apparent was unable to protect himself from slander.

Since eunuchs were in charge of issuing imperial edicts, one of the methods of manipulating power that they frequently employed was to announce or issue a false edict in the name of the emperor. False edicts were issued by powerful eunuchs to order the ministry of agriculture to supply funds, lumber, and convicts to build private homes and gardens for them (*HHS* 54:7a, 9a). In the coup d'état of 168, false edicts were issued to appoint one of the eunuchs to lead an army to arrest and kill the grand general, Tou Wu. Another general was also ordered to participate in the war against Tou (III, 66, 68; *HHS* 65:14b). Grand General Ho Chin was also summoned by a false edict of the empress dowager and killed by the eunuchs (III, 71).

Government officials had little direct access to an empress dowager, whereas eunuchs were the only men close to her, so the relationship between her and the eunuchs was much the same as between the emperor and the eunuchs. The eunuchs could avail themselves of this intimacy in order to enhance their own power; thus eunuchs were always most powerful when an empress dowager personally attended the court. For example, the fact that the power of the eunuchs was greatly increased when Empress Dowager Teng attended court was the subject of a complaint by a contemporary Han official (*HHS* 43:17b–18a, 78:3b). Actually, when an empress dowager nominally attended court, the government was either in the hands of members of the consort family or a group of eunuchs she trusted and relied upon.

Although the members of a consort family were blood relatives of an empress dowager, the eunuchs were still closer to her and had more opportunities to influence her. This accounts for the defeat of the consort family members. A nephew of Empress Dowager Teng was not allowed to enter the palace because a palace maid had slandered him. She formerly had been the Teng family's slave girl and was angry at Teng because he could not tolerate her impoliteness and had scolded her (*HHS* 10A:35b). Thus discord between an empress dowager and her relatives could be caused by a close attendant. The defeat of the two consort families, Tou and Ho, also shows that no matter how close the ties were between the empress dowager and her relatives, they always had less influence with her than a eunuch. Tou Wu, the father of the empress dowager, was unable to convince his daughter to remove all the eunuchs from their positions of power and have them killed. Her hesitation finally led to the coup in which Tou Wu was killed and she was removed from the palace (III, 66). Empress Dowager Ho also rejected her brother's proposal to kill all the powerful eunuchs. She did not dismiss them until she was forced to under the threat of military action. Her indecisiveness and the recall of the powerful eunuchs into the palace finally led to the death of her brother (III, 71).

Conflicts Between Eunuchs and the Officials

Traditionally, political power had been distributed between the officials and the consort family members, but the emergence of powerful eunuchs upset the established pattern. The officials, like the consort families, did not want their powers infringed upon by a new rival group; therefore, whenever the eunuchs came to power they met strong opposition from the officials. When Shih Hsien was appointed to the post of palace writer, an office in charge of memorials, Hsiao Wang-chih and other officials strongly opposed giving a eunuch such an important office (III, 32; *HS* 78:11a–b). Many other officials focused their attacks on the faults and unlawful activities of the powerful eunuchs (III, 32). The eunuchs, on the other hand, did everything possible to defend their newly acquired power and used every means to counterattack. Hsiao Wang-chih and many others were defeated and lost their lives (III, 32; *HS* 78:13a–14b). But, as we have seen, while this attempt by the eunuchs was the most notable one in the Early Han period, it was also relatively short-lived; the dismissal of Shih Hsien by Emperor Ch'eng marked the end of the eunuch threat to the power of the officials in the Early Han.

Eunuchs were more firmly established and more powerful in the Later Han, and thus the conflict between the two groups was also more intense. First of all, eunuchs were entrusted with more power, and in using it they grossly interfered with the exercise of the bureaucratic power of the officials. It was because of their growing power that Li Ku and others requested the removal of eunuchs from their positions (*HHS* 63:5a–b). Moreover, the appointment of relatives of eunuchs to the positions of grand administrators and prefects also produced a ceaseless conflict between the eunuch group and the local officials. The violence and unlawful actions of the eunuchs and their relatives made it very difficult to carry on routine administrative tasks, especially the administration of justice. Officials had to tolerate the situation or risk being punished for challenging the eunuchs. Many officials, central and local, who attempted to reduce the power of eunuchs or to charge them with their unlawful activities were punished and lost their lives (III, 64, 65, 69; *HHS* 66:11a, 16a–b, 29a–b, 33a–b).

The students of the Imperial Academy, who were potential members of officialdom, shared a common interest with the officials. They saw the rise of the eunuchs as a threat to the political order and the bureau-

cracy itself, so they joined the officials in the struggle against them.
When in 153 an inspector, Chu Mu, was dismissed and sentenced to
forced labor for his opposition to the eunuchs, several thousand students
presented memorials to Emperor Huan to request that the innocent
official be released. The request was granted (*HHS* 43:15b–17a). In
another instance, more than three hundred students presented memorials to appeal for the release of another official, Huang-fu Kuei 皇甫規,
who had offended the eunuchs and was sentenced to forced labor
(*HHS* 65:8b).

As the eunuchs became increasingly powerful and a threat to both
the consort families and the officials, men of the two groups began to
realize that they were not strong enough as individuals or separate
groups to challenge the powerful eunuchs. Effective opposition seemed
possible only by mutual support and joint action. A number of officials,
under the leadership of Li Ying, the colonel-director of retainers, did
everything in their power to curb the eunuchs, but their efforts had the
opposite result. The coalition, which was superior in number and,
apparently, in influence, certainly constituted a great threat to the
eunuchs. But it also had one important weakness: it was exposed to the
danger of being accused of being a clique. The formation of a clique
would very likely have been considered a threat to the emperor and
would not have been tolerated by him. The eunuchs centered their
attack precisely on this charge, which finally led to the proscription of
the officials and the imperial students.

The first proscription took place in 166. The leader of the officials,
Li Ying, who had killed a man closely associated with the eunuchs,
was accused by them of forming a clique with other officials and the
students. Li Ying, Tu Mi 杜密, and many others, numbering over two
hundred, were arrested by Emperor Huan. The empress's father,
Tou Wu, and other officials petitioned the emperor on behalf of the
accused officials, whereupon they were released. But they were forever
prohibited from entering officialdom (*HHS* 7:23b–24a, 67:5a–6a, and
35a, 69:1b–3b).

When Empress Dowager Tou attended the court in person and her
father, Tou Wu, was appointed grand general in 168, an alliance was
formed with the consort family and a number of officials as its core and
with students of the Imperial Academy, numbering more than thirty
thousand, as the main supporters. The group was determined to wipe
out the eunuchs once and for all (*HHS* 67:5a, 69:4a ff.). That year
an open conflict broke out that led instead to the downfall of the Tous

and the death of the grand tutor, Ch'en Fan, a leader of the officials
who was closely associated with Tou in the fight against the eunuchs.
A year later, Chang Chien 張儉, Li Ying, Tu Mi, and many other officials were again accused by the eunuchs of forming a clique and
threatening the security of the government. More than one hundred
officials were arrested and executed, and six to seven hundred officials
were dismissed and prevented forever from entering officialdom. This
second proscription marked the greatest victory of the eunuchs, for
they defeated both the consort family and the officials associated with
it. In 176 more than a thousand students of the Imperial Academy
were arrested, and all the kin, disciples, and former subordinate officials of the Partisans were forever prohibited from entering officialdom.
The Partisans were not pardoned until the Yellow Turban Rebellion
broke out in 184 (*HHS* 8:4a, 8b, and 14b, 67:6b–9b, 16a–b, and 29a–b).

Wealthy Merchants

Wealthy merchants and landlords, who possessed the major means of
production, the land, controlled the supply of capital in the market,
commanded the services of others, enjoyed a superior status, and associated closely with the nobles and officials, remained a power group
in the Later Han.

They were, in fact, very active in the power struggle against Wang
Mang, playing a positive role in re-establishing the ruling house of the
Later Han. Among the prominent large families in Nan-yang, where
Liu Hsiu's family and landed property were located, three were big
merchants and landlords. All three had marital ties with the renowned
Liu family, and became its strong supporters; in fact, together they
constituted the backbone of Liu Hsiu's force. Li T'ung, a member of
a prominent family that had been engaged in trade for generations
(II, 51), married Liu Hsiu's sister. But Li T'ung's background was not
exclusively in the sphere of trade. His father, Li Shou 李守, had served
as an official under Wang Mang. Li T'ung himself had previously
served as a petty official, but since his family was wealthy and his behavior was such that he acted as a "cock of the walk" in his village, he
felt unhappy about occupying a low position and therefore resigned.
Thus, notes the *Hou-Han-shu,* it was as a commoner that Li T'ung began
his rebellion (*HHS* 15:4b). For his decision to join Liu Hsiu's rebellion
against Wang Mang—a decision that resulted in the death of his father and sixty-four other family members—he was rewarded with

great success in his political career: he was appointed grand minister of works by Emperor Kuang-wu.

The Fan family, a merchant-landlord family with three hundred *ch'ing* of land (I, 40), also intermarried with the Lius. One girl of the Fan family married Liu Hsiu's father and another married one of his relatives, Liu Hung 劉弘. Fan Hung, the maternal uncle of Liu Hsiu, married the latter's paternal cousin (*HHS* 14:19b).

Liu Hsiu married a daughter of the Yin family, a wealthy landlord family that owned over seven hundred *ch'ing* of land (*HHS* 32:16b–17a, 10A:9a–b). Furthermore, the Yin family intermarried with the prominent Teng family, also of Nan-yang, members of which had been 2,000-picul officials for generations (*HHS* 10A:9b, 15:10b). The marital ties between these three wealthy families (the Fan, Yin, and Teng) and the Liu family clearly show the power and influence of the wealthy merchants and landlords at that time. Liu Hsiu eagerly sought their support, which derived from their economic power; such economic based support clearly contributed to his political success. These ties also made it possible for the families to be successful in their political careers. They gained political positions that helped them consolidate and enhance their economic power; for example, five members of the Fan family were made marquises, and the family received government gifts totaling fifty million cash (*HHS* 32:4a–b).

The description of the activities and power of wealthy merchants in the Early Han applies equally to their counterparts in the Later Han. It suffices here to quote a statement of Chung-ch'ang T'ung that sums up his assessment of the power and influence of the wealthy merchants in his time (*HHS* 49:25b–26a):

> The powerful men are engaged in trade. Their houses spread over all the divisions and commanderies. Their landed property extends in all directions. Although they do not even have the title of a petty officer, they wear the ornamented garments of officials. Although they are not even the head of a unit of five families, they have the services of one thousand households [which is equivalent to the total households] in a famous city. Their glories and pleasures surpass those of the feudal lords and their influence is equal to that of a grand administrator or a prefect. They are engaged in profitmaking. They are not punished when they break the law. The assassins and those who are willing to die for others devotedly offer their services to them.

With such power, they were really awe inspiring in the eyes of the people. There was a case in which two wealthy merchants, Kao and

Ts'ai, were feared, and therefore served, by the people of the community. To refuse to serve such families was to incur their hatred—this was the fate of a scholar who lived near the Kao and Ts'ai families but refused to associate with them (*HHS* 67:20b).

Yu-hsia

Pan Ku mentions that the administration of Emperor Kuang-wu and Emperor Ming aimed at suppressing the strong and supporting the weak and that, as a result, there were no powerful *yu-hsia* (*hao-chieh chih hsia* 豪桀之俠) in the local communities (*HS* 23:22a). There is no detailed information regarding the suppression of the strong, particularly the government policy dealing with *yu-hsia*. Perhaps there is some connection between Pan's statement and the data found in the *Hou-Han-shu* that in the early years of the reign of Emperor Kuang-wu the meshes of the law were loose and the various kings were fond of associating with guests; but in A.D. 52, when a king who had sent a guest to assassinate someone was imprisoned by the emperor, many guests of the various kings were executed, and consequently the kings began to observe the law.[132] The *Hou-Han-shu* also states that King Ying of Ch'u, who was fond of *yu-hsia*, associated with guests. Later, in A.D. 70, when the king was charged with perversion, more than a thousand persons were involved. They were either executed or moved by the government (*HHS* 2:21b, 42:7b and 9a–b). Besides imperial relatives, feudal lords, and officials, *hao-chieh* of the various commanderies and prefectures were involved in the case. Apparently *yu-hsia* were included in this category. It is probably true that the government was more strict in this period in an attempt to control the activities of the kings and their guests, and that as a result the nobles were more restrained in their association with the guests, particularly the dangerous *yu-hsia*.

But this does not mean that the *yu-hsia* as a group waned and disappeared in Han society. Pan Ku's statement quoted above seems to be exaggerated. There are indications that the group was still very active in society. As usual, many officials were known to be fond of *hsia* and engaged in *hsia*-type activities. Such persons are definitely found in the transitional period between Early and Later Han, for instance, Liu Yen (Po-sheng) (*HHS* 1A:1b), Tou Jung (23:1b), and Wei Ao's uncle,

---

[132] *HHS* 42:5b–6a. According to *HHS* 1B:27b, several thousand guests of various kings and marquises were put to death.

Wei Ts'ui 隗崔 (13:1a, 9b). Many officials in later days were known for
their *hsia* activities: Ma Yen, Ma Tun 馬敦,[133] Tu Pao 杜保,[134] Tung
Cho,[135] Yüan Shao,[136] and Yüan Shu.[137] Unfortunately there are no
biographies of *yu-hsia* in the *Hou-Han-shu*, so very little information
concerning this group is available, especially regarding the *yu-hsia*
among the common people. Fragmentary information is given only
incidentally in the biographies of certain well-known officials. However,
there is no reason to assume that there were no *yu-hsia* among the lesser
officials and the commoners. The *San-kuo-chih* mentions at least two
cases in which a subordinate official was a *hsia*[138] and three cases in
which the *hsia* were commoners.[139]

Moreover, *yu-hsia* remained a local power group in society. Relying
on physical force, like their counterparts in the earlier period, they
controlled the activities of others, frequently interfered with the government administration, and violated the law. There was a man named
Sun, who is described in the history as "powerful and *hsia*"; his followers and guests frequently violated the law. Robbers often took refuge in his home, and officers were unable to arrest them. Once a determined prefect led his men to surround the Sun family home, whereupon the family resisted arrest by fighting.[140] In another instance, a
subordinate official, who was "powerful and *hsia*," had a thousand
guest families under his control, and they were also robbers.[141] Another
subordinate official is said to have engaged in *hsia* and illicit activities.
When he was executed by the prefect, his followers and kinsmen gathered a force of a thousand men to attack the prefect.[142]

A *yu-hsia* who was able to command the obedience of his followers
often became the leader of a well-organized group and engaged in
hazardous adventures. Li T'ung 李通, a well-known *hsia* who led a
group of followers in an uprising during the time of the Yellow Turban

[133] Both were Ma Yüan's nephews. Ma Yüan, who was concerned over their
activities, wrote a letter to warn them (*HHS* 24:18b–20a).

[134] Tu Pao, a major of the elite cavalry (*yüeh-ch'i ssu-ma* 越騎司馬), was described by
Ma Yüan as a person engaged in *hsia* activities and fond of righteousness (*HHS*
42:20a).

[135] *HHS* 72:1a; *SKC*, Wei, 6:1a.
[136] *SKC*, Wei, 1:1b.
[137] *HHS* 68:10a, 74A:1b, note, 75:18b; *SKC*, Wei, 6:32a.
[138] *SKC*, Wei, 12:20b–21a; *SKC*, Wu, 15:1a.
[139] *SKC*, Wei, 11:14b, 18:2b–3a; *SKC*, Wu, 10:11b–12a.
[140] *SKC*, Wei, 11:14b.
[141] *SKC*, Wei, 12:20b–21a.
[142] *SKC*, Wu, 15:1a.

Rebellion, killed another powerful local leader and took over the two thousand families under his command. Li T'ung also captured a general of the Yellow Turbans. He joined Ts'ao Ts'ao and was subsequently made a general of the palace gentlemen.[143] Kan Ning was a *hsia* who gathered together a number of young daredevils and became their leader; they usually carried weapons when they traveled. They were friendly to the local officials and the people who treated them nicely, but robbed those who were not accommodating. They also deliberately committed crimes in the territory within the jurisdiction of the officials who had offended them. Kan engaged in this kind of activity for about twenty years; then he became interested in reading books.[144]

---

[143] *SKC*, Wei, 18:2b–3a. This Li T'ung is not to be confused with the Li T'ung of the same name who collaborated with Emperor Kuang-wu.

[144] *SKC*, Wu, 10:11b–12a.

Part Two: Documents of Han Social Structure

I

KINSHIP AND MARRIAGE

1. COLLECTIVE RESPONSIBILITY

In the twentieth year [of Duke Wen of Ch'in] the law for the first 746 B.C. time contained [the provision of] the punishment of the three tsu¹ [of the criminal]. [*SC* 5:6b]

¹ Thus Yang Chung said, "The government of Ch'in was cruel and severe. . . . When one man was guilty, [the punishment] was extended to his three *tsu*" (*HHS* 48:1b). There were different explanations of the meaning of three *tsu* 族. In the *I-li* Cheng explains that they were father's brothers, ego's brothers, and son's brothers (*ILCS* 6:6a). In the *Li-chi* Cheng says they were father, sons, and grandsons (*LCCS* 50:9b). Ju Shun comments that the three *tsu* included the father's clan, mother's clan, and wife's clan; and Yen agrees with him (*HS* 1B:12b). Chang Yen says it included the father and mother, siblings, and wife and sons (Pei).

Judging from other evidence in the *Shih-chi* and *Han-shu*, Chang's interpretation seems to be the most acceptable (Ch'eng Shu-te, *Han-lü k'ao*, in *Chiu-ch'ao lü-k'ao* [Shanghai: Commercial Press, 1927], 2:25, hereafter cited as *HLK; HLCI* 9:16b–17a). According to Han law, as referred to by K'ung Kuang, the commandant of justice, when discussing whether the divorced wife of Ch'un-yü Ch'ang 淳于長 should be included in the punishment for crimes of high treason and impiousness (無道), one's parents, wife, children, and siblings, whether old or young, had to be publicly executed (*HS* 81:19b). The Han code, quoted by Ju Shun himself, reads similarly except for the phrase "whether old or young," which was omitted (Yen: *HS* 5:3b). When Emperor Wen attempted to abrogate the law for the arrest and punishment of the criminal's wives and children, both he and the two chancellors mentioned the punishment of "fathers and mothers, wives, children, and siblings" (see I, 17). In fact, we know from the cases in which the punishment of extermination of the *tsu* is mentioned in detail that it included only the relatives mentioned above. In the case of Ch'ao Ts'o, his parents, wife, children, and siblings, without discrimination of age, were all executed (*HS* 49:25a). In Li Ling's 李陵 case, the list included his mother, wife, and children (*SC* 109:10b; *HS* 54:14a); it also included his younger brother(s), which must be an error, because Li Ling was a posthumous child (*SC* 109:8b–9a; *HS* 54:9a) and could not have had a younger brother.

In Chi Hui-yüeh's 紀恢説 case, the edict shows clearly that had Hui-yüeh, the son of the marquis of Hsiang-p'ing, not attempted to cause the death of his father by his intended rebellion, the marquis and his wife and other sons (i.e., the criminal's parents and siblings) would not have been pardoned and exempted from the joint punishment. Only Hui-yüeh and his wife and children were executed (*HS* 5:3b).

On three *tsu*, see also *HLCI* 9:17a; *CCLK*, pp. 58–59; A.F.P. Hulsewé, *Remnants of Han Law* (Leiden, 1955), I, 112 ff.

2. Fathers and Sons Encouraged to Live Apart

359 B.C.   [Shang Yang² urged Duke Hsiao of Ch'in to reform the law.] "Good," said Duke Hsiao, and he granted Wei³ Yang the [honorary rank of] chieftain of the multitude of the left.⁴ At last the law of reform was fixed upon. . . . Persons with two sons or more and not living separately were required to pay a double tax.⁵ [*SC* 68:3b–4a]

3. Sons Sent Away by Father

359 B.C.   [Chia I said in his memorial]:⁶ "The Lord of Shang abandoned propriety, discarded benevolence, and concentrated his attention upon the advancement of [national] attainments.⁷ After this had been practiced for two years, the customs of Ch'in deteriorated from day to day. Therefore, among the people of Ch'in, if the family was rich when a son reached adulthood, then he was sent away with a share [of the property]; if the family was poor when a son reached adulthood, then he was pawned out.⁸

---

² See *SC* 5:23b–25a, 68:1a–9b, and J. J. L. Duyvendak, *The Book of Lord Shang* (London, 1928), pp. 1–130.

³ Shang Yang was called Wei Yang because he was a member of the ruling family of the state of Wei (*SC* 68:1a).

⁴ "Chieftain of the multitude of the left," *tso-shu-chang* 左庶長, was, according to Yen, a title of the tenth rank (*HS* 58:9b).

⁵ The purpose of this law is not clear: the double tax might have been enacted to increase tax revenues or to enforce the law. Nor can we be sure that the size of the family was reduced in order to break the strength of the large families. But some concrete effects of this law can be seen. For example, in the *Chin-shu* it is said that in modifying the Han law the state of Wei (227–239) abolished the law that required sons to live separately from their fathers so that fathers and sons would not have to have separate property (*CS* 30:7a). This proves that the regulation set up by Ch'in in 359 B.C. was still kept in the Han Code and was not abolished until the Wei dynasty. The action of Lu Chia, who divided his property equally among his five sons during his lifetime (see I, 13) might have been a practical outcome of this law. Evidence also shows that this practice was common among the common people (see I, 3).

⁶ This memorial was presented by Chia I in 174 B.C.

⁷ This statement refers to Shang Yang's reforms and not to his personal behavior. Chia I's criticism of Shang Yang is a typical reaction of the Confucianists against the Legalists, who were considered cruel and were attacked for disregarding the moral principles of the Confucianists. The Confucianists emphasized morality and education rather than law and punishment (*HS* 48:20a–21b).

⁸ Ying Shao explains that the term *chui* 贅, which literally means "an excrescence," here refers to *chui hsü* 贅婿. According to him, *chui-hsü* was a poor man's son who was sent to his wife's family (*SC* 6:21b). Yen comments that such a man was called *chui hsü* because it was as abnormal for a man to enter his wife's family as for a tumor to

"When one lent a rake or hoe to his father, [the son] would assume the appearance of a benefactor. When a mother took [her child's] dust-pan or broom, [the daughter] would stand there and reprove her. [Daughters-in-law], while carrying their babies, squatted with their fathers-in-law. Whenever the daughter-in-law and the mother-in-law were not on good terms with one another, then, with sneers, they levied recriminations against each other."[9] [*HS* 48:15a]

4. FATHER, SONS, AND BROTHERS
NOT ALLOWED TO LIVE IN THE SAME ROOM

The Ch'in moved from Yung [to Hsien-yang] and made it its capi-   350 B.C.
tal.[10] A law prohibiting the people, father, sons, and brothers from living together in the same room was proclaimed.[11] [*SC* 68:5a]

---

grow on the human body. He also identifies *chui* with 質, "to pawn"; the man who was poor and unable to make a betrothal gift offered himself to the bride's family as a pledge (*HS* 64A:3b–4a, 48:15a).

Ch'ien Ta-hsin rejects Yen's second interpretation and refers to the same passage in the *Han-shu* (64A:3b), which states that people pawned their children (*chui tzu* 贅子) when the harvest was bad in order to get food and clothing. Ju Shun, commenting on this same term, says that the people of Huai-nan (south of the Huai River) frequently sold their children (*mai tzu* 賣子) to work as slaves and that they were called *chui tzu*, "pawned children"; if they were not redeemed within three years, they became male or female slaves. From this, Ch'ien concludes that *chui tzu* was a person who was pawned out for a limited time and whose status was little better than that of a bond servant. A son who was pawned out in this fashion and was not redeemed within a given time may have married his patron's daughter, and would then have been called *chui hsü*, "bond husband," a term that brought him the contempt of his fellows (*Ch'ien-yen-t'ang wen-chi*, in *Ch'ien-yen-t'ang ch'üan-shu* [Ch'ang-sha: Hung-shih chia-shu ch'ung-k'an, 1884], 12:3b–4a, hereafter cited as *CYTWC*). Ch'ien Mu, however, thinks that *chui hsü* was a male family slave who was given a female slave as his wife, not his master's daughter (*Hsien-Ch'in chu-tzu hsi nien k'ao-pien* [Shanghai: Commercial Press, 1935], p. 330).

Whatever the explanation, the *chui hsü* had an inferior status and were treated unfavorably by the government. Under the Ch'in and Han they were sent together with fugitives and merchants to guard the frontiers (II, 7, n. 21). According to Kung Yü, *chui hsü* were also prevented from entering officialdom during Emperor Wen's time (*HS* 72:16b).

[9] Shang Yang's reforms resulted in notable changes in the structure of the family and in interpersonal relationships. The double tax (see I, 2) discouraged the maintenance of large family units; and, as this statement by Chia I indicates, the rich and the poor had different ways of adjusting to the situation. The reorganization of the family into small units also made the children more independent. Such statesmen as Chia I condemned the new attitudes of individualism, which differed so blatantly from those principles of filial piety that had dominated the previous period.

[10] In the twelfth year of Duke Hsiao of Ch'in, 350 B.C. (*SC* 5:24a).

[11] The following remark was made by Shang Yang to Chao Liang 趙良 concerning

5. FATHER SELECTS A SON-IN-LAW

Ch'in   A man of Shan-fu, Old Gentleman Lü,[12] was a good friend of the
prefect of P'ei. In order to escape a feud he came to [the prefect] as his
guest and thus settled down there. When the eminent and distinguished
persons and officials of P'ei heard that the prefect had an important
guest, they all went to congratulate him. . . . Kao-tsu was chief of a
canton. . . . When his card was sent in, Old Gentleman Lü was greatly
surprised; he arose and welcomed him at the door. Old Gentleman Lü
liked to physiognomize people, and it was because he noticed Kao-tsu's
appearance and features that he greatly honored him. He escorted him
in and seated him in the seat [of honor].[13] . . . When the drinking drew
to an end,[14] Old Gentleman Lü looked at Kao-tsu in such a way as
definitely to detain him. After Kao-tsu had finished drinking, Old
Gentleman Lü said, "Your servant[15] from his youth has liked to physiognomize people. None of them has had [as auspicious] a physiognomy
as yours, Chi. You, Chi, should take care of yourself. Your servant has
a daughter whom he would like to make your maid of the dustpan and
broom."[16]

When the feast was over, Old Lady Lü was angry with Old Gentleman Lü, and said, "Previously you, sir, have always wanted to hold
this girl precious and give her [in marriage] to some distinguished person. The prefect of P'ei is your good friend. He has asked for her and
you would not give her to him. Why did you senselessly promise to give
her to Liu Chi?" Old Gentleman Lü replied, "This is not a thing that
children or women can understand." In the end he gave her to Kao-

---

his success in government: "Previously Ch'in had the culture of the Jung 戎 and Ti
翟(狄) barbarians. Fathers and sons were not separated; instead, they lived in the
same room. Now I have changed its culture and make a distinction between men and
women" (*SC* 68:7a). Apparently this law was supposed to remodel the family system
in the image of the traditional Chinese family (1) by maintaining a distance between
the father and his sons and (2) by discouraging immorality by preventing family
members of different sexes from sharing the same room.

   [12] Old Gentleman Lü was the father of Empress Lü. His personal name is not
known.

   [13] The *Han-shu* reads 坐上坐, "seated him in the seat of honor."

   [14] Wen Ying says that the phrase means that half of those who had been drinking
had departed, while the other half remained (*SC* 8:3b).

   [15] *Ch'en* 臣 is a humble expression referring to oneself.

   [16] 箕帚妾 means wife, because a woman was supposed to serve her husband and
keep the house clean with "dustpan and broom." In this context, 妾 is merely a
humble term for all women and not at all connected with the idea of "concubine."

tsu. The daughter of Old Gentleman Lü was [later] the Empress Lü and gave birth to Emperor Hsiao-hui and Princess Lu-yüan. [*SC* 8:3a–4a; *HS* 1A:2a–3a; Edouard Chavannes, *Les Mémoires historiques de Se-ma Ts'ien* (5 vols.; Paris, 1895–1905), II, 327–28]

6. Wife Abandons Husband and Remarries

Chang Erh[17] was a native of Ta-liang. During his youth he was early enough to be a guest of the prince of Wei, Wu-chi.[18] Chang Erh had once fled as a fugitive [from his native prefecture] and wandered in Wai-huang [of Ch'en-liu]. In Wai-huang there was a wealthy man's daughter who was very beautiful and who was married to a common, worthless man.[19] She ran away[20] from her husband and went to her father's guest. Her father's guest had long known Chang Erh. Then he said to the girl, "If you wish to have a worthy husband, go to Chang Erh." The girl followed his words and asked him to have her divorced [from her husband], and she then married Chang Erh.

Chang Erh at this time was able to entertain freely. The girl's family supplied him with a great deal of money. Thus he was able to have

---

[17] Chang Erh was a native of Wei. Because of their great repute, both he and Ch'en Yü were sought by Ch'in when it conquered Wei. They followed Ch'en Sheng when he revolted against Ch'in. He made them colonels and sent them to join Wu Ch'en 武臣 in taking over the territory of Chao. Following their advice, Wu Ch'en made himself king of Chao, and appointed Chang Erh as chancellor of state of the right. When Wu Ch'en was killed by a member of his army, Chang Erh and Ch'en Yü made Chao Hsieh 趙歇 king of Chao. But when Chang and the king of Chao were attacked by Chang Han 章邯, a Ch'in general, Ch'en Yü did not come to their aid. Chang Erh then joined Hsiang Yü and entered the capital of Ch'in, after which Hsiang made him king of Ch'ang-shan. Ch'en Yü, because he was given only a marquisate, attacked Chang Erh, who fled and joined Liu Pang, the later Emperor Kao. Ch'en Yü revolted against Han, and Chang killed him when he led Liu Pang's army for an offensive attack against him. Emperor Kao then made Chang the king of Chao (*SC* 89:1b ff.; *HS* 32:1a ff.).

[18] That is, the lord of Hsin-ling, who was the younger brother of King An-li of Wei 魏安釐. He died in 244 B.C.

[19] Literally the phrase 庸奴 means "worthless slave." But as this does not seem to be the meaning of this passage, we translate it as "worthless man." The wording of the *Han-shu* is a little different. The phrase 庸奴 is used as a transitive verb instead of as an adjective and noun. It reads, "She treated her husband as a worthless slave" (庸奴其夫).

[20] The word 亡 may also mean "lost," and Wang Mou and Wang Nien-sun explain its use in the passage above as "lost in death." We, however, follow Chu I-hsin and translate it "ran away" (*HSPC* 32:1a). The *Han-shu* reads, "ran away and went to a guest of her father" 亡邸父客.

guests[21] come from a great distance. He then became prefect of Wai-huang. His name was more known than before. [*SC* 89:1a–b; similar *HS* 32:1a]

7. Brothers Living Together

Before
209 B.C. The Imperial Chancellor Ch'en, whose name was P'ing,[22] was a native of Hu-yu district[23] of Yang-wu prefecture. When he was young, his family was poor. He was fond of study.[24] [The family] had thirty *mou* of land. He lived alone with his elder brother, Po. Po worked constantly in the fields, thus leaving P'ing free to visit and to study.[25]

P'ing was tall and good-looking. Someone inquired of Ch'en P'ing, saying, "Poor [as you are] what do you eat to get so stout?" His elder brother's wife, who resented P'ing's disregard for the livelihood of the family, said, "He just eats the husks of the threshed wheat. It is better not to have a brother-in-law at all than such a one." When Po heard this, he drove out his wife and divorced her.[26] [*SC* 56:1a; *HS* 40:11b]

---

[21] While Emperor Kao was still a commoner, he was a guest of Chang Erh (*SC* 89:1b; *HS* 32:1b).

[22] Ch'en P'ing (d. 179 B.C.) joined Emperor Kao in 205 B.C. and was made a chief commandant. He contributed much to the success of the emperor's campaign for power. In 201 B.C. he was granted the marquisate of Hu-yu. From 190 on he served Emperor Hui as an imperial chancellor of the left, and in 188 B.C. he was made imperial chancellor of the right. In 180 B.C. he was transferred to his previous post, but shortly thereafter he was made imperial chancellor (*SC* 56:1a–11a).

[23] Hu-yu 戶牖 district was located twenty *li* northwest of modern Lan-feng county in Honan. According to Hsü Kuang and the *Ch'en-liu feng-su chuan* quoted by Chang, Hu-yu was a district during Ch'in times and became a prefecture in Han times, subordinate to the Ch'en-liu commandery (*SC* 56:1a).

[24] The *Han-shu* states that he studied the methods of Huang-ti and Lao-tzu.

[25] It should be pointed out that although Ch'en P'ing was able to proceed with his visiting and studying because of his brother's sacrifice, both of them must have been very poor. Thirty Han *mou* equal about ten modern *mou*, the equivalent of a little over an acre. Such a small farm could hardly support three people. Therefore the phrase "free to visit and to study" should not be taken at face value. Probably Po just wanted to free P'ing from farm work so that he would have time for some kind of social activity when he was not studying. The poor income of the family also suggests that the education could not have been formal; nor could the visiting have been far from Ch'en P'ing's native community. He would have been able to travel to distant places only after his marriage to Chang Fu's granddaughter (see I, 8).

[26] The seven reasons for which a wife could be divorced were: lack of filial piety toward her husband's parents, barrenness, adultery, jealousy, incurable disease, loquacity, and theft (*TTLC* 13:6a; *KTCY* 6:6a; *KYCS* 8:10a). Po probably divorced his wife for loquacity (口多言). Although the phrase itself means "talkativeness," it seems to refer particularly to improper talk between relatives—the kind that sows

8. MARRIAGE CONSIDERATIONS

When Ch'en P'ing grew up and became of marriageable age,[27] no   <small>Before
209 B.C.</small>
one among the rich was willing to give him [his daughter]. P'ing also
was ashamed [to marry] a poor one.

Long afterwards, in Hu-yu there was among the rich men one named
Chang Fu.[28] Chang Fu's granddaughter had been married five times,
and her husbands had all died. There was no one who dared to marry
her,[29] but P'ing desired to have her. . . .

When there was a funeral in the community, P'ing, being poor,
served at the funeral, going there early and leaving late in order to help.
When Chang Fu saw him at a funeral, he alone looked at and admired
P'ing. P'ing also left late because of certain reasons, and Fu followed
P'ing to his house. His house was in a poor lane with its back against the
outer city wall[30] and had a worn-out straw mat for a door. But outside
the door there were many ruts from the carriages of prominent people.

When Chang Fu returned home, he addressed his son, Chung, saying,
"I wish to give my granddaughter to Ch'en P'ing." Chang Chung said,
"P'ing is poor and has no regular occupation.[31] The people in the whole
prefecture all laugh at his actions. Why then should we give him the
girl?" Fu said, "Can such a handsome man as Ch'en P'ing be poor and
low permanently?" Finally he gave the girl [to P'ing]. Because P'ing
was poor, he lent him the gifts for the betrothal,[32] and gave him money

---

discord in the close in-group and thus weakens the family as a whole. All explanations
of the term emphasize that it separates the relatives of the family (離親) (*TTLC*
13:6a; *KTCY* 6:6a; Ho: *KYCS* 8:10a).

[27] According to the *Li-chi*, the preferred age for marriage was thirty for men and
twenty for women (*LCCS* 1:8a). But it seems that many married younger; at least
they did in Han times. By the first century B.C. marriage must have taken place at an
early age, since Wang Chi complains about early marriages (*HS* 72:7b). Wang
Ch'ung (A.D. 27–97) remarks that the people of his time were not following this
preferred age for marriage; he thought that the ancients had not followed it either
(Lun-heng, SPTK ed., 18:16b–17a, hereafter cited as *LH)*.

[28] Ssu-ma says that *fu* 負 was used to designate an old woman, but in this context
it seems to be the name of a man. Wang Ming-sheng also believed that Chang Fu
張負 was the name of a man *(Shih-ch'i shih shang-ch'üeh* [Tung-ching-ts'ao t'ang,
1787], 4:3b, hereafter cited as *SCSSC)*.

[29] This was the usual attitude at that time. The death of all her husbands was
taken to indicate that such a woman would "destroy" anyone who married her. The
Lun-heng notes that the untimely death of a husband or wife usually happened because
of the "character" of the spouse (*LH* 3:3b). So no one dared to marry an "unlucky"
widow.

[30] Only the poorest people lived outside the outer city wall.

[31] For Ch'en's economic status, see I, 7.

[32] The offering of a gift to the prospective bride's family at the time of betrothal
(*na-cheng* 納徵 or *na-pi* 納幣) was one of the six rites observed in connection with

for the wine and meat[33] for the wedding feast. Fu instructed his grand-daughter, saying, "Do not be disrespectful in serving your [husband] because of his poverty. Serve the elder brother, Po, as if serving your father, and serve the elder brother's wife as your mother."[34] [*SC* 56:1a–2a; *HS* 40:11b–12a]

9. A JEALOUS EMPRESS

Empress Dowager Lü, who was the wife of Emperor Kao while he was still humble, gave birth to [the later] Emperor Hsiao-hui and to a daughter, [the later] Queen Dowager Lu-yüan.[35]

206 B.C.   When Emperor Kao became the king of Han, he took the concubine Ch'i of Ting-t'ao; she was loved and favored by him and gave birth to King Yin of Chao, Ju-i. The heir apparent was kind and weak. Emperor Kao considered him "not resembling myself," and intended to depose the heir apparent and to appoint Ju-i: "Ju-i resembles me." Concubine Ch'i won the emperor's favor and usually followed him east of [Han-ku] Pass. Weeping day and night, she hoped that her son would be appointed.

[At that time] Empress Lü was old; she was frequently left [in the capital] and seldom had a chance to see [the emperor. Thus their relationship] became more and more tenuous. After Ju-i had been appointed king of Chao, he almost replaced the heir apparent a number of times. Because of the struggle of high officials [to support the heir apparent] and the plot of the marquis of Liu,[36] the heir apparent was not replaced.

Empress Lü was unyielding and resolute. She helped Emperor Kao to pacify the world. . . .

195 B.C.   On the day *chia-ch'en* of the fourth month in the twelfth year Emperor

---

marriage. Wang Chi (d. 48 B.C.) remarked that betrothal gifts made it difficult for the poor to marry (*HS* 72:7b). See our forthcoming work on Han folkways.

[33] People usually had a wedding feast on that day. See the forthcoming work mentioned in note 32.

[34] Ordinarily one would expect a remark concerning the wife's attitude toward her parents-in-law. But since Ch'en had lost his parents and lived with his elder brother and his wife, they are mentioned instead. Pei suggests that she might have been Po's second wife.

[35] The Princess Lu-yüan married the marquis of Hsüan-p'ing, Chang Ao, the former king of Chao. She was given the posthumous title of "queen dowager" by Empress Lü (*SC* 9:1a).

[36] For the plot of Chang Liang, the marquis of Liu, see *SC* 55:10b–13a.

Kao died at Ch'ang-lo Palace. The heir apparent inherited the title and became emperor. . . .

Empress Lü greatly resented Lady Ch'i and her son, the king of Chao. Then she ordered [the officials of] the Yung-hsiang[37] to imprison[38] Lady Ch'i and summoned the king of Chao. The messenger went three times and returned. The chancellor of Chao, the marquis of Chien-p'ing, Chou Ch'ang, said to the messenger, "Emperor Kao entrusted me with the king of Chao. The king of Chao is young. I heard that the empress dowager resents Lady Ch'i and intends to summon the king of Chao and kill them together. I dare not send my lord. Moreover, the king is ill and unable to obey the edict." Empress Lü was very angry and thereupon sent someone to summon the chancellor of Chao. When the chancellor of Chao had been summoned and arrived in Ch'ang-an, someone was sent again to summon the king of Chao. The king was on his way and had not yet arrived. Emperor Hsiao-hui was kind and benevolent; knowing that the empress dowager was angry, he himself went to welcome the king of Chao at the Pa River. They entered the palace together. He kept the king of Chao with him, living, drinking, and eating together with him. The empress dowager wanted to kill the king, but there was no opportunity.

In the twelfth month of the first year of Hsiao-hui, the emperor went 194 B.C. to shoot in the early morning. The king was young and unable to get up early. Hearing that he was staying alone, the empress dowager sent a man to give him a poisoned drink. When Hsiao-hui returned at dawn, the king of Chao was already dead. . . .

The empress dowager then cut off the hands and feet of Lady Ch'i, took out her eyes, burned[39] her ears, gave her a silencing dose to drink, made her stay in a privy, and named her "human swine." Several days later Emperor Hsiao-hui was summoned to see the human swine. Upon seeing her and inquiring and learning that it was Lady Ch'i, Hsiao-hui wept loudly. Thereupon he became sick and was unable to get up for more than a year. [The emperor] sent someone to tell the empress

---

[37] The Yung-hsiang 永巷 was a long lane in which guilty palace ladies were kept in custody *(San-fu huang-t'u,* in *PCKTS,* pp. 23b–24a, hereafter cited as *SFHT).*

[38] Lady Ch'i's 戚姬 head was shaved, she wore an iron collar, was dressed in red cloth, and was made to pound rice *(HS* 97A:3b). Both garb and work were usual in the punishment of criminals.

[39] The *Shih-chi* contains the character 煇 meaning "to burn." The *Han-shu* reads 熏, which Yen explains as "to fumigate the ear with certain medicines to bring on deafness" *(HS* 97A:4a).

dowager, "This act is not that of a human being. I am the son of the empress dowager and so I will never be able to rule the empire." Thus Hsiao-hui drank daily and indulged in lustful pleasures and did not attend to government. Therefore he was ill.[40] [SC 9:1a–3a; cf. HS 97A:3a–4b]

10. A SELF-SUPPORTING FAMILY

206 B.C.   While the rich people vied with each other in extravagance, the Jen abstained, were frugal, and worked hard at farming and stockbreeding. While [other] people strove for land and cattle at low prices, the Jen were the only ones to take the dear and the best. [The family] remained rich for several generations. However, the family regulations of Mr. Jen were that nothing that was not produced from their own fields or cattle should be used for clothing or food; and that until the common work[41] was done, no one could drink wine or eat meat. Because of this, they became the model in their rural community. [SC 129:19a–b; HS 91: 9b–10a]

11. MANY TENS OF KINSMEN SENT TO ARMY

204 B.C.   In the third year, when the king of Han was in combat with Hsiang Yü between Ching and So,[42] the king frequently sent representatives to encourage the chancellor.[43] Pao said to the chancellor, "The king is exposing himself in the field and many times he sends men to encourage you. This is because he does not trust you. For your sake, the best way is to send your children, grandchildren, and your brothers[44] who are strong enough to hold arms to enlist in the army. Then the king will trust you."[45] Hsiao Ho took this advice. The king was delighted.

[40] He died seven years later in 188 B.C. (HS 97A:4b).

[41] *Kung shih* 公事 literally means "public business." Here it refers to the domestic work of the family, such as farm work, taking care of the cattle, making utensils, domestic routine, and so forth. The sharp contrast between "public" (family) and "private" (individual) activities is significant. The regulations of the Jen family show clearly that the individual interests of family members were discouraged.

[42] Ching 京 was in the east, south of Ying-yang, and So 索 was Jung-yang prefecture, which is equated with modern Ch'eng-kao county in Honan.

[43] That is, during the time when the chancellor, Hsiao Ho, was left behind in the capital to recruit forces and supply rations for the troops (SC 53:2a).

[44] The term *k'un-ti* 昆弟 may mean brothers as well as cousins. Since many tens of the Hsiaos were enlisted in the army and only about ten of Hsiao Ho's brothers were ennobled, together with his parents (SC 53:4a; HS 39:4b), it seems that *k'un-ti* was used here as a classificatory term.

[45] Obviously the word "encourage" used here cannot be taken at face value. Of

In the fifth year, when Hsiang Yü was killed and the whole nation 202 B.C.
was pacified, rewards were given according to each one's achievements.
As all the officials were boasting and arguing concerning their own
merit, the problem was not settled for more than a year. Emperor Kao,
considering that Hsiao Ho's merit was the greatest, made him the marquis of Tsan and granted him many fiefs.[46] All other officials who had
merit said, "We, wearing armor and holding weapons, engaged in
battles either for many tens or even more than one hundred times. We
attacked cities and seized places, some large and some small. Now
Hsiao Ho never had any merit in war, but was concerned only with
documents and discussions, without fighting. Yet, why is he in a position higher than all of us?" Emperor Kao said, ". . . Furthermore, all
of you merely gave yourselves to following me, at most [with] two or
three persons. Now Hsiao Ho's entire lineage,[47] amounting to many
tens, were following me. His merit is unforgettable." [*SC* 53:2a–3a;
HS 39:2b–3b]

12. Selection of Palace Ladies

Empress Dowager Tou was a native of Kuan-chin of the Ch'ing-ho *Ca.* 195–
commandery in the [old state of] Chao. In the time of Empress Dow- 190 B.C.
ager Lü, Lady Tou,[48] as a girl of good family, entered the palace to
serve the empress dowager.[49] When the empress dowager dismissed the
palace ladies to bestow them on the various kings, five to each king,
Lady Tou was on the list to be sent. . . . When she arrived at Tai, the
king of Tai[50] favored only Lady Tou. She bore a daughter, P'iao. Later
two sons were born.[51] [*SC* 49:5a; *HS* 97A:7b]

---

course the king wanted his chancellor to do his best, and sent him words of encouragement via his representatives; but these visits also gave the king a chance to check up
on his highest official. The dual purpose of the "friendly" mission seems to have been
well recognized.

[46] According to *HS* 39:2b, eight thousand households were granted to him.

[47] This statement gives a clue to the size of the lineage. If the "many tens" refer to
the adult males in Hsiao Ho's lineage, they would probably include more than three
generations. The cohesiveness of the group and the decisive authority of Hsiao Ho
are clearly indicated.

[48] The word *chi* 姬, here translated "lady," was a general term for the various
concubines (*HS* 4:1a).

[49] In the corresponding passage in the *Han-shu,* the phrase "to serve the empress
dowager" is omitted.

[50] The later Emperor Wen.

[51] The elder son, who later became Emperor Ching, was born in the seventh year

13. Equal Shares Given to Brothers

195–
188 B.C.   [Lu Chia] resigned on the ground of illness[52] and stayed at home. Because the land in Hao-chih prefecture[53] was fertile, he considered it a suitable place to live. He had five sons. He then took out the contents of his bag that he had received from the Yüeh during his mission[54] and sold them at a price of one thousand [catties of] gold. He divided [the money] among his sons, each son getting two hundred [catties of] gold, and ordered them to use it to earn their living.

Mr. Lu usually rode in a four-horse comfortable carriage and was followed by singers, dancers, lute-players, and attendants, ten people in all. His precious sword was worth one hundred [catties of] gold. He said to his sons, "Let me have an agreement with you. When I come to you, you will provide wine and food for my people and horses. After being fully satisfied for ten days, I will change to another place.[55] The family in which I die will get my precious sword, carriage, horses, and attendants. As I have to visit other friends, I will not make, in general, more than two or three visits in a year. Boredom would be caused by too many visits; you will not be disturbed by me for long."[56] [*SC* 97:8a–b; *HS* 43:7b]

14. Son Beaten by Father

193–
190 B.C.   [Ts'ao] Shen's son, Ch'u, was holding the post of palace grandee.[57] Wondering why the chancellor of state was not attending to his official

---

of Emperor Hui (189/188). Therefore, Tou Chi was probably selected for the palace at the beginning of Emperor Hui's reign.

[52] Lu Chia was sent by Emperor Kao in 196 B.C. (*HS* 1B:16a–b) to persuade the king of Nan-yüeh to become a subject of the Han government. As a reward for his successful mission, he was appointed grand palace grandee. He resigned from this position because he opposed empress dowager Lü's efforts to raise the Lü family to kingly status. For further information see II, 17, n. 58.

[53] Hao-chih 好畤 was a prefecture in Yu-fu-feng (*HS* 28A:13a).

[54] Because the king of Nan-yüeh liked Lu Chia very much, he had presented him with a bag that contained articles worth one thousand catties of gold and with other gifts also valued at one thousand catties of gold (*SC* 97:7b; *HS* 43:6b).

[55] Probably meaning that he would then visit one of the other sons (Yen: *HS* 43:7b).

[56] The *Han-shu* reads 數擊鮮毋久溷嬭也, instead of 數見不鮮無久思公爲也. Thus it would mean, "You should slaughter fresh meat for me, and I won't disturb you for long."

[57] At this time (193–190 B.C.) Ts'ao Shen 曹參 held the post of chancellor of state (*HS* 19B:2a).

duties[58] and thinking that [the chancellor] was dissatisfied with him, Emperor Hui said to Ch'u, "When you go back to your home, try to interrogate your father privately in an easy manner, saying, 'Emperor Kao has recently passed away. The emperor is young. You, Sir, are the chancellor, and you drink day after day without asking for instructions. How can you be concerned with the world?' But don't mention that I told this to you."

When Ch'u returned home on his day of rest,[59] waiting on [his father,] he remonstrated with Shen as if it were his own idea. Shen became angry and gave Ch'u two hundred strokes, and said, "Go and be in attendance at once. The affairs of the world are not what you can talk about."[60] [*SC* 54:7b; *HS* 39:12a]

15. MARRIAGE WITH ELDER SISTER'S DAUGHTER

The marquis of Hsüan-p'ing, [Chang] Ao,[61] had married the older   192 B.C. sister of Emperor [Hsiao-hui], the Princess Lu-yüan.[62] They had a daughter. When Emperor Hui ascended the throne, Empress Dowager Lü, wishing to double the [ties] of relationship, married the daughter

---

[58] The chancellor of state had for years followed the Taoist system of governing, which emphasized the principle of noninterference. His method of governing had worked successfully when he was chancellor of the kingdom of Ch'i, so he practiced the same doctrine when he became the chancellor of state. He spent all his time drinking and did not care about the administration of his office. Everyone who visited him was offered drink, and was thus prevented from giving any advice. He later explained to the emperor that since Hsiao Ho, his predecessor, had set up all the laws and regulations, it was not necessary to make any changes. His words convinced the young emperor, who permitted him to go on in his own way.

[59] *Hsi-mu* 洗沐, which occurred every five days, was the day of rest for officials.

[60] It was rather unusual for an emperor to act in this way instead of making the inquiry himself. Probably it was because Emperor Hui was still young (he was only thirteen years old when he ascended the throne) and did not know how to deal with the old, powerful chancellor (*HS* 2:1a, 4b). The emperor, according to Ssu-ma Ch'ien, was benevolent but weak (*SC* 9:1a).

[61] Chang Ao was the son of Chang Erh, the King of Chao. See I, 6, n. 17. He became king after the death of his father in 202 B.C., but in 198 B.C. he was accused of plotting a rebellion and was imprisoned. He was pardoned, but was deprived of his title when his chancellor proved that he himself had instigated the rebellious plot and that the king was completely unaware of it. Since Chang Ao was married to an imperial princess, he was made a marquis. He died in 182 B.C. (*SC* 89:11a–14a; *HS* 1B:12a–b, 32:8a–10a).

[62] Both Emperor Hsiao-hui and Princess Lu-yüan were born of the Empress Dowager Lü (*SC* 9:1a; *HS* 97A:3a).

of the princess to the emperor,[63] and made her empress.[64] [*HS* 97A:5b; similar *SC* 49:2b]

16. ABOLITION OF COLLECTIVE RESPONSIBILITY

187 B.C.   In the first year [of Empress Dowager Lü] . . . an edict said, "Previously Emperor Hsiao-hui said that he intended to abolish the punishment of the three *tsu*[65] and the ordinance against improper words,[66] but his deliberations had not yet been concluded when he died. Now We abolish these [punishments]." [*HS* 3:1b]

[63] Marriage to a sister's daughter was very unusual. Marriages of persons of different generations who were close relatives deviated from the regular pattern. This is one of three instances in Early and Later Han of generational lines being overridden by emperors. One emperor married his grandmother's first cousin's daughter, that is, her father's brother's son's daughter (see I, 36). In another case an emperor married his great-grandfather's wife's second cousin's granddaughter, that is, her grandfather's brother's grandson's granddaughter (see *HHS* 10B:12a). Of course, in this last case the relationship was very remote.

[64] In 192 B.C. (*HS* 2:4a).

[65] This was a Ch'in punishment that was carried over to Han; see I, 1.

[66] The term *yao-yen* 訞言 (or 妖言, *SC* 10:1a–b, *HS* 66:13a, *HHS* 3:18a; or 祅言, *HS* 21A:19a, 75:2a–b, *HHS* 5:10b) is explained by Yen as meaning "improper words" 過誤之言 (*HS* 3:1b). The case of Yang Yün suggests that most of the improper words were connected with the emperor. Yang was accused of using "improper words" because he had said that the emperor might die when there were certain omens, and that he wished the emperor to ask about the faults of Chieh and Chou, ancient tyrants, and that while he was looking at their pictures he found likenesses between the Ch'in and Han governments (*HS* 66:11a–13a).

Some other instances suggest that "improper words" were usually associated with slander 誹謗. In 178 B.C. an edict was issued by Emperor Wen, saying: "Now the law has punishments for slander and improper words. This causes [the various officials] to refrain from expressing their feeling fully, [with the result that] the emperor is then prevented from hearing his faults. How can we make the virtuous who are at far distances come? Let us abolish it. People sometimes make an agreement to curse their superior and later cease from doing so. They are considered great rebels by officials. When they have other kinds of words, the officials consider them slanderous. This is the stupidity of the little men, and they forfeit their lives because of their lack of knowledge. We do not approve of this. From now on those who transgress this law shall not be punished" (*HS* 4:9b–10a).

When Yang Yün was accused of using improper words, he was also accused of slandering the regime (*HS* 66:12a).

In most cases it seems that there is no clear-cut distinction between improper words and slander. Thus, in discussing the government of Ch'in, Lu Wen-shu said, "Those who remonstrated positively were called slanderers; those who [tried to] prevent the faults [of the ruler] were called [users of] improper words" (*HS* 51:28b).

The punishment for improper words and slander varied from dismissal from office (*HS* 66:13a; *HHS* 3:18a) and removal to the frontiers (*HHS* 5:10b) to the sentence of death (*HS* 75:1a–2a, 90:18a–19a; *HHS* 34:6a; 63:17a).

[In the twelfth month of the first year of Emperor Wen the emperor]   179 B.C.
completely abrogated all the statutes and orders for the enslavement of
wives and children and for punishing them with [the criminal].[67] [*HS*
4:5a]

17. REINTRODUCTION OF COLLECTIVE RESPONSIBILITY

From the rise of Han . . . among the death punishments, there were
still the ordinances of the extermination of the three *tsu*. . . . P'eng Yüeh,
Han Hsin, and some others all had received this kind of sentence. In the
first year of Empress Kao the punishment of the three *tsu* and the ordinance against improper words were then abolished.

In the second[68] year of Emperor Hsiao-wen, [the emperor] said again   179–
to the imperial chancellor, the grand commandant, and the imperial   178 B.C.
secretary: "The law, being the rectifier of the administration, is for the
purpose of prohibiting violence and protecting good men. Now these
criminals have already been sentenced, and yet We have their innocent
fathers and mothers, wives, children, and siblings punished and enslaved together.[69] We do not consider it proper. Discuss it." The left

---

Finally it should be pointed out that although the punishment against *yao-yen* was
abolished by Empress Dowager Lü and Emperor Wen in 187 and 178 B.C., actually
the law was still in practice in later days, as we see in the examples mentioned above.
Furthermore, in 7 B.C. an edict was issued by Emperor Ai to abolish the punishment
concerning slander (*HS* 11:3b). In the Later Han the punishment for improper words
and slander was also in practice (see *HLCI* 3:2a–7a; *CCLK*, pp. 124–25).

[67] For further information concerning our translation of this phrase, see I, 17.

[68] According to *SC* 10:5b and *HS* 4:5a (see I, 16), the year of abrogation was the
first year, 179 B.C.

[69] The phrase 坐之及收, if translated literally, would mean "to be punished and
arrested." The word "arrested" here seems to give little additional meaning to the
sentence. The parallel passage in the *Shih-chi* reads 坐之及為收帑, the word *nu* 帑
being explained by Ying Shao as "sons." Yen suggested that *nu* was a synonym for
nu 奴, "slave" (*HS* 4:5a–15). His opinion was reaffirmed by Tuan Yü-ts'ai when he
commented on the word in the *Shuo-wen* (*SWCTC* 7B:106–107). This can also be
proved by a statement in *HS* 6:2b that in 140 B.C. Emperor Wu pardoned the family
members of the rebels of Wu, Ch'u, and the Seven States who had been enslaved by
the government. Here the character *nu* 帑 was also used for the enslaved family
members. Ying Shao comments, "At the time of the rebellion of Wu, Ch'u, and the
Seven States the wives and children [of the rebels] were submerged and made
government male and female slaves" (*HS* 6:2a). If *nu* 帑 is interpreted in this way,
then *shou nu* 收帑 means "to enslave the family members" and the sentence from the
Shih-chi quoted above actually includes two actions:(1) the punishment with the criminals and (2) enslavement. Throughout the whole passage in the *Han-shu* the two
are mentioned separately. For a detailed discussion of this law see *HLCI* 10:5a–7b;
see also Hulsewé, *Remnants of Han Law*, I, 114.

Since *shou nu* is mentioned in the *Shih-chi* as well as in *HS* 4:5a (I, 16) whereas the

and right chancellors, Chou P'o and Ch'en P'ing, presented a memorial and said: "To have fathers and mothers, wives, children, and siblings punished and enslaved [with the criminal] is to frighten their minds, making it not easy for them to violate the law. This has been practiced for a long time. In our humble opinion, it would be better to keep to the old practice." Emperor Wen again said: "We hear that people will be honest if the law is proper; people will follow if this punishment is deserved. Furthermore, to rule people and to guide them to good is [the function of] officials. If you cannot guide them, and instead punish them by improper laws, it does harm to the people and is violent. We cannot see its advantage. You ought to give it full consideration."

Then P'ing and Po said: "Your Majesty bestows great benevolence upon the world by not enslaving the [family members] of criminals and not punishing those who are innocent. We cannot match Your great virtue. In accordance with Your edict, we ask to abrogate all the laws enslaving [criminals' family members] and making them mutually responsible."

The punishment of the three *tsu* came into practice again when Hsin Yüan-p'ing attempted treachery.[70] [*HS* 23:17b–18b; similar *SC* 10:5b–6a]

18. SUPPORTED BY ELDER BROTHER

197–
177 B.C. Chang Shih-chih,[71] whose style was Chi, was a native of Che-yang[72]

---

word *shou* is mentioned only in the present passage (both referring to the same incident), it seems that *shou* actually has the same meaning as *shou nu*. Probably the word *shou* or *shou lü* 收律, "the law of *shou*," was so understood at that time. The *Shih-chi* reads 除收帑諸相坐律令, whereas the above passage reads 盡除收律相坐法, but they mean the same thing.

According to Han law, among the family members only the wives and children of the criminals were made male and female slaves and had their faces tattooed (see *SKC*, Wei, 12:9a–b). It was reported in the early part of the third century that among the slaves whose ancestors were criminals there were those who were still tattooed and served in the government even after a hundred generations (*SKC*, Wei, 12:9a–b).

Something should be said concerning the abrogation of the punishment of enslavement. In 156 B.C. the enslaved family members of the rebels of Wu, Ch'u, and the Seven States were pardoned, which indicates that the punishment did not actually come to an end after the abolition act of 179.

[70] This event occurred in the seventh year of Emperor Wen, 163 B.C. For other cases occurring after the abolition act, see I, 1, n. 1, and *HLCI* 10:7b–8b.

[71] Chang Shih-chih reached the post of commandant of justice after several promotions. When Emperor Ching ascended the throne, he was demoted and appointed chancellor of the kingdom of Huai-nan (*HS* 50:1a–5b).

[72] Che-yang 者陽 prefecture was located in modern Fang-ch'eng county in Honan.

of the Nan-yang commandery. He lived with his elder brother Chung. He became a "mounted gentleman" by virtue of wealth.[73] Although he served Emperor Wen for ten years, he was given no chance for promotion, nor did he have a wide reputation. He said, "Remaining long in office, I have reduced Chung's property, [and yet my purpose] has not been achieved." Consequently he intended to resign and return home.[74] [*HS* 50:1a]

19. HUNDREDS OF CONCUBINES

After [Chang] Ts'ang[75] had been dismissed from the post of imperial   162 B.C. chancellor, he was old and had no teeth in his mouth. He drank milk and had women as his wet nurses. His wife and concubines numbered up to a hundred, and with those who had once been pregnant he would not have any intercourse again. Ts'ang died at the age of more than a hundred. [*SC* 96:6b; *HS* 42:6a]

20. REMARRIAGE

Empress Wang of Emperor Hsiao-ching was the mother of Emperor   Before 156 B.C. Wu. Her father, Wang Chung, was a native of Huai-li.[76] Her mother, Tsang Erh, was the granddaughter of Tsang T'u, the former king of Yen. She was the wife of Wang Chung. She bore a son, Hsin, and two daughters. Chung died. Tsang Erh remarried and became the wife of T'ien of Ch'ang-ling.[77] She bore [two] sons, Fen and Sheng.

---

[73] One of the qualifications for candidates for official appointment, according to a Han regulation, was the possession of a certain amount of wealth. In the early days one hundred thousand cash was set as the minimum. Considering that this standard was too high and that many scholars who did not possess enough property were blocked from becoming officials, Emperor Ching reduced the minimum to forty thousand in 142 B.C. (*HS* 5:9a). Ju Shun, who quotes the *Han-i-chu*, says that five hundred thousand was required for the post of gentleman in regular attendance (Yen: *HS* 50:1a). For more details on these qualifications, see Chapter 4, n. 4.

[74] He did not resign. He received a promotion through the recommendation of another official (*HS* 50:1a).

[75] Chang Ts'ang 張蒼 was an old follower of Emperor Kao, who made him the marquis of Pei-p'ing because of his military merit. He was skillful in calculation and astronomy, and in the office of the imperial chancellor held an important position in charge of the accounts presented by the various kingdoms and commanderies. He was later promoted to the post of grandee secretary. He became the imperial chancellor in 176 and was dismissed in 162 (*SC* 96:1a–2a, 5b–6b; *HS* 42:1a–b, 4b–5b).

[76] Huai-li 槐里 was located in modern Hsing county of Shensi.

[77] Ch'ang-ling 長陵 prefecture was located in the northeastern part of Hsien-yang of Shensi. It was the place where Emperor Kao was buried.

The elder daughter of Tsang Erh married and became the wife of Chin Wang-sun. A daughter was born. Tsang Erh performed a divination which said, "Both daughters will be noble." Intending to depend upon her two daughters, she took away [her daughter] from Chin. Chin was angry and did not want to divorce her. Then [Tsang Erh] presented her to the palace of the heir apparent.[78] The heir apparent favored and loved her.[79] Three daughters and a son were born.[80] . . .

156 B.C.
150 B.C.   [Emperor Ching] set up his wife [née] Wang as empress and her son as heir apparent.[81] Hsin, the older brother of the empress, was ennobled as marquis of Kai.[82] . . .

140 B.C.   After she had been empress for nine years, Emperor Ching died. When Emperor Wu ascended the throne, she was made the empress dowager. The mother of the empress dowager, Tsang Erh, was honored with the title of baronet of P'ing-yüan; T'ien Fen was ennobled as marquis of Wu-an, and [T'ien] Sheng as marquis of Chou-yang. Among the members of the Wang and T'ien families, those who became marquises were three. . . . Fen [later] reached [the post of] imperial chancellor. Wang Chung was posthumously honored with the title of Marquis Kung. A [funerary] park town[83] consisting of two hundred households was founded at Huai-li, and a chief and assistants were put in
136 B.C.   charge to guard it. When the baronet of P'ing-yüan died,[84] she was buried together with the T'ien family at Ch'ang-ling. A [funerary] park town like the one for Marquis Kung was also set up.

Su,[85] the daughter born to Chin Wang-sun by the empress dowager while she was a commoner, was staying with the common people. The

[78] The later Emperor Ching.

[79] The younger sister was also later sent to the palace of the heir apparent and was favored by him. She gave birth to four sons, who were all made kings (*HS* 97A:10b).

[80] The son, the later Emperor Wu, was born in 156 B.C. after Emperor Ching had ascended the throne.

[81] In 150 B.C. (*HS* 5:5a).

[82] In 145 B.C. (*HS* 18:4a).

[83] A funerary park town, *yüan-i* 園邑, was a town established by order of the emperor around a tomb, usually that of the parents of an empress. Two or three hundred households were moved there and a chief and assistants (*ch'eng* 丞) were appointed to guard the tomb and temple and to offer sacrifices. Cf. *SC* 49:4b, 5b; *HS* 97A:7a, 8a, 18a, 20b, 23b, 26a, 28a.

[84] In 136 B.C. (*HS* 6:3a).

[85] We follow the explanation of Ch'ien Ta-hsin and Wang Hsien-ch'ien, who assume that the character *su* 俗 was the name of the girl. Wang supports Ch'ien's interpretation by quoting the statement of Hsü Kuang, who said that her name was Su (*HSPC* 97A:10a). The story of the elder sister was not in Ssu-ma Ch'ien's text; it was a supplement by Chu, who said he had heard it from a scholar whose surname was Chung-li. The *Han-shu* includes it in the text.

matter was concealed. Shortly after Emperor Wu came to the throne, Han Yen[86] told him of it. The emperor said, "Why did you not speak of this earlier?" Then he got into a carriage and went personally to welcome her. Her home was in the small market place of [the city of] Ch'ang-ling. Going directly to the door, he sent his attendants in search of her. All the family members were frightened. The girl fled and hid herself.[87] [The attendants] helped her to come out and to make obeisance to [the emperor]. The emperor descended from the carriage, and standing[88] there said, "Elder sister, why do you hide yourself so entirely?" Taking her to the Ch'ang-lo Palace in the carriage, he went with her to visit the empress dowager. The empress dowager wept, and the girl also wept with emotion. The emperor presented wine and offered a toast, wishing [his mother's] health. And he granted to his elder sister ten million cash, three hundred male and female slaves, one hundred *ch'ing* of public land, and one mansion. The empress dowager thanked him and said, "The emperor has spent too much." Then he granted her a benefice[89] and gave her the honorary title of baronet of Hsiu-ch'eng. She had one son and one daughter. The daughter married a marquis.[90] The son had the honorific title of Tzu-chung of Hsiu-ch'eng. Because of [his relation to] the empress dowager he was overbearing in the capital. [*HS* 97A:9b–10a, 10b–11b; similar *SC* 49:7a–9b, 12a–13a]

21. WIDOW ELOPES AND REMARRIES

It happened that King Hsiao of Liang died.[91] [Ssu-ma] Hsiang-ju[92]   Ca. 144 B.C.

---

[86] Han Yen 韓嫣 had been studying with Emperor Wu before he ascended the throne and was very much in his favor (*HS* 93:3a–b).

[87] According to *SC* 49:12b, she hid herself under the bed.

[88] *SC* 49:12b has 泣, "to weep," instead of 立, "to stand." See also *HSPC* 97A:10a.

[89] "Benefice" is *t'ang-mu i* 湯沐邑. "*I*" means city, or in this case, a fief. *T'ang-mu* literally means "to bathe." In Chou times a feudal lord received in addition to his main fief a benefice called *t'ang-mu*, located near the imperial capital. Before proceeding to a court audience, he was supposed to stop there and perform his ablutions (*LCCS* 13:16a). The fiefs of the princesses of Han and probably also of Ch'in were small estates near the imperial capital (cf. *HS* 14:3a), and even though they had lost their original function, they were still called *t'ang-mu*.

[90] According to Chu, she became the queen of a king. Hsü Kuang says that she married the heir apparent of the king of Huai-nan, Liu An (*SC* 49:13a, P'ei; cf. *HS* 44:9b).

[91] In 144 B.C. *HS* 5:7a.

[92] Ssu-ma Hsiang-ju (179–117 B.C.) was one of the most famous poets of Han. He was a native of Ch'eng-tu in Shu commandery. Possessing a large amount of wealth, he went to Ch'ang-an where he became a gentleman at the imperial court and later

returned home. His family was poor and had nothing to live on. He was a good friend of the prefect of Lin-ch'iung, Wang Chi. Chi said, "Chang-ch'ing,[93] you left home and engaged in an official career for a long time and have not been successful. Come to my place."[94] Then Hsiang-ju went there and stayed in a canton outside the city. The prefect of Lin-ch'iung pretended to be respectful to him, going to visit Hsiang-ju every day. At first Hsiang-ju received him. Later he pretended to be ill and ordered the attendants to give his thanks to Chi [for his visit]. Chi was more respectful than before.[95]

In Lin-ch'iung there were many rich persons. Cho Wang-sun[96] had eight hundred household slaves. Ch'eng Cheng[97] also had several hundred. These two men said to each other, "The prefect has an honorable guest. Let us prepare dinner and invite him and also invite the prefect."

When the prefect arrived, Cho's guests numbered a hundred. At noon [men were sent] to invite Ssu-ma Chang-ch'ing. Chang-ch'ing apologized, [saying] that he was ill and unable to go. The prefect of Lin-ch'iung dared not eat any food. He himself went to welcome Hsiang-ju. Hsiang-ju could not refuse him. Then he made an effort to come. He was admired by all the guests.

After much wine had been drunk, the prefect of Lin-ch'iung rose to present a lute and said, "I hear that Chang-ch'ing is fond of it. I hope he will amuse himself by playing it." Hsiang-ju declined with thanks, but [then] played a couple of verses.

---

a military horseman regular attendant *(wu-ch'i ch'ang-shih* 武騎常侍) at the rank of 600 piculs. Emperor Ching did not care for poetry, and Hsiang-ju went to the kingdom of Liang where he was well-treated by King Hsiao. When the king died in 144 B.C., Ssu-ma Hsiang-ju returned to Shu, where he married Wen-chün 文君, the daughter of the rich iron manufacturer, Cho Wang-sun, as described here. Later, Emperor Wu was delighted with a prose-poem *(fu)* by Hsiang-ju and invited him to the capital, where he became a gentleman, and later, general of the palace gentlemen. He was later active in Southwest China, where, as a delegate of the Han court, he was able to persuade the Southwest Barbarians to submit to the Han. See *HS* 57A and B.

[93] Chang-ch'ing 長卿 was the style of Ssu-ma Hsiang-ju.

[94] As a guest. Both friendship and, although it is not stated here, Hsiang-ju's scholarship recommended this relationship despite his poverty and lack of success in an official career.

[95] Such formal behavior is not called for between good friends. The prefect's visits to Hsiang-ju were made in the hope that such acts would build up respect for his guest. Similarly, Hsiang-ju's refusal to see so important an official as the prefect would increase respect for him among his neighbors. In other words, it was a game of pretense between good friends to enhance the status of the poorer of the two.

[96] Cho Wang-sun was a rich iron manufacturer.

[97] Ch'eng Cheng was also a rich iron manufacturer of Lin-ch'iung.

At this time Cho Wang-sun had a daughter, Wen-chün, who had recently lost her husband. She was fond of music. Therefore Hsiang-ju pretended [to be playing] for the prefect to show his respect for him, but expressed his feelings by means of the lute to captivate her. When Hsiang-ju went to Lin-ch'iung, he was escorted by carriages and horses. He was very handsome in a calm, easy, and elegant manner. When he played the lute at Cho's banquet, Wen-chün peeped at him through the door. She was pleased and liked him, but she feared she could not have him as her mate.[98] When the banquet was finished, Hsiang-ju then sent someone to present a valuable gift to Wen-chün's attendant, through whom he expressed [what was in] his heart. Wen-chün ran away to meet Hsiang-ju that very night. Hsiang-ju then fled back [to Ch'eng-tu][99] with her. His home had nothing but the four standing walls.

Cho Wang-sun was extremely angry[100] and said, "My daughter is worthless. I am not hard-hearted enough to kill her, but I will not give her a single cash." Someone urged Wang-sun [not to act in this way]. Wang-sun did not take the advice.

Later on, Wen-chün was unhappy. "Chang-ch'ing," said she, "let us go to Lin-ch'iung. If we borrow money from my brother, it will still be enough to maintain our living. Why should we be as poor as this?"

Hsiang-ju went to Lin-ch'iung with her. He sold all his carriages and horses, bought a wine shop to sell wine and let Wen-chün take care of the stall. Hsiang-ju himself, wearing calf-nose trousers,[101] worked together with his hired labor washing the utensils in the market.

When Cho Wang-sun heard about this, he was ashamed of it. He closed his door and did not go out any more. The brother, cousins, and uncles [of Wen-chün], one after another, said to Wang-sun, "You have one son and two daughters. You are not lacking in wealth. Now Wen-chün has already lost her chastity to Ssu-ma Chang-ch'ing. Chang-ch'ing is tired of traveling. Although he is poor, his talent is dependable. And moreover, he is the guest of the prefect. Why do you disgrace him like this?" Having no alternative, Cho Wang-sun divided

---

[98] She may have been fearful either that the young man did not care for her or that her father would object to the marriage. Her fear was probably of her father, because she eloped with Hsiang-ju after he had declared himself through her personal servant.

[99] While the *Shih-chi* reads 馳歸, the *Han-shu* has 馳歸成都.

[100] Apparently Cho Wang-sun was angry at his daughter for neglecting to obtain his consent and particularly for eloping, which was an intolerable shame to the family.

[101] A kind of apron.

his property and gave Wen-chün one hundred slaves, a million cash, and her clothing, bed coverings, and other properties [which she had had] at the time of her [first] marriage.

Then Wen-chün returned to Ch'eng-tu with Hsiang-ju. They bought land and houses and became rich persons.[102] [*SC* 117:1b–3a; *HS* 57A: 1b–3a]

22. Cross-Cousin Marriage

141–
130 B.C. Empress Ch'en of Emperor Wu was the daughter of the elder princess, P'iao.[103] [*HS* 97A:11b]

23. No Relief from Brothers

Ca.
127 B.C. [Chu-fu] Yen[104] said: "Since my twenties for more than forty years I have been engaged in traveling and studying without success. My parents did not treat me as their son; my brothers did not receive me; my guests left me.[105] I have been in straits for a long time. . . ."

The emperor appointed Yen chancellor of Ch'i. When he arrived at

---

[102] More of this biography is translated in I, 24.

[103] P'iao 嫖 was the elder princess of Kuan-t'ao 館陶長公主, the elder sister of Emperor Ching. Their mother was Empress Tou of Emperor Wen (see I, 12). The princess married Ch'en Wu 陳午, by whom she had a daughter, whose name, according to the *Han-wu ku-shih,* quoted by Ssu-ma, was A-chiao 阿嬌. A-chiao was married to Emperor Ching's son, the later Emperor Wu, who was the heir apparent at the time. When Emperor Wu ascended the throne, she was made empress. She was dismissed in 130 B.C. (*SC* 49:5a–b, 10b–11a; *HS* 97A:7b–8a, 11b–12a).

[104] Chu-fu Yen was a native of Lin-tzu (modern Lin-tzu of Shantung) of the kingdom of Ch'i. He became adept in the technique of political persuasion, the so-called perpendicular and horizontal technique, a method used by those who argued either for or against a particular point in an effort to influence the attitudes of the political leaders of different states. Later he engaged in the study of the classics and taught in various schools. His attempts to establish a relationship with the princes of Ch'i were frustrated by scholars who refused to receive him.

In 134 B.C. he went to the capital. There he visited the Grand General Wei Ch'ing. On a number of occasions Wei brought his name to the attention of the emperor, but these friendly efforts brought no results. Finally, faced with destitution, Chu-fu Yen presented to the emperor a memorial that he himself had written. Upon reading it the emperor immediately appointed him gentleman of the palace. After several transfers he was made palace grandee. Yen became very influential, advising the emperor on different matters. He was appointed chancellor of the kingdom of Ch'i about 127 B.C. When he arrived there the king committed suicide because Yen knew about his incestuous behavior. The king's *tsu* were exterminated because of this. See *HS* 64A:16b–21a and 14:5a for the date of the king's death.

[105] The reason for their bad treatment was his social failure.

Ch'i, he assembled all his brothers and guests. He distributed five hundred catties of gold to them. Scolding them, he said: "When I was poor, my brothers did not give me any clothing or food, and my guests did not receive me into their homes. Now that I have become the chancellor of Ch'i, you, gentlemen, come to welcome me from a distance of a thousand *li*. I am going to break with you. Don't enter my door again." [*HS* 64A:20a–b]

24. DAUGHTER RECEIVES SHARE OF FATHER'S PROPERTY

Cho Wang-sun sighed, thinking that he had consented to his daughter's marriage to Ssu-ma Chang-ch'ing rather late.[106] Then he generously distributed a part of his property and gave it to his daughter. It was equal to that [given to] his son.[107] [*SC* 117:30a; *HS* 57B:3b–4a]

129 B.C.

25. FATHER BEATS SON

After Queen Ch'eng-shu died, the king[108] made Hsü-lai queen. Lady Chüeh was also favored by him. The two were jealous of each other. Lady Chüeh thereupon slandered Queen Hsü-lai to the heir apparent,[109] saying, "Hsü-lai commanded her slave girl to kill the heir apparent's mother by means of *ku*[110] magic." The heir apparent hated Hsü-lai. When Hsü-lai's elder brother came to Heng-shan, the heir apparent drank with him and wounded the queen's elder brother with a sword. The queen hated him and was furious; she frequently slandered

---

[106] This happened after Ssu-ma Hsiang-ju had been promoted to the post of general of the palace gentlemen and sent as an envoy to the Western Barbarians. Since Cho's daughter had eloped with Ssu-ma Hsiang-ju, the statement probably means that he regretted that he had waited so long before recognizing his daughter's marriage. See I, 21.

[107] As a rule, a daughter was entitled to enjoy part of her parent's wealth as a marriage dowry. Cho Wang-sun, who had one son and two daughters, had given Wen-chün one-eighth of his slaves and some cash in an earlier settlement. For a daughter to receive a share equal to her brother's seems rather atypical. Since no mention is made of an equal share for the other daughter, we do not know whether both daughters enjoyed the same privilege. But considering that the gift, which is described as a "generous distribution" in our text, was given only after Ssu-ma's political success had deeply impressed Cho, it would seem to be an exception.

[108] The king of Heng-shan, Tz'u 衡山王賜, was one of the grandsons of Emperor Kao.

[109] The heir apparent, Shuang 爽, was the son of Ch'eng-shu 乘舒.

[110] On *ku* 蠱, see Ch'ü T'ung-tsu, *Law and Society in Traditional China* (Paris and The Hague, 1961), p. 222.

the heir apparent to the king. . . . Therefore the king beat[111] the heir apparent many times.

In the fourth year of Yüan-shuo the queen's stepmother was wounded by someone. The king suspected that the heir apparent had sent a man to hurt her and beat the heir apparent. Later, when the king was sick, the heir apparent, pleading illness as an excuse, did not go to attend him. Hsiao, the queen, and Wu-ts'ai[112] slandered the heir apparent [saying] that the heir apparent was not really ill, that he himself said he was ill but had a joyful expression on his face. The king was extremely angry and wanted to depose the heir apparent and put his younger brother, Hsiao, in his place.

Knowing that the king had decided to depose the heir apparent, the queen hoped to set Hsiao aside also. The queen had an attendant who was skillful in dancing and was favored by the king. The queen wanted the attendant to have sexual relations with Hsiao in order to defame him, hoping thus to set aside both sons and put her own son, Kuang, in the place of the heir apparent. The heir apparent, Shuang, learned about it. Considering that the queen frequently slandered him without end, he intended to have illicit relations with her to close her lips. When the queen drank to [the heir apparent],[113] the heir apparent came forward to offer a toast, and taking advantage of this he leaned against the thigh of the queen and sought to sleep with her. The queen was angered and told the king. The king then summoned the heir apparent and wanted to bind him and beat him. Knowing that the king wanted to depose him and place his younger brother, Hsiao, in his place, the heir apparent then said to the king, "Hsiao had illicit intercourse with your female attendants,[114] and Wu-ts'ai had illicit intercourse with a slave.

---

[111] The *Han-shu* reads 繫笞, "to bind and beat," instead of 擊笞.

[112] Hsiao 孝 was the heir apparent's younger brother. Wu-ts'ai 無采 was his sister. All three were born of the same mother.

[113] The *Han-shu* reads 后飲太子太子前為壽.

[114] The terms *shih-che* 侍者, *yü-che* 御者, and *shih-yü* 侍御 all mean the same thing: an attendant. They were identical with the term *yü-pei*, the personal female slave. The texts of both the *Shih-chi* and the *Han-shu* use first the term *shih-che* and then *yü-che*; later when Hsiao was accused and executed, the term *yü-pei* is used (*SC* 118:12a; *HS* 44:17a). In another case in the *Han-shu* the biography of a marquis states that he had illicit relations with his father's *yü-pei*, but in the table only the term *yü* is used (*HS* 16:5a; 41:9b). However, the term *yü-pei* appears in *SC* 16:4b and 95:12b. In commenting on the terms *liang-jen* 良人 and *shih-yü* 侍御, Yen makes it clear that the former were concubines and the latter were female slaves (*HS* 97A:19b). This is an important statement in distinguishing the difference in status between a *shih-yü* and a concubine.

To have intercourse with a father's concubine was considered incest and therefore

Please make an effort to eat.[115] I am going to present a report to the emperor." Then he deserted the king and left. The king sent men to stop him, but no one was able to do so. Then the king himself, on horseback, pursued, and seized the heir apparent. The heir apparent used offensive language recklessly. The king fettered the heir apparent in the palace.[116] [*SC* 118:20a–21a; *HS* 44:15a–b]

---

a serious crime. A king who had illicit relations with his father's concubine and with his daughters committed suicide because he was accused of "perverting human relationships" (亂人倫) and his execution was demanded (*HS* 35:5b). In later dynasties, as evidenced in the codes of T'ang, Sung, Yüan, Ming, and Ch'ing, having illicit relations with a father's concubine was labeled "incest" (內亂) and in all laws except those of Yüan the punishment was death (Chang-sun Wu-chi, *T'ang-lü su-i*, Lan-ling Sun-shih ed., 1:21a, 26:13a, hereafter cited as *TLSI*; Tou I, *Sung hsing t'ung*, Liu-shih chia-yeh-t'ang ed., 1:10b, 26:15b, hereafter cited as *SHT*; Sung Lien *et al.*, *Yüan-shih*, Po-na ed., 104:3b, hereafter cited as *YS*; *Ming-lü chi-chieh fu-li* [Peking: Hsiu-ting fa-lü kuan, 1908], 1:5a, 25:6b, hereafter cited as *MLL*; *Ta Ch'ing lü-li hui-chi pien-lan* [Hu-pei: Hsien-chü, 1872), 4:19b, 33:21b, hereafter cited as *CLL*). In T'ang and Sung law the punishment for illicit intercourse with a female slave to whom one's father had granted his favors was three years' imprisonment, two degrees less severe than in the case of a concubine (*TLSI* 26:13a; *SHT* 26:15b). Such an offense was not included in the category of "incest."

The situation in Han is less clear because our knowledge of Han law is only fragmentary. Since a *shih-yü* or *yü-pei* did not have the status of a concubine, it seems unlikely that illicit intercourse with a father's personal female slave could have the implication of "incest," as Martin Wilbur suggests (*Slavery in China During the Former Han Dynasty* [Chicago, 1943], p. 331, n. 2). Of course, it would be arbitrary and dangerous to draw a conclusion based on the codes of later dynasties, even though the earlier codes might have had a considerable influence on the compilation of the later ones (cf. *HLCI*, preface, p. 1b, on the relation between the law of Han and T'ang). But in all the cases found in our texts none of the men found guilty of such an offense was accused of "perverting human relationships." It was considered ethically wrong and unlawful for a son to have relations with his father's *yü-pei* simply because her intimate relations with his father were known. It seems unlikely that no distinction was made between the punishment for having illicit intercourse with a father's concubine and his personal slave.

Considering that Hsiao was accused of having illicit intercourse with his father's personal slave and was executed (*SC* 118:12a; *HS* 44:17a), the death penalty seems to have been the punishment for such an offense. However, it should be noted that he and the king were involved in plotting a rebellion. The king took his own life. The queen and the heir apparent were also executed. There is another case in which a marquis who was accused of having illicit intercourse with his father's *yü-pei* committed suicide and his marquisate was abolished (*SC* 95:12b; *HS* 41:9b). It seems logical to assume that the marquis would not have committed suicide if such an offense did not call for a severe punishment. However, it should be pointed out that he was married to a princess, which may have been why he took his own life.

[115] The king obviously was too disturbed to eat.

[116] Two years later the king presented a memorial asking for the dismissal of the heir apparent and naming Hsiao in his place. When the heir apparent learned of it, he sent someone to the capital to accuse Hsiao of illegal actions. The king then accused the heir apparent. Previously the king had plotted rebellion with his elder

26. WIFE LEAVES POOR STUDENT

Before
126 B.C.   Chu Mai-ch'en,[117] whose style was Weng-tzu, was a native of Wu. His family was poor. He was fond of reading books and did not engage in managing property. He used to cut firewood and sell it to provide himself with food. He read aloud while he was carrying bundles of wood.

His wife also carried [wood] on her back and followed him. She frequently tried to stop Mai-ch'en from reading aloud on the road. Mai-ch'en read faster. His wife was ashamed of this and asked to leave him.[118] Mai-ch'en smiled and said, "I will become noble at the age of fifty. Now I am already more than forty. You have been suffering for many days. Wait until I am rich and noble; I will recompense you for your merit." His wife was angry and said, "People like you will eventually starve to death in a ditch. How can you become rich and noble?" Mai-ch'en could not detain her and let her go.

After that Mai-ch'en walked and recited alone on the road. [Once when] he was carrying wood among the graves [he met] his ex-wife and her [new] husband and family, who were offering a sacrifice before the tomb. Seeing that Mai-ch'en was hungry and cold, they called him and gave him food and drink. . . .

Ca.
123 B.C.   [Later on] the emperor appointed Mai-ch'en governor of the K'uai-chi commandery. . . . Hearing that the grand administrator was com-

---

brother, Liu An, the king of Huai-nan. When the plot was disclosed in 123 B.C., the king committed suicide. The heir apparent was executed because of the accusation by his father. The queen and Hsiao were also executed because of her black magic that caused the death of the former queen and because of his illicit intercourse with the king's maid (*SC* 118:19a–22b; *HS* 6:11a, 44:14a–17a).

[117] Chu Mai-ch'en was skilled in the writing of essays. Some years after his divorce he went to Ch'ang-an as a servant with an account bearer (*chi-li* 計吏) of the commandery government. There he met a man from his native place, Yen Chu 嚴助, who was an attendant within the palace at the court from about 132 B.C. (*HS* 64A:2a, 8a–11a) and who recommended him to the emperor. He was called to court to explain the *Ch'un-ch'iu* and the *Ch'u-tz'u*. His lecture was much appreciated by the emperor, who appointed him palace grandee. When the king of Tung-yüeh rebelled, because of Chu's good advice, Chu was promoted to the post of grand administrator of K'uai-chi to lead the army against the Tung-yüeh. His campaign was successful, and more than a year later, in 122 (see *HS* 64A:12a and 13a, 19B:6b), he was made chief commandant in charge of noble ranks (*chu-chüeh tu-wei* 主爵都尉). A few years later he was dismissed, but was subsequently given the position of chief official of the imperial chancellor (*ch'eng-hsiang chang-shih* 丞相長史). There were bad feelings between him and Chang T'ang, a high official, whom he accused of consorting with merchant families to his private benefit. Chang committed suicide in 115 B.C. (*HS* 6:15b), and Chu was put to death by the emperor when his charges were proven false. See II, 28.

[118] That is, asked to be divorced.

ing, the commandery sent people to clear the road. The prefects of the prefectures and officials all came to speed and welcome him. There were more than a hundred carriages. When he entered the territory of Wu he saw his ex-wife and her husband, who were repairing the road. Mai-ch'en stopped his carriage and ordered the carriage following to carry the couple to the grand administrator's official residence. He put them up in the garden and gave them food. One month later the wife committed suicide by hanging. Mai-ch'en gave money to her husband to bury her. [*HS* 64A:11a–13a]

27. A Widowed Princess Remarries

At this time the princess of P'ing-yang had lost her husband and lived alone.[119] Only a marquis could marry the princess.[120] She consulted with her attendants as to which one of the marquises of Ch'ang-an was qualified to be her husband. All of them mentioned the grand general.[121] The princess laughed and said, "This [man] came out of my family.[122] I frequently ordered him to ride and follow me when I was coming and going. How can I take him as my husband?" The attendants said, "Now the elder sister of the grand general is the empress,[123]

124 B.C.

[119] The *Han-shu* has a different version. It reads, "Formerly when [Wei] Ch'ing was honored and favored, the marquis of P'ing-yang, Ts'ao Shou 曹壽, had an incurable disease and went to his marquisate. The elder princess asked [her attendants] who was worthy among the marquises." However, according to the table of meritorious officials in the *Shih-chi* and *Han-shu*, Ts'ao Shih 曹時 became a marquis in 153 B.C., and his son Ts'ao Hsiang 曹襄 inherited the marquisate in 130 B.C. (*SC* 18:3a; *HS* 16:4a). Both Ssu-ma Ch'ien and Wang Hsien-ch'ien identify Ts'ao Shou with Ts'ao Shih (*SC* 18:3a–b; *HSPC* 55:17a).

Wei Ch'ing became the grand general in 124 B.C. Thus Ts'ao Shou (or Ts'ao Shih) had died several years before, and the *Shih-chi* is correct in saying that the princess was a widow at this time. Probably Ts'ao Shou had gone to his marquisate before his death and the princess had lived alone before she became a widow.

[120] Another story also makes reference to such a custom, stating that according to Han tradition a princess was usually married to a marquis (*HS* 68:3b, 97A:19a).

[121] Wei Ch'ing, the Marquis of Ch'ang-p'ing, at this time (124 B.C.) was at the peak of his career. He had just been appointed grand general and his marquisate had been increased by six thousand households (8,700 according to the *Han-shu*).

[122] Wei Ch'ing's father was a prefectural officer who was assigned to serve in the house of the marquis of P'ing-yang. He had illicit intercourse with one of the slave-servants of the marquis, and Ch'ing was born of this union. Ch'ing became a servant in the marquis's family and later an escorting horseman of the princess (*SC* 111:1a–b; *HS* 55:1a–b).

[123] Empress Ch'en was deposed in 130 B.C. (*HS* 6:5b), and after Wei Tzu-fu gave birth to a son she became empress in 128 B.C. (*SC* 49:9b–10b; *HS* 6:8a, 97A:12b–13a).

and his three sons are marquises. His honor and wealth shake the world. Why is the princess treating him lightly?"

The princess then consented and asked the empress to tell Emperor Wu. A decree was issued ordering General Wei to marry the princess of P'ing-yang. [*SC* 49:13b–14a; similar *HS* 55:14b]

28. WIFE DIVORCED BECAUSE OF PETTY THEFT

Before *ca.* 87 B.C.

Previously[124] when [Wang] Chi[125] was young, he studied and stayed in Ch'ang-an. His neighbor to the east had a large jujube tree that stretched over Chi's yard. Chi's wife picked some jujubes to feed Chi. Later Chi learned about it and divorced his wife.[126] Hearing this, the neighbor on the east wanted to cut down the jujube tree. The neighbors all stopped him and implored Chi firmly to take back his wife. [*HS* 72:8b]

29. FATHER KILLS SON

87 B.C.

At this time the Attendant Within the Palace Hu, the son of the Commandant of the Guard Wang Mang,[127] declared, "I, Hu, was always there when the emperor[128] passed. How could there be an edict ennobling these three men?[129] This group of children are ennobling themselves." Hearing this, Ho Kuang reprimanded Mang severely. Mang killed Hu with poison. [*HS* 68:2b]

30. LEGAL RESPONSIBILITY OF FAMILY HEAD

81 B.C.

In the seventh month in the fall of the sixth year of Shih-yüan the Office for the Wine Monopoly was abolished. It was ordered that the

---

[124] Before he was appointed commandant of the capital of the king of Ch'ang-i, Ho 賀, who became king in 87 B.C.

[125] Wang Chi was a famous scholar and a virtuous official. He died in 48 B.C.

[126] Theft was one of the seven conditions under which a man could divorce his wife. In this instance, however, the husband interpreted the prohibition too strictly. This was reflected in the attitude of the owner, who wanted to cut down his tree, and the neighbors, who urged Chi to take back his wife.

[127] This is not the powerful Wang Mang who made himself emperor in A.D. 9.

[128] Emperor Wu.

[129] While Emperor Wu was ill, he issued an edict ennobling Chin Mi-ti, Shang-kuan Chieh, and Ho Kuang, raising them to the rank of marquis.

people be allowed to assess their tax in accordance with the law and to sell wine at four cash per *sheng*.[130] [*HS* 7:4b]

31. A Wife's Decision in Political Affairs

Emperor Chao died. The king of Ch'ang-i[131] was summoned and ascended the throne. He was licentious and disorderly; the Grand General [Ho] Kuang, together with the General of Chariots and Cavalry Chang An-shih, planned and intended to dismiss the king and to put someone else on the throne. After their discussion had been settled, they sent the Grand Minister of Agriculture T'ien Yen-nien to report it to [Yang] Ch'ang.[132] Ch'ang was shocked and frightened and did not know what to say. His back was wet through with perspiration and he merely answered, "Yes, yes" respectfully.

Yen-nien got up and went to [the place for] changing clothing.

74 B.C.

[130] Ju Shun comments: "According to the law, for all those who must assess their tax, the head of a family, each one must in person assess [the value of] his goods (家長身各以其物占). If his assessment is not in accordance with the facts, or if the head of the family does not himself in person have it written down, in all [such cases] he is fined two catties of gold, and whatever goods have not been assessed in person are confiscated and their value in cash is brought to the government."

Two interpretations of the text are possible. If the statement about the tax is read as one sentence, the tax was assessed on the sale of wine only. This is the opinion of Liu Pin, who says: "To assess the tax in accordance with the law means that it was ordered that the people could sell wine and assess the profit that they made and pay their tax. If their assessment did not correspond with the facts, they were punished according to the law." The *tsu* 租 was the *shui* 税, the tax on wine sales (*HSPC* 7:5a–b). This interpretation is followed by Dubs (*HFHD*, II, 161–62). We also follow Liu's interpretation. However, if the text is read as two sentences, the assessment of the tax would refer to goods in general, not merely to the wine tax. This interpretation is also reasonable, because there was a general regulation under which merchants and artisans were required to assess the value of their goods in paying their tax (*HS* 24B:11b; Nancy Lee Swann, *Food and Money in Ancient China* [Princeton, 1950], pp. 280–83).

[131] Emperor Chao died without an heir. The king of Ch'ang-i, Liu Ho, was chosen by Ho Kuang as the successor, but he was on the throne for only twenty-seven days. Then his kingdom was abolished and he was merely given a fief of two thousand households. In 63 B.C. he was ennobled as marquis of Hai-hun with four thousand households; later he was deprived of three thousand of them (*HS* 8:3a, 63:16b–20b).

[132] Yang Ch'ang was at first a subordinate of the grand general. He was later promoted to the post of grand minister of agriculture and then grandee secretary. At this time he was holding the post of imperial chancellor. He died in 74 B.C., after Emperor Hsüan had ascended the throne (*HS* 66:9a–b).

Ch'ang's wife[133] said hurriedly to Ch'ang from the east side room,[134] "This is an important affair of the empire. Now the grand general has decided after deliberation and sent [one of the] Nine Ministers to report it to you, Sir Marquis.[135] If you, Sir Marquis, do not respond promptly, are not of the same mind with the grand general, and hesitate without decision, you will be killed first." When Yen-nien returned after changing his clothing, Ch'ang's wife, together with Yen-nien [and Ch'ang], all three, talked together and consented: "We shall obey the instruction and order of the grand general." Thereupon they together dismissed the king of Ch'ang-i and put Emperor Hsüan on the throne. [*HS* 66:9a–b]

32. BROTHERS DISPUTE OVER PROPERTY

58 B.C.   [Han Yen-shou][136] arrived at Kao-ling[137] as he was proceeding on a tour of inspection of the prefectures [under his jurisdiction]. There were [two] brothers who were having litigation over land and accusing each other. Yen-shou was deeply depressed and said, "I have the honor to fill the position and to be the example for the commandery; yet I have been unable to propagate and make manifest the influence of the teachings. [The situation has] come to the point that it causes the people to have disputes and litigation among kindred and it causes harm to public morals. Moreover, it has made the virtuous chief officials, the bailiffs, the thrice venerable, and the 'filially and brotherly respectful' be

---

[133] According to *HS* 66:10a–b, the mother of Yang Yün, the second son of Yang Ch'ang, was the daughter of Ssu-ma Ch'ien; but Yün had a stepmother who had no son. Since Yang Ch'ang died about a month after the incident (the dismissal of the king took place in the seventh month, and Yang Ch'ang died in the eighth month, see *HS* 8:3a–b), the wife mentioned in the passage above must have been the stepmother. Cf. *HSPC* 66:8b, Ho Cho's comment.

[134] According to Yen, 厢 was the side room either on the east or west of the main bedroom (*HS* 42:2b).

[135] According to Ju Shun, a marquis who held the post of imperial chancellor was addressed as *chün-hou* 君侯, Sir Marquis. Yen, quoting the example of Yang Yün, who was addressed as *chün-hou* by someone, thinks that all marquises might have been addressed in this manner, not only the imperial chancellor (*HS* 66:5a).

[136] Han Yen-shou 韓延壽, who had been grand administrator of three other commanderies, was appointed left adjunct (*tso-p'ing i* 左馮翊) in 59 B.C. The inspection tour took place more than a year after he had held the post. He was later involved in a case in which he and Grandee Secretary Hsiao Wang-chih brought accusations against each other. He was found guilty of violating the sumptuary laws, of distributing government funds without authorization, and of falsely accusing the grandee secretary, and was executed in 57 B.C. (*HS* 76:8b–13a).

[137] Kao-ling 高陵 was near the modern city of Kao-ling in eastern Shensi.

ashamed. The fault[138] is with the adjunct. I must start by resigning."[139]

On the same day he notified [the central government] by dispatch that he was ill and was not attending [official] affairs. He went and lay down in the relay station, closed his door, and reflected on his faults. The entire prefecture did not know what to do. The prefects, assistant prefects, bailiffs, and thrice venerable all bound themselves, waiting for punishment.[140] Then the kinsmen of the men who had the litigation reproached them one after the other. The two brothers, deeply repentant, both came to confess their fault, shaving their heads and baring their shoulders. They were willing to interchange their land with each other and [promised] not to dare to dispute again until death. [*HS* 76:11a]

33. FATHER INTENDS TO BEAT SON

[Ch'en Wan-nien's][141] son, Hsien, whose style was Tzu-k'ang, was   51–45 B.C. appointed gentleman when he was eighteen years old because of Wan-nien's recommendation.[142] His ability was unusual and he was unyielding and straightforward. He frequently discussed [government] affairs

---

[138] His attitude obviously was based upon the Confucianist idea of the role of moral influence in governing. Any offense among the people was a failure of the ruler either because of his bad influence or his failure to educate them. And the more exalted the status of the ruler, the greater his responsibility. Theoretically, all those who were inferior were under his influence. For this reason, Han Yen-shou was ashamed of himself and wanted to resign. For a discussion of the theory of moral influence in politics, see Ch'ü, *Law and Society*, pp. 247 ff.

[139] *I-ping* 移病 is a synonym for resign. It was called this because officials who intended to resign sent a letter (移書) telling of their illness. The document, which was official in nature, was known as 移. Since *i* also means "to move," the phrase may be interpreted as "to move to live in another place because of illness" 以病移居 (Yen: *HS* 58:1a).

[140] None of the officials was legally responsible for the disputes between the brothers. Their action was rather an expression of sharing the blame with their grand administrator.

[141] Ch'en Wan-nien 陳萬年 was at first only a petty official in the commandery government. He was later appointed a prefect of a prefecture, then grand administrator of Kuang-ling, and then grand keeper of equipages in 56 B.C. He was incorruptible and virtuous in his personal behavior. He was, however, skilled in serving influential persons, and was thus promoted to the position of grandee secretary in 51 B.C. upon the recommendation of the imperial chancellor, Ping Chi 丙吉, whom he served very well. He died seven years later (*HS* 66:16b–17a, 19B:12a–b).

[142] That is, appointed because of father's recommendation. According to the *Han-i-chu*, quoted by Ying Shao, a high official who ranked at 2,000 piculs or more and had been in office for three years was allowed to recommend one of his sons or brothers for the post of gentleman (*HS* 11:3b).

and satirized the [emperor's] intimate officials. Several tens of memorials were presented. He was promoted to the post of head of the Bureau of the Left.

Once when Wan-nien was ill, he called Hsien to his bedside and gave him instructions. He talked until midnight. Hsien fell asleep and his head touched the screen. Wan-nien became furious and wanted to strike him with his staff. He said, "I, your father, was instructing you, and yet you fell asleep and did not listen to my words. Why?" Hsien kowtowed, apologized, and said, "I already know what you are talking about; the main point is to instruct Hsien how to flatter." Wan-nien then did not say anything more. [*HS* 66:17a–b]

34. Divorce and Remarriage

Before
48 B.C.

[Wang Chin][143] was fond of wine and women. He took many concubines and had four daughters and eight sons. . . . Only Feng, Ch'ung, and Cheng-chün, the Empress Yüan,[144] belonged to the same mother. Their mother, who was the legal wife, was the daughter of a Li family of the Wei commandery. Later she was repudiated on the ground of jealousy,[145] remarried, and became the wife of Kou Pin of Ho-nei.

When Emperor Yüan died, the heir apparent ascended the throne; this was Emperor Hsiao-ch'eng. The empress was honored as empress dowager.[146] . . . The empress dowager's mother, Mother Li, the wife of Kou, had given birth to a son, whose name was Shen, and was a widow. [Previously] while Marquis Ch'ing, Chin, was still alive, the empress dowager[147] had ordered Chin to take back Mother Li. [*HS* 98:2a–b, 4a, 5a]

[143] While still a youth Wang Chin 王禁 studied law in Ch'ang-an and became a clerk of the commandant of justice. In 54 B.C. when his daughter Cheng-chün 政君, the later empress of Emperor Yüan, was eighteen, he presented her to the palace. In 48 B.C. after Emperor Yüan came to the throne, he made his father-in-law marquis of Yang-p'ing. Wang Chin died in 42 B.C. and was given the posthumous title of Marquis Ch'ing (*HS* 98:2a–3b).

[144] More than a year after she entered the palace, Cheng-chün was given to the heir apparent, the later Emperor Yüan, by Empress Hsüan. In 51 B.C. she gave birth to a son, the later Emperor Ch'eng. When the heir apparent ascended the throne, Cheng-chün was made "favored beauty" (*chieh-yü* 倢伃). Three days thereafter she was made empress (*HS* 98:3a–b).

[145] Jealousy was one of the seven causes for which a wife might be divorced. It was included among them, according to Ho Hsiu, because its presence made for friction in the family (*KYCS* 9:11b; *KTCY* 6:6a).

[146] In 33 B.C. (*HS* 10:1b).

[147] Cheng-chün became empress dowager in 33 B.C., and her father had died in 42 B.C., so she must have forced her father to take back her mother sometime after she became empress in 48 B.C.

35. The Wife Follows Her Husband

The wife of Pao Hsüan[148] of Po-hsi was a daughter of the Huan Before
15 B.C. family. Her style was Shao-chün. Hsüan once went to study with Shao-chün's father. Her father marveled at his simple and hard life; therefore he gave him his daughter in marriage. He provided a large dowry and gifts. Hsüan was displeased and said to his wife, "Shao-chün, you were born in riches and pride, and are accustomed to beautiful ornaments, but I am really poor and cannot match the courtesy." His wife said, "You, sir, cultivate virtue and live in simplicity, therefore my father sent me, your humble handmaid,[149] to serve you by holding the towel and comb.[150] Since I am at your service, I only follow your orders." Hsüan smiled and said, "If you can be like this, this is my will."

Then his wife returned to her family all her attendants, garments, and ornaments. She wore instead short clothes made of cloth. She and Hsüan, together pushing a small cart, returned to his village. [*HHS* 84:2a]

36. Marriage with Grandmother's Niece

Empress Fu of [Emperor] Hsiao-ai was the daughter of Queen Dowager Ting-t'ao's[151] paternal cousin.[152] When Emperor Ai was the King of Ting-t'ao, Queen Dowager Fu wished to double the [ties] of rela-

---

[148] Pao Hsüan later began his office career as a district bailiff (*se-fu* 嗇夫). He was appointed gentleman consultant (*i-lang* 議郎) upon the recommendation of Wang Shang (15–12 B.C.). He later became Grandee Remonstrant, and was promoted to the post of director of retainers in 2 B.C. He was dismissed in the same year. In the time of Emperor P'ing he was accused of receiving a guest whose arrest was sought by the government and was put into prison, where he committed suicide (*HS* 72:23b–29b).

[149] *Ch'ieh* 妾 is the conventional and courteous way for a woman to refer to herself when she is speaking before her husband or others. The use of such a humble term by a wife apparently underlines the woman's inferiority. A husband usually refers to himself as "I" when speaking before his spouse.

[150] This is also a conventional way for a wife to express her role in waiting upon her husband.

[151] She was an imperial concubine of Emperor Yüan, holding the title of brilliant companion. She was the mother of King Kung of T'ing-t'ao, the father of Emperor Ai, and was therefore called the Queen Dowager Ting-t'ao. After Emperor Ai ascended the throne, she was honored as revered empress dowager (*kung-huang-t'ai-hou* 恭皇太后), In 6 B.C. she was given the title *ti-t'ai-t'ai-hou* 帝太太后, and later that of *huang-t'ai-t'ai-hou* 皇太太后; both are the equivalent of empress dowager (*HS* 97B: 19a–21a).

[152] That is Fu Yen, the Queen dowager's father's brother's son (*HS* 97B:21a).

tionship and took her for a mate for the king. When the king entered
8 B.C. the [imperial house] and was made the heir apparent of Han, the daughter of the Fu family was made imperial concubine.¹⁵³ [*HS* 97B:23b]

37. Son Ordered to Commit Suicide

5–2 B.C.   [Wang] Mang¹⁵⁴ closed his door to protect himself.¹⁵⁵ His middle
son, Huo, killed a male slave. Mang scolded Huo severely and ordered
him to commit suicide. [*HS* 99A:4a]

38. Father Kills Son

A.D. 1   [Wang Mang] considered that Emperor P'ing was the successor of
Emperor Ch'eng and that no concern should be given to his private
[maternal] relatives.¹⁵⁶ Thus the emperor's mother and mother's family,
the Wei family, all remained in Chung-shan and were not permitted to
come to the capital. Mang's eldest son, Yü, disapproved of Mang's
isolation of the Wei family. Fearing that the emperor, when grown,
would hate them, Yü plotted together with Wu Chang and spread

---

¹⁵³ She became empress in 7 B.C. (*HS* 11:2a).

¹⁵⁴ Wang Mang was marquis of Hsin-tu. His fief was in the region of Hsin-yeh 新野
county (modern Honan) and had fifteen hundred households (*HS* 99A:1b).

¹⁵⁵ During this time Wang Mang was in retirement. He resigned from his post as
grand minister of war in 7 B.C. when Emperor Ai came to the throne and when the
emperor's grandmother, Fu, and his mother, Ting, were becoming more and more
influential. In 5 B.C. both Fu and Ting were given the titles of empress dowager, and
Wang Mang was accused by the imperial chancellor of having objected to the proposal to honor them in this way. He was commanded by the emperor to leave the
capital and go back to his fief. He remained there for three years, avoiding contact
with outsiders so that he would not become involved in political affairs that might
endanger him personally (*HS* 99A:3a–4a). Since Wang Mang was disliked by the
Empress Dowagers Fu and Ting, as well as by their relatives who were not in power
and many other high officials, any untoward act was liable to get him into trouble.
Probably this was why he took this incident so seriously that he even forced his son to
commit suicide. It seems unlikely that he did so because of his attitude against killing
slaves.

¹⁵⁶ Actually, Emperor P'ing succeeded Emperor Ai. The latter, who had no sons,
had followed Emperor Ch'eng, who also lacked direct male heirs. Both Emperor Ai
and Emperor P'ing were sons of Emperor Ch'eng's brothers, who held the rank of
kings. Since Wang Mang had been deprived of the reins of power for many years by
the families of Emperor Ai's mother and grandmother (the Ting and the Fu families),
he made every effort to prevent contacts between the family of Emperor P'ing's
mother and the imperial family.

blood[157] on Mang's gate at night as if it were a warning of the spirits in order to frighten Mang. [Wu] Chang hoped to use this opportunity to point out [to Mang] his errors. When the affair was disclosed, Mang killed Yü.[158] [*HS* 67:15a]

39. DIVORCE AND RECALL

[Chiang] Shih[159] served his mother very piously. His wife was very *Ca. A.D. 15* sincere in service and obedience. His mother liked to drink the water from the river. The water was about six or seven *li* away from the house. Frequently his wife went up to the stream to fetch the water. Once there was a storm and she could not get back on time. The mother was thirsty. Shih blamed [his wife] and sent her away.[160]

She then stayed at a neighbor's house. She spun day and night. She bought delicious foods and asked the neighbor woman to take them to her mother-in-law. After this had gone on for a long time, the mother-in-law was surprised and asked the reason. The neighbor woman told her the truth. The mother-in-law was ashamed of herself and called her back. She then served [even] more respectfully.

Later on the son went to fetch water from a distance and was drowned. Fearing that this might bring grief to her mother-in-law, she

[157] Actually it was the elder brother of Yü's wife, Lü K'uan 呂寬, who also participated in the plot and was sent by Yü 宇 to spread the blood (*HS* 99A:20a–b).

[158] According to Wang Mang's biography, he did not himself kill Yü. He arrested him and sent him to prison, where Yü drank poison and died. Yü's wife was also imprisoned and was executed after the birth of her child. Lü K'uan and hundreds of others were also put to death. Wang Mang memorialized that he did not dare to omit the punishment of his own son (*HS* 99A:20b–21a). Thus Wang Mang's son, strictly speaking, was killed legally by the government; therefore we cannot consider this a case of killing a son on the father's authority.

[159] Chiang Shih 姜詩 had a reputation for the greatest filial piety in his time. During the Red Eyebrow Rebellion the bandits who passed through his village, believing that it would anger the spirits and ghosts if the most filial of men were frightened, made their way quietly and without any show of arms. Since the harvest was bad, they offered him rice and meat. He took the gifts but buried them in the ground. In A.D. 60 he was recommended by the commandery government as "filially pious and incorrupt" and was sent to the capital. He was appointed gentleman of the palace and later became the prefect of Chiang-yang prefecture. He remained in this office until his death. His administration was effective and successful; the people of the prefecture instituted a sacrifice for him (*HHS* 84:4a–b).

[160] This action apparently was based on one of the seven traditional reasons for divorcing a wife. A woman was expected to serve her parents-in-law with all filial piety, and any failure to do so was grounds for divorce (*KYCS* 9:11b; *KTCY* 6:6a).

did not tell the truth, making an excuse that he was away studying.
[*HHS* 84:3b–4a]

40. Economic Functions of a Family

Fan Hung,[161] whose style was Mi-ch'ing, was a native of Hu-yang
of Nan-yang. He was the maternal uncle of Emperor Kuang-wu.[162] His
remote ancestor, Chung Shan-fu[163] of the Chou dynasty, was ennobled
as Fan;[164] therefore [the family] took it as their surname. [Fan's family]
was a distinguished one in the local community. His father, Chung,
whose style was Chün-yün, [and his forebears] had been skilled in farming for generations and were fond of business. Chung was gentle and
generous in character. There were [family] regulations, and for three
generations his family held their property in common. His children paid
him respect morning and evening as if they were in a government
[court].

He managed his property in such a way that nothing was wasted.
He assigned work to his slaves,[165] all in a suitable way. For this reason
both superiors and the inferiors could work hard, and their wealth and
profits doubled every year. He expanded his land to more than three
hundred *ch'ing*. The houses he built all had double halls and high
chambers. There were reservoirs[166] and canals irrigating [his fields]. He

---

[161] Fan Hung was appointed to the post of imperial court grandee in A.D. 25 and
was particularly honored by Emperor Kuang-wu, who bestowed upon him the rank
of "specially advanced," next only to that of the Three Ducal Ministers. In A.D. 29 he
was ennobled as marquis of Ch'ang-lo. Later his younger brother, his elder brother's
son, and his paternal cousin were also ennobled as marquises. He died in A.D. 51
(*HHS* 32:2b–4a).

[162] Emperor Kuang-wu's mother, Hsien-tu 嫺都, was the daughter of Fan Chung
(*HHS* 14:8a–b). Our text has the name T'ung 童, which is apparently an error for
Chung 重; the Palace edition has Chung.

[163] Chung Shan-fu 仲山甫 was a minister of King Hsüan of Chou (827–782 B.C.).

[164] Fan was located in modern Chi-yüan county in northern Honan.

[165] The term used in the text is *t'ung-li* 童隸.

[166] According to Li Tao-yüan, the reservoir was still known in his time as the
Reservoir of the Fan Family, although this family, because of financial reverses, no
longer owned it. It was located southwest of Hsin-yeh county (*HHS* 32:1b).

The *Shui-ching-chu*, quoted by Li, records a reservoir called Fan-shih 樊氏 Reservoir. The reservoir was "ten *li* from east to west and five *li* from south to north," and
was located east of the old mansion of the Fan family. According to a ditty of the time,

> The reservoir has a great expanse of water
> The land below it is good.
> After the Fan family lost their property
> The Yü 庾 family thereupon became prosperous.

(The present text of the *Shui-ching-chu* varies a little; see Li Tao-yüan, *Shui-ching-chu*
[Ssu-hsien chiang-she k'an-pen, 1892], 31:14a, hereafter cited as *SCC).*

raised fish in the ponds and bred cattle. Whatever was sought for was provided. Once he was going to make certain utensils. He first planted catalpa and lacquer trees. His contemporaries ridiculed him, but in later years he made use of all of them. Those who had laughed at him all came seeking to avail themselves of them. His wealth accumulated to a hundred million cash. He gave relief to his kinsmen and extended his kindness to those living in the same local community.

His daughter's sons, the Ho brothers, accused each other over property. Chung felt ashamed about that and gave them two *ch'ing* of land to bring an end to their quarrels and litigation. He was admired in his prefecture and selected to be thrice venerable.

Chung died at the age of more than eighty. He had lent many millions to the people. Before his death he made a will, [asking his family] to burn and destroy all the documents. All the debtors, being ashamed when they heard of it, came in a rush to pay their debts. Obeying Chung's will, his sons refused to take it. [*HHS* 32:1a–2a]

41. Kinsmen Mobilized for War

When Shih-tsu[167] crossed the Ho and came to Han-tan,[168] [Keng Ch'un][169] went to visit him. Shih-tsu treated him nicely. Seeing that the way in which [Kuang-wu's] generals led the army differed from that of other generals, [Ch'un] thereupon attempted to affiliate himself with [Kuang-wu]. He presented horses and many hundred rolls of silk. Shih-tsu went northward to Chung-shan[170] and asked Ch'un to remain in Han-tan.

While Wang Lang[171] was revolting and Shih-tsu was fleeing south-   A.D. 24

---

[167] Shih-tsu is the temple title of Emperor Kuang-wu.

[168] Modern Han-tan of southern Hopei.

[169] Keng Ch'un was from a distinguished family of Chü-lu. His father, Ai 耿艾, who first was governor under Wang Mang's regime, became grand administrator of Chinan when he submitted to Li I 李軼, a general of the Keng-shih emperor. Keng Ch'un was appointed chief commandant of cavalry by Li, who considered him out of the ordinary but also appointed him because of his family background. Keng Ch'un performed many deeds of military merit after he followed the later Emperor Kuang-wu. When Kuang-wu ascended the throne in A.D. 25, Keng was ennobled as marquis of Kao-yang, and in the following year he was appointed grand administrator of the Tung commandery. He died in A.D. 37 (*HHS* 21:11b–16b).

[170] Chung-shan 中山 is equated with modern Ting county of Hopei.

[171] Wang Lang ascended the throne in Han-tan in A.D. 24. In the following year Han-tan surrendered to Kuang-wu, and Wang Lang was killed (*HHS* 1A:11a ff.).

eastward from Chi,[172] Ch'un and his paternal first cousins, Hsin, Su, and Chih,[173] led their kinsmen and guests numbering more than two thousand people. Those who were old and sick carried coffins with them. They welcomed Kuang-wu at Yü.[174] Kuang-wu appointed Ch'un general of the van and made him district marquis of Keng. Hsin, Su, and Chih all became generals of the flank. . . .

In the meantime many commanderies and kingdoms were surrendering to Han-tan.[175] Fearing lest his kinsmen might change their minds, Ch'un sent Hsin and Su back to burn their houses. Shih-tsu asked him the reason for this. Ch'un replied, ". . . Now [Wang Lang in] Han-tan has ascended the throne, and many of the northern states are in a situation of doubt and uncertainty. Although I have had my entire lineage submit to you, even the old and weak following the army, yet I still fear that half of my kinsmen and guests might not be of the same mind. Therefore I burned the houses in order to break off any hopes of looking back."[176] Shih-tsu sighed and admired him. . . .

Ch'un's army was several *li* ahead of the other camps. He was attacked by bandits[177] in the night. Arrows fell like rain; many soldiers were killed and wounded. He ordered his troops not to move. A two thousand dare-to-die corps was chosen, each man being equipped with a strong bow and three arrows. They were ordered to go forward with gagged mouths and to make a detour in order to come out behind the bandits. [Arriving there], they shouted all at the same time and all the strong bows were released simultaneously; the bandits were frightened and withdrew. The army pursued them and defeated the bandits. Then he sent a horseman to report to Shih-tsu the next morning. Shih-tsu and many generals came to console him, asking whether he was in great trouble the preceding night. "Depending upon your majesty and vir-

---

[172] At this time Liu Hsiu, the later Kuang-wu, was in great distress. Wang Lang had ascended the throne in Han-tan, and a number of cities had surrendered to him. A reward was offered for the arrest of Liu Hsiu. Liu Hsiu went to Hsin-tu (located to the northeast of modern Chi of Hopei), where the grand administrator welcomed him. Thus Liu Hsiu was able to occupy several prefectures with the four thousand men he had recruited (*HHS* 1A:11b–12b).

[173] Keng Hsin 耿訢, Keng Su 耿宿, and Keng Chih 耿植 were later ennobled as marquises. Both Hsin and Chih became generals; Hsin was killed in action. Su became the grand administrator of the Tai commandery (*HHS* 21:16b–17a).

[174] Yü 育, according to Li, was a prefecture in Chi division.

[175] That is, Wang Lang who had his capital in Han-tan.

[176] That is, to keep them from having any desire to return home.

[177] The bandits were the Ch'ih-mei (Red Eyebrows), Ch'ing-tou 青犢, Shang-chiang 上江, Ta-t'ung 大彤, T'ieh-ch'ing 鐵脛, and Wu-fan 五幡. Altogether they numbered more than one hundred thousand men (*HHS* 21:13b).

tue," he replied, "we were lucky enough to preserve [our force]." "As the army should not move in the night we did not come to help you," said Shih-tsu. "With troops advancing and retreating without regularity, it is not good for all your kinsmen to stay in the army." Hence he appointed one of Ch'un's kinsmen, Keng Chi, to be the prefect of P'u-wu [prefecture],[178] and ordered all the kinsmen to live there. . . .

From these clansmen four became marquises,[179] three became marquises within the passes, and nine became 2,000-picul [officials]. [*HHS* 21:12b–14a, 17a]

42. Kinsmen Fight

While Wang Lang was revolting, [Liu] Chih and his brother Hsi and his cousin Hsin[180] led their kinsmen and guests, raising a troop of several thousand, and retained possession of Ch'ang-ch'eng.[181] Having heard of the return of Shih-tsu from Chi, they opened the gate to welcome him. [*HHS* 21:10b–11a]   A.D. 24

43. Husband and Mother-in-Law Influenced by Wife

Once, when [Yüeh] Yang-tzu[182] was walking on the road, he found a piece of gold that had been dropped by someone. He came back and gave it to his wife. His wife said, "I, your handmaid, have heard that a determined man does not drink the water from a Thief Spring,[183] and a pure man does not accept food which is given by someone impolitely.   Later Han

---

[178] P'u-wu 蒲吾, according to Li, was in the southern part of present Ling-shou in Hopei.

[179] The four were Keng Ch'un and his three cousins, Hsin, Su, and Chih.

[180] Liu Chih was then appointed general of the brave cavalry (*hsiao-ch'i chiang-chün* 驍騎將軍), Hsi 喜 and Hsin 歆 were appointed generals of the flank. All three were ennobled as marquises. In A.D. 26 Liu Chih was killed in action.

[181] Ch'ang-ch'eng 昌城, the native place of Liu Chih, was located in the northwest of modern Chi county of Hopei. Ch'ang-ch'eng, which appears as 昌成 in *HS* 28B, belonged to Hsin-tu kingdom in the Early Han; in the Later Han it belonged to An-p'ing 安平 kingdom and its name was changed from Ch'ang-ch'eng to Fu-ch'eng 阜城. See *HS* 28B:12b–13a; *HHC* 20:11b–12a; Wang Hsien-ch'ien, *Hou-Han-shu chi-chieh* (Ch'ang-sha: Wang-shih chiao-k'an ed., 1915), 21:6b, hereafter cited as *HHSCC*; Hsieh Shou-ch'ang *et al., Chung-kuo ku-chin ti-ming ta tz'u-tien* (Shanghai: Commercial Press, 1935), pp. 471–72, hereafter cited as *TMTTT*.

[182] The entire biography of Yüeh Yang-tzu 樂羊子 is translated here.

[183] This refers to a story told about Confucius. Once when Confucius was very thirsty, he passed by a spring called Thief Spring 盗泉. Since he disliked the name, he did not drink there (論語撰考讖, quoted in Li's commentary, *HHS* 84:13b).

How much worse is it to seek profit by picking up lost articles to stain one's behavior." Yang-tzu, being greatly shamed by this, then threw the gold into the field and went far away to find a teacher to study with. One year later he returned home. His wife knelt,[184] and asked the reason. Yang-tzu replied, "I was thinking [of you] because of my long absence. There was nothing else which should occasion wonderment."

His wife then took a knife, and going up to the loom, said: "This woven fabric came from the cocoons of silkworms and was produced by the shuttle and the loom. Threads accumulate into an inch, and inches accumulate into feet and to the roll. Now if I cut off this fabric, I shall lose what I have accomplished and waste days and months. You, in accumulating knowledge, should know from day to day what you lack in order to approach high virtue. If you return when your studies are but half finished, how does this differ from cutting off this fabric?"

Yang-tzu, being impressed by her statement, returned to finish his studies. He then did not come back for seven years. His wife always worked industriously to support her mother-in-law, and sometimes sent food far away to Yang-tzu.

Once a chicken from a neighboring house wandered into her garden. Her mother-in-law killed it stealthily and was going to eat it. The wife, with the chicken before her, did not take any food and wept. Her mother-in-law was astonished and asked the reason. The wife said, "I feel sad because of our poverty which makes us eat someone else's meat." Her mother-in-law then threw away the chicken.

Later, a robber, who intended to assault the wife, seized the mother-in-law first, accompanying his demand with a threat. When she heard this, the wife took a knife and came out. The bandit said, "If you lay down your knife and obey me, she will be safe; if you do not obey me, then I will kill your mother-in-law." The wife, looking upward, sighed, and cut her throat with her knife so that she died. The bandit did not kill the mother-in-law. [*HHS* 84:13b–14b]

44. ALL KINSMEN IN THE ARMY

A.D. 25   The emperor[185] frequently sent letters to console [K'ou Hsün].[186]

---

[184] It was customary at that time for people to squat on the ground. Whenever one wished to pay respect to another, he would raise himself to a kneeling position (Ch'ü Hsüan-ying, *Chung-kuo she-hui shih-liao ts'ung-ch'ao* [Ch'ang-sha: Commercial Press, 1937], II, 253–54). They did not kneel down from a standing position.

[185] Emperor Kuang-wu, who ascended the throne in A.D. 25.

[186] K'ou Hsün 寇恂 was a native of Ch'ang-p'ing. For generations his family had

Hsün's schoolmate, Tung Ch'ung, said to him, "The emperor has just ascended the throne; the nation has not yet been, unified and now you are holding a great commandery, internally winning the hearts of men and externally defeating Su Mao. Your power shocks the neighboring enemies, your accomplishments are known. This is the time for slanderers to look askance in hatred and malice. Formerly when Hsiao Ho was within the passes he took the advice of Pao, and Emperor Kao was delighted.[187] Now the army led by you includes all your kinsmen, brothers, and cousins.[188] Should you not take the precedent as a warning?" Hsün agreed with him. . . . Then he sent his brother's son, K'ou Chang, and his sister's son, Ku Ch'ung, to lead the cavalry as vanguards of the [emperor's] army. The emperor approved his action, and both were appointed generals of the flank. . . .

From among the younger brothers, brother's sons, and sister's sons of Hsün, eight became marquises because of their military merit. [*HHS* 16:27a–b, 31b–32a]

45. RELATIVES SUPPORTED

Hsüan Ping,[189] whose style was Chü-kung, was a native of Yün-yang prefecture of the Ping-i commandery. . . . He was appointed palace assistant imperial secretary in the first year of Chien-wu . . . and was A.D. 25 promoted to the post of colonel-director of retainers in the next year. . . . Ping by his nature was frugal. He always used a cloth comforter,

---

been famous. He was first the merit evaluator (*kung-ts'ao* 功曹) of his commandery. He persuaded the grand administrator to attach himself to Kuang-wu. He himself became a general of the flank. Later he was appointed grand administrator of Ho-nei and acting grand general when Kuang-wu occupied Ho-nei and engaged in fighting in the north. It was his responsibility not only to defend Ho-nei but also to supply arrows and food for Kuang-wu's army.

Meanwhile, Chu Wei 朱鮪, the grand general of the Keng-shih emperor, sent his generals, Su Mao 蘇茂 and Chia Ch'iang 賈彊, to attack Wen, a prefecture of Ho-nei, with over thirty thousand soldiers. Hsün defeated them. All the generals congratulated Kuang-wu, who then ascended the throne. It was at this time that Emperor Kuang-wu sent letters to console Hsün.

Hsün was dismissed in A.D. 26 but was reappointed several months later as grand administrator of the Ying-ch'uan commandery. In the same year, because of his military accomplishments in defeating Chia Ch'i 賈期, he was ennobled as marquis of Yung-nu with a fief of ten thousand households. In 31 he was appointed chief of police (*chih-chin-wu* 執金吾). He died in A.D. 36 (*HHS* 16:24a–32a).

[187] See I, 11.

[188] For the term *k'un-ti*, see I, 11, n. 44.

[189] Hsüan Ping 宣秉, whose official career is given in this passage, died in A.D. 30.

vegetable food, and earthenware. Once the emperor went to his home. Seeing [these things] he sighed, "The two Kungs of Ch'u[190] were no better than Hsüan Chü-kung of Yün-yang." Then cloth, silk, curtains, and many other utensils were bestowed upon him.[191] He was promoted to the post of chief assistant to the grand minister of the masses in the

A.D. 28 fourth year. The income from his salary was used to gather together his kinsmen and to support them. Land was given to those who were father-less and weak. He himself had not a saving of a single picul. [*HHS* 27:1a–2a]

46. Father Beats Son

A.D. 25–27 A fellow student of Wang Tan's[192] son, whose family was in Chung-shan, lost a parent. [The son] informed Tan that he intended to go there to condole with [his friend's family]. A group was got together and was about to leave; Tan was angry and beat[193] [his son]. He ordered [the son] to send some silk to offer as a sacrifice. Someone asked the reason. Tan said, "The difficulty of maintaining a friendship is not easy to speak of. . . . The end of [the friendship between] Ch'en and Chang was bad, and the conclusion of [that between] Hsiao and Chu was full

---

[190] The two Kungs are Kung Sheng 龔勝 and Kung She 龔舍 of the Early Han period; they were known for their frugality (Li: *HHS* 27:2a). Sheng was at first a subordinate in the commandery government and later was appointed a prefect through the recommendation of the local government. He was promoted to the post of grandee remonstrant during the time of Emperor Ai (6–1 B.C.) and was later appointed imperial court grandee. He resigned in A.D. 2. He committed suicide at the age of seventy-nine by refusing to take any food when Wang Mang had made himself emperor and sent messengers to force him to accept a position (*HS* 72:19a–23b).

She was a friend of Sheng and also became grandee remonstrant through his recommendation. Shortly after, he was dismissed because of illness. He was later appointed grand administrator of the T'ai-shan commandery by Emperor Ai, but resigned after several months and went home. After that he refused to take any official post and took up teaching as his profession. He died at the age of sixty-eight in *ca.* A.D. 6/7 (*HS* 72:18b–19a, 21b–22a).

Their frugality, however, is not mentioned in their biographies.

[191] The reason for the emperor's gifts was to express his admiration of Hsüan's frugality. The reward also served a practical purpose: to bring his living up to his status.

[192] Wang Tan was appointed junior tutor of the heir apparent *(t'ai-tzu shao-fu* 太子少傅) and later became grand tutor of the heir apparent.

[193] According to the *Tung-kuan Han-chi,* he beat his son fifty strokes (Li: *HHS* 27:5b).

of faults.[194] There are few who know how to preserve [their friend-ships]." [*HHS* 27:5a–b]

47. A Wife's Counsel

[Wang] Pa[195] had established high virtue in his youth. He was summoned several times by the government during the reign of Emperor Kuang-wu, but he refused to enter an official career. . . . His wife was A.D. 25–57 also admirable in her aims and actions.

Formerly Pa had made friends with a native of the same commandery, Ling-hu Tzu-po.[196] Later Tzu-po became the chancellor of Ch'u kingdom and his son became the merit evaluator in their commandery. Tzu-po then sent his son to deliver a letter to Pa. His carriage, horse, dress, and attendants, all were dignified. Pa's son was tilling in the fields. Hearing the guest arriving, he laid down his plough and came home. When he saw the young Ling-hu, he became downcast and ashamed of himself and could not look up. Observing this, Pa blushed. When the guest had left, he lay on the bed and did not get up for a long time. His wife was astonished and asked the reason. At first he did not tell her. When his wife asked how she was at fault, he said, "Tzu-po and I have never been alike. Just now I saw that his son is elegant in appearance and dress, and his behavior is fitting, whereas my son with his disheveled hair and few teeth knows no manners, and was ashamed when he saw a guest. Since father and son are deeply bound in affection, I automatically feel lost." His wife said, "During your youth you cultivated pure virtue, and were not concerned with splendor and

[194] Obviously Tan wanted to discourage the intimacy between his son and the friend because he thought that the course of friendship was very uncertain. To justify his action he referred to two well-known stories. For the story of Chang Erh and Ch'en Yü, who were originally such very good friends that they said they would die for one another, see I, 6, n. 17. The second story refers to Hsiao Yü 蕭育 and Chu Po, but no details are known (Li: *HHS* 27:5b; *HS* 78:16a–b).

[195] Wang Pa 王霸 was a native of T'ai-yüan 太原 (modern Shensi). When Wang Mang usurped the throne, Wang Pa gave up his official career and even severed his social ties with his friends. During the reign of Kuang-wu he was called to the court for official appointment. There he gave only his name before the emperor to avoid referring to himself as a vassal (稱臣). The minister of the masses, Hou Pa 侯霸, had intended to give up his rank for him, but was stopped from doing so by an official who said that the people of T'ai-yüan were prone to adhere to their own men and that Wang Pa was similarly disposed. Thereupon, Wang returned to his home, where he lived in retirement until he died. He refused to accept later summonses, although they were sent to him several times (*HHS* 83:8a–b).

[196] Ling-hu Tzu-po's 令狐子伯 biography is not recorded.

emoluments. Now how can the nobility of Tzu-po compare with your superiority? Why do you forget your old determination and become ashamed because of your children?" Pa got up, smiled, and said, "You are right." They then dwelt in seclusion for the rest of their lives. [*HHS* 84:2b–3b]

48. Relatives of Nine Degrees Supported

Sung Hung,[197] whose style was Chung-tzu, was a native of Ch'ang-an. . . . When Emperor Kuang-wu ascended the throne, he was appointed grand palace grandee. In the second year of Chien-wu . . . he became grand minister of works and was ennobled as marquis of Hsün-i. All that he obtained from his salary was distributed to support his kindred of the nine *tsu*.[198] No family property was left. [*HHS* 26:12a]

A.D. 26

[197] Sung Hung 宋弘 was an attendant within the palace during the reigns of Emperors Ch'eng and Ai (32–1 B.C.) and became provider of works (*kung-kung* 共工) in the time of Wang Mang. When the Red Eyebrow bandits occupied Ch'ang-an, he threw himself into the river to avoid a summons. When Emperor Kuang-wu ascended the throne, he was appointed grandee. In A.D. 26 he was made grand minister of works and was ennobled as marquis of Hsün-i. After holding this office for five years he was dismissed.

[198] What group of individuals was subsumed under the term "nine *tsu*" 九族 in ancient times was, and still is, a matter of debate. Scholars have generally offered two interpretations. One group says that the nine *tsu* include certain relatives with different surnames (i.e., of different clans) as well as the descendants of the paternal side. Hsia-hou Sheng 夏侯勝, Hsia-hou Chien 夏侯建, Ou-yang Sheng 歐陽生, and other scholars of the School of Modern Writing (so called because the texts they used employed square writing, a popular form of writing in Ch'in-Han times that differed from the pre-Ch'in *k'o-tou* writing 蝌蚪文 of the School of Ancient Writings) all belonged to this group. According to them the nine *tsu* comprised four paternal *tsu*, three maternal *tsu*, and two affinal *tsu*. The four paternal *tsu* include (1) the five *tsu*, that is, the five degrees of relationship, (2) father's married sisters and their sons, (3) ego's married sisters and their sons, and (4) ego's married daughters and their sons. The three maternal *tsu* include (1) mother's father's clan, (2) mother's mother's clan, and (3) mother's married sisters and their sons. The two affinal *tsu* include (1) wife's father's clan and (2) wife's mother's clan. See *Shang-shu chu-su, SPPY* ed., 2:5a, K'ung Ying-ta's commentary, hereafter cited as *SSCS; TCCS* 6:10b, K'ung Ying-ta's commentary.

Although the *Po-hu-t'ung* also includes relatives of different surnames in the nine *tsu*, and may for this reason be placed in the school just mentioned, the components of the different *tsu* are differently envisaged. For instance, the first of the four paternal *tsu* comprises all paternal kinsmen, not just individuals subsumed under the five degrees of relationship; and among the mother's *tsu* the clans of the mother's father and mother's mother are considered not as two but as a single *tsu*. The other two maternal *tsu*, according to this scheme, comprise the mother's brothers and sisters and the sons of mother's brothers and sisters (*PHT* 8:6b–7a).

Tu Yü claims that the nine *tsu* include mother's father, mother's mother, mother's

49. REMARRIAGE

The emperor's elder sister, the princess of Hu-yang, was newly A.D. 26–31
widowed. In order to learn her intentions the emperor discussed the
court officials with her. The princess said, "The dignified demeanor
and the moral capacity of Mr. Sung cannot be matched by any of the
other officials." The emperor said, "Let Us plan it."

Later [Sung] Hung was called in to see the emperor. The emperor
asked the princess to sit behind the screen. He said to Hung, "The
proverb says, 'Being noble one changes one's friends, being rich one
changes one's wife.'[199] Is that human feeling?" Hung said, "I have
heard that friends of poor and humble days must not be forgotten and
that a wife of the days of the husks of grain must not go down the

---

sisters' sons, wife's father, wife's mother, father's sisters' sons, sisters' sons, daughters'
sons, and ego's kinsmen (*TCCS* 6:10b, Tu Yü's commentary). This classification
differs from the two given above in one important respect. It includes only the sons
of father's sisters, of ego's sisters, of ego's daughters, and of mother's sisters. Father's
sisters, ego's sisters, ego's daughters, and mother's sisters are excluded because, according to Cheng Hsüan, a woman could only belong to the clan of her father and brothers
(commentary to *TCCS* 6:11b).

The School of Ancient Writing, on the other hand, insisted that the nine *tsu* comprised only individuals bearing the same surname. K'ung An-kuo, Ma Jung, and
Cheng Hsüan all agreed that the nine *tsu* included only those family members from
the great-great-grandfather's generation down to the great-great-grandson's generation (K'ung An-kuo's note, K'ung Ying-ta's commentary: *SSCS* 2:5a; K'ung Ying-
ta's commentary: *TCCS* 6:11b; Lu Te-ming, *Ching-tien shih-wen, TSCC* ed., 3:3a,
hereafter cited as *CTSW*). Later scholars, such as Lu Te-ming, Ku Yen-wu, and
Sun Hsing-yen, all support the statement of K'ung An-kuo, Ma, and Cheng (see
CTSW 3:3a; *JCLCS* 1:2a–3b; Sun Hsing-yen, *Shang-shu chin-ku wen chu-su*, in *PCKTS*
1A:7a, hereafter cited as *SSCKWS*).

Cheng's basic arguments rest on the following statements in the *Li-chi:* "In counting
kindred (and the mourning to be worn by them), the three closest degrees become
expanded into five, and those five again into nine" (James Legge, *The Texts of Confucianism: Sacred Books of the East*, ed. F. M. Müller [4 vols.; Oxford, 1879–85], II, 42).
He accepted this definition of the nine *tsu*, holding that the term *tsu* refers only to the
paternal clan (commentary to *TCCS* 6:11b; *SSCS* 2:5a).

Ku Yen-wu supports him strongly, claiming that the statement just quoted from
the *Li-chi* is an "unchangeable tenth power"; and he offers further evidence from the
Tso-chuan and from history that *tsu* only includes those with the same surname (*TCCS*
6:11b).

Sun Hsing-yen, quoting from the "Imperial Annals" of the *Han-shu* regarding the
function of the Office of the Superintendent of the Imperial House (*tsung-po* 宗伯)
(*HS* 1B:11a), concludes that in Han times the nine *tsu* comprised only individuals
bearing the same name (*SSCKWS* 1A:7a).

[199] This proverb of Han times reveals the effect of a rise in status and wealth upon
friendship and marriage.

hall."²⁰⁰ Then the emperor looked backward over his shoulder and said
to the princess, "The matter cannot be carried out."²⁰¹ [*HHS* 26:13b]

50. SON ORDERED TO COMMIT SUICIDE

A.D. 38–49   The petty official, T'an Chien, committed a theft in his prefecture.
The prefect of Hsia-ch'iu²⁰² ordered his retainers to retire and questioned him about the matter. Chien kowtowed and confessed his guilt.
Since [the prefect] could not bear to punish him, he sent him away for
a long retirement. When Chien's father heard this, he prepared wine
for Chien and said to him, "I hear that an unprincipled ruler destroys
people with the knife, whereas a principled ruler punishes people with
righteousness. Your guilt is your fate." Then he ordered Chien to take
the poison and he died. [*HHS* 41:14b]

51. SUPPORT OF KINDRED

A.D. 46   In the twenty-second year [of Chien-wu, Kuo Chi²⁰³] was appointed
grand palace grandee. An area with houses was given to him. Curtains,
cash, and rice were also given to fill his house. Chi then distributed
these things to his nine *tsu* without anything being left. [*HHS* 31:3b–4a]

52. A VIRTUOUS EMPRESS

After
A.D. 49   [Ma Yen]²⁰⁴ presented a memorial, saying, ". . . I hear that the heir

²⁰⁰ The phrase "go down the hall" 下堂 means to send the wife away from the
family, that is, to divorce her. The husks of grain were the food of the poor people;
consequently the "wife of the days of the husks of grain" means the wife of a poor
man. There were three conditions under which a wife should not be divorced: (1)
when she had shared her husband's previous poor estate, which is obviously the
condition operative in this case, (2) when she had been given in marriage by her
parents or some other person or persons, but now had no place to go, ostensibly
because no suitable member of her family was still alive to take care of her, and (3)
when she had observed the mourning period for her husband's parents (*TTLC*
13:6a; *KTCY* 6:6a; *KYCS* 8:10a).

²⁰¹ Both the statement of the emperor and of Sung Hung indicate that Sung already
had a wife and that he refused to put her aside to marry the princess.

²⁰² Hsia-ch'iu 瑕丘 prefecture was located in modern Shantung.

²⁰³ Kuo Chi 郭伋 received this appointment in A.D. 46 after a successful official
career. He died in A.D. 47.

²⁰⁴ Ma Yen was a nephew of Ma Yüan (see the next footnote) and a cousin of
Empress Ming. He lost his father when he was only seven years old. In A.D. 76 he
became general of the palace gentlemen of the five offices (*wu-kuan chung-lang-chiang*
五官中郎將) and later grand administrator of the Ch'en-liu commandery. He was
dismissed from his official post in 82 and died in 98 (cf. *HHS* 24:33a–37a; *TKHC*
12:7b–8b).

apparent and the kings do not yet have their mates. [Ma] Yüan[205] has three daughters. The eldest is fifteen, the next fourteen, and the youngest is thirteen. Their appearance, hair, and complexion are above the upper middle [grade]. All of them are filial, careful, agreeable, quiet, and polite. I hope a physiognomist[206] will be sent to examine whether they are agreeable. . . ." Thereupon the [later] empress[207] was selected and entered the heir apparent's palace. At that time she was thirteen years old. . . .

When Emperor Ming came to the throne, the empress was made honorable lady. During this time the daughter of the elder sister of the empress's stepmother,[208] Chia, was also selected for [the palace] and gave birth to Su-tsung. Because the empress had no child, Emperor [Ming] ordered her to take care of him, and said to her, "It is not necessary for one to give birth to a child oneself. But that which should cause worry is that [the child] may not be loved and nurtured thoroughly." Thereupon the empress fostered him with all her heart and became more wearied and worn than if it had been her own child. . . .

Considering that the imperial descendants were not many, the empress frequently was sad and sighed. She recommended her attendants [to the emperor] as if it were too late. When one of the palace ladies was presented to see the emperor, [the empress] frequently encouraged her. Those who had been favored several times she treated with more kind-

---

[205] During the reign of Wang Mang, Ma Yüan held the position of investigator of transgressions and later that of grand governor (Wang Mang's equivalent of the grand administrator) of Hsin-ch'eng (新成, the name given by Wang Mang to the Han-chung commandery). After he joined Emperor Kuang-wu he was made grand palace grandee in A.D. 33 and grand administrator of the Lung-hsi commandery in A.D. 36. In A.D. 41 he was appointed "billow-subduing general" *(fu-po chiang-chün* 伏波將軍) to subdue the rebels in the Chiao-chih commandery. He died in A.D. 49 during a military campaign (*HHS* 24:2a–26b).

[206] As a rule any girl who was under consideration as a member of the palace had to be examined by a physiognomist before a final decision was made. The *Hou-Han-shu* states: "According to Han law the people were always counted in the eighth month. The palace grandee and the assistant to the office of the side halls [*yeh-t'ing ch'eng* 掖廷丞], together with the physiognomists, were sent to examine the young girls of the good families of the prefecture of Lo-yang. Those whose age was above thirteen and below twenty, whose countenance and complexion were dignified, beautiful, and in accordance with the physiognomical requirements were conveyed back to the rear palace. Each was presented to the emperor after she had been selected and viewed as to whether she was satisfactory or not" (*HHS* 10A:4a). The physiognomist probably predicted whether the girl would bring luck to the imperial family and whether she would bear a son.

[207] That is, Empress Ming. She was the youngest daughter of Ma Yüan.

[208] That is, the first wife of her father. Her mother was his second wife.

ness. In the spring of the third year of Yung-ping . . . she was made
A.D. 60 empress. . . .

She always wore [garments of] thick silk,[209] and her skirt had no
border. . . . The emperor frequently visited the imperial parks and the
detached palaces. The empress always warned him about the wind, dew,
and fog. Her words and intent were sincere and perfect, and most of
them were accepted [by the emperor]. Once the emperor visited Cho-
lung [Park], and all the *ts'ai-jen*[210] were summoned; from the king of
Hsia-p'ei[211] down, all were at his side. They asked that the empress be
called. The emperor smiled and said, "That person is not fond of amusement. Even if she comes, she will not be happy. Therefore she seldom
participates in matters of travel and amusement." [*HHS* 10A:12b–14b]

53. EARNINGS OFFERED TO BROTHER

Second
half first
century
Cheng Chün,[212] whose style was Chung-yü, was a native of Jen-
ch'eng prefecture of Tung-p'ing kingdom. When he was young he was
fond of the writings of Huang-Lao.[213] His elder brother, who was a
functionary in the prefectural government, received a considerable
number of gifts. Chün several times urged him to put a stop to this, but
[his brother] refused to listen to him. [Chün] then went away and became a wage laborer. After more than a year he returned and offered
to his brother all the cash and silk that he had earned. [*HHS* 27:19a]

54. MARRIED AT FOURTEEN

Second
half first
century
[Pan Chao[214] wrote in her *Lessons for Women*,] "More than forty years

[209] *Ta-lien* 大練 was a kind of coarse silk.

[210] There was no such title as *ts'ai-jen* 才人 in the Han palace (*HS* 97A:2a–3a; *HHS*
10A:3b).

[211] The king of Hsia-p'ei was one of the sons of Emperor Ming (*HHS* 50:1a, 8a).

[212] Cheng Chün 鄭均, after having refused the invitations of the government of the
regional division and the commandery, of the minister of the masses, and of the
emperor, was specially summoned to the capital via government carriages in A.D. 78
and was induced to accept a post of master of writing and that of gentleman discussant. Although he resigned shortly afterwards, he continued to enjoy the emperor's
favor (*HHS* 27:19a–20a).

[213] The term Huang-Lao, an abbreviation for Huang-ti and Lao-tzu, was used to
designate Taoism in Han times. Tao-chia 道家, Huang-Lao, or the Method of
Huang-Lao (*SC* 54:6b, 56:1b) all mean the same thing.

[214] For Pan Chao, the sister of Pan Ku and Pan Ch'ao 班超, see Nancy Lee Swann,
Pan Chao: Foremost Woman Scholar of China (New York, 1932), pp. 3–74.

have passed since at the age of fourteen I took up the dustpan and broom[215] in the Ts'ao family." [*HHS* 84:6b]

55. DIVISION OF PROPERTY AMONG BROTHERS

Hsü Ching,[216] whose style was Shao-chang, was a native of Yang- A.D. 53–62
hsien of K'uai-chi. His grandfather, Wu, was recommended by the Grand Administrator Ti-wu Lun as "filially pious and incorrupt." Intending to make his two younger brothers, Yen and P'u, famous, as they were still unknown at that time, Wu made a proposal to them: "According to the rites *(li)*,[217] it is proper for the family to have separations and to live separately." Therefore, they divided the property into three parts. Wu took the fertile land, the big buildings, and the strong slaves for himself, while the two brothers got that which was inferior and fewer [in number]. All the local people praised the younger brothers for their ability to yield and despised Wu's covetousness. Because of this, Yen and P'u could be recommended.

Then Wu assembled his kinsmen, wept, and said, "I, being the eldest brother, am worthless and got my reputation and post to which I am not entitled. My two brothers, although full grown, had not yet obtained honor and rank. Therefore I asked for a division of the property and brought severe ridicule upon myself. Now the property through [proper] management has increased threefold." He then gave all this to the two brothers; he himself did not take any part of it. Hence he was praised by all the commandery.[218] [*HHS* 75:15b–16b]

---

[215] "To hold the dustpan and broom" is a humble phrase to designate a wife. It is obvious from this and other passages that in Han times girls married early, around thirteen or fourteen.

[216] Hsü Ching 許荊 (*fl. ca.* 89–105) while still young was a petty commandery official. Later he was recommended as "filially pious and incorrupt," and after several promotions became grand administrator of the Kuei-yang commandery. Finally he was appointed grandee remonstrant.

[217] Li claims that this refers to the *I-li*, which reads: "According to principle there should be no separation among brothers, but separations occur in order to make way for the private [interests] of the sons. A son would no longer be a son if he did not share his private [interests] with his father. Therefore there are the east compound, the west compound, the south compound, and the north compound. They share the same property, yet dwell apart. If they have a surplus, they offer it to the *tsung*; if there is not enough [for their own needs] they can ask from the *tsung*."

[218] This story seems to imply that it was not the division of property among brothers after the death of their parents, but the unequal distribution, that brought about adverse opinion. The eldest son was not justified in securing either a larger or a better share of the paternal estate.

56. Support of Kindred

A.D. 58–83   [Liang Sung][219] was fond of giving charity and was not engaged in managing property. His elder brother's wife, the princess of Wu-yin,[220] who gave support to the various [members of] Liang's [family], varying according to the degree of their relationship to her, especially respected Sung. Even if it were clothing, food, and utensils, [whatever she gave him] was more and better. Sung distributed all these things to his kindred, he himself using nothing. [*HHS* 34:7b]

57. A Severe Father

A.D. 58–92   Teng Hsün,[221] although broadminded and tolerant of others, was very severe to his family. All his brothers respected and feared him. When his sons came to call upon him, he never gave them a seat or received them with a mild countenance. [*HHS* 16:15a]

[219] Liang Sung 梁竦 was the second son of Liang T'ung, who was a grand administrator and ennobled as a marquis. Sung was exiled to Chiu-chen because his elder brother, Sung 松, had slandered Emperor Ming. The elder brother died in prison and later Sung was pardoned and allowed to return to his own commandery. He refused to enter upon any official career, but his two daughters became honorable ladies of Emperor Chang, one of them giving birth to the later Emperor Ho. Their favored positions made them the envy of the Tou family, also imperial relatives-in-law. Because of slanderous accusations, both daughters were killed and their father put into prison where he died (*HHS* 34:1a ff.).

[220] The princess of Wu-yin was the daughter of Emperor Kuang-wu. She was married to Liang Sung, who held the post of general of the palace gentlemen as rapid as tigers and later that of grand keeper of equipages. He was dismissed when it was disclosed that he had written to local officials asking for personal favors. In A.D. 59 he was accused of slandering the emperor in anonymous writings and was put in prison, where he died (*HHS* 34:6a).

[221] Teng Hsün was the sixth son of Teng Yü, the grand minister of the masses. Hsün, who at one time held the position of internuncio, was given the offices of "colonel who guards against the Wu-huan" (*hu Wu-han hsiao-wei* 護烏桓校尉) and grand administrator of Chang-yeh. While holding the post of "colonel who guards against the Ch'iang" (*hu Ch'iang hsiao-wei* 護羌校尉), he defeated the Ch'iang tribes. His daughter was selected for the palace and became an honorable lady of Emperor Ho and later, after Hsün's death, was made empress (*HHS* 16:11a–15a, 10A:23a–26b).

The *Tung-kuan Han-chi* has a similar description: "Hsün was humble and lenient to others. He treated the noble and the humble alike as old friends. His friends' sons, coming to him freely, were treated as his own sons. If they had faults, he would instruct and beat them" (Li: *HHS* 16:11a–b; *TKHC* 8:6a).

58. Brothers Living Together

Wei Pa,[222] whose style was Chiao-ching, was a native of Kou-yang of the Chi-yin commandery. [The family] had observed the *li* and [the rules of] righteousness for generations. Pa lost his parents during his youth and lived together with his brothers. The village community admired their harmony. During the Chien-ch'u period he was recom- A.D. 76–83 mended [under the category of] "filially pious and incorrupt."[223] [*HHS* 25:18a]

The family [of Ts'ui Yüan][224] was poor. He and his brothers lived A.D. 76–142 together for many decades. The local community was greatly influ- enced [by him]. He became a petty commandery official when he was over forty. [*HHS* 52:17b–18a]

59. People Return to Live with Parents

In about a year [Ho Ch'ang][225] was shifted to the post of grand ad- *Ca.* A.D. 90 ministrator of the Ju-nan commandery. . . . On the day of Li-ch'un[226] he usually called back the investigators of transgressions to the com-

---

[222] Wei Pa 魏霸 became the grand administrator of the Chü-lu commandery in the time of Emperor Ho (89–105). In 104 he was appointed grand court architect and in 106 held the post of grand minister of ceremonies. One year later he resigned be- cause of illness and then held the title of imperial court grandee (*HHS* 25:18a–b).

[223] The admiration inspired by this action implies that brothers rarely lived together after the death of their parents.

[224] Both Ts'ui Yüan's great-great-grandfather and great-grandfather were grand administrators. Because of illness, his grandfather did not enter officialdom. His father, Yin, famous for writing *fu*, was appointed by Tou Hsien, the general of chariots and cavalry, as his subordinate. Sometime thereafter he incurred the dislike of Tou Hsien and was demoted to the position of prefect, an offer he refused to accept. He then returned home. His son, Yüan, was given an appointment by Teng Tsun 鄧遵, the "general who crosses the Liao River" (*tu Liao chiang-chün* 度遼將軍), and Yen Hsien, the general of chariots and cavalry. When the latter was executed, Ts'ui Yüan was dismissed. Later he was made a prefect; ultimately he was promoted to the chancellorship of Chi-pei kingdom. He died in 142 at the age of sixty-six (*HHS* 52:1a ff.).

[225] Ho Ch'ang 何敞 had already held several minor positions, first as a subordinate of the grand commandant, then as attendant secretary, and then, in A.D. 89, he became grand tutor of Chi-nan kingdom.

[226] *Li-ch'un* is the day spring begins. It was a routine matter for the commandery grand administrator or the chancellor of a kingdom to make a trip of inspection through his subordinate prefectures in order to encourage farming and to give relief to the poor (*HHS* 28:5a).

mandery government[227] and sent various Confucian great officers to inspect the subordinate prefectures to honor those who were "filially pious" and "brotherly respectful" and who had behaved righteously and to examine the innocent prisoners according to the principles of the *Ch'un-ch'iu*.[228] Therefore no regret was expressed in the commandery, and the common people were influenced by his kindness and *li*. All those who lived separately [from their parents] went back to support their fathers and mothers or made up for their deficiencies by wearing mourning garments.[229] There were about two hundred people who declined property and yielded to others.[230] [*HHS* 43:32a–b]

60. WIVES AND SLAVES OWNED BY A KING

A.D. 93   [Liu Ch'ang,[231] King of Liang, in his petition to the throne said:] "Your servant, Ch'ang, has thirty-seven concubines; those who have no children want to go back to their original homes. I should like to select two hundred careful and self-restrained male and female slaves. As to the rest, the rapid as tigers guards,[232] the horse-escorts, the various artisans, the musicians, the Dark-green Heads, the male and female slaves,[233] the weapons and the crossbows, and the horses that I received [from the throne], they are to be returned to the original bureaus to which they belonged." [*HHS* 50:10b–11a]

[227] The function of the investigators of transgressions was to look for faults and crimes. Since the autumn and winter seasons were the only times when it was permitted to examine and punish criminals (cf. *HHC* 28:5a), no actions of this kind could take place after the day of Li-ch'un. Cf. *HHC* 4:2b; *HHS* 3:18b and 23a, 46:9a–11a; for further discussion see Ch'ü T'ung-tsu, *Chung-kuo fa-lü yü chung-kuo she-hui* (Shanghai: Commercial Press, 1947), pp. 206–7. Therefore the investigators were called back (see Li: *HHS* 43:32a–b).

[228] This was not unusual. Many officials in Early and Later Han judged law cases according to the principles embodied in the *Ch'un-ch'iu*. For details see *CCLK*, pp. 197 ff.

[229] Li explains that those people who had neglected to wear full mourning for their deceased parents now, influenced by Ho, put on mourning garments to compensate for their negligence.

[230] This apparently refers to relatives, especially brothers. The *Tung-kuan Han-chi* gives the number as 185 persons (*TKHC* 19:8b).

[231] Liu Ch'ang 劉暢 petitioned, after he had been impeached by the inspector of the regional division of Yü for subversive activities, to be permitted to return his estate to the emperor.

[232] The rapid as tiger guards were the imperial guards under the command of the general of the palace gentlemen as rapid as tigers.

[233] Here the Dark-green Heads and the male and female slaves are mentioned separately. For the Dark-green Heads, see II, 53, n. 160.

61. BROTHERS HOLD PROPERTY IN COMMON

Second
century
A.D.

Miao Yung,[234] whose style was Yü-kung, was a native of Chao-ling
of the Ju-nan commandery. All the four brothers, being orphaned during their youth, held the property in common. After they were all married, their wives asked for separation and quarreled with each other
frequently. Deeply depressed and exasperated, Yung closed his door
and struck his own cheek, saying [to himself], "Miao Yung, you have
cultivated yourself, behaved properly, learned the teachings of the
sages, with an attempt to improve the customs, and yet you are unable
to regulate the family." Having heard this, his younger brothers and
their wives all came to kowtow before him and to confess their fault.
Consequently they changed their behavior and treated each other cor-
dially and harmoniously.[235] [*HHS* 81:24b]

62. ANOTHER REASON FOR DIVORCE

Before
A.D. 106

Li Ch'ung,[236] whose style was Ta-hsün, was a native of Ch'en-liu.[237]
The family was poor. All the six brothers shared their food and clothing.
His wife said to Ch'ung privately: "Now we are so poor it is difficult to
be secure for long. I have some private property. I hope to separate
from them." Ch'ung pretended to acquiesce and said: "If you wish to
separate, we should prepare wine and a party to ask the people of the

[234] At this time Miao Yung had not yet entered upon an official career. Later he
became a petty officer in prefectural and commandery governments, first as master
of documents (*chu-pu* 主簿) of the prefectural government and later as clerk in the
bureau of decisions (*ch'üeh-ts'ao-shih* 決曹史) of the commandery government. He
was afterwards promoted to the position of prefect of Chung-mou prefecture of the
Ho-nan commandery. He died while holding this post.

[235] This story reveals that family property could be broken up after the death of the
parents. Cf. I, 55 and 63. Against what was probably a not unusual request on the
part of wives for a separation of households, Miao Yung's behavior and self-criticism,
while extreme, seem to have been effective in restoring family order, but actions such
as his were probably more typical of the intelligentsia than of the general population.

[236] Li Ch'ung 李充 was a scholar. He erected an elegant building in which he
lectured to his students. When he refused to accept the office of merit evaluator, the
grand administrator was so angered that he gave him the inferior post of chief of a
canton (*t'ing-chang* 亭長). During the reign of Emperor Ho he was appointed by the
court as erudite. Later he was promoted to the position of attendant within the palace.
Because of his strictness, he was disliked by the imperial relatives and probably for
this reason was transferred to the post of general of the palace gentlemen on the left.
He became "thrice venerable of the state" (*kuo san-lao* 國三老) at the age of eighty-
eight (*HHS* 81:23a–24b).

[237] Ch'en-liu prefecture was modern Ch'en-liu county in Honan.

local community and all the family members and relatives[238] to discuss this matter together."

Following his suggestion, his wife prepared wine and gave a feast for guests. Leaving his seat, Ch'ung knelt before his mother and said: "This woman does not behave well, urging Ch'ung to alienate his mother and brothers. Such a wrong[239] merits expulsion from this house." So he scolded her and drove her out the door. His wife left with tears in her eyes. All those who were present were shocked and reverential. Thereupon the meeting was dismissed and all left. [*HHS* 81:23a]

63. Generous Arrangement of Division of Family Property

A.D.
107–128

During the time of Emperor An, Hsieh Pao,[240] whose style was Meng-ch'ang, of the Ju-nan commandery was interested in learning and sincere in behavior. His extreme filial piety was well known at the time of the death of his mother. When his father married a second wife, [Pao] was disliked by his father and was told to live separately. Weeping and crying day and night, Pao did not want to leave. He was beaten with a stick [by his father]. As there was no other alternative, he lived in a hut outside [his father's] house. At dawn he came to clean [the house]. His father was angry and again drove him away. He then lived in a hut

---

[238] The original text reads *nei wai* 內外, "inside and outside." Since in ancient times women were not permitted to pass beyond the threshold of their apartments, and all domestic duties demanded of them were performed within these limits, "inside" refers to the female members of the family and "outside" to the male members (see *LCCS* 2:7b–8a; Chia: *CLCS* 3:11b).

[239] Dividing the family property among brothers was not uncommon in Han times, so the action taken by Li Ch'ung, which was unexpected by the neighbors and relatives, seems to have been too extreme and severe. In a similar case, wives who made the same suggestion were not divorced (see I, 61). The only difference is that Li had a parent living, whereas the brothers in the other case were orphans. Probably Li's wife would have been less subject to criticism if she had had no mother-in-law, because sons and their wives were expected to live with their parents and serve them.

It should be noted that Li did not condemn his wife for proposing to divide the family property but for "alienating his mother and brothers." This condemnation seems to be in accordance with "loquacity," which was included as one of the seven conditions for divorcing a wife because it created discord between close relatives (*KYCS* 9:11b; *KTCY* 6:6a).

[240] Hsieh Pao 薛包 was not interested in a political career. During the Chien-kuang period (A.D. 121) he was summoned to court and appointed attendant within the palace. He refused to take the post, making a pretext of illness and asking to be allowed to die at home. Leave was granted him by the emperor, permitting him to keep the official rank and be cured at home. He was over eighty when he died (*HHS* 39:3a–b).

near the village gate and did not fail to inquire after the health of his parents both in the morning and evening. More than a year later his parents felt ashamed and took him back. Afterwards [when his parents died] he wore six years' mourning[241] for them and was exceedingly sorrowful.

Shortly after, his younger brother's son asked for a division of property and a separate dwelling. Pao could not stop him. He then divided the property in half.[242] Among the male and female slaves he took the old ones, saying, "They have worked for me for a long time; you cannot command them." From the land and houses he took the deserted ones, saying, "These were cultivated by me during my youth; hence I am strongly attached to them." From the utensils he took the bad ones, saying, "These are the ones usually used by me. My body and my mouth are at ease with them."

His brother's son failed several times; he always gave something to assist him. [*HHS* 39:2b–3a]

64. Son Commits Suicide Because of Father's Anger

In the third year of Yüan-ch'u the king of P'eng-ch'eng, Kung, was angry at his son, Fu, because of certain incidents.[243] Fu committed suicide. [*HHS* 50:4b]   A.D. 116

65. Wife and Son Punished

Since the time of grandfather Yü,[244] the sons and grandsons [of the Teng family] had been taught to obey the laws and regulations. Taking   Ca. A.D. 110

[241] That is, three years' mourning for his father and another three years for his stepmother.

[242] This story implies that uncles and nephews did not usually live together after the death of their common ancestor. A nephew who had lost his father was not only justified in asking for separation but also had the right to demand equal shares from his uncle, since family property was usually divided equally among the brothers. The nephew was asking for that to which his father was entitled.

[243] The *Tung-kuan Han-chi* says: "The former wife of Kung's son T'ing died. Fu insulted T'ing's concubine. Kung was angry and confined him in the stable. Fu escaped in the night, going to P'eng-ch'eng prefecture, intending to present a memorial to the emperor. Kung sent his attending officials and Dark-green Heads to ask him to come back and then scolded him. Fu then committed suicide" (*TKHC* 7:9a).

[244] Teng Yü was an important political and military aide of Kuang-wu during his campaign for the imperial throne. Immediately after his accession to the throne in

the example of the Tou[245] as a serious warning, the whole lineage was restricted and restrained. They closed the gate and lived quietly. [Teng] Chih's[246] son, Feng, an attendant within the palace, once wrote to Chang K'an, a gentleman of the masters of writing, recommending that Ma Jung, a gentleman of the palace, should have a post in the ministry of the master of writing.[247] Furthermore, Jen Shang, the general of the palace gentlemen, had presented a horse to Feng. Later, Shang was arrested and sent to the commandant of justice because of his corruption connected with the army food supply. Fearing that the matter (i.e., accepting the horse) would be discovered, Feng first confessed to Chih. Chih was afraid of the empress dowager. He then shaved off the hair[248] of his wife and Feng to acknowledge the fault. All the world admired him. [*HHS* 16:19b–20a]

66. A Virtuous Empress

The name of Empress Liang, [whose posthumous title was] Shun-lieh, was Na. She was the daughter of the grand general [Liang] Shang. . . .

A.D. 128   In the third year of Yung-chien she was selected for the inner palace together with her paternal aunt.[249] At that time she was thirteen years old. When the physiognomist Mao T'ung saw the [later] empress, he was astonished and bowed twice and said, "This is the so-called 'sun-

---

A.D. 25 the emperor made Teng grand minister of the masses and marquis of Tsan with a fief of ten thousand households. In A.D. 37, after the empire was pacified, he was enfeoffed as marquis of Kao-mi with a fief of four counties, but no longer held his high office. When Emperor Ming came to the throne, Teng Yü was made grand tutor, but died in the same year. His descendants and relatives were favored because of his services (*HHS* 16:1a–10b).

245 For the Tou family, see III, 54.

246 Teng Chih was the grandson of Teng Yü. His younger sister was the empress of Emperor Ho, and later the empress dowager. Because of her influence Chih and his three brothers all held prominent positions; however, all of them steadily refused to accept the title of marquis that was granted to them.

247 According to Li, *t'ai-ko* 臺閣 refers to the office of the masters of writing, that is, the ministry of the masters of writing (*HHS* 49:32b).

The recommendation was improper and unlawful because as an attendant within the palace, Teng Feng 鄧鳳 had no authority to interfere with the administration of the office of the masters of writing. Obviously he was trying to use his personal influence in asking favors of Chang K'an 張龕.

248 To shave off the hair and put an iron collar around the neck was a kind of punishment. See II, 13, and n. 49. Apparently in this case Teng Chih shaved the head of his wife and son as an acknowledgment of guilt.

249 Her father's younger sister.

corner and half-moon.'²⁵⁰ Your physiognomy is noble beyond anything that your servant has ever seen." The grand astrologer divined by means of tortoise shell and obtained a *chao*²⁵¹ of *shou-fang*,²⁵² and again he divined by the stalks of the plant and obtained [a change from] *k'un* to *pi*.²⁵³ Thereupon she was made an honorable lady.²⁵⁴

Frequently she was especially called to wait on the emperor and she refused gracefully, saying before the emperor, "To bestow broadly is the virtue of the male, and not to monopolize is the principle of the female. Grasshoppers²⁵⁵ are the origin of all blessings. I hope Your Majesty will consider spreading the clouds and the rain equally and will take note of the order in a series of fish,²⁵⁶ so that your humble concubine will be free from the worry of guilt and slander." Thereupon the emperor paid more respect to her. In the first year of Yang-chia . . . the honorable lady was made empress. [*HHS* 10B:4b–5b]

²⁵⁰ In the terminology of physiognomy, the left side of the forehead is called the "sun-corner" (日角) and the right side the "moon-corner" (月角). According to the *Book of Physiognomy*, written by a famous physiognomist Chu Chien-p'ing 朱建平 at the end of the Later Han, it was the sign of an emperor when both corners projected (*WH* 54:22b; cf. *HHS* 1A:1b). The so-called 日角偃月 would then be a person who has a sun-corner on the left and a moon-corner on the right and thus has a very unusual physiognomy inferior only to that of an emperor.

However, according to Ssu-ma Hsi, a man of the era of the Warring States, 犀角偃月 instead of 日角偃月 was the physiognomy of an empress. Pao Piao comments that 犀角 is the bone on the top of the head and 偃月 is the bone of the forehead (*Chan-kuo ts'e*, *SPTK* ed., 10:17a, hereafter cited as *CKT*). Probably the name 犀角 is given to such a sign because the bone projects like the horn of a rhinoceros. Kuo P'u describes the rhinoceros as having three horns, one of them on the top of its head (*EYCS* 10:9b). If so, 犀角偃月 signifies a woman who has a projecting bone on the top of her head and a projection on her right forehead.

²⁵¹ The result of a divination was called *chao* 兆.

²⁵² *Shou-fang* 壽房 is the name of the particular *chao* or result, but no concrete details are known.

²⁵³ *Pi* 比 is the name of a hexagram (*kua* 卦). It is a combination of *k'un* ☷ and *kan* ☵ in the form ䷇. It was considered a lucky hexagram. See *Chou-i chu-su*, *SPPY* ed., 2:6b–8b, hereafter cited as *CICS*; Legge, *Texts of Confucianism*, II, 73–75.

²⁵⁴ Honorable lady was the highest rank of an imperial concubine.

²⁵⁵ The grasshopper (螽斯) is notable for its high fertility. The name was therefore invoked in a poem, which, according to the *Shih-hsü*, suggested that an empress or an imperial concubine would have a great number of children if she, like the grasshopper, was not jealous (*Mao-shih chu-su*, *SPPY* ed., 1(2):7b–8a, hereafter cited as *MSCS*).

²⁵⁶ In the *Book of Changes* the hexagram *pa* 剝 is given thus ䷖, a form that symbolizes five females under one male. The females, who were compared to a series of fish, were palace maids who received the favors of the emperor one after the other in a set order. This was considered good. See *CICS* 3:9b–10b; Legge, *Texts of Confucianism*, II, 105–6.

67. A MODEL WIFE

Before
A.D. 144   The wife of Hsü Sheng of Wu was a daughter of the Lü family. Her
style was Jung. Sheng was a gambler in his youth, paying no attention
to his morals or behavior. Jung was industrious [in caring for] the family
property to support her mother-in-law. She frequently urged Sheng to
study. Whenever he was at fault, she always admonished him with tears.
Jung's father became increasingly angry at Sheng and summoned Jung,
intending to marry her to someone else. Jung sighed and said, "Whatever my fate, it is not right to be separated and remarried." She refused to go back after all.

Sheng was deeply impressed and determined to improve himself.
Then he found a teacher and studied far away [from his home]. Thus
he established his reputation. Later he was summoned for appointment
by the government of the regional division and was killed by a bandit
when he was passing along the road at Shou-ch'un.[257] The bandit was
arrested by the Inspector Yin Yüeh.[258] While Jung was on her way to
receive her husband's coffin, she heard this and went to the regional
division and asked to satisfy her revenge by having her enemy [turned
over to her]. Yüeh allowed this. Then Jung beheaded [the bandit] and
took [the head] to sacrifice to the spirit of her husband.

Later her commandery was attacked by bandits. A bandit intended
to assault her. Jung leaped a wall to escape. The bandit drew his knife
and pursued her. The bandit said to her, "Obey me, and you will live;
if not, you will die." Jung said, "Righteousness [decrees that] I not disgrace myself in the hands of bandits." She was killed. [*HHS* 84:16a–17a]

68. ADMISSION OF FAULT TO INDICATE AUTHORITY

Second
half of
second
century   Ch'ou Lan[259] always restrained himself by observing the rites even
in his private life. When his wife and sons had committed any fault, he
usually took off his hat [260] and reproved himself. After his wife and sons

---

[257] Shou-ch'un 壽春 was located in modern Shou county, Anhui.

[258] Yin Yüeh 尹耀, who was the inspector of Yang division, was killed by bandits
in 144 (*HHS* 6:23a).

[259] Ch'ou Lan 仇覽 was chief of a canton for a number of years. He was later
appointed master of documents of the prefectural government and sent by the prefect
to study in the Imperial Academy. When he completed his studies he returned home,
but he refused to accept any official appointment (*HHS* 76:24b–26a).

[260] To take off one's hat, usually in the presence of a superior or an elder, was a way
of acknowledging one's fault. For examples, see *HS* 50:2a–b.

had come to the courtyard to apologize, they did not dare to ascend to the main room[261] until he had put on his hat. The members of his family were never able to observe any change in his countenance or voice because of pleasure or anger. [*HHS* 76:26a–b]

69. Property Not Divided for Three Generations

[Ts'ai Yung][262] lived with his uncles and first cousins. For three generations they had not div:ded their property.[263] His righteousness was highly admired by the local community. [*HHS* 60B:2a]

A.D.
159–192

70. Suicide as a Protest Against Remarriage

The wife of Yin Yü of the Nan-yang commandery was the daughter of Hsün Shuang[264] of the commandery Ying-ch'uan. Her name was Ts'ai; her style was Nü-hsün. She was wise and clever and had literary talent. She married Yin when she was seventeen. When she was nineteen a daughter was born and Yü died. While Ts'ai was still young she guarded herself carefully lest she be compelled by her family [to marry again].

A.D.
166–190

[261] The *t'ang* 堂 is the main room of the house, and is higher than the other rooms.

[262] Ts'ai Yung, whose style was Po-chieh, was a native of Ch'en-liu prefecture of Honan. He was an outstanding scholar of the classics and also an expert in mathematics, astronomy, and music. Later he became a gentleman of the palace, and during his term of office he was active in collating and correcting books. He was promoted to the position of gentleman discussant, and in 175 in order to correct the errata in the six classics he wrote them on stone tablets, which were erected in front of the Imperial Academy. He was disliked by a number of officials and the powerful eunuch, Ch'eng Huang 程璜, and therefore was slandered and imprisoned. He was exiled to Shuo-fang in 178 and was pardoned the following year. When Tung Cho came into power, Ts'ai was forced to accept an appointment and was promoted to the post of general of the palace gentlemen of the left in 190 and was ennobled district marquis of Kao-yang. Two years later, because of his political affiliation with Tung Cho, he was killed by Wang Yün 王允.

[263] This passage and I, 40, are the only two known instances in Han times of three generations living together and sharing the family property in common. This, together with the fact that such a family was highly admired by the local community, suggests that large households were comparatively rare at that time; otherwise they would not have been mentioned in the history. Note that even brothers rarely lived together in Han times and that this, too, inspired admiration. See I, 58; cf. also I, 61 and I, 62.

[264] Hsün Shuang's family was well known. His father, Shu, was famous for his learning and was respected by both Li Ku and Li Ying, who regarded him as their teacher. All of Shu's eight sons, including Shuang, were famous. They were known as the Eight Dragons. Shuang, being a great scholar, was summoned several times to court and finally became minister of works (*HHS* 62:1a ff.).

Later, Kuo I,[265] a native of the same commandery as she, lost his wife. Shuang promised that he could marry Ts'ai. Accordingly he pretended to be very ill and asked Ts'ai to come back. Lacking any alternative, Ts'ai returned. She carried a knife with her, vowing to herself [never to marry again]. Shuang ordered the girl slaves to take away her knife, embraced her, and took her into the carriage. He still worried that this might make her angry and indignant, and she was guarded very strictly.

When she arrived at the house of Kuo, she then feigned happiness and said to her attendants: "Originally I made up my mind to be buried with Yin, yet I am unable to escape from compulsion and consequently it comes to this. My original intention is unfulfilled. What shall I do then?" She then ordered the four lamps to be lit, adorned herself richly, asked [Kuo] I to come in that they might meet and have a talk. Her words were without end. Then she was respected and feared by [Kuo] I, who did not dare to possess her. At dawn he left. Ts'ai then ordered her attendants to prepare a bath for her. Having entered the room, she asked the attendants to leave and [started to] write on the door with powder, "Corpse to be returned to Yin." The character "Yin" was not completed because she feared that someone might come. She strangled herself with the belt of her dress. Her attendants were negligent and failed to care for her. When they went to see her she had died. Her contemporaries were mournful. [*HHS* 84:20a–b]

71. DESERTION

Ca.
A.D. 169 Huang Yün was known for his talent. . . . Yüan Wei, the minister of the masses, intended to find a husband for his niece. When he saw Yün he sighed and said, "I would be content if I could have such a son-in-law." Having heard this, Yün divorced his wife, Hsia-hou, and sent her away. She said to her mother-in-law, "Now I am going to be deserted and will leave the Huangs forever. Please let me have a chance to meet the relatives to bid them farewell."

Then more than three hundred guests were assembled. In the midst [of those who were] seated the wife pulled up her sleeves and enumer-

---

[265] Kuo I 郭奕 was the son of Kuo Chia 郭嘉, who was the military libationer of the minister of works *(ssu-k'ung chün chi-chiu* 司空軍祭酒) and had also been made canton marquis of Wei-yang with a grant of two hundred households. After Chia's death eight hundred households were added to his fief, to which Kuo I succeeded, as well as to the marquisate. Kuo I was appointed literary scholar of the heir apparent, *(t'ai-tzu wen-hsüeh* 太子文學) (*SKC*, Wei, 14:8b–12a).

ated fifteen cases of Yün's secret and crooked conduct. Having completed her talk, she got into the carriage and went away. Because of this Yün was ostracized [266] during his time. [*HHS* 68:6a–b]

72. A FAMILY OF SIXTY MEMBERS

[Chang] Hsien[267] went to the Fu-feng commandery. The administrator sent [Su] Pu-wei[268] to welcome him. Pu-wei was immediately arrested, and his whole family[269] of more than sixty persons were all killed. Thus the Su declined greatly. [*HHS* 31:21a]   A.D. 172–73

---

[266] That is, kept from official position. Since entry to a political career depended most frequently upon recommendation by imperial or commandery officials who based their evaluations on a candidate's ability to qualify as "wise, virtuous, square, and upright" or "filially pious and incorrupt," individuals who were known to be immoral or corrupt would have been unable to obtain office through this means. In the present case, and as it often did, social ostracism seems to have led to political ostracism.

[267] Chang Hsien 張賢 was a subordinate officer of Tuan Ying, the colonel-director of retainers, who sent him to kill Su Pu-wei.

[268] Su Pu-wei's 蘇不韋 family had a notable history. Su Chien 蘇建, Pu-wei's ancestor in the eleventh generation, was a colonel in the expeditionary force that fought against the Hsiung-nu under the command of Wei Ch'ing, the grand general. Because of his merit in this campaign, Su Chien was made a marquis in 124 B.C. Later, while holding the title of general of the right, he participated again in an attack on the Hsiung-nu—this time, however, without success. His army was lost and he himself was demoted to the status of commoner. Ultimately he became the grand administrator of the Tai commandery.

Su Wu 蘇武, one of Su Chien's three sons, was sent with the rank of general of the gentlemen of the palace as a special envoy to the Hsiung-nu, who detained him for nineteen years (*HS* 54:15b–23b).

Pu-wei's ancestor in the sixth generation, Ch'un 純, who held the position of chief commandant custodian of the imperial equipages (*feng-chü tu-wei* 奉車都尉), was made a marquis because of his meritorious fight against the northern Hsiung-nu and the Chü-shih in 73/74. He became grand administrator of Nan-yang (*HHS* 31:17b).

Ch'un's grandson, Chang 章, the brother of Pu-wei's great-grandfather, was also an official; see III, 61.

Pu-wei's father, Ch'ien 謙, was the investigator of transgressions of the commandery. Later he was promoted to the position of grand administrator of Chin-ch'eng. After his dismissal from this office, he was killed by Li Hao 李暠, the colonel-director of retainers, for personal reasons. Pu-wei failed to take vengeance upon Li Hao directly; instead he murdered his concubine and son, exhumed and decapitated his father's corpse, offering it as a sacrifice to his own father. Tuan Ying, an intimate friend of Li Hao, hated Pu-wei and killed him. At the time of his death Pu-wei was the head of the five offices (*wu-kuan-yüan* 五官掾) of the Fu-feng commandery (*HHS* 31:17a–21a).

[269] The original statement is 一門六十餘人. *Men* 門 is used interchangeably with the term "family." Literally it means "door."

73. Vow Not to Remarry

The wife of Liu Chang-ch'ing of P'ei was the daughter of Huan Luan of the same commandery. Luan's [life] is mentioned in his biography above. She bore a son. When the child was five years old, Chang-ch'ing died. In order to be above suspicion [of wishing to remarry], the wife never returned to her father's home. Her son died at the age of fifteen.

Fearing that [remarriage] was unavoidable, she cut off her ear, in advance [of any pressure to remarry] in order to vow to herself [not to marry again]. The wives of her husband's lineage consoled her and together said to her: "Your family has no such idea. Even if they should have, you can still express your true feelings through your aunts and sisters. Why do you regard righteousness so highly and your body so lightly?" She replied: "In the past, the learning of my ancestor, the *Wu-keng*,[270] was followed by scholars, and he was honored as the teacher of the emperor. Since the *Wu-keng*, generation after generation, there has been no deterioration [of the family]. All the men are famous for their loyalty and filial piety; all the women are praised because of their chastity and submission. The *Shih* says, 'Disgrace not your ancestors; cultivate your virtue.' Therefore I cut myself in advance in order to manifest my intent."

175–179 A.D.   The chancellor of P'ei, Wang Chi, memorialized concerning her eminent behavior and distinguished her village gate by marking it "Righteously Behaving Widow Huan." Whenever there was a sacrifice in the prefecture, the sacrificial meats were sent to her.[271] [*HHS* 84:18b–19a]

74. Five Degrees of Relationship

A.D. 176   An edict was again given to all divisional and commandery govern-

---

[270] The *Wu-keng* 五更 (a title given to elders who were honored by the emperor) refers to Huan Jung 桓榮, her great-great-grandfather. Jung was appointed lesser tutor of the heir apparent by Emperor Kuang-wu. Thus he was honored as the teacher of the emperor when Emperor Ming ascended the throne and was appointed *Wu-keng*. Later he was ennobled as a marquis within the passes.

Huan's family was famous for generations after Huan Jung. Jung's son, Yü, also became the teacher of Emperors Chang and Ho and was promoted to the post of grand minister of ceremonies. Yü's son, Yen 焉, was the teacher of Emperors An and Shun. He was appointed grand tutor and then grand commandant. Huan Luan 桓鸞, the father of the girl in this example, was the son of Yen's younger brother. At first he was a prefect and was then promoted to the position of gentleman discussant (*HHS* 37:1a–11b).

[271] Sacrificial meat was given only to honorable persons.

ments to re-examine the students, former subordinate officials, fathers, sons, and brothers of the Partisans.[272] All those who had been holding official positions were then dismissed and posted on the proscription list. The interdiction extended to all kinsmen[273] within the five degrees of relationship.[274]

[272] This passage refers to the political intrigue that occurred during the reigns of Emperors Huan and Ling. See III, 65, n. 376. The edict of 176 was issued because of a memorial presented by Ts'ao Luan 曹鸞 in defense of the Partisans, which had angered the emperor (*HHS* 8:8b; 67:7b–8a).

[273] According to the "Annals" of Emperor Ling, the proscription had already been extended to the kinsmen within the five degrees of relationship in the year 169 (*HHS* 8:4a), and this was not mentioned in connection with the investigation of the Partisans in 176, as our text states.

[274] Li comments that the five degrees of relationship (*wu shu* 五屬) are identical with the five degrees of mourning. Since the mourning garment was differentiated according to the nearness or remoteness of the kindred, it served as a practical index for degrees of relationship for a long time; it was the only index before the modern Chinese law introduced the new system of degrees of relationship based upon canon law. It defines the proximity or distance (degree of relationship) as well as the scope of kinship.

The five degrees of mourning are: (1) *chan-ts'ui* 斬衰, (2) *tzu-ts'ui* 齊衰, (3) *ta-kung* 大功, (4) *hsiao-kung* 小功, (5) *ssu-ma* 緦麻. The terms are found in many Han works such as the *I-li* (*chüan* 11 *passim*), *Li-chi* (*chüan* 9, 18, 20), *Po-hu-t'ung* (10:6a), and *Huai-nan-tzu* (11:9a); although the *Huai-nan-tzu* merely mentions "garments of five ts'ui," the commentary gives the terms of mourning of three years, one year, nine months, five months, and three months (*HNT* 11:9a). This is in accordance with the statement of the *I-li*. Since the *Huai-nan-tzu* is an early Han work (it was a cooperative work of the guests of the king of Huai-nan, An, 164–122 B.C.; see Kao Hsiu's preface in *Huai-nan-tzu*, p. 2a; cf. *HS* 44:8b; Hu Shih, *Huai-nan-wang shu* [Shanghai: Hsin-yüeh shu-tien, 1931], pp. 3–10) and the commentator Kao Hsiu was also a Han man who wrote his commentary in the years 205–212 A.D. (see his preface in *HNT*, p. 2a), it is likely that the five degrees of mourning were already in practice in Han times.

The length of the term and the kind of clothing for each degree, based upon the *I-li*, are summarized as follows:

1. *Chan-ts'ui* 斬衰	Unhemmed coarse hempen garment	three years (nominally, but actually only twenty-five months)
2. *Tzu-ts'ui* 齊衰	Coarse hempen garment with hem	three years one year three months
3. *Ta-kung* 大功	Garment of fine hempen cloth	nine months
4. *Hsiao-kung* 小功	Garment of finer hempen cloth	five months
5. *Ssu-ma* 緦麻	Garment of finest hempen cloth	three months

The kinds of mourning to be worn by various degrees of kindred, according to the same source, are summarized as follows:

    1. *Chan ts'ui:*

        For father 父

> By father for his eldest son by his principal wife 父為長子
>
> By an adopted son for his father by adoption 為人後者
>
> By a wife for her husband 妻為夫
>
> By a concubine for her master 妾為君
>
> By an unmarried daughter still living in the paternal home for her father 女子在室為父
>
> By a married daughter who has been divorced and dwells in the paternal home for her father 子嫁反在父之室

2. *Tzu-ts'ui:*

   a. Three years

> For mother after the death of the father 父卒則為母
>
> For a stepmother 繼母
>
> For a foster mother (a childless concubine who, by the command of her master, takes care of a motherless child of another concubine) 慈母
>
> By a mother for the eldest son 母為長子

   b. One year *(ch'i)*

     (1) With a staff:

> For mother when the father is still alive 父在為母
>
> For the wife 妻

     (2) Without a staff:

> For paternal grandparents 祖父母
>
> For father's brothers and their wives 世父母
>
> For brothers 昆弟
>
> For all sons other than the eldest son by the principal wife 為衆子
>
> For brothers' sons 昆弟之子
>
> For the eldest grandson by the principal wife 適孫
>
> By an adopted son for his natural father and mother 為人後者為其父母
>
> For a stepfather if living in his house 繼父同居者
>
> By a concubine for her master's wife 妾為女君
>
> For husband's parents 婦為舅姑
>
> For a son of one's husband's brother 夫之昆弟之子
>
> By a woman for her paternal grandparents 女子子為其祖父母

   c. Three months

> For a stepfather if not living in his house 繼父不同居者
>
> For paternal great-grandparents 曾祖父母
>
> By a woman, married or unmarried, for her paternal great-grandfather 女子子嫁者未嫁者為曾祖父母

3. *Ta-kung:*

> For father's brothers' sons and unmarried daughters 從父昆弟
>
> For all grandsons other than the eldest one of the principal wife 庶孫
>
> For the wife of the eldest son of the principal wife 適婦
>
> For husband's paternal grandparents and for his paternal uncles and their wives 夫之祖父母世父母叔父母
>
> By a woman, married or unmarried, for her paternal uncles and their wives, her paternal aunts, and her own sisters 女子子嫁者未嫁者為世父母叔父母姑姊妹

4. *Hsiao-kung:*

> For paternal grandfather's brothers and their wives 從祖祖父母
>
> For paternal grandfather's brothers' sons and their wives 從祖父母
>
> For brothers' grandsons 兄弟之孫 (報)
>
> For father's brothers' grandsons 從父兄弟之子 (報) (De Groot and J. Steele were wrong in not including the last two. *Pao* 報 means

    reciprocal, that is, the grandfather's brothers and their wives as well as the grandfather's brothers' sons and their wives also wore the same mourning reciprocally for their brothers' grandsons or their father's brothers' grandsons; see *ILCS* 33:1a: K'ung's commentary)

For paternal grandfather's brothers' grandsons 從祖昆弟

For husband's paternal aunts and sisters 夫之姑姉妹

By the wives of brothers for each other 女弟姒婦報

5. *Ssu-ma:*

For paternal great-grandfather's brothers and their wives 族曾祖父母

For paternal great-grandfather's brothers' sons and their wives 族祖父母

For paternal great-grandfather's brothers' grandsons and their wives 族父母

For paternal great-grandfather's brothers' great-grandsons 族兄弟

For paternal grandfather's brothers' great-grandsons 從祖昆弟之子

For great-grandsons 曾孫

For paternal grandfather's sisters 父之姑

For husband's paternal grandfather's brothers and their wives and for husband's grandfather's brothers' sons and their wives 夫之諸祖父母報

For husband's paternal uncle's sons' wives 夫之從父兄弟之妻

ILCS, chüan 28–33. For English translation, see J. J. M. de Groot, *The Religious System of China* (6 vols.; Leiden, 1892–1910), II, 506 ff., and John Steele, *The I-li, or Book of Etiquette and Ceremonial* (2 vols.; London, 1917), II, 9 ff.

Since our present aim is merely to show the scope of kinships and the degree of relationship among kinsmen, we include only those who bear the same family name. Minor differences, owing to the political status of the man who wore the mourning, which were not applicable in Han institutions, are excluded. It should also be noted that wives of the various family members were considered members of the group and were not considered affinals in Chinese families; and a married daughter was not included unless she was divorced and lived again in her father's home.

This table clearly shows that the extent of kinship was extended to the offspring of great-great-grandfathers only (great-great-grandfather as the common ancestor), with *ssu-ma* as its limitation. Beyond this limit kinship came to an end.

A similar explanation is found in the *Li-chi*, which reads: "For parties four generations removed (from the same common ancestor) the mourning was reduced to that worn for three months, and this was the limit of wearing the hempen cloth. If the generations were five, the shoulders were bared and the cincture assumed; in this way the mourning within the circle of the same [family name] was gradually reduced. After the sixth generation the bond of kinship was held to be at an end" (*LCCS* 34:4b; Legge, *Texts of Confucianism*, II, 63).

As great-great-grandfather and great-great-grandson are not enumerated in *I-li* 11, we are confronted with a problem: Are they included in the mourning group? Some scholars, such as Yüan Chün (Chin), Shen K'uo (Sung), Li Ju-kuei (Sung), and Ku Yen-wu (Ch'ing), argue that one had to wear mourning for his direct ancestors even if they were ten generations removed. The term *tseng-tsu* 曾祖, "great grandfather," in the text of the *I-li* is not applied in its narrow sense; all remoter ancestors, one or more generations above the great-grandfather, are included, hence *tzu-ts'ui* (second degree) is the mourning for all remote ancestors. See *TT* 90:493; Shen K'uo, *Meng-hsi pi-t'an, TSCC* ed., 3:14, hereafter cited as *MHPT;* Li Ju-kuei, *I-Li chi-shih,* in *WYT,* 18:5a–b, hereafter cited as *ILS; JCLCS* 5:30a–b.

Their argument is not very strong because there is no evidence to support it, and it contradicts the statement of the *Li-chi*. If there is no limitation for direct ancestors, then the number "nine" in the statement of the *Li-chi* is meaningless (see below).

There are other scholars who assume that the mourning worn for direct ancestors extended only to the great-great-grandfather. Basing himself on the statement of the *I-li*, Cheng Hsüan made the following statement: "Five being the limit of mourning, then *ssu-ma* should be the mourning for the great-great-grandfather, and *hsiao-kung* for great-grandfather. One year being the mourning for grandfather, then *ta-kung* should be worn for the great-grandfather and *hsiao-kung* for great-great-grandfather. Since both the great-great-grandfather and the great-grandfather have the difference of *hsiao-kung*, the mourning worn by their great-great grandsons and great-grandsons should be the same" (*ILCS* 31:6b).

His argument of including only the great-great-grandfather may be supported by the following statement of the *Li-chi*: "In counting kindred (and the mourning to be worn for them), the three closest degrees become expanded into five, and these five again into nine. Mourning diminished as the degrees ascended or descended, and the collateral branches also were correspondingly less mourned for; the mourning for kindred thus came to an end" (*LCCS* 32:3b; Legge, *Texts of Confucianism*, II, 42). Counting from the son, the three refer to father, son (self), and son's son; adding the grandfather and grandson, we have five. The great-grandfather and the great-great-grandfather on one end, and great-grandson and great-great-grandson on the other end, make nine. See Cheng's commentary: *LCCS* 32:3b.

Basing ourselves on this statement, we may reach the conclusion that great-great-grandfather is included in the *wu-fu;* with this assumption in mind, we are able to re-examine the statement of the *Li-chi* quoted above. The phrase "four generations removed" should not only refer to the clansmen but should also be applicable to the ancestors and descendants. In this way the prescribed number of generations (four and nine) and the prescribed limit of mourning *(ssu-ma)* is understandable. Taking "self" as a starting point:

Four generations of ascendants (F, F′F, F′F′F, and F′F′F′F) plus four generations of descendants (S, S′S, S′S′S, and S′S′S′S) including himself, make nine. The two statements differ in words, but mean practically the same thing.	Mourning reduced	↑	IV
			III
			II
			I
	IV, III, II, I		SELF 9
			I
	Mourning reduced		II
			III
		↓	IV

If great-great-grandfather is not included, then there will be only three generations instead of four, and the total number of nine cannot be reached.

But there are some other problems that seem to contradict our interpretation. First, what is the status of great-great-grandson? He was not enumerated in the text of the *I-li*. Since *ssu-ma* is known as the last (marginal) mourning, and it is already worn for the great-grandson, then there is no place for the great-great-grandson. But this explanation again is contradictory to the statements of the *Li-chi*. If he is excluded, then there will be only three descending generations instead of four, and the total number will be eight instead of nine. The only possible answer is to assume that the mourning for great-great-grandson is the same as for great-grandson: *ssu-ma*. This practically was the system defined by the *K'ai-yüan li* in T'ang times (see *TT* 134:702) and followed by the Sung, Yüan, Ming, and Ch'ing dynasties.

The other problem is connected with the status of brother's great-grandson and father's brothers' great-grandsons' son. They were not enumerated in the list of the *I-li*. But theoretically, since *hsiao-kung* is worn for brother's grandson and for father's

In the second year of Kuang-ho, Ho Hai, the chief of Shan-lu, [pre- A.D. 179
fecture] presented a memorial, saying, "According to the *Book of Rites,*
cousins of the same great-grandfather[275] should live separately with
individual property. Their affections are weak and their relationship is
remote. Yet now the proscription of the Partisans is extended to all the
five *tsu*.[276] It is in conflict with the teachings of the *Book* and not in accordance with normal tradition."

The emperor became aware of the situation. Thus all those family
members descended from a grandfather's father and more remote
relatives were excluded from the proscription. [*HHS* 67:8a]

75. FATHER BEATS SON

[Ts'ui] Lieh was well known in the northern commanderies. He had   A.D. 178–179
held the office of commandery administrator and had been one of the
Nine Ministers. At that time Emperor Ling put up a notice at the Hung-
tu Gate [announcing] the sale of official ranks and titles.[277] From the
posts of the Three Ducal Ministers, the Nine Ministers, and [the chief
executives of] regional divisions or commanderies down to the [wearers]
of yellow seal-cords,[278] [the prices] varied at different rates. . . .

---

brother's grandson, one more generation should be extended descendantly. This is
the reason that the *K'ai-yüan li* added *ssu-ma* for the two relatives mentioned above
(*TT* 134:701). However, it is hard to say whether the omission in the *I-li* is accidental.

[275] 從祖 refers to the following relatives whose degree of mourning is *hsiao-kung*:
paternal grandfather's brothers (從祖祖父), paternal grandfather's brothers' sons
(從祖父), paternal grandfather's brothers' grandsons (從祖兄弟), brother's grandsons
(兄弟之孫), and father's brothers' grandsons (從父兄弟); see the table above. Thus
HHS 8:11b reads, "All those family members from the *hsiao-kung* and below [小功以
下] were removed from the proscription."

The proscription for other closer relatives (namely, from the *ta-kung* and above)
remained in effect until 184 when the Yellow Turban Rebellion started. Then all the
Partisans, upon the suggestion of Lü Ch'iang 呂彊, a eunuch holding the post of
regular palace attendant, were pardoned, and those families that had been exiled
were allowed to return to their native commanderies (*HHS* 8:15a, 67:8a–b).

[276] In Chinese classical usage the word *tsu* has several meanings. One is identical
with "lineage" and includes all the members. Sometimes it refers only to the generations represented in the lineage. When used thus, a number usually precedes it. Nine
tsu therefore is "nine generations," or all generations from the paternal great-great-
grandparents down to the great-great-grandsons. We find also such an expression as
three *tsu* (*HS* 1B:14b and 15b, 34:13b, 37:1a and 4a). However, when "five *tsu*" is
used it refers to the five degrees of mourning, and it is in this sense that the phrase is
employed in this passage.

[277] The selling of official ranks commenced in 179 (*HHS* 8:11a).

[278] Copper seals and yellow seal-cords were worn by officials from the rank of
"equivalent to 200 piculs" up to those with a rank of 400 piculs (*HS* 19A:16b).

Lieh, through the emperor's governess, paid five million[279] for the post of minister of the masses. . . . Hence Lieh's reputation was suddenly lowered.

After a lapse of time, he himself did not feel easy. Then he asked his son, Chün, in an easy manner, "I am in the position of a ducal minister. How is public opinion [about it]?" Chün replied, "You had a good name during your youth and held the offices of minister and administrator. Those who discuss [the matter] do not think that you should not be a ducal minister. Now you have risen to the position, and the world is disappointed." "What is the reason?" asked Lieh. Chün replied, "They dislike the smell of copper."

Lieh was angry and raised his stick to strike him. At this time Chün was general of the palace gentlemen as rapid as tigers and was wearing a military cap adorned with pheasant feathers. He ran away in great distress. Lieh scolded him and said, "You, dead soldier! Is it filial to run away when your father beats you?" Chün replied, "Shun serving his father in this way accepted [the punishment] when the stick was small, but ran away when the stick was large.[280] It cannot be considered as unfilial." Lieh was ashamed of himself and stopped. [*HHS* 52:27a–28b]

76. A Lineage Migrates

A.D. 190's   Hsün Yü,[281] whose style was Wen-jo, was a native of Ying-yin of

[279] According to *HHS* 8:11a, the price for the post of a ducal minister was ten million cash and that of one of the nine ministers was five million. The amount paid by Ts'ui Lieh was thus only half the regular price. His biography mentions that the emperor regretted not having asked for ten million (*HHS* 52:27b).

[280] This story is found in the *K'ung-tzu chia-yü*. Shun ran away so that his father would not have a reputation for unrighteousness in case he were killed (*KTCY* 4:5b–6a).

[281] Hsün Yü 荀彧 (163–212) first attached himself to Yüan Shao, then from 191 until his death to Yüan's opponent, Ts'ao Ts'ao, becoming his trusted adviser. Hsün Yü was promoted to the position of attendant within the palace and acting prefect of the masters of writing in 196 when Emperor Hsien was removed from Lo-yang to Hsü. The defeat of Lü Pu, Yüan Shao, and the pacification of Ho-pei were the result of his plans and advice. In recognition of his services he was ennobled canton marquis of Wan-sui and was given one thousand households. On Ts'ao Ts'ao's recommendation another thousand households were added to the original gift. However, Yü lost favor with him when he objected to Tung Chao's 董昭 proposal to make Ts'ao Ts'ao a duke and honor him with nine bestowals (九錫). During Ts'ao Ts'ao's campaign against Sun Ch'üan 孫權, he kept Yü in his army as a military adviser. While on his way Yü became ill. Ts'ao Ts'ao sent him a present of food, but when the box was opened it was found to be empty. Yü thereupon took poison and died (*HHS* 70:25a ff.).

Ying-ch'uan. He was the grandson of Hsün Shu,[282] the prefect of Lang-ling.[283] His father, K'un,[284] was the chancellor of Chi-nan kingdom. . . .

In the sixth year of Chung-p'ing [of Emperor Ling, Yü] was recom-   A.D. 189
mended as "filially pious and incorrupt" and later appointed prefect of Kang-fu.[285] During the rebellion of Tung Cho[286] he gave up his office and returned to his native place. In the meantime Han Jung, a native of the same province, was moving his kinsmen and relatives, amounting to more than a thousand households, to the west hill of Mi[287] in order to escape trouble.

Yü told his elders, "Ying-ch'uan is a place having communication with all directions; it usually becomes a military key-point when there is war. Mi, though small, is unable to avoid great distress. We should keep away from it." Cherishing their native place, most of the men were unable to move.

It happened that the shepherd of Chi province was Han Fu,[288] of the same commandery; he sent horsemen to welcome [Yü into his jurisdiction]. Yü then led his kinsmen to Han Fu. Those who remained [in the commandery] were for the most part killed by Li Chüeh, Tung Cho's general. [*HHS* 70:24a–b]

[282] Hsün Shu was appointed gentleman of the palace, and was then promoted to the post of prefect of Tang-t'u during the time of Emperor An (107–125). Later he was dismissed from his post and returned home. When Empress Dowager Liang came to power (144–150), he was recognized as "wise and virtuous" and "square and upright." He satirized the arrogant general Liang Chi, the younger brother of the empress dowager, in his examination paper and as a result was disliked by the general and sent out as chancellor of the marquis of Lang-ling. Shortly thereafter he gave up his post and returned home. He died in 149. All his eight sons were men of high reputation and were called by their contemporaries the Eight Dragons (*HHS* 62:1a–2a).

[283] Lang-ling 朗陵 is the present Ch'üeh-shan county of Honan. According to Hsün Shu's biography, he was the chancellor of the marquis of Lang-ling and not a prefect, as our text reads.

[284] Hsün K'un 荀緄 was the second son of Hsün Shu (*HHS* 62:2a).

[285] Kang-fu 亢父 was located fifty *li* south of modern Chi-ning, Shantung.

[286] When Emperor Ling died in 189, Tung Cho led his troops to the capital, deposed the young emperor, and put Emperor Hsien on the throne. In the following year Yüan Shao, Han Fu 韓馥, Sun Chien, and many others led their troops to attack Tung Cho.

[287] Mi is the present Mi county of Honan.

[288] Han Fu was among the group of administrators and shepherds who raised troops against Tung Cho, under the leadership of Yüan Shao. (The office of shepherds of provinces replaced that of the former inspectors of regional divisions; the change in name reflects a shift from a censorial role to a fully administrative one.) Han was later forced by Yüan Shao to yield his post to him. He went to Chang Miao 張邈, the grand administrator of Ch'en-liu. He committed suicide when Yüan sent someone to visit Chang and he suspected they were plotting against him (*HHS* 64A:3b–9a).

77. REMARRIAGE

The wife of Tung Shih of Ch'en-liu was the daughter of Ts'ai Yung[289] of the same province. Her name was Yen, her style Wen-chi. She was widely learned, talented, and eloquent. She was also skilled in music. She married Wei Chung-tao of Ho-tung. Her husband died, and they had no son. She then went back to her father's home.

A.D.
190–193During the Hsing-p'ing[290] period the world was being destroyed and was in disorder. Wen-chi was seized by the mounted [northern] barbarians,[291] and was taken by the king of Tso-hsien of the southern Hsiung-nu. She stayed with the barbarians for twelve years and bore two sons.[292] Ts'ao Ts'ao formerly had been friendly with Ts'ai Yung. Grieving for Ts'ai's lack of descendants, he then sent a messenger to ransom her with gold and jade and married her to Shih. Shih was chief commandant of garrison fields. [*HHS* 84:22a]

78. SIZE OF A LINEAGE—ONE HUNDRED PERSONS

[Yüan Shu][293] sent his general, Sun Ts'e,[294] to attack [Lu] K'ang.[295] The city was surrounded; circle after circle was firmly defended. . . . A.D. 194 After being besieged for two years, the city was finally taken. One

[289] For Ts'ai Yung, see I, 69.

[290] The invasion of the Hsiung-nu took place after the death of Emperor Ling (189). The reign period should be Ch'u-p'ing, not Hsing-p'ing (see Hui Tung, *Hou-Han-shu pu-chu*, *TSCC* ed., 84:14a, hereafter cited as *HHSPC*). Therefore, we give the date as 190–193.

[291] The word *hu* refers to the northern barbarians, that is, the Hsiung-nu.

[292] According to the poem written by Wen-chi, her sons were left with the Hsiung-nu (*HHS* 84:24a).

[293] Yüan Shu was one of the warlords who arose at the end of the Later Han dynasty. In 190 he became grand administrator of Nan-yang; from there he rebelled against Tung Cho and began a campaign for the throne. He assumed the title of emperor in 197 and died in 199 (*HHS* 75:8a–14b).

[294] Sun Ts'e was the eldest son of Sun Chien, who was the "general who destroys the caitiffs" (*p'o-lu chiang-chün* 破虜將軍) under the command of Yüan Shu. Sun Chien was killed during the war in 192/193, and later the command of his private troops was given to Sun Ts'e by Yüan. After he had conquered and occupied Chiang-tung, Sun Ts'e disassociated himself from Yüan and was appointed "general who punishes the refractory" (*t'ao-ni chiang-chün* 討逆將軍) and ennobled as marquis of Wu by Ts'ao Ts'ao. He was murdered in A.D. 200 at the age of twenty-six by the guests of Hsü Kung 許貢, whom he had killed.

[295] Lu K'ang was a native of Wu; for generations his family had been a famous one. His great-great-grandfather, Hung 閎, was the prefect of the masters of writing in the time of Emperor Kuang-wu (25–57). His grandfather, Hsü 續, was the head of the staff (*men-hsia-yüan* 門下掾) of Wu commandery. Both of his paternal uncles, Ch'ou 稠

month later [Lu K'ang] fell sick and died at the age of seventy. Of his kinsmen, who numbered more than one hundred, nearly half were dead from starvation and destitution. [*HHS* 31:26b–27a]

---

and Feng 逢, were grand administrators (*HHS* 81:20a–21b). In 178 Lu K'ang became grand administrator of Wu-ling; in 192 he was administrator of Lu-chiang with the title of "loyal and righteous general" (*chung-i chiang-chün* 忠義將軍). It was at this time that Yüan Shu was defeated by Ts'ao Ts'ao and Yüan Shao; and when K'ang refused to help Shu by sending supplies, Shu sent his General Sun Ts'e to besiege the city of Lu-chiang.

II

SOCIAL CLASSES

1. SLAVES EMPLOYED IN PRIVATE ENTERPRISES

Third
century
B.C.
It was the custom of Ch'i to look down upon male slaves.[1] Tiao
Chien[2] alone liked and valued them. Truculent and cunning slaves were
considered a bane by the people, but Tiao Chien alone took them in
and employed them in seeking profits from fishing, salt, and trade.
Some of them[3] had carriages and horsemen and associated with administrators [of commanderies] and chancellors [of kingdoms]. However,
he entrusted more and more to them. Eventually by their help he became rich to the amount of several thousand myriad [of cash]. Therefore, it was said, "Rather to be with Tiao than to have noble rank."[4]

---

[1] The two characters in the term *nu lo* 奴虜 mean "male slaves" and "captives"
respectively. Wilbur translates them thus and remarks on their close association
(Martin Wilbur, *Slavery in China During the Former Han Dynasty* [Chicago, 1943],
p. 281). However, *lo* 虜 may also mean "slaves."

[2] Tiao Chien (the *Han-shu* has 刁 instead of 刁, but the pronunciation was the same)
is mentioned only in this passage.

[3] Duyvendak, who considers that Tiao Chien should be regarded as the subject
throughout the paragraph, suggests that it was Tiao Chien himself, not the slaves,
who traveled and associated with administrators. For this reason he understands the
character *huo* 或 as "sometimes" (J. J. L. Duyvendak, "A Scribal Error?," *Orientalia
Neerlandica* (Leiden, 1948), pp. 454–55). However, we understand *huo* as the subject
of the sentence with the meaning of "some" and as referring to the slaves (similar
examples are found in the Chinese classics, e.g., 或謂孔子曰 "Someone addressed
Confucius" [*LYCS* 2:4a] and 或問禘之説 "Someone asked the meaning of the great
sacrifice" [*LYCS* 3:4a]). The preceding sentence states that slaves were employed in
seeking profits from fishing, salt, and trade, and the following sentence, "However, he
entrusted . . ." also refers to slaves. It seems illogical and meaningless for the interven-
ing sentence suddenly to refer to Tiao Chien himself. What connection could there
be between his riding and visiting and the employment of slaves? And why is the
word 然, "however," used in this following sentence: 然愈益任之? We agree with
Meng K'ang's interpretation that it was some of the slaves who traveled and associated with administrators and chancellors. There is nothing wrong grammatically with
this reading and logically it is not unreasonable to suppose that slaves, traveling with
carriages and retinue, should associate with high officials.

[4] The original sentence in both the *Shih-chi* and the *Han-shu* reads: 寧爵毋 (or 無)
刁 (or 刀), literally, "Rather to have rank than to be with Tiao." Meng K'ang tries
to explain the seeming contradiction as follows: "Tiao Chien was able to keep strong

male slaves, and some of the slaves had carriages and horsemen and became intimate with administrators and chancellors. The slaves said to themselves, 'Would we rather be freed and become commoners with rank or stay and be the slaves of Tiao?' " Meng holds that *wu* 毋 (or 無) was merely an interjection (exclamatory auxiliary word). Chou Shou-ch'ang rejects this interpretation, arguing that an idiomatic expression should not be so complicated. He suggests instead, "Would we rather have the honor of a rank and not have the wealth of Tiao?" (for the various views see *HSPC* 91:10a).

Neither wording is acceptable. Both convert the original statement into a question that, if the import of the whole passage is considered, demands a negative answer. Various examples can be cited from the classics to show that when a sentence begins with the word *ning* 寧, and the word *hu* 乎 or *yeh* 耶 appears at the end of the second phrase, it is an interrogative sentence (see P'ei Hsüeh-hai, *Ku-shu hsü-tzu chi-shih* [Shanghai: Commercial Press, 1935], pp. 504–5). When neither *hu* nor *yeh* appears, the sentence is declarative. This is the case in the present text. It should be noted that *ning* always means "prefer" or "rather than" whether the sentence is declarative or interrogative. When both phrases begin with *ning*, or when the first phrase begins with *ning* and the second with *chiang* 將, alternative choices are indicated. Thus 寧其死為留骨而貴乎, 寧其生而曳尾于塗中乎 *(CT* 6:27b) means "Would you prefer to die a noble or live and be humble like a dog hanging its tail in the street?" When one phrase begins with *ning* and the other with *yü-ch'i* 與其 or *wu* 無, as in our text, one choice is definitely preferable. *Wu* or *yü-ch'i* always means "not preferred." Thus 與其奢也寧儉 means "It is better to be sparing than extravagant," and 寧僭 無濫 "Rather to be excessive [in reward] than to be excessive [in punishment]" (*TCCS* 37:7a–b). The sentence in the passage above, 寧爵無刁, which has exactly the same construction as this last sentence, would then mean "Rather to have rank than to be with Tiao." This, however, controverts the sense of our passage as a whole.

Duyvendak, as previously noted, suggests that the subject of our whole passage, including the sentence under discussion, is Tiao Chien and that the character *tiao* 刁 should be *li* 力, "labor" in the phrase *"ning chüeh wu* Tiao." Thus he translates: "Therefore he said: '(Do you suppose that) I would rather have noble rank and no labour!' " (Duyvendak, "A Scribal Error?," pp. 454–55). Although there is close similarity between the characters *tiao* 刁 and *li* 力, and a scribal error is quite possible, certain objections to this substitution can be made. First, there is no grammatical reason, as Duyvendak holds, that the subject of consecutive sentences in a passage must remain the same, nor is there any specific indication that Tiao Chien is the subject of the sentence in question. It therefore seems more logical either to hold that the slaves are the subject, as assumed by Meng K'ang and accepted by Wilbur (*Slavery in China,* pp. 281–82), or to regard the sentence as a popular saying, as suggested by Chou Shou-ch'ang and accepted by us. Had Tiao Chien been the subject, the sentence would not have started with 故曰, "Therefore said." Second, Duyvendak's interpretation involves two assumptions: (1) that there is a scribal error, and (2) that the sentence is an interrogative one. The occurrence of the character *li* in other sentences in the passage in no way guarantees that it should also appear in this one. On the other hand, since the passage refers to Tiao and his slaves, it would be more meaningful if the word were *tiao* 刁. Furthermore, to make the phrase an interrogative one and to presume a negative answer is also questionable procedure; our objections to Meng K'ang's and Chou Shou-ch'ang's interpretations as indicated above also apply here.

Erroneously understanding Meng K'ang's commentary to mean "Would we want to be freed and become plebeians with honorary rank if we had to stop being Tiao Chien's slaves?," Wilbur translates the phrase in question "Rather no noble rank [than to be] without Tiao" (cf. Wilbur, *Slavery in China,* p. 281, and Duyvendak, "A

It means that he was able to make strong male slaves self-sufficient[5] while using their energies to the utmost. [*SC* 129:18b; *HS* 91:9a]

2. TREATMENT OF SLAVES

Ch'in   [Wang Mang[6] said, "Ch'in] also established markets [for the sale] of male and female slaves, putting them in the same pens with oxen and horses. They were controlled by the common people who had arbitrary authority over their lives. The treacherous and brutal people profited by exploiting this authority. They even seized and sold other people's wives and children. It was contrary to the intention of Heaven, and it confused the basic relations of mankind."[7] [*HS* 99B:9b]

Scribal Error?," pp. 451–54). It is also well to point out here that the word "no" does not appear in the Chinese and that *ning* cannot mean "rather no."

None of the foregoing explanations of the phrase seems satisfactory. However, the sentence becomes both grammatical and meaningful if we make a textual inversion and if instead of *ning chüeh wu Tiao* we read *ning Tiao wu chüeh*, "Rather to be with Tiao than to have noble rank."

[5] Suggesting that the word *jao* 饒 has also the meaning of "to be liberal," "to be tolerant," Duyvendak translates, "Which means that Tiao Chien was able to cause overbearing slaves, while sacrificing themselves, to exert their strength to the utmost" (Duyvendak, "A Scribal Error?," p. 455). However, the usage of *jao jen* 饒人, "to pardon others," "to cede to others," is a colloquial one; see *K'ang-hsi tzu-tien* (hereafter cited as *KHTT*), *sub* 饒. The word *jao* in Ch'in–Han texts has only the meaning of "abundance" or "affluence." Even when the phrase *jao jen* is used, the implication is the same, e.g., 能饒人以爵邑 "You, Great King, can enrich others by giving ranks and fiefs to them" (*SC* 56:4b; *HS* 40:14b). Moreover, even in colloquial expressions the Chinese do not say *tzu jao* 自饒 in the sense of "ceding oneself" or "of being liberal to oneself."

This document does not tell us by what means these slaves were able to enrich themselves. Probably there was an agreement between the master and his slaves that a certain percentage of the profit was given to them as a reward for their services. This seems to constitute the incentive that encouraged them to be "self-sufficient while using their energies to the utmost." It is also possible that as business agents for their master they were able to acquire benefit by various means. In any case, the employment of slaves in commerce and industry for their master's and their own benefit was not uncommon in the history of slavery. Parallels are found in the Neo-Babylonian and Late Assyrian periods. Furthermore, the right of a slave to accumulate private property was widely recognized. See Isaac Mendelsohn, *Slavery in the Ancient Near East* (New York, 1949), pp. 66 ff.

[6] Wang Mang, who seized the throne at the end of the Early Han, ruled from A.D. 9 to 23. He discussed the treatment of slaves in former times because he tried—unsuccessfully—to improve their position.

[7] According to Confucius the five basic relations are the relation between ruler and subject, between father and son, between elder and younger brothers, between husband and wife, and between friend and friend.

3. A Merchant Seeks Political Power

Lü Pu-wei was a big merchant in Yang-ti.[8] He traveled here and Ch'in
there, bought at low prices and sold at high prices. His family property
amounted to a thousand catties of gold.

In the fortieth year of King Chao of Ch'in, the heir apparent died. 265 B.C.
In the forty-second year, the second son, An-kuo Chün, was made
heir apparent.

An-kuo Chün had more than twenty sons. An-kuo Chün had a
favorite concubine whom he made his legal wife, calling her Wife
Hua-yang. Wife Hua-yang had no son. An-kuo Chün's middle son was
Tzu-ch'u. Tzu-ch'u's mother, Hsia Chi, received no favor [from An-kuo
Chün]. Tzu-ch'u was Ch'in's hostage son in Chao. . . . Since Tzuch'u
was a grandson[9] born of a concubine and was held as a hostage by a
feudal state, his carriages and expenses were not generously provided
for, and his living conditions were embarrassing. He was not satisfied.

Lü Pu-wei traded in Han-tan. Seeing [Tzu-ch'u], he pitied him and
said [to himself], "Here is a wonderful commodity to get hold of."
Thereupon he went to see Tzu-ch'u and said to him, "I can enlarge
your gate."[10] Tzu-ch'u smiled and said, "Enlarge your own gate. [Why
should] you want to enlarge my gate?" Lü Pu-wei said, "You don't
know it, but my gate can be enlarged only by enlarging your gate. . . .
I heard that An-kuo Chün loves Wife Hua-yang. Wife Hua-yang has
no son; but when it comes to establishing an heir, only Hua-yang can
do it. Now you have more than twenty brothers and you are the middle
one and are not favored [by your father]. You have been a hostage in
this feudal state for a long time. When the great king dies and An-kuo
Chün becomes king, there will be no hope for you to compete for the
position of heir apparent with the elder son and the other sons who have
stayed before him day and night." Tzu-ch'u said, "Right. Then what
should I do?" Lü Pu-wei said, "You are poor and are here as a guest.
You don't have [enough wealth] to present gifts to your parents or to
associate with guests. Although I, Pu-wei, am poor, I am willing to
spend a thousand [catties of] gold for you to go to the west [to Ch'in]
to serve An-kuo Chün and Wife Hua-yang in order to have you adopted

[8] Yang-ti 陽翟 is modern Yü county of Honan.

[9] Grandson of King Chao of Ch'in.

[10] Since the higher a man's status, the larger his gate, the phrase "to enlarge the
gate" means "to raise one's status." It is interesting to note here that an individual's
way of life was determined in the main by his political status; the rich merchant
could enlarge his gate only by enlarging the gate of the prince.

as heir." Tzu-ch'u then bowed his head and said, "If it works out as you plan, I should like to divide the state of Ch'in and share it with you."

Lü Pu-wei thereupon gave five hundred [catties of] gold to Tzu-ch'u for his expenses and [for the cost of] associating with guests. And with another five hundred [catties of] gold he bought rare commodities and curios, which he took with him when he went westward to Ch'in. He asked to visit the elder sister of Wife Hua yang and [through her] he presented all these things to Wife Hua-yang. Then he spoke about the virtue and wisdom of Tzu-ch'u, his association with the feudal lords and guests from all over the world, and said that [Tzu-ch'u] was always saying, "I, Ch'u, consider the Wife as my heaven."[11] [He said that Tzu-ch'u] wept day and night thinking of the heir apparent and the Wife. The Wife was very pleased. Pu-wei then asked the elder sister to urge her, saying,". . . Now you, Madam, serve the heir apparent. You are very much loved by him but have no son. Why not associate yourself now, in good time, with one of the sons who is virtuous and filial adopting him as your heir and trusting him as your own son?[12] While your husband is alive you will be honored; when your husband [dies after his] hundredth year, your son will be king and you will never lose your power. . . . Now Tzu-ch'u is virtuous, and he himself knows that he is a middle son and that as a secondary son he does not qualify as heir. Again, his mother is not favored [by An-kuo Chün]; she attaches herself to you, Madam. If you, Madam, really choose him now as heir, then you, Madam, will be favored in Ch'in throughout your life." Wife Hua-yang considered this right. . . . [She said to An-kuo Chün], "I should like to adopt Tzu-ch'u as heir in order to depend upon him [in my later life]." An-kuo Chün consented to it. . . . An-kuo Chün and the Wife then sent a generous gift to Tzu-ch'u and asked Lü Pu-wei to be his tutor.[13] Because of this, Tzu-ch'u had more repute among the feudal lords.

Lü Pu-wei took a girl of Han-tan, who was extremely beautiful and skilled in dancing, and lived with her. [Later] he knew that she was

[11] That is, as his mother. Parents were usually considered as heaven.

[12] This sentence seems to be incomplete.

[13] It should be noted that the tutor was a merchant. This suggests that the status of merchants at this time was not so inferior as it was during the Han dynasty. We do not know how much education Lü Pu-wei had. It is likely that the term tutor was used in its broadest sense. Later a scholarly work, *Lü-shih ch'un-ch'iu*, was compiled by Lü's guests under his plan. This indicates that Lü was a man of considerable knowledge in classics and literature, if not highly educated.

pregnant. While Tzu-ch'u was drinking with Pu-wei, he saw her and was pleased by her. Then he stood up, made a toast, and asked to have her. Lü Pu-wei was angry, but considering that he had already ruined his family for Tzu-ch'u in the hope of hooking a rare fish, he then offered the girl. The girl concealed her pregnancy. When her time arrived, she gave birth to a son, Cheng.[14] Tzu-ch'u then made the girl his wife.

In the fiftieth year of King Chao of Ch'in, Wang Ch'i was sent to surround Han-tan with a great force. [Officials of the state of] Chao wanted to kill Tzu-ch'u. Tzu-ch'u plotted with Pu-wei and bribed the guard with six hundred catties of gold and was thus able to escape. He fled to the Ch'in army and consequently was able to get back to Ch'in. [Officials of the state of] Chao wanted to kill Tzu-ch'u's wife and son. Tzu-ch'u's wife was the daughter of a powerful family of Chao. She was able to hide herself. For this reason, the mother and son succeeded in remaining alive till the end. 257 B.C.

In the fifty-sixth year of King Chao of Ch'in, [the king] died, and the heir apparent, An-kuo Chün, became king. Wife Hua-yang became queen and Tzu-ch'u the heir apparent. [The state of] Chao then sent back Tzu-ch'u's wife and son, Cheng, to Ch'in. 251 B.C.

The king of Ch'in was on the throne for one year and then died. His posthumous title was King Hsiao-wen. The heir apparent, Tzu-ch'u, succeeding him, ascended the throne; he was King Chuang-hsiang. . . .

In the first year of Chuang-hsiang, Lü Pu-wei was made chancellor, ennobled as marquis of Wen-hsin, and enfeoffed with a hundred thousand households in Lo-yang in Honan. King Chuang-hsiang was on the throne for three years and died. The heir apparent, Cheng, became king. [*SC* 85:1a–4b] 249 B.C.   246 B.C.

4. Ten Thousand Slaves Owned by a Chancellor

When the Heir Apparent Cheng became king, he honored Lü Pu-wei [with the position of] chancellor and addressed him as "Uncle." The king of Ch'in was young.[15] The empress dowager secretly had private relations with Lü Pu-wei from time to time.[16] Pu-wei had ten thousand household slaves. . . . 246 B.C.

---

[14] Cheng 政 became the First Emperor of Ch'in.

[15] Cheng, who later became the First Emperor of Ch'in, was thirteen years old when he ascended the throne.

[16] For earlier aspects of their relationship, see II, 3.

As the First Emperor grew older, the empress dowager [still] did not cease her lewdness. Lü Pu-wei, fearing that misfortune would strike him, . . . then presented Lao Ai to her. . . . The empress dowager had illicit intercourse with him and loved him very much.[17] . . . Lao Ai frequently attended her. The gifts bestowed [upon him] were tremendous. All matters were decided by Lao Ai. Lao Ai's household slaves numbered several thousand. [*SC* 85:4b–6a]

5. NUMBER OF SLAVES OWNED BY A BUSINESSMAN

After
228 B.C.   The [Cho family] grew so rich that it possessed a thousand[18] slaves. Their delight in parks and hunting was equal to that of a ruler of the people. [*SC* 129:17b; similar *HS* 91:8a]

6. GREAT STOCKBREEDER

221–
210 B.C.   Wu-chih Lo raised livestock. . . . The First Emperor of Ch'in ordered that Lo be considered equal to an enfeoffed lord with permission to visit the court with the ministers at appointed times. [*SC* 129:6b; *HS* 91:5b]

7. MERCHANTS SENT TO GUARD THE FRONTIERS

215/214
B.C.   In the thirty-third year [of the First Emperor], those who had been fugitives, adopted sons-in-law,[19] and merchants[20] were sent to conquer Lu-liang territory, which was made into the commanderies of Kuei-lin, Hsiang, and Nan-hai. The convicted ones[21] were sent to guard [them]. [*SC* 6:21b]

---

[17] Lü Pu-wei and the empress dowager generously bribed the official in charge of castration to report falsely that Lao Ai 嫪毐 was a eunuch so that he could stay in the palace and attend the empress dowager. In 238 B.C. the emperor discovered that Lao Ai was not a eunuch and that he was planning a rebellion. Lao Ai and his clan were executed, but Lü Pu-wei, because of the services he had previously rendered the emperor's father, was only dismissed from office. He committed suicide in 235 B.C.

[18] The *Han-shu* gives the number as eight hundred.

[19] For the *chui hsü*, see I, 3, n. 8.

[20] It is interesting to note that the social status of merchants was so inferior that they were sent with convicts to the frontiers. Even the children of merchants were classed as an inferior group.

[21] In Ch'in times the "convicted ones" (*che* 謫 or 適 or 讁) were persons who were guilty of crimes against the government or society, or who were for some reason or another considered undesirable. Classification as "convicted ones" did not, to judge from the data on hand, necessarily entail prosecution in a court of law.

The passage above mentions the fugitives, the adopted sons-in-law, the merchants, and the "convicted ones." Were the "convicted ones" a fourth group or a general

8. Convicts

[Chou Wen][22] claimed himself to be an expert in military affairs. King Ch'en[23] gave him the seal of a general to attack in the west.[24] On his way he gathered his troops and arrived at the pass[25] with one thousand chariots and several hundred thousand soldiers. He reached Hsi[26]

209 B.C.

---

category under which the other three were subsumed? *SC* 6:22a states that in the following year (213 B.C.), "the officials who had been unfair in deciding law cases were condemned to build the Great Wall and to undertake construction in the territory of the southern Yüeh" (the Momiziyama and Sanjo editions have "city" instead of "territory"). Whether these officials were considered "convicted ones" is not made clear in the *Shih-chi* texts.

A memorial presented by Ch'ao Ts'o criticizing the garrison service of Ch'in throws some light on the problem. Ch'ao Ts'o noted that the following groups were sent as garrison soldiers to the territory of Yang-yüeh: (1) officials guilty of crimes, (2) adopted sons-in-law, (3) merchants, (4) those who had once been entered on the market register, (5) those whose parents or grandparents had once been entered on the market register, and (6) those who live on the left side of a village. Ch'ao Ts'o's list covers all the categories mentioned in our passage except the fugitives. In addition it includes the children and grandchildren of merchants and those who lived on the left side of a village. Ch'ao Ts'o's memorial was presented in 169 B.C., that is, about seventy years before the *Shih-chi* was composed, but Ssu-ma Ch'ien's record is based on actual historical documents. Whatever their differences, both should be considered. Read together, they illuminate each other and the complex issue involved.

HS 6:28a speaks of the "seven classes of convicted ones" (七科讁) who in 97 B.C. were sent as soldiers to attack the Hsiung-nu; see II, 32, and cf. Dubs, *HFHD*, II, 108, n. 35. 2. According to Chang Yen, quoted by Yen, these were: (1) officials guilty of crimes, (2) fugitives, (3) adopted sons-in-law, (4) merchants, (5) those who had formerly been entered on the market register, (6) those whose parents had been entered on the market register, and (7) those whose grandparents had been entered on the market register.

We do not know whether the Ch'in had an identical arrangement. But we are safe in holding with Ssu-ma Ch'ien that the law regulating the seven classes of convicted ones of Han was rooted in Ch'in practice (*SC* 6:22a). Ch'ao Ts'o and Chang Yen agree in all but one category, the former having omitted the fugitives and added "those who lived on the left side of a village." Thus we may assume with considerable certainty that the "convicted ones" included all the undesirables mentioned above: fugitives, merchants, and adopted sons-in-law (all these were sent as soldiers to conquer the south) as well as those officials found guilty of misdoings in 213 B.C.

[22] Wen was the style of Chou Chang 周章 who had served in Hsiang Yen's 項燕 army as a military diviner; his main function was to divine the lucky days for military action.

[23] That is, Ch'en Sheng, king of Ch'u.

[24] The *Han-shu* reads "to attack Ch'in in the west."

[25] The Han-ku Pass.

[26] The Hsi River, which is located east of Lin-tung.

and camped there. Ch'in ordered the Privy Treasurer Chang Han[27] to free the convict-laborers[28] of Li Mountain and those born as male

[27] Chang Han later defeated Ch'en Sheng, Hsiang Liang, and Wei Chiu 魏咎, but submitted finally to Hsiang Yü. It was Chang Han who suggested that the Li Mountain convicts be freed and sent to fight the troops of Chou Chang, who was approaching the capital; it was too late to mobilize the troops of the neighboring prefectures (*SC* 6:35a).

[28] These convicts, *t'u*, have frequently been identified as government-owned slaves. Based upon the statement in the *Chou-li* that reads, "Among the [government] slaves, the men were sent [to work as] convicted laborers and the women were sent to pound [rice] and dry [straw]" (*CLCS* 36:5b), Cheng Hsüan and Hsü Shen both make the point that slaves, male as well as female, were criminals in ancient times (*CLCS* 36:5b; *SWCTC* 13:20). Ying Shao also says, "Originally in ancient times there were no male and female [private] slaves. All male and female slaves were law-violators" (*FSTI* [A], 37:4a). The *Li-chi* comments, "The male and female convicts 徒 are generally called slaves 奴" (*HS* 23:9b).

It is difficult to decide whether the convicts in Ch'in and Han were still government slaves. A positive assertion was made by Liang Ch'i-ch'ao and many others who claimed that convicts who were subjected to the following servitudes were considered government slaves until released (Liang Ch'i-ch'ao, "Chung-kuo nu-li chih-tu," *THHP*, II [1925], 532; Lao Kan, "Han-tai nu-li chih-tu chi-lüeh," *LSYY*, V [1935], 8; Wu Po-lun, "Hsi Han nu-li k'ao," *Shih-huo*, I, No. 1 [1935], 278; Ma Fei-pai, "Ch'in Han ching-chi shih liao," Part 6: "Nu-li chih-tu," *Shih-huo*, III, No. 8 [1936], 385, 389; Ma Ch'eng-feng, *Chung-kuo ching-chi shih* [2nd ed., 2 vols.; Ch'ang-sha: Commercial Press, 1939], II, 246).

One-year convicts:	Male—frontier guard and forced labor
	Female—forced labor 復作
Two-year convicts:	Male—*ssu-k'ou* 司寇, guard
	Female—labor as *ssu-k'ou* 作如司寇
Three-year convicts:	Male—to cut wood for sacrifices 鬼薪
	Female—to pound rice for sacrifices 白粲
Four-year convicts:	Male—unshaved and to build city walls at dawn 完城旦
	Female—unshaved and to pound rice 完舂
Five-year convicts:	Male—shaved, wearing the iron collar, and to build city walls at dawn 髡鉗城旦
	Female—shaved, wearing the iron collar, and to pound rice 舂

(See also *HCI* B:9a–b; cf. *HS* 2:2b, Ying and Meng's comments; Li and Meng's comments: *HS* 8:1b, 23:14a; *HHS* 45:21b, 56:2b; *HLCI* 9:1a–6b; *CCLK*, pp. 51–55; Hulsewé, *Remnants of Han Law*, I, 128–32).

Liang's view was rejected by Wu Ching-ch'ao, who based his argument on the fact that *t'u*, "convicts," in Han were but petty offenders and as such were forced into servitude for a few years only. They were prisoners, not slaves (Wu Ching-ch'ao, "Hsi-Han she-hui chieh-chi chih-tu," *THHP*, X, No. 3 [1935], 18). Both he and Wang Shih-chieh pointed out that it was the family members of the criminals who were converted into government slaves (Wang Shih-chieh, "Chung-kuo nu-pei chih-tu," *She-hui k'e-hsüeh chi-k'an*, III, No. 3 [1925], 306–7).

Wilbur also argues that *t'u* were not slaves. After a careful examination of a number of passages in which the terms *t'u* and *nu*, "slaves," are associated, he discovered that two of the passages indicate a clear distinction between the two terms, that one is indecisive, and that two others can be taken to mean "convict slaves" (Wilbur,

Slavery in China, pp. 81–82). We agree with him that *t'u-nu* cannot reasonably be considered a compound term. An exhaustive study of the passages in the *Han-shu* that contain the term *t'u* gives clear evidence that this term is always used alone when it means "convict"; in not a single case was the compound term used (*HS* 2:3b, 7:5b and 9a, 8:12a and 16a, 9:5b and 7a, 10:3b, 6a–b, 7b, and 12b–13a, 11:5a, 12:4a). Moreover, a five-year convict who wore an iron collar was called "iron-collared convict" (*HS* 55:1b). If the convict subject to the longest term of servitude was called a convict, it is certain that those who were serving shorter sentences would not be called "slaves." These observations are in harmony with those passages that clearly distinguish between convict and slave. Though few in number, they support our assumption that whenever *t'u* and *nu* are mentioned together they refer to separate categories of persons. We should hesitate, therefore, to be diverted from this conclusion by two or three ambiguous cases in which these two characters can be taken to mean "convict slaves."

It should be pointed out that only the family members of criminals were appropriated by the government and made government slaves, as suggested by Wang Shih-chieh and Wu Ching-ch'ao. About the second decade of the first century numerous families who had been guilty of casting coins, as well as those who were held responsible collectively, were made government male and female slaves (see II, 47, 49; *HS* 99C:12a). It is, however, important to distinguish between those criminals who were appropriated by the government as government slaves and those who served out their prison sentences as convict-laborers. One of the passages in the *Han-shu* reads: "[Wang Mang] then made the law less severe. Those who secretly cast [*huo-*] *ch'üan* 貨泉 and [*huo-*] *pu* 貨布 coins were to be seized with their wives and children and made government male and female slaves. The officials and [the people] from the related five [families held collectively responsible] who knew but did not expose them were subject to the same punishment. Those who criticized and sabotaged the *pao-huo* were to be sentenced to one year of hard labor if they were common people . . ." (see *HS* 24B:24b). This passage clearly shows a distinction between the two and supports our argument that these convict-laborers who were sentenced to one to five years were not included in the category of government slaves.

In addition, this passage suggests that convicts were sentenced to a definite period, whereas the servitude of government slaves had no set limits. There are many instances in which *t'u* were pardoned by the emperor, either on a national or local basis (*HS* 8:12a, 9:5b and 7a, 10:3b, 6a, and 6b, 11:5a, 12:4a). On the other hand, government slaves were rarely manumitted. However, in 160 B.C. an edict was issued by Emperor Wen freeing all slaves (*HS* 4:16a–b), and in 7 B.C. another edict, issued by Emperor Ai, stated that "government male and female slaves who were fifty years of age or older were to be dismissed and made commoners" (*HS* 11:3b). These decrees indicate that the manumission of *t'u* and government slaves received separate consideration. Moreover, the second underlines the age limitations imposed even when government slaves were manumitted.

But despite the real differences between convicts and government slaves, certain similarities should not be overlooked. Both the five-year convicts and slaves had their heads shaved, and both wore the iron collar (see above, and cf. *SC* 100: 1a–b, 104:1b; *HS* 37:1a–b, 5b), and it would seem that the treatment accorded each group was more or less the same. Both slaves and convicts were, as a rule, assigned to similar services. Both could be sent to war to fight side by side and under the same officer (see *SC* 6:14a, 92:18b; *HS* 31:4a, 34:13a, 24B:25a, 99C:5a; *HCIPI* A:4a). All of these facts lead us to conclude that during his term of punishment a convict's status was not unlike that of a slave.

slaves[29] and send them all to attack the army of Ch'u, which was completely defeated. [*SC* 48:4b–5a; *HS* 31:4a]

9. Process for Killing a Slave

209 B.C.   T'ien Tan,[30] in order to deceive [the prefect],[31] bound up his male slave and, followed by young men, went to the court; he [pretended that he] wished to petition [for permission] to kill his slave.[32] When he saw the prefect of Ti, he then attacked and killed the prefect. [*SC* 94:1a; *HS* 33:2a–b]

10. Butcher's Son a General

207 B.C.   The Lord of P'ei[33] wanted to attack Ch'in's army below the Yao

[29] *Nu ch'an tzu* 奴產子 is explained by Fu Ch'ien (P'ei) as children of household slaves. Yen says "*nu ch'an tzu* are like those whom people now call house-born slaves" 家生奴 (*HS* 31:4a). Obviously, children of slaves were slaves until freed.

In the "Imperial Annals" of Ch'in the same story is recorded, but the house-born slaves are not mentioned (*SC* 6:35a).

[30] For T'ien Tan, see III, 5.

[31] He was planning to kill the prefect in order to be able to start a rebellion.

[32] To judge from this passage, at this time a slave could be killed only with the approval of the government. Fu Ch'ien comments: "Formerly to kill a male or female slave one had [first] to report the case to the government. Tan intended to kill the prefect; therefore, in order to deceive him, he bound up his male slave so that he could petition [the prefect]" (P'ei).

The term *yeh-sha* 謁殺, which means "to petition to kill," might have two meanings: either to petition the authorities for permission for the master himself to kill his slave, or to petition the authorities and ask them to kill his slave. The same term appears in a Chin (A.D. 265–419) law: "If a male or female slave strikes his master, the latter is allowed to petition to kill him or her" (*CS* 30:10a). Since Ch'in law was mainly followed in Han law (see *CS* 30:5a–b), and since the law of Wei and Chin was codified according to the model of Han (*CS* 30:5a, 6a–8b), we believe that this practice of Ch'in, as described in our passage, was still in practice in the Chin dynasty. Unfortunately, the actual meaning of *yeh-sha* in the *Chin-shu* is as ambiguous as in the *Shih-chi* and *Han-shu*. The problem therefore remains unsolved.

The term *yeh-sha* is not found in the law of later dynasties, but there are similar regulations concerning the killing of a slave. In T'ang and Sung there was a law that reads: "If a male or female slave is guilty and if the master kills him or her without asking the government, the master is to be given one hundred strokes" (*TLSI* 22:3b; *SHT* 22:3b). The same provision also appeared in the Ming and Ch'ing codes, but with one minor revision: instead of "asking" 請, the character 告, "report" or "petition," is used (*MLL* 20:25b; *CLL* 28:3b). The Liao law is clearly different in this aspect. An edict reads: "If a male or female slave is guilty [of a crime calling for] the punishment of death, he or she is to be sent to the authorities; the master is not allowed to kill him or her at his own will" (*Liao-shih*, 61:5a–b).

[33] Liu Pang, the later Emperor Kao.

Pass with twenty thousand soldiers. [Chang] Liang[34] said, "Ch'in's forces are still strong and must not be underestimated. I have heard that their general is the son of a butcher. Merchants are easily moved by profit. I hope you will remain in camp. Let Li I-chi[35] take the great treasure to induce the Ch'in general [to make peace]." In fact, the Ch'in general was willing to make peace [with Han] and to cooperate with them in attacking Hsien-yang to the west.[36] [*HS* 40:2b–3a]

11. A SLAVE BECOMES AN OFFICIAL

Luan Pu[37] was a native of Liang. Formerly when the king of Liang, P'eng Yüeh, was a commoner,[38] he was frequently in the company of Pu. Being poor and distressed, [Pu] hired himself out in Ch'i as a waiter in a wineshop.[39] Several years later P'eng Yüeh left; he went to Chü-yeh where he became a bandit. Pu was kidnapped and sold by someone as a slave in Yen; he avenged the grievances of his master. The Yen general, Tsang T'u,[40] elevated him to the post of chief commandant.

Before 206 B.C.

[34] Chang Liang was a native of the old state of Han where his forebears had served as ministers. In 207 B.C., with the support of Hsiang Liang, uncle of Hsiang Yü, Chang Liang set up Han Ch'eng 韓成 as king of Han, he himself holding the position of minister of the masses. In the struggle against Ch'in, Chang Liang commanded the troops of Han and followed Liu Pang into Hsien-yang. In 206 B.C. Liu Pang was made the king of Han. Later that year Hsiang Yü put Han Ch'eng to death, whereupon Chang Liang rejoined Liu Pang, becoming one of his chief assistants. After Emperor Kao's accession to the throne, Chang was enfeoffed as the marquis of Liu (*HS* 40:1a–7b).

[35] Li I-chi was one of Emperor Kao's military and political advisers in the early days of his campaign. In 204 B.C., through diplomatic maneuver, he brought the king of Ch'i, T'ien Kuang, to submission (*HS* 43:1a–5a).

[36] According to *HS* 1A:13b, this event took place in 207 B.C.

[37] Luan Pu was appointed chief commandant by Emperor Kao after the king of Liang, P'eng Yüeh, was accused of rebellion and executed. He became the chancellor of Yen during the time of Emperor Wen and was later given the post of general. In 154 B.C. he was ennobled as marquis of Yü because of his military merit in the campaign against the Wu, who had rebelled (*SC* 100:5b; *HS* 37:5a).

[38] According to Ssu-ma, *chia-jen* 家人 was a man staying at home without an official post, that is, a commoner (cf. also Yen: *HS* 37:4a; Wang: *HSPC* 37:3b). The term is synonymous with *shu-jen* 庶人, "common people." Thus in the biography of Wei Pao 魏豹, the *Shih-chi* reads "*chia-jen*" while the *Han-shu* has "*shu-jen*" (*SC* 90:1a; *HS* 33:1a). Wang Hsien-ch'ien comments that the two terms had the same meaning (*HSPC* 33:1a).

[39] According to P'ei, *chiu jen pao* 酒人保 is a guaranteed laborer in a wineshop. A waiter in a wineshop is still called *chiu-pao* 酒保. The *Han-shu* has 酒家保, the meaning of which is the same.

[40] Tsang T'u, a general of the state of Yen, joined Hsiang Yü in the revolt against Ch'in. In 206 B.C. he was made king of Yen and retained this rank even after the

206 B.C.   Later Tsang T'u was made the king of Yen and he appointed Pu a
202 B.C. general. When Tsang T'u rebelled, Han attacked Yen and captured
Pu. Hearing of this, the king of Liang, P'eng Yüeh, then asked the
emperor [to be allowed] to redeem Pu and make him the grandee of
Liang. [*SC* 100:4a–b; *HS* 37:4a]

12. CHILDREN SOLD BY PARENTS

205 B.C.   When Han arose, it inherited the misery of the Ch'in. The various
feudal lords[41] rose up simultaneously, the people lost their occupations,
and there was a great famine. The grain [cost] five thousand [cash] a
picul; the people ate human flesh, and more than one-half of the
population died. Kao-tsu then ordered that people might sell their
children and go to Shu and Han[42] for food.[43] (*HS* 24A:7b]

13. MARKS OF SLAVERY

Chi Pu,[44] was a native of Ch'u. He was famous in Ch'u for his
courage[45] and activities in redressing wrongs.[46] Hsiang Chi[47] had him

death of Hsiang Yü. He later rebelled against Emperor Kao and was captured and
killed in 202 B.C. (*SC* 7:20a and 21b, 8:30a; *HS* 1A:18b, 1B:6b).

[41] In 207 B.C. the feudal lords (*chu hou* 諸侯) set themselves up as kings and rebelled
against Ch'in. Thus *SC* 6:37b reads, "Yen, Chao, Ch'i, Ch'u, Han, and Wei all were
[re-] established as kingdoms. From the east of the [Han-ku] Pass almost [every
place] rebelled against the Ch'in officials and took part with the feudal lords. All the
feudal lords led their troops westward."

[42] In 205 B.C. war and famine occurred in the area of Kuan-chung. *HS* 1A:24b
reads: "There was a great famine in Kuan-chung. A picul of rice [cost] ten thousand
cash and people ate human flesh. People were ordered to go to Shu and Han for food."
Shu and Han had been given to the king of Han by Hsiang Yü in 206 B.C. (*HS*
1A:18a).

[43] In 202 B.C. an edict to free those who had sold themselves into slavery because of
famine and hunger was issued; see II, 14.

[44] Chi Pu was pardoned and appointed by Emperor Kao through the efforts of Chu
Chia, who procured a recommendation from the lord of T'eng, Hsia-hou Ying
夏侯嬰. Chi became grand administrator of the Ho-tung commandery during the
time of Emperor Wen (*SC* 100:1b–3a; *HS* 37:1b–2b).

[45] *Ch'i* 氣 may be generally defined as "spirit." In exploring the relation between
chih 志, "will," and *ch'i*, Mencius mentions that will is the leader of the spirit and that
the latter pervades and animates the body. He also talked about the vast spirit he was
nourishing (*MTCS* 3A:5a). However, *ch'i* may refer to a specific spirit, namely,
courage or bravery. In discussing and comparing the different ways of nourishing
their courage in the cases of Pei-kung Yu 北宮黝, Meng Shih-she 孟施舍, and Tseng
Ts'an 曾參, Mencius remarks that what was maintained by Meng, which was his
ch'i, was inferior to what Tseng maintained, which was the principle and of greater
importance (*MTCS* 3A:4a–5a). Hsiang Yü, who was so proud of his bravery and

lead his troops, and [Chi Pu] frequently harassed the king of Han. After Hsiang Yü was killed, Kao-tsu offered a thousand [catties] of gold for the arrest of Chi Pu; anyone who dared to harbor and hide him would be punished [by the extermination of his] three *tsu*.[48] Pu hid in [the family of] Chou at Pu-yang. Chou said, "Han searches for you, General, and their anxious pursuit will soon come to your servant's family. If you, General, will listen to your servant, your servant will venture to present a plan; if not, he would like to cut his throat beforehand." Pu consented to it. Thereupon [Chou] shaved Chi Pu's head, put an iron collar on him,[49] dressed him in coarse clothes, put him in a funeral

203–
202 B.C.

---

military art, sang on the eve of the day he was surrounded by the Han troops, "My strength is able to uproot a mountain and my *ch'i* is capping the world" (*SC* 7:32a; *HS* 31:24a).

The use of the term *ch'i* in the sense of bravery or courage seems to have been common in Han times. As illustrated in the present passage, as well as in some others, *ch'i* is as a rule ascribed to redressers-of-wrongs (*SC* 100:1a and 3b, 120:2a, 129:8b and 9b; *HS* 28B:27b and 33b, 37:3b, 50:7b; *HHS* 69:12a). This interesting combination suggests that *ch'i* must be a kind of spirit that constitutes the basic qualification for being a redresser-of-wrongs. Apparently *ch'i* here refers to bravery and courage, which are virtues of a man whose task it is to rescue others or to redress a wrong and who never breaks his word even at the expense of his life. In the biography of Chi Pu (in the second sentence of this translation) the phrase 為氣任俠 occurs (the parallel passage in the *Han-shu* omits the character *ch'i*, which may be a clerical error); it also states that his younger brother, Chi Hsin, was known for his *ch'i* in the area within the passes and was a redresser-of-wrongs. Then it is stated both in the *Shih-chi* and the *Han-shu* that Chi Hsin was famous for his bravery and Chi Pu for keeping his promises. Ssu-ma Ch'ien also makes the remark that even with the existence of Hsiang Yü's *ch'i*, Chi Pu was still able to be renowned in Ch'u for his bravery 勇 (*SC* 100:1a, 3b, 4a, 5b; *HS* 37:1a, 3b, 7a). This indicates clearly that what was meant by *ch'i* was the spirit of bravery or courage. The two characters *yung* 勇 (bravery) and *ch'i* are used interchangeably in the texts mentioned above.

[46] For the meaning of *hsieh*, see III, 1, n. 2.

[47] That is, Hsiang Yü.

[48] See I, 1, n. 1.

[49] *K'un ch'ien*, to shave off the hair and put an iron collar around the neck, was a kind of punishment from the time of Ch'in on (*HC* 1B:9b; *HLCI* 9:6b; *CCLK*, p. 51; cf. B. Schindler, "Preliminary Account of the Work of Henri Maspero Concerning the Chinese Documents on Wood and on Paper Discovered by Sir Aurel Stein on His Third Expedition to Central Asia," *Asia Major*, N.S., I, No. 1 (1949), 224; Hulsewé, *Remnants of Han Law*, I, 129). According to the Ch'in and Han law, shaving the head and wearing an iron collar was a regular punishment for male and female criminals who were serving five-year sentences (see II, 8, n. 28). Since Emperor Wen abolished the three kinds of mutilations (tattooing, cutting off the nose, cutting off the feet) in 167 B.C., *k'un ch'ien* had been used as a substitute for tattooing (*HS* 23:13b). Thus *k'un ch'ien* was a severe punishment, next in degree to the death sentence. Chung-ch'ang T'ung once wrote in an essay: "Since the abolition of mutilating punishments, there have been no grades for light and severe [punishments]. Next to death we have *k'un ch'ien* and next to *k'un ch'ien* we have whipping and beating" (*HHS* 49:26a–b).

cart,⁵⁰ and sent him, together with several tens of his household slaves,⁵¹

As shown here and in other cases, *k'un ch'ien* was also applied to slaves. When the king of Chao, Chang Ao, was arrested in 198 B.C., the central government warned his officials not to follow their king to the capital. However, Meng Shu 孟舒, T'ien Shu 田舒, and some ten other Chao officials, dressed in red, with shaved heads and iron collars around their necks, and disguised as the king's household slaves, followed him to Ch'ang-an (*SC* 104:1b; *HS* 1B:12a–b). Chi Pu's case seems to indicate that shaving the head and wearing an iron collar were regular marks for a slave.

It is interesting to note that certain classes of convicts were similarly accoutered. According to the *Feng-su t'ung-i,* those guilty of crimes who were sent to build the Great Wall by the First Emperor of Ch'in were ordered to have their heads shaved and to wear red clothing (Yü Shih-nan, *Pei-t'ang shu-ch'ao* [Nan-hai: K'ung-shih san-shih-san wan chüan t'ang chiao-chu ch'ung-k'an, 1888], 45:3a, hereafter cited as *PTSC*). According to the Han law, shaving the head and wearing an iron collar was a regular punishment for male and female criminals who were serving a five-year sentence (see II, 8, n. 28).

⁵⁰ Fu Ch'ien says that this cart had a broad track. Li Chi thinks it was an ox-cart covered with willows (P'ei). Both Cheng and Chin Cho, quoted by Yen, consider it a funeral cart (*HS* 37:1a; *HSPC* 37:1a).

⁵¹ *T'ung* 童 (or 僮) was a synonym for slave. The *Shuo-wen* in defining the term notes that "males who are criminals are called *nu* [slaves]; *nu* are called *t'ung;* females are called *ch'ieh*" (*SWCTC* 3A:66). This fits the various statements that criminals were the earliest slaves. Ying Shao says: "In the ancient system there did not exist male and female slaves. The male and female slaves were all violators of the law" (*FSTI* [A], 37:4a). Cheng Hsüan comments, "The male and female slaves of the present day were the criminals of ancient days" (*CLCS* 36:5b). The *Shuo-wen's* explanation is based on the original meaning of the word, which was "crime," and this is part of the character *t'ung.* Although we cannot assume that *t'ung* and *nu* were necessarily criminals in the Han period (cf. II, 8, n. 28; Wilbur, *Slavery in China,* p. 67, n. 2), the definition that *t'ung* are *nu* remains authoritative.

Specific examples show clearly that private slaves were also called *t'ung.* And it is also clear that *t'ung* and *nu* were used interchangeably. When Chia I discussed the selling of slaves, he used the term *t'ung* instead of *nu* (II, 19; *HS* 48:14a). Wang Pao's essay *Contract for a T'ung* was about a slave. Sometimes both terms appear together (*HS* 82:8b, 98:9b).

However, the term *t'ung* does not always refer to male slaves. Chia I said, "Nowadays when people sell their *t'ung,* they dress them up in embroidered clothes and silk shoes with braided trimmings on the edges. . . . These were in ancient times the garments of the empress. . . . And yet the common people are allowed to use them to clothe their female slaves" (see II, 19). It is clear that the *t'ung* described here were female slaves. Wei Ch'ing's father had illicit intercourse with a female attendant of his master's family, who gave birth to Ch'ing. In the *Shih-chi* she is called *ch'ieh,* "female attendant or slave," whereas in the *Han-shu* the term *t'ung* is used (*SC* 111:1a; *HS* 55:1a). When Wang Mang's wife was wearing a short garment and a cloth apron, she was mistaken by various ladies for a *t'ung* (*HS* 99A:2b). Yen comments that "*t'ung* is a general term for *pei-ch'ieh* 婢妾, female slave" (*HS* 55:1a).

Since the term *t'ung* may refer to both male and female slaves, a more comprehensive definition was given by Meng K'ang: "*T'ung* are *nu pei* [male and female slaves]" (*HS* 91:7a). Ju Shun also remarked, "*T'ung* means *li* 隸, male attendants and *ch'ieh*" (*HS* 48:14a).

Although *t'ung* may mean "youth," it is important to note that when it is used to

to Chu Chia[52] of Lu to be sold. Chu Chia knew in his heart that [the slave] was Chi Pu; then he bought him and put him on his land.[53] He instructed his son, saying, "In matters pertaining to the fields listen to this slave and you must eat together with him." [*SC* 100:1a–b; *HS* 37:1a–b]

14. SLAVES FREED BY EDICT

In the fifth month of the summer [of the fifth year of Emperor Kao] 202 B.C.
the soldiers were all demobilized and returned to their homes. An edict was issued, saying, ". . . People who because of hunger sold themselves to others as male and female slaves shall all be freed and become commoners." [*HS* 1B:4a–b]

15. DECREES DISCRIMINATING AGAINST MERCHANTS

After the empire had been pacified, then Kao-tsu, in order to humil- 199 B.C.
iate the merchants, decreed that they were not to wear silk or to ride in carriages. He increased their taxes.

mean "slave" the age connotation is absent (cf. Wilbur, *Slavery in China*, p. 67). The two characters 僮 and 童 are used interchangeably in the *Shih-chi* and *Han-shu* (see Wilbur, p. 67, n. 1). However, originally there was a strict distinction in usage in Han times; the interchangeability of the two characters in the *Shih-chi* and the *Han-shu* may be the result of revision because of a change in later usage (*SWCTC* 3A:66). According to the *Shuo-wen*, 僮 meant a youth not yet capped (*SWCTC* 8A:2), whereas 童 belonged to a different radical and referred specifically to slaves (*SWCTC* 3A:66). An examination of the various cases in our texts reveals that none of them has the meaning of youth. The ten thousand *t'ung* owned by Lü Pu-wei (see II, 4), the thousand owned by Cho (see II, 5), and the seven hundred owned by Chang An-shih (see II, 36) could not all have been young slaves. In Wang Pao's *Contract for a T'ung* the *t'ung* was a bearded male slave (*Ch'üan Han wen*, in *Ch'üan shang-ku san-tai Ch'in Han san-kuo liu-ch'ao wen* [Huang-kang Wang-shih ed., 1894], 42:11b, hereafter cited as *CHW*).

Tuan Yü-ts'ai points out that in modern usage 僮 is reserved for slaves, whereas 童 refers to youth; in the earlier usage it was just the opposite (*SWCTC* 3A:66, 8A:2). The mixing up of youth and slave seems merely to be the result of the confusion of changing usage. Thus Yen Shih-ku's commentary that "*t'ung* are servants who had not been capped," that is, who had not yet been initiated (Shih Yu, *Chi chiu p'ien*, *TSCC* ed., 3:183, hereafter cited as *CCP*), reflects a notion based on later usage and should not be accepted as a definition applicable to Han times.

[52] Chu Chia was a famous redresser-of-wrongs, *yu-hsia*, of modern Shantung. He spent most of his money to bring relief to others, while he himself had few material demands. At great personal risk he hid and saved more than a hundred people. See III, 1.

[53] *HS* 37:1b reads "*t'ien-she*" 田舍, "farm hut," instead of *t'ien*.

195–
180 B C

During the time of Emperor Hsiao-hui and Empress Kao, because the empire had just been pacified, the regulations for merchants were again relaxed, but the descendants of the people of the market were still not allowed to become officials. [*SC* 30:1b, *HS* 24B:3a–b]

16. Merchants—Generals

197 B.C.

Thereupon the emperor asked who were the generals of Ch'en Hsi.[54] He received the reply: "They are Wang Huang and Wan-ch'iu Ch'en, both of them formerly merchants." The emperor said, "I know how [to deal with them]." Thereupon he offered rewards of one thousand [catties of] gold each for [Wang] Huang, [Wan-ch'iu] Ch'en, and others.[55]

197/
196 B.C.

In the winter of the eleventh year the Han army attacked and beheaded Ch'en Hsi's general, Hou Ch'ang . . . below Ch'ü-mi.[56] Those under the command of Wang Huang and Wan-ch'iu Ch'en received the reward, delivering them both alive. Therefore the army of Ch'en Hsi was defeated. [*SC* 93:8b–9a]

17. Slaves Presented as a Gift

187–
180 B.C.

Ch'en P'ing[57] thereupon presented Mr. Lu[58] with one hundred male

---

[54] Ch'en Hsi was the chancellor of Chao. In 197 B.C. (we follow *SC* 8:34b and *HS* 1B:13a in reading "the tenth year" instead of "the seventh year" of our text), together with Wang Huang 王黃 and others, he rebelled and made himself the Great King. One year later his army was defeated and he himself was captured and beheaded (*SC* 93:7b–9b; cf. *SC* 8:34b–35a, 36b–37a; *HS* 1B:13a–14a, 18a).

[55] *SC* 8:35a states: "Thereupon he used a great amount of gold to entice Hsi's generals. Many of the generals of Hsi submitted." The parallel version of *HS* 1B:14a reads *kou* 購, "to offer a reward" instead of *tan* 啗, "to entice."

[56] The text actually says "Hou Ch'ang 侯敞 and Wang Huang," but in view of what follows, Wang's name does not belong here.

[57] Ch'en P'ing was imperial chancellor of the right at this time. He died in 179 B.C. (*HS* 4:7a; see I, 7 and 8).

[58] Lu Chia was one of the early followers of Emperor Kao. He persuaded the king of Nan-yüeh to remain loyal to the Han government, and as a reward he was appointed grand palace grandee. He resigned from this post during the reign of Emperor Hui because he disapproved of Empress Dowager Lü's policy of placing increasing power in the hands of the Lü family. After the death of Emperor Hui a considerable number of Lü family members had been given kingdoms; Ch'en P'ing feared that they would undermine the security of the imperial family. Lu Chia advised Ch'en P'ing to be friendly and cooperate with Chou P'o, the grand commandant, in the hope that the influence of the Lü family could be weakened. Ch'en P'ing accepted this advice and in return gave him the gifts mentioned above. The joint efforts of Ch'en P'ing and Chou P'o succeeded in destroying the Lü family and in putting Emperor Wen on the throne. Lu Chia was again appointed grand palace grandee on Ch'en's recommendation (*SC* 97:6a–9b; *HS* 43:5a–8b).

and female salves, fifty carriages with horses, and five million cash for living expenses.[59] Having these, Mr. Lu associated with the dukes and ministers of the Han court, and his renown increased very much.[60] [*SC* 97:9b; *HS* 43:8b]

18. The Wealth and Power of Businessmen

[Ch'ao Ts'o also presented a memorial to the emperor, saying], "As to the traveling and resident merchants, the big ones hoard goods and get one hundred per cent profit, while the small ones sit in a row [at the market] and do retailing. [With their profits] they get hold of rare goods, and every day wander about in the markets of the big cities. Taking advantage of the emperor's urgent needs, they always sell their goods at double [their value]. Therefore, even though their men neither till nor weed, and their women neither rear silkworms nor weave, they wear only variegated silk and eat only good grain and meat. They do not suffer the hardships of the peasant, but they enjoy the products of the land. By means of their wealth they associate with kings and marquises. Their power surpasses that of the officials. They compete with each other in wealth. They travel around a thousand *li*, one following immediately after the other. They ride in well-built carriages and drive fat horses. They wear silk on their feet and trail the *kao* silk behind them. This is the reason why the merchants encroach upon and swallow the peasant, and why the peasants abandon their homes and become wanderers.

"Now the law despises merchants, but the merchants have become rich and noble; it honors farmers, but the farmers have become poor

178 B.C.

---

[59] *Yin shih fei* 飲食費 literally means "expenses for drinking and eating." Wilbur raises an important question: Did Ch'en P'ing draw upon his personal resources, or, as chancellor, upon the government treasury when he made these gifts (Wilbur, *Slavery in China*, p.278, n.4)? No final answer can be given on the basis of the text, but it should be noted that when *nu* or *pei* 婢 is used alone, it usually means "private slaves," whereas "government slaves" are usually called *kuan nu* 官奴, *kuan pei* 官婢, or *kuan nu-pei* 官奴婢 (*HS* 4:16a–b, 23:13a, 44:12a, 68:9a, 77:16b, 97B:5b, 94B:14b). Cho Wang-sun, a wealthy merchant, is known to have once given one hundred slaves to his son-in-law, Ssu-ma Hsiang-ju; see II, 24. It seems quite within the realm of possibility that Ch'en P'ing, who enjoyed the income of a fief of thirty thousand households (cf. *SC* 56:7b, 97:9a; *HS* 40:17a, 43:8a), was rich enough to make a similar gift.

[60] Meng K'ang interprets *chi* 籍 in the phrase *ming sheng chi shen* as *lang chi*, "having a bad reputation." Chou Shou-ch'ang suggests that *chi* 籍 should be *chieh* 藉, which means "to avail oneself, to rely on, by means of." The sentence would then read "because of this his renown increased very much" (*HSPC* 43:9a).

and mean. Thus what is valued by the people is despised by the ruler; and what is scorned by the officials is honored by the law. The ruler and the people oppose each other, and good and bad are reversed. To wish that the country be rich and that the law be upheld is impossible." [*HS* 24A:11b–12a]

19. SLAVE MARKET

174–
169 B.C.　　[Chia I presented a memorial, saying,] "Nowadays when people sell their slaves,[61] they dress them up in embroidered clothes and silk shoes with braided trimmings on the edges, and put them in pens.[62] These were in ancient times the garments of the empress of the Son of Heaven that were to be used in the ancestral temples, not for ordinary wear. And yet the common people are allowed to use them to clothe their female slaves.[63] [Garments of] white silk gauze on the outer side and

[61] The word *t'ung* here is a synonym for slave; see II, 13, n. 51. To judge from the general context, the slaves referred to here were women. The text gives no clue as to the functions of the slaves in question. But the fineness of their raiment suggests that these women were either entertainers, proficient in music and dance, or personal attendants who gave sexual satisfaction to their masters.

[62] Fu Ch'ien says that *hsien* 閑 was an enclosure where male and female slaves were kept, pending sale.

[63] The phrase *pei ch'ieh* usually means "girl slaves and concubines." However, *ch'ieh* can also mean "a female slave." For instance, the *Shuo-wen* states, "Males who are criminals are called *nu* [slaves]; *nu* are called *t'ung*; females are called *ch'ieh*" (*SWCTC* 3A:66), and defines *ch'ieh* as "the female criminals who render services and are close to the lord" (*SWCTC* 3A:66). Frequently *ch'ieh* is associated with other synonyms for slaves, as in *ch'en ch'ieh* 臣妾, the *ch'en* meaning "male attendant, male servant," and being a synonym for "slave"; or as in *tsang-hu pei ch'ieh* 臧獲婢妾 (*HS* 62:20b), *tsang* being another term for *nu*, and *hu* being another term for *pei* in certain areas (see Liang Ch'i-ch'ao, "Chung-kuo nu-li chih-tu," *THHP*, II [1925] 527; Wilbur, *Slavery in China*, pp. 68–69).

In neither case should *ch'ieh* be translated as "concubine." Similarly the *pei-ch'ieh* of our passage must be considered a compound meaning "female slaves" and not "female slaves and concubines."

Our translation in no way implies that a master had no sexual rights over his female slaves. The term *fu-pei* refers to a female slave who assists her master in affairs of his clothes and bed (Yen: *HS* 72:10a). These obviously are intimate services, and the phrase "affairs of clothes and bed" seems to be a euphemism for sexual relations. Thus Yen says that *fu* also means "close favorite" 近幸 (*ibid.*). *Yü-pei*, the attending woman slave, also seems to have served her master intimately. There are cases in which a son was accused and punished for having had illicit intercourse with his father's *fu-pei* or *yü-pei*. An imperial chancellor was accused and dismissed on these grounds (*HS* 82:3a). A marquis committed suicide because of such an accusation (*HS* 41:9b), and the son of a king was executed for the same reason (*HS* 44:17a). If the *fu-pei* or *yü-pei* were merely ordinary slaves of the family, the sons' actions would not have been

linings of light white silk with braided trimmings on the edges, the more beautiful being embroidered with the design of the ax and other patterns—these were in ancient times the garments of the Son of Heaven. Now the rich people and great merchants, when they are preparing a great entertainment and inviting guests, use [the material] to cover the walls. What was used in ancient times to serve an emperor and an empress was moderate and proper. Now the common people are allowed to use the emperor's clothes for the walls of their rooms, and the singers[64] and the mean[65] are allowed to use the decorations of the empress. How can the empire not be exhausted? [*HS* 48:14a–b]

20. DAUGHTER REQUESTS BECOMING A GOVERNMENT SLAVE

In the fifth month [in the thirteenth year of Ch'ien of Hsiao-wen]   167 B.C. the prefect of T'ai-ts'ang of Ch'i, Mr. Ch'un-yü[66] was found guilty and had to be punished. An imperial order was issued to arrest him and transfer and imprison him in Ch'ang-an. Mr. T'ai-ts'ang[67] had no son but had five daughters. When Mr. T'ai-ts'ang was expecting the arrest, he cursed his daughters, saying, "When one has children but no sons, one is helpless in case of an emergency." His youngest daughter, T'i-ying, felt grieved and wept. Thereupon she followed her father to Ch'ang-an and presented a memorandum to the emperor, saying, "Your servant's father, being an official, is considered incorruptible and just by all [the people] in Ch'i. Now he has violated the law and will be punished. Your servant grieves that when one is dead he cannot live again, and when one is punished [the dismembered part] cannot be reattached.[68] Although later he may wish to reform himself, there is no

---

considered such serious offenses. Obviously the severe punishment was based on the notion that having sexual intercourse with father's concubines or "intimate" female slaves, whose sexual relations with the father were understood, was considered incest.

Thus, the *pei-ch'ieh* were female slaves, not concubines, and their status was different. Yen makes an important statement when he comments, "*Liang-jen* means concubine; the *shih-yü* [same as *yü-pei*] includes female slaves" (*HS* 97A:19b).

[64] *Ch'ang yu* 倡優. According to Yen: *HS* 52:9b, *ch'ang* are musicians and *yu* are comedians.

[65] *Hsia chien* 下賤, "the mean," refer to the slaves.

[66] Neither the *Shih-chi* nor the *Han-shu* mentions the given name of the prefect. However, we learn from *SC* 105:7b–11a that it was Ch'un-yü I 淳于意 and that he was a noted physician who, after being released on the petition of his daughter, devoted himself entirely to the practice of medicine.

[67] Because he was the prefect of T'ai-ts'ang, he was addressed as T'ai-ts'ang Kung. *Kung* is a term of respect.

[68] Here the punishment referred specifically to the punishment by mutilation:

way to follow. Your servant wishes to be made a government slave in order to redeem her father from his punishment and to give him a chance to reform himself."[69] [*SC* 10:13a–b; *HS* 23:12b–13a]

21. GOVERNMENT SLAVES FREED

160 B.C.   In the fifth month [in the fourth year of the Hou reign period of Emperor Wen] a general amnesty [was proclaimed], and government male and female slaves were set free to become commoners. [*HS* 4:16a–b]

22. PIG BREEDER BECOMES IMPERIAL CHANCELLOR

Kung-sun Hung[70] was a native of Hsüeh of Tzu-ch'uan. When he was young he was a jail officer. He was found guilty [of some crime] and dismissed. Since his family was poor, he raised pigs on the sea 160 B.C.   shore. When he was more than forty years old he began to study the various interpretations of the *Ch'un-ch'iu*. When Emperor Wu ascended 140 B.C.   the throne, he called for the "men of virtue and wisdom" and the "men of letters." At this time Hung was sixty years old. He was summoned to court as a "man of virtue and wisdom" and was made an erudite.

He was sent as an emissary to the Hsiung-nu, but upon his return his report was not in accord with the wishes of the emperor. His Majesty became angry and considered him incapable. Hung thereupon reported he was ill and was dismissed and returned home.

130 B.C.   In the fifth year of Yüan-kuang [the court] again summoned "men of virtue and wisdom" and "men of letters." Tzu-ch'uan kingdom again recommended Hung. Hung declined and said, "The last time I was sent to the west, I was dismissed because of my lack of ability. I hope you will select someone else from among the people of the kingdom." They strongly recommended Hung. Hung went to the grand minister of ceremonies. His Majesty himself gave the examination questions[71] for the various scholars. . . .

---

tattooing the face, cutting off the nose or feet, and castration. Emperor Wen described these punishments referred to in our text as "cutting off the limbs and carving the skin and flesh" 斷支體刻肌膚 (*SC* 10:14a; *HS* 23:13b).

[69] Because of the petition, not only was Ch'un-yü I pardoned, but also the punishments by mutilation (with the exception of castration) were abolished (*SC* 10:14a, 105:8b; *HS* 4:13a, 23:13b; cf. *HLCI* 9:7a–13b; *CCLK*, pp. 44 ff.).

[70] Kung-sun Hung held the post of imperial chancellor until his death in 121 B.C. at the age of eighty (*HS* 58:8a, 19B:6a–b).

[71] The examination questions, given by the emperor to the various scholars who

At the time, those who answered [the questions] numbered more than one hundred persons. The grand minister of ceremonies memorialized to place [Kung-sun] Hung in the low grade. When the answers were presented to [the emperor], the Son of Heaven promoted Hung's answers to be the first. He was summoned to see [the emperor]. His appearance was very handsome. He was appointed erudite and "waiting-for-edict at the Golden-Horse Gate." . . .

Thereupon His Majesty observed that [Kung-sun Hung] was careful and sincere in behavior, that he had more than eloquence (i.e., he debated with ease), and that he was familiar with the documents of the law and yet supplemented them with the method of Confucianism. His Majesty liked him. Within a year he was promoted to the post of clerk of the left of the capital region. . . .   126 B.C.

During the time of Yüan-shou he replaced Hsieh Tse as the imperial   125 B.C. chancellor. In former times the Han court had been in the habit of appointing a marquis as imperial chancellor; but Hung had no title. Thereupon His Majesty issued an edict, saying: ". . . Ennoble the Imperial Chancellor Hung as marquis of P'ing-chin with a fief of six hundred and fifty households from the P'ing-chin district of Kao-ch'eng prefecture." Afterwards this became a precedent; ennobling the imperial chancellor began with Hung. [*HS* 58:1a, 4a–6b]

23. SLAVES AND MILITARY SERVICE

At the time when Wu and Ch'u[72] rebelled, the marquis of Ying-yin,   154 B.C. Kuan Ho,[73] was a general under the command of the grand comman-

---

were summoned to the court to answer them, were called *ts'e* 策, and the answers to these questions were called *tui-ts'e* 對策. Those whose answers were considered satisfactory by the emperor were appointed officials. However, this kind of examination was different from the regular examination system introduced in Sui and T'ang in that it was held only when the emperor saw the need of it and ordered the various commanderies and kingdoms and the high officials in the central government to recommend "men of virtue and wisdom" or scholars with the qualification of straightforward speech to him. Only those who were thus recommended were given the privilege of taking the examinations. See *HHHY* 44:1a–2b.

[72] In 154 B.C. (*HS* 5:4a).

[73] Kuan Ho 灌河 was the son of Kuan Ying 灌嬰. Kuan Ying had been a follower of Emperor Kao from the very beginning of his campaign for power. After Emperor Kao ascended the throne, he bestowed on Kuan Ying the marquisate of Ying-yin. In 177 B.C. he was made the imperial chancellor, and died the following year (*SC* 95:12b–17a).

dant. He requested that Kuan Meng[74] be appointed a colonel. [Kuan]
Fu[75] was with his father as [an officer of] one thousand men. Kuan
Meng was old; but the marquis of Ying-yin insisted on his request.
[Meng] felt depressed and discontented.[76] Therefore, he usually attacked the strong center [of the enemy] when there was a battle. Consequently, he was killed in the midst of the Wu army. According to
military law, when father and son both joined the army, in case of
death [the survivor] was permitted to return home with the coffin.
Kuan Fu was unwilling to return home with the coffin. He said coura-
geously, "I wish to get the head of the King of Wu or that of a general
to avenge my father." Thereupon Kuan Fu put on his armor, took his
lance, and called for those brave men in the army who were close to
him. Several tens of men volunteered to follow him, but when they got
outside the gates of the ramparts none dared to advance. Two men only,
together with more than ten horsemen who were their attendant male
slaves, galloped into the Wu army. Reaching the flag of a Wu general,
they killed and wounded several tens of people. Unable to go forward,
they rushed back and entered the Han ramparts. All lost their male
slaves,[77] and only one horseman returned with [Kuan Fu]. Fu had ten
or more serious wounds on is body. Fortunately, he had some precious
medicines, and therefore he did not die. [*SC* 107:6a–b; *HS* 52:5a–b]

24. SLAVES OWNED BY BUSINESSMAN

Ca.
142 B.C.   In Lin-ch'iung there were many rich people. Cho Wang-sun[78] had
eight hundred[79] household slaves,[80] and Ch'eng Cheng also had several

[74] Kuan Meng 灌孟, the father of Kuan Fu as noted below, had been a guest of
Kuan Ying. Because of this connection he had become a high official. He therefore
changed his surname from Chang to Kuan.

[75] For further details about Kuan Fu, see III, 16.

[76] Wang Hsien-ch'ien comments that the grand commandant, who considered
that Kuan Meng was too old to fight, was unwilling to give him the appointment. He
finally consented because of Kuan Ying's insistence. This was the reason for Kuan
Meng's despondency (*HSPC* 52:6a).

[77] The slaves were probably killed in action. The story shows that a personal slave
could not desert his master in a critical situation. If the master left the scene of battle,
the slave would leave with him. When he stayed, his slave stayed also.

[78] Cho Wang-sun's ancestors had been wealthy iron manufacturers for generations.
The family had moved to Lin-ch'iung in 228 B.C.

[79] Cho Wang-sun's father and grandfather were known to have had substantial
slaveholdings some eighty years earlier. According to *SC* 129:17a–b, their slaves
numbered one thousand (the parallel passage in the *Han-shu* says eight hundred).
These figures throw an interesting light on the stability of wealth in business families
in Han times.

80 Instead of *chia-t'ung* 家僮, "household slaves," the *Han-shu* uses the term *t'ung-k'o*, which is usually defined as "slaves and guests" or "slave-guests." This raises the question: Was the term a compound, or did it refer to two distinct categories of persons (cf. Wilbur, *Slavery in China*, pp. 185–86, n. 1)? A similar problem arises with the term *nu k'o* (see III, 29, n. 160). Since *t'ung* and *nu* were used interchangeably (see II, 13, n. 51), and since *t'ung k'o* and *nu k'o* were also used as synonyms (a passage in the *San-kuo-chih*, Shu, 8:6b–7a reads: "[Mi Chu's] 麋竺 *t'ung k'o* numbered ten thousand," while a second reference to the same fact reads: "he presented two thousand *nu k'o*"), the cases of *nu k'o* and *t'ung k'o* are best treated together.

The present passage in the *Han-shu*, which uses the term *t'ung k'o* at first, speaks only of *t'ung* when noting the one hundred slaves given to Cho's daughter. This may be interpreted in two ways: either Cho owned both slaves and guests, but gave only slaves to his daughter, or the terms *t'ung k'o* and *t'ung* are interchangeable. Another case in the *San-kuo-chih* mentions that Mi Chu owned ten thousand *t'ung k'o* and offered two thousand *nu k'o* to Liu Pei (*SKC*, Shu, 8:6b–7a). Here again it may be interpreted in two ways, depending on whether *t'ung k'o* and *nu k'o* are understood as slaves and guests or slave-guests. There are also other instances in which it is not clear whether *nu k'o* is a compound term or two separate terms. For example the *Han-shu* mentions that the *nu k'o* of a powerful family went to a market with their weapons (III, 26). Again, a passage in the *Hou-Han-shu* states that the *nu k'o* of Tou Ching 竇景 relied upon his influence and oppressed the ordinary people (III, 57). In a passage in *San-kuo-chih* an official suggested building a dam, and the empress warned him that the *nu k'o* would secretly take the government bamboo and wood (*SKC*, Wei, 5:11b). It is mentioned in the *Wei-lüeh* that when someone intruded upon Ting Mi 丁謐 while he was lying on his bed, he called his *nu k'o* and said, "Who is this fellow? Order him to leave quickly" (*SKC*, Wei, 9:23b, note). The expression *nu k'o* also appears in a memorial of Tung Chao, a top official in the Wei dynasty (*SKC*, Wei, 14:20a).

But there are instances where we find a more or less clear distinction between slaves and guests. A passage in the *Han-shu* mentions that the paramour of a princess sent his guest to shoot and kill a former grand administrator. The guest hid in a hut of the princess, and the prefect led his men to arrest him. The princess, escorted by a large number of male slaves and guests, rushed there, and they shot the prefect's functionaries. She then accused the police chief of the prefect of wounding the male slaves of her household (III, 29). The *Wu-shu* mentions that Kan Ning led his eight hundred *t'ung k'o* to Huang Tsu, and that many of his guests deserted, having been won over by Huang; later, when Kan became a prefect, he was able to induce some of these runaway guests to return (quoted in *SKC*, Wu, 10:11a, note). This passage suggests that Kan had both slaves and guests, but only the guests ran away. The *Chiang piao chuan* says that Hsü Kung's *nu k'o* hid themselves among the people, intending to avenge him. One day while Sun Ts'e was hunting he met three men who were Hsü's guests and who forthwith killed him (quoted in *SKC*, Wu, 1:16a, note). It seems that both slaves and guests were engaged in a mission of vengeance, but that only three of the guests found an opportunity to kill their patron's enemy.

The following passages indicate clearly that *nu* and *k'o* are two distinct terms, not a compound term. The *Han-shu* mentions that when Emperor Ch'eng went out incognito, he was usually escorted by his private *nu k'o*. Ku Yung 谷永 said, in a memorial reproaching the emperor, that the emperor "gathered together frivolous and improper persons to be private guests (*ssu k'o* 私客) . . . and kept private male slaves (*ssu-nu* 私奴), carriages, and horses in the Northern Palace" (*HS* 27 *chung* A:11b–12a). Obviously, he distinguished between the two classes of people. In a memorial addressed to Emperor Ai, Pao Hsüan complained that the emperor bestowed upon his consort relatives and his favorite, Tung Hsien, an enormous amount of money,

hundred. . . . [Cho Wang-sun] gave Wen-chün[81] one hundred slaves, a million cash, and clothes, bed coverings, and other properties [which she had had] at the time of her [former] marriage. [*SC* 117:1b, 3a; *HS* 57A:1b, 3a]

---

thus causing their slave attendants (*nu-tsung* 奴從) and guests *(pin-k'o)* to consume wine and meat as if they were soup and bean leaves (*HS* 72:26a). It is interesting to note that Pao mentioned *nu-tsung* and *pin-k'o* separately instead of *nu k'o*. This is an indication that the term *nu k'o*, although appearing to be loose and vague, really meant both *nu* and *k'o*. The most unequivocal statement in this respect was made by Ts'ui Shih, a scholar of the second century, who once remarked that when a prefect had no male slave he would take a guest, and that such a guest was paid one thousand cash monthly (*CSCY* 45:10a). This statement indicates that slaves and guests were not one and the same: whereas one was not free, the other came under the category of hired labor. (For a discussion of *ku-yung* 雇傭, hired labor, which Lao Kan identifies as *k'o*, see Lao Kan, "Han-tai ti ku-yung chih-tu," *LSYY*, XXIII [1951], 77–87; *idem, Chü-yen Han-chien* [Taipei, 1960], pp. 56–57.)

To summarize: In some contexts we cannot definitely say whether the term *nu k'o* is a compound or two separate words; either alternative makes sense. But in most cases there is a fairly clear distinction between slaves and guests. The ambiguity of the usage leads some writers to believe the term to be a compound (Chü Ch'ing-yüan, "San-kuo shih-tai ti 'k'o'," *Shih-huo*, III, No. 4 [1936], 16), but as we review the passages cited above, such an assumption seems highly questionable. In fact the ambiguity usually derives from lack of information in the context; whenever details are available the ambiguity disappears. The weight of evidence favors the conclusion that slaves and guests are two categories of persons (cf. Wilbur, *Slavery in China*, pp. 185–86, n. 1; T'ao Hsi-sheng, "Hsi Han shih-tai ti k'o," *Shih-huo*, V, No. 1 [1937], 1). This distinction was strictly observed by some Han writers, Ts'ui Shih and others.

But the fact that slaves and guests were frequently mentioned together in the texts should not be overlooked. We believe that it was the similar status and function of these two groups that led to such usage. Guests were also attached to their patrons personally, although they were not considered "property" in the sense that slaves were. The cases of the Cho family (II, 5) and of Mi Chu (*SKC*, Shu, 8:6b–7a), who were said to have "owned" hundreds of slaves and guests, imply rights of possession over both categories. This is even more clearly shown in Hsü Ling's 徐陵 case: after his death some of his *t'ung k'o* and lands were seized by others (*SKC*, Wu, 12:6b, note quoting the *K'uai-chi tien lu*). Ts'ui Shih's statement that either a slave or guest might be called upon to perform personal services and the evidence that slaves and guests were both engaged in building a dam show that both groups could be called upon for similar tasks and the tasks could be of a menial nature. Military and other dangerous tasks were also assigned to slaves and guests (*SKC*, Wei, 11:92; *SKC*, Wu, 1:10a). In view of these many similarities, it is understandable that slaves and guests are frequently mentioned together. See Lao Kan, "Han-tai ti ku-yung chih-tu," pp. 83–84, and *Chü-yen Han-chien*, p. 57.

[81] Cho Wen-chün was Cho's widowed daughter who eloped with Ssu-ma Hsiang-ju, the great poet. See I, 21.

25. STUDENT WAGE LABORER

Ni K'uan[82] was a native of Ch'ien-sheng. He studied the *Shang-shu*, Before 126 B.C. serving Ou-yang Shen[83] as a disciple. Through selection by the commanderies and kingdoms he was sent to the office of the erudites.[84] He studied under K'ung An-kuo.[85] Since he was poor and without means he acted for some time as cook for his fellow students and often worked as a wage laborer, carrying the classics with him while he hoed. Whenever he was resting, he read. His concentration on his studies was thus.

By shooting the examination questions[86] he became master of precedents. . . . When [Chang] T'ang was the grandee secretary[87] he made 120–116 B.C. K'uan a bureau head and recommended him to the post of attendant imperial secretary. Meeting the emperor, [K'uan] talked about the classics. The emperor liked him and asked him about one chapter of the *Shang-shu*. He was promoted to be palace grandee and then trans-

---

[82] Ni K'uan, until he was recommended by Chang T'ang, held an inferior position. He was a petty officer under the commandant of justice, but since he had little knowledge of the law he was put in charge of the livestock belonging to the office of the erudites. Once when the department's subordinates were unable to write a satisfactory memorial, K'uan did so. The result so pleased Chang T'ang and the emperor that K'uan was made a bureau head under the commandant of justice, Chang T'ang (*HS* 58:11a–12a).

[83] Ou-yang Sheng, also a native of Ch'ien-sheng, was a student of Fu Sheng, an erudite in the Ch'in dynasty who secretly hid his books inside a wall when the government ordered all books to be burned. He was the only Han scholar who knew the text and meaning of the *Shang-shu* (*HS* 88:10b–11b).

[84] In the time of Emperor Wu it was decreed that persons over eighteen were to be selected by the office of the grand minister of ceremonies and made the students of the erudites. It was also decided that persons in the various localities who were interested in literature, revered their elders and superiors, respected the government and education, were in accord with the villagers, and whose behavior was not contradictory to the moral standard were to be selected by the local governments and sent to the office of the grand minister of ceremonies; and they were also allowed to study under the erudites as students (*HS* 88:4a). Ni K'uan belonged to the second category.

[85] K'ung An-kuo, a famous commentator of the *Shang-shu,* was said to be a descendant of Confucius in the thirteenth generation. At this time he was an erudite.

[86] The students who studied under the erudites were given an examination after one year of study. Questions covering various problems were written down on tablets, placed into different groups, and labeled *chia k'o* 甲科, *i k'o* 乙科, and *ping k'o* 丙科. They were put together and those who were taking the examination were asked to select a topic by shooting a dart at them *(she-ts'e* 射策). Those who passed the examination were then made officials (see *HS* 88:4b–6a, 26a–b; Yen: *HS* 78:2a; *HSPC* 81:1b). *She-ts'e* should not be confused with *tui-ts'e* 對策, for which see 22, n. 71, of this section.

[87] See *HS* 6:15b, 19B:6b for the date.

113 B.C. ferred to the post of left clerk of the capital region. . . . K'uan was
110 B.C. appointed grandee secretary.[88] [*HS* 58:11a, 12a, 13a]

26. PEOPLE ENCOURAGED TO CONTRIBUTE SLAVES TO THE GOVERNMENT

Ca.
126 B.C.   [At that time] the treasuries were all empty.[89] Thereupon people
were asked to contribute male and female slaves [to the government],
and thereby be exempted from corvée for life or become gentlemen, or
[if they were already gentlemen] receive an increase in rank.[90] [*SC*
30:4b; *HS* 24B:6b]

27. GOVERNMENT SLAVES

123 B.C.   Then the king[91] ordered the government slaves to go to his palace to
make the emperor's seal. . . . [*SC* 118:16b; *HS* 44:12a]

28. CONNECTION BETWEEN OFFICIAL AND MERCHANT

Previously [Chang T'ang][92] was a petty official and carried on specu-

[88] *HS* 58:14a says that he held the office for nine years. According to *HS* 19B:7b,
he held this post for only eight years. This is correct since he was appointed in the
first year of Yüan-feng (110 B.C.) and died in the twelfth month of the second year of
T'ai-ch'u (102 B.C.) (*HS* 6:26a).

[89] According to *SC* 30:3b–4b and *HS* 24B:6a–b, this was owing to the opening of
the road to the Southwest Barbarians, in which tens of thousands of workers were
engaged (130–126 B.C.), and the guarding and building of the city wall of Shuo-fang
by a hundred thousand men after the territory had been taken from the Huns. In 127
B.C. the territory was taken by Wei Ch'ing and a hundred thousand people were
moved there. In the next year the city wall was built (*HS* 6:9a–b).

[90] Yen says, "Commoners who contributed male and female slaves would be
exempted for life. Those who were already gentlemen would have an increase in their
rank." However, a different explanation, quoted by Yen, states, "Those who contributed only a small number of male and female slaves would be exempted for life,
those who contributed many could become gentlemen, and those who were formerly
gentlemen would have an increase in rank" (*HS* 24B:6b).

[91] The king of Huai-nan, whose name was Liu An, at this time was planning to
rebel. He started by forging government seals. The plot was discovered, the king
committed suicide, and his partisans (several ten thousands) were all executed (*SC*
118:19a; *HS* 6:11a, 44:17a).

[92] Chang T'ang was one of the few outstanding statesmen of the Han dynasty who,
despite the many difficulties involved, fought for a strong central government. Rising
from the post of a small official of Ch'ang-an prefecture, he was a staunch supporter
of the economic and political reforms of Emperor Wu, such as the introduction of a
new monetary system, government monopoly of salt and iron production, and suppression of great merchants, as well as powerful and wealth-grabbing families. In

lative trading.[93] He made friends with the rich merchants of Ch'ang-an, such as T'ien Chia, Yü Weng-shu, and the like. When he became [one of the] nine ministers, he received and associated with famous scholars   120 B.C. and officials of the empire. Although he was not in agreement with them in his heart, yet he pretended to admire them. . . .

T'ang's guest, T'ien Chia, although a merchant, had a virtuous character. Previously, at the time when T'ang was a petty official, they had associated with each other because of financial matters. When T'ang became a high official, Chia, by urging T'ang on to righteous deeds and [reproving him for] his faults, had the spirit of a meritorious scholar. . . .

[Chang] T'ang several times acted for the imperial chancellor. Knowing that these three chief clerks[94] had always been honored [in holding high posts], he frequently insulted and humiliated them.[95] Therefore the three chief clerks conspired together and said [to the imperial chancellor, Yen Ch'ing-ti], "Previously T'ang made an agreement that he and you were to apologize [to His Majesty] and afterwards he betrayed you and wants to charge you with the affair of the imperial temple.[96] This [indicates his] intention to replace you. We know

---

[93] 126 B.C. while holding the office of grand palace grandee, he, together with Chao Yü 趙禹, worked out laws for establishing a more rigid control over government functionaries. In 126 B.C. he was made commandant of justice. In 120 B.C. he was promoted to the position of grandee secretary (*HS* 19B:6b). Having become a victim of a court conspiracy, he committed suicide in the eleventh month of the second year of Yüan-ting, 116 B.C. (*SC* 122:5b ff.; *HS* 59:1a ff., 6:15b).

[93] This reading of the phrase *kan-mu* 乾沒 follows Shen Ch'in-han's interpretation of it (see *HSPC* 59:2a).

[94] According to the context, the three chief clerks (*chang-shih* 長史) were under the imperial chancellor, but according to *HS* 19A:3a, the imperial chancellor had only two chief clerks. Yen, therefore, is led to believe that one of the three must have been an acting chief clerk (*HS* 59:6a). The three were Chu Mai-ch'en, Wang Ch'ao 王朝, and Pien T'ung 邊通.

The three clerks had all held positions higher than those held by Chang T'ang in the past. All three had been demoted to the post of chief clerk while Chang had been promoted to the post of grandee secretary, a rank which almost equaled that of the imperial chancellor.

[95] His insulting attitude and behavior toward the three clerks, which caused them to hate and conspire against him, is also mentioned in *HS* 59:5b–6a, 64A:13a–b.

[96] That is, the stealing of the money buried in the tomb of Emperor Wen. The imperial chancellor, Yen Ch'ing-ti 嚴青翟, made an agreement with Chang T'ang that they would apologize in the presence of the emperor. When they were in the court, Chang T'ang considered that it was the duty of the imperial chancellor to tour the imperial tombs every season; he therefore did not apologize. The imperial secretaries were ordered by the emperor to investigate the case. Chang T'ang thereupon intended to accuse Yen of having had knowledge of the case in advance. The imperial chancellor considered this a threat to him (*SC* 122:10a; *HS* 59:6a).

T'ang's secret affairs." They sent officials to arrest and investigate T'ang, witnesses, T'ien Hsin[97] and others. They charged: "Whenever T'ang was about to present his proposals to the throne, Hsin always knew it beforehand. Then he hoarded goods to acquire wealth which he would share with T'ang." And they [also charged him] with other unlawful acts. Many of the accusations reached the emperor's ear. His Majesty asked T'ang [about them], saying, "Whatever I did, the merchants always knew it beforehand and hoarded more goods. It seems that there was someone who told them my plans." T'ang did not apologize, but, pretending to be surprised, said, "There certainly must be."[98] [*SC* 122:6b, 9a, 10b–11a; *HS* 59:1b–2a, 4b, 6a]

29. STOCKBREEDER BECOMES AN OFFICIAL

Pu Shih was a native of the Honan commandery. He made farming and stockbreeding his occupation. . . . After some ten years his sheep amounted to more than a thousand. He bought land and houses. . . .

At this time Han was engaged in the affairs with the Hsiung-nu. [Pu] Shih presented a memorial to the emperor stating that he was willing to contribute half of his family property for frontier [expenses]. . . . The emperor did not reply to him. Several years later Shih was then dismissed. Shih returned home and again engaged in farming and stockbreeding. More than a year later when Hun-yeh of the Hsiung-nu 121 B.C. surrendered,[99] the government expenses were heavy, and its granaries and treasuries were empty. The poor people were moving in great numbers;[100] they all looked to the government for supplies. The govern-

[97] T'ien Hsin 田信 was a merchant who was close to Chang T'ang.

[98] There is reason to believe that Chang T'ang was falsely accused by the chief clerks. When he died his whole property amounted to not more than five hundred catties of gold, a sum that was an accumulation of his salary and grants from the emperor. Moreover, immediately after T'ang committed suicide (in 116 B.C.) Emperor Wu put the three chief clerks to death; and the imperial chancellor, Yen Ch'ing-ti, committed suicide.

[99] The Hsiung-nu who surrendered numbered more than forty thousand. For the expenses of receiving, rewarding, and supporting the surrendered Hsiung-nu, see *HS* 24B:8a–b.

[100] This took place in 119 B.C. A year before there had been a great flood in the area within the passes. The granaries in the various commanderies and kingdoms were exhausted and the wealthy were asked to lend money and grain for the poor. The relief, however, was far from sufficient. Then 725,000 dispossessed people were ordered to be moved from their homes to the following places: (1) west to Lung-hsi, Pei-ti (in modern eastern Kansu), and Shang (in northern Shensi) commanderies; (2) north to Hsi-ho (in southern Sui-yüan) and the area of Hsin-ch'in-chung (in

ment was unable to meet all the needs. Shih again took two hundred thousand cash to the grand administrator of Honan to provide for the expenses of the migrating people. [The administrator of] Honan presented to the emperor the names of the rich people who had contributed to the poor.[101] The emperor knew the name [Pu] Shih, and said, "This is the man who wanted to contribute half of his family property for the frontier [expenses]." Thereupon Shih was given [the privilege of] exempting from labor service four hundred men.[102] Shih again gave them all to the government. At that time the powerful and rich persons all strove to conceal their wealth, and only Shih was willing to contribute to the expenses. Thereupon the emperor considered that after all Shih was a sincere man,[103] then he summoned Shih, appointed him a palace gentleman, bestowed upon him the rank of chieftain of the multitude of the left, and granted him ten *ch'ing* of land. The matter was announced all over the empire to honor and show [the merit of Pu Shih] and to encourage the people. At first Shih was not willing to be a gentleman. The emperor said, "I have sheep in the Shang-lin Park. I should like to have you as a shepherd for them." Then Shih became a gentleman; he wore plain cloth clothes and straw shoes and acted as shepherd of the sheep. A year later all the sheep had become fatter and more numerous. When the emperor passed by the sheep pastures, he was satisfied. Shih said, "It should be the same for the ruling of people, not for sheep only. They should have a regular life, and the bad ones should be removed in order not to destroy the group." The emperor was sur-

---

southern Sui-yüan), which had been acquired from the Hsiung-nu after the submission of the king of Hun-yeh; (3) south to K'uai-chi (in eastern Kiangsu and western Chekiang). It is reported in the *Han-shu* that this large-scale migration of the poor people, which cost the government a hundred millions, was a heavy burden on the empire and that white metal money made of silver and tin was made to meet the expenses. Cf. *SC* 30:7a, 110:25a; *HS* 6:13a–b, 24B:8b–10a.

[101] *HS* 6:13a and 24B:8b report that in 120 b.c. an appeal was made to wealthy persons to lend to the poor who were suffering from the flood, and the names of those who contributed were to be reported to the emperor by the local governments.

[102] The meaning of this sentence is not clear. Su Lin comments: "外繇 means 'to guard the frontier.' Every man contributes three hundred cash; this is called 過更. Shih was given one hundred twenty thousand cash every year. Someone says that [the sentence means that] besides labor service he was allowed to have four hundred men exempted from labor service." Yen considers the last explanation correct.

[103] When Pu Shih asked to contribute half of his family property for frontier expenses, the emperor asked the opinion of the imperial chancellor, Kung-sun Hung, who replied that Pu Shih's action was not in accordance with human feeling, that he was an unlawful man; he suggested that the emperor should not accept the contribution. Apparently the emperor, who had been influenced by the imperial chancellor (who died in 121 b.c.), was now convinced of Pu Shih's sincerity.

prised at his words and wanted to make him try to govern people. He was appinted prefect of Hou-shih. [The people of] Hou-shih were glad to have him. He was transferred to the post of prefect of Ch'eng-kao and had the best record for grain transportation. Because he was honest and loyal, the emperor made him grand tutor and later chancellor of the king of Ch'i.[104] [*HS* 58:8b–10a; similar *SC* 30:11b–12b]

30. MERCHANTS AND MANUFACTURERS BECOME OFFICIALS

119 B.C.   Thereupon, Tung-kuo Hsien-yang and K'ung Chin were made assistants to the grand minister of agriculture in charge of the affairs concerning salt and iron.[105] Sang Hung-yang, because of his knowledge of mathematics, was employed and made the attendant in the palace. Hsien-yang was a great salt manufacturer of Ch'i, and K'ung Chin was a great manufacturer of iron in Nan-yang. Both of them acquired property amounting to a thousand [catties of] gold. Therefore Cheng Tang-shih mentioned and recommended them to the emperor. Hung-yang was the son of a merchant in Lo-yang who, because of his mental ability in calculation, became the attendant in the palace at the age of thirteen. [*SC* 30:9a; *HS* 24B:10a–b]

31. FUNCTION OF GOVERNMENT SLAVES

Ca.
113 B.C.   The confiscated male and female slaves[106] were distributed among the various parks to tend dogs, horses, birds, and animals,[107] and were

104 In 112 he was ennobled as Kuan-nei marquis and in the following year was summoned to the capital and appointed grandee secretary. But a year later he lost favor with the emperor because he disagreed with the policies for handling salt and iron. He was dismissed from this post and demoted to grand tutor of the heir apparent (*HS* 58:10b–11a).

105 Through the suggestion of Tung-kuo Hsien-yang and K'ung Chin, government offices were established in various places to administer the affairs concerning the monopoly of salt and iron. Those who had formerly been rich salt and iron manufacturers were made government functionaries. It was reported by Ssu-ma Ch'ien and Pan Ku that there were many merchants among the officials.

106 These slaves were confiscated, together with land and other property, from the merchants who failed to pay the *min ch'ien* 緡錢, a tax on their property. See *HS* 24B:11b–12a, 13b–14a; Nancy Lee Swann, *Food and Money in Ancient China* (Princeton, 1950), pp. 279–82, 294–96.

107 In the Shang-lin Park male and female slaves cared for the deer (*HCI* B:8a). We have no over-all figure for the number of slaves used in the parks for this and related purposes. But according to the *Han-i-chu*, quoted by Ju Shun, there were in the thirty-six parks along the northern and western frontiers thirty thousand slaves, male and female, to take care of three hundred thousand horses (*HS* 5:7b).

given to the various offices.[108] The various offices increased [in size] and the newly established ones were numerous.[109] The convicts and male and female slaves were numerous; they were sent down the Ho to transport four million piculs [of grain, which,] together with [the grain] bought by the offices themselves was then sufficient [to support them]. [*SC* 30:15b; *HS* 24B:14b]

32. Merchants Drafted into Expeditionary Force

In the first month of the spring of the fourth year [of T'ien-han] . . . 97 B.C. the seven classes of the convicted ones[110] in the empire and the brave warriors were moblized. [*HS* 6:27b]

33. Illicit Relations with a Male Slave

In the early days [Ho] Kuang[111] favored his slave superintendent,[112] Ca. 86–66 B.C. Feng Tzu-tu, with whom he often discussed matters. When Hsien[113] became a widow, she had illicit relations with Tzu-tu. [*HS* 68:14b]

34. Powerful Merchants Against a Minister

The rich men who lost wealth[114] all held a grudge against him and 74– 72 B.C. offered money to seek out a crime [committed by T'ien] Yen-nien.[115]

---

[108] From various sources, we know that there were government male and female slaves in the bureaus within the palace (*HCI* B:4a), in the office of the imperial chancellor (*HCI* A:9a–b), in the office of the grand minister of agriculture (*HS* 24A:7a), and in the office of the chief of police (*HS* 77:16b). In the office of the grand provisioner alone there were three thousand male and female slaves (*HCIPI* A:4a).

[109] The *Han-shu* has 雜 instead of 新. In that case the sentence would mean "The offices became increasingly complex and many were instituted."

[110] See II, 7, n. 21.

[111] Ho Kuang was the regent from 86 to 68 B.C. See III, 26, n. 149.

[112] According to Yen, *chien-nu* was a slave who managed the family affairs. Other slaves of the family were under his supervision. Cf. II, 53, n. 160.

[113] Hsien 顯 was the wife of Ho Kuang. She was executed in 66 B.C. because of plots for a rebellion.

[114] Before the death of Emperor Chao, the two rich Chiao and Chia families of Mao-ling had secretly hoarded charcoal and other burial materials valued at tens of millions. After the emperor's death, T'ien Yen-nien memorialized that their way of making a profit was improper and that the hoarded materials should be confiscated. His petition was approved. See *HS* 90:14b.

[115] T'ien Yen-nien held the office of grand minister of agriculture at this time (*HS* 19B:10b). For further details about T'ien, see III, 27.

Previously when the grand minister of agriculture had hired thirty thousand ox-wagons from the people to transport gravel from under the Pien Bridge to [Emperor Chao's] tomb, the charge for one wagon was a thousand cash. Yen-nien, when he presented the account book, falsely increased the charge to two thousand for each wagon, the total being sixty million. He embezzled half of it. The Chiao and Chia families [now] charged him with this matter. [The case] was handed down to the office of the imperial chancellor. The imperial chancellor examined it and memorialized that Yen-nien's stealing of thirty million when he himself was in charge was an improper action. . . . Emissaries were sent to summon Yen-nien to go to the commandant of justice. When he heard the beating of the drum,[116] he cut his throat and died.[117] [HS 90:14b–15a, 15b]

35. CHANCELLOR'S WIFE QUESTIONED ON DEATH OF SLAVE

67 B.C. In the seventh month of the third year of Ti-chieh the imperial chancellor's[118] attendant female slave,[119] having committed some fault, hanged herself. [Chao] Kuang-han heard of this and suspected that [the female slave] had been killed by the imperial chancellor's wife because of jealousy.[120]. . . Then he himself led functionaries and guards-

[116] According to Chin Cho, it was customary to beat a drum when a messenger arrived with an edict (Yen).

[117] In 72 B.C. (*HS* 8:5b).

[118] The imperial chancellor was Wei Hsiang 魏相. He had been the grand administrator of Honan for years. After Emperor Hsüan ascended the throne he was promoted to the post of grand minister of agriculture and one year later, in 72 B.C., to grandee secretary. His suggestion on reducing the power of the Ho family after the death of Ho Kuang pleased the emperor, who appointed him imperial chancellor and enfeoffed him as marquis of Kao-p'ing in 67 B.C. He remained in this post until his death in 59 B.C. (*HS* 74:1a–7b, 19B:11a–12a).

[119] For *fu-pei*, see II, 19, n. 63.

[120] Chao Kuang-han was then the governor of Ching-chao. Before he held this office he had been prefect of price equalization and standardization *(p'ing-chun-ling* 平準令) under the minister of agriculture and grand administrator of the Ying-ch'uan commandery. He was a brilliant administrator, quick to suppress or recommend the extermination of powerful families who had oppressed others or acted illegally. See III, 30, 31.

His accusation of the chancellor's wife climaxed a series of incidents. Sometime previously one of Kuang-han's guests who had been privately selling wine in the Ch'ang-an market was driven out of the market by a clerk of the chancellor. The guest thought that a certain Su Hsien 蘇賢 had reported the affair to the authorities. Kuang-han sought to aid his guest by having one of his subordinates accuse Su Hsien of being a "mounted warrior" who had failed to appear at his camp. The decision went against the subordinate, who was executed; and his superior, Kuang-han, was

men and unexpectedly entered the mansion of the chancellor· He called forth [the chancellor's] wife to kneel down in front of the hall to answer questions. He arrested more than ten male and female slaves and left with them. He charged [the imperial chancellor's wife] with having killed a female slave. The imperial chancellor, Wei Hsing, presented a memorial, saying, "My wife really did not kill the female slave. . . . I hope an able commissioner will be sent to investigate the case of your servant Hsiang's family, which has been examined by Kuang-han."

The case was assigned to the commandant of justice for investigation. In reality the imperial chancellor himself had scolded and beaten his attendant female slave because of a fault; she had left and gone to an outer hose where she had died. It was not as Kuang-han had said. . . . Kuang-han was sentenced to be cut in two at the waist.[121] [*HS* 76:5a–6a; similar *SC* 96:10a–b] 65 B.C.

36. HOUSEHOLD SLAVES ENGAGED IN PRODUCTION

[Chang] An-shih,[122] although he had been honored as a minister and marquis and had a fief of ten thousand households,[123] dressed in thick 67–62 B.C.

---

reduced one degree in rank. Suspecting that Jung Hsü 榮畜, a man from the same prefecture as Su Hsien, had instigated the countersuit, Kuang-han had him killed. Kuang-han was again accused, the case being referred to the imperial chancellor and the grandee secretary for investigation. Kuang-han then sent a trusted man to act as gate guard at the chancellor's residence, hoping to uncover illegal actions on the part of the chancellor or his household. Learning of the slave girl's death, Kuang-han sought to blackmail the chancellor into discontinuing his investigation. The chancellor, however, speeded up the case against Kuang-han. It was then that Kuang-han accused the chancellor's wife and investigated her for having killed the slave girl. When the examination established her innocence, Chao Kuang-han was accused of blackmailing a high official, killing innocent persons, and failing to report the facts (*HS* 76:1a–6a).

[121] Cf. *HS* 19B:11a.

[122] Chang An-shih, the son of Chang T'ang, a grandee secretary, was ennobled as marquis of Fu-p'ing in 75 B.C. His position was second only to the grand general, Ho Kuang.

In 80 B.C. Chang was made general of the right; in 74 B.C. he was promoted to the post of general of chariots and cavalry. In 67 B.C., a year after the death of Ho Kuang, he was given the highest posts in the central government at that time: grand minister of war and general of chariots and cavalry (later transferred to grand minister of war and general of the guards) and concurrently in charge of the affairs of the masters of writing. He held this post until he died in 62 .BC. (*HS* 59:7a–11b, 19B:10a–b and 11b).

[123] At first his fief comprised only 3,040 households. By 73 B.C., when Emperor Hsüan came to the throne, the number had been increased to 13,640 (*HS* 59:7b, 18:5b).

black silk, and his wife herself reeled [the silk] and wove it. His seven hundred household slaves were all skilled in handicrafts and engaged in [such] work. At home he managed his estate, piling up the smallest things, and therefore was able to increase his wealth and was richer than the Grand General [Ho] Kuang. [*HS* 59:11a]

37. FARMER'S SON BECOMES CHANCELLOR

Before
56 B.C.

K'uang Heng, whose style was Chih-kuei, was a native of Ch'eng prefecture of the Tung-hai commandery. His father was a farmer [as his forefathers had been] for generations. Coming to his time, Heng was fond of studying. Because he was from a poor family, he hired himself out to work in order to provide for his expenses. His energy particularly exceeded that of other persons. . . .

Heng shot the *chia* group of the examination questions, and since [his answers] were not in accordance with the instructions, he was appointed master of precedents [of the office of] the grand minister of ceremonies[124] and then transferred to the post of man of letters of the P'ing-yüan commandery. Many scholars presented memorials to the emperor, recommending [K'uang] Heng, saying that his knowledge of the classics was rarely paralleled among his contemporaries, that now he was made a man of letters and had taken up office, that all the [students of the] younger generation in the capital wanted to follow Heng to the commandery of P'ing-yüan, and that Heng should not be in a distant place. The case was handed down to the grand tutor of the heir apparent, Hsiao Wang-chih, and the privy treasurer, Liang Ch'iu-ho; they asked Heng to answer [questions about] the various basic meanings in the *Book of Poetry*. His answers were very brilliant. [Hsiao] Wang-chih memorialized that [K'uang] Heng was accomplished in classical studies and that his interpretations were the way of a master and worth reading. Emperor Hsüan did not employ many Confucianists, and Heng was sent back to his post [in P'ing-yüan]. But the heir

---

[124] For the meaning of shooting the examination questions, *she ts'e*, see II, 25, n. 86. The examination questions were arranged in three groups labeled *chia k'o, i k'o,* and *ping k'o*. Yen explains that K'uang Heng shot at the *chia k'o* questions, but his answers were not in accordance with the instructions given in the *chia k'o (Shih-chi* 96:12a reads 不中科 instead of 不應令); therefore he was merely appointed master of precedents, instead of gentleman of the palace, the post usually accorded to those who passed the *chia k'o* examination. According to *SC* 96:12a, K'uang Heng, who was not talented, failed to pass the examination many times, and finally passed the *ping k'o* on the ninth attempt (cf. *HSPC* 81:1b).

apparent, who saw the answer of [K'uang] Heng, admired it privately. When Emperor Hsüan died and Emperor Yüan had just ascended the throne, the Marquis of Yüeh-ling, Shih Kao,[125] because of being a member of the consort family, was made grand minister of war and general of chariots and cavalry and took charge of the affairs of the masters of writing. . . . Shih Kao appointed [K'uang] Heng a clerk in the Bureau of Deliberations and recommended Heng to His Majesty. His Majesty made him gentleman of the palace and he was then promoted to the post of "erudite who serves in the palace."

At this time there was a portent of an eclipse of the sun and an earthquake. His Majesty asked him about the merits and faults in the government. Heng presented a memorial. . . . His Majesty was pleased with his statement and he was promoted to the post of imperial court grandee and junior tutor of the heir apparent. . . .

Having been junior tutor for several years, [K'uang] Heng presented a number of memorials to state [what he considered was] convenient and proper. Besides, when government affairs were discussed in the court, he answered in accordance with the principles of the classics, and his statements were mostly of propriety and righteousness. His Majesty considered him capable of being a minister. He was therefore made superintendent of the imperial court and grandee secretary.

In the third year of Chien-chao he replaced Wei Hsüan-ch'eng in the post of imperial chancellor and was ennobled as marquis of Lo-an with a fief of six hundred households. [*HS* 81:1a–b, 2b, 5b–6a, 8a]   36 B.C.

38. RICH MERCHANTS BECOME OFFICIALS

From [the time of Emperor] Yüan and [Emperor] Ch'eng to that of   *Ca.* 48 B.C.–A.D. 23
Wang Mang the rich men of the capital region . . . were men of tremendous wealth in the world. Fan Chia had fifty millions and the others [each] had a hundred million. Wang sun [Ta-]ch'ing, who used his wealth to support men of distinction, associated with powerful and distinguished persons. Wang Mang made him the supervisor of markets of the capital, which was the prefect supervisor of the eastern market of Han [*HS* 91:10b–11a]

---

[125] Shih Kao was Emperor Hsüan's grandmother's brother's son. He became grand minister of war and general of chariots and cavalry when Emperor Yüan ascended the throne (*HS* 81:1b, 97A:21a–b).

39. NUMBER OF GOVERNMENT SLAVES

44 B.C.   [Kung Yü,[126] in his memorial,] also [said] that the government male
and female slaves, more than one hundred thousand people,[127] were
idle and without work,[128] that [the government] was taxing the good
people to support them at an annual expense of five to six hundred
million; that they ought to be freed and become common people, be
fed from the granaries, and be ordered to replace the garrison soldiers

[126] Kung Yü (124–44 B.C.) held various offices before he was made grandee remonstrant (*chien ta-fu* 諫大夫) in 48 B.C. While holding this position he presented a
memorial to Emperor Yüan urging him to reduce expenses; this advice was accepted
in part. Later Kung Yü was promoted to the post of imperial court grandee. In 44
B.C. he was again promoted, this time to the office of grandee secretary. He died
shortly thereafter. Limited though his tenure was, he presented many memorials, the
more important among them dealing with such problems as the lowering of the tax-
able age, the promotion of agriculture, and the abolition of metal currency.

[127] Wilbur, *Slavery in China*, pp. 398–400, raises the question of the reliability of
this figure, but reaches the conclusion that it is in accord with the history of the Early
Han. First, as pointed out by Wilbur, Kung Yü held an important position at court;
since he was an able and experienced executive, it seems entirely reasonable to assume
that he had access to the best information regarding the number of government slaves
as well as the number of government artisans and the expenses of the different bureaus,
all specifically mentioned in his memorial and all important to the proper management of the state. We agree with Wilbur that necessary as these figures are to the
business of administration "one hundred thousand" may well be a rough estimate.

Wilbur's general conclusion can be further justified by viewing Kung Yü's figure
in relation to other figures on slavery in the *Han-shu* and related texts. According to
the *Han-i-chu*, quoted by Ju Shun, thirty thousand male and female government slaves
cared for three hundred thousand horses in the thirty-six grazing grounds along the
northern and western frontiers (*HS* 5:7b). If thirty thousand slaves were used in the
frontier parks, it seems reasonable to assume that a substantial number were also
employed in the parks in the interior. We know that in 113 B.C. many slaves who were
confiscated from the merchants were sent to the various parks to rear dogs, horses,
birds, and other animals. See II, 31.

In 113 B.C. it was also reported that four million piculs of grain, together with grain
bought by the bureaus, were used to provide for numerous convicts and male and
female government slaves. See II, 31. Assuming that eighteen piculs of food were
consumed per annum by each individual—it was said (*HS* 24A:6a–b) that one and
one-half piculs were consumed per month by an individual—four million piculs would
feed about two hundred thousand persons. We cannot say how many of those supported by the four million piculs were convicts and how many were slaves; but our
estimated totals—although derived from a text dated 113 B.C.—give plausibility to
Kung Yü's figure.

[128] Similar ideas were expressed by other Han officials. For example, one of those
involved in the debates on the salt and iron monopolies said, "Now the government
keeps numerous male and female slaves. They sit and receive their clothes and food.
. . . The common people are not free from work from dawn to evening; [the govern-
ment] male and female slaves cross their hands and idle about" (*YTL* 6:8a).

east of the [Han-ku] Pass and to mount the beacons[129] and barriers on the northern frontiers to keep watch. [*HS* 72:16a–b]

40. Officials Not Allowed to Trade

[Kung Yü in his memorial] also expressed the hope that the families 44 B.C. of the officials close [to the emperor], starting with those of the various bureaus[130] and the attendants within the palace and the higher ones, would be prohibited by order from trading privately and from competing with the people for profits; that anyone violating the order should be immediately dismissed from his official post, deprived of his rank, and not allowed to hold any government office. [*HS* 72:16b]

41. Merchant Relying on the Power of a Marquis

In a few years [Lo P'ou][131] acquired more than ten millions. P'ou 32–1 B.C. used half his [profits] to bribe the marquises of Ch'ü-yang and Ting-ling.[132] Relying upon their power, he sold merchandise on credit and lent out money in the commanderies and kingdoms; and not one of the people dared default payment. He monopolized the profits of the salt wells. What he made in a year doubled his investment. Thus he increased his wealth. [*HS* 91:8a–b]

42. Wealthy Merchants Become Officials

After the family of Shih Shih[133] had declined, during the time of 32 B.C.–A.D. 23

---

[129] For *t'ing* 亭 at the frontier, see Lao Kan, "Shih Han-tai chih t'ing-chang yü feng-sui," *LSYY*, XIX (1948), 501–22.

[130] According to Chin Cho, the various functionaries and those who held the posts of "officials who concurrently serve in the palace" who daily attended the court, in charge of the affairs of the office of masters of writing and the presentation of the reports to the throne 諸吏給事中日上朝謁平尚書奏事, were divided into two bureaus (*ts'ao* 曹), the left bureau and the right bureau (*HS* 19A:13b). Both bureaus were occupied by men of the 2,000-picul rank (*HCI* A:3b–4a). For comments on 右左曹 and 諸史, see Shen Ch'in-han, *Han-shu su-cheng* (Che-chiang kuan shu-chü, 1900), 5A:14a–b, hereafter cited as *HSSC; HSPC* 19A:24a–b.

The bureau members and attendants within the palace were called close officials because all of them served within the palace and were close to the emperor (cf. *HSPC* 19A:24a).

[131] Lo P'ou was a big merchant in the time of Emperors Ch'eng and Ai.

[132] That is, Wang Ken and Ch'un-yü Ch'ang, the son of the sister of Emperor Yüan's empress.

[133] Shih Shih 師史 had been a wealthy merchant of Lo-yang.

[Emperors] Ch'eng and Ai and Wang Mang, Chang Ch'ang-shu and Hsieh Tzu-chung of Lo-yang had a wealth of a hundred millions [each]. [Wang] Mang made both of them officials under the grand minister of agriculture,[134] intending to imitate Emperor Wu,[135] but he could not derive any advantage [from the arrangements]. [*HS* 91:9b]

43. Official's Family Refuses to Pay Tax

Ca. 26 B.C.   [Ho] Wu and his brothers, five men in all, were officials[136] in the [Shu] commandery government. [The authorities of] the commandery and the prefecture respected and feared them. The family of Hsien, Wu's younger brother, had its name on the market register.[137] They often did not pay their tax.[138] Therefore the prefectural government several times failed to present the amount of tax [required]. [*HS* 86:1b]

44. Merchants Not Allowed To Be Officials

7 B.C   [The responsible ministers suggested that] no merchant should be allowed to hold title to land or become an official; violators should be punished according to the law.[139] [*HS* 11:3b]

[134] In A.D. 9, the year of the founding of his dynasty, Wang Mang changed the title of the grand minister of agriculture (the state treasurer) to *hsi-ho* 義和 and then to *na-yen* 納言 (*HS* 99B:4a). The word "officials" is an inadequate translation of the character *shih*. Wang Mang classified the officials with ranks from 100 piculs up to 600 piculs into five groups of *shih*, designated respectively as the *shu-shih* 庶士 (100 piculs), the *hsia-shih* 下士 (300 piculs), the *chung-shih* 中士 (400 piculs), the *ming-shih* 命士 (500 piculs), and the *yüan-shih* 元士 (600 piculs). We do not know to which class of *shih* Chang and Hsieh belonged.

[135] Yen comments that the author refers to the employment of Pu Shih, Tung-kuo Hsien-yang, and K'ung Chin by Emperor Wu as officials. However, Pu Shih was not a merchant (see II, 29) and therefore should not have been included. Sang Hung-yang, who was from a merchant family and who became grandee secretary, should be substituted for Pu Shih.

[136] This was shortly before Ho Wu was recommended as a "man of wisdom and virtue" by the Grand Keeper of Equipages Wang Yin, who held this post from 26 B.C. to 23 B.C. (*HS* 19B:15a).

[137] Everyone who had a shop in the market was registered (cf. II, 7, n. 21). The fact that Wu's family appeared on the registration list (*shih-ch'i* 市籍) indicates that some families of officials engaged in business.

[138] Obviously the tax here refers to the *shih-tsu* 市租, the market tax paid by the merchants who had a business in the market. Chu-fu Yen remarked that the market tax of Lin-tzu, a city of one hundred thousand households, amounted to a thousand catties of gold (*HS* 38:11a).

[139] This is part of the suggestions presented by the ministers in reply to an edict of Emperor Ai. Such a prohibition had already been formulated in the time of Emperor Kao (II, 15). It is probable that Emperor Wu's appointment of merchants to official posts led to the discussion of this question.

45. EMANCIPATION OF GOVERNMENT SLAVES

[The responsible ministers suggested[140] that] the male and female government slaves fifty years of age and up were to be set free and become commoners. [*HS* 11:3b] 7 B.C.

46. MERCHANTS BECOME OFFICIALS

The *hsi-ho* (i.e., state treasurer under Wang Mang) appointed *ming-shih* officials[141] to supervise the Five Equalizations and the Six Controls, several persons for each commandery. All of them employed the wealthy merchants, Hsieh Tzu-chung and Chang Ch'ang-shu from Lo-yang, Hsing Wei from Lin-tzu, and others, who traveled in the relay carriages and searched for profits, their ways crossing throughout the empire. Availing themselves of the opportunity, they collaborated with the [officials of the] commanderies and prefectures in unlawful activities, preparing many false accounts. The treasury was not filled, and the people were ever more distressed. [*HS* 24B:23b] A.D. 10

47. CRIMINALS AND SLAVES

When one family cast coins, five families were held responsible; they would be seized and made male and female slaves. [*HS* 99B:17b] A.D. 10

48. LAW CONCERNING THE BUYING AND SELLING OF SLAVES

Thereupon [Wang Mang] issued an edict, saying, ". . . Let those who violate the law in illegally buying and selling the common people[142] be temporarily free from prosecution." [*HS* 99B:23b–24a] A.D. 12

49. CRIMINALS AND SLAVES

Those who secretly cast the [*huo*]-*ch'üan* and the [*huo*]-*pu* were to be A.D. 14

---

[140] See II, 44, n. 139.

[141] On the officials of the *ming-shih* rank, see II, 42, n. 134.

[142] This refers to the law promulgated in A.D. 9 that prohibited the buying and selling of slaves (*HS* 99B:9a–10b, 24A:19b). The *Han-shu* reports that the nobles, officials, and people who were punished for selling or buying slaves and land and casting coins were numerous. Wang Mang was advised that the ancient *ching t'ien* 井田 system could not be restored and enforced. He therefore issued this edict to abolish the law concerning the buying or selling of slaves and land (*HS* 99B:10b, 23b–24a).

seized with their wives and children and made government male and female slaves. The officials and [the people] from the related five [families held collectively responsible] who knew but did not expose them were subject to the same punishment. [*HS* 24B:24b]

A.D. 21   When the people violated the law and cast coins, those belonging to the related five families were sentenced together and were seized by the government to become male and female slaves. The men were transported in the cage-carts while the children and women went on foot; they had iron chains with locks[143] around their necks. Those sent to the office for coinage were numbered by the hundred thousands. Those who arrived, husbands and wives, had their mates exchanged. Those who died through grief and suffering were six or seven out of ten. [*HS* 99C:15a]

50. GUESTS

A.D. 22   In the third year of Ti-huang there was a great famine in Nan-yang. Most of the guests of the various families became petty robbers. [*HHS* 1A:2a]

Ca.
A.D. 22   At the end of [the rule of] Wang Mang, because his guests broke the law, [Wu Han][144] then fled and went to the Yü-yang [commandery]. [*HHS* 18:1a]

51. BUSINESSMEN AND POLITICS

Li T'ung, whose style was Tz'u-yüan, was a native of Wan of Nan-yang. For generations his family had been famous for engaging in trade. His father, Shou, who was nine feet tall and had an extraordinary appearance, was very strict and stern. At home he lived as if at court. Formerly he served Liu Hsin. He was fond of astronomy and the prognostication records. He was the honored director of imperial rela-

---

[143] According to Yen, *lang-tang* 琅當 is a long chain. Wang Hsien-ch'ien says the term means "to lock" (*HSPC* 99C:13a).

[144] Wu Han 吳漢 was a native of Wan, the capital of the Nan-yang commandery. He was a canton chief when this incident occurred. After he had become a fugitive he supported himself by selling horses. He was appointed a prefect by a commissioner of the Keng-shih emperor. Wu Han, however, deserted the Keng-shih emperor and attached himself to the future Emperor Kuang-wu who appointed him grand general; he was later appointed grand minister of war by Emperor Kuang-wu. Wu succeeded in defeating the various antagonistic forces and finally brought about the downfall of Kung-sun Shu. He died in A.D. 44 (*HHS* 18:1a ff.).

tives of Wang Mang.[145] T'ung [himself] was also subordinate to the Wu-wei general. [Later] he was appointed to the post of assistant prefect of Wu prefecture, being renowned for his ability.

At the end of [Wang] Mang's time the people were in sorrow and distress. T'ung frequently heard Shou quoting the prophecy: "The Liu will revive; the Li will be the assistant." He always kept this in mind, and, moreover, because at home he was rich and had leisure and was dominant in his rural community, he did not care to be a government official; hence he voluntarily retired and returned home.

When the Hsia-chiang and Hsin-shih[146] armies rebelled, Nan-yang   _{A.D. 22} was stirred up. T'ung's cousin, [Li] I, who was fond of being involved in affairs, then consulted with [T'ung] and said, "Now disturbance is everywhere. The Hsin dynasty will be destroyed and Han will revive. Among the imperial families [of Liu] in Nan-yang, only Liu Po-sheng[147] and his brother are men who love and tolerate others and with whom it is possible to plan great affairs." T'ung laughed and said, "This is what I have in my mind." Just at that time Kuang-wu was at Wan to avoid trouble.[148] When T'ung heard of this, he then sent [Li] I to welcome Kuang-wu.

Kuang-wu thought that T'ung was a gentleman who admired him.

---

[145] According to Li, in A.D. 5 Wang Mang, while regent, set up the director of imperial relatives *(tsung-shih* 宗師*)* in the commanderies and kingdoms to supervise the affairs of the imperial relatives. As a mark of respect this official was entitled honored director of imperial relatives *(tsung ch'ing shih* 宗卿師*)*. However, Hu San-hsing comments that while the director of imperial relatives was set up by Wang Mang (presumably during his regency), the position of honored director of imperial relatives was established by Wang Mang only after he had seized the throne. See Ssu-ma Kuang, *Tzu-chih t'ung-chien, SPPY* ed., 36:8b and 38:121a, hereafter cited as *TCTC.*

[146] The armies of Hsia-chiang 下江 and Hsin-shih 新市 were made up of the two rebellious forces led by Wang Ch'ang 王常, Ch'eng Tan 成丹, Wang K'uang, Wang Feng, Ma Wu 馬武, and others. For details see Hans Bielenstein, "The Restoration of the Han Dynasty," *Bulletin of the Museum of Far Eastern Antiquities,* No. 26 (1954), pp. 136 ff.

[147] Liu Po-sheng, whose name was Yen (Po-sheng being his style), was the elder brother of the future Emperor Kuang-wu. It was he who started the revolt and organized the attacking forces. He defeated Wang Mang's troops and occupied the city of Wan. He was appointed grand minister of the masses by the Keng-shih emperor in 23 and was killed by him in the same year, because Po-sheng was more powerful and had many supporters. For these reasons the Keng-shih emperor feared that he might be his political rival in the future *(HHS* 14:1a–5b, 1A:4a and 8b).

[148] According to the *Hsü-Han-shu,* quoted by Li, the guests of his elder brother, Liu Po-sheng, had robbed the people, and Kuang-wu had to run away from the officials of his native prefecture, Ts'ai-yang, to Hsin-yeh. At this time, as stated in the *Tung-kuan Han-chi,* the Nan-yang commandery was suffering from a famine caused by drought. But the fields of the future Emperor Kuang-wu yielded a good harvest. He therefore went to Wan to sell his grain *(HHS* 1A:2a).

Therefore he went to visit him. When they met each other, they talked for the whole day, holding each others' hands with the greatest pleasure. T'ung then explained the prophecy. Kuang-wu at first had no such intention and did not dare to think that he could be [the man of the prophecy]. At this time Shou was in Ch'ang-an. Kuang-wu then, seeking to observe [the reaction of] T'ung, said, "Even if it is so, what would happen to the honored director of imperial relatives?" T'ung replied, "It has been arranged." Thereupon he fully explained his plan. When Kuang-wu completely understood T'ung's intent, they consequently made an agreement and settled upon a plot.[149]

They expected to hold the grandee of Ch'ien-tui and the subordinate rectifier[150] by force on the day of the military review of the horsemen by the military officials and thus to command the group. Then [T'ung] asked Kuang-wu to return to Ch'ung-ling with [Li] I to raise an army for support. And he sent his nephew Chi to Ch'ang-an to inform Shou. Chi became ill and died on the way. . . . [Wang Mang executed Shou], and the family members of Shou who were in Ch'ang-an were all killed. [The government officials of] Nan-yang also executed the family members of T'ung and his brothers, numbering sixty-four. All the corpses were burned in the market of Wan. At the same time, Han troops[151] were also gathered in great number. T'ung met Kuang-wu and Li I at Chi-yang. Thereupon together they defeated the Ch'ien-tui forces and killed Chen Fu and Liang Ch'iu-tz'u.

A.D. 23   When the Keng-shih emperor[152] ascended the throne, he made T'ung the grand general who is a pillar of the state and ennobled him as the marquis of Fu-han. [T'ung] followed him to Ch'ang-an and was promoted to the post of grand general and ennobled as king of Hsi-p'ing. [Li] I[153] was made King of Wu-yin and T'ung's younger cousin, Sung,[154] was appointed imperial chancellor. . . . T'ung married Kuang-

---

[149] According to *HHS* 1A:2a–b, Kuang-wu decided to revolt against Wang Mang in the tenth month of the third year of Ti-huang (October/November, A.D. 22).

[150] Grandee and subordinate rectifier were the titles used by Wang Mang for the grand administrator and chief commandant of a commandery. Ch'ien-tui (literally: the front regiment) was Wang Mang's name for the Nan-yang commandery. The two officials in this case were Chen Fu 甄阜 and Liang Ch'iu-tz'u 梁丘賜.

[151] That is, the forces led by Liu Po-sheng and Kuang-wu.

[152] Keng-shih was the reign title of Liu Hsüan 劉玄, whose style was Sheng-kung; he was the cousin of Kuang-wu. He was put on the throne by the leaders of the rebelling forces and killed by the Red Eyebrows in A.D. 24. See *HHS* 11:1a ff.

[153] Li I was later killed by Chu Wei (*HHS* 15:5a).

[154] Li Sung 李軼 was killed in action when the Keng-shih emperor was defeated (*HHS* 15:5a).

wu's younger sister, Po-chi, the [later] princess of Ning-p'ing. When Kuang-wu ascended the throne he made T'ung the commandant of the guard. In the second year of Chien-wu, [T'ung] was ennobled as mar- A.D. 26 quis of Ku-shih and appointed grand minister of agriculture.[155] [*HHS* 15:1a–3b]

52. Runner Recommended as Official

[Fan Shih's][156] friend, K'ung Sung of Nan-yang, whose family was Ca. A.D. 25–27 poor and whose parents were old, then changed his name and surname and hired himself out as a street runner of A-li [village] of Hsin-yeh prefecture. When Shih was making a tour of inspection[157] over the circuit region and arrived at Hsin-yeh, Sung was selected by the prefecture to be the forerunning horseman to welcome Shih. Recognizing him at a glance, Shih called Sung, and grasping his arm, said, "Are you not K'ung Chung-shan?"[158] He sighed in front of him and talked about their past life, saying, "Formerly you and I both dragged our long robes and gathered at the Imperial Academy. Now I, receiving favors from the nation, have attained the post of shepherd and head while you, carrying virtue in your heart, conceal yourself and stay among the runners. Is it not sad?" Sung said, ". . . Poverty is proper for a scholar. Why is it humbling?"

Shih ordered the prefecture to replace Sung. Sung, considering that the previous labor had not been completed, did not consent to leave. While staying in A-li, Sung was upright and strict in morals; all the youngsters in the street were submissive to the [transforming influence of] his instruction. Thereupon he was summoned by [one of] the offices of the [three ducal] ministers[159] and went to the capital. . . . Sung reached the post of grand administrator of Nan-hai. [*HHS* 81:16a–b]

---

[155] In A.D. 20 Li T'ung was appointed grand minister of works. He was modest, did not crave power, and frequently asked to resign from this post; but he held it two years before he was permitted to resign. He died in A.D. 42 (*HHS* 15:4b–5a).

[156] Fan Shih 范式 was at that time inspector of Ching Division. Later he was promoted to the post of grand administrator of Lu-chiang commandery (*HHS* 81:16a–b).

[157] It was the duty of the inspector to go to the commanderies and kingdoms to investigate the local officials' handling of general administrative and judicial matters. See *HS* 19A:15a–b; *HHS* 28:1b.

[158] Chung-shan was the style of K'ung Sung 孔嵩.

[159] "Offices of the Ministers" (*kung fu* 公府) refers to any one of the offices of the three ducal ministers, that is, the grand minister of war (or grand commandant), the minister of the masses, and the minister of works.

53. Slave Becomes an Official

Li Shan, whose style was Tz'u-sun, was a native of Yü-yang [prefecture] of Nan-yang. Originally he was a Dark-green Head[160] of Li Yüan A.D. 25–26 of the same prefecture. During the Chien-wu period there was an

[160] Ying Shao, Chin Cho, Wei Chao, and Fu Ch'ien all comment that soldiers wore blue-green kerchiefs and were therefore given the name *ts'ang-t'ou* 蒼頭, the "Dark-green Heads" (*SC* 7:3b, 48:8a; *HS* 31:6b). A different explanation is given by Meng K'ang, who states that all inferiors were classed as "dark" and that black was their color. However, since the common people were called *li-min* 黎民 or *ch'ien-shou* 黔首, *li* and *ch'ien* meaning black, slaves were called *ts'ang-t'ou* to differentiate them from the free people (*HS* 72:26b). Ts'an also associates *ts'ang-t'ou* with slaves, but gives an explanation based on a quotation from the *Han-chiu-i* that reads: "The government male slaves were selected to render the services of writing and accounting, attending the attendants within the palace and below. They were dark-green heads, wearing blue-green kerchiefs" (*HS* 72:26b; cf. *HCI* B:2b). The quotation in the *Han-shu* omits the word "selected."

Shida Fudōmaro, a Japanese scholar, points out that in its early usage *ts'ang-t'ou* was connected with soldiers and these men were personal bodyguards. He assumes that the status of these soldiers was at first free but that they gradually took up domestic duties and became slaves ("Kandai no dorei seido sō tō ni tsuite," *Rekishigaku kenkyū*, II, No. 1 [1934], 20–29). If his assumption is correct, then the contradiction between the two explanations would disappear. However, as correctly pointed out by another Japanese scholar, Utsunomiya Seikichi, there is no evidence to support the assumption that *ts'ang-t'ou chün* was the predecessor of *ts'ang-t'ou*. Nor is there evidence that *ts'ang-t'ou* was used in the sense of private troops. (*Kandai shakai keizai shi kenkyū* [Tokyo, 1954], pp. 239–43). The name *ts'ang-t'ou* might be given to soldiers, as suggested by Ying Shao and Fu Ch'ien, just because of the kind of kerchiefs they wore (*HS* 31:6b). However, we should not confuse *ts'ang-t'ou chün* with *ts'ang-t'ou*. As far as the usage is concerned, the second term always refers to slaves, not soldiers or private troops.

The quotation from the *Han-chiu-i* cited above reveals that *ts'ang-t'ou* were government slaves. However, the term is also widely used to designate private male slaves (*HS* 68:14b, 72:26a–b, 86:12a; *HHS* 10A:16a, 26:14b, 77:3b, 78:16b and 30b, 81:16b–17a, 82B:3b). In some passages, such as *HHS* 12:15b–16a, 26:14b–15a and 16b, 77:3b–4a, the term is used interchangeably with *nu*, "slaves." The term *ts'ang-t'ou-nu* also suggests that they were slaves (*HS* 68:14b). *HHS* 78:30b speaks of many *ts'ang-t'ou* who, in welcoming a guest, were led by a *chien-nu*,"slave-superintendent," a leader under whom only slaves would be placed.

However, there is one instance in which *ts'ang-t'ou* and male and female slaves are mentioned together (*HS* 86:12a). This makes us consider the question whether the two were identical. Probably *ts'ang-t'ou* was a special kind of male slave who was assigned special functions. The quotation from the *Han-chiu-i* shows that they were selected to render the services of writing and accounting. The *ts'ang-t'ou* in Ma Fang's family were elegantly clothed in garments with white collars and sleeves and with green sleevelets over their arms (*HHS* 10A:16a), a costume obviously unsuited for menial labor. It seems that *ts'ang-t'ou*, whether owned by the government or by private families, were slaves of skilled ability, such as writing or accounting. It is said in the *Hou-Han-shu* that many of the ennobled powerful eunuchs bought and adopted *ts'ang-t'ou* as their sons to inherit their titles (*HHS* 78:16b).

epidemic, and the members of [Li] Yüan's family died one after the other, [leaving] only an orphan child, Hsü, who had been born only several tens of days before. However, [the family] property [amounted to] ten millions. All the male and female slaves secretly planned together, intending to kill Hsü and to divide his property. [Li] Shan deeply pitied the Li family, but it was out of his power to control [the situation]. Thereupon he secretly carried Hsü on his back, fled away and hid in the territory of Hsia-ch'iu [prefecture] of Shan-yang. He personally chewed food to nourish [the infant]. Milk was produced in his breasts. He gave the dry [place to the child] and he himself took the wet [place]. He suffered all kinds of hardships. Although Hsü was a child in arms, [Li Shan] served him [in a way] not different from that for an adult master. When there was some affair, he always knelt, requested, and reported, and then put it in practice. [The people in] the village were all influenced by his behavior and followed each other in cultivating righteousness. When Hsü was ten years old, [Li] Shan returned to the native prefecture with him to manage the old property. He accused the male and female slaves before the chief officials, who arrested and killed all of them.

At that time Chung Li-i was the prefect of Hsia-ch'iu; he presented a memorial to the emperor to recommend the behavior of [Li] Shan. [Emperor] Kuang-wu issued an edict to appoint both [Li] Shan and [Li] Hsü members of the retinue of the heir apparent.

During the time of Hsien-tsung, [Li] Shan was summoned by [one of] A.D. 58-75 the offices of the [three] ministers, and because he was able to manage a troublesome [post], he was promoted twice and became the grand administrator of Jih-nan. On his way from the capital to his office, the road went through Yü-yang and passed by Li Yüan's grave. When he arrived at a place one *li* distant [from the grave] he removed his court garment, took a hoe and dug up grass. When he prostrated himself before the grave, he wept very sadly. He personally cooked and held the sacrificial utensils to perform the sacrifice. He wept tears and said, "Master and Mistress, Shan is here." He [remained there], mourned to the utmost for several days, and then left.

Upon arrival at his post, he governed with love and benevolence and won [the hearts of those who had] strange customs.[161] He was shifted to

[161] The Jih-nan commandery, which consisted of five prefectures with a population of 100,676 (69,485 in the Early Han), was located on the eastern coast of modern Annam. Its customs were different from those of China proper; therefore, "strange customs" are mentioned in the text.

the post of grand administrator of Chiu-chiang. Before he arrived at [his post], he became sick and died on the way. [Li] Hsü reached [the post of] chancellor of Ho-chien. [*HHS* 81:16b–17b]

54. Emancipation of Private Slaves

A.D. 26   On the day *kuei-wei* [of the fifth month in the second year of Chien-wu] an edict was issued saying, "As to those peoples' wives who have been remarried and children who have been sold,[162] if they wish to return to their fathers and mothers, let them do so. Whoever dares to hold them shall be punished according to the law." [*HHS* 1A:27a]

55. Scholar as a Hired Laborer Becomes an Official

End of Early Han   Wei Li, whose style was Tzu-ch'an, was a native of Hsiu-wu of Ho-nei. The family was poor. He was fond of learning. While studying he had no food to eat. He used to hire himself out in order to support himself.

A.D. 9–23
A.D. 26   In the time of Wang Mang he became an official in the commandery and later held the post of governor of a province. In the second year of Chien-wu he was summoned by the office of the grand minister of the masses, Teng Yü.[163] He was recommended as able to manage a troublesome [post] and was appointed attendant imperial secretary and prefect of Hsiang-ch'eng. He became renowned for his administration, and was

Ca. A.D. 40   promoted to the post of grand administrator of Kuei-yang.[164] [*HHS* 76:3a]

---

[162] Under the pressure of poverty a husband might give his wife to another and parents might sell their children.

[163] Teng Yü (2–58) was an important political and military aide of Kuang-wu during his campaign for the throne. Immediately after his accession in A.D. 25, the emperor made Teng grand minister of the masses and marquis of Tsan with a fief of ten thousand households. In A.D. 37, after the empire was pacified, he was enfeoffed as marquis of Kao-mi with a fief of four prefectures, but no longer held his ministerial position. When Emperor Ming came to the throne, Teng became grand tutor, but died in the same year. His descendants and relatives were favored because of his services (*HHS* 16:1a–10b).

[164] Wei Li 衛颯 held this post for ten years. In A.D. 49 Emperor Kuang-wu wanted to appoint him privy treasurer, but he was unable to accept because of illness. Two years later he was granted one hundred thousand cash. He died in retirement (*HHS* 76:4a).

56. THE INFLUENCE OF MONEYLENDERS

[Huan T'an[165] in his memorial said], "Now many of the rich travel-   *Ca.* A.D. 26
ing merchants and the big resident merchants lend money. Young men
of the families of medium means work for them as trusty runners, and
serve them as diligently as their servants. They collect an interest equal
to the revenue of an enfeoffed lord. For this reason the people admire
and imitate them, enjoying food without tilling the land. They even go
so far as to circulate in great number articles of luxury, thereby debauch-
ing people's eyes and ears." [*HHS* 28A:4b–5b]

57. SLAVE KILLS HIS MASTER

In the spring of the fifth year [of Chien-wu, P'eng] Ch'ung[166] was   A.D. 29
fasting and alone in his private side room. The Dark-green Head,[167]
Tzu-mi, and others, altogether three persons, taking advantage of
Ch'ung's being asleep, together bound him to his bed and informed the
officials who were outside that the Great King[168] was fasting and ordered
all the officials to take a rest. They falsely claimed that they had been
ordered by Ch'ung to arrest and bind the male and female slaves and
put them in two different places.

They also called Ch'ung's wife by a summons purporting to be from
him. The wife entered and was greatly frightened.[169] Ch'ung hurriedly
exclaimed, "Be quick to prepare the bags for the generals."[17] Thereupon two male slaves went inside with his wife to take the precious
things, and one male slave remained to watch Ch'ung. Ch'ung said to

[165] Huan T'an, a noted scholar, was recommended by the grand minister of works,
Sung Hung (26–30), and was made a gentleman discussant. Shortly after this memorial was written Huan was demoted because he opposed the emperor with regard to
questions arising over the building of the Spirit Tower; he died on the way to his new
position.

[166] P'eng Ch'ung was made acting grand administrator of the Yü-yang commandery
by the Keng-shih emperor when he ascended the throne. Later he followed Kuang-
wu and was given the rank of marquis with the title of grand general. Not satisfied
with this appointment, he rebelled in A.D. 26. In the following year he occupied the
city of Chi and made himself king of Yen (*HHS* 12:12b–15b).

[167] See II, 53, n. 160.

[168] He had made himself king of Yen.

[169] According to the *Tung-kuan Han-chi,* she was frightened and said, "The slaves
are rebelling." The slaves took her by the hair and slapped her on the cheeks (*TKHC*
23:7b).

[170] Li comments that Ch'ung called them "generals" because he hoped that they
would be pleased and release him.

the male slave who was guarding him, "You, my young boy, have always been beloved by me. Now you are only forced by Tzu-mi. Release my bonds. I will marry my daughter, Chu, to you, and all the wealth and property in my family will be given to you." The young male slave was going to release him, but looking outside the door, he saw that Tzu-mi was listening and did not dare to do so. Then [the two slaves] gathered gold, jade, clothing, and other articles, bringing them to the place of Ch'ung, packed, and loaded them on the backs of six horses. They ordered [Ch'ung's] wife to sew two silk bags. In the evening they untied Ch'ung's hands and ordered him to write a note to inform the general of the city gate, "Now I send Tzu-mi and others to enter Tzu-hou Lan-ch'ing's[171] place. Be quick to open the gate and let them out. Do not detain them." When the note was ready, they immediately beheaded Ch'ung and his wife and put their heads in the bags. Holding the note, they ran out the gate and went to the court. They were all ennobled [with the title of] unrighteous marquis.[172] [*HHS* 12:15b–16b]

58. Emancipation of Government Slaves

A.D. 30   On the day *ting-mao*[173] of the eleventh month [of the sixth year of Chien-wu] it was decreed that those officials and people who had been seized and made male and female slaves at the time of Wang Mang not in accordance with the old law were all to be freed and to become common people. [*HHS* 1B:3a–b]

A.D. 31   On the day *chia-yin* [of the fifth month of the seventh year of Chien-wu] it was decreed that those officials and people who had been made male and female slaves or concubines through famine, disorder, or capture by the bandits of Ch'ing and Hsü,[174] if they wished to go [free] or remain, were to be permitted to do so without restriction. Anyone

---

[171] Tzu-hou Lan-ch'ing 子后蘭卿 was a younger cousin of P'eng Ch'ung. He was distrusted by P'eng because he had been sent back by Emperor Kuang-wu. Therefore P'eng ordered him to lead the army outside the city (*HHS* 12:14b–15b).

[172] The title "unrighteous marquis" is of interest. Since P'eng Ch'ung was a rebel, the act of the slaves in killing him was considered meritorious, but at the same time the act of murdering a master was not approved (cf. *TKHC* 23:7b–8a).

[173] According to Hoang (Pierre Hoang, *Concordance des chronologies néoméniques chinoise et européenne* [Shanghai, 1910], p. 111) there was no day *ting-mao* in the eleventh month of the sixth year of Chien-wu.

[174] That is, the Red Eyebrow bandits, who were for the most part in Ch'ing and Hsü regional divisions (modern Shantung, Kiangsu, and Anhui).

daring to bar their return by duress was to be convicted under the law of The Selling of People.[175] [*HHS* 1B:5a–b]

59. TREATMENT OF SLAVES

On the day *chi-mao* in the second month of the spring of the eleventh A.D. 35 year [of Chien-wu] a decree was issued, saying, "It is the nature of Heaven and Earth that mankind is noble. Those who kill male or female slaves shall not have their punishment reduced." [*HHS* 1B:8b]

On the day *kuei-hai* [in the eighth month of the eleventh year of A.D. 35 Chien-wu] a decree was issued, saying, "Anyone daring to burn a male or female slave will be punished according to the law, and those who are burnt will be freed and permitted to become common people." [*HHS* 1B:9b]

60. ABOLISHMENT OF SPECIAL PUNISHMENT FOR SLAVES

On the day *jen-wu* in the tenth month in the winter [of the eleventh A.D. 35 year of Chien-wu] it was decreed that the law for executing in the marketplace male and female slaves who had shot and wounded people should be abolished. [*HHS* 1B:9b]

61. EMANCIPATION OF SLAVES IN SZECHWAN AND KANSU

On the day *kuei-yu* in the third month [of the twelfth year of Chien- A.D. 36 wu] it was decreed that of the people of the Lung[-hsi] and Shu commanderies[176] who had been seized and made male and female slaves, all those who had themselves made a complaint and those whom the judges failed to report should be freed and become common people. [*HHS* 1B:10a]

[175] According to the law, seizing and selling people, or selling and buying them by mutual agreement, to make them male and female slaves was punishable by death (see note to *HHSCC* 1B:4b).

[176] Lung refers to the Lung-hsi commandery (in modern Kansu), which was occupied by Wei Ao, who rebelled against Han in A.D. 30 and died in 33. This edict was issued shortly after the submission of Wei Ao's son, Wei Ch'un 隗純, and his generals in the winter of A.D. 34 (*HHS* 1B:2a, 7a, and 8a, 13:14a–b and 19a).

Shu refers to the Shu commandery (in modern Szechwan). In the years A.D. 35 and 36 the Han army was waging war against Kung-sun Shu, the ruler of Shu. This edict was issued shortly before the defeat of Kung-sun Shu, who died in the eleventh month of 36 (see *HHS* 1B:10b, 13:32a). Obviously it was an attempt to win the hearts of the people of Lung-hsi and Shu in order to speed up the conquest.

A.D. 38   On the day *chia-yin* in the twelfth month of the winter [of the thirteenth year of Chien-wu] it was decreed that all the people of I province[177] who had been seized and made male and female slaves since the
eighth year [of Chien-wu][178] were to be freed and made commoners.
Those who, depending upon [others], had become concubines and who
now wished to leave were to be allowed to do so. Those who dared to
detain them would be sentenced in the same way as those in the two
provinces of Ch'ing and Hsü according to the law of seizing people.[179]
[*HHS* 1B:13a]

A.D. 39   On the day *kuei-mao* in the twelfth month [of the fourteenth year of
Chien-wu] it was decreed that all the male and female slaves of the two
provinces of I and Liang[180] who since the eighth year [of Chien-wu][181]
had themselves made a complaint before the officials in the place where
they were staying were to be freed and made commoners. Those who
had sold themselves did not have to pay back the money. [*HHS*
1B:13b–14a]

62. A Thousand Slaves Owned by a Family of Officials

A.D. 37–59   The Tou[182] family had one ducal minister,[183] two marquises,[184] three

[177] I province included Shu and other commanderies.

[178] The reason for antedating this order to the eighth year of Chien-wu (A.D. 32) is
not clear. Li comments that this refers to the time of Kung-sun Shu. However, it
should be noted that Kung-sun Shu had been the ruler of Shu since A.D. 24 (first as
king of Shu, then as emperor of his Ch'eng-chia 成家 dynasty). A major military
campaign was launched against Wei Ao in A.D. 31, the same year in which he was
appointed king of Shuo-ning by Kung-sun Shu. In A.D. 32 Kung-sun Shu sent troops
to rescue the besieged Wei Ao and to help him reoccupy T'ien-shui and Lung-hsi
(*HHS* 1A:14b and 18b, 1B:4b and 6a–b, 13:15b, 16a–19a, 22b, 23b, and 29b).
However, since neither T'ien-shui nor Lung-hsi was in I province, the date A.D. 32
does not seem connected with these operations. There is even some doubt as to the
meaning of "I-chou," here rendered "I province." There was also a *commandery*
named "I-chou" (same characters), but since this decree subsequently refers to other
provinces, we assume that I-chou indicates the province. This edict was issued one
year after the conquest of Shu and the death of Kung-sun Shu (*HHS* 1B:8b–10b,
13:30a–32a).

[179] See II, 58, n. 175. A marquis was executed because he had seized another's
wife (*HHSCC* 1B:10b).

[180] Liang province (roughly, modern Kansu) included, among others, the commanderies of T'ien-shui and Lung-hsi; see note 178 above.

[181] See note 178 above.

[182] For the family of Tou Jung, see III, 54.

[183] This refers to Tou Jung who held the post of grand minister of works, one of the
three ducal ministers in the court, from A.D. 37 to 44.

[184] Tou Jung was marquis of An-feng, and his younger brother Yu was marquis of
Hsien-ch'in (*HHS* 23:12b).

princesses,[185] and four 2,000-picul officials,[186] all at the same time. The government offices and mansions [of these members] from the grandfather down to the grandsons faced one another in the imperial capital. Their male and female slaves numbered a thousand. There was none among the imperial relatives and consort families and the meritorious officials who could match this family. [*HHS* 23:14b]

63. POWERFUL SLAVE KILLS A COMMONER

At this time,[187] a Dark-green Head[188] of the princess of Hu-yang[189] killed a man in the daytime and hid in the home of the princess; the officials were not able to seize him. [Later] when the princess went out and the male slave was escorting her in the carriage, Tung Hsüan[190] awaited them at Hsia-men canton. He then stopped the carriage, held the horse, and drew lines on the ground with his knife, loudly enumerating the faults of the princess. He shouted at the male slave, made him descend from the carriage, and then killed him. The princess at once returned to the palace and complained to the emperor. The emperor was very angry, summoned Hsüan, and wanted to have him beaten to

Before
A.D. 44

---

[185] Three members of the family, Jung's eldest son, Mu, Mu's son, Hsün, and Yu's son, Ku, all married princesses; see III, 54, n. 289.

[186] The four 2,000-picul posts held by the family, according to Li, were: (1) commandant of the guard, held by Tou Jung, (2) colonel of the guards of the city gates, held by Tou Yu and later by Mu after Yu's death, (3) "colonel who guards against the Ch'iang," held by Tou Lin 寶林, Jung's cousin's son, (4) general of the palace gentlemen, held by Tou Ku (*HHS* 23:14a–b, 16b).

[187] Ts'ai Mao's 蔡茂 biography mentions that he presented a memorial to praise the uprightness of Tung Hsüan 董宣 in killing the slave of the princess and to request that persons associated with the consort families should be dealt with more strictly. Ts'ai was the grand administrator of Kuang-han when Tung's case occurred, being promoted to the post of minister of the masses in A.D. 44 (*HHS* 26:16a–b). We therefore date the events of this passage as taking place before A.D. 44.

[188] See II, 53, n. 160. In the following sentence, the Dark-green Head is called *nu*, which suggests the interchangeability of the two terms.

[189] The princess of Hu-yang, whose name was Huang, was the eldest of the three daughters of Emperor Kuang-wu's father. She was ennobled as princess in A.D. 26 (*HHS* 14:8b).

[190] Tung Hsüan had been the chancellor of Pei-hai kingdom. He was arrested and sentenced to death because of the many killings involved in the extermination of one of the powerful families, but he was pardoned by the emperor. Sometime later he was appointed grand administrator of the Chiang-hsia commandery, only to be dismissed again when he insulted an official who was a member of the consort family. At the time of the present incident he was sixty-nine years old and prefect of Lo-yang. He remained in this office until his death some five years later. At his death his property consisted of several piculs of wheat and a worn-out carriage (*HHS* 77:2b–4b).

death. Hsüan kowtowed and said, "I ask to say some words before my death." The emperor said, "What would you like to say?" Hsüan said, "Your Majesty revives [the Han dynasty] with His sage virtue, and yet is lenient to the killing of [one of the] good people by a slave. How can [Your Majesty] govern the empire? Your servant need not be beaten. I request permission to kill myself." He then hit his head on a pillar. The blood was flowing all over his face. The emperor ordered a lesser attendant of the Yellow Gate[191] to hold him and ordered Hsüan to kowtow and apologize to the princess. Hsüan did not obey. [The emperor ordered them] to force him to bow his head. With his two hands resting on the ground, Hsüan after all was unwilling to prostrate himself. The princess said [to the emperor], "Wen-shu,[192] when you were a commoner[193] you hid the fugitives and [criminals sentenced to] death, and the officials did not dare to come to your gate. Now you are the Son of Heaven; can your majesty not influence a prefect?" The emperor laughed and said, "The Son of Heaven is not the same as a commoner." Then he ordered the unyielding prefect out and bestowed on him three hundred thousand cash. Hsüan gave them all to his subordinates. [*HHS* 77:3b–4b]

64. SLAVES GRANTED BY EMPEROR

A.D. 64   After the funeral[194] Ts'ang[195] then went back to his kingdom. [Em-

---

[191] The position of lesser attendant of the Yellow Gate was held by a eunuch.

[192] Wen-shu was the style of Emperor Kuang-wu (*HHS* 1A:1a).

[193] *Pai-i* 白衣 means "white clothes"; they were worn by humble persons in Han times. According to Yen, *pai-i* refers to those humble persons who served in the government as runners (Yen: *HS* 72:20b). One instance is recorded in which white clothes were worn by the private slaves and guests of Emperor Ch'eng when he went out incognito (*HS* 10:9a, note). Merchants also wore white clothes (*SKC*, Wu, 9:21b).

However, commoners were usually referred to as *pai-i*, as shown in the present passage. Since commoners were allowed to wear green and blue (see *HS* 10:14a), it seems unlikely that white was the only color worn by the commoners and it is doubtful that many of them actually did wear white clothes as suggested by Ku Yen-wu (*JCLCS* 24:24a–b). Instances seem to suggest that *pai-i* was merely a conventional expression applicable to all the people who were not officials, including the potential candidates for officialdom, the scholars (*SC* 121:3b; *HHS* 52:14b, 70:22a). The term was used loosely as a synonym for commoners as against officials, probably because officials usually wore more colorful garments. In one instance a scholar who had been a student in the Imperial Academy was referred to by this term by a high official who pointed out that it was improper for an emperor to receive a *pai-i* (*HHS* 52:14b).

[194] The funeral of the empress dowager, the mother of Emperor Ming and Liu Ts'ang 劉蒼.

[195] Liu Ts'ang was King Hsien of Tung-p'ing. He was one of the sons of Emperor Kuang-wu and was made king in A.D. 41. When Emperor Ming, his brother by the same mother, ascended the throne, he was appointed general of the flash cavalry. He resigned in A.D. 62.

peror Ming] gave him a special grant of five hundred palace ladies and male and female slaves. [*HHS* 42:15b]

65. SORCERER'S FAMILY

When [Kao] Feng[196] was old, he still followed his bent and was not tired [of studying]. His fame was widespread. The grand administrator summoned him several times [for appointment to office]. Fearing that he might not be able to escape from [the appointment], he then announced that originally his was a sorcerer's family and that he was not qualified to be an official. He also pretended to have litigation over land with his widowed sister-in-law. Thereupon he did not become an official.

Before
A.D. 76

During the Chien-ch'u reign period the grand court architect, Jen Wei, recommended Feng [to the court] as a "straight speaker."[197] Arriving at the office of the official carriages,[198] he pretended to be ill, escaped, and returned. He gave all his property to the orphan son of his older brother. He hid himself in the guise of a fisherman and died at home. [*HHS* 83:14b–15a]

A.D. 76–84

66. PIG HERDER BECOMES STUDENT AND OFFICIAL

Ch'eng Kung, whose style was Shao-tzu, was a native of Ku-mu of Lang-ya. He lost his father when he was a child. At eight years of age he herded pigs for others. In the village there was a man, Hsü Tzu-sheng, who gave instruction in the *Ch'un-ch'iu* classic to several hundred students. Kung passed there and rested beside the house. He liked the instruction and therefore approached to hear about the classic; then he asked to stay there as a student.[199] For his fellow students he gathered

First half
of first
century
A.D.

---

[196] According to Kao's biography, his family was engaged in farming. He was a student in his youth, and later became a famous scholar and teacher (*HHS* 83:14b–15a).

[197] "Straight speaker" or "those who are able to speak out frankly and to admonish [the emperor] fully" was one of the several categories under which scholars might be named by officials and recommended for office. See *HS* 4:8b and 14b, 6:1a–b, 8:9a, 9:4a and 8b–9a, 10:4b and 14b, 11:7b; *HHS* 3:6a and 10a, 4:12a, 5:4a and 12b, 6:3b, 7:3a, 6b, and 10b.

[198] All those who were summoned to the court by the dispatch carriages reported to the office of the prefect of official carriages at the major's gate *(kung-chü ssu-ma ling* 公車司馬令) on their arrival. See *HS* 10:4b; *HHS* 1B:5a, 3:10a, 4:12a, 5:12b.

[199] According to the *Hsü-Han-shu,* quoted by Li, when Ch'eng Kung 承宮 passed by Hsü Tzu-sheng's 徐子盛 house, he so enjoyed the lecture that he left the pigs and

firewood and worked hard. For several years he studied diligently without ever being tired. After he thoroughly understood the classics, he
then returned home and taught. Faced with the disorder[200] in the
empire, he led his students to Han-chung and took refuge there. Later,
with his wife and children he went to Meng-yin Mountain and worked
hard, tilling and sowing. When the *ho* millet and the *shu* millet were
about to ripen, someone claimed [the crop]. Kung did not dispute with
him but yielded it and went away. Because of this, he became famous.

He was summoned repeatedly by the three offices[201] and declined.
A.D. 58–76 During the Yung-p'ing period he was summoned to the office of the
official carriages.[202] When the emperor went to the Imperial Academy,
he called Kung and made him an erudite. [Later] he was promoted to
the post of general of the palace gentlemen of the left. . . . In the
seventeenth year [of Yung-p'ing] he was appointed libationer in attendance in the palace. He died in the first year of Chien-ch'u. [*HHS*
27:17b–18b]

67. More Than One Thousand Slaves Owned

A.D. 76–83 [Ma] Fang and his younger brother both were noble and prosperous.[203] Each of them had over a thousand male and female slaves,
and their property was valued in millions. Both of them bought the
extremely fertile and good land in the capital region. They also built
mansions and buildings on a large scale. . . . Guests from all four directions rushed to gather there. Tu Tu[204] of Ching-chao and several hun-

---

remained to listen. The owner of the pigs found Kung after a search and wanted to
beat him. The students prevented the owner from beating Ch'eng and kept him with
them.

[200] This refers to the wars and rebellions during the latter part of Wang Mang's
reign and the early years of the Later Han before the empire was unified.

[201] The three offices refer to the three highest offices in the central government: the
grand commandant, the minister of the masses, and the minister of works.

[202] On this office see II, 65, n. 198.

[203] Ma Fang and Ma Kuang were sons of Ma Yüan, the famous "billow-subduing
general" of the time of Emperor Kuang-wu. Their sister was the empress of Emperor
Ming. When Emperor Chang came to the throne, Ma Fang was given the post of
general of chariots and cavalry and at the same time held the office of colonel of the
guards of the city gates. His brother, Ma Kuang, was also promoted to the post of
chief of police. In A.D. 79 they were made marquises, each with a fief of six thousand
households. After the death of the empress dowager they were accused of living too
luxuriously and were dismissed from office. Ma Kuang was reappointed but committed suicide in A.D. 90 because he had been falsely accused of being a rebel (*HHS*
24:29b–32b).

[204] Tu Tu 杜篤 was known as a man of outstanding literary ability. He died about
A.D. 78 (*HHS* 80A:1b–12b).

dred other persons were permanent food-consuming guests and stayed
in their houses. Many inspectors, grand administrators, and prefects
came from their family. [*HHS* 24:31b–32a]

68. Number of Slaves Owned by a King

Henceforth K'ang[205] built up a huge fortune and erected palaces and $\quad$ A.D. 83
houses on a large scale. His male and female slaves numbered fourteen
hundred, the horses in his stable twelve hundred, and his private land
eight hundred *ch'ing*. [*HHS* 42:10b]

69. Slaves from the Western Regions

The Western Regions were prosperous and rich and abounded in $\quad$ After
$\quad$ A.D. 89
precious things. The attending sons[206] of the various states, the supervisor of the emissaries,[207] and the barbarian merchants frequently
presented to [Li] Hsün[208] male and female slaves, horses of [Ta]
Yüan,[209] gold, silver, spices, woolen cloth, and other things. He accepted
none of them. [*HHS* 51:1b–2a]

[205] Liu K'ang 劉康, king of Chi-nan, was a son of Emperor Kuang-wu.

[206] The "attending sons" were the sons of the rulers of the various states in the
Western Regions who were sent to China to attend the emperor after these states had
submitted to Han (*HHS* 88:2a). Actually they were hostages. After Pan Ch'ao con-
quered the Western Regions in A.D. 94, at least fifty states submitted and sent hostages
(*HHS* 88:3a; cf. Yang Lien-sheng, "Hostages in Chinese History," *Harvard Journal of
Asiatic Studies*, XV [1952], 509 ff.).

[207] The supervisor of emissaries (*tu-shih* 督使), according to Li, supervised the
emissaries of the barbarian states.

[208] Li Hsün studied the *Shih-ching* with comments by Han Ying 韓嬰 and became a
leacher of several hundred students. He was appointed attendant imperial secretary,
tater promoted to the post of inspector of Yen regional division, and then made grand
administrator of Chang-yeh. The gifts mentioned above were made to him after his
appointment as internuncio and lieutenant-colonel (*fu-hsiao-wei* 副校尉) of the
Western Regions, in which capacity he supervised the various states of the Western
Regions and guarded against attacks. He was later promoted to the post of grand
administrator of Wu-wei and then found guilty of a crime and dismissed. He returned
to his village on foot and stayed in a grass hut, making his living by plaiting mats;
there were also some students with him at the time. He died at his home at the age
of ninety-six (*HHS* 51:1a–2b).

[209] Ta-yüan 大宛, one of the states of the Western Regions, was famous for its
horses. To obtain these horses Emperor Wu sent an expeditionary force against Ta-
yüan in 104 B.C.

70. MERCHANTS ENLISTED IN EXPEDITIONARY FORCE

A.D. 94   In the autumn of the sixth year [of Yung-yüan, Pan] Ch'ao[210] thereupon mobilized the soldiers of eight countries, Chiu-tzu, Shan-shan,[211]
and others, totaling seventy thousand, and officers, soldiers, and traveling merchants, [numbering] one thousand four hundred, to attack
Yen-ch'i.[212] [*HHS* 47:12b–13a]

71. SCHOLAR WAGE LABORER REFUSES GOVERNMENT INVITATION

Second
century
A.D.

Hou Chin, whose style was Tzu-yü, was a native of Tun-huang.
While he was young he lost his father and was poor, living in the house
of a clansman. By nature he was devoted to study. He frequently hired
himself out to make a living. Returning in the evening, he always made
a wood fire in order to read. He always cultivated himself by the rules
of propriety. When he was alone in his room, he acted as though he
were facing an austere guest.

Many times he was summoned by his province and commandery and
he was summoned by the office of the official carriages[213] under the
category of "having propriety."[214] Each time he pretended to be ill and
did not go. . . . He moved to a mountain, where he devoted himself to
meditation and writing.[215] [*HHS* 80B:21a]

[210] Pan Ch'ao (32–103) without much military assistance brought more than fifty
of the western countries to submission. He was made marquis of Ting-yüan in A.D.
95. See Édouard Chavannes, "Trois Généraux chinois de la dynastie des Han orientaux," *T'oung Pao*, VII (1906), 210–69.

[211] Chiu-tzu 龜茲 is now the city of K'u-ch'e, situated at the confluence of the
Muzart River and the K'u-ch'e River at the foot of the Tien Shan. Shan-shan or
Charkhlik is roughly modern Shanshan in eastern Sinkiang. See Frederick John
Teggart, *Rome and China: A Study of Correlations in Historical Events* (Berkeley, 1939),
p. 113; Édouard Chavannes, "Les Pays d'Occident d'après le Wei-lio," *T'oung Pao*,
VI (1905), 531 ff.

[212] Yen-ch'i 焉耆, the city presently called Karachahr (in Turki meaning "black
town" [Teggart, *Rome and China*, p. 110; Chavannes, "Pays d'Occident," p. 531]) is to
the south of the Tien Shan, a few miles to the north of the place where the Yulduz
River flows into the Bagrach Kol.

[213] For the office of the official carriages, see II, 65, n. 198.

[214] "Having propriety" was one of the several additional categories introduced in
the Later Han under which scholars might be recommended for office. Usually such
scholars were required to answer examination questions, *tui ts'e*. However, in exceptional cases, as shown in the case of Hsü Chih 徐穉, one might be given an official
appointment immediately after the recommendation without being examined (cf.
HHS 53:7b, 61:33b; *THHY* 26:10a–11a).

[215] Hou Chin 侯瑾 was the author of the *Huang-te-chuan* and many miscellaneous
essays (*HHS* 80B:21a–b).

72. Eight Hundred Slaves Owned by an Official

[Che] Kuo[216] was the grand administrator of Yü-lin. . . . Kuo had a Second century A.D. wealth of two hundred thousand [cash] and eight hundred household slaves. [*HHS* 82A:18b]

73. Barbarians Submerged into Slavery

The Shao-ho tribe of the submitted Ch'iang people[217] of the An-ting A.D. 102 commandery compelled the various Ch'iang, numbering several hundred persons, to revolt. The forces of the commandery attacked and exterminated them. The weak[218] were all seized and made male and female slaves. [*HHS* 87:20a]

74. Emancipation of Government Slaves

On the day *i-hai* [of the second month if the fourth year of Yung- A.D. 110 ch'u] it was decreed that each of those who had been sentenced to be moved to the borders since the Chien-ch'u period [A.D. 76–84] because of improper words[219] or other crimes, was to be returned to his own commandery and those who had been made male and female slaves by the government were to be freed and made commoners. [*HHS* 5:10b]

75. Wage Laborer Becomes a Scholar

Ti-wu Fang, whose style was Chung-mou, was a native of Ch'ang- Before A.D. 126 ling of Ching-chao. He was the grandson of a remote paternal cousin of [Ti-wu] Lun,[220] the minister of works. In his youth he became an

---

[216] Because Che Kuo's great grandfather, Chang Chiang 張江, was the Marquis of Che, the family changed its surname to Che.

[217] The Ch'iang were composed of many tribes, of which the Shao-ho was one. The Ch'iang people who had been conquered by Ma Yüan in the early years of the Later Han frequently invaded the Han border in what is now Kansu from the time of Emperor An. They were a menace to the Han empire. A large number who submitted were moved to various commanderies in Kansu and lived together with the Chinese (see *HHS* 87:10b–11a, 21a). In 101, defeated by the Han army, more than six thousand Ch'iang people submitted and were moved to Han-yang, An-ting, and Lung-hsi. Those who lived in An-ting rebelled in the following year (*HHS* 87:19b–20a). Revolts of this kind were frequent among those who had submitted to Han.

[218] That is, the young women and immature boys.

[219] For "improper words," see I, 16, n. 66.

[220] Ti-wu Lun began his career as a low-ranking subordinate under the governor of the capital region. In A.D. 51 he was recommended as "filially pious and incorrupt"

orphan and was poor. He used to hire himself out as a farmer laborer in order to support his elder brother and his sister-in-law. Whenever he had leisure, he studied literature.

He became a merit evaluator in the commandery government. He was recommended as "filially pious and incorrupt" and was appointed prefect of Hsin-tu prefecture. . . . [Later] he was promoted to the post of grand administrator of the Chang-yeh commandery.[221] [*HHS* 76;20a–b]

76. Pig Breeding a Humble Occupation

Before
A.D. 141
Wu Yu, whose style was Chi-ying, was a native of Ch'ang-yüan of Ch'en-liu. His father, Hui, was the grand administrator of Nan-hai. Yu, at the age of twelve, accompanied [his father] to the office. . . . When he was twenty, he lost his father. Although there was not [a saving of a] single jar[222] or a picul in his home, he refused to accept any aid or gift. He usually herded pigs in the marsh of Ch'ang-yüan and read the classics while walking. Once he met an old friend of his father who said to him, "You are the son of a 2,000-picul official and yet you engage in such a mean occupation. Even though you have no sense of shame, how about your father?" Yu apologized but persisted in his intent as before.

Later, he was recommended as "filially pious and incorrupt" [by the commandery government]. At his departure the commandery government held a sacrifice to the Spirit of the Road[223] for him. . . .

---

and two years later became grand administrator of the K'uai-chi commandery. After holding a number of important offices, he became minister of works in A.D. 75 (*HHS* 41:1a ff.).

[221] Then Ti-wu Fang 第五訪 was appointed grand administrator of the Nan-yang commandery, and in 155 he was transferred to the post of colonel who guards against the Ch'iang, which he held until his death in 159 (*HHS* 87:36b–37a).

[222] According to Ying Shao, a small jar with the capacity of two *hu* was called a *tan* 檐 (or 擔 or 儋) by the people of Ch'i. *Tan* also has the meaning of the weight which can be carried on one's shoulder (*HS* 45:5a).

[223] *Tsu* 祖 was the sacrifice to the Spirit of the Road (祖道 or 行神) held before a traveler set out on his journey to insure his safety while en route. It was also called *tao* 道, "road," sacrifice or *pa* 軷, "to cross the mountain," sacrifice. The three are synonymous (*MSCS* 2 (3):4a–b; Cheng and Chia: *ILCS* 24:3b–3a; Tu and Kung: *TCCS* 44:3b). According to the *Feng-su t'ung-i*, Hsiu 修, the son of Kung Kung 共工, who was fond of traveling, was the spirit worshipped (*FSTI* 8:9a). However, some authors identify the spirit as Lei-tsu 纍祖, the son of Huang-ti (Yen K'o-chün, comp., *Ch'üan Hou-Han wen* in *Ch'üan shang-ku san-tai Ch'in Han san-kuo liu-ch'ao wen* [Huang-kang Wang-shih ed., 1894], 47:7a, hereafter cited as *CHHW;* Yen: *HS* 53:3a). During the sacrifice, soil was piled on the road to signify a hill and a tablet to present to the spirit was made of straw and thorns. Wine and dried meat were offered and

Yu, being characterized as of the "four conducts"[224] by the superintendent of the imperial court, was promoted to the post of chancellor of the marquis of Chiao-tung.[225] [*HHS* 64:1a–2b]

77. POWERFUL SLAVE

[Liang] Chi's[226] beloved superintendent male slave, Ch'in Kung, became an official and reached the post of prefect of the grand granary.[227] He could go into the place where Shou[228] lived. When seeing Kung, Shou always dismissed her attendants, pretending to discuss affairs, and had illicit relations with him. Being in favor both within and without,[229] Kung's awe and power shook the world. All the inspectors and 2,000-picul [officials] visited him to bid him farewell when they left. [*HHS* 34:17a–b]

A.D. 141–159

78. THOUSANDS OF COMMONERS ENSLAVED

[Liang Chi] sometimes seized good people and made all of them male

A.D. 141–159

---

then a farewell feast was held there by those who came to see the traveler off. Finally the carriage ran over the piled-up soil and started on the journey, symbolizing that there was no obstacle on the way. (See *ILCS* 19:3b–4a, 24:2b–3a; *CLCS* 32:9a; *LCCS* 17:5b; *TCCS* 44:3b–4a; *SWCTC* 15:102–3; *TYTT* A:10a; Ssu-ma: *SC* 59:2a; Yen: *HS* 71:4b, 53:3a, 66:5a; Li: *HHS* 64:2a.) Since a farewell feast followed the sacrifice the *tsu* also served a social purpose.

[224] According to Han regulations, those with the rank of gentleman who had merit, had been in service for a long time, and had revealed outstanding talent and virtue were to be recommended by the superintendent of the imperial court as men of "abundant talent" and the "four conducts" (*HHS* 61:31a–b). The "four conducts" were honesty, simplicity, modesty, and frugality (*HHS* 64:2b; *Han-kuan-i*, quoted by Yen).

[225] After nine years in Chiao-tung Wu Yu 吳祐 was promoted to the post of chancellor of the kingdom of Ch'i and later was made chief clerk by the grand general, Liang Chi. He resigned when he disagreed with Liang Chi, who attempted to accuse Li Ku falsely (see II, 80). Wu went home and spent his leisure in caring for his garden and vegetables and in teaching the classics. He died at the age of ninety-eight. His eldest son, Feng 鳳, later became the grand administrator of Lo-lang, and his youngest son, K'ai 愷, was a prefect (*HHS* 64:4a–b).

[226] See III, 63.

[227] The grand granary had one prefect under the direction of the ministry of agriculture. He had the rank of a 600-picul official. He received the grain that had been transported from the various commanderies and kingdoms of the empire (*HHC* 26:2a).

[228] Shou was Liang Chi's wife.

[229] That is, he was the favorite both of Liang Chi and his wife.

and female slaves, to the number of several thousand persons. He called them "self-sold persons."²³⁰ [*HHS* 34:19b]

79. BUSINESSMEN NOT QUALIFIED TO BECOME OFFICIALS

A.D.
141–219   Wang Lieh, whose style was Yen-fang,²³¹ was a native of T'ai-yüan. When he was young, he studied under the tutorship of Ch'en Shih.²³² He was known in his village because of his righteous behavior. Once a man stole a cow and was caught by the owner. The thief apologized and said, "I will take any kind of punishment, but, please, do not let Wang Yen-fang know of it." Hearing this, Lieh sent a man to thank him and presented him with a roll of cloth.²³³ . . .

Those who had disputes about what was right and wrong would take up the matter with Lieh; some turned back when they were half way and some turned back when they saw his house. Such was the effect of his virtue over people.

He was recommended as "filially pious and incorrupt" and was summoned at the same time by the offices of the three ministers. He declined everything. Meeting with the disorders of the Yellow Turbans
A.D.
184–192   and Tung Cho, he then fled to Liao-tung. The barbarians honored and respected him. The grand administrator, Kung-sun Tu,²³⁴ treated him as a brother and asked his advice on government matters. He wanted to make him chief clerk. Lieh then debased himself by becoming a merchant and was thus able to avoid appointment. Hearing of his high

---

²³⁰ He called these people "self-sold persons" in order to justify his behavior.

²³¹ According to the *Wei-chih*, Wang Lieh's style was Yen-k'ao (*SKC*, Wei, 11:23a-b).

²³² Ch'en Shih 陳寔, who was a native of Hsü, came from a poor and humble family. In his youth he became a minor official in the prefectural government. His devotion to study greatly impressed the prefect, who sent him to study in the Imperial Academy. Later Ch'en became a prefect. In 166 he was involved in the case of the Partisans and surrendered himself to imprisonment. After he was released he became a subordinate of Tou Wu, the grand general. After the execution of the Partisans in 169, he did not enter officialdom again. Although he never reached high office, his reputation was so high that he was usually considered as a qualified candidate for the post of a high-ranking minister. He declined to accept any appointment and died in 187, at the age of eighty-four. More than thirty thousand persons attended his funeral. He was posthumously designated as *wen-fan hsien-sheng* 文範先生 by the public (*HHS* 62:17b–20b).

²³³ As a token of encouragement and in the hope that the thief had reformed, in which hope he proved to be right (*HHS* 81:35b–36a).

²³⁴ Kung-sun Tu 公孫度 later made himself marquis of Liao-tung (A.D. 190). On Ts'ao Ts'ao's recommendation he was made the Wu-wei general and the marquis of Yung-ning district. He died in 204 (*HHS* 74B:11b–12a; *SKC*, Wei, 8:12b–14a).

repute, Ts'ao Ts'ao sent to summon him, but he did not come. In the
twenty-fourth year of Chien-an, he died at the age of seventy-eight in
Liao-tung. [*HHS* 81:35b–36a]   A.D. 219

80. Minister Accused of Appointing Businessmen

Formerly, in the time of Emperor Shun, many among the appointed A.D.
144–146 officials were not appointed in sequence. When [Li] Ku[235] was in charge of government matters, he presented a memorial petitioning for the dismissal of more than one hundred [such officials]. Since these persons hated him and at the same time wanted to please [Liang] Chi,[236] they together presented an urgent memorial to charge Ku falsely, saying, ". . . he selected a great number of merchant-small men[237] and appointed them prefects or clerks." [*HHS* 63:13a–b]

[235] Li Ku was the son of Li Ho 李郃, the minister of the masses. In 133 he was recommended, answered the examination questions, and was appointed gentleman discussant. His answers greatly displeased the emperor's wet nurse and the powerful eunuchs, who then accused him of a certain crime. He was proved innocent and appointed prefect, a post which he refused to take. He returned home and shortly thereafter was appointed attendant official and palace gentleman *(ts'ung-shih chung-lang* 從事中郎) by Liang Shang, the grand general. Later he held the posts of inspector of Ching Division, grand administrator of T'ai-shan, and then grand court architect *(chiang-tso ta-chiang* 將作大匠). He became grand commandant in 145. On the death of the three-year-old Emperor Ch'ung, Li Ku and Liang Chi, the grand general, disagreed with each other in the selection of an emperor. Those officials who disliked Li and attempted to please Liang accused Li of recommending his students for office, of receiving bribes in making appointments, and of appointing his relatives, acquaint-ances, and a number of merchants, as mentioned in our text. However, the accusation was turned down by the empress dowager, Liang Chi's younger sister. After the nine-year-old Emperor Chih had been murdered by Liang Chi, there was again a dispute between Li and Liang concerning the appointment of a new emperor. Li Ku was dismissed in 146 and Emperor Huan was put on the throne by Liang Chi. Li was later falsely charged by Liang of plotting with Liu Wen 劉文 and Liu Wei 劉鮪 to make the king of Ch'ing-ho, whom Li had nominated in the earlier conferences, the emperor. Li Ku was imprisoned and put to death in 147. Two of his sons were also arrested and put to death in prison (*HHS* 63:1a ff.).

[236] Liang Chi was at that time the grand general. He disliked Li Ku and envied him (see note 235).

[237] *Ku-shu* 賈豎, "merchant-small man," was a term of insult, the word *shu* meaning "boy" (*TCCS* 26:15b). When such expressions as *shu-tzu* 豎子 or *shu-ju* 豎儒 are applied to an adult, they have the meaning of immaturity or stupidity (*SC* 7:17b; *HS* 1A:25b, 43:2a). *Shu* also means "small servant" (*HNT* 18:4b). The term *ku-shu* appears quite frequently in Han texts (see *SC* 107:12b; *HS* 52:11a, 66:14b). Its popularity reflects the general attitude toward businessmen at this time.

81. Scholar-Hermit

Before
A.D. 142

[Chang] K'ai,[238] whose style was Kung-ch'ao, specialized in the *Ch'un-ch'iu* of the Yen school[239] and the *Shang-shu* in ancient characters. His disciples frequently numbered up to a hundred, and guests admired him. From the mature scholars of his father's lineage [to others], all called at his door. Carriages and horses blocked the street and the attendants and followers had no place to rest. Thereupon many families of eunuchs and nobles erected inns in the lane to serve the passing guests for profit. K'ai disliked such things and frequently moved to avoid them. His family was poor[240] and he had no means for taking up an occupation. He frequently rode in a donkey-wagon and went to the prefectural [seat] to sell drugs. As soon as he obtained enough for his food he returned to his village.

He was recommended as "abundantly talented" by the colonel-director of the retainers and appointed prefect of Ch'ang-ling prefecture. He did not go to the post and dwelt in seclusion in the Hung-nung Mountains. Scholars followed him there so that a market grew up at the place where he lived. Later on, therefore, there was the Kung-ch'ao Market south of the Hua-yin Mountains.

He was summoned many times by the five offices[241] and was recommended as "wise and virtuous" and "square and upright" but he
A.D. 142   did not accept. In the first year of Han-an, Emperor Shun sent a special edict to inform the Governor of Honan, saying, "The former prefect of Ch'ang-ling, Chang K'ai, is a man whose behavior emulates that of

[238] Chang K'ai's 張楷 father, Chang Pa 張霸, also a famous scholar, had been grand administrator of the K'uai-chi commandery sometime between 89 and 105 and later attendant within the palace. He died at the age of seventy (*HHS* 36:25b–27a).

[239] The founder of the school was Yen P'eng-tsu 嚴彭祖, who was a student of Kuei Hung 眭弘, the leading authority in the study of the *Ch'un-ch'iu* (for Kuei Hung, see *HS* 75:1a–b). After the death of their teacher, P'eng-tsu and Yen An-lo 顏安樂 each established his own school, and thereafter the study of the *Kung-yang Ch'un-ch'iu* was divided into two different schools. Yen P'eng-tsu was an erudite during the time of Emperor Hsüan (73–48 B.C.) and later became the grand tutor of the heir apparent (see *HS* 88:22a–b).

The fact that Chang K'ai was a specialist in the Yen school was obviously owing to the influence of his father, who had studied Yen's *Ch'un-ch'iu* from Fan Shu 樊鯈, later re-editing the work edited by Fan. The book was given the title, *The Study of the Chang Family* 張氏學 (*HHS* 36:26a–b).

[240] Since his father had been a 2,000-picul official and did not die until he was old, the family could not have been poor during the father's lifetime. Probably the un-corrupt father had not left much property.

[241] The five offices were those of the grand tutor, the grand commandant, the minister of the masses, the minister of works, and the grand general (Li: *HHS* 36:27b).

Yüan Hsien,[242] whose resolution matches that of I and Ch'i,[243] and who values noble status lightly and enjoys humility. While hiding in the lonely marsh, his high intent is so firm that he alone rises far above the ordinary. Previously [the government] summoned him several times, but he hesitated to come. Is this because the officials who are in charge are in the habit of being insufficiently polite to the virtuous, thus making it difficult for him to come?" At the time the commandery government [wanted to] send him [to the capital] with courtesy, but K'ai again reported himself sick and did not go. . . .

In the third year of Chien-ho an edict was issued to invite him with A.D. 149 the "comfortable carriage" and with all the courtesies.[244] K'ai refused because of serious illness and did not go. At the age of seventy he died at home.

His son, Ling, whose style was Ch'u-ch'ung, was an official and attained the rank of master of writing. Ling's younger brother . . . Hsüan, whose style was Ch'u-hsü, was a profound thinker and had great ability. He did not become an official because of the disorders of the time. The minister of works, Chang Wen, [tried to] appoint him with courtesy several times but could not get him. . . . He dwelt in seclusion in Lu-yang Mountain. When Tung Cho held the reins of A.D. 185-192 government, he heard about him and nominated him to be a bureau head and recommended him as an attendant imperial secretary [but Hsüan] did not accept. Cho exercised his authority through military force, and, having no alternative, he was forced to set off. When he reached Lun-shih prefecture he became ill and died on the way. [*HHS* 36:27a–30a]

82. Book Dealer

Liu Liang,[245] whose style was Man-shan, and who had another name,

---

[242] Yüan Hsien 原憲 was a disciple of Confucius and was poor and virtuous.

[243] I and Ch'i refer to the two brothers, Po-i and Shu-ch'i, the sons of Ku-chu Chün of the Shang dynasty. When Shang was overthrown by Chou, they were ashamed to eat grain produced in the land of the Chou. They escaped to Shou-yang Mountain, where they starved to death.

[244] "With courtesies" refers to the rolls of black silk offered as a present to honor the man to whom they were presented. Sometimes a jade *pi* or a goat was also included (see *HS* 88:15b–16a; *HHS* 53:4a, 61:43a). In Early and Later Han times, renowned scholars of extraordinary virtue or accomplishments were invited to the court with "comfortable carriages" and with the courtesies of such presents (see *HHHY* 44:9b; *THHY* 27:6a–10b).

[245] Liu Liang 劉梁 was famous for the writing of essays, one of which is included in his biography. When he held the post of chief of Pei-hsin-ch'eng, he established a

Ch'en, was a native of Ning-yang prefecture of Tung-p'ing. Liang was
a descendant of the imperial house. When he was young he lost his
father[246] and was poor. He sold books in the market to support
himself. . . .

A.D.
147–168   During the time of Emperor Huan he was recommended as "filially
pious and incorrupt" and appointed chief of Pei-hsin-ch'eng. . . . He
was especially summoned and appointed gentleman of the masters of
writing. [*HHS* 80B:9a, 12b–13a]

83. A Distinguished Scholar

Ca. A.D.
157–165   More than ten years had passed since [Cheng] Hsüan[247] had gone
away to study. Then he returned to his village.[248] His family was poor;
he took up his residence in Tung-lai[249] and cultivated land there.[250]

---

house for public lectures where several hundred students assembled. He frequently
went there to instruct and examine them. He died during the Kuang-ho period (176–
184) (*HHS* 80B:9a–13a).

[246] No information about his father is available.

[247] Cheng Hsüan (127–200) had been a village bailiff when he was young. He
disliked the job and instead went to study at the Imperial Academy. He spent more
than ten years traveling around widely and studied under various teachers, including
the most famous scholar of his time, Ma Jung.

Cheng never entered an official career. Shortly after he had returned home he was
involved in the political conflict between the eunuchs and a number of officials and
was prohibited from entering an official career for fourteen years. After the proscription had been raised in 184, he was recommended and appointed many times, including appointment to the post of grand minister of agriculture, but he declined them
all. Instead he devoted his energy to study and teaching. His commentaries on various
texts, *Chou-i, Shang-shu, Shih-ching, I-li,* and others, were the most authoritative in
China.

In 200, when Yüan Shao engaged in a war with Ts'ao Ts'ao, Cheng was forced by
Yüan to take part on his side. Cheng was ill at that time and died on the way at the
age of seventy-four (*HHS* 35:15b–21b; cf. 67:17a).

[248] Cheng Hsüan was born in 127. Basing himself upon a statement in the *Shih-shuo
Hsin-yü,* that says that Cheng left home at the age of twenty-one (Chinese way of
counting), Liu Ju-lin puts the date of his leaving home at 147 and the date of going
to Fu-feng to study with Ma Jung at 154 (Liu Ju-lin, *Han-Chin hsüeh-shu pien-nien*
[Shanghai, 1935], 5:94, 108–9, hereafter cited as *HCHSPN).* Cheng stayed three
years at Fu-feng before he returned home. If the last date of Liu is correct, then
Cheng returned about 157. This, however, is contradictory to Cheng's own statement
that he was over forty when he returned home (*HHS* 35:19a). It is our opinion that
"more than ten years" may mean any number between eleven and nineteen. If he
stayed away for nineteen years, then the year he returned would be 165 and his age
would be thirty-nine, a figure quite close to forty. It seems safe to assume that Cheng
returned home between 157 and 165.

[249] Tung-lai, roughly equivalent to modern Huang county, northeastern Shantung,
was several hundred *li* distant from Cheng Hsüan's native place, Kao-mi prefecture
of Pei-hai kingdom (roughly modern Kao-mi in eastern Shantung).

The students who followed him already numbered several hundreds to a thousand. . . .

Toward the end of Emperor Ling's [reign], when the proscription against the Partisans was released,[251] the grand general, Ho Chin,[252] heard about him and summoned him. Because Chin was a powerful consort relative, the provincial and commandery governments did not dare to disobey his will. Therefore they forced Hsüan [to go]. Having no other alternative, he went. Chin prepared a small table and a staff[253] for him and treated him with unusual politeness. Hsüan did not accept the official garments but visited [Chin] wearing a kerchief.[254] He stayed overnight and escaped. At this time he was sixty years of age. . . .

[250] The text reads *k'o keng Tung-lai* 客耕東萊, literally, "to cultivate land in Tung-lai as a non-native," for Cheng Hsüan was a native of Kao-mi. This statement raises an interesting problem as to the life and activities of the so-called poor scholars. Although the text says that Cheng's family was poor and he cultivated land in Tung-lai, it is dubious that Cheng actually supported himself by farming. As he was followed by several hundred students, it is reasonable to assume that he was supported by them, since they paid tuition to him.

An interesting account is given by Cheng himself in a written instruction to his son; it reads, "I rent land to till in order to amuse myself in the mornings and evenings," 假田播殖以娛朝夕 (*HHS* 35:18b–19a). *Chia t'ien*, literally "to rent land from others," thus means to become a tenant farmer; see Yen's commentary on *fen t'ien chieh chia* 分田劫假, which is understood by him as "a poor man who rents land from the rich" (*HS* 24A:19b). But this seems unlikely in Cheng's case, for according to his own statement he merely took up farming in his spare time as a hobby and did not really farm to make a living. His statement, "my family previously was poor" (*HHS* 35:18b), also indicates that his family was no longer a poor one after he had become a distinguished scholar.

[251] The proscription against the Partisans refers to the so-called *tang-ku*, which prohibited those officials and scholars who were labeled Partisans from entering officialdom. This was the result of an open conflict between a group of officials and the students of the Imperial Academy and the eunuchs, who were the victors. The proscription was issued by Emperor Huan in 166 and removed in 184 by Emperor Ling after the outbreak of the Yellow Turban Rebellion (see *HHS* 7:23b, 8:14b–15a, 67:4a–8b). For more details about the Partisans, see III, 65, n. 376.

[252] Ho Chin, the grand general, was a brother of Empress Ho. See II, 85, n. 267.

[253] Articles regularly set out to show respect for an elder. The staff would support him while walking, the table while sitting. In Chou times, according to the *Li-chi*, an important official above the age of seventy would be given such articles by his sovereign (*LCCS* 1:9a–10b).

[254] *Fu chin* 幅巾 means "to wear a kerchief around one's head instead of a hat" (see Li: *HHS* 29:9a). Since hats were worn only by officials, whereas commoners wore kerchiefs (see Pi Yuan, *Shih-ming su-cheng*, in *CHTTS*, 4:23b, hereafter cited as *SMSC*), Cheng Hsüan's appearance in a kerchief and without the official garments indicated that he did not intend to become an official. An analogous case is that of Pao Yung, a general under the Keng-shih emperor, who wore a kerchief when he went to see Emperor Kuang-wu after learning of Keng-shih's death and after dismissing his own troops and giving up his military title (*HHS* 29:9a). Han K'ang, who was

Later, the general of the rear, Yüan Wei, memorialized to appoint him attendant within the palace. He did not go because of the death of his father. The chancellor of the kingdom, K'ung Jung, highly respected Hsüan and, shuffling his shoes,²⁵⁵ paid a visit to [Hsüan's] house. He told [the officials of] Kao-mi prefecture to set up a district for Hsüan, saying, ". . . Let the district of Mr. Cheng be called Cheng-kung district. . . . The village gate and the road should be extended so that the high carriages²⁵⁶ can pass, and let [the gate] be called T'ung-te Gate." When Tung Cho moved the capital to Ch'ang-an, the ministers recommended Hsüan for chancellor of the kingdom of Chao. He did not come because of the interruption in communications. . . .

A.D. 196   In the first year of Chien-an he returned to Kao-mi from Hsü province. He met Yellow Turban Bandits on the way, numbering in the myriads. When they saw Hsüan, they all bowed to him and made an agreement among themselves not to dare to enter the territory of [Hsüan's] prefecture. . . .

At that time the grand general, Yüan Shao,²⁵⁷ was leading the army of Chi province. He sent messengers to invite Hsüan and brought together a large number of guests. Hsüan was the last to arrive, and then [the host] motioned him to take the seat of honor. . . . [Yüan] Shao then recommended Hsüan as "abundantly talented" and memorialized to appoint him general of the palace gentlemen of the left. He declined

---

summoned by Emperor Huan to court but who insisted on being a hermit, also wore a kerchief (*HHS* 83:16b–17a).

²⁵⁵ "To shuffle one's shoes" (*hsi lü* 屣履) is a figurative way of saying that a person is so anxious to visit a virtuous man that he has not the patience to put his shoes on in the usual fashion. The upper part of the cloth shoe at the back, instead of being pulled over one's heel, is folded in and under the heel.

²⁵⁶ High carriages were used by the officials. The ordinary village gate was too low and narrow to permit them to pass through. For this reason, K'ung Jung ordered the road broadened and the gate made higher for Cheng. There is a case in which a petty official, who believed that some of his descendants would become high officials, told the village elders when they were planning to rebuild the village gate to make it high enough to permit a four-horse carriage with high top to pass through (*HS* 91:9a).

²⁵⁷ Yüan Shao came from a family of high officials and was the friend of many officials in the capital. He was a close associate of Ho Chin and participated in the battles against the eunuchs at the end of the reign of Emperor Ling. Although Yüan recommended that Ho summon Tung Cho to the capital, because his forces were needed in the battles then going on at court, Yüan later (A.D. 190) became a leader of the forces against Tung Cho. In 196 Yüan became grand commandant, and in the following year, grand general. By this time Yüan Shao was one of the most powerful figures in China and on several occasions was urged to declare himself emperor. But he was no match for Ts'ao Ts'ao and after suffering several defeats, Yüan died of illness in A.D. 202 (*HHS* 74A:1a–33b).

both. The office of the official carriages summoned him to be the grand minister of agriculture and gave him a "comfortable carriage." Wherever he passed, he was welcomed and speeded on his way by the local authorities. Hsüan then, because of illness, asked to go home. [*HHS* 35:16b–18b, 20b–21a]

84. Farmer Refuses to Accept Official Position

Hsü Chih,[258] whose style was Ju-tzu, was a native of Nan-ch'ang of Yü-chang. Since his family was poor, he always tilled the fields and grew grain himself, refusing to eat anything that was not produced by his own labor. He was respectful, frugal, righteous, and humble. Those who lived where he did were won over by his virtues.

He was summoned several times by the office of the ministers,[259] but he declined. When Ch'en Fan was the grand administrator,[260] he invited him to be merit evaluator. Chih did not accept.[261] Having paid a visit to [Fan], he then left. Fan did not receive any guests while he was in the commandery; only when Chih came did he especially set up a couch, hanging it up when [Chih] left.[262] Later Chih was recommended under the category of "having propriety"[263] and was appointed at his home the grand administrator of T'ai-yüan commandery. He did not accept.

In the second year of Yen-hsi, Ch'en Fan, the prefect of the masters A.D. 159 of writing, Hu Kuang, the supervisor, and others presented a memorial recommending Chih and others.[264] . . . With "comfortable carriages" and [rolls of] black silk, Emperor Huan then summoned them with all

---

[258] According to Hsieh Ch'eng's *Hou-Han-shu,* Hsü Chih studied the classics, various techniques of magic and divination, astronomy, and the apocryphal texts (Li: *HHS* 53:7a).

[259] For the office of the ministers, see II, 52, n. 159.

[260] For Ch'en Fan, see III, 65, n. 377.

[261] The original sentence reads 不免之, "unable to avoid" or "not to decline." Ho Cho suggests that the word might be *chiu* 就, "to accept," instead of *mien* 免, "to decline" (*HHSPC* 53:6a). This seems more reasonable.

[262] That is, the couch (*t'a* 榻) was reserved for Hsü Chih only. Ch'en did the same thing for Chou Ch'ou 周璆 when he was the grand administrator of Lo-an (*HHS* 66:1b). According to Fu Ch'ien, a *t'a* was smaller than a *ch'uang* 牀, bed. The size of the former was three and a half feet, the latter eight feet (Hsü Chien *et al., Ch'u hsüeh chi* [Ning-shou-t'ang ed., 1607], 25:86, hereafter cited as *CHC).* Judging from the size, it is obvious that a *t'a* was used only for sitting.

[263] For this category of recommendation, see II, 71, n. 214.

[264] The other candidates recommended were Chiang Hung 姜肱, Yüan Hung 袁閎, Wei Chu 韋著, and Li T'an 李曇.

the courtesies. Not one of them came. ... In the beginning of Emperor Ling's reign, when the emperor intended to invite Chih with a [carriage with] rush-covered wheels, he died. At this time he was seventy-two.

His son, Yin, whose style was Chi-teng, and who seriously practiced filial piety and brotherly kindness, also lived in seclusion and did not enter an official career. The grand administrator, Hua Hsin,[265] asked with courtesy to see him. Firmly saying that he was ill, he did not go. At the end of Han there were bandits everywhere; they all respected the propriety and behavior of Yin and agreed with each other not to attack his village. He died during the Chien-an period. [*HHS* 53:7a–8a, 9a–b]

A.D. 192–194 (margin)

A.D. 196–219 (margin)

85. A BUTCHER'S DAUGHTER BECOMES EMPRESS

Empress Ho whose [temple title] was Ling-ssu and whose given name was unknown,[266] was a native of Yüan of the Nan-yang commandery. Her family originally were butchers. She entered the palace through selection.[267] She was seven feet and one inch tall. She gave birth to Prince Pien. . . . She was appointed honorable lady[268] and was very much favored [by the emperor]. By nature she was strong and jealous. All the ladies in the inner palace were afraid of her.

A.D. 180 (margin)

In the third year of Kuang-ho she was made empress. In the following year the father of the empress, Chen, was posthumously honored with the title of general of chariots and cavalry and ennobled as Hsüan-te

---

[265] Hua Hsin 華歆 was appointed grand administrator when Ma Mi-ti 馬日磾 was grand tutor (192–194) (*SKC*, Wei, 13:11a–b). Hua Hsin lost his position in 194 when Sun Ts'e conquered and occupied the area of Chiang-tung and appointed Sun Pen administrator (*SKC*, Wu, 1:10b–11a). Later he was summoned by Ts'ao Ts'ao and appointed gentleman discussant. In 216 he was promoted to the post of grandee secretary and became minister of the masses in 220 when Ts'ao P'i ascended the throne (*SKC*, Wei, 13:12a–b).

[266] Literally, "whose given name was so-and-so."

[267] For the selection of girls of good family in the eighth month, see I, 52, n. 206. According to the *Feng-su t'ung-i*, quoted by Li, her family bribed the man in charge to put her on the list. Whether or not this information is reliable is impossible to determine. The fact that the officials in charge of the selection included her suggests that her family was considered a "good family," as otherwise they would not have dared to do so.

Her brother, Chin, later became grand general and was ennobled as marquis of Shen. Her younger brother, Miao, was general of chariots and cavalry, and also a marquis. Ho Chin was the political leader in the fight against the powerful eunuchs; see III, 71.

[268] Honorable lady was the rank next to the empress (*HHS* 10A:3b).

marquis of Wu-yang. Thereupon the mother of the empress, Hsing, was ennobled as baronet of Wu-hang.[269] [*HHS* 10B:16a–b]

86. EMPEROR LING IMITATES THE MERCHANTS

In this year the emperor set up market stands in the rear palace and A.D. 181
ordered all the chosen ladies[270] to sell goods and furthermore to steal
from and struggle against one another. The emperor dressed in merchant's garments[271] and drank and feasted and made merry. [*HHS* 8:13b]

87. STUDENTS FOLLOW A PIG BREEDER

Sun Ch'i,[272] whose style was Chung-yü, was a native of Ch'eng-wu Before A.D. 189
of the Chi-yin commandery. When he was young he was a student
specializing in the study of the *I* by Ching [Fang] and the *Shang-shu* in
ancient characters. His family was poor. He served his mother in a most
filial manner. He herded pigs in a large swamp in order to provide for
her. Those who came from afar to study with him all carried the classics
to the edge of the fields to be with him. . . .

The commandery government recommended him as "square and upright" and sent officials with sheep and wine to extend an invitation to
Ch'i. But Ch'i drove his pigs into the grass and did not cast a glance at
them. The minister of the masses, Huang Wan,[273] especially summoned A.D. 189

[269] When her son, Prince Pien, ascended the throne in 189, the empress dowager
personally attended the court to rule with the assistance of her elder brother, Ho
Chin. After Tung Cho had dismissed the young emperor and put Prince Hsieh
(Emperor Hsien) on the throne, the empress dowager was poisoned by Tung Cho.
Her mother was also put to death.

[270] The chosen ladies (*ts'ai nü* 采女) were one class of the emperor's concubines
during the Later Han (*HHS* 10A:3b). Hui Tung says that the word *ts'ai* means "to
select" (*HHSPC* 5:1b).

[271] This passage gives no description of the merchant's garments. A passage in the
San-kuo-chih mentions that when Lü Meng 呂蒙 attacked Kuan Yü's 關羽 base in the
Nan commandery, he ordered his troops to wear white clothes and disguise themselves
as merchants (*SKC*, Wu, 9:21b). Since government runners and commoners also
wore white clothes (see II, 63, n. 193), the passage in the *San-kuo-chih* suggests that the
garments worn by merchants must have had a special style.

[272] Sun Ch'i must have been very famous as a scholar and a man of integrity, for
when the Yellow Turban Bandits passed through his village they agreed not to attack
his house (*HHS* 79A:11a–b).

[273] Huang Wan 黃琬 held this post from the ninth to the twelfth month in 189
(*HHSPP*, p. 1901).

him. He did not go and remained at home until his death. [*HHS* 79A:11a–b]

88. Farmer Refuses Official Appointment

P'ang Kung[274] was a native of Hsiang-yang of the Nan commandery. He lived south of Mount Hsien,[275] and he had never entered the city. He and his wife treated each other with respect as if they were guests. The inspector of Ching division, Liu Piao,[276] several times invited him [to take a government office], but failed to obtain his consent. Thereupon he went to pay him a visit and said, "Isn't it better to preserve the world intact than to preserve oneself intact?" P'ang Kung smiled and said, "A wild swan nests at the top of a high [tree in the] forest; in the evening it has a place to rest. A sea turtle digs a hole at the bottom of deep waters; in the evening it has a place to rest. Now, having one's own place and choosing to remain there[277] is also the 'nest' and the 'hole' of human beings. The principal thing is that each one has his own [place to] rest. It is not the world which has to be preserved intact." Thereupon he dropped his cultivating implement on the ridge of the field. His wife and children were weeding in front of him. Piao pointed to them and asked, "If you, sir, stay in the fields and refuse to take an office and receive a salary, what will you leave in the future to your descendants?" P'ang Kung said, "All the people nowadays leave them danger, but I alone leave them security. What I leave may be different, but you cannot say that I leave them nothing." Piao sighed and left. [*HHS* 83:22a–23a]

A.D. 190–192 *(margin)*

[274] P'ang Kung's 龐公 name, according to the *Hsiang-yang chi*, was Te-kung 德公. His son, Shan-jen 山人, who married the elder sister of Chu-ko Liang 諸葛亮, was an official of the Wei dynasty of the Three Kingdoms (*HHS* 83:22a–b, 22b–23a).

[275] Mount Hsien is located east of modern Hsiang-yang county.

[276] Liu Piao 劉表, a member of the imperial family, held the position of inspector of Ching division from 190–192. Then he was promoted, by a change in the names of that office, to shepherd of Ching division with the title of "general who subdues the south" (*chen-nan chiang-chün* 鎮南將軍) and was made marquis of Ch'eng-wu. He was ill and died in 208 before Ts'ao Ts'ao arrived with his troops. His younger son, Liu Tsung 劉琮, who succeeded to his father's post, then submitted to Ts'ao (*HHS* 74B:12a–18b; 9:5a–b; *SKC*, Wei, 6:35a–38b).

[277] "Having one's own place and choosing to remain there" is a free translation of 趣舍行止, which, if translated literally, would be very misleading.

III

POWERFUL FAMILIES

1. A REDRESSER-OF-WRONGS

Chu Chia[1] of [the old state of] Lu was a contemporary of Kao-tsu. While the people of Lu were all indoctrinated with Confucianism, Chu Chia became known as a redresser-of-wrongs.[2] The outstanding men whom he hid and rescued numbered a hundred; as for the others, they could not be counted. However, he never boasted of his ability nor displayed his virtue.[3] He was afraid lest what he had done for others be made known.

In succoring those in need he began with the poor and humble. At home he had no surplus of wealth. For clothing he never had a complete set of one color; for meals he never had more than one variety; and for riding he had but a small ox. He devoted himself to rushing to the distress of other people, considering it more important than his own interests. He secretly delivered General Chi Pu[4] from danger, but after Pu became honorable and noble [Chu] did not see him for the rest of his life. There was no person from the [Han-ku] Pass to the east who did not stretch out his neck[5] and long for his friendship. [SC 124:3a–b; HS 92:2b–3a]

2. POWERFUL FAMILIES REMOVED

One hundred twenty thousand households of powerful and wealthy [221 B.C.] men were moved to Hsien-yang.[6] [SC 6:13b]

---

[1] Chu Chia is more a man of Ch'in than of Han.

[2] Ju Shun comments that the word *jen* 任 means "to trust each other" and that *hsia (hsieh)* means "to agree in what is right and wrong." Yen understood the former to mean "by resort to strength" and the latter "to assist." When combined the phrase means "to assist people by means of force" (Yen, HS 37:1a).

Actually the terms, *jen-hsia, hsia, yu-hsia,* and *ch'ing-hsia* all mean the same thing, except that *yu* and *ch'ing* have the additional meaning of "wandering" and "light" respectively. For a fuller discussion see the section on *Yu-hsia* in Chapter 5.

[3] HS 92:3a reads *yin* 歙 "does not display," instead of 歙.

[4] See II, 13.

[5] An idiom indicating an eagerness to greet someone.

[6] Hsien-yang was the imperial capital of Ch'in.

3. Powerful Persons

^{Han}   The Han inherited the violence remaining from the Warring States. There were many powerful and cunning individuals. Of these the engrossers[7] were oppressive in the cities, while the outstandingly brave ones were domineering in the rural communities. [*HHS* 77:1a]

4. A Eunuch Replaces the Imperial Chancellor

210 B.C.   In the seventh month of this year the First Emperor arrived at Sha-ch'iu and became very ill. He ordered Chao Kao[8] to write a letter, to be given to Prince Fu-su,[9] saying, "Put the troops under the command of Meng T'ien.[10] You come to Hsien-yang for the funeral and bury me." The letter was already sealed but had not yet been handed over to the messenger when the First Emperor died. Both the letter and the seal were in the hands of Chao Kao. Only [the emperor's] son, Hu-hai, the Imperial Chancellor Li Ssu, Chao Kao, and five or six favorite eunuchs knew of the First Emperor's death. All the rest of the various officials knew nothing about this.

Considering that the emperor had died outside [the capital] and had not actually [appointed] an heir apparent, Li Ssu therefore kept [the death] a secret, and put the [body of the] emperor in the sleeping carriage.[11] The various officials memorialized [government] affairs and

[7] The term *ping-chien* or *chien-ping* suggests a person whose extraordinary wealth and power enabled him to encroach upon the people. Literally, it means to swallow up, to engulf, and thus to grab the property of others.

[8] Chao Kao was a distant relative of the royal family of Ch'in. According to the *Shih-chi*, he and several of his brothers were born in the Yin-kung—a place where newly castrated men were kept for a hundred days for healing and rest—and their mother had suffered punishment, so her descendants were low and humble for generations. Hsü Kuang remarks that they were made eunuchs.

According to Liu, quoted by Ssu-ma, Chao Kao's father was castrated and his mother was made a slave. She had illicit intercourse, but all her sons by others had the surname Chao. All were then castrated. Chao Kao was energetic and familiar with the law, and for this reason he was appointed prefect of the office of palace carriages (*chung-chü fu-ling* 中車府令) by the First Emperor. He served Prince Hu-hai and taught him to make judicial decisions. Later Chao Kao committed a serious crime and was sentenced to death, but was pardoned by the emperor and resumed his office (*SC* 88:1b–2a). For further details about his life, see III, 7.

[9] Prince Fu-su was the oldest son of the First Emperor. He should have succeeded him but, as we shall see, Chao Kao plotted against him.

[10] Meng T'ien 蒙恬 was the leading Ch'in general of the time. He was currently in command of forces on the northern frontier (*SC* 88:1a ff.).

[11] According to Meng K'ang, the sleeping carriage (*wen-liang chü* 轀輬車) was one with windows that could be closed to keep it warm or opened to keep it cool. Ju Shun comments that the carriage was large and had feather decorations.

presented food as usual, and the eunuchs always approved the various memorialized affairs from inside the sleeping carriage.

Chao Kao thereupon retained the letter and seal which had been granted to Fu-su and said to Prince Hu-hai, "The emperor died without issuing any edict to enfeof his various sons as kings,[12] and only granted a letter to his eldest son. When the eldest son arrives, he will be set up as emperor, and you have not a foot or an inch of land. What can you do?" Hu-hai said, "I have heard long ago that an enlightened ruler knows his ministers and that an enlightened father knows his sons. My father died and did not ennoble his various sons. What can I say about it?" Chao Kao said, "It is not so. Now the preservation or loss of the empire's power lies with you, myself Kao, and the imperial chancellor. I hope you will plan for it. Besides, to have others as one's subjects or to be the subject of others, to control others or to be controlled by others, how can [these two] be spoken of on the same day?" . . . After Hu-hai had agreed with the words of [Chao] Kao, Kao said, "If we do not plan together with the imperial chancellor, the matter may not succeed. Let me, your servant, consult with the imperial chancellor on your behalf."

[Chao] Kao thereupon said to the Imperial Chancellor [Li] Ssu, "The emperor died and gave a letter to his eldest son, [ordering him] to meet for the funeral at Hsien-yang and making him the heir. The letter has not been sent. Now no one knows about the death of the emperor, and the letter that was granted to the eldest son together with the tally and the seal are all at Hu-hai's place. To fix upon the heir apparent depends upon the mouths of you, Sir Marquis,[13] and Kao. What do you think about this matter?" [Li] Ssu said, "How can [you speak] these words that will ruin the empire? These are not matters to be discussed by subjects."

[Chao] Kao said, "You, Sir Marquis, judge yourself whether your ability is superior to Meng T'ien's, whether your merit is more than Meng T'ien's, whether in making farsighted and unfailing plans you are better than Meng T'ien, whether you have [caused] less hatred in the empire than Meng T'ien, and whether [the emperor's] eldest son befriends and trusts you more than Meng T'ien." [Li] Ssu said, "In

---

[12] Upon the suggestion of Li Ssu the First Emperor had considered the establishment of feudal states a disadvantage. Therefore, none of his sons was made a king.

[13] *Chün-hou,* literally "sir-marquis," was, according to Ju Shun, a term addressed to an imperial chancellor who was at the same time a marquis. Yen, however, thinks that any marquis could be addressed as *chün-hou* (*HS* 66:5a).

none of these five can I come up to Meng T'ien. But why do you, sir, blame me so severely?"

[Chao] Kao said, "Originally, I, Kao, was a servant among the inner officials but was fortunate enough to be able to enter the Ch'in palace by means [of my knowledge in] the writing of documents. I have been in charge of affairs for more than twenty years and I have never seen that any of the dismissed imperial chancellors and the meritorious officials of the Ch'in have [been able to retain] the ennoblement for two generations. In the end they all perished through execution. You, sir, know all the twenty and more sons of the emperor. The eldest son is firm and resolute, martial and brave; he trusts people and encourages the soldiers. When he ascends the throne, he will certainly employ Meng T'ien as imperial chancellor. It is quite clear that you, Sir Marquis, eventually will not [be able to] preserve your marquis seal and will have to return to your native village. After I, Kao, received an edict to teach Hu-hai, I made him study legal matters for several years. I have never found a fault in him. He is kind and sincere; he regards wealth lightly and yet regards scholars with esteem; he distinguishes [what is right and wrong] in his heart and yet is pliant in his speech; he fulfills politeness and respects scholars. None of the various sons of the Ch'in can match him. He can be the heir. You, sir, plan and settle it." . . .

[Chao] Kao said, "When the superior and the inferior[14] agree, [the matter] can be permanent; when within and without[15] become one, the matter has no outside and inside. If you, sir, listen to my plan, you will have the marquisate forever, and for generations [your descendants] will designate themselves *ku*.[16] Thereby you will have the longevity of a lofty pine tree and the wisdom of Confucius and Mo-tzu. Now if you disregard this [plan] and do not agree, the distress will be extended to your descendants. This is sufficient to make the blood run cold. One who knows how to adjust well turns distress into blessing. Sir, where are you going to stand?" . . . Thereupon [Li] Ssu listened to [Chao] Kao. Kao then reported to Hu-hai, saying, "Your servant begs to receive the brilliant order of you, the heir apparent, and report it to

[14] Here the superior and the inferior apparently refer to the future emperor, Prince Hu-hai, and the imperial chancellor.

[15] Within and without refer to Chao Kao and the imperial chancellor respectively. It implies the control within the palace by the eunuch and the control outside the palace by the imperial chancellor and the union of the two.

[16] When speaking of himself, a marquis usually designated himself as *ku* (cf. *LCCS* 30:14a).

the imperial chancellor. How would the Imperial Chancellor Ssu dare not to receive your order?"

Thereupon [Chao Kao and Li Ssu] plotted together, forging an edict [that they pretended] to have received from the First Emperor, which ordered the imperial chancellor to appoint [the emperor's] son, Hu-hai, heir apparent. They also composed a letter, to be given to the eldest son, Fu-su, saying, "We[17] are taking a tour all over the empire and worshipping the various deities of the famous mountains in order to prolong Our life. Now you, Fu-su, together with General Meng T'ien, leading several hundred thousand troops, have been stationed on the frontier for more than ten years, and have been unable to advance; many of the soldiers have been wasted [and you have] not had the merit of a single foot or inch. Yet you frequently presented memorials slandering in direct words what we have been doing. Because you are unable to withdraw and to return to become the heir apparent, you are resentful day and night. Fu-su as a son is unfilial. Let him be granted a sword to commit suicide. General Meng T'ien, who is staying with Fu-su outside [the capital], has not been correcting him. He must have known of [Fu-su's] plot. As a minister he is disloyal. Let him be granted death and let his troops be put under the command of Deputy-General Wang Li." The letter was sealed with the seal of the emperor. A guest of Hu-hai was sent to carry the letter and to grant it to Fu-su in Shang province. . . .

[Fu-su] then committed suicide. Meng T'ien was not willing to die. The messenger then put him under the custody of officials and imprisoned him in Yang-chou. The messenger returned and reported. Hu-hai, [Li] Ssu, and [Chao] Kao were exceedingly happy. When they arrived at Hsien-yang, they announced the death [of the emperor] and made the heir apparent the Emperor of the Second Generation. He made Chao Kao the prefect of the palace gentlemen[18] and regular attendant and in charge of the affairs within the palace. . . ..

[Chao Kao said to the Second Emperor], "The various princes and the great officials have been suspicious of our plan at Sha-ch'iu. And all the various princes are the emperor's elder brothers. Besides, the great officials were installed by the late emperor. Now Your Majesty has just been enthroned. These men are discontented and none of them has submitted. I am afraid that they will rebel. Moreover, although

---

[17] Meaning the First Emperor.

[18] According to *SC* 6:31b, Chao Kao was appointed prefect of the gentlemen of the palace (*lang-chung-ling* 郎中令) in 209 B.C.

Meng T'ien is already dead, Meng I[19] is leading troops and staying outside.[20] Your servant is troubled and worried and fears that we won't last long. Because of this how can Your Majesty be happy?" The Second Emperor said, "What shall we do?"

Chao Kao said, "Make the laws strict and the punishments severe. Order that those who are guilty be sentenced, together with those who are collectively responsible, to the death penalty and let it extend to the whole clan. Annihilate the great officials and keep your relatives at a distance. Enrich the poor and honor the humble. Remove the old officials of the late emperor completely and install instead those who have been intimate with and trusted by Your Majesty and be close to them. In this way secret gratitude will come to Your Majesty, mischief will be eliminated, and treacherous plots will be blocked. There will be no one of the various ministers who is not covered by Your benefits and who has not received Your great kindness; then Your Majesty will sleep on a high pillow[21] and can indulge Your will in [peaceful] living and happiness. No other plan is better than this."

The Second Emperor approved of Kao's words. Then the law was changed. Thereupon the various ministers and the various princes when found guilty were always handed over to [Chao] Kao who was ordered to try and examine them. The great ministers, Meng I and others, were killed. Twelve princes were executed in the market of Hsien-yang and ten princesses were torn to pieces and killed at Tu; their wealth and property were confiscated by the government. Those who were involved and punished as jointly responsible were innumerable. [*SC* 87:8a–10a, 11a–13a]

Previously when Chao Kao was the prefect of the palace gentlemen, those who were killed by him and those whom he requited for personal

---

[19] Meng I 蒙毅, who was the younger brother of Meng T'ien, was a high minister close to the First Emperor. Previously he had been ordered by the emperor to try Chao Kao, who had committed a serious crime, for which Meng I sentenced him to death. After Meng T'ien had been arrested, Chao Kao accused Meng I of urging the First Emperor not to appoint Hu-hai the heir apparent, and for this reason he was imprisoned and put to death. Meng T'ien was forced to commit suicide shortly thereafter (*SC* 88:1a–5b). See the following note.

[20] Two points are wrong in this statement. First, according to the biography of Meng T'ien, Meng I was killed before his elder brother died (see *SC* 88:2b–4b; cf. n. 19 of this document). Second, Meng I was a minister who usually attended at the side of the First Emperor and had never been a general with troops under his command. It was Meng T'ien who commanded three hundred thousand troops, which were stationed on the northern frontier. Apparently the names of the Meng brothers were transposed by mistake.

[21] An expression for peaceful rest.

hatred were very numerous. Fearing that the great officials who entered the court to memorialize affairs might slander him, he thereupon advised the Second Emperor, saying,[22] "What makes the Son of Heaven noble is that only his voice is heard and that none of the officials can see his face. Therefore he designates himself as *chen*.[23] Moreover, Your Majesty is rich in springs and autumns[24] and is not always completely familiar with all affairs. Now You sit in the court and if a censure or a recommendation is improper, the fault will be shown to the great ministers. This is not the way to manifest Your divine brilliance to the empire. If Your Majesty inside the palace folds Your hands high[25] [against Your breast] and together with Your servant and the palace attendants who are familiar with the laws wait for affairs, when affairs come they can be considered. In this way then the great ministers will not dare to memorialize doubtful affairs and the empire will consider you a sage ruler." The Second Emperor adopted his plan. Then he did not sit in the court to receive the great ministers, but stayed inside the palace. Chao Kao frequently attended [the emperor] in the palace and took charge of affairs. Affairs were all decided by Chao Kao.

Having heard that Li Ssu had mentioned [and complained] about this, [Chao] Kao then visited the imperial chancellor and said, "The various bandits[26] to the east of [Han-ku] Pass are numerous. Now the emperor urgently mobilizes labor services to build the A-p'ang Palace and accumulates dogs, horses, and useless articles. I, Your subject, have intended to admonish, but my position is humble. This is really a matter for you, Sir Marquis. You, sir, why do you not admonish [the

---

[22] In 208 B.C. (*SC* 6:35a–b).

[23] *Chen*, the imperial "I" (see *TYTT* A:1b–2a; Chapter 4, p. 000).

[24] That is, young in age, having many springs and autumns to come.

[25] 深拱, to fold one's hands high against the breast is an expression that means to govern in good order while at ease and without effort. According to Yen, 深 has the meaning of 高 in this phrase (*HS* 45:4a).

[26] Here the bandits refer to the various rebellious forces. At this time the Ch'in general, Chang Han, and others had already defeated and caused the deaths of Chou Chang, Ch'en Sheng, Wei Chiu, and T'ien Tan. However, Hsiang Liang, Hsiang Chi (Yü), and Liu Pang, all under the command of King Huai of Ch'u, still had a large number of troops. Besides, Chao, Yen, and Ch'i had also set up kings and had rebelled against Ch'in (*SC* 6:34b–35a, 7:7a, 48:4b–7b, 89:5b, 90:1a–b, 94:1a–b; *HS* 31:4a–6b and 12a–b, 32:3a–4a, 33:1a–b and 2b–3a).

SC 6:35a mentions the killing of Hsiang Liang when Chao Kao advised the Second Emperor not to attend the court. However, it should be pointed out that the death of Hsiang Liang took place after Li Ssu had been imprisoned. Li Ssu was punished by the five punishments in the seventh month of the second year of the Second Emperor (*SC* 87:22b). Hsiang Liang, who killed Li Yu 李由 in the eighth month, was defeated and killed by Chang Han in the ninth month (*HS* 1A:9a–b).

emperor]?" Li Ssu said, "It certainly is. I have wanted to speak about it for a long time. Now His Majesty does not sit in the court. His Majesty stays deep in the palace. What I want to say [to the emperor] I am unable to transmit. I want to see [the emperor] but he has no leisure." Chao Kao said to him, "If you, sir, really can admonish I beg to watch His Majesty's leisure time for you, Sir Marquis, and to inform you, sir."

Thereupon Chao Kao waited until the Second Emperor was drinking and enjoying music, with women in front of him, and sent someone to inform the imperial chancellor that His Majesty was at leisure and that the matter could be memorialized. The imperial chancellor arrived at the palace gate and asked for a visit. This happened three times. The Second Emperor was angry and said, "I usually have plenty of leisure days and the imperial chancellor does not come. Just when I am at rest, the imperial chancellor comes immediately to ask about [government] affairs. Is it that the imperial chancellor [considers that] I am young and therefore regards me lightly?" Chao Kao thereupon said, "If this is so, then it is dangerous. The imperial chancellor participated in the plot at Sha-ch'iu. Now Your Majesty has been made emperor and yet the nobility of the imperial chancellor has not been increased, which was his intention; also he expected to split the country and to become a king. But if Your Majesty does not ask me, Your servant, then I, Your servant, dare not say it. The imperial chancellor's eldest son, Li Yu, is the administrator of San-ch'uan. The bandits of Ch'u, Ch'en Sheng,[27] and others are all men of the neighboring prefectures of the imperial chancellor. Therefore the bandits of Ch'u publicly pass through the city of San-ch'uan and the administrator is unwilling to attack them.[28] I, Kao, heard that documents have been exchanged between one and the other. I have not got the details; therefore I did not dare to report. Furthermore, the imperial chancellor stays outside [the palace] and his power surpasses that of Your Majesty." The Second Emperor considered that this was right and wanted to investigate the imperial chancellor. Lest it might not be true, he thereupon sent someone to investigate the administrator of San-ch'uan with regard to the situation between him and the bandits.

Li Ssu heard about this. At this time the Second Emperor was in the Kan-ch'üan [Palace] and was just watching the competitive games[29] and

---

[27] Ch'en Sheng was the man who led the first uprising against the Ch'in.

[28] This was a false accusation; Li Yu was defeated and killed by Hsiang Liang in 208 B.C. (*SC* 7:6b–7a; *HS* 31:12a).

[29] *Chiao-ti* 角抵 or 觳抵 was a kind of game dating back to the period of the Warring

comedy plays.[30] Li Ssu was unable to visit [the emperor]. Thereupon he presented a memorial stating the faults of Chao Kao. . . . The Second Emperor had previously believed [the words of] Chao Kao. Fearing that Li Ssu would kill [Chao Kao], he thereupon privately informed Chao Kao. Kao said, "Kao is the only one with whom the imperial chancellor is concerned. When Kao dies, the imperial chancellor will then do what T'ien Ch'ang[31] did." Thereupon the Second Emperor said, "Put Li Ssu into the custody of the prefect of the palace gentlemen." Chao Kao investigated Li Ssu. Li Ssu was arrested, bound, and put in jail. . . .

Thereupon the Second Emperor ordered [Chao] Kao to investigate the case of the imperial chancellor and to punish his crime. [Chao Kao] questioned [Li] Ssu about the situation regarding the rebellious plot of Ssu and his son, Yu. All of their clansmen and guests were arrested. Chao Kao examined [Li] Ssu; the beating numbered more than a thousand [strokes]. [Li Ssu] could not bear the pain, and he himself falsely confessed. [Li] Ssu did not die[32] because he was confident of his own eloquence and merit, and truly had no intention to rebel. Hoping that he would be able to present a memorial to make a statement for

---

States. *HS* 23:5a records that during this period, "The ceremony of military training was gradually increased and made into a game with the purpose of showing off to one another. The Ch'in changed the name [of the game] and called it *chiao-ti*."

Ying Shao states that *chiao* 角 means "contest of skill" 角技 and *ti* 抵 means "to butt against each other" 相抵觸 (Yen: *HS* 6:22b). Wen Ying considers *chiao-ti* "all kinds of amusements." He interprets the meaning of the term as "two persons match each other in a contest of strength and skill and in the art of archery and driving" *(loc. cit.)*. Yen Shih-ku rejects Ying Shao's suggestion of butting, and thinks that it merely means "to encounter each other."

It is not possible to know the details of this ancient game, but judging from its military origin and the meaning of the term itself, we are inclined to believe that it was a kind of game in which strength and athletic skill were shown. Thus Wang Hsien-ch'ien likens the game to the *kuan-chiao* 貫跤, "wrestling" of his day (*HSPC* 6:27b). We hesitate to use the term "wrestling," since it might involve other kinds of athletic contests, as suggested by Wen Ying. Dr. Dubs translates it as "competitive game" (*HFHD*, II, 129), which is a very suitable rendering.

[30] The *Shuo-wen* explains *p'ai* 俳 as plays, *hsi* 戲 (*SWCTC* 8A:61), *yu* 優 as *ch'ang* 倡, and the latter is explained as music, *yüeh* 樂 (*SWCTC* 8A:44, 61). According to Yen, however, *ch'ang* refers to musicians, whereas *p'ai yu* or *yu* refers to comedies (*HS* 52:9b; 68:8b). Tuan Yü-ts'ai suggests that in effect the three are one thing; when talking about the play it is called *p'ai*, about music *ch'ang* or *yu* (*SWCTC* 8A:61).

[31] T'ien Ch'ang 田常 was one of the two chancellors of Duke Chien of Ch'i. He and his clan revolted and killed the other chancellor and the ruler. He then put Duke Chien's younger brother on the throne, and he himself became the chancellor. After three generations his great-grandson, T'ien Ho 田和, then replaced the old ruling family and became the marquis of Ch'i with the approval of the Chou Emperor (*SC* 46:4a–7a).

[32] That is, did not commit suicide.

himself and hoping that the Second Emperor would apprehend and pardon him, Li Ssu then presented a memorial from the jail. . . .

When the memorial was presented, Chao Kao ordered the officials to reject it and not to memorialize it, saying, "How can a prisoner present a memorial?"

Chao Kao ordered more than ten of his guests to pretend to be imperial secretaries, internuncios, and palace attendants and to go to reinvestigate [Li] Ssu in turn. [Li] Ssu every time replied with the truth and [Chao Kao] always sent someone to beat him again. Afterwards, the Second Emperor sent someone to examine [Li] Ssu. Thinking that [the situation] was the same as before, [Li] Ssu eventually did not dare to reiterate his statement and acknowledged himself guilty. At the moment when the memorial was presented to him, the Second Emperor was pleased and said, "But for Sir Chao, I would probably have been deceived by the imperial chancellor." . . .

208 B.C. In the seventh month of the second year of the Second Emperor all five punishments[33] were inflicted on [Li] Ssu and he was sentenced to be cut in two at the waist in the marketplace of Hsien-yang. . . . His three *tsu* were exterminated.

After the death of Li Ssu, the Second Emperor appointed Chao Kao[34] the *chung ch'eng-hsiang*.[35] All affairs, whether large or small, were always decided by [Chao] Kao.[36] [*SC* 87:18a–19b, 20b–21b, 22b–23a]

---

[33] According to the Treatise on Punishments in the *Han-shu*, those who were sentenced to the extermination of the three *tsu* were first punished by tattooing on the face, cutting off the nose, and cutting off the left and right feet. They were then beaten to death, beheaded, and had the head hung on a pole, and had their bones and flesh ground in the market. Those who were guilty of slandering the emperor also had their tongues removed before they were killed. This was called "complete with five punishments." Both P'eng Yüeh and Han Hsin suffered this kind of punishment (*HS* 23: 17b). Apparently this Han punishment was copied from Ch'in practice. Li Ssu was subject to the extermination of the three *tsu;* he suffered all the five punishments besides being cut in two at the waist. According to *SC* 6:36b–37a, he was given the five punishments in the second year of the Second Emperor and was executed in the next year.

[34] In the winter of the third year of the Second Emperor, 208–207 B.C. (*SC* 6:37a).

[35] *Chung-ch'eng-hsiang* 中丞相 is, literally, inner imperial chancellor. The term was given because a eunuch was appointed imperial chancellor. However, the character *chung*, "inner," is not mentioned in the "Annals of the First Emperor of Ch'in." It merely says: "Chao Kao became the imperial chancellor." He was also addressed as "imperial chancellor" (*SC* 6:37a, 38b).

[36] Cf. Derk Bodde, *China's First Unifier: A Study of the Ch'in Dynasty as Seen in the Life of Li Ssu* (Leiden: E. J. Brill, 1938), pp. 26–35, 44–46, 48–52.

5. An Old Ruling Family

T'ien Tan, a native of Ti, belonged to the T'ien lineage of the king of the former state of Ch'i. Tan's cousins, T'ien Jung and Jung's younger brother T'ien Heng, were both powerful and their lineage was strong, and [thus] they were able to win the hearts of other people.

Just at the time when Ch'en She[37] rebelled and became the king of 209 B.C.
Ch'u, he sent Chou Shih to pacify the land of Wei. [Chou Shih], going north, arrived at Ti; [the officials of] Ti closed [the gates] to the city and defended it. . . . [T'ien Tan] visited the prefect of Ti and thereupon attacked and killed the prefect. He summoned the powerful officers and the young men and said, "All the feudal lords have rebelled against Ch'in and have made themselves rulers. Since ancient times Ch'i has been a state. Tan, who belongs to the T'ien family, should be the king." He thereupon made himself king of Ch'i and sent troops to attack Chou Shih. Chou Shih's army withdrew. T'ien Tan then led his army to the east to pacify the territory of Ch'i. . . . Chang Han,[38] attacking in the night with his [troops] gagged, inflicted a heavy defeat on the armies of Ch'i and Wei and killed T'ien Tan at Lin-chi. Tan's younger cousin, T'ien Jung, collected Tan's surviving soldiers and went to Tung-a.

When the people of Ch'i heard that King T'ien Tan was killed, they made T'ien Chia, the younger brother of the former king of Ch'i, Chien, the king of Ch'i with T'ien Chiao as chancellor and T'ien Chien as general. . . . T'ien Jung was angry because Chia had been made king of Ch'i. He then came back with his troops, attacked, and drove away the king of Ch'i, Chia. . . . T'ien Jung thereupon made T'ien 208 B.C.
Tan's son, Shih, king of Ch'i with Jung as chancellor and T'ien Heng as general. They pacified the territory of Ch'i. . . . [*SC* 94:1a–2a; *HS* 33:2a–3a]

After Hsiang Yü had saved [the kingdom of] Chao, subdued Chang 206 B.C.
Han and others, gone westward to exterminate [the people in] Hsien-yang, overthrown [the empire of] Ch'in, and appointed the various kings and marquises, he thereupon transferred the king of Ch'i, T'ien Shih, to be the king of Chiao-tung, with its capital at Chi-mo. The Ch'i general, T'ien Tu, followed him and together they saved Chao and thereupon entered the [Han-ku] Pass; therefore he appointed

---

[37] She is the style of Ch'en Sheng. See *SC* 48:1a ff.

[38] Chang Han was a general of Ch'in who defeated and killed Hsiang Liang and besieged Chü-lu, a city of Chao. After Hsiang Yü had defeated the Ch'in troops, he submitted to Hsiang Yü and was made the king of Yung. He committed suicide in 205 B.C. when he was attacked by Liu Pang (*SC* 7:7a, 12b, and 18b, 8:20a and 22b).

[T'ien] Tu to be king of Ch'i, with its capital at Lin-tzu. The grandson of Chien, the former king of Ch'i, T'ien An, occupied several cities of Chi-pei, and leading his troops he submitted to Hsiang Yü when Hsiang Yü crossed the [Yellow] River to save Chao. Hsiang Yü appointed T'ien An the king of Chi-pei, with its capital at Po-yang.

Because T'ien Jung had been ungrateful[39] to Hsiang Liang in not consenting to send troops to aid Ch'u and Chao in attacking Ch'in, he did not get to become a king. The Chao general, Ch'en Yü,[40] also failed to fulfill his duty and did not get to become a king. Both of the two men hated King Hsiang. After King Hsiang had returned and the various feudal lords had each gone to their kingdoms, T'ien Jung sent someone to lead troops to aid Ch'en Yü, asking him to rebel in the territory of Chao. And [T'ien] Jung also sent an army to obstruct and attack T'ien Tu. T'ien Tu fled to Ch'u. T'ien Jung detained Shih, the king of Ch'i, and asked him not to go to Chiao-tung. The attendants of Shih said, "King Hsiang is very strong and cruel. You, King, should go to Chiao-tung. If you do not go to your kingdom it will be dangerous." Shih was frightened and fled to his kingdom. T'ien Jung was angry; he pursued, attacked, and killed the king of Ch'i, Shih, at Chi-mo. On his return, he attacked and killed the king of Chi-pei, An. Thereupon T'ien Jung made himself the king of Ch'i and had all the territory of the three Ch'i[41] under his control.

205 B.C.   When King Hsiang heard this, he was very angry and went northward to attack Ch'i. The army of the king of Ch'i, T'ien Jung, was defeated, and [the king] fled to P'ing-yüan. The people of P'ing-yüan killed Jung. King Hsiang then burned and destroyed the cities of Ch'i. He killed all the people where he passed. The people of Ch'i gathered and rebelled against him. Jung's younger brother, Heng, brought together the dispersed soldiers of Ch'i to the number of many tens of thousands, and counterattacked Hsiang Yü at Ch'eng-yang. And [at that time] the king of Han, leading the various feudal lords, defeated

---

[39] When Hsiang Liang asked T'ien Jung to join in the fight against Ch'in, T'ien requested the officials of Ch'u to kill T'ien Chia, the former king of Ch'i who was driven away by T'ien Jung and was taking refuge in Ch'u; he also requested the officials of Chao to kill T'ien Chiao and T'ien Chien. The officials of both Ch'u and Chao refused. T'ien Jung therefore did not send troops to aid the Ch'u forces. Shortly afterwards Hsiang Liang was defeated and killed by the Ch'in army (*SC* 7:6a–b, 94:2a–b).

[40] Because Ch'en Yü had not followed Hsiang into Han-ku Pass to conquer Ch'in, he was only made a marquis by Hsiang Yü (*SC* 7:20b, 89:9a–10a; *HS* 32:6b–7a).

[41] That is, the territory of the three kingdoms of Ch'i: Ch'i, Chiao-tung, and Chi-pei.

Ch'u and entered P'eng-ch'eng. Hearing this, Hsiang Yü then ceased his attack on Ch'i and returned to attack Han at P'eng-ch'eng. Thereupon he continuously fought with Han, as they opposed each other in Jung-yang. Therefore T'ien Heng was able to retake the cities and towns of Ch'i. He made T'ien Jung's son, Kuang, the king of Ch'i and he himself became chancellor. He took charge of government affairs and all matters, great or small, were determined by [him as] chancellor. . . .

The Han general, Han Hsin, led his army to the east to attack Ch'i. 204 B.C. . . . He captured the king of Ch'i, Kuang. . . . Hearing that the king of Ch'i had died, Heng made himself king of Ch'i and returned to attack [Kuan] Ying.[42] Ying defeated Heng's army at Ying. T'ien Heng fled to Liang and attached himself to P'eng Yüeh.[43] . . . More than a year later, Han overthrew Hsiang Chi (i.e., Hsiang Yü), and the king of Han set himself up as emperor and made Peng Yüeh the king of Liang. T'ien Heng, who was afraid of being executed, went to the sea with more than five hundred of his followers and stayed on an island. When Emperor Kao heard of this, he considered that since T'ien Heng and his brothers were the first to pacify [the territory of] Ch'i and that since many of the worthy men of Ch'i had followed him, it was to be feared that [Heng] would later make trouble if he stayed on the sea and was not taken. He then sent an emissary to pardon T'ien Heng's crime and to summon him to court . . . saying, "When T'ien Heng comes, the big one will be made a king and the small ones will be made marquises.[44] If he does not come, the troops will be sent to inflict punishment upon them."

Then T'ien Heng, together with two of his guests, rode in the relay carriage toward Lo-yang. When he was still thirty *li* away, he arrived at the relay carriage station of Shih district. [T'ien] Heng asked the emissary to excuse him and said, "When a subject is going to see the Son of Heaven, he should take a bath." He stopped there and stayed. He said to his guests, "At the beginning I, Heng, and the king of Han both faced the south[45] and designated ourselves as *ku*.[46] Now the king of Han has become the Son of Heaven but I, Heng, have become a ruined captive and am going to face the north to serve him. My shame

[42] Kuan Ying was a Han general (see *SC* 95:12b; *HS* 41:10a).

[43] P'eng Yüeh was the king of Liang.

[44] Yen suggests that the big one refers to T'ien Heng and the small ones to his followers.

[45] A ruler always sat facing the south, and a subject visiting his ruler sat facing north.

[46] See III, 4, n. 16.

is extreme. . . . Moreover, the reason that His Majesty wants to see me is that he merely wants to have a look at my countenance. Now His Majesty is in Lo-yang. Now if my head is cut off and it is hastily taken a distance of thirty *li*, the features [of my head] shall not yet be putrid and can still be observed." Thereupon he cut his own throat and ordered his guests to bear his head and, following the emissary and riding fast, to memorialize [its presentation] to Emperor Kao. . . . [Emperor Kao] appointed the two guests chief commandants and mobilizing two thousand men [for the funeral], he buried T'ien Heng according to the ceremony for a king. After the funeral the two guests each dug a hole beside the grave mound and cut their own throats, following [Heng] under [the ground].

When Emperor Kao heard of this, he was thereupon greatly startled, considering that all the guests of T'ien Heng were virtuous. Hearing that the rest of them, still numbering five hundred persons, were staying on the sea he sent emissaries to summon them. Upon their arrival, when they heard that T'ien Heng had died, all of them also committed suicide. [*SC* 94:2b–6a; *HS* 33:3b ff.]

6. An Old Powerful Family

Hsiang Chi was a native of Hsia-hsiang. His style was Yü. At the time he started the revolt, he was twenty-four. His uncle was Hsiang Liang. Liang's father, Hsiang Yen, was a general of Ch'u who was killed by the Ch'in general, Wang Chien. The Hsiang had for generations been generals of Ch'u. They were enfeoffed at Hsiang; consequently they took the surname Hsiang. . . .

Ch'en Ying,[47] who was formerly a clerk of the prefect of Tung-yang, lived in the prefecture. He was always honest and careful and was considered "the elder."

208 B.C.   The young men of Tung-yang killed the prefect. They gathered together, numbering several thousands of men. They wished to have a leader, but could not find anyone who was competent. They then asked Ch'en Ying. Ying declined on the ground of inability. Thereupon they compelled Ying to be the leader. Followers in the prefecture amounted to twenty thousand. These young people wanted to make Ying king. . . . Ying did not dare to be king, and said to his army officials, "The

[47] Ch'en Ying later became a general under the command of Hsiang Liang. After the defeat and death of Hsiang Yü, he surrendered to Han and was made a marquis in 201 B.C. because of his military merit (*HS* 16:5b).

Hsiang family has for generations been a family of generals; it is famous in Ch'u. Now if we wish to launch an important undertaking, there is no man but [one of the Hsiang family] who can be the general. If we rely on this famous lineage, it is certain that we can overthrow Ch'in." Thereupon the people followed his advice and placed the army under Hsiang Liang's command. [*SC* 7:1a, 3b–4a; *HS* 31:8a, 9b–10a]

7. A EUNUCH MURDERS THE EMPEROR

On the day *chi-hai* of the eighth month [in the third year of the Second Emperor] Chao Kao[48] intended to rebel. Fearing that the various officials would not consent, he first made a test. He brought a deer, presented it to the Second Emperor, and said, "This is a horse." The Second Emperor laughed and said, "Is not the imperial chancellor making a mistake? He calls a deer a horse." He asked the attendants. Some of the attendants kept silent, some said it was a horse to flatter and obey Chao Kao, and some said it was a deer. [Chao] Kao then secretly injured those who said it was a deer by applying the law against them. Afterwards the various officials all feared [Chao] Kao. . . . 207 B.C.

The Second Emperor dreamed that a white tiger bit the left outside horse of [his carriage] and killed it. He was unhappy in his heart. He considered it uncanny and asked the dream diviner, who divined and said, "The [spirit of] the Ching River is creating an evil influence." The Second Emperor thereupon fasted at Wang-i Palace, intending to offer a sacrifice to the Ching [River] and to drown four white horses. He sent messengers to reprimand [Chao] Kao about the matter of the bandits.[49] Kao was frightened and then secretly consulted with his son-in-law, the prefect of Hsien-yang, Yen Lo, and his younger brother, Chao Ch'eng, saying, "His Majesty does not listen to admonitions. Now the matter becomes urgent and he intends to lay the distress on our lineage. I want to replace His Majesty and set up Prince Tzu-ying

---

[48] At this time Chao Kao, the powerful eunuch, had already been appointed imperial chancellor.

[49] Here the bandits refer to the rebellious forces. Chao Kao had previously said to the emperor that these bandits were not worth worrying about. Now the Ch'in general, Chang Han, had been defeated and was surrounded by Hsiang Yü. Nearly all the territory east of the Han-ku Pass was occupied by the rebel forces, and Liu Pang was advancing toward the west. Chao Kao was frightened and feigned illness to avoid seeing the emperor. Thus a messenger was sent by the emperor to reprimand Chao Kao (*SC* 6:37a–b; *HS* 1A:13b).

instead. Tzu-ying is kind and thrifty and all the people honor his words."
He ordered the prefect of the gentlemen of the palace[50] to respond
within. Falsely announcing that there were great bandits, he ordered
[Yen] Lo to summon officers to send soldiers to chase [the bandits]. He
took [Yen] Lo's mother by force and put her in Miss Kao's residence.[51]
He sent [Yen] Lo to lead the officers and soldiers, numbering more
than one thousand men. When they arrived at the hall gate of Wang-i
Palace, they bound the prefect of the guard and the supervisor, and
said, "The bandits entered here. Why did you not stop them?" The
prefect of the guard said, "At all the posts around [the palace] I have
placed soldiers who are very alert. How could the bandits dare to
enter the palace?" [Yen] Lo then beheaded the prefect of the guard
and directly led the officers who entered [the palace] shooting. The
gentlemen and the eunuchs were greatly frightened. Some fled and
some resisted; those who resisted were always killed. The dead
[amounted] to tens of men. The prefect of the gentlemen of the palace
and [Yen] Lo entered together and shot at the curtain where His
Majesty was sitting. The Second Emperor became angry and summoned
his attendants. All the attendants were terrified and did not fight.

At the side [of the emperor] there was one eunuch who was in attendance and did not dare to leave. The Second Emperor went inside
and said to him, "Why didn't you, sir, tell me earlier? And now it has
come to this." The eunuch said, "I, Your servant, did not dare to mention it; thus, I, Your servant, am able to preserve [myself]. If I, Your
servant, had told you earlier, I would have been killed. How could I
[have lived] up to the present." Yen Lo advanced, went close to the
Second Emperor, and enumerated [his wrong doings], saying, "You
sir,[52] are arrogant and unrestrained; you kill [people] and are not in
accordance with the Way. All in the empire are rebelling against you,
sir. You, sir, make a plan for yourself." The Second Emperor said,
"Is it possible to see the imperial chancellor?" [Yen] Lo said, "No."
The Second Emperor said, "I should like to have one commandery
and become a king." This was not granted. He then said, "I should

---

[50] The post of prefect of the gentlemen of the palace had previously been held by
Chao Kao. Apparently the post was given to someone else, since Chao had been
appointed imperial chancellor. According to Hsü Kuang, Chao Kao's younger
brother, Chao Ch'eng 趙成, was the prefect at this time (P'ei: *SC* 6:38a).

[51] Apparently he did not trust Yen Lo 閻樂 entirely and therefore kept his mother
as hostage.

[52] Here the term 足下, a conventional address used between men of equal status,
was used instead of 陛下 "Your Majesty."

like to be a ten thousand household marquis." This was not granted. He said, "I and my wife and children would like to be commoners [with a status] like those of the various princes." Yen Lo said, "I, Your subject, received the order from the imperial chancellor to kill you, sir, on behalf of the [people of the] empire. Although you, sir, have many words, I dare not report [it to the imperial chancellor]." He motioned for his soldiers to advance. The Second Emperor committed suicide. Yen Lo returned and reported to Chao Kao.[53]

Chao Kao then summoned all the various great officials and the princes, informed them of the circumstances of the killing of the Second Emperor, and said, "Originally Ch'in was a kingdom. The First Emperor became the ruler of the empire; therefore he proclaimed himself emperor. Now the six kingdoms have re-established themselves. The territory of Ch'in becomes smaller and smaller, and yet being an emperor in name without the reality is impossible. It is proper to become a king as it was originally." Thereupon he installed the Second Emperor's elder brother's son, Prince Tzu-ying, as the king of Ch'in.[54] The Second Emperor was buried according to [the ceremony for] commoners, in the I-ch'un Park south of Tu. [Chao Kao] ordered Tzu-ying to fast, and then to visit the [imperial ancestral] temple to receive the seal of the king.

Having fasted for five days, Tzu-ying plotted together with his two sons, saying, "The imperial chancellor, [Chao] Kao, killed the Second Emperor in the Wang-i Palace. He fears that he will be killed by the various ministers. I heard that Chao Kao has made an agreement with Ch'u to exterminate the royal family of Ch'in and to become the king of the area within the passes. Now he tells me to fast and to visit the [ancestral] temple. Thus, he wants to kill me in the temple. If I declare myself ill and do not go, the imperial chancellor must come by himself. When he comes, we will then kill him." [Chao] Kao sent someone to invite Tzu-ying, and several men were sent [in succession]. Tzu-ying

[53] A different report is found in *Shih-chi* 87, which states that Chao Kao falsely issued an edict to order the imperial guards to wear plain clothes and to face the palace with arms in their hands. Then Chao Kao reported to the emperor that the bandits had arrived, and he forced the emperor to commit suicide (*SC* 87:23b).

[54] According to *SC* 87:23b, Chao Kao intended to make himself ruler. It states that after the death of the emperor, Chao Kao took the emperor's seal and wore it. The various officials did not follow him in ascending to the palace and three times the palace hall seemed to be in danger of collapsing (cf. Bodde, *China's First Unifier*, p. 53). Chao Kao himself realized that Heaven had not given him the mandate and that the various officials would not consent. Then he summoned the First Emperor's grandson (the text has younger brother, which is an error) and gave him the seal.

did not go. [Chao] Kao, as was expected, went in person and said, "[The matter] of the ancestral temple is an important affair. Why do you, King, not go?" Tzu-ying thereupon stabbed and killed[55] [Chao] Kao in the palace for fasting, exterminated the three *tsu*[56] of Kao's family, and exposed their corpses in Hsien-yang.[57] [*SC* 6:37a–39b]

8. Old Powerful Families Moved to the Capital

199 B.C.   [Liu Ching said to Emperor Kao], "The area of Ch'in has been devastated recently. Its population is small and its land is fertile; it can be filled with more [people]. When the feudal lords[58] first rose [in revolt], no one except the T'ien of Ch'i, the Chao, Ch'ü, and Ching of Ch'u were able to arise.[59] Now although Your Majesty has Your capital in Kuan-chung, yet its population is small; in the north it is close to the Hu invaders;[60] in the east there are the strong lineages of the six [old] states.[61] If some day there should be an emergency, Your Majesty would not be able to sleep on Your high pillow.[62] Your subject wishes that Your Majesty would move the various T'ien of Ch'i, the Chao, the

---

[55] According to *SC* 87:23b, however, it was a eunuch of Tzu-ying, Han T'an 韓談, who stabbed and killed Chao Kao under the instruction of Tzu-ying. Before the plot was put into action, Han was consulted by Tzu-ying.

[56] For the extermination of the three *tsu*, see I, 1, n. 1.

[57] Cf. Édouard Chavannes, *Les Mémoires historiques de Se-ma Ts'ien* (5 vols.; Paris, 1895–1905), II, 211–17.

[58] That is, the men who revolted against the sovereignty of Ch'in. Most of them made themselves kings.

[59] The *Han-shu* reads *yü* 與, "to participate," instead of *hsing* 興, "to arise."

The rebel leaders who were members of the old ruling families of the old states were (1) T'ien Tan, who became king of Ch'i (those who succeeded him in Ch'i were all five from the T'ien family, see III, 5); (2) Ching Chü, who was king of Ch'u (*SC* 7:4a; *HS* 1A:8a); (3) Huai Hsin 懷心, grandson of King Huai of Ch'u, who was king of Ch'u (*SC* 7:5b; *HS* 1A:8b, 31:11a); (4) Han Ch'eng, king of Han (*HS* 1A:20a); (5) Chao Hsieh, king of Chao (*HS* 1A:8a); (6) Wei Chiu and Wei Pao, kings of Wei (*SC* 48:6a, 90:1a; *HS* 31:5b, 33:1a).

However, the man who first started the rebellion, Ch'en Sheng, and who declared himself king of Chang-ch'u, was a man of humble origin. Besides Ch'en, Wu Ch'en, the king of Chao, and Han Kuang 韓廣, the king of Yen, had no connections with the old ruling families.

[60] According to Liu Ching, the nearest distance between the Hsiung-nu and Ch'ang-an was 700 *li*. Horsemen with light equipment could cover this distance in a day and a night.

[61] That is, Ch'i, Ch'u, Yen, Han, Chao, and Wei.

[62] The *Han-shu* reads *an* 安, "comfortable," "peaceful," instead of "high" *kao* 高. See III, 4, n. 21.

Ch'ü, and the Ching of Ch'u,[63] the descendants of [the old states of] Yen, Chao, Han, and Wei, and other famous families[64] of powerful and awe-inspiring persons[65] [and make them] take up residence in Kuan-chung. If there is no trouble [inside the empire], they could be used in preparation for defense against the Hu. Should the feudal lords[66] revolt, then they could be led to launch an attack to the east. This is the way to strengthen the trunk and weaken the branches." The emperor said, "Good." He then ordered Liu Ching to move those mentioned above, more than one hundred thousand persons, to Kuan-chung. [*SC* 99:5a; *HS* 43:13b–14a]

9. TRANSFER OF OLD POWERFUL FAMILIES

In the eleventh month [of the ninth year of Emperor Kao] the emperor moved[67] the great lineages of Ch'i and Ch'u—the people of five surnames of Chao, Ch'ü, Ching, Huai, and T'ien[68]—to Kuan-chung[69] and gave them good land and houses. [*HS* 1B:12a]

199 B.C.

[63] According to Yen (*HS* 43:13b), the Chao, Ch'ü, Ching, and T'ien were lineages of the kings of the old feudal states of Ch'u and Ch'i. The clan of Huai, which is not mentioned here, was also included among the big lineages of Ch'u that were moved to Kuan-chung. See III, 9, and n. 68 of that passage.

[64] An example of this category may be found in III, 10.

[65] The term "powerful and awe-inspiring persons" 豪傑 or 傑 originally meant men who were regarded as above the multitude in intellect and ability. According to *Huai-nan-tzu*, there were four degrees of these elites: *ying* 英, those superior to ten thousand men; *tsun* 俊, those superior to a thousand men; *hao*, those superior to one hundred men; and *chieh*, those superior to ten men (*HNT* 20:10b). Gradually the term was used to mean a person who was awe-inspiring and able to command obedience from others. It implies that he could assume a certain kind of leadership. However, the various uses of this term have given it various connotations that can only be determined by the context. The person described as a *hao-chieh* might be a political or military leader, a redresser-of-wrongs, or any influential person. In general, it signifies a person who possesses considerable personal power because of his position and influence in a locality. Since there is no exact equivalent in English, I have arbitrarily translated it as "powerful and awe-inspiring persons."

[66] The feudal lords referred to here were various kings and marquises ennobled by Han. They were all located east of Kuan-chung.

[67] This followed Lou (Liu) Ching's suggestion; see III, 8.

[68] In the biography of Lou (Liu) Ching, the number of persons specified under the category of powerful families of the old feudal states is given as one hundred thousand; see III, 8. Obviously powerful families of states other than those mentioned were also moved. It is probable that the five mentioned here were the most outstanding among the families of the old states.

[69] According to the "Treatise on Geography" in the *Han-shu*, the families of the T'ien of Ch'i, and Chao, Ch'ü, Ching of Ch'u, as well as those of the meritorious officials, were moved to Ch'ang-ling (the imperial mausoleum of Emperor Kao). Apparently these families were distributed in the area of Kuan-chung, with the mausoleum as one of the centers.

10. FAMILY OF OLD NOBLES

Lien Fan,[70] whose style was Shu-tu, was a native of Tu-ling of Ching-chao. He was a descendant of Lien P'o, a general of the state of Chao.

Ca. 198 B.C. When the Han arose, because the Lien family was of a powerful lineage,[71] it was moved there from K'u-hsing.[72] For generations [members of the family] were administrators of border commanderies. Because some of them were buried in Hsiang-wu in the Lung-hsi commandery, they held official positions [as being natives from] there. [Fan's] great-grandfather, Pao, was the general of the right during the time of [em-

32–1 B.C. perors] Ch'eng and Ai. His grandfather, Tan, was grand minister of war and shepherd of the regional division of Yung[73] during the time of

A.D. 9–23 Wang Mang. They were all famous in Early Han. [*HHS* 31:11b–12a]

11. POWERFUL PERSONS

Before 197 B.C. Coming to the time when Han arose, the net of the law was loose and had not yet been rectified. Therefore the chancellor of Tai, Ch'en Hsi,[74] had a thousand escort chariots. And [the king of] Wu, Pi,[75] and [the king of] Huai-nan[76] all invited guests to the number of a thousand [each]. The members of the consort family and the high ministers such as [the marquis of] Wei-ch'i[77] and the [marquis of] Wu-an[78] emulated

---

[70] Lien Fan 廉范 (*fl.* 58–83) lost his father while still in his early teens. He entered his official career as merit evaluator in a commandery government. He later became the governor of Yün-chung (*HHS* 31:11b–15a).

[71] Apparently moving the Lien family was a result of Lou (Liu) Ching's suggestion to move the various powerful families in order to put them under direct control. The Lien family obviously fell within the category of "famous families of powerful and awe-inspiring persons" mentioned by Lou. See III, 8.

[72] K'u-hsing 苦陘 was located in what is now Wu-chi county in central western Hopei.

[73] Wang Mang changed the name of I 益 division to Yung 庸 circuit (*HHS* 31:12a).

[74] Ch'en Hsi revolted in 197 B.C.; see II, 16. A detailed report of his gathering of guests and establishing power is given in *SC* 93:7b–8a.

[75] Liu Pi 劉濞, king of Wu, harbored a large number of fugitives and convicts in his kingdom. All his guests were made military officials to lead his troops when he rebelled in 154 B.C. (*SC* 106:2a, 3b–4a, 9a, 11a, 12a; *HS* 35:4b, 5b–6a, 12a–b).

[76] Liu An, king of Huai-nan, was fond of books and guests. He kept many guests and men specializing in magical sciences to a number of several thousand persons. Books on general matters and on magic were compiled by them. All his guests were arrested and killed when his plot to rebel was disclosed in 122 B.C. He committed suicide (*HS* 44:8b, 13a–14a).

[77] The marquis of Wei-ch'i was Tou Ying, who became grand general in 154 B.C. and imperial chancellor in 140/139 B.C. He was fond of guests and was very generous to them (*HS* 52:1a–b, 3a; III, 16, n. 105).

[78] The marquis of Wu-an was T'ien Fen, who became grand commandant in 140/139 B.C. and imperial chancellor in 135 B.C. (*HS* 52:3a; III, 16, n. 102).

one another in the imperial capital. The wandering redressers-of-wrong among the commoners, such as Chü Meng and Kuo Hsieh,[79] rushed about in the rural communities. Their power spread over the regional divisions, and their might made the dukes and marquises bow. The masses honored their names and achievements and longed for and admired them. . . .

From the time of the [marquis of] Wei-ch'i, the [marquis of] Wu-an, and [the king of] Huai-nan on, . . . the powerful and awe-inspiring persons in the commanderies and kingdoms could be found everywhere. In the imperial capital the imperial relatives and relatives-in-law followed immediately one after the other. This indeed is a normal phenomenon both in the past and the present and is not particularly worth mentioning.

Only in the time of Emperor Ch'eng [does the situation change]; 32–37 B.C. the emperor's mother's family, the Wang family,[80] was very prosperous with many guests, with Lou Hu as their leader.[81] And in the time of Wang Mang, among the high officials Ch'en Tsun was cock of the walk and among the redressers-of-wrongs of the rural communities Yüan She[82] was the first. [*HS* 92:1b–2b]

12. A REDRESSER-OF-WRONGS

In Lo-yang there was [a man named] Chü Meng. While the people of Chou[83] made their livelihood by means of trading, Chü Meng was known to the feudal lords because of his activities as a redresser-of-wrongs.[84] At the time when Wu and Ch'u rebelled, the marquis of 154 B.C. T'iao[85] was grand commandant. When riding in a relay carriage and about to reach Honan, he met Chü Meng. He was pleased and said,

---

[79] On Chü Meng and Kuo Hsieh, see III, 12 and 20.

[80] Wang Mang's family.

[81] Lou Hu was an extraordinarily talented man and a distinguished orator. He won the respect of all the guests of the Wang family. He held the position of grandee remonstrant and was grand administrator of a commandery. When Wang Mang came to power, he was given the title of marquis (*HS* 92:7a–9a).

[82] For Yüan She, see III, 47.

[83] Chou signifies the imperial domain of Eastern Chou, that is, present day central Honan.

[84] *Jen-hsia;* see III, 1, n. 2.

[85] The marquis of T'iao was Chou Ya-fu, the son of Chou Po. Between 156 and 154 B.C. Chou Ya-fu held the post of general of chariots and cavalry. In 154 B.C., during the rebellion, he was promoted to the post of grand commandant. He held the post of imperial chancellor from 150 to 147 B.C. (*SC* 57:7a–12a; *HS* 40:26a–30a).

"Wu and Ch'u have started a big affair, but, since they did not try to get Meng, I am sure they will not be able to accomplish anything." When great uprisings occurred in the world, the ministers got hold of [Meng] just as they got hold of an enemy country.

Chü Meng's activities were for the most part like those of Chu Chia,[86] but he was fond of *po*[87] and of most of the young men's amusements.

When Chü Meng's mother died, those who came from remote places to attend the funeral rode in about a thousand carriages, but when Chü Meng [himself] died, his family did not have property [worth] even ten [catties of] gold left. [*SC* 124:3b–4a; *HS* 92:3a–b]

13. POWERFUL FAMILY EXTERMINATED

Before
150 B.C.   The Hsien of Chi-nan were a lineage of more than three hundred families. They were powerful and cunning. None of the 2,000-picul [officials][88] could control them. Therefore Emperor Ching appointed [Chih] Tu[89] to the post of grand administrator of Chi-nan. On his arrival he immediately exterminated the chief offenders from the Hsien clan, together with their families.[90] The rest [were so frightened] that their legs trembled. [*SC* 122:2a–b; *HS* 90:2a–b]

14. LOCAL POWERFUL PERSONS EXECUTED

Ca. 150–
141 B.C.   A native of Fu-li,[91] Wang Meng, was also famous for his activities in redressing wrongs in the region between the Chiang and the Huai [rivers].

[86] For Chu Chia, see III, 1.

[87] *Po*, i.e., *liu-po* 六博, is a kind of game played by two persons. For details, see Yang Lien-sheng, "A Note on the So-called TLV Mirrors and the Game *Liu-po*," *Harvard Journal of Asiatic Studies*, IX (1947), 202–6; *idem*, "An Additional Note on the Ancient Game *Liu-po*," *HJAS*, XVI (1952), 124–39.

[88] That is, the grand administrators of the commandery.

[89] Chih Tu was an official famous for his honesty and courage. In 150 he was appointed commandant of the capital (*HS* 19B:4b). He was strict in enforcing the law and did not spare the nobles and high officials. In 148 he investigated the case of the king of Lin-chiang, the son of Emperor Ching, who then committed suicide (*HS* 5:5b). This angered the empress dowager, and Chih was dismissed. Later when Chih Tu was holding the post of grand administrator of Yen-men and violated a certain law, she insisted that Chih be executed although Emperor Ching considered him a loyal official and wanted to pardon him (*HS* 90:2b–3a; cf. 53:3a).

[90] The phrase *tsu-mieh* 族滅 means literally "to exterminate by family or clan." For a discussion of this punishment, see I, 1, n. 1.

[91] Fu-li was located in modern Su-hsien in northern Anhui.

At that time the Hsien [family] of Chi-nan and Chou Yung of Ch'en were also known for their domination. When Emperor Ching heard of them, he sent out a commissioner and killed all the persons of this kind. Later the Pai [families] of the Tai commandery, Han Wu-pi of [the old state of] Liang, Hsüeh K'uang of Yang-chai,[92] and Han Ju of Shan[93] came forth again in large numbers. [*SC* 124:4a; *HS* 92:3b]

15. A POWERFUL OFFICIAL DISMISSED

After the death of Chih Tu[94] many of the imperial relatives around Ch'ang-an were violent and violated the law. Thereupon His Majesty summoned Ning Ch'eng and appointed him commandant of the capital.[95] In his administration he imitated Chih Tu, but he was not as incorrupt as [Chih Tu]. Nevertheless, the imperial relatives and the powerful and outstanding persons were all terrified. 148 B.C. 144 B.C.

When Emperor Wu ascended the throne, [Ning Ch'eng] was transferred to the position of clerk of the capital region. Many of the imperial relatives-in-law censured Ch'eng's faults. He was found guilty and had his head shaved and a collar put around his neck.

At this time, when any of the Nine Ministers was found guilty and sentenced to death, he was put to death; only a few had suffered physical punishment. Ch'eng suffered an extremely severe punishment.[96] Considering that he would never again be given an office, he broke the chain, falsely carved a passport,[97] got through the pass,[98] and returned home. He said, "If an official fails to attain [a position of] 2,000 piculs, or if a merchant fails to acquire [a fortune of] ten million cash, how can he equal others?" Then he borrowed money and purchased more than one thousand *ch'ing* of land with reservoirs. He rented land to the poor people, and thus obtained the services of several thousand families.

[92] Yang-chai was located in modern central Honan.

[93] According to Hsü Kuang, Shan 陝 should be written Ch'i 郟, which was a prefecture belonging to the Ying-ch'uan commandery. According to Yen (*HS* 92:3b), Shan was Shan-hsien 陝縣 of Shan Chou 陝州 of T'ang. Shan-hsien is modern Shanhsien in western Honan.

[94] For Chih Tu, see III, 13.

[95] In 144 B.C. (*HS* 19B:5a).

[96] That is, he had his head shaved and an iron collar placed around his neck, as noted above. This was a punishment imposed on those who were condemned to a five-year sentence and sent to build city walls or to pound rice. See II, 13, n. 51.

[97] During the time of Han, it was necessary to show a passport (*ch'uan* 傳) at the passes.

[98] The Han-ku Pass.

A few years later he met with a general amnesty. He acquired property worth several thousand [catties of] gold.[99] He engaged in activities of redressing wrongs and dominated the officials by finding fault with them. When he went out, he was followed by several tens of mounted attendants. In making use of the people his authority superseded that of a commandery administrator. [*SC* 122:3b–4a; *HS* 90:3b–4a]

16. A FORMER POWERFUL OFFICIAL

Ca.
135 B.C.

Kuan Fu[100] was stern and upright. He was unrestrained when drunk. He did not like to flatter a person to his face. To those noble relatives who in their power were superior to him he did not want to show politeness and always treated them with contempt. Those who were inferior to him he treated as equals, and the poorer and more humble they were the more he showed them respect. . . . Fu did not like literary studies, but took pleasure in acting as a redresser-of-wrongs. He was a man of his word. Those with whom he associated were all powerful and awe-inspiring persons and men of great cunning. His family property grew to several tens of millions. The guests who ate his food numbered from several tens to a hundred each day. He had reservoirs and fields and gardens. The members of his lineage and his guests strove for power and profits and were overbearing in Ying-ch'uan. The children of Ying-ch'uan sang:

> While the Ying River is clear
> The Kuan family will be secure;
> When the Ying River is muddy
> The Kuan family will be exterminated. . . .

In the spring of the fourth year[101] of Yüan-kuang the imperial chan-

99 The *Han-shu* has several tens of millions.

100 Kuan Fu and his father both fought in the campaign against the kingdom of Wu. The father was killed, and the son, seeking revenge, hurled himself against the enemy and was badly injured (II, 23). He was appointed general of the gentlemen of the palace, chancellor of Tai, grand administrator of Huai-yang, and later, in 140 B.C., grand keeper of equipages. The following year, while drunk, he struck his companion, Tou Fu 竇甫, a cousin of Empress Dowager Tou. Emperor Wu, fearing Kuan's execution by the empress dowager, removed him from the capital and gave him the post of chancellor of the kingdom of Yen. Several years later Kuan was dismissed from office because he had violated the law, and he again took up residence in Ch'ang-an.

101 According to Hsü Kuang, quoted by P'ei, the fourth year should be the third year.

cellor[102] told [the emperor] that Kuan Fu's family in Ying-ch'uan was so violent that the people were in distress, and he petitioned for an investigation. His Majesty said, "This is an affair of the imperial chancellor. Why do you petition for it?" [Kuan] Fu seized on the private affairs of the imperial chancellor, accusing him of making profit by corrupt practices, of receiving gold from the king of Huai-nan,[103] and of having conversations with [the latter]. The guests [of the two] acted as intermediaries and the [dispute] was closed.

In the summer the imperial chancellor took the daughter of the king of Yen[104] as his wife. There was an edict of the Empress Dowager [Wang] ordering all the marquises and the members of the imperial family to go to congratulate him. The marquis of Wei-ch'i[105] went to see Kuan Fu . . . and forced [Fu] to go along with him. . . . When the marquis of Wei-ch'i was leaving [the feast], he signaled to Kuan Fu to go out. [The marquis of] Wu-an[106] thereupon became furious and said, "This is my fault for having been arrogant to Kuan Fu." Then he ordered his horsemen to detain Kuan Fu. . . . He accused Kuan Fu of insulting a guest[107] and of not respecting [the command of the empress dowager]. He imprisoned him in the Chü-shih[108] and then investigated former matters [concerning him]. Officers were sent by groups to arrest the various members of the Kuan family. All of them were sentenced to be executed in the market place. . . .

[The marquis of Wei-ch'i] said [to Emperor Wu] that Kuan Fu had been drunk and had eaten to the full and that the affair was not serious

---

[102] T'ien Fen was a half-brother by the same mother of Empress Wang, the wife of Emperor Ching (I, 20). When Emperor Wu ascended the throne, T'ien Fen was ennobled as marquis of Wu-an. When Tou Ying was imperial chancellor, he held the position of grand commandant. In 139 B.C. he was dismissed from this office by Empress Dowager Tou at the time Tou Ying lost his post. After the death of Empress Dowager Tou, in 135, he was appointed imperial chancellor (SC 107:2b–4b; HS 52:2b–4a).

[103] Liu An, who rebelled in 122 B.C. See I, 25, n. 116, and II, 27, n. 91.

[104] According to Yen, the king of Yen was Liu Chia 劉嘉, the son of Liu Che 劉澤.

[105] Tou Ying. He was the grand general and was ennobled as the marquis of Wei-ch'i after the Rebellion of the Seven Kingdoms was put down. In 140 B.C. he was promoted to the post of imperial chancellor, but a few months later he was dismissed because his aunt, the Empress Dowager Tou, disliked him. From then on, until his execution in 131 B.C., he lived in retirement and became a fast friend of Kuan Fu, who had also lost his political influence.

[106] T'ien Fen, the imperial chancellor.

[107] At the feast Kuan Fu considered that his friend, the marquis of Wei-ch'i, had not been treated with sufficient respect. He then insulted the imperial chancellor and one of the guests.

[108] Chü-shih 居室 was a prison supervised by the privy treasurer (HS 19A:8b).

enough for execution. His Majesty considered him right, bestowed food upon him, and said, "Argue it in the East Court."[109] [The marquis of] Wei-ch'i went to the East Court and highly praised the virtue of Kuan Fu; he said that Kuan Fu was at fault [only] because of his drunkenness and his eating to the full, and that the imperial chancellor had falsely charged him with other affairs. [The marquis of] Wu-an again made the accusation that Kuan Fu's behavior was violent and unrestrained, and that his crime was one of great perversion and impiety. [The marquis of] Wei-ch'i, considering that there was no other alternative, then mentioned the faults of the imperial chancellor. . . . Thereupon His Majesty asked the court officials which of the two men was right. The grandee secretary, Han An-kuo, said, ". . . The imperial chancellor also said that Kuan Fu associates with treacherous and cunning persons and encroaches on the small people, that at his home there are accumulated a hundred millions, that [the family] is violent in Ying-ch'uan, that he oppresses the imperial lineage and encroaches upon the bones and flesh.[110] . . . The imperial chancellor's words are also right. . . ."

. . . During the reign of Emperor Ching [the marquis of] Wei-ch'i had received an imperial mandate which said, "Whenever there is something inconvenient, you are allowed to discuss it and present it to the emperor. . . ." Wei-ch'i then ordered his nephew to present a memorial, mentioning the point, and hoped that he might be called to see the emperor. . . . Then Wei-ch'i was accused of making a false mandate[111] in the name of the late emperor and was sentenced to be executed.

132 B.C.   In the tenth month of the fifth year[112] [of Yüan-kuang] all the family members of Kuan Fu were executed. . . . [The marquis of Wei-ch'i] was executed in the city of Wei on the last day of the twelfth month. [*SC* 107:7a, 9a, 10a–b, 11a–b, 12b, 13a–b; *HS* 52:5a–11b]

---

[109] According to Ju Shun, the East Court refers to the court of the empress dowager.

[110] That is, one's kindred. Here it refers to the imperial lineage. Semantically the two phrases are practically identical.

[111] The mandate was given to Tou Ying by Emperor Ching personally. Since no duplicate was found in the office of the masters of writing, the mandate privately kept in Tou's family was considered a false one.

[112] Hsü Kuang, quoted by Pei, doubts that it was the fifth year. Ssu-ma agrees with him and states that Hsü Kuang's argument is based on the "Annals of Emperor Wu," which record the execution of the marquis of Wei-ch'i in the winter of the fourth year of Yüan-kuang (cf. *HS* 6:5b).

17. ESTATE OF A MARQUIS

[The marquis of] Wu-an[113] from this time on[114] became more and more overbearing. The residence he built was superior to all other mansions. His fields and gardens were the most fertile. The [bearers of the] utensils and articles that he bought from the commanderies and prefectures formed a continuous line on the roads. In his front hall he set up bells and drums, and hoisted a banner on a curved pole.[115] The women in his inner halls numbered a hundred. All the feudal lords offered him gold, jade, dogs, horses, and curios, which were countless.[116] [*SC* 107:5b; *HS* 52:4b]

135 B.C.

18. POWERFUL FAMILIES MOVED BY THE GOVERNMENT

[Chu-fu Yen][117] also advised the emperor, saying, "Mao-ling has just been established. Throughout the empire the families of the powerful and awe-inspiring persons and of the engrossers, who inflame the masses, should all be moved to Mao-ling.[118] Within, this will strengthen the capital region, and without, this will eliminate the treacherous and cunning persons. This is called getting rid of the harmful without using punishments."

The emperor again followed his suggestion.[119] [*HS* 64A:19b]

127 B.C.

19. POWERFUL FAMILIES MOVED

The powerful and awe-inspiring persons of the various command-

127 B.C.

[113] T'ien Fen, who was then the imperial chancellor.

[114] After the death of Empress Dowager Tou, when he was appointed imperial chancellor.

[115] According to Ju Shun and Su Liu, the *ch'ü chan* 曲旃 was a silk banner mounted on a pole that curved at the end. It could be used only by high officials.

[116] T'ien Fen himself once acknowledged in the presence of the emperor that he was fond of music, dogs, horses, land, houses, musicians, comedians, and skillful artisans (*SC* 107:10b–11a; *HS* 52:9b).

[117] When he made this suggestion, Chu-fu Yen was a palace grandee. He was a staunch supporter of the absolute concentration of power in the hands of the central government; see I, 23, and n. 104.

[118] Mao-ling, Emperor Wu's mausoleum, was built in 138 B.C. It was located eighty *li* northwest of Ch'ang-an (*SFHT*, p. 55).

[119] It should be pointed out that this idea was not initiated by Chu-fu and that this was not the first time people were moved to an imperial mausoleum. Emperor Kao had moved the powerful families of the old states and the families of meritorious officials to his mausoleum, Ch'ang-ling; see III, 9, n. 69.

eries and kingdoms and those whose wealth was three million [cash] or more were moved to Mao-ling. [*HS* 6:9a]

20. A Powerful Redresser-of-Wrongs

Before
125 B.C.
180–
157 B.C.

Kuo Hsieh, who was a native of Chih[120] and whose style was Weng-po, was the son of the daughter of Hsü Fu,[121] a skillful physiognomist. Hsieh's father was executed in the time of Emperor Hsiao-wen because he engaged in the activities of the redressers-of-wrongs. Hsieh was small and short, but energetic and fierce. He drank no wine. When he was young, he was secretly malevolent and sentimentally moved.[122] Those whom he killed because they displeased him were very numerous. He lent his life to avenging his friends. He hid fugitives, acted illegally, robbed ceaselessly, cast coins [illegally], and violated graves. His offenses were countless. . . .

As Hsieh grew older, he changed his intentions and became frugal. He repaid injustice with kindness and gave generously with little hope of return. However, his own pleasure in acting as a redresser-of-wrongs was even greater. When he saved the life of another, he did not boast of his merit. His secret malevolence was rooted in his heart; it emerged suddenly as before whenever there was an angry look [exchanged]. The young men, admiring his behavior, frequently took vengeance on his behalf without his knowledge. . . .

Whenever Hsieh entered or left, all the people got out of his way. [Once] there was one man who squatted and looked at him. Hsieh sent someone to ask his name and surname. Certain guests wanted to kill him. Hsieh said, "While I stayed at my own native place I was not respected; this must be because my virtue has not been cultivated. What is wrong with him?" Then he secretly told a clerk of the [prefectural] commandant, "I think highly of this man. Whenever his term comes to render labor service, see that he is exempted."[123]

[120] Chih was located in modern Chi-yüan, Honan.

[121] The character *fu* 負 can be read as a proper name or as meaning "woman." In the latter case it is written interchangeably with *fu* 媍. *HS* 40:26a also mentions a physiognomist Hsü Fu 許負.

[122] The *Han-shu* reads *kan-k'ai* 感概 instead of *k'ai* 慨. Wang Hsien-ch'ien thinks that the omission in the *Shih-chi* was an error. The phrase *kan-k'ai* is explained by Yen as meaning "to be moved in spirit and establish integrity" 感意氣而立節概. However, Wang Hsien-ch'ien, who points out that 感概 should be 感慨, which means "sentimentally moved" (*HSPC* 92:3b–4a), rejects Yen's interpretation.

[123] *Chien-keng* 踐更 is one of the three technical terms referring to one month's labor service rendered by adults. Ju Shun defined it as "hired service" (*HS* 7:8a). This is

Repeatedly it was time for labor service, and after several terms had passed and the officers had not sought him, the man, being astonished, asked the reason. He was informed that it was Hsieh who had had him released. The man who had squatted then bared his shoulder and apologized. Hearing this, the young men felt even more admiration for Hsieh's behavior.

[Once] there were two natives of Lo-yang who hated each other. The virtuous and powerful persons in the city who attempted to act as arbitrators amounted to ten, but they were never heeded. Then a guest visited Kuo Hsieh. Hsieh visited the two enemy families in the night. The enemy families yielded and listened to Hsieh. Hsieh then said to the enemy families, "I heard that you did not listen to most of the gentlemen of Lo-yang who were arbitrators here. Now, fortunately, you listen to Hsieh. Why should Hsieh take away power from the local virtuous persons of another prefecture?" He left in the night without letting anyone know of it and said, "Don't wait for me. Wait until I have left, ask the powerful persons of Lo-yang to act as arbitrators and then listen to them." . . . The young men in the city and the virtuous and powerful men of the neighboring prefectures came to his door in the middle of the night with more than ten carriages and asked for Hsieh's guests in order to keep and support them.[124]

When the powerful and wealthy persons were moved to Mao-ling, Hsieh's family being poor did not fall in this category of wealth.[125] But the officials were afraid and did not dare not to move him. General Wei[126] spoke [to the emperor] about him, saying that Kuo Hsieh's family was poor and did not belong to those who should be moved. His Majesty said, "This commoner is so powerful that he can make you, General, speak for him. This shows that his family is not poor." Hsieh's

---

considered erroneous by Hamaguchi Shigekuni, Lao Kan, and other modern scholars. We follow the definition of Fu Ch'ien who said that *chien-keng* meant "to go on duty personally" 自行為卒 (*SC* 106:3a; *HS* 35:5b). For a detailed discussion, see Hamaguchi Shigekuni, "Senkō to kakō—Nyojun setsu no hihan," *Tōyō gakuhō*, XIX, No. 3 (1931), 84:107; *idem*, "Senkō to kakō—Nyojun setsu no hihan ho i," *Tōyō gakuhō*, XX, No. 2 (1932), 140–46; Lao Kan, "Han-tai ping-chih chi Han-chien chung ti ping-chih," *LSYY*, X (1948) 43–45; Yang Lien-sheng, "Schedules of Work and Rest in Imperial China," *Harvard Journal of Asiatic Studies*, XVIII (1955), 301–25.

[124] Ju Shun comments that Kuo Hsieh always kept numerous fugitives and that these young men of similar interests knew that fugitives usually approached Hsieh for protection. Therefore, they came with carriages to welcome them and take them away (*SC* 64:6a. Yen holds a similar view; see *HS* 92:5b).

[125] The criterion of wealth was three million and over.

[126] Wei Ch'ing was general of chariots and cavalry at that time (*HS* 55:2a, 3b–4a).

family was then moved. The notables who saw him off contributed more than ten million [cash].

Yang Chi-chu's son, a native of Chih, who was a bureau head of the prefectural [government], recommended the transfer of Hsieh.[127] Hsieh's older brother's son cut off the head of bureau head Yang. Hence the Yang family and the Kuo family became enemies.

Hsieh entered [Han-ku] Pass. The virtuous and powerful persons within the pass, regardless of whether or not they knew him, hearing of his fame, strove joyfully to associate with Hsieh. Hsieh was short and small, and he drank no wine. When he went out, he never had [an escort of] horsemen.

Later Yang Chi-chu was killed.[128] Yang Chi-chu's family presented a memorial. Someone killed [the person carrying the memorial] at the [palace] gate. When His Majesty was informed about it, he thereupon ordered officials to arrest Hsieh. Hsieh escaped. . . .

After a long time Hsieh was captured. He was thoroughly examined about his unlawful actions. All those who were killed by Hsieh were murdered before the pardon.[129] There was a Confucian scholar in Chih who was once in attendance at the seat of a commissioner. One of the guests praised Kuo Hsieh. The scholar said, "Kuo Hsieh purposely violated the public law by his evil deeds. How can he be considered virtuous?" Upon hearing this, one of Hsieh's guests killed the scholar and cut off his tongue. The officers blamed Hsieh for this. Actually Hsieh did not know who the murderer was. Till the end it was not known who the murderer was.

An official memorialized that Hsieh was not guilty. The Grandee Secretary Kung-sun Hung[130] gave his opinion, saying, "Hsieh, a commoner, acts as a redresser-of-wrongs and exercises power. He kills people because of an angry look. Although Hsieh does not know about [the murder], this crime is greater than if Hsieh himself had killed the man. He is guilty of great perversion and impiety." Thereupon Kuo Hsieh and his family were exterminated. [*SC* 124:4b–7a; similar *HS* 92:3b–6b]

---

[127] The *Han-shu* reads 扄之 instead of 舉徒解. It means that the bureau head blocked the contribution so that Kuo Hsieh was unable to get it.

[128] According to the *Han-shu*, Yang Chi-chu 楊季主 was killed by a man of the same city.

[129] As a rule, men who committed crimes before a general amnesty were exempt from punishment.

[130] Kung-sun Hung held the post of grandee secretary from 127 to 125 B.C. (*HS* 19B:6a–b).

21. Local Redressers-of-Wrongs

After this[131] those who engaged in activities of redressing wrongs were very numerous. They were imperious and not worth enumerating. However, Fan Chung-tzu of Ch'ang-an, Chao Wang-sun of Huai-li, and Kao Kung-tzu of Ch'ang-ling in Kuan-chung, Kuo Kung-chung of Hsio-ho, Lu Kung-ju of T'ai-yüan, Ni Ch'ang-ch'ing of Lin-huai, and T'ien[132] Chün-ju of Tung-yang, though they were engaged in activities of redressing wrongs, yet they were sincere and had the spirit of a yielding gentleman.[133]

As regards those such as the Yao in the north, the Tu in the west, Ch'ou Ching in the south, Chao T'a-yü [styled] Kung-tzu in the east, and Chao T'iao of Nan-yang, each of them was nothing but a Robber Chih[134] living among the people. How can they be worth mentioning? These are the people about whom old Chu Chia[135] would have felt shame. [*SC* 124:7a–b; *HS* 92:6b]

After 125 B.C.

22. Powerful Families Exterminated

When His Majesty heard of it, he promoted [Wang Wen-shu] to the position of grand administrator in Ho-nei.[136]

Before 119 B.C.

During the time he was in Kuang-p'ing he had known all the powerful and lawless families of Ho-nei. When he went [to his new post], he reached it in the ninth month. He ordered that fifty private horses in the commandery be prepared for a relay service going from Ho-nei

---

[131] That is, after Kuo Hsieh's death, which occurred about 127–125 B.C.

[132] The *Han-shu* has Ch'en 陳 instead of T'ien 田.

[133] Yielding was a virtue highly emphasized by the Confucians. In the eyes of Confucius' disciples it was one of the virtues possessed by the Great Master (*LYCS* 1:4a). Confucius once remarked that a gentleman has no contentions (*LYCS* 3:2b). He also mentions the importance of *li* and yielding in ruling a country (*LYCS* 4:2b).

[134] Robber Chih was described by Ssu-ma Ch'ien as one who killed innocent people daily, ate their livers, behaved tyrannically and recklessly, gathered thousands of followers around him, and acted contrary to all that was reasonable and right (*SC* 61:8b).

[135] For Chu Chia, see III, 1.

[136] Wang Wen-shu in his youth frequently engaged in unlawful activities. Later he became a subordinate of the commandant of justice and then was promoted to the post of chief commandant of Kuang-p'ing. Because of his success in wiping out bandits, the emperor considered him an able official and appointed him grand administrator of Ho-nei and then commandant of the capital in 119 B.C. After holding several other government posts, he committed suicide in 104 B.C. when he was found guilty of receiving a bribe and of other unlawful activities (see *HS* 90:7b–9b, 19B:6b–8a).

to Ch'ang-an.[137] He controlled his functionaries in the same way as during his days in Kuang-p'ing.[138]

He arrested the powerful and cunning persons in the commandery. The powerful and cunning persons in the commandery who were implicated and charged numbered more than a thousand families. He presented a memorandum to the throne, asking for the extermination of the *tsu*[139] in the cases of the principal offenders and the death penalty for the persons involved in the cases of small offenders, and that the entire family [property of the convicted ones] be confiscated and [used] to compensate for what they had stolen.[140] [*SC* 122:14b; *HS* 90:8a]

23. Chancellor Opposed by Redresser-of-Wrongs

103 b.c.   [Kung-sun] Ho succeeded Shih Ch'ing and eight years later became the imperial chancellor[141] and was ennobled as Ko-i Marquis. . . . Ho's son, Ching-sheng, replaced Ho as grand keeper of equipages. Both father and son were holding positions as ministers. Ching-sheng, being

[137] According to the law, punishments were applied before the twelfth month. After the day *li-ch'un*, there were no further sentences (*HHC* 4:2a–b). As Wang arrived at his post in the ninth month, the relay service was established to speed up the report and the approval of the sentences so that punishments could be administered in time.

[138] Wang Wen-shu, while holding the office of chief commandant in Kuang-p'ing kingdom, appointed bold and powerful persons, who had committed serious offenses, as his subordinates. Since he was in possession of their crime records, Wang was able to control and manipulate them. They would not be investigated if they succeeded in wiping out the bandits. Otherwise, they would be executed. For this reason it was said that robbers and bandits were wiped out of the area (*SC* 122:14b; *HS* 90:7b–8a).

[139] For the punishment of the three *tsu*, see I, 1, n. 1.

[140] Because of his special relay service, two or three days after he had sent his memorandum he received the answer of the emperor granting him his request. He proceeded rapidly with the application of the law and the commandery was cleaned up before the twelfth month.

[141] Kung-sun Ho's grandfather was a marquis. In his youth Ho was a horseman and achieved merit several times. When Emperor Wu was still the heir apparent, Ho held the post of member of the retinue of the heir apparent. After Emperor Wu ascended the throne, he was made grand keeper of equipages, and a few years later he became general of chariots and cavalry and participated in the military campaign against the Hsiung-nu under the command of the Grand General Wei Ch'ing. Because of his military merit he was ennobled marquis. However, he had no merit in the next two campaigns and lost his marquisate. When in 103 he was appointed imperial chancellor, he at first refused to accept the appointment because three of Emperor Wu's chancellors had lost their lives. (Li Ts'ai 李蔡 and Yen Ch'ing-ti were found guilty and committed suicide. Chao Chou 趙周 was imprisoned and died there.) Ho feared that the same fate might befall him. However, his effort to refuse was in vain (*HS* 66:1a–b; cf. *HS* 19B:5b, 7a–8a).

the son of an elder sister of the empress,[142] was arrogant and extravagant
and engaged in lawless conduct. During the Cheng-ho period he spent   92 B.C.
without authority nineteen million cash belonging to the Northern
Army.[143] The matter was discovered and he was imprisoned.

At that time an imperial edict was issued for the arrest of Chu An-shih
of Yang-ling, but it was impossible to capture him. The emperor wanted
him urgently. Ho himself offered to track down and arrest An-shih in
order to redeem the guilt of Ching-sheng. The emperor acquiesced.
Afterwards he, in fact, captured An-shih.

An-shih was a great redresser-of-wrongs in the capital. Hearing that
Ho was using him to ransom his son [from punishment], he laughed and
said, "The misfortune of the imperial chancellor shall now involve his
whole lineage. The bamboo of the Nan Shan will not be sufficient to
put down my statement [of accusation], nor will the wood of Yü Valley
be enough for the hand shackles I shall cause to be made." Thereupon
An-shih presented a letter to the emperor from prison, accusing Ching-
sheng of having had illicit intercourse with the princess of Yang-
shih,[144] of causing men to offer magical sacrifice to curse the emperor,
of going up to Kan-ch'üan Palace to bury a human image in the imperial highway, and of cursing with evil words. It was handed down
to the officials in charge who ordered Ho to be investigated and his
guilt looked into thoroughly. Therefore the father and son died in
prison. The calamity that the *wu-ku* [affair][145] brought upon the [im-
perial] family[146] was set in motion by Chu An-shih and was completed
by Chiang Ch'ung so that the princess, the empress, and the heir apparent all perished.

In the spring of the second year of Cheng-ho in an edict to the at-   91 B.C.
tendant secretary [the emperor said], "The former imperial chancellor,
Ho, relying on his old relations [with the emperor], took advantage of

[142] Kung-sun Ho's wife, Wei Chün-ju 衛君孺, was an elder sister of Empress Wei
(*HS* 66:1a).

[143] The Cheng-ho period covered the years 92–88 B.C. But according to the "Imperial Annals," Kung-sun Ho and his son were imprisoned and died in prison in the
first month of the second year of Cheng-ho, 91 B.C. (*HS* 6:29b). Therefore his son
could have spent the government money only in the year 92 B.C.

[144] The princess of Yang-shih was the daughter of Emperor Wu by Empress Wei
(*HS* 66:2a, 6:29b; Yen).

[145] For details concerning *wu-ku,* see Ch'ü T'ung-tsu, *Law and Society in Traditional
China* (Paris and The Hague, 1961), p. 222, n. 100.

[146] Here 家族 refers to the imperial family, not the family and lineage of Kung-
sun; cf. J. J. M. De Groot's translation, *The Religious System of China* (6 vols.; Leiden,
1892–1910), II, 829.

his high position and acted viciously. He set up good fields to benefit his descendants and guests. He did not care about the masses." [*HS* 66:1b–2b]

24. Powerful Persons Associated with Bandits

^{99/}
98 B.C.   In the eleventh month in the winter [of the second year of T'ien-han] a decree was issued to the chief commandant of [Han-ku] Pass, saying, "Now many of the powerful and awe-inspiring persons [in Kuan-chung] are making allies of the bandits at a far distance in the east. Let those going out and coming in be carefully examined." [*HS* 6:27b]

25. The Environs of an Imperial Palace Settled

96 B.C.   In the first month of the spring in the first year of T'ai-shih . . . the powerful and awe-inspiring persons among the officials and the common people from the [various] commanderies and kingdoms were moved to Mao-ling and Yün-ling.[147] [*HS* 6:28a–b]

26. Slaves of a Powerful Family

87–75 B.C.   At this time[148] the Grand General Ho Kuang[149] was in charge of the

[147] According to Yen, Yün-ling was not established during the reign of Emperor Wu (140–87 B.C.), but after his successor, Emperor Chao, ascended the throne in 87 B.C. at the mausoleum of Emperor Chao's deceased mother (cf. *HS* 7:1b, 97A:18a; *SFHT*, p. 57). The place mentioned in our text should therefore be Yün-yang. The commentator assumes that the people were transferred to Yün-yang because Kan-ch'üan Palace was located there. Yün-yang is equivalent to the northern part of modern Ching-yang county in central Shensi.

[148] At the time that Yin Weng-kuei 尹翁歸 was made a market official and before he had been chosen as an aide by the grand governor of Ho-tung, T'ien Yen-nien (cf. III, 27).

[149] Ho Kuang, who was the half-brother of Ho Ch'ü-ping, the general of the flash cavalry, became a gentleman on the recommendation of Ho Ch'ü-ping. After the death of the latter, he was promoted to the post of chief commandant custodian of the imperial equipages and imperial court grandee. After more than twenty years of service he won the confidence of Emperor Wu and was made grand minister of war and grand general in 87 B.C. Upon the death of Emperor Wu he was entrusted with the responsibility of helping and supporting the emperor's youngest son, the future Emperor Chao. Throughout Emperor Chao's reign (87–74 B.C.), Ho held the regency, virtually exercising the highest authority in the state. His daughter's daughter was made the empress. When Emperor Chao died, Ho placed the king of Ch'ang-i on the throne. The king was found to be dissolute and full of faults and was dethroned by the empress dowager at the request of Ho Kuang, who called a council and memorialized its decision to her. Emperor Hsüan was then put on the throne and Ho Kuang, whose younger daughter became the empress, held the regency until his death in 68 B.C.

During his lifetime his son, Yü, and his grandnephews, Shan and Yün, attained high posts; see III, 34, n. 199.

government. The male slaves and guests of the various Ho of P'ing-yang[150] carried weapons into the market, fought and created disturbances, and the officers could not stop them. [*HS* 76:6a]

27. DESCENDANTS OF OLD NOBLES

T'ien Yen-nien, whose style was Tzu-ping, belonged to one of the [87–75 B.C.] T'ien families of the old state of Ch'i, which had been moved to Yang-ling.[151] Because of his talent and ability Yen-nien served in the office of the grand general. Ho Kuang[152] valued him. He was promoted to the post of chief secretary and then made grand administrator of the Ho-tung commandery. Selecting Yin Weng-kuei[153] and others as his claws and teeth, he executed and exterminated the powerful and strong persons. Thus the depraved persons did not dare to be active.[154] [*HS* 90:14a]

28. RICH PEOPLE TRANSFERRED

In the sixth month in the summer [of the fourth year of Shih-yüan] ... [83 B.C.] the rich people of the Three Adjuncts were moved to Yün-ling and granted one hundred thousand cash per household. [*HS* 7:3a]

29. POWERFUL PERSONS

[Ting] Wai-jen[155] was arrogant. He hated the former governor of [81–80 B.C.]

[150] P'ing-yang was the native place of the Ho family.

[151] According to Yen, they were moved by Emperor Kao to the region that later became Yang-ling prefecture. Yang-ling was where Emperor Ching's mausoleum had been built in 152 B.C. (*HS* 5:4b). For the transfer of the important and noble families of the old states in the time of Emperor Kao, see III, 8 and 9.

[152] Ho Kuang was appointed grand minister of war and grand general in 87 B.C. (*HS* 19B:9b).

[153] Yin Weng-kuei was a subordinate of T'ien whose ability was highly admired by T'ien. For further details, see III, 36.

[154] Shortly afterwards, in 75 B.C., T'ien Yen-nien 田延年 was promoted to the post of grand minister of agriculture. When Ho Kuang called a council to deliberate about the dethronement of the newly established emperor, the previous king of Ch'ang-i, T'ien strongly supported the proposal of Ho, threatening with death any official who disagreed with Ho. Because of this he was ennobled marquis of Yang-ch'eng. In 72 B.C. he was accused by the rich and powerful merchants of corruption and committed suicide before being taken to prison. See also II, 34.

[155] Ting Wai-jen 丁外人 was the paramour of the princess of O-i, Emperor Chao's elder sister and the wife of the marquis of Kai (*HS* 7:5b–6a). In 80 B.C. he was ex-

Ching-chao, Fan Fu,[156] and sent one of his guests to shoot and kill him.[157] The guest hid in a hut of the princess,[158] and the government functionaries did not dare arrest him. The prefect of Wei-ch'eng, [Hu] Chien, led the functionaries and soldiers to surround [the hut] in order to arrest him. The prince of Kai, hearing the news, rushed there with Wai-jen and General Shang-kuan,[159] escorted by a large number of male slaves and guests,[160] to shoot the functionaries who were surrounding [the hut]. Then the functionaries dispersed and ran away. The princess ordered the supervisor to accuse the police chief of the prefect of Wei-ch'eng of wounding male slaves of the princess's household. [Hu] Chien reported that the police chief was not guilty. The princess of Kai was angry and ordered someone to present a memorial accusing Chien of insulting the elder princess, shooting at the gate of her residence, and deliberately not investigating the case thoroughly in order to avoid [handing down] a sentence when he knew that his functionaries had wounded her male slaves. The Grand General Ho Kuang shelved the memorial. Later when Kuang was ill, Shang-kuan administered [the government] as his substitute[161] and sent officials to arrest Chien. Chien killed himself. Officials and people all considered that an injustice had been done. Up to the present there still is in Wei-ch'eng a shrine for him. [*HS* 67:4a–b]

---

ecuted together with Shang-kuan Chieh and Shang-kuan An when their plot to murder Ho Kuang, to dismiss Emperor Chao, and to put the king of Yen, Emperor Chao's elder brother, on the throne was disclosed. The princess then committed suicide (*HS* 68:3b–5a).

[156] Fan Fu 樊福 was governor of Ching-chao in 81 B.C. (*HS* 19B:10a).

[157] That guests were expected to carry out assignments as dangerous and illegal as this underlines the obligatory nature of their service.

[158] The princess of O-i.

[159] Shang-kuan An, who was the father of the empress, was the general of the flash cavalry. He and Ting Wai-jen became close friends because Shang-kuan's daughter entered the palace through the princess. Both An and his father, Chieh, the general of the left, had attempted in vain to make Ting a marquis or an official. Both the father and the son were executed when their plot to rebel was disclosed (*HS* 68:3a–b, 5a).

[160] The phrase *nu k'o* may be considered a compound meaning "slave-guests" or two separate characters meaning "slaves and guests." For further discussion of this problem, see II, 24, n. 80. It may be noted that in two instances the two characters are used separately: Ting Wai-jen sent a *k'o*, guest, to murder the official, and the princess accused the prefect of wounding her *nu*, slaves.

[161] When Ho Kuang was absent from the office, Shang-kuan Chieh usually acted as his surrogate (*HS* 68:3b).

30. A Powerful Officer

Because his administration was remarkable [Chao Kuang-han] was promoted to the post of commandant of the capital and acting governor of Ching-chao.

It happened that Emperor Chao died, and Tu Chien of Hsin-feng 74 B.C. was a subaltern official of Ching-chao supervising the construction work of the tomb at P'ing-ling. Chien had long been powerful and acted as a redresser-of-wrongs. His guests engaged in illicit profit-making. Hearing this, Kuang-han warned him; he did not reform. Thereupon he was arrested and sentenced under the law. Well-known eunuchs[162] and powerful and famous persons[163] asked pardon for him by every means. Until the end [Kuang-han] never listened to any of them. [Chien's] kinsmen and guests planned to take him away by force. Kuang-han knew all about the plot, the names of the principal [participants][164] and their daily activities.[165] He sent officers to inform them, saying, "If your plot is thus, then your families will also be exterminated." He ordered several officers to put Chien to death in the marketplace. No one dared to approach. The people of the capital praised him.[166] [*HS* 76:1a–b]

31. Cooperation Between Powerful Families

[Chao Kuang-han] was transferred to the post of grand adminis- 74–72 B.C. trator of Ying-ch'uan. The kinsmen of the great families of the com-

---

[162] Yen comments that *chung-kuei-jen* 中貴人 were those nobles who were in the central court. Here we follow the interpretation of Fu Ch'an and Liu Feng-shih (*HSPC* 76:1b).

[163] Yen comments that 豪長者 means powerful persons 豪傑 and those famous for their virtue 有名德之人.

[164] Chou Shou-ch'ang suggests that 主名 refers to the name of the kinsmen and guests in question (*HSPC* 76:1b). Actually the term means the name of the principal offender in a crime (cf. *HS* 76:19b–20a). Here it refers to the principal offenders-to-be who plotted to take the prisoner away by force.

[165] The phrase 起居 is explained by Yen as meaning the place where one lives and the manner in which one intends to act. Considering Yen's interpretation too dogmatic, Chou Shou-ch'ang suggests that it merely means motion and rest. In the biography of Chang Ch'ang, we find the expression 主名區處; Yen explains the phrase 區處 as "the place where one lives" (*HS* 76:20a). This example seems to support the view of Chou. Since the phrase 起居, which literally means "rising and resting," generally refers to routine activities in connection with one's daily life, we therefore translate it as "daily activities."

[166] Chao Kuang-han's biography is continued in III, 31. See also, II, 35, and n. 120.

mandery, the Yüan and the Ch'u, were overbearing and unrestrained. Their guests violated the law and acted as bandits. None of the previous 2,000-picul [officials] had been able to control or seize them. Several months after Kuang-han arrived he executed the chief offenders of the Yüan and the Ch'u. [The people] in the commandery were shaken with fear.

Formerly the powerful and awe-inspiring persons and the great families of Yin-ch'uan were intermarrying, and the officials were in the habit of forming cliques. Kuang-han regarded this as an evil. He encouraged and selected those among them who could be used to receive his instructions.[167] They were sent out to investigate the cases and when the names of the guilty ones were obtained [Kuang-han] exercised the law and punished [the offenders].

Then Kuang-han purposely divulged the statement of the man [who had investigated the case] in order to make them hate each other. He also instructed the officers to prepare some jars.[168] When a letter of prosecution was received, he scraped off[169] the name of the accuser and pretended it was a statement made by the powerful and awe-inspiring persons and the young people of the great families. Later all the families of the great and large lineages became enemies, and the evil cliques were dissolved. The customs were greatly changed. The officials and the people accused each other, and Kuang-han used them as his ears and eyes. Thus robbers and bandits did not take any action. When they took action, they were seized immediately.[170] [*HS* 76:1b–2a]

32. A EUNUCH COMES INTO POWER

Shih Hsien, whose style was Chun-fang, was a native of Chi-nan. Hung Kung was a native of Pei. Both of them violated the law, were castrated, and became palace attendants within the Yellow Gate

[167] Fu Chien comments that the phrase *shou-chi* 受記 means to accept the records of lawsuits. Basing himself upon a similar statement in the biography of Chang Ch'ang, Chu I-hsin points out that the phrase means to receive instructions from the grand administrator (*HSPC* 76:1b–2a).

[168] A written accusation was placed in a jar, which was so constructed that a document once deposited could not be removed without breaking the jar (see note: *HSPC* 76:2a).

[169] At this time all statements were written on bamboo tablets.

[170] Afterwards, in the fall of 72 B.C., Chao Kuang-han was sent to lead the soldiers against the Hsiung-nu. Upon his return the following year he was again made governor of Ching-chao (*HS* 19B:11a). In 67 B.C. Chao was found guilty of falsely accusing the imperial chancellor and was executed (see II, 35).

when they were young. They were selected and became palace masters of writing.[171] In the time of Emperor Hsüan, they were appointed scribes of the palace.[172] [Hung] Kung was familiar with laws, ordinances, and traditional practices, was good at making memorials, and was able to fulfill his functions. [Hung] Kung became the prefect [of the palace writers][173] and [Shih] Hsien was the supervisor [of the palace writers].

Several years after Emperor Yüan ascended the throne, [Hung] Kung died and [Shih] Hsien took his place as prefect of the palace writers. At this time Emperor Yüan was ill and did not personally attend to government matters, [but] he was extremely interested in music. Considering that [Shih] Hsien had long attended to [court] affairs, was a eunuch and had no outside connections,[174] was devoted to [his business], and could be trusted and employed, [the emperor] thereupon entrusted him with the government affairs. [All affairs], whether large or small, were reported through [Shih] Hsien for [the emperor's] decision. His honor and favor dominated the court and all officials served [Shih] Hsien respectfully.

[Shih] Hsien as a man was clever and quick and accustomed to dealing with affairs. He was able to find out the hidden will of the ruler.

---

[171] According to Wang Hsien-ch'ien, the palace masters of writing, *chung-shang-shu* 中尚書, concurrently had charge of the duties of the masters of writing (*HSPC* 19A:16a).

[172] Scribes of the palace, *chung-shu-kuan* 中書官, refers to the internuncios of the palace writers, or palace writers. The *Han-chiu-i* mentions that Han installed the scribes of the palace to take charge of the affairs of the masters of writing (*HCI* A:3a; *HKI* A:20b).

[173] Prefect of the palace writers, the abbreviated form for the title prefect of the internuncios of the palace writers, serving under the privy treasurer, was a eunuch charged with the duty of handling government documents. In the early years of Han this duty was entrusted to the master of writing, a post held by regular officials. Emperor Wu began to assign the duty to the eunuchs, creating the post of prefect of the internuncios of the palace writers (originally prefect of the palace internuncios). Since the eunuchs shared the same duty with the masters of writing, they were referred to as palace masters of writing; see note 171 of this document. The later office was abolished by Emperor Ch'eng in 29 B.C., and, reverting to the old pattern, the duty of handling documents was exclusively assigned to ordinary officials instead of the eunuchs. The title of the office of prefect of the internuncios of palace writers was then changed back to prefect of the palace internuncios. For details see *HS* 78:11a–b, 93:4b–5a; *HHC* 26:8a; *HCI* A:3a; *HCIPI* A:4b; *HKI* A:20b; *HSPC* 19A:15a, 16a, 17a; Lao Kan, "Lun Han-tai ti nei-ch'ao yü wai-ch'ao," *LSYY*, XIII (1948), 265–66.

[174] Yen explains that 中人無外黨 means that the eunuchs had few kinsmen and were without relatives through marriage (*HS* 93:4b). However, it might also mean that they were isolated within the palace and hence had no outside connection with officials and others.

Being extremely malicious inside, he held to perverse arguments to strike at and injure others. Those who opposed [his will] and exchanged angry looks with him were always charged with serious offenses.

48–44 B.C.   During the Ch'u-yüan period the general of the van, Hsiao Wang-chih,[175] the imperial court grandee, Chou K'an,[176] and the superintendent of the imperial clan, Liu Keng-sheng,[177] all became "officials who concurrently serve in the palace,"[178] and [Hsiao] Wang-chih took charge of the affairs of the masters of writing. Knowing that [Shih] Hsien was monopolizing power and being pernicious, they advised that the [office of] masters of writing was the fundamental of the officialdom and the key part of the government and that it should [therefore] be occupied by [persons of] intelligence and justice. [They also advised] that [the precedent of] Emperor Wu, who played around

[175] Hsiao Wang-chih, an outstanding scholar, started his official career as a gentleman. Later he was promoted to the posts of privy treasurer, grand administrator, and grandee secretary. Shortly afterwards he was accused of being impolite to the imperial chancellor and was demoted to the post of grand tutor of the heir apparent. In the last days of the reign of Emperor Hsüan he was appointed general of the van and assigned to aid the young emperor in taking charge of the affairs of the masters of writing, together with the grand minister of war and general of chariots and cavalry, Shih Kao, and another official, Chou K'an 周堪 (see note 176 below). His request to dismiss the eunuchs from the office of masters of writing greatly displeased the eunuchs, Hung Kung and Shih Hsien. They then asked someone to accuse Hsiao of forming a clique with Chou K'an and Liu Keng-sheng 劉更生 in grasping power and attempting to dismiss Shih Kao from the government. As a result, Hsiao was dismissed and Chou and Liu were degraded to the status of commoners. Later. Hsiao's son presented a memorial to state his grievance. Hsiao Wang-chih was thereupon accused by Hung Kung and Shih Hsien of not acknowledging his fault and of instructing his son to present a memorial in order to put the blame on the emperor, They suggested to the emperor that Hsiao should be imprisoned. Before he could be arrested, he committed suicide, in 46 B.C. (*HS* 78:1a–14b).

[176] Chou K'an, who had been the junior tutor of the heir apparent, was appointed imperial court grandee by Emperor Hsüan to aid the young emperor, together with Shih Kao and Hsiao Wang-chih. He and Liu Keng-sheng were imprisoned and degraded to the status of commoners after they were accused by Shih Hsien (*HS* 78:10b–13b; see also note 181 below).

[177] Liu Keng-sheng, a member of the imperial family who held the post of "mounted attendant without specified appointment" and grandee remonstrant, became an "official who concurrently serves in the palace" (on this title, see note 178 below), upon the suggestion of Hsiao Wang-chih. He was later shifted to the post of superintendent of the imperial clan (*tsung-cheng* 宗正). When he was accused with Hsiao Wang-chih and Chou K'an, he was dismissed and made a commoner (*HS* 78:11b–13b).

[178] *Chi-shih-chung*, which literally means "to render service within the palace" (here rendered "official who concurrently serves in the palace"), was a post given to a person holding at the same time some regular post. The duty of the holder was to attend at the side of the emperor (*HSPC* 19A:24b, text and notes; Hu Kuang, *Han-kuan chieh-ku*, in *PCKTS*, p. 46, hereafter cited as *HKCK; HCI* A:2a).

and amused himself in the inner apartments [of the palace] and therefore employed eunuchs [to take charge of the masters of writing], was
not an ancient tradition, and that it was [therefore] proper to dismiss
those eunuchs [who held the office of] palace writers in order to be in
accordance with the ancient [rule] that men who had suffered punishment[179] should not be close to [the ruler]. Emperor Yüan did not consent. Thereafter they greatly opposed [Shih] Hsien and afterwards　46 B.C.
they were all ruined by him.[180] [Hsiao] Wang-chih committed suicide
and [Chou] K'an and [Liu] Keng-sheng were dismissed and prohibited
from being employed. The statements [regarding these men] are in the
biography of [Hsiao] Wang-chih.

Later, the Grand Palace Grandee Chang Meng,[181] the Grand Admin-
istrator of Wei Commandery Ching Fang,[182] the Palace Assistant
Imperial Secretary Ch'en Hsien,[183] and the Expectant Appointee
Chia Chüan-chih[184] all had mentioned the faults of [Shih] Hsien when

[179] Here *hsing-jen* 刑人, "one who had been punished," refers particularly to a man
who had suffered castration.

[180] See notes 175, 176, and 177 of this document.

[181] Chang Meng 張猛 was a disciple of Chou K'an. After Chou's demotion and
Hsiao Wang-chih's suicide, the emperor was grieved at Hsiao's death and appointed
Chou superintendent of the imperial court and Chang Meng imperial court
grandee and an "official who concurrently serves in the palace." Chang Meng was
later impeached and demoted to prefect of Huai-li; Chou K'an was demoted at the
same time to the position of grand administrator of Ho-tung. Later, when a calamity
occurred, Chang Meng became grand palace grandee and an "official who concurrently serves in the palace" and Chou K'an was appointed imperial court grandee.
Shortly thereafter, Chou K'an died and Shih Hsien slandered Chang Meng, who was
forced to commit suicide (*HS* 36:9b, 19b–20b).

[182] Ching Fang, who was a friend of Chang Po 張博, the maternal uncle of the king
of Huai-yang, had attempted to ask the latter to urge the emperor to dismiss Shih
Hsien. Ching Fang was accused by Shih Hsien of cooperating with Chang Po in
slandering the government and deluding the king. As a result both Ching and Chang
were executed (*HS* 76:6a–11b).

[183] Ch'en Hsien became a gentleman because of his father, Ch'en Wan-nien, who
was a grandee secretary. Ch'en Hsien was later promoted to the post of palace assistant imperial secretary. He once told his friend Chu Yün 朱雲, who was a mag-
istrate and who was being charged with cruelty and killing innocent persons, to present a memorial to explain the matter. Ch'en was then accused by Shih Hsien of giving
out information, imprisoned, and sentenced to having his head shaved and building
the city wall. During Emperor Ch'eng's time he was reappointed and later appointed
to the posts of grand administrator and then privy treasurer. He was later accused by
the imperial chancellor, Chai Fang-chin 翟方進, of being cruel, corrupt, and seeking
recommendation for appointment. He was dismissed and died at home (*HS* 66:17a–
19a).

[184] Chia Chüan-chih 賈捐之 was unable to procure official appointment because
he frequently mentioned the faults of Shih Hsien. Cooperating with a prefect, the two
planned to support and recommend each other in order to gain high official posts.
This was learned by Shih Hsien, who accused him of it and caused him to be given
the death penalty (*HS* 64A:14a–20a).

they presented sealed memorials[185] or were summoned to see [the emperor]. [Shih] Hsien looked for their crimes. [Ching] Fang and [Chia] Chüan-chih were executed in the market, [Chang] Meng committed suicide at [the Office of the] Official Carriages, and [Ch'en] Hsien was punished for his crime by [being sentenced to] having his head shaved and to [building] the city wall at dawn.[186] And Cheng Ling and Su Chien,[187] who secured the private letters of [Shih] Hsien and memorialized them [to the emperor], were [accused of] some other matters and put to death. Thereafter [the officials], from the ministers on down, feared [Shih] Hsien and dared not be unrestrained. [Shih] Hsien and the supervisor of the palace writers, Lao Liang, and the privy treasurer, Wu-lu Ch'ung-tsung, associated with each other and became partisans and friends. All those who attached themselves to them were given honorable posts. . . .

Seeing that the general of the left, Feng Feng-shih, and his son[188] were both ministers of renown and that moreover his daughter was a brilliant companion, [Shih] Hsien intended to attach himself to them, and recommended the brilliant companion's elder brother, the internuncio [Feng] Ch'ün[189] as being cultivated and [said that it] was proper for him to attend the emperor. The emperor summoned him, intending to make him a palace attendant. Ch'ün begged to make a statement during the leisure[190] [time of the emperor]. Having heard Ch'ün say that [Shih] Hsien was grasping power, the emperor was greatly angered, dismissed Ch'ün and made him return to his office of gentleman.[191]

Afterwards the post of grandee secretary was unoccupied[192] and the various officials all recommended Ch'ün's elder brother, Yeh-wang,[193]

---

[185] Usually memorials were unsealed, but officials were allowed to seal their memorials in a black bag when the matter was confidential. This was called *feng-shih* 封事 (cf. *TYTT* A:6a; *HHS* 60B:21b).

[186] For details, see notes 181–184 of this document.

[187] This is not the Su Chien 蘇建 who had been ennobled marquis of P'ing-ling because of his military merit in attacking the Hsiung-nu during Emperor Wu's time.

[188] Feng Feng-shih 馮奉世 had nine sons, four of whom had held official posts. The son referred to here is Feng Yeh-wang who, at the time, held the post of grand herald (*ta-hung-lu* 大鴻臚), one of the Nine Ministers at the court (*HS* 79:7b–8a).

[189] Feng Ch'ün 馮逡 was later promoted to the post of grand administrator of Lung-hsi. He was over forty when he died (*HS* 79:10a–b).

[190] The purpose of 請間, "to beg to make a statement during the emperor's leisure," is to have a confidential talk without the presence of others.

[191] Liu Pin suggests that 歸郎官 might be 歸放官. If his suggestion is correct, then the sentence means "to be dismissed and return to his original post."

[192] At this time, Li Yen-shou 李延壽, the grandee secretary, died (*HS* 79:8a).

[193] For Feng Yeh-wang, see n. 188 above.

[saying that his] behavior and ability were the first [among the offi-
cials]. The emperor asked [the opinion of Shih] Hsien. Hsien said,
"None of the Nine Ministers is superior to Yeh-wang. But Yeh-wang
is the elder brother of the brilliant companion. I, Your servant, am
afraid that [the persons of] future generations will consider that Your
Majesty neglects many virtuous [men], being partial to a relative of
[one in] the inner palace and making him [one of the] Three Ministers."
The emperor said, "Good. I did not see this." Thereupon an edict was
issued praising Yeh-wang, but he was disregarded instead of being
employed. a [full] statement is in the biography of Yeh-wang.

　[Shih] Hsien himself, knowing in his heart that he was grasping
power and that authority was in his hands, was afraid that someday
the emperor might adopt the eyes and ears[194] of those who attended at
his side, and that they would be able to separate him and [the emperor].
Thereupon, at times he returned to honesty and used truth to prove
[his honesty]. Once [Shih] Hsien was sent to some officials for the collection [of certain items]. [Shih] Hsien first personally reported that
he might be late and that the [day] clepsydra would be exhausted and
the palace gates closed. He requested that an edict be prepared ordering the officials to open the gate. The emperor consented. [Shih] Hsien
purposely came back in the night, announced the edict to open the gate,
and entered. Someone eventually presented a memorial charging [Shih]
Hsien with acting on his own authority and issuing a false edict to
open the palace gate. Having heard about this, the emperor smiled and
showed the memorial to [Shih] Hsien. Hsien thereupon wept and said,
"Your Majesty grants favor to me, Your humble servant, by mistake
and entrusts me with affairs. There is not a single one of Your subordinates who does not envy me and want to ruin me. Things of this kind
are more than a single [case] and only You, the intelligent Ruler, know
it. Your foolish servant is small and humble and indeed I alone am not
able to please ten thousand persons and to bear the blame of the whole
empire. I, Your servant, am willing to return the key post [of the court]
and accept the cleaning and sweeping services in the inner [apartment
of the] palace. And I would die without regret. Only Your Majesty
will pity me and make the decision to save the life of Your small servant." The emperor considered that he was right and pitied him. Frequently [the emperor] comforted and encouraged [Shih] Hsien and
gave him more grants. The grants and gifts [given by the various offi-
cials] amounted to a wealth of a hundred millions.

194 That is, those who watched him and reported to the emperor.

Formerly [Shih] Hsien had heard that among many people there was a great deal of talk saying that he had killed the general of the van, Hsiao Wang-chih. Wang-chih was a contemporary scholar of reputation. [Shih] Hsien feared that the scholars in the empire would denounce him and was distressed about it. At this time, Kung Yü of Lang-ya, a scholar who had a knowledge of the classics and was well known for his integrity, was the grandee remonstrant. [Shih] Hsien sent someone to give his regards and he himself made great efforts to become closer to [Kung Yü]. Hsien thereupon recommended Yü to the emperor. Later [Yü] reached the position of one of the Nine Ministers[195] and became grandee secretary. [Shih Hsien] observed all the due courtesies [with Yü]. Thereupon those who discussed [such things] praised [Shih] Hsien, considering that he had not envied and slandered [Hsiao] Wang-chih. The trickery and deceits of [Shih] Hsien in order to save himself and to obtain the confidence of the ruler were all of this kind.

Emperor Yüan was ill and lay [in bed] during his later years. King Kung of Ting-t'ao was loved by and a favorite of [the emperor]. [Shih] Hsien contributed much of his effort[196] to supporting and protecting the heir apparent. When Emperor Yüan died and Emperor Ch'eng ascended the throne, Hsien was shifted to the post of grand keeper of the palace equipages of Chang-hsin [Palace] with the rank of fully 2,000 piculs. [Shih] lost his close association with [the emperor] and was separated from power. Several months later the imperial chancellor and the grandee secretary memorialized item by item the old crimes of [Shih] Hsien and [also charged] his associates, Lao Liang and Ch'en Shun; both of them were dismissed from their offices. [Shih] Hsien together with his family[197] was moved and sent back to his native commandery. Being full of sorrow, he could not eat and was ill and died on the way. Those who had associated with Hsien and became officials because of him were all dismissed. The privy treasurer, Wu-lu Ch'ung-

[195] Kung Yü had held the post of privy treasurer before he became the grandee secretary (*HS* 72:15a).

[196] Certain editions have 有功, "have merit," instead of 有力 (*HSPC* 93:6a).

[197] We do not know whether Shih Hsien had been married and had a son before he became a eunuch or whether he married after he became a eunuch and adopted a son. However, it should be pointed out, as noted by Ch'ien Ta-chao, that many eunuchs married and that such abnormal inhuman unions were frequently complained of by their contemporaries as interfering with the natural harmony of heaven and earth (*HSPC* 93:6a–b, note). In the biography of the eunuchs in the *Hou-Han-shu* there is mention of many eunuchs who took beautiful girls from good families and made them concubines (*HHS* 78:16b).

tsung, was demoted [to the post of] grand administrator of Hsüan-tu, and the palace assistant of the imperial secretary, I Chia, became chief commandant of Yen-men. [*HS* 93:4b–7a]

33. Settlement Around an Imperial Tomb

In the first month in the spring in the first year of Pen-shih [the gov- 73 B.C. ernment] mustered those officials and common people of the command- eries and kingdoms whose wealth was one million [cash] or more and moved them to P'ing-ling.[198] [*HS* 8:3b]

34. Slaves of Powerful Families

Later, the male slaves of the two families [of Ho[199] and Wei[200]] quar- 67 B.C. reled over the right of way. The Ho male slaves entered the office of the grandee secretary, intending to kick down his door. The secretary kowtowed and apologized. Then they left. Someone told the Ho fam- ily about it. Hsien[201] and others for the first time knew what it was to worry.[202] [*HS* 68:15a]

[198] P'ing-ling, the mausoleum of Emperor Chao, was located seventy *li* northwest of Ch'ang-an (*SFHT*, p. 55).

[199] The Grand General Ho Kuang had died in 68 B.C.; see III, 26, and n. 149. Ho's son, Yü, who had been general of the palace gentlemen inherited the marquisate of Po-lu and was made the general of the right upon his father's death; he later held the position of grand minister of war. Ho Kuang's grandnephews, Yün and Shan, also held important posts. Ho Yün was the general of the palace gentlemen and marquis of Kuan-yang. Ho Shan, while holding the position of chief commandant custodian of the imperial equipages with the title of marquis of Lo-p'ing, was vested with authority to supervise the affairs of the masters of writing. At this time the Ho was the most important family of Han. However, the family power was reduced when in 67 B.C. Emperor Hsüan decreed that memorials to the throne should not pass through the office of the masters of writing, thus seriously restricting Ho Shan's auth- ority; and Ho Yü, though holding the honorable title of grand minister of war, was forced to give up the armies under his command. Other relatives and in-laws of the Ho family also suffered demotions or restrictions of one kind or another. In 66 B.C. the family planned to rebel. When the plot was discovered, Yün and Shan committed suicide. Yü and other family members, including his mother, were all executed. Empress Ho thereupon was dismissed and later committed suicide (*HS* 68:12a–18b).

[200] Wei Hsiang was grandee secretary at this time. He became imperial chancellor in 67 B.C. (*HS* 19B:11b).

[201] Hsien was the second wife of Ho Kuang. Yen quoted Chin Cho, who cited the *Han-yü*, to state that she had been a female slave and was made Ho's wife after the death of his first wife (*HS* 68:14b). She bribed a female physician to poison Empress Hsü of Emperor Hsüan and succeeded in marrying her daughter—who was later made empress—to the emperor. Because of this murder the emperor greatly reduced

35. Powerful Families Moved by the Government

65 B.C.   In the spring of the first year of Yüan-k'ang . . . [the families of] the imperial chancellor, the generals, the marquises, the officials of 2,000 piculs, and those whose property amounted to a million [cash] were moved to Tu-ling.²⁰³ [*HS* 8:11b–12a]

36. A Powerful Man

65 B.C.   The great and powerful man of the Tung-hai commandery, Hsü Chung-sun of T'an,²⁰⁴ carried on unlawful and cunning activities and brought disorder on the administration of the officials. [The people in] the commandery suffered because of him.

The 2,000-picul officials tried to arrest him, but he always extricated himself through power and intrigue. [The officials] never could control him. When [Yin] Weng-kuei arrived,²⁰⁵ he sentenced Chung-sun to be executed in the marketplace. The whole commandery trembled with fear, and nobody dared to transgress the prohibitions of the law. Thereupon the Tung-hai commandery was in great peace.²⁰⁶ [*HS* 76:7a–b]

---

the power of the Ho family. This led to the rebellion of the family. Hsien was executed, together with all the members of the Ho family, in 66 B.C. when their plans for rebellion were discovered (*HS* 8:11a, 68:14b–18b, 97A:25a–27a).

²⁰² After the death of Ho Kuang, Emperor Hsüan began to take an active part in government affairs. Wei Hsiang, the grandee secretary, was assigned to take charge of the affairs in the palace. Hsien, aware of this, fully realized that any misconduct on the part of the family might lead to prosecutions. She was therefore concerned when the Ho slaves behaved in the way described in the above passage (*HS* 68:14b–15a).

²⁰³ Tu-ling, the mausoleum of Emperor Hsüan, was located south of the imperial capital, Ch'ang-an (*SFHT*, p. 56).

²⁰⁴ T'an 郯 was located in modern T'an-ch'eng county in southern Shantung.

²⁰⁵ Yin Weng-kuei was a petty jail officer who had a knowledge of law. His unusual ability greatly impressed Grand Administrator T'ien Yen-nien, and he was appointed his subordinate; see III, 27, n. 153. He was later promoted to the post of chief commandant of Hung-nung and then grand administrator of T'ung-hai, a post he was holding when the incident took place. It was said that he knew who was honest and who was vicious in the commandery and that such a record was in his possession. In 65 B.C. (*HS* 19B:11b) he was promoted to the post of acting grand administrator of Yu-fu-feng, which he held until his death in 62 B.C. He was also famous for his impartiality and his integrity. He left no property to his family when he died. These qualities so much impressed Emperor Hsüan that a special edict was issued and a hundred catties of gold were bestowed on Yin's son. His three sons all became grand administrators, and one of them was appointed general of the rear (*HS* 76:6a–8a).

²⁰⁶ Ssu-ma dates this event in 65 B.C. (*TCTC* 25: 13a). According to Yin Weng-kuei's biography it should be placed a little earlier.

37. POWERFUL FAMILIES PROTECT ROBBERS
AND ARE FEARED BY OFFICIALS

On his return [Yen Yen-nien][207] was appointed grand administrator   61 B.C.
of the Cho commandery. At that time there had been for several terms
no able grand administrator in this commandery. Because of this, Pi
Yeh-po and other natives of Cho disregarded the laws and created
disorder. There were great families, the Western Kao and the Eastern
Kao.[208] Everyone from the commandery officials down feared and
avoided them, and no one dared to come up against them. All said,
"Rather be ungrateful to the 2,000-picul official[209] than to be ungrateful
to the powerful and great families."

Their guests were unrestrained and practiced robbery. If discovered,
they entered the houses of the Kao, and the officials did not dare to
pursue them. The cases gradually increased daily. On the roads only
with the bow stretched and the sword unsheathed did one dare to
proceed. Thus was the disorder.

When Yen-nien arrived, he sent a bureau head, Chao Hsiu of Li-wu,
to examine the cases of the Kao family, and they were found guilty
[and deserving] of the death penalty. As Yen-nien had only recently
become general,[210] Hsiu was fearful in his heart and made two [state-
ments for] prosecution, intending to report the less severe one first in
order to observe the will of Yen-nien, and then to present the more
severe one if he were angry.

Yen-nein knew that he would act like this. When Bureau Head Chao
came and reported the less severe one, Yen-nien searched inside his
clothes and got the severe indictment. Thereupon [Hsiu] was arrested
and sent to prison. He was imprisoned in the night and taken to the

[207] Yen Yen-nien had learned law when he was young and had been a subordinate
in the office of the grandee secretary and a prefect. On his return from an expedition
against the Ch'iang people under General Hsü Yen-shou in 61 B.C. (*HS* 8:16b) he was
appointed to the post of grand administrator of the Cho commandery and then of
Ho-nei. He was so severe in punishment that he was called by the nickname
"butcher," and for this reason the emperor changed his mind concerning his appointment as grand administrator of Feng-i. His mother was also very unhappy about
his way of governing and refused to see her son. Later he was accused by a subordinate, who thought him unfriendly, of having made defamatory remarks regarding
political affairs of the court. He was executed.

[208] Yen says they were called Western and Eastern Kao depending on the location
of their residences.

[209] That is, the grand administrator.

[210] The grand administrator was called the commandery general because he was
also in charge of military affairs (Yen: *HS* 90:16b).

marketplace in the morning and executed before those whom he had prosecuted had died. All the officials had their legs trembling. Then he sent other officials to examine the two Kao [families] separately and to trace their evils thoroughly. Many tens of each [family] were executed. All in the province were frightened, and no one picked up things on the road.

58 B.C.   Three years later he was transferred to the post of grand administrator of the Ho-nei commandery and was granted twenty catties of gold [by the emperor]. The powerful and strong persons held their breath, and there were no robbers in the countryside. Awe of him shook the neighboring commanderies. His governing was devoted to destroying and suppressing the powerful and strong persons and to supporting and aiding the poor and weak. The poor and weak, even when they violated the law, would be excused by means of distorted statements. The powerful and awe-inspiring persons when they encroached on the small people would be charged by means of a legal statement. [*HS* 90:16a–17a]

38. REDRESSERS-OF-WRONGS IN THE CAPITAL

47–27 B.C.   [Kung-sheng Hsing, the thrice venerable of Hu prefecture, presented a memorial, saying], "The powerful persons of old and the great and cunning individuals of Ch'ang-an, such as Chia Wan of the Eastern Market,[211] Chü Chang from west of the city, Chang Chin, the arrow maker, Chao Fang, the wine producer, Yang Chang of Tu-liang [prefecture], and others, had all associated with evil persons, formed gangs, and kept lawbreaking people. They violated the imperial laws above and caused disorder in the official administration below. They encroached upon others, made them serve, and exploited the small people. They were wolves of the people. They outlasted several 2,000-picul [officials] and for twenty years they could not be seized. [Wang] Tsun[212] investigated and punished them with the proper law and all admitted their crimes. The treacherous and evil doings were brought to an end. Officials and people were happy and confident." [*HS* 76:27a]

---

[211] According to the *Miao-chi*, quoted in *San-fu huang-t'u*, there were nine markets in Ch'ang-an in Han times (*SFHT* [A], 2:1a). The Eastern Market is where Ch'ao Ts'o was executed (*SC* 101:9b; *HS* 49:25a) and where Ssu-ma Chi-chu 司馬季主 practiced divination (*SC* 127:1b). The *Hou-Han-shu* (11:9b) mentions the existence in A.D. 25 of east and west markets.

[212] At this time Wang Tsun was governor of Ching-chao. He was appointed to this post in 29 B.C. and was dismissed two years later (*HS* 19B:14b). Since the powerful

Chü Chang, whose style was Tzu-hsia, was a native of Ch'ang-an. Ch'ang-an was in full prosperity, and in every street there were powerful redressers-of-wrongs. Chang lived at the Willow Market located west of the city; the people called him Chü Tzu-hsia of west of the city. He was staff supervisor[213] of the governor of Ching-chao. When he attended [the governor] and went to the imperial palace, the attendants within the palace, feudal lords, and other nobles strove to salute Chang, while none of them spoke to the governor of Ching-chao. . . .

He was closely associated with the prefect of the palace writers,[214] Shih Hsien.[215] He also profited from Hsien's power. At his door the hubs of carriages were always in contact with each other. . . .

During the Ho-p'ing [reign period], when Wang Tsun held the office of governor of Ching-chao, he arrested and killed the powerful

---

individuals had avoided capture for some twenty years, their illegal activities must have started sometime around 47 B.C.

Wang Tsun's official career was full of ups and downs. He had been a prefect. He was later promoted to the post of grand administrator of An-ting, but was dismissed after a short time because he was too severe in applying punishments. He was then appointed a colonel in charge of the army transportation and was again dismissed. Upon the recommendation of a grand administrator, Wang Tsun was appointed prefect and later promoted to the post of inspector of I division. Because of his accomplishments, he was appointed chancellor of Tung-p'ing kingdom. However, he was disliked by the mother of the king to such an extent that she threatened to commit suicide if the chancellor was not dismissed. For this reason, he lost his post and was made a commoner. Upon the recommendation of the Grand General Wang Feng, he was again appointed and promoted to the post of colonel-director of retainers. He brought an accusation against the imperial chancellor and the grandee secretary and was therefore demoted to the post of prefect. During this time there was a group of bandits in the area of Nan Shan whom the officials were unable to pacify. Wang Tsun was recommended and appointed grandee remonstrant and acting commandant of the capital and also in charge of the affairs of the governor of Ching-chao, that is, of the capital. The bandits were subdued within months, and so he was promoted to the post of imperial court grandee and acting governor of Ching-chao and later made governor of Ching-chao. He was accused of being impolite to imperial emissaries and was dismissed. Later he was appointed inspector of Hsü Division, then grand administrator of the Tung commandery, a post he held until his death (*HS* 76:21a–29b).

[213] The staff supervisor (*men-hsia-tu* 門下督) was an official in the commandery government who served under the grand administrator. His duties are unknown; Ch'iang Ju-hsün is of the opinion that he was a military officer (Ch'iang Ju-hsün, *Han chou chün hsien li chih k'ao*, in *Ch'iu-i-chai ch'üan-chi* [1898], A:17b–18a, hereafter cited as *CCHLCK*).

[214] On the prefect of the palace writers, see III, 32, n. 173.

[215] Shih Hsien was a powerful eunuch who held the post of prefect of the internuncios of the palace writers in Emperor Yüan's time. He lost this post when Emperor Ch'eng decided to dismiss eunuchs from this position. The title was then changed to prefect of palace internuncios (*HSPC* 10:4b–5a, 19A:17a; *HHC* 26:8a; for Shih Hsien, see III, 32).

redressers-of-wrongs. He killed [Chü] Chang and Chang Hui, the arrow maker, and Chao Chün-tu and Chia Tzu-kuang, the wine dealers. All of them were well-known powerful persons of Ch'ang-an who took vengeance and kept assassins.[216] [*HS* 92:6b–7b]

39. POWERFUL AND RICH FAMILIES MOVED

20 B.C.   [Ch'en T'ang] thereupon presented a memorandum, saying,[217] "The *ch'u-ling*[218] is the most fertile and the best [region] in the territory of the capital region. A prefecture should be established there. For more than thirty years the people throughout the empire have not been moved to an imperial mausoleum.[219] The wealthy people east of the pass have become more and more numerous. Most of them occupy the good land and make the poor serve them. They should be moved to the *ch'u-ling* in order to strengthen the capital region and weaken the

[216] As early as the Ch'un-ch'iu and Warring States periods there were groups of assassins, *tz'u-k'o* 刺客, who, either because of obligation or by request, committed murder for others for political reasons or personal revenge (*SC, chüan* 86). Professional assassins seem to emerge in Han times. As shown by this text, they could be professionals who were supported as guests. In some cases they were hired assassins (*HS* 49:6b–7a; III, 42, n. 228).

[217] At that time Ch'en T'ang 陳湯 was a subordinate in the office of the grand general. Later he was accused of receiving bribes and of other crimes and was made a commoner and moved to the frontier. Many years later he was permitted to return to the capital and died there (*HS* 70:17b–21b).

[218] According to Fu Chien, before an imperial mausoleum was named it was designated a *ch'u-ling* 初陵 (*HS* 9:10a). His explanation is supported by the fact that the mausoleums of Emperor Yüan and Emperor Ai were also called *ch'u-ling* at first (*HS* 10:3b and 8b–9a, 11:5b–6a). Our text refers to the mausoleum of Emperor Ch'eng. The site was selected in 31 B.C., but construction on the tomb was stopped several years later when the emperor became interested in another site. In 20 B.C., following the suggestion of Ch'en, Ch'ang-ling prefecture was set up and work on the *ch'u-ling* was again started. After five years, work was stopped. The original plan to build the mausoleum in three years could not be carried out because the construction was too expensive and the people's energy exhausted (*HS* 10:3b, 8b–9a, and 10b–11a, 70:18b–19a). Eventually Emperor Ch'eng was entombed in Yen-ling, which was situated in Fu-feng, 62 *li* from Ch'ang-an (*HS* 10:16a; *SFHT* [A], 6:5a).

[219] To move the people to where an imperial tomb was being built, thus making the place a prefecture, was an old practice. However, the practice was suspended by Emperor Yüan in 40 B.C. when he issued an edict saying that in order to make it possible for the people to live peaceably at their native places they were not to be moved to the site of projected mausoleums (*HS* 9:10b, 70:18a); so only twenty years had elapsed since the edict not to move people had been issued. But previous to this edict Emperor Hsüan had transferred the people to his mausoleum in 65 B.C. (*HS* 8:11b–12a), that is, forty-five years before Ch'en presented this memorial. Apparently Ch'en had in mind that the people had not been moved to a mausoleum since 65 B.C.

feudal lords.[220] This will also make it possible for the people from the families of medium means and lower to be equalized in wealth. T'ang is willing, together with his wife and children and family dependents, to move to the *ch'u-ling* in order to lead [the people] of the empire."

Thereupon the Son of Heaven followed his suggestion.[221] [*HS* 70:18a–b]

40. MONOPOLY BY POWERFUL FAMILIES

At that time Ch'ang-ling[222] was under construction and the city of the imperial mausoleum was being built. Many of the offspring and the guests of the imperial relatives-in-law and close ministers cornered and monopolized [the market for building materials] and engaged in illicit profiteering. [Chai] Fang-chin led his subordinates in investigating the cases and discovered a great amount of illegal possessions[223] worth several tens of millions.[224] [*HS* 84:4b]

20–18 B.C.

---

[220] The basic reason for the policy of moving the families of high officials, wealthy men, and other powerful persons to the various mausoleums was to put them under the direct control of the central government and reduce the potentially powerful elements in the various localities (*HS* 28B:18b–19a, 64A:19b). However, Ch'en was merely using this conventional argument to convince the emperor to build the mausoleum and move the people there; actually his hidden motive was self-interest. It was Hsieh Wan-nien 解萬年, the grand court architect, who suggested to Ch'en T'ang that if the mausoleum was built, Hsieh would be rewarded with ennoblement or promotion, and if Ch'en requested that his family be moved there, land and a house would be granted to him, too (*HS* 70:18a–b).

[221] Thus, in 19 B.C., five thousand households of powerful and outstanding persons of the various provinces and kingdoms, whose property was equal to over five million cash, were ordered to be moved. Graveyards and houses were also granted to the imperial chancellor, the grandee secretary, generals, marquises, princesses, and full 2,000-picul officials (*HS* 10:9b, 70:18b). However, when the construction of the mausoleum was suspended in 16 B.C., an edict was issued that officials and people were not to be moved and that houses newly erected by the people there were to be abandoned (*HS* 10:11a, 70:19a). From this time on, people were no longer moved to the mausoleum areas. Thus an edict was issued by Emperor Ai in 5 B.C., when his mausoleum was under construction, that people were not to be moved there (*HS* 11:5b–6a).

[222] Ch'ang-ling was a prefecture where Emperor Ch'eng had planned to build his mausoleum, but the tomb was never finished. See III, 39, n. 218.

[223] The character 贜 means either a "bribe" or "stolen property."

[224] Chai Fang-chin was then the director of justice of the imperial chancellor. It was his duty to prosecute those engaged in illegal activities. The emperor was very pleased with his investigation and promoted him to the post of governor of Ching-chao in 18 B.C. (*HS* 19B:15b–16a).

41. GUESTS ENGAGE IN ROBBERY

20–16 B.C.   [His Majesty] then ordered the masters of writing to question the colonel-director of retainers and the governor of Ching-chao as to whether or not they knew . . . that the marquis of Hung-yang, [Wang] Li,[225] and his sons had been hiding depraved persons and fugitives and that their guests had been engaging in group robberies But both the director of retainers and the governor tolerated that and did not memorialize to have them punished.[226] [*HS* 98:11a]

42. BRAVOS KILL OFFICIALS

16–8 B.C.   During [the reign periods of] Yung-shih and Yüan-yen, His Majesty was indolent in civil administration. The imperial relatives-in-law were arrogant and unrestrained. The elder and younger sons of [the marquis of] Hung-yang[227] associated with the reckless redressers-of-wrongs and hid fugitives.

And the great and powerful persons of the Pei-ti commandery, Hao Shang and others, taking revenge, killed the prefect of I-ch'ü and his wife and children, six persons. They went back and forth in Ch'ang-an. The imperial chancellor and the secretaries sent their subordinates to search for the gang members. An edict was issued for their arrest, but it took a long time to capture them.

In Ch'ang-an the depraved and cunning persons gradually increased. The young men of the local communities killed officials to avenge others in return for a reward.[228] Together they made pellets, and [each

---

[225] Wang Li was one of the half-brothers of Empress Dowager Wang and the maternal uncle of Emperor Ch'eng.

[226] Emperor Ch'eng discovered all this, as well as the misconduct of his other maternal uncles, after he started to go out incognito in 20 B.C. However, he could not bear to have his uncles punished and pardoned them after Wang Li and his sons admitted their guilt and apologized (*HS* 98:10b–11b, 10:9a, 18:8a).

[227] According to Teng Chan, Hung-yang was the surname of a man with the style Chang-chung; Ju Shun explains that Hung-yang was the name of a prefecture, Chang being the surname and Chung the style of a man. At variance with this, Yen comments that Hung-yang was a family name, whereas Chang was the style of the elder and Chung that of the younger brother. But Yen also quotes a statement suggesting that the phrase means the "elder and younger sons of Wang Li, the marquis of Hung-yang." Since the preceding sentence dealt with the relatives-in-law and the activities of the marquis and his son described here are consistent with those of another passage (cf. III, 41), and since both have the statement, "hide fugitives," we feel that Yen's second interpretation is the most plausible.

[228] Yen suggests that they killed the officials either to satisfy a grudge of their own or to carry out revenge for someone who rewarded them for it.

one] chose one.[229] The one who got the red pellet was to kill a military officer, the one who got the black was to kill a civil official, [and the one who got] the white was to take care of the funerals.[230]

Inside the city at dusk, the dust rose. They attacked and robbed passers-by. The dead and wounded lay crosswise on the streets. The [alarm] drum sounded incessantly. [*HS* 90:20a–b]

43. POWERFUL SLAVES OF A POWERFUL FAMILY

Thereupon Imperial Chancellor [Hsüeh] Hsüan and Grandee Secretary [Chai] Fang-chin[231] memorialized that [Chang] Fang[232] was arrogant, extravagant, licentious, and unrestrained. Previously Attend- 15 B.C.

---

[229] Wang Nien-sun says that the two characters 為彈 were probably not in the original text (Wang Nien-sun, *Tu-shu tsa-chih* [Chin-ling shu-chü, 1870], 6:91, hereafter cited as *TSTC)*. He points out that the phrasing is repetitious because 丸 and 彈 have the same meaning.

[230] That is, the funerals of his friends who were killed by officials or others.

[231] Chai Fang-chin held the post of grandee secretary from the third to the eighth month of the second year of Yung-shih, 15 B.C. (*HS* 19B:16a).

[232] Chang Fang's family had been high officials for many generations. His great-great-great-grandfather, Chang T'ang, was grandee secretary. T'ang's son, An-shih, was appointed grand minister of war and general of chariots and cavalry and ennobled as marquis of Fu-p'ing by Emperor Hsüan. An-shih's son, Yen-shou, was grand keeper of equipages of the bureau of the left and inherited the title of marquis on the death of his father. His grandson, Fang's father, Lin 臨, married the princess of Ching-wu, the sister of Emperor Yüan. Fang himself married the daughter of the younger brother of Empress Hsü, wife of Emperor Ch'eng. He inherited the marquisate in 32 B.C. and was appointed attendant within the palace and general of the palace gentlemen. He was so intimate with the emperor, his cousin, that he could sit and sleep in his room; he frequently accompanied him on his incognito trips and to cockfights and horse races.

Because of the activities exposed in the memorial, the emperor, at the empress dowager's insistence, was forced to send him from the court. Fang was made chief commandant of the Pei-ti commandery. He was recalled a number of times, but each time, at the insistence of the empress dowager and also of the ministers, he was sent away again. After Emperor Ch'eng's death in 7 B.C. Chang Fang is said to have died of grief.

The Chang family was a very powerful one from the time of Emperor Hsüan (73 B.C.) to the end of the Early Han. There were more than ten members who held the posts of attendant within the palace, regular palace attendant, and other high positions. Moreover, according to Pan Ku, the Changs were the only family of the nobility who retained their marquisate for so long a time. Even during Wang Mang's reign, Fang's son, Ch'un, held a marquisate. At the beginning of the Later Han he was grand minister of works and had the title of marquis of Wu-shih (*HS* 59:3a, 7a–8b, 10a, 12a–15a; cf. also *HS* 18:5b, which erroneously states that Fang was marquis for thirty-six years. It should read twenty-six, because he succeeded his father in 32 B.C. and his son inherited the marquisate in 6 B.C.).

ant Imperial Secretary Hsiu and others, four in all, had been commissioned to go to [Chang] Fang's house to arrest the criminals designated by name. At this time Fang was in. The male slaves and attendants closed the gate, set up weapons and crossbows, shot at the officers, resisted the commissioners, and did not allow them to enter.

Learning that a man, Li Yu-chün, planned to present his daughter [to the court, Fang] sent Ching Wu, the superintendent of musicians of the office of music, to take her by force, but he failed. He then sent his male slaves, K'ang and others, to the man's house. They injured three persons.

He also hated Mang, the patrolman of the office of music, because of some governmental affairs, and sent his senior male slaves, Chün and others to a total of more than forty, grouped together and equipped with weapons and crossbows; they entered the office of music in the daytime, attacked and shot up the offices, tied up the juniors of the chief official, and smashed the furnishings. All those in the offices fled and hid. Mang himself shaved his head, wore an iron collar, and dressed in russet clothes,[233] and together with the chief official and clerks, T'iao and others, all barefoot,[234] kowtowed and apologized to Fang. Fang then stopped.

His slaves and attendants and relatives, all relying on his power, were cruel and tyrannical. They even tried to take the wife of an official, and when they were unable to get her, they killed the husband. If they hated a person, they ruthlessly killed his relatives. They then always escaped and entered Fang's house and could not be captured. [*HS* 59:13a–b]

44. Land Occupied

Before
11 B.C.

At that time the emperor's maternal uncle, [Wang] Li, the marquis of Hung-yang, sent his guest to seize and reclaim, through Li Shang, the grand administrator of the Nan commandery, several hundred *ch'ing* of uncultivated land, a considerable part of which was made up of land around the lake,[235] which was rented by people from the privy

---

[233] These were the signs of a criminal. Obviously the man humiliated himself in this way in order to plead his guilt and apologize.

[234] Also an expression of self-humiliation.

[235] The term 陂澤 is found in the *Shih-ching*, being interpreted as the shore which blocks the water 陂澤障也 (*Shih-ching chu-su, SPPY* ed., 12:16a). Yen explains 大澤之陂 in *HS* 1A:1a as meaning the "shore of a great pond." However, according to the *Shuo-wen*, 陂 also means pond or lake. Tuan comments that while 陂 refers to the shore and 池 to the pond, actually they mean the same thing, "the pond and the shore" (*SWCTC* 14B:3–4).

treasury. He roughly opened up the land,[236] and presented a memorial expressing his willingness to offer the land to the government. An edict was issued to the grand administrator of the commandery to appraise the land and pay him its value. He received more than a hundred million cash over the current price.[237] [*HS* 77:11b–12a]

45. LOCAL BRAVOS

Chao Chi and Li K'uan, reckless redressers-of-wrongs, kept many guests. By means of their physical strength they encroached upon the rural communities, went so far as to rape people's wives and daughters, and got hold of officials [by learning] their faults. They acted without restraint all over the whole commandery. When they heard that [Ho] Ping[238] was about to come, they both fled.   6–1 B.C.

When Ping arrived at his office, he sought out officials who were brave and were familiar with the law, altogether ten persons. He asked the civil officials to investigate the cases of the three men[239] and the military officials to arrest them. He instructed them and said, ". . . Chao and Li are cruel and vicious. Even though they are far away we should get their heads to comfort the people. . . ." [The officials] also caught Chao and Li in another commandery and brought back their heads. [*HS* 77:18b–19a]

[236] According to Yen, although the marquis of Hung-yang said that the land he had seized was uncultivated, actually that part that was rented by the people from the privy treasury was cultivated.

[237] This happened sometime between 15 and 11 B.C., while Wang Li's brother, Wang Shang, held the post of grand minister of war (*HS* 19B:16b) and probably not long before his death.

[238] Ho Ping 何並 had been a prefect of Ch'ang-ling. He became famous because he was strict with the unlawful imperial relatives-in-law. He was then promoted to the posts of grand administrator of Lung-hsi and then of Ying-ch'uan. Chao and Li fled because they knew that the newly appointed governor was strict and severe. Ho Ping held this post until his death.

[239] The other man was Chung Wei 鍾威, a subordinate in the commandery government, who had been guilty of receiving bribes. His brother, Yüan 元, the commandant of justice at this time, had asked Ho Ping to reduce his brother's sentence. Ho refused. When Ho arrived at his office he instructed his subordinates that since the crime of Chung Wei had been committed before a recent amnesty, Chung was to be sent into the Han-ku Pass and that he was to be arrested only if he refused to do so. Relying on the influence of his brother, Chung Wei stopped at Lo-yang, outside the pass, and so was killed by Ho's subordinates (*HS* 77:18b–19a).

46. A POWERFUL OFFICIAL

2 B.C.   [Wang Chia[240] also memorialized], "Whenever there are receptions of guests, weddings, and meeting of relatives in [Tung] Hsien's[241] house,[242] all the officials in the government pay tribute to him. [Your Majesty] granted to his Dark-green Heads and male and female slaves[243] as much as a hundred thousand cash each. Imperial emissaries were sent to supervise matters, [but they] took goods from the markets, and all the merchants were shocked. The people on the roads were clamoring, and all the officials were confused." [*HS* 86:12a]

---

[240] Wang Chia, who had been a grand administrator and grandee secretary, was at this time the imperial chancellor. This memorial warning the emperor that Tung Hsien should not be treated with such great favor greatly displeased the emperor. Later when the emperor issued an edict to add two thousand more households to Tung's fief, Wang rejected the edict and memorialized that the grant was improper. This angered the emperor. Wang's memorial recommending Liang Hsiang 梁相, the dismissed commandant of justice, also displeased the emperor. It was thereupon ordered that the imperial chancellor be arrested and investigated. Wang refused to eat in prison and died there about twenty days later (*HS* 86:6a ff.).

[241] Tung Hsien's father, Tung Kung 董恭, was an imperial secretary through whose recommendation Hsien was appointed member of the retinue of the heir apparent. When Emperor Ai ascended the throne, he was appointed gentleman with the function of reporting the time, standing below the Imperial Hall. Because of his good looks, which greatly impressed the emperor, he was in 5 B.C. made gentleman of the Yellow Gate, a post that brought him close to his ruler. Shortly thereafter, he became chief commandant of escorting cavalry (*fu-ma tu-wei* 駙馬都尉). He was greatly in favor and often shared the sleeping quarters of the emperor, and his wife also was permitted to remain inside the palace.

His younger sister was made brilliant companion, his father was promoted to the post of commandant of the guard, and his brother and father-in-law were also made high officials. Tung Hsien was ennobled as marquis of Kao-an and in 1 B.C. at the age of twenty-two he was appointed grand minister of war to replace Ting Ming, the emperor's maternal uncle. His power surpassed that of the two consort families, Fu and Ting. He was loved so much by the emperor, who had no son, that the emperor even considered making Tung his successor. However, immediately after the death of Emperor Ai, he was dismissed by Empress Dowager Wang and Wang Mang, who came into power again. He and his wife then both committed suicide. His family property was confiscated and sold by the government; it was worth four billion three hundred million cash (*HS* 93:9b–15b, 19B:18a).

[242] Tung Hsien's luxurious residence was constructed by order of the emperor, who ordered construction to be supervised by the grand court architect, a post then held by Tung's father-in-law. The building was extremely luxurious and was furnished with precious articles that were even superior to those used by the emperor. According to the memorial of K'ung Kuang, who accused Tung Hsien after his death, the construction of Tung's residence and tomb cost one hundred million cash, and thus the government treasury was exhausted (*HS* 93:10b and 15a, cf. 86:11b–12a).

[243] Cf. *HS* 93:10b.

47. A RETIRED OFFICIAL BECOMES A REDRESSER-OF-WRONGS

Formerly [Yüan] She's[244] paternal uncle was murdered by the Ch'in *Ca.* A.D. 1–4 family of Mao-ling. After having stayed at Ku-k'ou for about half a year, She brought impeachment against himself and was dismissed from his office. He intended to avenge [his uncle]. Certain powerful and awe-inspiring persons of Ku-k'ou killed the Ch'in family for him. He went into hiding, and after more than a year it happened that there was an amnesty and he came out. Various powerful persons of the commanderies and kingdoms and those of Ch'ang-an and the five mausoleum [prefectures],[245] who had courage and integrity, all admired and attached themselves to him. She then humbled himself in dealing with others. Men, both virtuous and unworthy, thronged near his gate. The village where he stayed was full of guests.

Someone censured She, saying, "You originally were an official and you are a descendant of a 2,000-picul [official]. When you bound your hair[246] and cultivated yourself, you became renowned, observing the mourning [for your father], declining the funeral gift, and practicing politeness and yielding. Even though you avenged [your uncle] and seized your enemy, you were still not far from benevolence and righteousness. Why do you then indulge yourself and become a man recklessly redressing wrongs?"

She replied, "Have you alone never seen the widow of a common family? At first when she controls herself, her mind admires Po-chi of Sung,[247] and the filial woman, Ch'en.[248] When once she is unfortunately

[244] The style of Yüan She was Chü-hsien. His grandfather, because he was a powerful person, was moved from Yang-tse to Mao-ling during the time of Emperor Wu. His father was grand administrator of Nan-yang in the reign of Emperor Ai. It was customary when such an official died for other officials to present funeral gifts to the man's family; sometimes these amounted to over ten million cash. When Yüan She's father died, Yüan returned the funeral gifts and went into mourning for three years, which at the time was not common. Because of these filial actions Yüan became well known and when the mourning period was ended he was recommended for office and became prefect of Ku-k'ou, located in modern Li-ch'üan, Shensi (*HS* 92:13a–b).

[245] The five mausoleum prefectures, according to Yen, were Ch'ang-ling, An-ling, Yang-ling, Mao-ling, and P'ing-ling.

[246] A rite of initiation usually occurring at the age of twenty when an adolescent boy first tied up his hair and put on his cap. Tied-up hair became a figurative way of speaking of a young man of twenty.

[247] Po-chi, the daughter of Duke Hsüan of Lü, married Duke Kung of Sung. One night during her widowhood a fire broke out in her house. Her attendants urged her to flee, but true to the tradition that a woman should not leave the hall at night unless accompanied by her governess and tutor she refused to leave and was burned to death (Yen: *HS* 92:14a).

insulted by a bandit, she will then be lewd and indolent. She knows that it is not in accordance with propriety, yet she is unable to return to [her former chastity]. I am like that."

She thought to himself that it was unfilial to enjoy fame in his lifetime for declining the funeral gift given by Nan-yang [commandery officials], and for allowing his forebears' tomb to be frugal and simple. Thereupon he built the tomb-house on a large scale, with buildings around it with double doors. . . . All the expenses were put upon the rich people and the elders. But his own clothes, carriages, and horses were merely sufficient, and his wife and sons were poor in their home. He devoted himself wholly to the affairs of relieving the poor and giving to the people in distress.

Once someone prepared wine and invited She. When She entered the village gate, a guest informed him of the illness of the mother of one of She's acquaintances; she was sick and was resting in a house in the village. She immediately went to pay a visit. When he knocked at the door, the family was lamenting. Then he entered to present his condolences and inquired about the funeral. The family had nothing. She said, "Sweep clean and wash [the corpse] only and await my return." [She] went to his host, sighed in front of the guests, and said, "While someone's parent is lying on the ground and is not being put into a coffin, how can She enjoy this? I should like my wine and food taken away." The guests vied with each other asking what articles should be procured. She then sat on the edge of the mat,[249] scraped [wooden] tablets,[250] writing down all the robes, comforters, coffin, down to objects to be put into the mouth, and distributed [the tablets] to the various guests. The various guests rushed to buy [the things]. When the sun was setting, they all gathered. She personally checked [everything]. . . . Then carrying the coffin and other things and followed by the guests, he went to the bereaved family, put the corpse in the coffin, encouraged [the guests], and finished the interment. His way of assisting the needy and of treating people was like this. Later someone slandered She, saying, "He is the leader of the vicious people." The son of the bereaved family immediately stabbed and killed the speaker.

---

[248] The filial woman, Ch'en, supported her mother-in-law after her husband's death. Her parents wanted to take her away and remarry her. They did not force this plan when they learned that she would commit suicide to avoid remarriage *(ibid.)*.

[249] Yen comments that it was customary for a man to sit in this manner when mourning.

[250] At this time paper had not yet been invented.

The majority of [She's] guests broke the law, and their offenses and faults were frequently presented to and known by the high authorities. Wang Mang arrested [She] several times and wanted to put him to death, but he was always pardoned and released again. She was frightened and sought to be a clerk of a bureau head in a minister's office, wishing thus to escape his guests. At the time of the death of Empress Dowager Wen-mu[251] he held the office of "colonel who inters." Then A.D. 13 he became a gentleman of the palace and was later dismissed from office.

She intended to visit the tomb [of his father][252] but he did not want to meet his guests; he secretly made an arrangement to meet only his old friends. She drove to Mao-ling in a single carriage, entered the village at sunset, then hid himself, and did not see anyone. He sent a male slave to the market to buy meat. The male slave, relying upon She's influence, quarreled with the butcher, wounded him by cutting [him with a knife], and fled. At the time, the acting prefect of Mao-ling, Mr. Yin, had recently taken office, and She had not yet visited him. Hearing of this, [the prefect] was furious. Knowing that She was a famous and powerful man, he wanted to make an example of him to the public in order to refine the customs. He sent two officers to keep guard on She by force. By noon the male slave had not appeared, and the officers intended to kill She immediately and leave. She was in distress and did not know what to do. Just then those who had made an appointment with She to visit the tomb arrived with several tens of carriages. All of them were powerful persons. All together they urged Mr. Yin [to release She], but Mr. Yin did not listen to them. The various powerful persons then said, "Yüan Chü-hsien's male slave broke the law and has not been captured. If we make She bare his shoulder, bind himself, pierce his ear with an arrow,[253] and come to the gate of the court to acknowledge his guilt to you, Sir, it would be sufficient for your authority." Mr. Yin consented. She apologized according to the agreement, [was permitted] to re-dress, and was sent away.

[251] This is the title of Empress Dowager Wang, the aunt of Wang Mang. When he came to the throne he changed the title grand empress dowager to Empress Dowager Wen-mu of the Hsin dynasty (*HS* 98:17b, 19a).

[252] It has been suggested that this might have been Emperor Wu's tomb, Mao-ling; see Martin Wilbur, *Slavery in China During the Former Han Dynasty* (Chicago, 1943), p. 459. However, it would have been most unusual for a commoner to be permitted to visit an emperor's tomb. Moreover, the term *chung* 冢, "tomb," is used in our text, not *ling*, "mausoleum." Mao-ling was Yüan She's place of origin and his father's tomb was located there.

[253] This was the attitude of a prisoner of war showing complete surrender.

Formerly She had made friends with a wealthy man of Hsin-feng, Ch'i T'ai-po. The younger [half-]brother of T'ai-po by the same mother, Wang Yu-kung, always envied She. At this time he was a subordinate of the prefect and advised Mr. Yin, saying, "You, Sir, being an acting prefect, humiliated Yüan She by what you did; one day, when the real prefect comes, you will again be in a single carriage and go back to become a subordinate of a commandery government. She's assassins are [numerous] as the clouds, and when they kill people no one ever knows the name of the murderer. It makes your heart freeze. She built the tomb-house extravagantly and beyond the regulations,[254] and his offenses and evil acts are manifest and known to the emperor. Now for your plans, nothing would be better than to destroy She's tomb-house and memorialize his past crimes point by point. You, Sir, will certainly become a real prefect, and because of that She will not dare to hate you." Mr. Yin followed his plan. [Wang] Mang eventually made him the real prefect. From that time on She hated Wang Yu-kung. He selected some of his guests and sent his eldest son, Ch'u, followed by twenty carriages, to attack the family of Wang Yu-kung. Yu-kung's mother was also the mother of Ch'i T'ai-po. When the various guests saw her, all bowed and said to each other, "Do not frighten Mrs. Ch'i." Then they killed Yu-kung's father and his son [that is, Yu-kung himself],[255] cut off the heads of the two and left.

She's nature was very similar to that of Kuo Hsieh,[256] who outwardly was gentle, kind, and humble, but inwardly concealed his feelings and

[254] Han law regulated the size and structure of a tomb and tomb-house in accordance with one's political rank and status. The mound for a marquis could be four feet high, and the one for a marquis within the passes down to the ones for commoners were proportionately lower (*CLCS* 22:1b). The *Li-chi* states that no mound at all marked the grave of a commoner (*LCCS* 12:6b; cf. *YTL* 6:5b). That these restrictions were real and strict may be seen from the story of Empress Dowager Ma, whose complaint that her mother's burial mound was slightly over the prescribed height led her brother to have it reduced immediately (*HHS* 10A:18a). Two marquises in the Later Han were also punished for similar violations; one had his head shaved and the other had his marquisate reduced (*CFL* 3:9a). The case here indicates that the regulations applied to the tomb-house as well as to the burial mound.

[255] Yen explains that the sentence means that Wang Yu-kung's 游公 father and Yu-kung were killed. Liu Pin, however, says that the father and son referred to are Yu-kung and his son. A later subcommentator, Chou Shou-ch'ang, points out that although Yu-kung and Ch'i T'ai-po had the same mother, the surname of Yu-kung's father was Wang, whereas the admonition was not to frighten Mrs. Ch'i. This indicates that the murderers did not intend to show any leniency to Mr. Wang, Yu-kung's father. On this basis, Chou follows Yen in the interpretation of the passage (*HSPC* 92:14b), and so do we.

[256] For Kuo Hsieh, see III, 20.

enjoyed murder. Many who offended him by an angry look in the dusty [market] were killed by him.[257] At the end of Wang Mang's [reign], when the soldiers of the east arose,[258] most of the younger members of the various Wang [families] recommended She as one who could be used because he was able to make people willing to die for him. Mang thereupon summoned him for an audience, reproved him for his guilt and evil doings, pardoned him, and appointed him grand governor of Chen-jung, the grand administrator of T'ien-shui.[259]

Shortly after She took office, [the forces of] Ch'ang-an[260] were defeated and those in the commanderies and prefectures who held unauthorized titles[261] raised troops [and] attacked and killed the 2,000-picul [officials] and chief officials in order to support Han. All those who held the unauthorized titles had usually heard of the renown of She; they vied with each other in asking the whereabouts of Governor Yüan, and visited him. At this time, those inspectors and the commissioners of [Wang] Mang who were attached to She were able to save their lives.[262] She was transferred and sent to Ch'ang-an. The Hsi-p'i general   A.D. 23 of the Keng-shih [emperor], Shen-t'u Chien, made a request to see She, whom he valued highly. The former prefect of Mao-ling, Mr. Yin, who had destroyed the tomb-house of She was the master of documents of Chien. Originally She did not hate him. When She went out from Chien's house, Mr. Yin purposely intercepted him, bowed, and said, "Now the world has changed; there should no longer be any hatred between us." She said, "Mr. Yin, why do you treat me as if I were fishmeat [that is, not a man]?" Because of this, She was angry with him and ordered his guest to stab and kill the master of documents. She planned to run away. Being secretly ashamed[263] of this, Shen-t'u Chien

---

[257] We follow the interpretations of Wang Nien-sun and Wang Hsien-ch'ien for this passage; see *HSPC,* 92:14b, and cf. *HHS* 66:18b.

[258] This refers to the various rebellious forces east of Han-ku Pass.

[259] The two phrases, grand governor of Chen-jung and grand administrator of T'ien-shui, refer to the same office. Wang Mang changed the name of the T'ien-shui commandery to Chen-jung and also changed the official title, grand administrator, to grand governor. Ch'ien Ta-hsin suggests that the second phrase was originally a note that was later incorporated into the text through a copyist's error (*HSPC* 92:14b–15a).

[260] That is, the government forces of Wang Mang.

[261] Those who rose against Wang Mang usually claimed that they were generals (*HS* 99C:24a, 31b; *HHS* 11:3a) but since no such titles had been conferred or authorized by the sovereign, they were called "false" or "unauthorized" titles (假號). See *SC* 7:10a, 92:11b–12a.

[262] That is, they were under the protection of Yüan She.

[263] He was ashamed of not being able to protect his subordinates. The assault was an insult to him.

said deceitfully, "I want to [cooperate] with Yüan Chü-hsien in pacify-
ing the Three Adjuncts. Why should I change my mind because of one
official?" The guests [of the two parties] exchanged words with each
other [and it was decided that] She was to enter the prison of his own
volition in order to apologize to Chien who approved of this. The guests
whose carriages amounted to several tens²⁶⁴ altogether escorted She on
his way to the prison. Chien sent troops, intercepted, and took She
from his carriage. The escorting carriages dispersed and ran away.
Thereupon She was beheaded and [his head] hung in the market at
Ch'ang-an. [*HS* 92:13b–17a]

48. AN OLD POWERFUL FAMILY

Feng Fang,²⁶⁵ whose style was Hsiao-sun, was a native of Hu-yang of
the Nan-yang commandery. One of his ancestors belonged to a branch
of [the ruling family of the old state of] Wei and had held the fief²⁶⁶ of
the City of Feng, and therefore took [its name] for his name. After
Ch'in conquered Wei, [the family] was moved to Hu-yang and stood
out as the distinguished family of the commandery.

Ca.
A.D. 22   At the end of Wang Mang's [reign] the people throughout the empire
revolted. Fang then gathered together his guests, summoned powerful
and awe-inspiring persons, and made camps and moats to wait for the
person to whom he would offer allegiance. [*HHS* 33:11b–12a]

49. MILITARY FORCE OF FAMILY MEMBERS AND GUESTS

Yin Shih,²⁶⁷ whose style was Tz'u-po, was a native of Hsin-yeh of
Nan-yang. He was an elder half-brother of Empress Kuang-lieh [by her

²⁶⁴ We follow the Palace edition in reading "ten" instead of the "thousand" of our
text.

²⁶⁵ Feng Fang 馮魴 later made himself a subject of Emperor Kuang-wu, who
appointed him a prefect in A.D. 27. He held the office of grand keeper of equipages in
A.D. 51 and that of minister of works in A.D. 56. He had the rank of a *hsiang* marquis
of Yang-i. In 61 he was dismissed and also deprived of his noble rank. Three years
later he was reappointed to office, and later his noble rank was also restored. He died
in A.D. 85 at the age of eighty-six (*HHS* 33:12b–14a).

²⁶⁶ According to Liu Pin, the word *ts'ai* 菜 is an error for *ts'ai* 采, "fief" (*HHSCC*
33:7a).

²⁶⁷ Yin Shih held a number of high positions during the reign of Emperor Kuang-
wu and had the rank of marquis. In A.D. 58 he was appointed to the post of chief of
police of the capital region. He died in A.D. 59 (*HHS* 32:12b–13a).

father's] first wife. His ancestors were descendants of Kuan Chung.[268] Kuan Chung's grandson of the seventh generation, Hsiu, moved from Ch'i to Ch'u, where he became a grandee of Yin,[269] from which the family name [of Yin] was derived. During the transitional period from Ch'in to Han, the family for the first time set up their home in Hsin-yeh.

When Liu Po-sheng[270] raised his Righteous Army, Shih was traveling and studying at Ch'ang-an. Having heard of this, he gave up his study, returned home, and led his relatives of the younger generation, his kinsmen, and guests, more than one thousand men, and went to Po-sheng. Po-sheng then appointed Shih to the post of colonel. [*HHS* 32:12a–b] A.D. 22

50. MILITARY POWER OF STRONG FAMILIES

Soon after the Keng-shih [emperor] was enthroned the Three Supporting Districts continuously suffered from war and banditry. The people were disturbed and frightened. The strong lineages and big families all kept large bodies of men to protect their camps. Not one of them was willing to be the first to submit. [*HHS* 31:1b] A.D. 23

After Keng-shih came to the throne the great family Li of Wu-yin[271] occupied the city and refused to submit. [*HHS* 26:21a]

After [Emperor] Kuang-wu came to the throne [Li Chang][272] was appointed prefect of Yang-p'ing.[273] At that time the powerful and awe-inspiring persons of Chao and Wei usually guarded [their areas] and assembled [men]. In Ch'ing-ho the big family of Chao Kang then erected a walled stronghold on the boundary of the prefecture, made armor and weapons, and inflicted injuries on the people wherever [Kang] was.[274] When [Li] Chang arrived, he then prepared a banquet and invited Kang. Wearing a decorated sword and a feathered coat, A.D. 25

---

[268] Kuan Chung was the famous statesman who helped Duke Huan of Ch'i establish his hegemony over the feudal states.

[269] Yin was located in modern Kuang-hua county in the extreme north of Hupei.

[270] Liu Po-sheng was the elder brother of Emperor Kuang-wu. For a biographical sketch, see II, 51, n. 147.

[271] We have no further information about the influential Li of Wu-yin except that they later submitted. The city of Wu-yin was located ten *li* north of the modern city of Pi-yang in northern Honan.

[272] Li Chang's ancestors had been 2,000-picul officials for five generations. Li was a follower of Emperor Kuang-wu before he ascended the throne.

[273] Yang-p'ing was located in modern Hsing county in western Shantung.

[274] According to Hui Tung, the sentence 為在所害 means 所在為人害 "he inflicted injury on the people wherever he was" (*HHSPC* 77:4a).

Kang arrived, followed by more than one hundred men. Chang drank with him face to face. Soon after, he beheaded Kang with his sword. The followers were also all killed by hidden soldiers. Then he rushed to [Kang's] walled stronghold, attacked, and destroyed it. From then on officials and people were at peace. . . .

A.D. 38   Within the year [Li Chang] was appointed attendant imperial secretary and then sent out to be grand administrator of the Lang-ya commandery.[275] At that time Hsia Ch'ang-ssu and others, the big families of An-ch'iu[276] of the Pei-hai commandery, rebelled. They put the grand administrator, Ch'u Hsing, in custody and occupied the city of Ying-ling.[277] On hearing this, Chang immediately mobilized a thousand soldiers to rush to attack them.[278] . . . He led the soldiers to the city of An-ch'iu, called for brave men to burn the gate of the city, fought with Ch'ang-ssu, and beheaded him. He killed more than three hundred men, got more than five hundred head of oxen and horses, and returned.[279] [*HHS* 77:6b–7a]

A.D. 26   At that time the Red Eyebrows and Yen Ch'en[280] despotically disturbed the Three Supporting Districts. All the big families of the commanderies and prefectures possessed numerous soldiers. [*HHS* 17:7b]

A.D. 36   At the time that [Jen Yen][281] arrived at the Wu-wei commandery,

[275] Lang-ya commandery was located in modern Shantung. Li Chang was made administrator in A.D. 38 when the previous administrator, Ch'en Chün 陳俊, was transferred to another post (*HHS* 18:19a).

[276] An-ch'iu was located in modern An-ch'iu county in Shantung.

[277] Ying-ling, a prefecture in the Pei-hai commandery, was located about 50 *li* southeast of modern Ch'ang-lo, Shantung.

[278] It was unlawful for Li Chang as grand administrator of a commandery to dispatch troops on his own authority to go into the territory of the neighboring commandery. When Li was warned by his subordinates, he replied that he would not regret this action even if he were punished by death. He later reported the case to the court and was not punished (*HHS* 77:7a–b).

[279] Later, in A.D. 40, he was charged with inaccuracy in measuring the people's land and was dismissed.

[280] Yen Ch'en 延岑 was leader of one of the rebellious forces that occupied the area of Han-chung. He defeated the Red Eyebrows and made himself the king of Wu-an. In A.D. 29 he was defeated by Han troops and submitted to Kung-sun Shu, who appointed him grand minister of war and ennobled him as king of Ju-ning. In 36, when Kung-sun Shu was defeated by Wu Han, Emperor Kuang-wu's grand minister of war, Yen submitted and was executed (*HHS* 1A:15a, 1B:10b, 11:21b–22a, 13:25a and 32a, 17:10a, 18:20b–21a).

[281] Jen Yen 任延 was appointed chief commandant of the K'uai-chi commandery by the Keng-shih emperor in A.D. 23, when he was only nineteen years old. He was appointed grand administrator of Chiu-chen by Emperor Kuang-wu. Later he was transferred to the post of grand administrator of Wu-wei. (This was probably in A.D. 36, since up to this year this post was held by Liang T'ung; *HHS* 34:1b–2a.) He was demoted to the post of a prefect because he executed the Ch'iang people without first

the Chief Clerk Who Leads Troops T'ien Kan, was a [member of the] big family of the commandery. His relatives in the younger generation and his guests were despotically harmful to the people. Yen arrested Kan and put him in prison. Father and son and the guests who were executed according to the law were five or six persons. Kan's youngest son, Shang, then gathered several hundred frivolous persons and made himself general. In the night he came and attacked [the capital of] the commandery. Yen immediately sent out troops and defeated him. [*HHS* 76:7a–b]

51. RULER SET UP BY POWERFUL PERSONS

[Liu Lin][282] thereupon conspired with the great and powerful men of the kingdom of Chao, Li Yü, Chang Ts'an, and others, and together they put [Wang] Lang[283] on the throne. . . . In the twelfth month of the first year of Keng-shih, Lin and the others then led several hundreds of A.D. 24 carriages and horsemen, entered the city of Han-tan in the morning, and stopped at the king's palace. They made Lang the Son of Heaven. Lin became the imperial chancellor, Li Yü the grand minister of war, and Chang Ts'an, grand general. Generals were sent separately to attack and conquer the [various cities in] Yu and I divisions. [*HHS* 12:1b–2a]

52. POWERFUL FAMILIES AND LABOR SERVICE

Previously the powerful individuals and the great families, wishing to A.D. 39–43

---

reporting to the government. He was again appointed grand administrator, this time of Ying-ch'uan, by Emperor Ming, and in A.D. 59 he was transferred to the post of grand administrator of Ho-nei, a position he held for nine years until his death (*HHS* 76:4b–8a).

[282] Liu Lin 劉林 was the son of King Mu of Chao. He liked magic and associated with powerful and cunning persons.

[283] Wang Lang, whose other name was Ch'ang, was a native of Han-tan in Chao. He had been a professional diviner and physiognomist who believed that someone in the area of Ho-pei was going to be emperor. When Wang Mang was usurping the throne, a man announced that he was Tzu-yü, the son of Emperor Ch'eng by a concubine. Wang Mang had the man arrested and killed. Thereupon Wang Lang claimed that he was the real Tzu-yü. Liu Lin, who was a close friend of Wang Lang, was convinced that this was true. Therefore, he and other powerful persons put Wang Lang on the throne. Liu Hsiu, the future Emperor Kuang-wu, who was at that time under the command of the Keng-shih emperor, refused to subject himself to Wang Lang; he attacked and occupied the city of Han-tan a few months later. Wang escaped but was pursued and killed (*HHS* 12:1a–4a, 1A:11a and 13b–14a).

take advantage of the labor service on the reservoir, vied with each other in their desire to monopolize it in their locality. [Hsü] Yang[284] did not listen to any one of them. Consequently they together accused Yang of accepting a bribe. [Teng] Ch'en then had Yang arrested and imprisoned.[285] [*HHS* 82A:8a–b]

53. A POWERFUL RETIRED OFFICIAL

A.D. 41   [Chao Hsi][286] was appointed prefect of Huai. Li Tzu-ch'un, of the great family [of the prefecture], formerly the chancellor of Lang-ya kingdom, was powerful and cunning, encroached upon and did harm to the people. When Hsi arrived, he heard that [Li's] two grandsons had committed a murder, and though the case had not yet been opened, he investigated the offense thoroughly and arrested and examined Tzu-ch'un. The two grandsons committed suicide. The people of the capital who asked for leniency on behalf of Li numbered several tens; [Hsi] did not listen to any of them.

At this time the king of Chao, Liang,[287] was ill and about to die. The emperor personally went to visit the king and asked what he wanted to say. The king said, "Li Tzu-ch'un and I have always been friendly with each other. Now he is guilty and the prefect of Huai, Chao Hsi, is going to execute him. I beg that his life be saved." The emperor said, "When an official is carrying out the law, it must not be bent. Ask for something else that you wish." The king did not say anything more. After he died, the emperor was moved by memories of the king of Chao. Thereupon he pardoned and released Tzu-ch'un. In the same year Hsi was pro-

[284] Hsü Yang 許楊, who was an expert in occult arts, was appointed by Teng Ch'en, the grand administrator, as a subordinate official in charge of water works and entrusted with the duty of the construction of the reservoir.

[285] Yang was found innocent and was released the same day.

[286] Chao Hsi 趙憙 had been appointed general of the palace gentlemen by the Keng-shih emperor. He was made prefect of Huai by Emperor Kuang-wu. In A.D. 51 he was promoted to the post of grand commandant with the title of Kuan-nei marquis. When Emperor Chang ascended the throne, Chao was appointed grand tutor. He died at the age of eighty-four in the year 80 (*HHS* 26:21b–25a).

[287] The king of Chao, Liu Liang, who was the paternal uncle of Emperor Kuang-wu, had been a prefect in Emperor P'ing's time. When Liu Po-sheng and Liu Hsiu revolted and were defeated by Wang Mang's army, Liang's wife and two sons were killed. In A.D. 26 he was made the king of Kuang-yang and in 29 the king of Chao. In 37 he was degraded to the rank of duke of Chao, a rank he held until his death in A.D. 41 (*HHS* 14:11a–12a). Thus it is erroneous to refer to him as king of Chao at this time. The "Annals of Kuang-wu" read, "In the first month of the seventeenth year of Chien-wu the duke of Chao, Liang, died" (*HHS* 1B:17a).

moted to the post of grand administrator of P'ing-yüan. [*HHS* 26:22b–23a]

54. THE POWERFUL FAMILY TOU

[Tou] Jung was on duty with the imperial guards for more than ten A.D. 60 years.[288] When he grew old, his sons and grandsons became self-indulgent and very often violated the law. [Tou] Mu and others[289] then associated with frivolous people, asked the good office of [the authorities of] the commanderies and prefectures, and interfered with and disturbed the government. Because their fief was in An-feng,[290] and wishing that the old kingdom of Lu-an[291] should all be occupied by their relatives-in-law, they thereupon forged a mandate in the name of Empress Dowager Yin, ordering the marquis of Lu-an, Liu Yü, to divorce his wife. Then they married [Mu's] daughter to him.

In the fifth year of [Yung-p'ing] the family of Yü's [former] wife A.D. 61 presented a memorial to report the case. The emperor was very angry and then dismissed Mu and the others from all their positions. The

---

[288] Tou Jung had been a major under the "strong-crossbow general" during A.D. 6 and 7. In A.D. 21 Wang Mang made him general of the P'o River. He surrendered to the Keng-shih emperor in 23 and was made the chief commandant of the dependent state of Chang-yeh. Thereby he was able to establish himself in what is now Kansu corridor, where his progenitors had been officials, and in 25 he organized the five commanderies of Wu-wei, Chang-yeh, Chiu-ch'üan, Tun-huang, and Chin-ch'eng into one unit, of which he became the head. In 29 he established contact with Emperor Kuang-wu, who appointed him to the position of shepherd of Liang division. In A.D. 32 he helped Emperor Kuang-wu eliminate Wei Ao, and thereupon was granted the title of marquis of An-feng. A few years later he was made the shepherd of Chi division, and in 37 was transferred to the post of grand minister of works. In A.D. 44 he was dismissed, but later he was granted the title of "specially advanced." In 47 he held the post of commandant of the guard at the same time he held the post of grand court architect. He asked to be allowed to resign and was ordered to return home to rest in 56 when his cousin's son, Lin, was found guilty and executed (*HHS* 23:1a–16a).

[289] Tou Mu was Jung's eldest son. He married the princess of Nei-huang and held the post of colonel of the guards of the city gates. Mu's son, Hsün, married a daughter of Liu Ch'iang 劉疆, King Kung of Tung-hai, the princess of Pi-yang. Tou Jung's brother's son, Ku, married a daughter of Emperor Kuang-wu, the princess of Nieh-yang (*HHS* 23:14b; see also II, 62). Since the princess of Nei-huang is not listed in *HHS* 10, where all the daughters of the various empresses are listed, Ch'ien Ta-hsin and Chou Shou-ch'ang assume that she was the daughter of a king (*HHSCC* 23:9a).

[290] Tou Jung was ennobled as the marquis of An-feng 安豐. His fief covered four prefectures in modern An-hui: An-feng, Yang-ch'üan, Liao-an, and An-feng 安風 (*HHS* 23:12a–b).

[291] All of these prefectures belonged to the former kingdom of Lu-an *(Shan-hai ching*, in *CHTTS*, 22:13a, hereafter cited as *SHC)*.

various Tou who were holding the position of gentlemen or other official posts were all [ordered] to return to their native commandery, together with the members of their families. Only Jung was [allowed] to remain in the capital.²⁹² [*HHS* 23:15a–b]

55. Monopoly and Exploitation

A.D. 68   The emperor had wanted to establish the Permanent Stabilization Granary.²⁹³ The majority of the ministers who discussed the matter considered it advantageous. [Liu] Pan²⁹⁴ answered that it would be disadvantageous to establish the Permanent Stabilization Granary, because although outwardly it seemed to benefit the people, inwardly it actually caused the exploitation of the people because the powerful and awe-inspiring persons acted illegally in taking advantage of it and the small people were not able to be equitably treated through it. The establishment of it would not be advantageous. The emperor then gave up the idea. [*HHS* 39:13b]

56. Powerful Official Seizes Land from a Princess

A.D. 78–88   Both the elder and the younger brothers [Tou]²⁹⁵ were close to and

²⁹² Shortly afterwards Tou Mu and other family members were allowed to return to live in the capital. Tou Jung died shortly thereafter at the age of seventy-eight. Several years later Tou Mu and the family members were ordered to go back to their native commandery. Because Mu had bribed a petty official, he and his son, Hsüan 宣, were put in prison, where they died. Tou Hsün, who was allowed to stay in the capital, also died in prison (*HHS* 23:15b). The family came into power again when Tou Hsün's daughter became the empress; her brothers, Hsien, and others occupied prominent posts. See III, 56 and 57.

²⁹³ The Ch'ang-p'ing granary was established in 54 B.C.

²⁹⁴ Liu Pan 劉般, who was Emperor Hsüan's great-great-grandson, was the acting chief of police of the capital at this time.

²⁹⁵ Tou Hsien and his younger brother, Tou Tu 竇篤, were sons of Tou Hsün; see III, 54, and notes. The family came into power again when Hsien's younger sister became empress in A.D. 78. Hsien held the office of general of the palace gentlemen as rapid as tigers and at the same time that of attendant within the palace. Tu was the attendant gentleman at the Yellow Gate.

In A.D. 88 Tou Hsien was appointed general of chariots and cavalry and in the next year led an expeditionary force against the Northern Hsiung-nu. He defeated them severely; more than two hundred thousand men surrendered. He pursued the fleeing enemy and reached Yen-jan Mountain, 3,000 *li* beyond the frontier. The Northern Shan-yü submitted to the Han and sent his younger brother to present tribute to the Han court. For his victory Tou Hsien was appointed grand general and ennobled as marquis. At first he declined firmly both honors, but then accepted them. His three

favored by [the emperor]. They both served in the imperial palace. The grants [bestowed upon them] accumulated. Their favor and honor increased every day. From the feudal kings' daughters[296] and the Yin and the Ma[297] [down] to other families, there was no one who was not afraid of them. Relying upon the influence of the imperial palace,[298] Hsien then demanded the garden of the princess of Hsin-shui[299] at a low price. Intimidated, the princess did not dare to dispute with him.[300] [*HHS* 23:19a]

57. POWERFUL OFFICIALS

After Tou Hsien had gone,[301] his younger brothers Tu, the commandant of the guard, and Ching, the chief of police, each seized power. They openly sent their guests to block the roads in the capital and seize the wealth of the people. Moreover, Ching without authorization sent out envoys riding the relay horses to distribute dispatches to the commanderies along the border to mobilize the crack cavalry and those who were adept at shooting from horseback and those who had talent and strength.

Each of the three commanderies, Yü-yang, Yen-men, and Shang-ku, sent officials to hand over [these cavalry and men] to Ching's residence. The government officials were afraid of him and no one dared to tell about this. [Yüan] An[302] then accused Ching of mobilizing the frontier

*Ca.
A.D. 89*

---

younger brothers were made marquises, holding at the same time high official posts; see also III, 57.

The increasing power of the Tou family made the fourteen-year-old Emperor Ho very uneasy. In 92 he took back the seal of the grand general from Tou Hsien, made him a marquis, and sent him and his three brothers back to their fiefs. Hsien, Tu, and Ching were all forced to commit suicide (*HHS* 23:18b ff.; cf. 3:7b, 4:8a–b).

[296] According to Chang Yen, *wang-chu* 王主, was the daughter of a prince (Yen, *HS* 10:2a).

[297] The Yin family was the family of Empress Yin, the second empress of Kuangwu and the mother of Emperor Ming.

The Ma family was the family of Empress Ma of Emperor Ming.

[298] The side building within the palace where the empress and the palace ladies lived was called *yeh-t'ing* 掖庭. Here the term obviously refers to the empress, the Tou brothers' sister, the source of the power upon which they relied.

[299] The princess of Hsin-shui was Emperor Ming's daughter (*HHS* 10B:26a).

[300] This was later found out by Emperor Chang, who became very angry. Empress Tou apologized for her brother. He was therefore not punished, but was ordered to return the land to the princess.

[301] Tou Hsien, then the general of chariots and cavalry, was sent to direct the expedition against the Hsiung-nu in A.D. 88. See III, 56, n. 295.

[302] Yüan An, who had been a grand administrator, grand keeper of equipages, and minister of works, was now holding the post of minister of the masses. He died in A.D. 92 (*HHS* 45:1b ff.).

soldiers without authorization and of thus frightening and deluding the officials and the people. [He also accused] the 2,000-picul officials of obeying Ching's orders immediately without waiting for the [presentation] of a tally and he [proposed that] they should be subject to open execution. He also memorialized that the colonel-director of retainers and the governor of Honan were assenting to the noble relatives without the righteousness of fulfilling their duty, and asked for their dismissal from their offices and an investigation of their guilt. Both [memorials] remained without answer.

Hsien, Ching, and the others became more and more arrogant every day; they placed their close adherents and guests in all the famous cities and great commanderies,[303] where they collected taxes. The officials and the people offered bribes. The rest of the divisions and commanderies, observing how the wind blew, also followed them. [*HHS* 45:4a–b]

A.D. 91   After [Tou] Hsien had quelled the Hsiung-nu, his awe-inspiring fame was even greater. . . . From that time on the ministers in the court were in dread of him and observing the way the wind blew, followed his wishes. [Tou] Tu was elevated to the position of the "specially advanced"[304] and was entitled to recommend officials. The ceremony for his audience with the emperor equaled that of the Three Dukes. [Tou] Ching was the chief of police and [Tou] Huai[305] was the superintendent of the imperial court.[306] Their power and position were so awe-inspiring that they shook the capital region. Although they were all haughty and overbearing, Ching was the worst. His slaves, guests, and *t'i-ch'i*,[307] relying on his influence, oppressed and exploited the small people. They

---

[303] According to Li Hsien, who quoted Yüan Shan-sung, the governor of Honan and the grand administrators of the Han-yang and Nan-yang commanderies were at that time their guests.

[304] "Specially advanced" was a rank given only to a marquis who was especially respected by the court. The rank was second only to that of the Three Ducal Ministers or Three Dukes, the three highest ministers in the government. Cf. *TT* 34:193B.

[305] Tou Huai 竇瓌, another younger brother of Hsien, had been a grand administrator and had been ennobled as a marquis. Because he was the only person among the Tou brothers who was able to restrain himself, he was merely sent back to his marquisate but was not forced to commit suicide (*HHS* 23:25a–27b).

[306] The superintendent of the imperial court was the minister in charge of the guards at the gates of the imperial palace. He took part in the ceremony of the sacrifice to Heaven (*HHC* 25:4a).

[307] The *t'i-ch'i* 緹騎 were soldiers of the chief of police outside the imperial palace. There were two hundred of them (*HHC* 27:1a–b). Li Tsu-mao, citing the *Shuo-wen* to the effect that 緹 was a kind of silk fabric of cinnabar-yellow color, suggests that the *t'i-ch'i* soldiers were so called because their clothes were made of this fabric (Wang Hsien-ch'ien, *Hsü-Han-chih chi-chieh,* in *HHSCC* 27:1b, hereafter cited as *HHCCC*).

took by force the property of others, freed without authority the criminals,[308] and married and seized women and girls. The merchants shut up [their shops] as if they were avoiding enemies. The authorities in charge were afraid of him and not one dared to impeach him. [*HHS* 23:25b–26a]

58. A Eunuch Made Marquis

At this time[309] Empress Dowager Tou was holding the reins of government and the empress [dowager's] elder brother, the Grand General [Tou] Hsien,[310] and others were usurping power and authority. There was not a single court official, superior or inferior, who did not adhere to him. Yet [Cheng] Chung[311] alone was devoted to the imperial family with all his heart and did not serve the powerful clique.[312] The emperor was intimate with him and trusted him. When Hsien and his brothers planned to rebel,[313] Chung thereupon initiated a plan to execute them. Because of his merit, he was promoted to the post of minister of the empress.[314] When merits were mentioned in edicts, and rewards were

A.D. 89–92

A.D. 92

[308] That is, by force while they were still in the custody of the government. The prisoners might have been guests, slaves, or members of the Tou family, or anyone closely associated with them, who had committed a crime. The Tou family sheltered and protected such miscreants.

[309] At the beginning of Emperor Ho's reign.

[310] For Tou Hsien, see III, 56 and 57.

[311] Cheng Chung, a eunuch, held the posts of regular palace attendant and prefect of the palace parks (*kou-tun-ling* 鉤盾令).

[312] This refers to the powerful group attached to the Tou family.

[313] It is not clear what the plan was. The "Annals of Emperor Ho" mentions only that Tou Hsien secretly planned to murder the emperor and rebel (*HHS* 4:8a; cf. 10A:21a). According to Tou's biography, Teng Tieh 鄧疊, his younger brother Teng Lei 鄧磊, Kuo Chü 郭舉 (Tou Hsien's son-in-law), and Kuo Huang 郭璜 (Chü's father) associated together. Kuo Chü and Teng's mother, Yüan, had entrée to the palace and won the favor of Empress Dowager Tou. They planned to assassinate the emperor. The emperor, who was aware of the plot, consulted with Cheng Chung and decided to kill them. However, as Tou Hsien and Teng Tieh were with their troops in Liang division at this time, the emperor did not order the arrest and execution of the men of the Teng and Kuo families until Tou Hsien and Teng Tieh returned to the capital with their troops in 92 (*HHS* 23:26b–27a). Since nothing is mentioned about Tou's rebellion (except his arrogance and tyranny), it seems that the Tou were not involved in the rebellion, if there was such a plan.

[314] The Ch'ang-ch'iu Palace was the palace occupied by an empress (*HHS* 10A: 13b). The duty of the grand minister of the empress *(ta-ch'ang ch'iu* 大長秋), a 2,000-picul post, was to announce her messages and to escort her when she was not in the palace. In the Early Han eunuchs as well as ordinary officials were appointed to the post. In the Later Han it was held only by eunuchs (*HHC* 27:2a).

granted, he always refused the most and accepted the least. Thereupon he frequently participated in the discussion of [government] affairs. The exercise of power in the hands of eunuchs began with Chung.

A.D. 102   In the fourteenth year [of Yung-yüan] the emperor thought of Chung's excellent merit and ennobled him as *hsiang* marquis of Ch'ao
A.D. 107 with a fief of fifteen hundred households. In the first year of Yung-ch'u
A.D. 114 three hundred more households were granted to him by Empress Ho-hsi.[315] He died in the first year of Yüan-ch'u. His adopted son, Hung, inherited [his rank and fief]. [*HHS* 78:6a–b]

59. A Deposed Heir Apparent Placed on the Throne by Eunuchs

A.D.
106–121   During this time Empress Dowager Teng personally attended the court and Emperor [An] himself did not participate in the government in person. The Lesser Attendant of the Yellow Gate Li Jun and the emperor's wet nurse Wang Sheng[316] together often slandered the empress dowager's elder brother, the Chief of Police [Teng] Hui and others,[317] saying that they wanted to dethrone the emperor and put the king of P'ing-yüan, [Liu] Te,[318] on the throne. The emperor was always angry and afraid.

[315] Empress Ho-hsi was Empress Teng, Emperor Ho's wife.

[316] Wang Sheng 王聖, who was given the title Baronet Yeh-wang, was the first wet nurse to be ennobled in the history of Han. This example was then followed by Emperors Shun and Ling (*HHS* 15:20a, 61:7b, 63:2a–3a). Wang Sheng was so favored by the emperor that a great residence was constructed for her by order of the emperor.

[317] It should be pointed out here that among the Teng brothers, Ching 景 died before 106, Hung 弘 in 115, and both Hui 悝 and Ch'ang 閶 in 118 (*HHS* 16:16a, 19a–b). Actually Teng Chih was the only one personally faced with the accusation. Thus it is mentioned in *HHS* 55:14a that Teng Chih and his brother were accused; Teng Hui was involved in the accusation, since it was made retroactively. According to *HHS* 16:20b, Hui, Hung, and Ch'ang were posthumously slandered in 121 upon the death of Empress Dowager Teng; the emperor, becoming angry, retroactively ordered the sons of Ching, Hung, Hui, and Ch'ang to be deprived of their marquisates and made commoners. Teng Chih, who had not participated in the plot, was merely deprived of the title "specially advanced" and permitted to keep his marquisate. This last fact further justifies the statement in our passage concerning the accusation of Teng Hui.

[318] Liu Te 劉德 was the king of An-p'ing, not of P'ing-yüan. The Liu Te 劉得 who had been king of P'ing-yüan for six years had died in 119 without an heir. Then another marquis, Liu I 劉翼, a brother of Liu Te, was made king of P'ing-yüan in 120 (*HHS* 5:21b and 22b; 55:13a, 14a, and 16a). Apparently Liu Te 德 was mistaken for Liu Te 得 because of similarity of sound. Since Teng Hui and his brothers were accused of planning to put the king of P'ing-yüan on the throne, and since Teng Hui and Teng Ch'ang died in the year 118, it seems that they could have conspired with

When the empress dowager died, [the emperor] then punished the _{A.D. 121}
Teng family[319] and demoted the king of P'ing-yüan. He ennobled [Li]
Jun as *hsiang* marquis of Yung. And the Lesser Attendant of the Yellow
Gate, Chiang Ching, advanced himself by means of slander and flattery.
Formerly he had welcomed the emperor at his residence,[320] and for this
merit he was ennobled as *tu-hsiang* marquis. Each of them had a fief of
three hundred households. Jun and Ching were both promoted [to the
post of] regular palace attendant and Chiang Ching was concurrently
made minister of the empress. Together with the Regular Palace
Attendant Fan Feng, the Prefect of the Attendants of the Yellow Gate
Liu An, the Prefect of the Imperial Palace Parks Ch'en Ta, Wang
Sheng, and Sheng's daughter, Po-jung,[321] they created disturbances
within and without [the palace] and vied with each other in extravagance and cruelty. Furthermore, the emperor's maternal uncle, the
Grand General Keng Pao,[322] and the empress' older brother, the Grand
Herald Yen Hsien,[323] also adhered to them and formed a clique. Con-

---

Liu Te 得 only, not with Liu I. However, according to *HHS* 55:14a, the wet nurse
and the eunuchs slandered the Teng brothers and the king of P'ing-yüan, Liu I,
accusing them of plotting to rebel; the king was then demoted to the rank of a *tu-
hsiang* marquis. So it is possible that Liu I was involved instead of Liu Te. On
these grounds, Ho Cho thinks that Liu Te was a mistake for Liu Chi (*HHSCC* 78:5a–
b).

[319] The members of the Teng family were not executed; but they were all deprived
of their ranks, dismissed from their official positions, and ordered to return to their
native place. Their property was confiscated, and many of them committed suicide
(*HHS* 16:20b–21a).

[320] Emperor An, the son of King Ch'ing of Ch'ing-ho, was a grandson of Emperor
Chang. When the infant emperor, Emperor Shang, died, the later Emperor An was
made a marquis by Empress Dowager Teng and put on the throne. He was thirteen
years old. However, according to the "Annals," it was the General of Chariots and
Cavalry Teng Chih who was sent to welcome the new emperor from the king's residence (*HHS* 5:1a–b). Probably Chiang Ching was among the eunuchs who were sent
to welcome the emperor.

[321] Po-jung, the daughter of the wet nurse, Wang Sheng, could enter the palace to
visit her mother. It was through her that bribes from the various officials were arranged. Apparently, as seen in the memorial of Yang Chen accusing Wang of making
connections with the officials, many persons received official appointments by means
of bribery (see note 324 below).

She was the wife of Liu Huai 劉瓌, the paternal cousin of the deceased marquis of
Chao-yang, Liu Hu 劉護. Because of this marital connection, Liu Huai was able to
inherit the marquisate from Liu Hu even though Liu Hu had a younger brother
(*HHS* 54:3a–5a).

[322] Keng Pao's younger sister was the wife of the king of Ch'ing-ho. She was the
legal mother of Emperor An. His real mother was Concubine Tso (*HHS* 55:7b).

[323] Yen Hsien gradually came into power after the death of Empress Dowager
Teng. When Emperor An died in 125 and Empress Dowager Yen personally attended

sequently they unjustly killed the Grand Commandant Yang Chen[324] and deposed the heir apparent,[325] making him the king of Chi-yin.

A.D. 125   In the following year Emperor [An] died and the *hsiang* marquis of Pei was made the Son of Heaven.[326] [Yen] Hsien and others then monopolized the court and strove for power. Thereupon they hinted to the officials to present a memorial to execute Fan Feng and to dismiss Keng Pao. Wang Sheng and her associates were all killed or moved.[327]

---

the court, Yen Hsien was appointed general of chariots and cavalry. His brothers, Ching 景, Yao 耀, and Yen 晏 held important military posts (*HHS* 10B:2a–3b).

[324] Yang Chen had been made minister of the masses in 120, and in 123 was appointed grand commandant. His memorial that accused the wet nurse, Wang Sheng, and her daughter of their unlawful activities and requested the emperor to show them less favor greatly displeased the emperor. He also charged the powerful eunuch, Fan Feng, with making a false edict in ordering the government bureaus to build private residences for him. Yang was falsely accused by Fan before Yang's memorial reached the throne, and Yang was dismissed from his post. Soon after, the Grand General Keng Pao, who was cooperating with Fan Feng, accused Yang of unwillingness to acknowledge his fault. Yang was ordered to return to his native place, where he committed suicide (*HHS* 54:1a–9b).

[325] The heir apparent was deposed by Emperor An, who was convinced by the slander of the empress (who herself had no son), Fan Feng, and Chiang Ching. The latter had caused the death of the heir apparent's wet nurse (*HHS* 10B:2a–b, 15:20a–21b).

[326] The *hsiang* marquis of Pei was the son of King Hui of Chi-pei. He was selected by the Empress Dowager Yen with the agreement of her brother, Yen Hsien, because he was young and could be easily controlled (*HHS* 5:30b, 10B:3a). The young marquis ascended the throne in the third month and died in the tenth month of the same year (*HHS* 5:30b–31a).

[327] A violent struggle for power underlines this story. Keng Pao, the maternal uncle of Emperor An, was still holding the post of grand general, while Yen Hsien was the general of chariots and cavalry under the protection of Empress Dowager Yen. Keng's post was superior to Yen's, and Keng had been in power a long time. This was in direct conflict with the rising Yen family. Yen was envious of Keng and attempted to remove him from power. Keng was accused of associating with Fan Feng, Wang Sheng, and others and was demoted to the rank of a *t'ing* marquis and sent back to his fief, where he committed suicide (*HHS* 10B:3a–b).

The Yen family had been on good terms with the eunuch Fan Feng and Wang Sheng and her daughter. Empress Dowager Yen cooperated with them in the attempt to dismiss the heir apparent. Apparently the group was closer to Keng Pao (*HHS* 10B:2a–3a, 54:9a–b). Besides, a group that had been in power for a long time was probably considered a potential threat by the Yen family.

As a result of the accusation, Fan Feng and two other officials, Hsieh Yün 謝惲 and Chou Kuang 周廣, were put in jail and died there. Wang Sheng and her daughter Yung were banished to Yen-men and Yung's husband, Fan Yen 樊嚴, who was an attendant gentleman of the Yellow Gate, was also sentenced to have his head shaved and wear the iron collar (*HHS* 10B:3a–b). The other daughter, Po-jung, the wife of Liu Huai, was not involved.

It should be pointed out here that in the process of the power struggle Yen Hsien was by no means in conflict with all the eunuchs, as were Tou Wu and Ho Chin; see

In the tenth month the *hsiang* marquis of Pei was seriously ill. [Sun] Ch'eng[328] said to Hsing Ch'ü, the chief of the internuncios of the king of Chi-yin: "The king is the legal successor and has not lost his virtue. The deceased emperor listened to slander and thus he (the king) was deposed. If the *hsiang* marquis of Pei does not recover and if we altogether put an end to Chiang Ching and Yen Hsien, the affair might be successful." Ch'ü and others agreed with him. Furthermore, the Palace Attendant within the Yellow Gate, Wang K'ang of Nan-yang, who had formerly been a clerk in the administration of the heir apparent, frequently felt sad and angry, and also the Assistant Grand Provisioner of Ch'ang-lo [Palace], Wang Kuo of Ching-chao, both adhered to Ch'eng. On the twenty-seventh day the *hsiang* marquis of Pei died. Yen Hsien informed the empress dowager to summon the sons of the kings to select the successor to the emperor. Before they had time to arrive, on the second day of the eleventh month, Ch'eng, together with eighteen persons, Wang K'ang and others, then assembled and made plans under the West Bell.[329] All of them took an oath by cutting off a piece of their clothing.[330] In the night of the fourth day Ch'eng and others met together in the Ch'ung-te Palace and from there entered the

---

III, 66 and 71. He was still cooperating with other powerful eunuchs: Chiang Ching, Li Jun 李閏, Liu An, and Ch'en Ta 陳達. Here we also see a split among the eunuchs themselves and their attachment to one or the other consort family. Fan Feng was closely attached to Keng Pao. Chiang Ching, who had been in cooperation with Fan Feng in an attempt to depose the heir apparent (*HHS* 10B:2a–b), belonged to the clique of Yen Hsien. Apparently he did not oppose the execution of Fan Feng. It was he who cooperated with Yen and persuaded him to select another successor when the young emperor, the former *hsiang* marquis of Pei, was seriously ill (*HHS* 10B:3b). On the other hand, Sun Ch'eng (see next note) and his group, who had no connection with Yen, acted as a rival group to the grand general, as well as to the powerful eunuchs closely associated with him. The split among the eunuchs shows how much each group was seeking the opportunity, whenever possible, to gain power.

[328] Sun Ch'eng, a eunuch, held the post of palace attendant within the Yellow Gate and was assigned to render services in the Ch'ang-lo Palace, the palace of the empress. In 132 he was appointed chief commandant custodian of the imperial equipages, whose duty it was to take charge of the carriages used by the emperor (*HHC* 25:6b), and he was given the title of "specially advanced." Upon his death he was posthumously given the title of general of chariots and cavalry, a superior military rank that had never before been given to a eunuch (*HHS* 78:7b, 12a).

[329] In the Palace edition *chung* 鍾 is written 鐘, which has the same meaning. Probably there was a bell located there and consequently the place was given the name West Bell. It was here that the deposed heir apparent, the king of Chi-yin, lived (*HHSCC* 78:6a).

[330] In order to make an oath solemn, certain ritual in one form or another usually accompanied the plain words of the oath. To cut off or break something implied that one would suffer the same fate if he were to break his oath. For another form of ritual in taking an oath, see III, 64, n. 361.

Chang-t'ai Gate. At this time Chiang Ching, Liu An, Li Jun, Ch'en Ta, and others were sitting together below the gate of the palace. Ch'eng and Wang K'ang approached together and beheaded Ching, An, and Ta. . . . Then they raised their weapons and forced Jun, saying, "Now we shall put the king of Chi-yin on the throne. Don't vacillate." Jun said, "All right." Thereupon they assisted Jun to rise and together they welcomed the king of Chi-yin under the West Bell and put him on the throne. This was Emperor Shun.[331]

[The emperor] summoned [officials], from the prefect of the masters of writing and the supervisor down, to follow his carriage to the Terrace of Clouds of the South Palace. Ch'eng and others remained to guard the palace gates and block [the connection between] within and without [the palace].

At that time Yen Hsien was within the palace. He was worried and distressed and did not know what to do. The Lesser Attendant of the Yellow Gate Fan Teng persuaded Hsien to mobilize the troops. In the name of the empress dowager's edict [Hsien] summoned the Colonel of the Elite Cavalry Feng Shih and the General of the Gentlemen as Rapid as Tigers Yen Ch'ung and stationed them at the Shuo-p'ing Gate to stop Ch'eng and others. He induced Shih to enter the palace. The empress dowager sent someone to give him a seal and said, "Anyone who can get the king of Chi-yin will be ennobled as a marquis of ten thousand households and the one who gets Li Jun will become a marquis of five thousand households." Considering that the men led by Shih were few, Hsien sent him together with Teng to meet the officers and soldiers outside the left side gate. Shih, taking advantage of this, fought and killed Teng and returned to his camp to defend it.

Hsien's younger brother, the Commandant of the Guard, Ching, hurriedly returned from the palace to the outside office[332] to assemble troops. When he arrived at the Sheng-te Gate, Ch'eng summoned the various masters of writing and ordered them to arrest Ching. Kuo Chen, a master of writing, at this time was lying in bed ill. Upon hearing this, he immediately led the on-duty Forest of Feathers Imperial Guards and went out the South Chih-chü Gate. There he met Ching who was followed by officers and troops and who bared his knife and shouted, "Do not oppose the weapons." Chen thereupon descended from his carriage, held the tally, and announced the edict. Ching said, "What edict?" He

[331] He was then eleven years old (*HHS* 6:2a).

[332] According to Hu San-hsing, the outside office refers to the office of the commandant of the guard (*TCTC* 51:3b).

then struck at Chen [with his knife] but missed him. Chen drew his sword and struck Ching, who fell from his carriage. [Chen's] followers pierced his breast with a lance. Then they seized him and sent him to the jail of the commandant of justice. He died the same night. The next morning [the emperor] ordered attendant imperial secretaries to arrest Hsien and others[333] and sent them to jail. Thereupon [the matter] was settled.

An edict was issued, saying, "To exhibit merit and to record good is the general principle of the past and the present. The former Regular Palace Attendant and Grand Keeper of Equipages of Ch'ang-lo [Palace] Chiang Ching, the Prefect of the Yellow Gate Liu An, the Prefect of Palace Parks Ch'en Ta, and the former General of Chariots and Cavalry Yen Hsien and his brothers made evil and rebellious plans and overturned and put in disorder the empire. The Palace Attendants Within the Yellow Gate Sun Ch'eng and Wang K'ang, the Assistant Grand Provisioner of Ch'ang-lo Palace Wang Kuo, the Palace Attendants Within the Yellow Gate Huang Lung, P'eng K'ai, Meng Shu, Li Chien, Wang Ch'eng, Chang Hsien, Shih Fan, Ma Kuo, Wang Tao, Li Yüan, Yang T'o, Ch'en Yü, Chao Feng, Li Kang, Wei Meng, and Miao Kuang cherished loyalty and were aroused with indignation. They put forth effort and consulted together and thereupon wiped out the big evil and settled the imperial family. Is it not said in the *Shih*[*-ching*] that 'not a single statement is not answered and not a single virtue is not rewarded'? Ch'eng was the leader in the plot and K'ang and Kuo assisted and cooperated. Let: [Sun] Ch'eng be ennobled as marquis of Fou-yang with a fief of ten thousand households; [Wang] K'ang be the marquis of Hua-jung and [Wang] Kuo be the marquis of Li, each with [a fief of] nine thousand households; Huang Lung be the marquis of Hsiang-nan with [a fief of] five thousand households; P'eng K'ai be the marquis of Hsi-p'ing-ch'ang, Meng Shu be the marquis of Chung-lu, and Li Chien be the marquis of Fu-yang, each with [a fief] of four thousand two hundred households; Wang Ch'eng be the marquis of Kuang-tsung, Chang Hsien be the marquis of Chu-a, Shih Fan be the marquis of Lin-chü, Ma Kuo be the marquis of Kuang-p'ing, Wang Tao be the marquis of Fan-hsien, Li Yüan be the marquis of Pao-hsin, Yang T'o be the marquis of Shan-tu, Ch'en Yü be the marquis of Hsia-chün, Chao Feng be the marquis of Hsi-hsien, Li Kang be the marquis of Chih-chiang, each with [a fief of] four thousand households; Wei

---

[333] Yen Hsien and his two other younger brothers and their associates were all executed (*HHS* 6:3a, 10B:4a).

Meng be the marquis of I-ling with [a fief of] two thousand households; Miao Kuang be the marquis of Tung-a with [a fief of] one thousand households." These were the nineteen marquises.[334] In addition, they were granted carriages, horses, gold, silver, cash, and silk, each according to his rank. Because Li Jun did not participate in the plan at the beginning, he therefore was not ennobled. Then [Sun] Ch'eng was promoted and appointed chief commandant of cavalry.[335] [*HHS* 78:7b–11b]

60. Powerful Families Ask for Illegal Protection

A.D.
107–125   Tso Hsiung, whose style was Po-hao, was a native of Nieh-yang of the Nan commandery. During Emperor An's time he was recommended as "filially pious and incorrupt" and was soon promoted to the post of inspector of Chi division. In this division there were many powerful families who liked to make requests and ask for favors.[336] Hsiung always shut his door and did not deal with them. [*HHS* 61:1a]

61. Official Dismissed Because of Suppressing the Powerful

A.D.
126–144   [Su Chang][337] was moved to the post of inspector of Ping division. On the charge that in suppressing the powerful individuals he went counter to the imperial will, he was dismissed. [*HHS* 31:18a]

[334] This was the first time that eunuchs were ennobled with full marquisates. Previously they had merely been given the rank of *hsiang* or *t'ing* marquis (*HHS* 78:6a, 7a, 8a, 13b; cf. *HHS* 78, *chiaɔ pu* 1b–2a). Emperor Shun also set up a rule that the adopted son of a eunuch was allowed to inherit his noble rank (*HHS* 78:12a–b).

[335] The chief commandant of cavalry was a high-ranking military official in charge of the horsemen of the Forest of Feathers Cavalry, *yü-lin-ch'i* 羽林騎 (*HHC* 25:6b). This was the first time that a eunuch received such a military post. Later two others of the nineteen eunuchs, Wang Tao and Li Yüan, were appointed to the same post (*HHS* 78:12a).

[336] These included requests for office, for pardon or exemption from punishment, or for illegal protection for their relatives and guests.

[337] Su Chang had been the prefect of Wu-yüan and then inspector of Chi division before he was appointed to the position mentioned above. He was known as a very upright and impartial official. When he was holding the post of inspector, he played the host with great courtesy to one of his friends who was a grand administrator and whom he had been investigating for corruption, but on the next day he arrested the administrator and punished him. He said that on the first day he drank with the grand administrator as an old friend, and on the next day he performed the role of an inspector. After his dismissal he retired and refused to accept the appointment of governor of Honan (*HHS* 31:18a–b).

62. Encroaching Upon Commoners

At that time[338] the powerful families in the Three Supporting Districts A.D. 140–154 frequently encroached upon and oppressed the small people. [*HHS* 51:11a]

63. Family of Powerful Officials

[Liang] Chi[339] followed [Sun] Shou's[340] advice, and many of the A.D. 141–159

---

[338] At the time when Ch'en Kuei 陳龜 was holding the post of governor of Ching-chao.

[339] The Liang family had been a powerful family for generations. Liang Chi's great-great-grandfather, T'ung, was a grand administrator and a marquis. T'ung's elder son, Sung, whose wife was the daughter of Emperor Kuang-wu, was found guilty of slandering the court and died in prison. Sung, the younger brother, was the father of an honorable lady, the mother of the later Emperor Ho. Because of the birth of this child, Empress Tou, who had no son herself, and her family accused the honorable lady of slander and thus brought about the death of the concubine and her father. However, the Liang family came into power again when Empress Dowager Tou died. The Honorable Lady Liang was posthumously honored with the title of empress, and the three sons of Sung, the younger brother, were ennobled as marquises and appointed officials.

The power of the Liang family reached a new climax when both the sister and the daughter of Liang Shang, the grandson of Liang Sung, were selected as imperial concubines of Emperor Shun. Shang was promoted to the post of palace attendant and colonel of the garrison cavalry (*t'un-ch'i hsiao-wei* 屯騎校尉). In A.D. 132 his daughter was made empress and he was appointed chief of police. Two years later he was appointed grand general. Liang Shang, though he occupied the most powerful post, was modest, generous to the poor, and did not use his influence and power to interfere with the law. He sought to appoint virtuous men in the government.

Liang Chi, the son of Shang, already had held the post of chief of police and later governor of Honan while his father was still alive. He was immediately appointed grand general by Shun upon the death of his father. Chi's younger brother, Pu-i 不疑, then replaced him in his post of governor of Honan. Liang Chi was at the peak of his power when the child emperor, Emperor Ch'ung, ascended the throne; Chi's younger sister, Empress Dowager Liang, personally attended the court and ordered him to take charge of the office of master of writing together with that of the grand tutor and grand commandant. When Emperor Ch'ung died, Liang Chi put the young Emperor Chih on the throne, but poisoned him the same year. He then enthroned Emperor Huan, who married Liang's younger sister, who was made empress. In 147, thirteen thousand more households were granted to his fief, which in 150 was enlarged to thirty thousand households. Further honor was granted to him by the grateful emperor, who gave him the privilege of occupying a separate seat in the court. All other honors connected with his presence in the court were the same as those given to Hsiao Ho.

Both his two younger brothers, Pu-i and Meng, 蒙, and his son, Yin, were ennobled marquises. Yin became governor of Honan at the age of sixteen. Later Pu-i's son and Yin's son were also ennobled.

But Liang Chi's excessive grasping of power and his despotic and tyrannical behavior were too much for the emperor. With the assistance of five eunuchs the emperor

Liang who were holding government posts were dismissed. On the surface it was because of modesty and deference, but actually it was to honor the Sun family. The relatives [of the Sun family], who by taking falsely the name [of the Liang family][341] held such positions as attendant within the palace, minister, colonel,[342] administrator of a commandery, and superior official in a prefecture,[343] numbered more than ten persons. All were covetous and cruel. Each of them sent out his private guests to make a list of the wealthy men in the prefecture under his control and charged them with some crime, shut them up in prison, and had them flogged to force them to offer money for redemption. Those who offered a small amount of their wealth even met with death or exile.

There was a man in Fu-feng whose name was Shih-sun Fen. He was wealthy but stingy. [Liang] Chi thereupon made him a gift of four horses and asked for a loan of fifty millions. Fen gave him thirty millions. Chi was enraged and then reported to [the authorities] of the commandery and prefecture that Fen's mother was his slave [in charge of] storage and that she had stolen ten bushels of white pearls and a thousand catties of purple gold and had run away. Fen and his brothers were then arrested and tortured. They died in prison. All of his property, which was appraised at one hundred seventy millions, was confiscated.

Of the things that were exacted [by the central government] from the four directions and that were sent in as tribute or offerings at regular times, the best were first presented to Chi's house. Those that were given to the emperor were only of the second grade. Officials and people who

---

ordered a eunuch to surround Chi's residence with a thousand soldiers; Liang was deprived of the seal of the grand general and demoted to the rank of marquis of a capital district. Liang Chi and his wife committed suicide the same day. Liang Yin, who was still holding the post of governor of Honan, was executed together with all the members of the Liang and Sun families. Liang Chi's property, which was confiscated and sold by the government, was worth more than three billion cash. This fund made it possible for the government to reduce the empire's tax by half (*HHS* 34:1a ff.; cf. 7:14a, 10B:6a–b and 9b–10b).

[340] Sun Shou 孫壽 was the wife of Liang Chi. She was ennobled as baronet of Hsiang-ch'eng with an annual income from her rents of fifty million cash.

[341] That is, Liang Chi's family name. Chi was then the grand general and directed practically all the political affairs of the empire.

[342] The colonels were the commanders of the five *hsiao* or five divisions, the garrison cavalry, the elite cavalry, the infantry (*pu-ping* 步兵), the *Ch'ang shui* (a place name, literally "long river," used by the Hu "barbarians"), and the "shooters at sounds" (*she-sheng* 射聲), all of whom served as imperial guards (*HHC* 27:7b–8a).

[343] The term *chang-li* 長吏 may refer to all officials above the rank of 600 piculs (*HS* 5:7a) or to senior officials of a prefecture from the rank of 400 piculs down to 200 piculs (*HS* 19A:16a).

came carrying gifts to ask for offices or to request pardons when found guilty were in sight of each other on the road.

Chi also sent guests to go beyond the border to communicate with foreign countries and to search extensively for rare objects. When they were traveling on their way they recruited prostitutes and drivers. And the messengers, relying on [Chi's] power, were also arrogant and cruel. They married and seized the wives and daughters of other people and beat the officers and runners. They were hated wherever they were.

Chi then built a mansion on a large scale, and Shou also constructed houses opposite it across the street. . . . Moreover, he established a tremendous park to which he shipped soil to build hills. . . . He also considerably extended forests and parks and imposed prohibitions like those of the imperial family. They stretched to Hung-nung in the west, adjoined Ying-yang in the east, reached Lu-yang in the south, and extended to the Ho and the Ch'i [rivers] in the north.[344] They included mountains and swamps and were girdled by hilly wildernesses. The circumference of the enclosure amounted to almost a thousand *li*. He also established a rabbit park south of the Ho and west of the [imperial] city that extended for several tens of *li*. He mobilized the laborers and convicts of the prefectures under his control to build storied belvederes.

The completion of the work took several years. He sent out urgent orders to wherever there were [rabbits] to exact live rabbits, and marked their hair in order to identify them. The punishment of anyone who hurt [the rabbits] was up to the death penalty. Once there was a foreign merchant from the Western Regions who did not know the prohibitions and by mistake killed a rabbit. Accusations were made by one against the other [of the merchants]. Those who were given the death sentence numbered more than ten persons. . . .

All the officials who were promoted or summoned had to call at Chi's gate to present a written document thanking him for his benevolence before they dared to go to the office of the master of writing. Wu Shu, a native of Hsia-p'i, was appointed prefect of Yüan and paid a farewell visit to Chi before leaving for his post. Chi's guests were spreading all over the territory of the prefecture. He asked the favor of Shu's protection for them. Shu replied, ". . . Since I have been in attendance at this seat I have not heard you mention a single virtuous

---

[344] The city of Hung-nung was located thirty *li* southwest of modern Ling-pao county in western Honan. Ying-yang was located north of the modern city in northern Honan below the Yellow River. Lu-yang was located south of the modern city of Lu-shan in central Honan. The Ch'i River was in the extreme northern part of Honan.

man, and most of those you have recommended to me are improper men. I really dare not heed this." Chi remained silent and displeased. When he arrived at the prefecture, Shu then executed several tens of Chi's guests who were injuring the people. Therefore [Chi] hated him deeply. Later Shu was appointed inspector of Ching division. On the point of leaving he called on Chi to bid him farewell. Chi prepared wine for him, using this to poison him. When Shu left, he died in his carriage.

Hou Meng, the grand administrator of Liao-tung, did not visit Chi when he was appointed for the first time. Taking the pretext of some other matter, [Chi] had him sentenced to be cut in two at the waist.

At that time the palace gentleman, Yüan Chu of Ju-nan, who was nineteen years old, seeing that Chi was so cruel and unrestrained, could not overcome his anger. He then went to the capital to present a memorial [to accuse Chi]. . . . Chi heard of this and sent men to arrest Chu secretly. Chu then changed his name, later pretended to be ill, and had a false report of his death circulated. A dummy was made of reeds tied together, and a coffin was bought and the funeral performed. Chi investigated the matter and found out that it was a deception. He searched for him secretly and beat him to death. . . .

At this time there were Ho Chieh and Hu Wu of T'ai-yüan. . . . They were friends of Chu. Formerly Chieh and others together signed and presented a memorial to the offices of the three highest ministers, recommending the notable scholars of the empire, and they had not visited Chi. Chi resented this because of the previous matter and also suspected that they were associates of Chu. He commanded the officials of the capital to issue urgent orders to arrest those who had presented the memorial and have them killed. Consequently Wu's family was executed and more than sixty people lost their lives. Chieh at first escaped. Knowing that it was impossible to avoid [capture], he then carried a coffin to Chi's home and presented a document there. When the document was taken in, he took poison and died.[345] Therefore his family was spared. . . .

In the family of Chi there were seven marquises,[346] three em-

---

[345] In A.D. 159 (*HHS* 7:14a).

[346] According to Hu San-hsing, the seven marquises of the Liang family were: (1) Liang Chi's grandfather Yung 雍, marquis of Ch'eng-shih, (2) Liang Chi, marquis of Hsiang-i, (3) Chi's younger brother, Pu-i, marquis of Ying-yang, (4) another brother Meng, marquis of Hsi-p'ing, (5) Pu-i's son Ma 馬, marquis of Ying-yin, (6) Chi's son Yin, marquis of Hsiang-i, (7) and Yin's son Tao 桃, marquis of Ch'eng-fu (*TCTC* 54:5a).

presses,[347] six honorable ladies,[348] two grand generals,[349] seven *fu-jen*,[350] and daughters, altogether seven, who had fiefs and the title of baronet bestowed on them,[351] and three who were married to princesses.[352] The rest who held the positions of minister, general, governor,[353] and colonel numbered fifty-seven persons.

Actually there were five more marquises in the family. Liang T'ung, Chi's great-great-grandfather, was ennobled as marquis of Ch'eng-i and later as marquis of Kao-shan. Both T'ung's brother, Hsün 巡, and his paternal cousin, T'eng 騰, were also ennobled as marquises within the passes. Furthermore, Liang Yung's two brothers, T'ang 棠 and Ti 翟, were marquises of Lo-p'ing and Shan-fu respectively. And Liang Sung, Chi's great-grandfather, was made a marquis posthumously (*HHS* 34:2a, 10b–11a).

[347] The three who became empresses were: (1) Liang Sung's daughter, who was the mother of Emperor Ho and who was posthumously honored with the title of empress, (2) Liang Shang's daughter, the empress of Emperor Shun, who was the empress dowager and personally attended the court after the emperor's death, and (3) the empress of Emperor Huan, the younger sister of the empress dowager (*HHS* 34:8a, 10a, and 11b; 10B:4b ff. and 9b ff.).

[348] The honorable ladies were the imperial concubines who ranked just below the empress (*HHS* 10A:3b). Only three can be identified: Liang Sung's two daughters and Liang Shang's sister (*HHS* 34:8a, 11b).

[349] Liang Chi and his father, Shang.

[350] According to Ju Shun, the wife of a marquis was called Wife (*HS* 4:11b: Yen). This term is part of an older system recorded in the *Li-chi* (*LCCS* 5:7a).

[351] Baronet or *feng-chün* 封君, the enfeoffed lords or ladies, refers to those whose noble rank was inferior to the marquises and who received income from their fiefs (*shih-i* 食邑 or *t'ang-mu i*). Ku Yen-wu holds that *kuan-nei* marquises were called *feng-chün* (*JCLCS* 22:5b). His statement is supported by a case in which an official who was ennobled *kuan-nei* marquis was granted a fief of eight hundred households and was given the title Pao-ch'eng *chün* (*HS* 81:17a). However, in another instance, Lou Ching first received the title *feng-ch'un chün* and later was ennobled a *kuan-nei* marquis and granted a fief of two thousand households (*HS* 43:12a–b).

In the Early Han the title *chün* was granted to both sexes (see *HHHY* 34:356–57, 361). A woman who possessed such a title was usually the mother of an emperor's mother or a princess (*HHHY* 34:356). In the Later Han such a title was not only given to the mother of an empress dowager or an empress, but also to a wet nurse of an emperor. It was rather exceptional for an empress's brother's wife and other female relatives (as in the case of Liang Chi) to be honored with the title of baronet. A woman possessing the title of baronet was entitled to the privilege of having an annual income from the households granted to her (*HS* 97A:11b and 23a, 97B:26b–27a, 98:15a, 99A:21b; *HHS* 10B:11a, 61:7b). Liang Chi's wife received an annual income of fifty million cash (*HHS* 34:16a).

[352] Liang Sung, who married the Princess Wu-yin, the daughter of Emperor Kuang-wu, is the only known case (*HHS* 10B:24b, 34:6a).

[353] According to Hu San-hsing, "minister" refers to the Nine Ministers; "general" to the general of the gentlemen of the palace; and "governor" to the governor of Honan (*TCTC* 54:5a). The last post was successively held by the Liang family for more than thirty years. It was first held by Liang Chi, then by his brother Pu-i, and lastly by Chi's son Yin (*HHS* 34:15a–b, 22b).

[Liang Chi] was in power for more than twenty years.[354] He flourished and prospered to the utmost. Awe of him spread within and without [the palace]. All the officials looked with sidelong glances, and none of them dared to disobey his orders. The Son of Heaven maintained his self-respect[355] and was unable personally to participate [in government affairs]. [*HHS* 34:17b–23a]

64. A Powerful Consort Family Wiped Out by Eunuchs

_{A.D.}
147–159   In the earlier years of the reign of Emperor Huan, [Shan] Ch'ao, [Hsü] Huang, and [Chü] Yüan were regular palace attendants, and [Tso] Kuan and [T'ang] Heng were clerks of the lesser attendant of the Yellow Gate. Previously the two younger sisters of Liang Chi had been made the empresses of the two emperors Shun and Huan, and Chi had succeeded his father, Shang, as grand general. [The family] had been a powerful consort family for two generations.[356] Its power shook the empire.

A.D. 159   After he had executed the Grand Commandant Li Ku,[357] Tu Ch'iao,[358] and others, Chi became more arrogant and overbearing than ever. The empress, relying upon his influence, was envious and unrestrained, and many people were injured by her. All persons, superiors and inferiors, held their tongues, and none of them mentioned it. The emperor, who had been oppressed and afraid for a long time, always felt disquieted. He did not dare to plot against [Chi] lest word would leak out.

---

[354] Hu San-hsing suggests that this counts only the years Liang Chi was holding the post of grand general (A.D. 141–159); actually the time was nineteen years (*TCTC* 54:7a). In fact, he had earlier held many other important posts, including governor of Honan, a post assigned to him in 136 (*HHS* 34:15a).

[355] Referring to Emperor Shun's government without exertion, Confucius remarks that all Shun had to do was "to maintain his dignity (self-respect) and [sit] facing the south" (*LYCS* 15:1b). Here the same phrase is used, but whereas Emperor Shun did not have to do anything, Emperor Huan was not permitted to participate in government affairs.

[356] See III, 63, n. 339.

[357] For Li Ku, see II, 80.

[358] Tu Ch'iao, who had held the posts of grand administrator, attendant within the palace, minister of agriculture, and grand herald, became grand commandant in 147, a post from which he was dismissed three months later because of an earthquake. When Liu Wen and Liu Wei plotted to make the king of Ch'ing-ho emperor, Liang Chi, who was on bad terms with Tu Ch'iao, then took this opportunity to accuse him falsely of associating with the rebellious party, a case in which Li Ku was also involved (cf. II, 80). He was arrested and died in prison in 147 (*HHS* 63:22a–24a; see also 7:4a–b).

In the second year of Yen-hsi the empress died. When the emperor went to the privy, he called only [T'ang] Heng and asked who among the intimate attendants were not on good terms with the outside household.[359] Heng replied, "Shan Ch'ao and Tso Kuan formerly went to visit the governor of Honan, [Liang] Pu-i. They were slightly informal in their politeness and respect. Pu-i arrested their brothers and sent them to jail in Lo-yang. The two went to his residence to apologize and then [their brothers] were released. Hsü Huang and Chü Yüan are often privately angry at the indulgence and arrogance of the outside household, but their mouths do not dare to mention it." Thereupon the emperor called [Shan] Ch'ao and [Tso] Kuan to enter the room and said to them, "General Liang and his brother grasp power firmly in the imperial court and oppress and use force on the outside and the inside.[360] [Officials] from ministers on down follow their hints and will. Now We want to execute them. What do you, the regular attendants, think?" Ch'ao and the others replied, "Surely they are the evil rebels of the empire and should have been executed long since. Yet we, Your subjects, are weak and inferior and do not know what is the sage mind [of Your Majesty]." The emperor said, "If it is so, you, the regular attendants, plan it secretly." They replied, "It is not difficult to plan against them, but we fear that Your Majesty might be hesitant in your heart." The emperor said, "The evil ministers are oppressing the empire; they should suffer their punishment. How could there be any doubt?" Thereupon he also summoned [Hsü] Huang, [Chü] Yüan, and others, altogether five persons, and then made the decision. The emperor bit the arm of [Shan] Ch'ao until it bled, and took the oath.[361] Thereupon an edict was issued to arrest [Liang] Chi and his kinsmen, relatives, and associates and have them all executed.

---

[359] The outside household 外舍, according to Li, refers to the consort family.

[360] "Outside and inside" probably refers to the palace and the government offices respectively.

[361] Blood was usually used in making an oath. According to the *Huai-nan-tzu*, to cut the arm in taking an oath was the custom among the people of Yüeh, whereas the people of China proper were accustomed to smearing animal blood on their mouths (*HNT* 11:7b). This is not the only mention in Chinese history of the human arm being bitten or cut in taking an oath. The *Tso-chuan* tells of a girl who cut the arm of a duke in making him take an oath to seal his promise to make her his wife (*TCCS* 10:12b). In another case a son bit his own arm in making an oath before his mother that he would not return if he failed to become a high official (*SC* 65:5a). Judging from the statement in the *Huai-nan-tzu,* together with a comparison of various cases documented in history, it is obvious that it was more common to use animal blood and may be considered as typical in China. Probably when a human arm was bitten it was either because animal blood was not available, as in the case of the son who bid farewell to his mother outside the city wall; or for the sake of secrecy when two lovers

[Tso] Kuan and [T'ang] Heng were promoted to the post of regular palace attendants. [Shan] Ch'ao was ennobled as marquis of Hsin-feng with [a fief of] twenty thousand households; [Hsü] Huang, as marquis of Wu-yüan; [Chü] Yüan, as marquis of Tung-wu-yang, each with fifteen thousand households, and each was granted fifteen million cash. [Tso] Kuan was ennobled as marquis of Shang-ts'ai and [T'ang] Heng as marquis of Ju-yang, each with thirteen thousand households and each was granted thirteen million cash. The five persons were ennobled on the same day; therefore they were commonly called the "five marquises." Besides, the lesser attendants of the Yellow Gate, Liu P'u, Chao Chung, and others, altogether eight persons, were ennobled as *hsiang* marquises. From then on the power was in the hands of the eunuchs and the disorder in the court increased daily.

When [Shan] Ch'ao became ill, the emperor sent an emissary to appoint him general of chariots and cavalry[362] at his residence. In the following year he died. . . .

[The four remaining marquises] all competed in building residences. The storied buildings were magnificent and elegant, and [the construction] extremely skillful. Gold, silver, felt, and feather decorations were used for dogs and horses. They took many beautiful girls of the good people as concubines, whose precious ornaments were all elegant and extravagant, imitating the standards of the palace ladies. Their servants and attendants rode in ox carriages and were followed by rows of horsemen. They also brought up their remote relatives or asked [to make a boy] of a different surname their heir, or bought a Dark-green Head[363] and made him their son—all this in order to hand down their

---

were entering into a secret betrothal, as in the case of the duke; or when a group was secretly plotting a rebellion or a political conspiracy, as in the passage above. On more formal occasions, such as the forming of a political or military alliance, animal blood was used.

[362] This was the first time a eunuch was appointed general of chariots and cavalry during his lifetime. Previously Sun Ch'eng had been posthumously honored with such a title; see III, 59, n. 328. However, it was merely an honor and Shan Ch'ao, because he was sick, did not have the opportunity to perform the duties of the post. That this prominent post was given to a eunuch either posthumously or while he was ill and that he was not expected actually to take charge of the office is seen more clearly in the case of Ts'ao Chieh, another powerful eunuch. He was appointed general of chariots and cavalry and again appointed regular palace attendant (*HHS* 78:20b). The only exception is the case of Chao Chung 趙忠, who was appointed to this position and actually held the post for more than one hundred days. However, this happened many years later (186) and was rather exceptional (*HHS* 8:18a–b, 78:34a; III, 69, n. 423).

[363] Adopting a person with a different surname is certainly not in accord with the traditional practice, which only permitted a person to adopt a child from his own lineage. On eunuchs buying and adopting Dark-green Heads, see II, 53, n. 160.

marquisates and pass on their noble rank. The elder and younger brothers and relatives all became chief executives of divisions or commanderies. They sought for[364] [the properties of] the people and did not act differently from robbers.

[Shan] Ch'ao's younger brother, An, was grand administrator of Ho-tung, and his younger brother's son, K'uang, was grand administrator of Chi-yin. [Hsü] Huang's younger brother, Sheng, was grand administrator of Ho-nei, [Tso] Kuan's younger brother, Min, was grand administrator of Ch'en-liu. [Chü] Yüan's elder brother, Kung, was the chancellor of Pei. All of them encroached upon and injured others in the places where they stayed. [Hsü] Huang's elder brother's son, Hsüan, who was the prefect of Hsia-p'ei, was most cruel and tyrannical. Previously he had asked to have the daughter of Li Kao of Hsia-p'ei, the former grand administrator of Ju-nan, and was unable to get her. Upon his arrival at [Hsia-p'ei] prefecture, he then led his officials and runners to Kao's home, carried his daughter back, and shot her to death for fun. He buried her in the office [grounds]. At this time Hsia-p'ei prefecture was under the jurisdiction of Tung-hai, and Huang Fu of Ju-nan was the chancellor of Tung-hai. Someone accused Hsüan. Thereupon Fu arrested the family members of Hsüan and investigated them young and old. His subordinates all firmly remonstrated and urged him [to stop the investigation]. Fu said, "Hsü Hsüan is the evil of the empire. If I kill him today and if I am punished by death tomorrow, it will be sufficient to close my eyes."[365] Thereupon he investigated the crimes of Hsüan, executed him in the marketplace, and exposed his corpse to show it to the people. All in the commandery were shaking and trembling. Huang then stated his grievance before the emperor. The emperor was extremely angry. Fu was sentenced to have his head shaved and to wear an iron collar and sent to do hard labor under [the direction of] the colonel of the right.[366]

The kinsmen and guests of the five marquises were tyrannical all over the empire. Being unable to bear their command, the people

[364] Wang Nien-sun explains *ku chiao* 辜榷 (also written 辜較) as meaning 總括財利, "to collect wealth together" (*HSPC* 66:15b; cf. *HHS* 78, *chiao pu* 2b); 榷 also has the meaning of monopoly.

[365] That is, to die without regret.

[366] The convicts and laborers belonging to the office of the grand court architect were divided into two groups and were under the supervision of the colonel of the left, *tso-hsiao* 左校, and the colonel of the right, *yu-hsiao* 右校, respectively. The grand court architect was in charge of the construction of the imperial temples, palaces, tombs, various kinds of construction works, and the planting of trees along the highways (*HHC* 27:6a–b).

A.D. 164 arose and became bandits. In the seventh year [of Yen-hsi, T'ang] Heng died and he was also [posthumously] granted [the title of] general of chariots and cavalry, following the precedent set by [Shan] Ch'ao. When [Hsü] Huang died, cash and hemp cloth were given [by the emperor] for funeral expenses and a graveyard was also granted. In the following year the colonel-director of retainers Han Yen memorialized and charged [Tso] Kuan with his crimes and evil doings, and also [charged] his elder brother, the grand keeper of equipages and *hsiang* marquis of Nan, Ch'eng, with asking favors from the division and commandery governments, accumulating [money], and engaging in illicit activities, and [charged] his guests with being unrestrained and offending officials and people. Both Kuan and Ch'eng committed suicide. Yen also memorialized about the corruption of [Chü] Yüan's elder brother, the chancellor of Pei, Kung. [Kung] was summoned to the commandant of justice- [Chü] Yüan went to the jail, apologized, and returned to the emperor the seal and seal ribbon of the marquis of Tung-wu. An edict was issued to demote him to the [rank of] *tu-hsiang* marquis. [*HHS* 78:14b–17b]

65. POWERFUL EUNUCHS

Hou Lan, a native of Fang-tung in Shan-yang, was a regular palace attendant during the early years of Emperor Huan. He advanced [to this post] because of his flattery and treachery. Relying upon his power, he was greedy and unrestrained. The bribes received by him were counted by the millions.

A.D. 162 During the Yen-hsi period, because of military campaigns for successive years, the state treasury was exhausted. Then the government borrowed from the salaries of the officials and from the taxes due to the kings and marquises.[367] [Hou] Lan also offered five thousand rolls of *chien* silk.[368] He was granted the rank of marquis within the passes; and under the pretext that he had achieved merit because of his participation in the plan to exterminate Liang Chi, he was promoted to the rank of *hsiang* marquis of Kao.[369]

[367] In the fifth year of Yen-hsi, A.D. 162 (*HHS* 7:19a).

[368] According to Hsü Shen, *chien* 縑 is a kind of *tseng* 繒 woven with double silk threads (*SWCTC* 13A:21). Liu Hsi says that the silk threads of *chien* are double the number used in the *chuan* 絹. He also notes that *chien* silk is impervious to water (*SMSC* 4:19a).

[369] The real instigators of the plot against Liang Chi were five other eunuchs, who were made prefectural marquises; see III, 64. Hou Lan 侯覽 had not actually taken part in this plan and therefore was ennobled with the rank of district *(hsiang)* marquis.

Tuan Kuei, a lesser attendant at the Yellow Gate, had his home in the Chi-yin commandery. Both he and Lan established landed property that was situated close to the territory of Chi-pei kingdom. Their servants and guests encroached upon the people and robbed travelers.

T'eng Yen, the chancellor of Chi-pei kingdom, arrested all of them, killed several tens of persons, and exposed the corpses on the road. Lan and Kuei were infuriated and carried the matter to the emperor. Yen, found guilty of killing many innocent people, was summoned to the commandant of justice and dismissed. . . . Because of this Lan and others became even more unrestrained.

Lan's elder brother, Shen,[370] was the Inspector of I division. He always made false charges of rebellion against those among the people who were rich, exterminated them, and confiscated their property, which altogether amounted to hundreds of thousands of cash. The Grand Commandant Yang Ping[371] presented a memorial to the em- A.D. 163–165 peror [against Shen]. Shen was sent [to the capital] in a cage cart[372] but committed suicide on the way. The governor of Ching-chao, Yüan Feng, investigated Shen's more than three hundred carriages at the inn. All were full of gold, silver, brocade, silk, and precious curios; their numbers were countless.

Lan, because of this case, was dismissed, but soon afterwards he was reinstated in his previous office.

In the second year of Chien-ning [Hou Lan's] mother died. He re- A.D. 169 turned home and constructed a burial ground and a tomb on a large scale. Chang Chien, a [commandery] investigator of transgressions, charged Lan with being greedy and extravagant, having no regard for the property of others, and having in all asked permission to seize other people's residences, numbering three hundred and eighty-one sites, and land amounting to one hundred and eighteen *ch'ing*. [He also charged that Lan] had built sixteen residences, all of which were high and storied and had ponds and parks, and that the halls and towers facing one another were decorated with exquisite designs and red varnish and the like, and that the structures were very deep and imitated the standard of the imperial palace. [The charge said] that he had also

---

[370] According to *HHS* 54:16b, Shen 謇 was Lan's younger brother.

[371] Yang Ping held the post of grand commandant from 163 until his death in 165 (*HHS* 7:19a, 21a).

[372] The cage cart was a vehicle originally used to transport animals, but it was used throughout the Han to transfer political prisoners. See Lo Jung-pang's forthcoming work on transportation and communication in the Han.

constructed a tomb for himself with a stone outer coffin, double *ch'üeh*,[373] and a high *wu*[374] of a hundred feet in height, and that he had demolished the houses of others, and dug open their graves, that he had captured good people, married and seized their wives and children, and that he [had committed] many other crimes. He requested the death sentence for him.

But Lan watched and intercepted the memorial; it was not presented to the emperor. Chien then demolished Lan's tomb and houses, confiscated his property, and reported his guilt. He also memorialized that when Lan's mother was alive she associated with guests and intervened in [the political affairs of] the commanderies and kingdoms. Again [this memorial] was not presented to the throne. Thereupon Lan falsely accused Chien[375] of being associated with the Partisans,[376] and

---

[373] The *ch'üeh* 闕 were two stone monuments placed before the tomb of a noble or an official. On these were engraved his name and the official positions and titles he had held (Li Fu-sun, *Han Wei Liu-ch'ao mu-ming tsuan-li*, in *Huai-lu ts'ung-shu* [Hsing-su-ts'ao t'ang ts'ang-pan, 1887], 3:1a ff., hereafter cited as *HWLCMM*).

[374] According to Li, the *wu* was a circular hall below the corridor.

[375] According to the "Biographies of the Partisans," however, Chang Chien and twenty-three other persons of the same district were accused by Chu Ping 朱並, who wanted to please Hou Lan (*HHS* 67:6b–7a, 29a). It is possible that Chu made the the accusation with the knowledge and support of Hou Lan.

[376] The Partisan movement was a political intrigue that occurred during the reigns of Emperors Huan and Ling when the eunuchs held the reins of power and when the conflict between them and their opponents, a number of officials led by Tou Wu, Ch'en Fan, and Li Ying, and the students of the Imperial Academy, whose leaders were Kuo Lin-tsung 郭林宗 and Chia Wei-chieh 賈偉節, was at its peak. In 166, Li Ying, who was holding the post of colonel-director of retainers, was accused by Lao Hsiu 牢修 of associating with the students of the Imperial Academy, of forming cliques, and slandering the imperial court. This greatly angered Emperor Huan, who ordered the arrest of the Partisans all over the empire. Li Ying, Ch'en Shih, and others, altogether more than two hundred persons, were listed as Partisans and imprisoned in 167. At the request of Tou Wu and Ho Hsü 霍諝 they were released the following year, but all were proscribed from official appointment for life. The names of all the Partisans were listed in the government records.

In 169, when Chang Chien charged the eunuch Hou Lan and his mother with their illegal activities, Chang and twenty-three others were then accused of being Partisans. An edict was issued by Emperor Ling to arrest Chang and the others. All those who were involved in the trial of 166 were again accused by some officials under the direction of the eunuchs. (According to *HHS* 8:42 and 78:19a–b, it was Hou Lan who promoted the accusation and caused the death of the Partisans. However, *HHS* 67:7a–b states that it was another eunuch, Ts'ao Chieh, who hinted to the officials to accuse Li and the others.) Thereupon Li Ying, Tu Mi, and others, numbering more than one hundred persons, were put in prison, where they died. Their wives and sons were moved to the frontier. The family members, students, and previous subordinates of the Partisans were dismissed and prohibited from official appointment. Altogether six to seven hundred persons were involved in the accusation.

[he also accused] the former privy treasurer of the Ch'ang-lo Palace,[377] Li Ying,[378] the grand keeper of equipages, Tu Mi,[379] and others, who were all exterminated.[380] . . .

In the first year of Hsi-p'ing the authorities presented a memorial A.D. 172 that Lan was grasping for power, and that he was arrogant and extravagant. An order was issued to take back his seal and seal cord. He committed suicide. [*HHS* 78:18a–19b]

The prohibition against the Partisans came to an end in 184 with the uprising of the Yellow Turban Rebellion. Lü Ch'iang, one of the regular palace attendants who did not cooperate with Ts'ao Chieh and Wang Fu, warned the emperor that the Partisans had been treated unfairly and that this might lead them to cooperate with the rebel forces. The emperor was convinced; a pardon was granted to all the Partisans, and their family members who had been moved were allowed to return to their native places. See *HHS* 7:23b–24a, 8:4a, 8b, and 14b–15a, 67:4a–8a, 14b–15a, 16a–b, and 29a–b, 78:18b–19b.

[377] The post of privy treasurer of the Ch'ang-lo Palace was held by a eunuch in charge of the affairs of the Ch'ang-lo Palace, which was occupied by the mother of an emperor. The duties corresponded to those of the minister of the empress, who was in charge of the empress's palace. See *HHS* 10A:7b, 10B:8b; *HHC* 27:3b–4a; *HKI* A:26a. The fact that an ordinary official was at this time appointed to such a post was apparently connected with the policy of Tou Wu and Ch'en Fan, who were planning to wipe out the powerful eunuchs (see *HHS* 67:16a). However, this was not the only case in which a noneunuch held this post (see *HHS* 10A:7b).

[378] Li Ying, who had been grand administrator of various commanderies and in other high-ranking posts, was an important figure among the Partisans. In 166 when he was holding the post of colonel-director of retainers, he was accused by Lao Hsiu, whose teacher had been killed by Li, of associating with the students of the Imperial Academy, of forming cliques, and of slandering the imperial court. In 167 (*HHS* 7:23b) he and more than two hundred persons were imprisoned, but were released the following year. In 168 Li Ying was made privy treasurer of Ch'ang-lo Palace. He was dismissed when Tou Wu and Ch'en Fan were killed by the eunuchs (see III, 66 and 68, n. 416). In 169 when Chang Chien and others were accused of being Partisans, Li Ying was again accused and imprisoned. Li Ying died during the trial (*HHS* 67:10a–16b).

[379] Tu Mi had been grand administrator in several commanderies and chancellor of Pei-hai. During this time many family members of the powerful eunuchs held posts as prefects in the various commanderies. Tu was very strict with them and arrested those who were guilty of unlawful acts. He was later promoted to governor of Honan and then to grand keeper of equipages. He was involved in the Partisan movement and was accordingly dismissed. He was honored when his name was included among the *pa-chün* 八俊, the Eight Eminent Ones, that is, leaders of the Partisan group. When Ch'en Fan became grand tutor, Tu was reappointed grand keeper of equipages. When in 169 the Partisans were again being arrested and investigated, he committed suicide before he was seized (*HHS* 67:6a–b, 17a–18a).

[380] Chang Chien was able to escape and fled to a place outside the border, where he remained until 184 when the Partisans were pardoned (*HHS* 67:29a–b).

66. War Between Eunuchs and Consort Family and the Partisans

Tou Wu, whose style was Yu-p'ing, was a native of P'ing-ling in Fu-feng and was a great-great-grandson of Marquis Tai of An-feng, [Tou] Jung. His father, Feng, was the grand administrator of Ting-hsiang. . . .

A.D. 165

In the eighth year of Yen-hsi his eldest daughter was selected to enter the palace. Emperor Huan made her an honorable lady and appointed Wu a gentleman of the palace. In the winter the honorable lady was set up as empress and Wu was promoted to the post of colonel of the elite cavalry and enfeoffed as marquis of Huai-li [with a fief of] five thousand households. In the following year in the winter he was appointed colonel of the guards of the city gates. While he held office he frequently named to office scholars of reputation. He purified himself and hated evil. Courtesies and presents were not brought to him. . . .

At this time there were many faults in the government of the state, and eunuchs were specially favored. Li Ying, Tu Mi, and others were involved in the matter of the Partisans[381] and were arrested and investigated. In the first year of Yung-k'ang [Tou] Wu presented a memorial

A.D. 167

admonishing [the emperor].[382] . . . When his memorial had been presented, he thereupon pretended illness, and returned to the emperor the seals and seal cords of the colonel of the guards of the city gates and of the marquis of Huai-li. The emperor did not accept [his resignation] and issued an edict pardoning Li Ying, Tu Mi, and the others. Those prisoners in the various prisons of the Huang-men Pei-shih,[383] Jo-lu,[384] and Tu-nei[385] whose crimes were light were all freed.

[381] For the Partisans, see III, 65, n. 376.

[382] He requested the release of the Partisans and the punishment of the eunuchs.

[383] Meng Kang identifies Huang-men Pei-shih jail 獄黃門北寺 with Jo-lu jail 獄若盧 (*HS* 82:4b–5a). Since both are mentioned in our passage, this explanation does not seem acceptable (cf. *HLCI* 6:14b). Some passages in the *Hou-Han-shu* mention Huang-men Pei-shih jail (*HHS* 67:14b and 24a, 81:33a), while others mention Pei-shih jail (*HHS* 69:6a, 7a). In one case, Shan Ping 山冰, who was newly appointed prefect of the Yellow Gate *(huang-men ling)*, 黃門令, was ordered by Tou Wu to put the eunuch Cheng Li 鄭颯 in the Pei-shih jail (*HHS* 69:6a). In another case the rebellious eunuchs appointed Wang Fu the prefect of the Yellow Gate and he then went to the Pei-shih jail to arrest Shan Ping and to release Cheng Li (*HHS* 69:7a). It is clear from these two cases that Huang-men Pei-shih or Pei-shih jail was a jail belonging to the Yellow Gate and under the jurisdiction of the prefect of the Yellow Gate. Hu San-hsing remarks that this jail was set up by the eunuchs after they had come into power (*TCTC* 55:20a).

[384] The Jo-lu was an office under the privy treasurer. According to the *Han-chiu-i*, the chief of the Jo-lu jail was in charge of storing weapons and investigating generals, chancellors, and other high officials (cf. *HS* 19A:8b and note; *HHS* 4:17a: Li; *HCI* 6:10b–11a).

[385] The *tu-nei* 都內 was an office under the minister of agriculture (*HS* 19A:8a). According to Li, the office was in charge of storing.

In the winter the emperor died without an heir. [Tou] Wu summoned the attendant imperial secretary Liu Shu of Ho-chieh [kingdom], consulted with him, and inquired about which of the king's sons who were marquises in this kingdom were the most worthy. Shu praised the *t'ing* marquis of Chieh-tu, [Liu] Hung. Wu entered [the palace] and spoke to the empress dowager, who thereupon summoned [Liu Hung] and enthroned him. This was emperor Ling. Wu was appointed grand general, regularly living in the palace.

After [the emperor] had ascended the throne, the merit for making the decision [to put him on the throne] was considered and [Tou] Wu was again ennobled as marquis of Wen-hsi. His son, Chi, [was ennobled as] marquis of Wei-yang and appointed attendant within the palace; his elder brother's son, Shao, [was ennobled as] marquis of Hu and promoted to the post of colonel of the infantry, and Shao's younger brother, Ching, [was ennobled as] marquis of Hsi-hsiang and made attendant within the palace and supervisor of the cavalry of the left of the Forest of Feathers Guards.

When Wu was assisting in the administration of court affairs, he frequently had the intention of executing and destroying the eunuchs. The Grand Tutor Ch'en Fan[386] had also had such a plan for a long time. Once when they were meeting in the hall of the court, Fan privately said to Wu, "The Regular Palace Attendants Ts'ao Chieh,[387] Wang Fu,[388] and others since the time of the late emperor have controlled and manipulated the authority of the state, defiling and disturbing the empire everywhere. The people cry out, putting the blame on them. If you now do not execute Chieh and the others, later on it will certainly be difficult to handle them." Wu wholly agreed, and Fan, greatly pleased, pressed his hand on his [sitting] mat and arose.

[Tou] Wu thereupon inducted men of the same mind, Yin Hsün[389] to the position of prefect of the masters of writing, Liu Yü to that of

---

[386] Ch'en Fan was one of the officials who led the group of Partisans.

[387] For Ts'ao Chieh, see III, 68.

[388] For Wang Fu, see III, 68.

[389] Yin Hsün, who belonged to a family that had held official positions for generations, reached the position of prefect of the masters of writing after several promotions. Later because of his participation in the plot against Liang Chi, he was ennobled as a *tu-hsiang* marquis and made grand administrator of Ju-nan. He was dismissed from the second post because he presented a memorial to defend Fan P'ang 范滂 and Yüan Chung 袁忠, who were involved in the case of the Partisans. He was later promoted to the posts of grand court architect and grand minister of agriculture. He was imprisoned in 168 because of his connection with Tou Wu, and committed suicide (*HHS* 67:27a–b).

attendant within the palace, and Feng Shu to that of colonel of the garrison cavalry. He also summoned the empire's scholars who had been dismissed and excluded: the former [Colonel-]Director of Retainers Li Ying, the Superintendent of the Imperial Clan Liu Meng,[390] the Grand Keeper of Equipages Tu Mi, the Grand Administrator of Lu-chiang Chu Yü,[391] and others and installed them in the court. He asked the former Grand Administrator of Yüeh-sui Hsün I[392] to be attendant officer and palace gentleman, and appointed Ch'en Shih[393] of Ying-ch'uan to be his subordinate. Together they made plans and decisions. Thereupon the extraordinary men of the empire knew of their intention, and there was not one of them who did not stretch out his neck and stand on his toes, thinking eagerly of contributing his intelligence and strength.

A.D. 168   It happened that in the fifth month [of the first year of Chien-ning] there was an eclipse of the sun. [Ch'en] Fan again advised [Tou] Wu, saying, ". . . Now you may take advantage of the eclipse of the sun and dismiss the eunuchs in order to stop [the evil effects] of the [astrological] changes in heaven. Moreover, the Lady Chao[394] and the female masters of writing[395] day and night confuse the empress dowager's mind. It is necessary to dismiss them. I hope that you, Grand General, will consider this matter."

[Tou] Wu then spoke to the empress dowager, saying, "It has been a rule that the regular attendants of the Yellow Gate only serve in the interior of the palace, taking charge of the doors and controlling the property and wealth of the offices within the palace.[396] Now they are allowed to participate in government affairs and are given powerful positions and authority. Their junior relatives are distributed [in the various localities] and are engaged particularly in covetousness and tyranny. The empire is crying out just because of them. Therefore it

---

[390] For Liu Meng, see III, 68.

[391] Chu Yü 朱寓 who later held the post of colonel-director of retainers was imprisoned with other Partisans in 169 and died in prison (*HHS* 67:7b, 9a). He is not to be confused with the eunuch Chu Yü 朱瑀 mentioned below.

[392] Hsün I, the later chancellor of P'ei, was very strict to the relatives and guests of the eunuchs. Many of them who had committed crimes were put to death. He was arrested with other Partisans in 169 and died in prison (*HHS* 62:2b, 67:7a–b).

[393] For Ch'en Shih, see II, 79, n. 232.

[394] Chao Jao 趙嬈, the wet nurse of Emperor Ling.

[395] The "female masters of writing" is understood by Li to mean the eunuchs.

[396] According to Hu San-hsing, 近署財物 refers to the property in the palace treasury (*chung-tsang-fu* 中藏府), imperial manufactory (*shang-fang* 尚方), and various offices within the palace. All of them were under the supervision of the privy treasurer of the emperor (*HHSCC* 69:3b).

would be proper to execute and dismiss them in order to purify the court."

The empress dowager replied, "According to tradition from the beginning of the Han, this has been [the situation] for generations. Only those who have committed crimes should be executed. Why should they all be dismissed?"

At this time the Regular Attendant Within the Palace Kuan Pa, who had considerable talent, had arbitrary authority within the palace. [Tou] Wu first reported [on the need] to execute [Kuan] Pa together with the Regular Attendant Within the Palace Su K'ang and others. They were examined and died.[397] Several times Wu again urged [the empress dowager] to execute Ts'ao Chieh and others. The empress dowager hesitated and could not bear it. Hence the matter was delayed and no action was taken. . . .

[In the eighth month Tou Wu and Ch'en Fan] decided that they should act. Thereupon Chu Yü was made colonel-director of retainers, Liu Yu, the governor of Honan, and Yü Ch'i, the prefect of Lo-yang. Wu then submitted a memorial requesting the dismissal of the Prefect of the Yellow Gate Wei Piao and his replacement by Shan Ping, a close associate [of Wu] who was lesser attendant of the Yellow Gate.[398] He had Ping memorialize [the names of] those who had for a long time been knavish and most degenerate. The Master of Writing of Ch'ang-lo [Palace] Cheng Li was sent to Pei-shih jail.[399]

[Ch'en] Fan said to [Tou] Wu, "This man Ts'ao ought to be immediately arrested and killed. Why should he be investigated again?" Wu did not follow [his advice]. He ordered [Shan] Ping, together with Yin Hsün and the Attendant Imperial Secretary Chu Chin to examine [Cheng] Li. His confession involved Ts'ao Chieh and Wang Fu. Hsün and Ping immediately submitted a memorial [requesting] the arrest of [Ts'ao] Chieh and the others, and sent Liu Yü to take the memorial to the palace.

At that time [Tou] Wu had gone out to spend the night, returning to his official residence. Those who had charge of writing in the palace first informed the clerk of the Five Offices of Ch'ang-lo [Palace, the

---

[397] Here we follow the interpretation of Hui Tung, who says that 竟死 means 考竟而死, "died after being examined" (*HHSCC* 69:3b).

[398] The lesser attendant of the Yellow Gate was a 600-picul post held by a eunuch whose duty it was to attend the emperor, accept the memorials presented by the masters of writing, and maintain communications between the outside court and the emperor when the emperor was in the inner palace (*HHC* 26:5b–6a).

[399] That is, the Huang-men Pei-shih jail. See note 383 of this document.

eunuch,] Chu Yü 朱瑀. Yü stealthily opened the memorial of Wu. He cursed and said, "The palace officials who have acted unrestrainedly may be executed, but what crime have we committed, and must we all be executed with our families?" Thereupon he called out loudly, saying, "Ch'en Fan and Tou Wu have memorialized to inform the empress dowager to dethrone the emperor; they are rebellious." Then in the night he summoned those with whom he had been friendly and who were strong: the clerks of the attendant office of the Ch'ang-lo [Palace], Kung P'u, Chang Liang, and others, seventeen men [in all]. They smeared their mouths with blood and together took an oath to execute [Tou] Wu and the others.

When Ts'ao Chieh heard of it, he was startled, arose, and informed the emperor, saying, "[The matters] are very urgent outside. I beg [Your Majesty] to go out and to go to the Te-yang Front Hall." He ordered the emperor to draw his sword and to jump [as he went], and had his wet nurse Chao Jao and others act as escort around him. He took the credentials[400] and blocked the doors of the forbidden palace. He summoned the subordinates at the office of the masters of writing, and, intimidating them with a naked blade, made them write an imperial edict appointing Wang Fu prefect of the Yellow Gate. Carrying a verge, [Wang Fu] went to the prison of Pei-shih to arrest Yin Hsün and Shan Ping. Ping was suspicious and did not accept the imperial edict; Fu struck and killed him. Thereupon he killed Hsün, released Cheng Li, and returned. Together they used force upon the empress dowager and seized from her the imperial seal and documents.[401] They ordered the palace internuncio to guard the Southern Palace, close the doors, and block the elevated double roadways[402] [to the Northern Palace], and asked Cheng Li and others, carrying verges, together with the attendant imperial secretaries and internuncios to go to arrest [Tou] Wu and the others.

[400] According to the *Hsü-Han-chih, Han-kuan-i,* and *Han-kuan chieh-ku,* all those who served and lived in the palace had their names on a list, which was kept at the palace gate. Before they were permitted to enter, their names had to be checked, and a wooden credential on which was branded the name of the palace in which the individual served was examined. For those who did not live in the palace and were summoned to the palace for a special mission a *ch'i* 棨 credential was used as a passport (*HHCCC* 25:9a; *HHS* 69:6b, note; *HKCK*, p. 3b; *HCI* A:13b).

[401] Liu Pin suggests that since the empress dowager was not in possession of the seal and documents, the term 璽書 is a mistake for 璽綬, "the seal and the seal cord." The "Annals" reads "seal and cord" instead of seal and documents (*HHSCC* 69:4b, note; *HHS* 6:3a).

[402] On the elevated double roadways, see the forthcoming work on Han transportation and communications by Lo Jung-pang.

[Tou] Wu did not accept the imperial edict, and galloped into the camp of the foot soldiers. With [Tou] Shao they together shot and killed the messengers. They summoned and assembled the soldiers of the five divisions of the Northern Army,[403] [numbering] several thousand men, and encamped in a capital canton.[404] He issued a command to the soldiers,[405] saying, "The regular attendants of the Yellow Gate have rebelled. Those who make their best efforts will be enfeoffed as marquises with heavy rewards."

An imperial edict[406] made the Privy Treasurer Chou Ching the acting general of chariots and cavalry; he was to carry a verge and, together with the General of the Palace Gentlemen Who Guard Against the Hsiung-nu Chang Huan,[407] lead the troops of the five camps[408] to punish [Tou] Wu. When the night scale of the water clock was at its end, Wang Fu led the Rapid as Tigers[409] and the Forest of Feathers[410]

---

[403] On the five divisions, see III, 63, n. 342.

[404] The capital cantons were cantons located in or near administrative centers; for example, commandery and prefectural capital cities had capital cantons. In Lo-yang there were capital cantons on the major avenues and at each of the twelve city gates (see the forthcoming work on Han transportation and communications by Lo Jung-pang). The context here does not tell us which capital canton is referred to, but the next paragraph indicates that this capital canton was probably located just outside the palace.

[405] We follow *HHSCC* 69:4b in reading 土 instead of the 七 of our text.

[406] Obviously the edict was issued by the eunuchs in the name of the emperor. In the biography of Chang Huan 張奐, it is said that the eunuchs issued a feigned edict to order Chang and Chou Ching 周靖 to arrest Tou Wu (*HHS* 65:14b).

[407] Chang Huan was not on the side of the eunuchs. At this time he had just returned to the capital from the frontier and was not aware of recent political developments. He thought the edict to arrest Tou Wu was actually issued by the emperor. After Tou was executed, Chang was promoted to the posts of privy treasurer and grand minister of agriculture and ennobled as marquis because of his merit. He was ashamed of being deceived by the eunuchs and refused to accept the ennoblement. Instead he asserted the innocence of Tou Wu and Ch'en Fan and suggested to the emperor that they should be reburied with honor, that their family members should be allowed to return, and that their associates who had been prohibited from officialdom should be pardoned. Because of this he was disliked by the eunuchs and their group and was falsely accused of being associated with the Partisans; he was dismissed and prohibited from entering officialdom. He returned home, engaged in teaching and writing, and died in retirement at the age of seventy-eight in 181 (*HHS* 65:11a–18a).

[408] The five camps refers to the five divisions of the Northern Army previously mentioned. See III, 63, n. 342.

[409] The Rapid as Tigers Guards were imperial guards under the command of the general of the palace gentlemen as rapid as tigers (*HS* 19A:6b; *HHC* 25:5a–b; *HKI* A:11a–b).

[410] The Forest of Feathers (*yü-lin* 羽林) Guards were imperial horsemen whose duty it was to escort the emperor while hunting or on tour and to guard the palace. They

[Guards], the stable grooms and the sword- and lance-[bearing] soldiers [under the command of the] captains of the capital,[411] altogether more than a thousand men, and encamped at the Vermilion Bird Gate where they joined with [Chang] Huan and the others. At dawn they all encamped below the [palace] and formed a battle array opposite Wu. As Fu's troops gradually increased, his soldiers called out loudly to Wu's army, saying, "Tou Wu is a rebel. You are all imperial soldiers and should guard the palaces. Why do you follow a rebel? For those who first surrender there will be rewards."

[The troops of] the five camps were accustomed to fearing and obeying the eunuchs. Consequently Wu's army gradually went over to Fu. Between dawn and the time for eating[412] almost all of [Wu's] troops surrendered. Wu and Shao fled. When the armies pursued and surrounded them, they both committed suicide. Their heads were suspended on stakes in a capital canton in Lo-yang. Their kinsmen, guests, and relatives by marriage were all arrested and executed, and Liu Yü and Feng Shu were exterminated with their clans. Wu's family members were exiled to Jih-nan. The empress dowager was moved to the Cloud Tower. At this time evil fellows gained their goal and the scholars and officials all lost their spirit. [*HHS* 69:1a–b, 3b–8a]

67. OFFICIAL ACCUSED

A.D.
165–172   [Ch'en Ch'iu] was transferred to the post of grand administrator of the Nan-yang commandery. Because he investigated and exposed [the faults of] powerful and influential [individuals], he was slandered by the influential families. He was summoned by the commandant of justice to account for his crimes.[413] [*HHS* 56:20a]

were under the command of the general of the palace gentlemen of the Forest of Feathers Guards (*HS* 19A:6a; *HHC* 25:5b–6a; *HKI* A:11b–12a).

[411] There were two captains of the capital, *tu-hou* 都侯, one of the left and one of the right. Each had a number of soldiers bearing swords and lances under his command. The captain of the capital of the right had 22 officers and 416 soldiers; the captain of the capital of the left had 28 officers and 383 soldiers. Their duty was to guard the palace and to arrest those who were wanted by the emperor (*HHC* 2:9a; *Han-kuan*, in *PCKTS*, pp. 3a–b, hereafter cited as *HK*).

[412] Hui Tung explains that "the time for eating" 食時 means mid-morning (*HHSCC* 69:5a).

[413] Previously Ch'en Ch'iu 陳球 had been grand administrator of the Ling-ling commandery in 165 (*HHS* 7:21a) and then of the Wei commandery. He was pardoned after his summons to the commandant of justice. He later held the posts of commandant of justice, minister of works, grand commandant, and finally privy treasurer of Yang-lo Palace. In 179, together with Liu Ho, the minister of the masses,

68. Government Under the Control of Eunuchs

Ts'ao Chieh, whose style was Han-feng, was from Hsin-yeh of Nan-yang. Originally he was a native of the Wei commandery, and [members of his family] had been 2,000-picul officials for generations.[414] In the early years of the reign of Emperor Shun he was promoted from horseman of Hsi-yuan to lesser attendant of the Yellow Gate. In Emperor Huan's time he was promoted to the posts of regular palace attendant and chief commandant custodian of the imperial equipages.

In the first year of Chien-ning he held the verge and led the palace   A.D. 168
attendants within the Yellow Gate and the Rapid as Tigers and Forest of Feathers [Guards], altogether one thousand men, to the north to welcome Emperor Ling. He accompanied the emperor and rode into the palace. When the emperor ascended the throne, because of [his merit in] settling the scheme,[415] he was ennobled as *hsiang* marquis of Ch'ang-an with a fief of six hundred households. At this time Empress Dowager Tou personally attended the court. The empress [dowager's] father, the Grand General Tou Wu, and the Grand Tutor Ch'en Fan plotted to kill the eunuchs. Chieh and a clerk of the Five Offices of Ch'ang-lo [Palace], Chu Yü, the clerks of the Office of Attendants, Kung P'u and Chang Liang, the Palace Attendant Within the Yellow Gate Wang Tsun, the Internuncio of Ch'ang-lo [Palace] T'eng Shih, and others, altogether seventeen persons, together issued a false edict to make the supervisor of meals of Ch'ang-lo [Palace], Wang Fu, the prefect of the Yellow Gate, and ordered him to lead soldiers to kill [Tou] Wu and [Ch'en] Fan.[416] The matter is already completely

---

he planned to kill the powerful eunuchs, Ts'ao Chieh and others. Their plot was discovered by the eunuchs, and Ch'en Ch'iu, Liu Ho, Liu Na 劉納, and Yang Ch'iu were accused; Ch'en died in prison at the age of 62 (*HHS* 56:19b–24a).

[414] This is the only information concerning the family background of those in the "Biography of the Eunuchs." Although the background of other eunuchs is unknown, we have reason to believe that it was exceptional for a member of a prominent family, as claimed in this case, to become a eunuch. It seems that most of the eunuchs came from not wealthy and nonofficial families.

[415] Actually Emperor Ling, who had been a *t'ing* marquis, was put on the throne by Empress Dowager Tou and her father, Tou Wu (*HHS* 8:1a, 10B:12a, 69:3b–4a). Ts'ao Chieh did not participate in the consultation. He was probably ennobled because he was the leading eunuch who was sent to welcome the newly appointed emperor. Another official, Liu Shu, who recommended the *t'ing* marquis to Tou Wu, was given a tally and sent to welcome the emperor (*HHS* 8:1a–b, 69:3b–4a).

[416] See III, 66, for the story of Tou Wu's death by suicide when his troops surrendered to the eunuchs without fighting. Ch'en Fan, who was more than seventy years old at this time, upon hearing of the death of Tou Wu drew his knife and entered

[recorded] in the biographies of [Ch'en] Fan and [Tou] Wu. [Ts'ao] Chieh was promoted to the post of commandant of the guards of Ch'ang-lo [Palace], ennobled as marquis of Yü-yang, and his fief was increased to three thousand households; [Wang] Fu was promoted to the post of regular palace attendant and held the post of prefect of the Yellow Gate as before; [Chu] Yü was ennobled as *tu-hsiang* marquis with a fief of fifteen hundred households; [Kung] P'u, [Chang] Liang, and others, altogether five persosn, each were ennobled with [a fief of] three hundred households. All the other eleven persons were ennobled as marquises within the passes with an annual rent of two thousand piculs. . . .

A.D. 169   In the second year [of Chien-ning] Chieh was very ill, and an edict was issued to appoint him general of chariots and cavalry. Shortly thereafter he recovered from his illness and returned to the emperor the seal and seal ribbon. He was dismissed and again became regular palace attendant with the title of "specially advanced" and a salary of fully 2,000 piculs. Later he was transferred to the post of minister of the empress.

A.D. 172   In the first year of Hsi-p'ing Empress Dowager Tou died. Someone wrote on the Ch'iao-ch'üeh Gate [of the palace] saying that the empire was in great disorder, that Ts'ao Chieh and Wang Fu had secretly murdered the empress dowager,[417] that the Regular Attendant Hou Lan had killed many Partisans, that all the ministers drew their salary like corpses,[418] and none of them spoke loyally. Thereupon an edict was issued to order the Colonel-Director of Retainers Liu Meng to search for and arrest the [writer]. In ten days there was one meeting.[419] Con-

---

the palace gate, together with a group of his subordinates and students, stating that the eunuchs were the rebels, not Tou Wu. Ch'en was arrested by Wang Fu and sent to prison, where he was murdered (*HHS* 66:14a–15a).

[417] Empress Dowager Tou was moved from the palace to the Cloud Terrace of the Southern Palace after her father had failed to wipe out the eunuchs and had died. According to her biography, Ts'ao Chieh and Wang Fu had slandered and caused the death of another eunuch, Tung Meng 董萌, who had attempted to improve the relationship between the emperor and the empress dowager. Apparently the two were trying to keep her away from the emperor and from returning to her palace. She died at the Cloud Terrace after she had been confined there for almost four years (*HHS* 8:3a and 5b, 10B:12b–13a).

[418] *Shih lu* 尸禄 means to take the salary without performing the expected duties, just as a corpse occupying an official post.

[419] The meaning of 十日一會 is not quite clear here. In view of what follows, it probably means that Liu Meng did not wish to prosecute the case and, in spite of the gravity of the charge, he called only one meeting in ten days to discuss it. It is possible that the sentence should be understood as part of the orders to the colonel-director of retainers, Liu Meng, that is, he was ordered to meet the higher authority concerned and to report the progress of the investigation and arrests every ten days.

sidering that the libelous writing was a frank statement, Meng was unwilling to make hasty arrests. After more than a month the name of the principal [criminal] had not been obtained. Meng was punished by demotion to the post of grandee remonstrant, and the palace assistant imperial secretary, Tuan Ying, replaced Meng. Then [men] were sent in all directions to search for and arrest [suspects]. And among the students who had traveled around and studied at the Imperial Academy, those who were jailed numbered more than one thousand persons. [Ts'ao] Chieh and the others hated [Liu] Meng even more than before and ordered [Tuan] Ying to charge him with some other matter. Meng was punished for an offense and was sent to the colonel of the left.[420] Many of the court officials spoke on his account. Thereupon he was exempted from punishment and was again summoned by the [prefect of] the Major's Gate.[421]

[Ts'ao] Chieh and Wang Fu and others then falsely accused Emperor Huan's younger brother, the king of Po-hai, Hui, of planning to rebel, and he was executed. There were twelve men who were ennobled because of this merit. Fu was ennobled as marquis of K'uan-chün. Chieh had his fief increased by forty-six hundred households; altogether with those previously held there were seventy-six hundred households. Their fathers, elder brothers, and junior relatives, all became ministers, colonels of various [posts], inspectors, grand administrators, and prefects; they were distributed all over the empire.

[Ts'ao] Chieh's younger brother, P'o-shih, was the colonel of the elite cavalry. The wife of a squadron leader in the elite cavalry camp was beautiful. P'o-shih asked to have her. The squadron leader did not dare to disobey. His wife was determined not to consent to go; therefore she committed suicide. P'o-shih's licentiousness, tyranny, and perversion were mostly of this kind.

In the second year of Kuang-ho the Colonel-Director of Retainers A.D. 179 Yang Ch'iu memorialized to execute Wang Fu and his sons, the privy treasurer of Ch'ang-lo [Palace], Meng,[422] and the chancellor of P'ei, Chi. All of them died in prison. [*HHS* 78:19b–21b]

---

[420] That is, to be sent to the colonel of the left to serve as a convict laborer (see III, 64, n. 366).

[421] The Major's Gate refers to the prefect of the official carriages of the Major's Gate who was in charge of the Major's Gate of the palace. It was his duty to receive memorials presented by the people and to take charge of affairs in connection with the summoning of officials and others whom the emperor wanted to see (*HKI* A:13b).

[422] According to *HHS* 77:14a–b, Wang Meng 王萌 was the privy treasurer of Yung-lo Palace.

69. EUNUCH'S INFLUENCE IN OFFICIAL APPOINTMENT

A.D.
168–189

During the time of Emperor Ling both [Chang] Jang and [Chao] Chung[423] were promoted to the post of regular palace attendant and ennobled as marquises. They and Ts'ao Chieh and Wang Fu closely associated together. After the death of Chieh, Chung was the acting minister of the empress. Jang had a superintendent slave who was in charge of domestic affairs. He made wide connections and practiced bribery. His majesty was awe inspiring.

Meng T'o, a native of Fu-feng, who had plenty of wealth, made friends with the slaves [of Chang Jang], exhausted [his wealth] in offering presents to them, and none of them was neglected. All the slaves were grateful to him. They asked T'o, saying, "What do you, sir, want? Our power will be able to procure it for you." [T'o] said, "I hope that you will give me a salute." At that time the carriages of the guests who sought to visit [Chang] Jang were usually [numbered] from several hundreds to a thousand. When T'o went to visit Jang, he arrived late and was unable to proceed. Then the superintendent slave led the various Dark-green Heads to welcome and salute him on the road. They then all together led [T'o's] carriage into the gate. All the guests were startled. Considering that T'o was on good terms with Jang, they all strove to bribe him with precious articles. T'o presented a part of them to Jang. Jang was greatly pleased and then made T'o the inspector of Liang division.

At this time [Chang Jang and others], altogether twelve men, were all made regular palace attendants, ennobled as marquises, and were honored and favored [by the emperor]. Their fathers, elder brothers, and junior relatives were distributed all over the divisions and commanderies.[424] Wherever they were, they were covetous and cruel and injurious to the people. [*HHS* 78:30a–31a]

---

[423] Chang Jang and Chao Chung were the two powerful eunuchs who induced the emperor to exact money from officials and people. When a part of the palace was destroyed by fire, they suggested increasing the land tax all over the empire to make up the fund. Their proposal to ask those officials who had been newly appointed or promoted to another post to contribute a sum for the army and the repair of the palace was also adopted by the emperor. The emperor was so fond of money and so grateful to the two eunuchs that he considered them his parents. Chao Chung was appointed general of chariots and cavalry and held the post for more than one hundred days, when he was dismissed. For further details, see III, 71.

[424] That is, they were appointed as local officials in the various regions and commanderies.

70. Powerful Families Seize Land

[Yüan K'ang] was promoted to the post of grand administrator of *Ca.* A.D. 169
the T'ai-shan commandery. Most of the powerful families in the commandery acted unlawfully. When he arrived, K'ang inspired awe and
showed displeasure. He proclaimed strict orders. No one ventured to
violate them. The lands and houses that had previously been seized
were all immediately given back.[425] [*HHS* 67:33a]

71. The Massacre of the Eunuchs

Ho Chin, whose style was Sui-kao, was a man of Yüan of Nan-yang.
His younger sister by a different mother was selected to enter the imperial palace, became an honorable lady, and secured the favor of Emperor Ling, who appointed Chin gentleman of the palace. He was
promoted to the post of general of the palace gentlemen as rapid as
tigers and sent out as grand administrator of Ying-ch'uan.

In the second year[426] of Kuang-ho the honorable lady was established　A.D. 181
as empress. [The emperor] summoned Chin to enter [the court] and
appointed him palace attendant, grand court architect, and governor
of Honan. In the first year of Chung-p'ing the Yellow Turban Bandits,
Chang Chiao and others, rose up, and Chin was made the grand
general. . . .

At this time[427] [the emperor] set up eight colonels of the Western　A.D. 188
Park. The Lesser Attendant of the Yellow Gate Chien Shih[428] was made
colonel of the Upper Army, the General of the Palace Gentlemen as
Rapid as Tigers Yüan Shao[429] was made colonel of the Middle Army,

[425] Prior to this appointment, Yüan K'ang 苑康 held the post of prefect. In 169,
while he was the grand administrator, many of the relatives and guests of a powerful
eunuch, Hou Lan, who had been investigated by Chang Chien (see III, 65), fled to
the territory of the T'ai-shan commandery. Yüan K'ang arrested them. Because of
this, Hou Lan hated him and accused him falsely. He was dismissed and died in
retirement (*HHS* 67:33a–b).

[426] According to the "Annals of Emperor Ling" and the "Biography of Empress
Ho," the latter was made empress in the twelfth month of the third year (not the
second) of Kuang-ho, that is in 181 (*HHS* 8:12b, 10B:16a).

[427] In the fifth year of Chung-p'ing (*HHS* 8:20b).

[428] Chien Shih 蹇碩 was the only eunuch among the eight colonels. He was also the
first eunuch who was actually given military power during his lifetime. Previously
the title of general of chariots and cavalry was merely given to a eunuch posthumously
or during illness (see III, 64, n. 362).

[429] Yüan Shao came from a family whose members had held ministerial positions
for generations. In 189 he held the position of colonel-director of retainers and as-

the Chief Commandant of the Garrison Cavalry[430] Pao Hung was made colonel of the Lower Army, the Gentleman Consultant Ts'ao Ts'ao[431] was made colonel of the Controlling Army, Chao Yung was made colonel of the Assisting Army, and Ch'un-yü Ch'iung was made colonel of the Helping Army. There were also left and right colonels.[432] Since the emperor thought that Chien Shih was stout and strong and versed in military tactics, he particularly trusted him and made him marshal supervising [the officials from] the colonel-director of retainers on down. Even the grand general[433] was subordinate to him. . . .

Previously Empress Ho had given birth to Prince Pien and the Honorable Lady Wang had given birth to Prince Hsieh.[434] All the officials asked [Emperor Ling] to set up the heir apparent. The emperor considered that Pien was light and frivolous, without majestic deportment, and unsuitable to become the ruler of men. However, Empress [Ho] had [the emperor's] favor and [Ho] Chin also possessed important power. So for a long time [the emperor] did not make a decision.

A.D. 189   In the sixth year [of Chung-p'ing], when the emperor was seriously ill, he entrusted [Prince] Hsieh to Chien Shih. Shih had already received [the imperial] testamentory edict and, moreover, he had usually thought light of and envied Ho [Chin] and his younger brother.[435]

---

sisted Ho Chin in his campaign against the eunuchs. Yüan suggested summoning Tung Cho and his troops to the capital, but because of a disagreement with Tung he fled from the capital. In 190 Yüan assisted Han Fu and later usurped his position as shepherd of Chi division. After defeating Kung-sun Tsan, Yüan controlled four regional divisions and had thousands of men in his armies. He became the most powerful rival of Ts'ao Ts'ao, who defeated him in 200. Yüan died in 202 (*HHS* 74A).

[430] Liu Pin points out that there was no such title as chief commandant of the garrison cavalry in Han times and that instead it should be colonel of the garrison cavalry (*HHSCC* 69:6b).

[431] Ts'ao Ts'ao was the founder of the Wei dynasty. Although he did not become emperor, he was posthumously honored in 220 with the title of "Emperor Wu" when his son, Emperor Wen, ascended the throne (*SKC*, Wei, 2:15a). He also held the temple title T'ai-tsu 太祖, a conventional title for the first emperor of a dynasty. The author of the *San-kuo-chih* follows this nomenclature, calling his family the imperial house.

[432] According to the *Shan-yang-kung tsai-chi*, quoted by Li, Chao Yung 趙融 was the left colonel of the Assisting Army; Feng Fang was the right colonel of the Assisting Army. Hsia Mou 夏牟 was the left colonel, and Ch'un-yü Ch'iung 淳于瓊 was the right colonel (*HHS* 8:20b, 74A:2a).

[433] Ho Chin was holding the post of grand general.

[434] Liu Hsieh, the later Emperor Hsien, was put on the throne in 189 at the age of nine after the young emperor, Liu Pien, had been killed by Tung Cho. The title of Liu Hsieh's mother as given here is apparently a mistake for "beautiful lady"; other references to her, including a biographical sketch in *HHS* 10B consistently read "beautiful lady."

[435] Ho Miao, who held the post of general of chariots and cavalry.

When the emperor died, Shih was within [the palace]. He wanted first to execute [Ho] Chin and then enthrone Hsieh. When [Ho] Chin entered from without, Shih's major, P'an Yin, who was an old acquaintance of Chin, welcomed and eyed him [significantly]. Chin was startled, galloped away, and returned to his camp by a short way; he led his troops to encamp in the lodges of the hundred commanderies.[436] Thereupon he pronounced himself ill and did not go into [the palace]. [Chien] Shih's plot was not carried out. Prince Pien thereupon ascended the throne.[437]

Empress Dowager Ho attended court [as regent]. [Ho] Chin and the Grand Tutor Yüan Wei assisted her in the government and took charge of the affairs of the masters of writing.

[Ho] Chin had known for a long time that the empire was suffering from the eunuchs, and at the same time he was angry with Chien Shih for his plot against himself. Therefore, when he had seized the power of the court, he planned secretly to execute him. Yüan Shao had also had this plan for a long time; through the medium of an intimate guest of [Ho] Chin, Chang Chin, he urged [Ho Chin], saying, "The power of the regular attendants of the Yellow Gate has been great for a long time. Moreover, they have made connections with the empress dowager of the Ch'ang-lo [Palace][438] and are engaged in making illicit profits.[439] It would be proper for you, General, to select 'men of wisdom and virtue' [for office] in order to put the empire in order and to remove the injurious elements of the empire."

[Ho] Chin agreed with his words. Considering also that the Yüan family had for successive generations been favored [by the emperors]

---

[436] According to Hu San-hsing, the commanderies and the kingdoms in the empire numbered more than one hundred; all of them established lodges in the capital. They were called the lodges for the hundred commanderies (*po-chün-ti* 百郡邸) because all of them were grouped together as one (*TCTC* 59:5b).

[437] The seventeen-year-old prince was on the throne only five months; then he was dethroned by Tung Cho and made king of Hung-nung. Consequently, he had no temple title and was spoken of by historians as Shao-ti 少帝, the Young Emperor. He was murdered by Tung Cho in 190 (*HHS* 8:21b and 23a, 9:2b).

[438] This refers to Empress Dowager Tung, the wife of the *t'ing* marquis of Chieh-tu, Liu Chang 劉萇, and the mother of Emperor Ling. When her son ascended the throne, she was given the title of honorable lady of Shen-yüan and later was given the title of filial and benevolent empress. The name Ch'ang-lo must be an error, since she lived in the Yung-lo Palace (*HHS* 10B:13a–14a).

[439] Empress Dowager Tung was accused by Ho Chin and other top-ranking officials of sending the eunuchs, Hsia Yün 夏惲, Feng Hsü 封諝, and others to communicate with the various divisional and commandery governments to obtain precious things and bribes (*HHS* 10B:14a).

and that all were honorable,[440] and that all within the seas turned to them, and that [Yüan] Shao had long been good at caring for gentlemen so that he was able to secure powerful persons and employ them, and that [Shao's paternal] cousin, the General of the Palace Gentlemen as Rapid as Tigers [Yüan] Shu,[441] also esteemed courage and the activities of the redressers-of-wrongs, he therefore treated both of them generously. Thereupon he also widely summoned scholars of knowledge and plans: P'ang Chi, Ho Yung, Hsün Yu, and others; together they had the same aim.

Chien Shih was suspicious and [his mind] was not at rest. He sent a letter to the Regular Palace Attendant Chao Chung and others, saying, "The grand general and his younger brother are grasping the state's [power] and control the court. Now they have plotted with the Partisans of the empire to execute [the attendants] who were on the right and left[442] of the late emperor and to sweep away and annihilate us. Only because I, Shih, control the imperial guards, do they still hesitate. It is now proper to close [the doors of the] palace[443] and hasten to seize and execute them."

The Regular Palace Attendant Kuo Sheng[444] was a man from the same province as [Ho] Chin. Sheng had contributed to the Empress Dowager [Ho's] and Chin's nobility and their gaining of favor [from the emperor]. Hence Sheng was close to and trusted the Ho. Thereupon, together with Chao Chung and others, he decided not to follow [Chien] Shih's plot and to show the letter to Chin. Chin then ordered the prefect of the Yellow Gate to arrest Shih and execute him. Then he took over the command of [Chien Shih's] encamped troops.

[440] The *San-kuo-chih* says that since the time of Yüan An, Shao's great-great grandfather, four generations had held the posts of the Three Ducal Ministers (*SKC*, Wei, 6:14b). According to the *Hou-Han-shu*, Yüan An was the minister of works and minister of the masses; An's son Ch'ang was minister of works. Ch'ang's elder brother's son T'ang was minister of works, minister of the masses and grand commandant. One of T'ang's sons, Ch'eng (the father of Shao), was general of the palace gentlemen of the left; another son, Feng (father of Shu), was minister of works; and a third son, Wei 隗, was grand tutor (*HHS* 45:3b, 8a–9a; cf. Hua Chiao's *Han-shu*, quoted in *SKC*, Wei, 6:14b; Chao I-ch'ing, *San-kuo-chih chu-pu* [Pei-ching Ta-hsüeh reproduction of the Kuang-ya shu-chü ed., 1935], 6:12b).

[441] Yüan Shu was one of the warlords who arose at the end of the Later Han dynasty. In 190 he was made grand administrator of Nan-yang, where he rebelled against Tung Cho and began a campaign for the throne. He assumed the title of emperor in 197 and died in 198 (*HHS* 75:8a–14b).

[442] The close attendants refer to the eunuchs.

[443] Hu San-hsing explains 上閤 as the door of the palace (*TCTC* 59:6a).

[444] Kuo Sheng 郭勝 was one of the twelve eunuchs who were made marquises by Emperor Ling (*HHS* 78:30b–31a).

Yüan Shao again advised Chin, saying, ". . . Now the Deceased Emperor[445] is in the Front Hall. It would be proper for you, General, to receive an imperial edict to have you head the palace troops and it would not be proper for you lightly to go out of or into the palaces." Chin agreed heartily with him; he pronounced himself ill and did not enter [the palace] to join the mourning ceremonies and also did not accompany [the funeral] to the imperial mausoleum.[446]

Thereupon, with [Yüan] Shao he settled his arrangements and told the empress dowager about his plans. The empress dowager would not agree, saying, "That the eunuchs should have general control in the palace has been [the practice] from ancient times to the present and is the tradition of the House of Han. It cannot be done away with. Moreover, the late emperor has but recently left the empire. How could I, in brilliant [attire],[447] consider [government] business together with the scholars?"

[Ho] Chin could hardly oppose the idea of the empress dowager, but he also wished to execute those [eunuchs] who had been most unrestrained. [Yüan] Shao held that the eunuchs were intimate with the sovereign and took out and brought in the [imperial] orders. If now they were not all done away with, later there would certainly be a calamity.

However, the mother of the empress dowager, the baronet of Wuyang,[448] together with [Ho] Miao, had several times received gifts from the various eunuchs. Knowing that Chin wanted to execute the [eunuchs], they several times reported to the empress dowager and protected the eunuchs. They also said that the grand general would arbitrarily kill those on her right and left and would seize [the imperial] authority in order to weaken the dynasty. The empress dowager suspected him and considered that they were right.

Some of the eunuchs had been in the palace for several decades, had been ennobled as marquises, had been honorable and favored, and were firmly [established both] within and without [the court]. [Ho] Chin

---

[445] According to *Feng-su t'ung-i*, an emperor who had died recently and had not yet been given a posthumous title, that is, a temple title, was spoken of as *ta-hsing huang-ti* 大行皇帝 (Li: *HHS* 5:2b).

[446] The Wen Mausoleum of Emperor Ling (*HHS* 8:22a).

[447] Li quotes the *Shih-ching* and *Ch'u-tz'u* to explain that 楚楚 means a state of brilliancy. Hui Tung gives a different explanation; he holds that it means sorrow. Li's commentary is supported by Wang Hsien-ch'ien (*HHSCC* 69:8a), who suggests that because of the emperor's death, the empress dowager did not feel that she could appear in brilliant court attire.

[448] Her name was Hsing (*HHS* 10B:16b).

had newly taken an important post and had long respected and been afraid of them. Although outwardly he had gathered a great reputation, inwardly he could not decide. Hence the matter was not settled for a long time.

[Yüan] Shao and the others again made a plan for him to summon many brave generals from all directions, together with the various powerful and outstanding persons, and have them together lead troops toward the imperial capital in order to intimidate the empress dowager. [Ho] Chin agreed. . . . Thereupon he summoned from the west the General of the Van Tung Cho to encamp within the pass in Shang-lin Park. Moreover, he sent a subordinate from his office, Wang K'uang of T'ai-shan, to mobilize in the east the strong crossbowmen of his commandery. He also summoned the grand administrator of Tung, Ch'iao Mao, to encamp at Ch'ang-kao, and ordered the Martial and Fierce Chief Commandant Ting Yüan to burn Meng-chin. The fire shone into the city of [Lo-yang]. All had as their slogan the execution of the eunuchs.

The empress dowager still would not agree. [Ho] Miao said to [Ho] Chin, "At first, when we altogether came from Nan-yang, we were all poor and humble. By relying upon those within the palace,[449] we have become honorable and rich. State affairs are not easy matters. Water when upset cannot be collected again. You should ponder deeply about it and make peace with those in the inner palace."

[Ho] Chin's intentions were even more undecided than before; [Yüan] Shao, fearing that Chin would change his plan, intimidated him, saying, "The struggle has already begun and the issues have been revealed. If the matter is delayed, adverse changes will be brought about. Why do you, General, want to wait and not decide promptly?"

[Ho] Chin thereupon made [Yüan] Shao colonel-director of retainers, giving him a verge,[450] with the power to act arbitrarily in making

---

[449] "Those within the palace" refers to the eunuchs. According to the *Feng-su t'ung-i*, the Ho family had offered a bribe to those who were in charge of selecting the imperial ladies, and thus their daughter was included in the list; see II, 85, n. 267. Hu San-hsing comments that Empress Ho entered the palace by means of the eunuchs and because of this the Ho brothers were able to become honorable and rich (*TCTC* 59:9a). Moreover, Empress Ho was saved from being dismissed by the effort of some of the eunuchs; see note 456 of this document.

[450] In the early years of Early Han the colonel-director of retainers was authorized to have a verge, but from Emperor Yüan's time on this position no longer carried the privilege. Now under the particular circumstances, according to Hu San-hsing, a verge was given specially to the newly appointed colonel-director in order to increase his authority (*HHC* 27:9a–b; *TCTC* 59:9b).

attacks and decisions. The Attendant Official and Palace Gentleman Wang Yün became the governor of Honan. [Yüan] Shao ordered the military officials of Lo-yang who knew stratagems to investigate the eunuchs and urged Tung Cho and others to gallop by post horses, intending to advance troops to the P'ing-lo Hall.

The empress dowager thereupon became afraid and dismissed all the regular palace attendants and the lesser attendants of the Yellow Gate and sent them to return to their village homes. Only those who ordinarily had been close to [Ho] Chin were retained to guard the palace.

The various regular attendants and lesser attendants of the Yellow Gate all went to [Ho] Chin to beg pardon for their crimes and submitted themselves to his disposition. Chin said to them, "The whole empire is in an uproar just because it is concerned with you, sirs. Now Tung Cho is coming soon. Why, sirs, didn't you go to your fiefs earlier?" Yüan Shao urged Chin two or three times to execute them immediately. Chin did not consent. Shao also wrote letters to the regional divisions and commanderies, falsely announcing Chin's intention [to kill the eunuchs] and ordering them to arrest and investigate the relatives of the eunuchs.

When [Ho] Chin's plans leaked out, to a great extent because of the many elapsed days, the eunuchs were frightened and thought of bringing about a [radical] change. Chang Jang's[451] [adopted] son's wife was the younger sister of the empress dowager. Jang kowtowed to his daughter-in-law and said, "Your old servant has offended and must return to his private house, together with you, my daughter-in-law. Yet I have received grace from [the imperial family] for generations. Now that we must go far away from the palaces to which my heart is attached, I wish that I could enter and serve again for one time and be permitted for a short moment to look upon the faces of the empress dowager and His Majesty, after which I shall retire to my ditches to die without regret." The daughter-in-law spoke to the baronet of Wu-yang, who entered [the palace] and told the empress dowager. She then issued an edict that all the regular attendants might again enter to serve her.

In the eighth month [Ho] Chin entered the Ch'ang-lo [Palace] to speak to the empress dowager to beg that he might execute all the [eunuchs] from the regular attendants on down and select gentlemen of the three offices[452] to enter and have charge of the eunuchs'

---

451 For Chang Jang, see III, 69.

452 The gentlemen of the three hffices (*san-shu lang* 三署郎) refers to the gentlemen who served in the office of the five offices, the left office, and the right office

quarters. The eunuchs said to each other, "The grand general pronounced himself ill and did not attend the mourning ceremonies nor accompany the [imperial] funeral. Now he suddenly enters the palace. What has he in mind? Is an affair like that of Tou [Wu][453] occurring again?"

Chang Jang and others also sent people to listen in hiding and heard all their words. Then they led the Regular Attendants Tuan Kuei, Pi Lan, and others, several tens [in all], bearing weapons, and they furtively entered by side doors, and lay in ambush within the palace.[454] When [Ho] Chin came out, they thereupon falsely summoned Chin by an edict of the empress dowager to enter and sit at the entrance[455] of the palace. [Chang] Jang and others reprimanded Chin, saying, "It is not for our crime alone that the empire is in disorder. The Late Emperor was once so displeased with the empress dowager that she was almost completely ruined.[456] We wept and rescued her and each of us paid out thousands or tens of thousands of our family property as presents to pacify and please the emperor. We merely wanted our households to rely upon you, Minister, and now you intend to destroy us and our class. Is not this too much? You, Minister, say that within the palace we are filthy. But who are the loyal and pure ones among the Ministers?" Thereupon the Supervisor of the Imperial Manufactory Ch'ü Mu pulled out his sword and decapitated Chin in front of the Chia-te Hall.[457]

---

under the supervision of the general of the palace gentlemen of the five offices, general of the palace gentlemen of the left, and general of the palace gentlemen of the right. They were of four ranks: palace gentlemen, gentlemen consultants, attendant gentlemen, and gentlemen of the palace. Except for the gentlemen consultants, their duty was to serve as guards below the steps of the palace hall and also at the doors of the various palace halls (*HHS* 4:24b; *HHC* 25:4b–5a; *HKI* A:10b–11a, 12b).

[453] Tou Wu, the father of Empress Dowager Tou, had intended to wipe out the powerful eunuchs but was defeated and killed by them in 168; see III, 66.

[454] According to Ts'ai Yung, *sheng-chung* 省中 stands for the original *chin-chung* 禁中, meaning the palace. Because the given name of the father of Empress Yüan was Chin, this character was tabooed, and the character *sheng* 省 was used instead (Yen: *HS* 7:1b; *TYTT* A:3a–b; *SFHT* 6:5b).

[455] The Palace edition reads *ko* 閤 instead of *ta* 闥. According to Han Ying, *ta* is the place between the door and the screen (*MSCS* 5(1):7b). Yen understands it as a small door in the palace or a door screen (*HS* 41:5a). For the meaning of *ko*, see note 459 below.

[456] When an imperial concubine, the Beautiful Lady Wang, gave birth to Prince Hsieh, Empress Ho poisoned her. Emperor Ling was extremely angry and wanted to dismiss the empress. This was stopped by a group of eunuchs who begged pardon for her (*HHS* 10B:16b).

[457] The Chia-te Hall was in the Southern Palace (*HHS* 8:21b).

[Chang] Jang, [Tuan] Kuei, and the others made an imperial edict to appoint the former Grand Commandant Fan Ling colonel-director of retainers and the Privy Treasurer Hsü Hsiang governor of Honan. When the masters of writing received the order for the edict, they doubted it and said, "We beg that the grand general come out and discuss this with us." A palace attendant within the Yellow Gate threw the head of Chin at a master of writing and said, "Ho Chin plotted to rebel and has already been executed."

Wu K'uang and Chang Chang, who were generals of [Ho] Chin's units,[458] had always been close to and favored by him. They were outside [the palace]. When they heard that Chin had been killed, they

---

[458] The term "units," *pu-ch'ü*, was first used in connection with the army, both *pu* and *ch'ü* being units in the Han military organization; see Lo Jung-pang's forthcoming work on the Han military. At the end of the Later Han *pu-ch'ü* came to be a special term for private troops. In the latter part of the second century A.D. the area within the passes was torn by war and general disturbances, and great numbers of people emigrated to other places. When they returned several years later, they found themselves without means of support; and being enlisted by certain generals into their private forces, they became their *pu-ch'ü*.

Wei Chi pointed out in a letter to Hsün Yü that this made these generals very powerful and that they would be a threat to the government (see *SKC*, Wei, 21:11b–12a). Moreover, reasons of security and protection also called for joining the organization of *pu-ch'ü*. Evidence seems to show that only a large organized force was strong enough to protect itself from all possible attacks, both from troops and from bandits.

As a rule, at the death of a father his son took over this *pu-ch'ü* (see *HHS* 75:11a; *SKC*, Shu, 6:6b; *SKC*, Wu, 1:8a, 10:4a–b). In the case of the Li family, Li Ch'ien's troops were taken over by his son, Li Cheng 李整, and after Cheng's death by Li Ch'ien's brother's son, Li Tien (*SKC*, Wei, 18:1a).

The Li case seems to imply that Ch'ien's *pu-ch'ü* was made up of guests; but it was the family, and not the individual, that constituted the basic unit of the *pu-ch'ü* (cf. *SKC*, Wei, 3:3a). Thus women as well as men were included in it (see *SKC*, Wu, 1:13b, 10:4b). This is understandable. People were ready to become a person's *pu-ch'ü* because it was the only way to get their living and protection during the period of disorder and war. Their families were in the same situation and needed the same protection. And in those days war and banditry accelerated the rate of physical mobility to such an extent that to join the army, with one's family members, was the only practical means of protecting one's self and family. This was also true in Chin times (*CS* 100:13b).

Pu-ch'ü still appeared in Wei, Chin, and the Northern and Southern dynasties as private troops—the family remaining the basic unit of the organization. The members of the *pu-ch'ü* owned by a single individual might be as many as several thousand persons or even ten thousand families (*CS* 100:13b–14b; *Liang-shu* 28:12b, 39:9b; *Ch'en-shu* 13:7a). However, as time went on the status of *pu-ch'ü* gradually deteriorated, until they were little better than slaves. An edict issued in 577 by Emperor Wu of Northern Chou ordered that all those commoners who had been enslaved should be manumitted; if, however, their masters wanted to have them living with him, he could keep them as *pu-ch'ü* and *k'o-nü* 客女 (*Chou-shu*, Po-na ed., 6:18a). This indicates

wanted to lead their troops into the palace. But the side doors[459] were closed. Yüan Shu with [Wu] K'uang together chopped at and attacked them. The palace attendants within the Yellow Gate, holding weapons, guarded the side doors. When the sun was going down, [Yüan] Shu then set fire to the Gate of the Nine Dragons of the Southern Palace and the Eastern and Western Palaces, intending to compel [Chang] Jang and the others to come out.

[Chang] Jang and the others entered and told the empress dowager, saying, "The troops of the grand general have rebelled and are burning the palaces. They are attacking the entrance of the office of the masters of writing."[460] Thereupon they took the empress dowager, the Son of Heaven, the king of Ch'en-liu,[461] and forcing the official subordinates within the palace[462] [to come along], they fled by the elevated double

that by the end of the Northern and Southern dynasties the *pu-ch'ü* had a status more or less similar to that of slaves.

Pu-ch'ü definitely became semislaves in T'ang and Sung and were treated as such. Their status was somewhat superior to that of the ordinary private slaves. The latter were considered by law as property, while the former were not. A *pu-ch'ü* thus could not be sold (*TLSI* 2:14b, 17:1b, 18:5b; *SHT* 2:15b, 17:2a, 18:6a). The comparative status of *pu-ch'ü* and slaves is also seen in marital and criminal laws. A slave could marry only within his own group, whereas a *pu-ch'ü* could marry a commoner, a woman of his own group, or a female slave (*TLSI* 6:7b–8a, 14:6b; *SHT* 6:6b–7a, 14:6b). In criminal law, the punishment for a commoner who injured or killed a *pu-ch'ü* was heavier than the punishment for injuring or killing a slave, but less severe than if the victim was a commoner. On the other hand, the punishment for a *pu-ch'ü* who injured or killed a commoner was less severe than if the aggressor was a slave. Moreover, a *pu-ch'ü* who injured or killed a slave was punished in the same way as a commoner who injured or killed a *pu-ch'ü*, whereas the punishment for a slave who injured or killed a *pu-ch'ü* was the same as for a *pu-ch'ü* who was guilty of injuring or killing a commoner (*TLSI* 22:2b–3a; *SHT* 22:2b). The punishment for a master who killed his *pu-ch'ü* was also one degree heavier than for killing a slave. However, a master was exempted from punishment if he punished a faulty slave or *pu-ch'ü* and caused his death accidentally. However, *pu-ch'ü* and slaves were given the same punishment for assaulting their masters (*TLSI* 22:3b–5a; *SHT* 22:3b–4b).

The *pu-ch'ü* disappeared after Sung. Such a term is not found in the laws of Yüan, Ming, or Ch'ing.

For a more detailed discussion on *pu-ch'ü*, see Shen Chia-pen, *Hsing-chih fen k'ao*, in *Shen Chi-i hsien-sheng i-shu chia-pien* (1929), 15:29b–35a; Ho Shih-chi, "Pu-ch'ü k'ao," *Kuo-hsüeh lun-ts'ung*, I, No. 1 (1927), 125–49; Yang Chung-i, "Pu-ch'ü yen-ko lüeh-k'ao," *Shih-huo*, I, No. 3 (1935), 97–107; Niida Noboru, *Shina mibumpō shi* (Tokyo: Tōhō Bunka Gakuin, 1942), pp. 865–80.

[459] According to the *Shuo-wen*, a *ko* was a door at the side of a gate (*SWCTC* 12A: 15a). Yen comments that *ko* is a small door (*HS* 58:6b).

[460] The office of the masters of writing was located in the palace within the Shen-hsien Gate 神仙門 (*HHSCC* 69:10a).

[461] The king of Ch'en-liu was Prince Hsieh, the future Emperor Hsien, who was put on the throne by Tung Cho in 190 after the Young Emperor was dethroned.

[462] 省内官屬 refers to those officials who served in the palace.

roadways to the Northern Palace. The Master of Writing Lu Chih, holding a lance, [stood] below a window of the double roadways, looked up, and reprimanded Tuan Kuei. Tuan Kuei and the others became afraid and released the empress dowager. The empress dowager took refuge in the roadways and thus got free.

Yüan Shao with his uncle Wei[463] forged an imperial edict summoning Fan Ling and Hsü Hsiang and beheaded them. [Ho] Miao and [Yüan] Shao then led their troops and encamped below the Vermilion Bird Tower Gate. They arrested Chao Chung and the others and beheaded them.

Wu K'uang and others had always hated [Ho] Miao because he did not agree with [Ho] Chin, and they also suspected that he had plotted with the eunuchs. So they gave an order in the army, saying, "The one who murdered the grand general was the [general of] chariots and cavalry. Are you, soldiers and officers, able to take revenge?" [Ho] Chin had always been benevolent and gracious [to his army] and the soldiers all wept, saying, "We are willing to die for him." [Wu] K'uang then led his troops and with the younger brother of Tung Cho, the Chief Commandant Custodian of the Imperial Equipages, [Tung] Min, attacked and killed [Ho] Miao, exposing his corpse in the park.

[Yüan] Shao then closed the gates of the Northern Palace and commanded his troops to arrest the eunuchs regardless of whether they were young or old, and kill them all. As some men who had no beards died by mistake, others exposed their bodies and in this way were able to escape. Those who [died[464] numbered] more than two thousand.

[Yüan] Shao then advanced his troops to the palaces. Some climbed up the building at the Tuan Gate[465] in order to attack the palace. Chang Jang, Tuan Kuei, and the others were hard pressed; therefore they took the emperor with the king of Ch'en-liu, and several tens of persons and walked out the Ku Gate,[466] and ran to the Hsiao-p'ing Ford.

[463] Yüan Wei was the grand tutor and took charge of the affairs of the masters of writing with Ho Chin. He was killed with his kinsmen in 190 by Tung Cho, when Wei's nephew, Yüan Shao, raised troops to attack Tung (*HHS* 9:3a, 74A:4a).

[464] Basing himself on a similar passage in the *San-kuo-chih*, which states that more than two thousand eunuchs were killed (*SKC*, Wei, 6:16a), Hui Tung points out that the character *ssu* 死, "to die," has been omitted from the text. Otherwise, according to Liu Pin, the two sentences would become one sentence that would have an entirely different meaning and would be very illogical—"those who had no beard and escaped death by exposing their bodies numbered more than two thousand" (*HHSCC* 69: 10b).

[465] The Tuan Gate was the main south gate of the palace (*TCTC* 59:11a).

[466] The Ku Gate was the main north gate of Lo-yang.

The ministers all went out of the P'ing-lo Hall, but none of them was able to follow. Only the Master of Writing Lu Chih galloped by night to the [Yellow] River. Wang Yün sent the head of the central division of Honan, Min Kung, to follow after [Lu] Chih. When [Min] Kung arrived, he beheaded several persons with his sword. The rest all threw themselves into the river and died.[467] The next day the ministers and all the officials welcomed the Son of Heaven back to the palace. [Min] Kung was made a gentleman of the palace and enfeoffed as *tu-t'ing* marquis.

Tung Cho then dethroned the emperor.[468] He also oppressed and killed the empress dowager and killed the baronet of Wu-yang. The Ho family then vanished and the House of Han from this time on also was ruined and in disorder. [*HHS* 69:9b, 10b–18b]

---

[467] Chang Jang was among those who drowned themselves in the river (*HHS* 78:34a–b).

[468] Three days after the emperor's return to the palace (*HHS* 8:23a).

BIBLIOGRAPHY

The following abbreviations have been used in compiling the bibliography:

CHTTS	Pi Yüan 畢沅 (compiler). *Ching-hsün t'ang ts'ung-shu* 經訓堂叢書.
LSYC	*Li-shih yen-chiu* 歷史研究.
LSYY	*Li-shih yü-yen yen-chiu-so chi-k'an* 歷史語言研究所集刊.
PCKTS	*P'ing-chin kuan ts'ung-shu* 平津館叢書, 1885.
SPPY	*Ssu-pu pei-yao.*
SPTK	*Ssu-pu ts'ung-k'an.*
THHP	*Tsing-hua hsüeh-pao* 清華學報.
TSCC	*Ts'ung-shu chi-ch'eng* 叢書集成.
WYT	*Wu-ying tien chü-chen pan ts'ung-shu* 武英殿聚珍板叢書.
	Fukien: Pu-cheng shih-shu k'an-pen, 1895.

TRADITIONAL CHINESE WORKS

CCFL	Tung Chung-shu 董仲舒. *Ch'un-ch'iu fan-lu* 春秋繁露. *SPPY* ed.
CCHLCK	Ch'iang Ju-hsün 強汝詢. *Han chou chün hsien li chih k'ao* 漢州郡縣吏制考 in *Ch'iu-i-chai ch'üan-chi* 求益齋全集, 1898.
CCLK	Ch'eng Shu-te 程樹德. *Chiu-ch'ao lü-k'ao* 九朝律考. 2 vols. Shanghai: Commercial Press, 1927.
CCP	Shih Yu 史游. *Chi chiu p'ien* 急就篇 (顏師古注, 王應麟補注), *TSCC* ed.
CFL	Wang Fu 王符. *Chien-fu lun* 潛夫論. *SPTK* ed.
CHC	Hsü Chien *et al.* 徐堅等. *Ch'u hsüeh chi* 初學記. Ning-shou-t'ang ed., 1607.

[507]

CHHW Yen K'o-chün 嚴可均 (compiler). *Ch'üan Hou-Han wen* 全後漢文 in *Ch'üan shang-ku san-tai Ch'in Han san-kuo liu-ch'ao wen* 全上古三代秦漢三國六朝文. Huang-kang Wang-shih ed., 1894.

CHW Yen K'o-chün (compiler). *Ch'üan Han wen* 全漢文 in *Ch'üan shang-ku san-tai Ch'in Han san-kuo liu-ch'ao wen*. Huang-kang Wang-shih ed., 1894.

CHYTP Sun K'ai 孫楷. *Ch'in hui-yao* 秦會要; *ting-pu* 訂補 by Hsü Fu 徐復. Shanghai, 1955.

CICS *Chou-i chu-su* 周易注疏. *SPPY* ed.

CKT *Chan-kuo ts'e* 戰國策. *SPTK* ed.

CLCS *Chou-li chu-su* 周禮注疏. *SPPY* ed.

CLL(HL) *Ta Ch'ing lü-li hui-chi pien-lan* 大清律例彙輯便覽. Hupei: Hsien-chü, 1872.

CS Fang Ch'iao *et al.* 房喬等 *Chin-shu* 晉書. Po-na ed.

CSCY Wei Cheng *et al.* 魏徵. *Ch'ün-shu chih-yao* 羣書治要. *SPTK* ed.

CSTP Wang Ch'ang 王昶. *Chin-shih ts'ui-pien* 金石萃編. Ching-hsün t'ang ed. 經訓堂, 1805.

CT *Chuang-tzu* 莊子. *SPPY* ed.

CTSW Lu Te-ming 陸德明. *Ching-tien shih-wen* 經典釋文. *TSCC* ed.

CYTWC Ch'ien Ta-hsin 錢大昕. *Ch'ien-yen-t'ang wen-chi* 潛研堂文集 in *Ch'ien-yen-t'ang ch'üan-shu* 潛研堂全書. Ch'ang-sha: Hung-shih chia-shu ch'ung-k'an, 1884.

Ch'en Yao Ssu-lien 姚思廉. *Ch'en-shu* 陳書. Po-na ed.

Chou Ling-hu Te-fen 令狐德棻. *Chou-shu* 周書. Po-na ed.

EYCS *Erh-ya chu-su* 爾雅注疏. *SPPY* ed.

FSTI Ying Shao 應劭. *Feng-su t'ung-i* 風俗通義. *SPTK* ed.

FSTI (A) Ying Shao. *Feng-su t'ung-i* in *CHHW*.

HC Hsün Yüeh 荀悅. *Han-chi* 漢紀. *SPTK* ed.

HCFK Shen Chia-pen 沈家本. *Hsing-chih fen k'ao* 刑制分考 in *Shen Chi-i hsien-sheng i-shu chia-pien* 沈寄簃先生遺書甲編 (under heading *Li-tai hsing-fa k'ao* 歷代刑法考). 1929.

HCHSPN Liu Ju-lin 劉汝霖. *Han Chin hsüeh-shu pien-nien* 漢晉學術編年. Shanghai, 1835.

HCI Wei Hung 衛宏. *Han-chiu-i* 漢舊儀. *PCKTS*.

HCIPI Wei Hung. *Han-chiu-i pu-i* 漢舊儀補遺, compiled by Sun Hsing-yen 孫星衍. *PCKTS*.

HFT *Han-fei-tzu* 韓非子. *SPTK* ed.

HHC Ssu-ma Piao 司馬彪. *Hsü-Han-chih* 續漢志. Po-na ed.

HHCCC Wang Hsien-ch'ien 王先謙. *Hsü-Han-chih chi-chieh* 續漢志集解 in *HHSCC*.

HHHY Hsü T'ien-lin 徐天麟. *Hsi-Han hui-yao* 西漢會要. *TSCC* ed.

HHS Fan Yeh 范曄. *Hou-Han-shu* 後漢書. Po-na ed.

HHSCC Wang Hsien-ch'ien 王先謙. *Hou-Han-shu chi-chieh* 後漢書集解. Ch'ang-sha: Wang-shih chiao-k'an pen, 1915.

HHSPC Hui Tung 惠棟. *Hou-Han-shu pu-chu* 後漢書補註. *TSCC* ed.

HHSPP Ch'ien Ta-chao 錢大昭. "Hou-Han-shu pu-piao" 後漢書補表 in *Erh-shih-wu shih pu-pien* 二十五史補編. Shanghai: K'ai-ming shu-tien, 1936–37.

HK　　　*Han-kuan* 漢官, compiled by Sun Hsing-yen 孫星衍. *PCKTS*.

HKCK　 Hu Kuang 胡廣. *Han-kuan chieh-ku* 漢官解詁, compiled by Sun Hsing-yen. *PCKTS*.

HKI　　Ying Shao 應劭. *Han-kuan-i* 漢官儀, compiled by Sun Hsing-yen. *PCKTS*.

HKTI　 Ts'ai Chih 蔡質. *Han-kuan tien-chih i-shih hsüan-yung* 漢官典職儀式選用, compiled by Sun Hsing-yen. *PCKTS*.

HLCC　 Tu Kuei-ch'ih 杜貴墀. *Han-lü chi-cheng* 漢律輯證. Preface dated 1843.

HLCI　 Shen Chia-pen 沈家本. *Han-lü che-i* 漢律摭遺 in *Shen chi-i hsien-sheng i-shu chia-pien* 沈寄簃先生遺書甲編, 1929.

HLK　　Ch'eng Shu-te 程樹德. *Han-lü k'ao* 漢律考 in *Chiu-ch'ao lü-k'ao* 九朝律考. Shanghai: Commercial Press, 1927.

HNT　　Liu An 劉安. *Huai-nan hung-lieh chieh* 淮南鴻烈解. *SPTK* ed. [*Huai-nan-tzu*]

HS　　　Pan Ku 班固. *Han-shu* 漢書. Po-na ed.

Hsin　　Chia I 賈誼. *Hsin-shu* 新書. *SPPY* ed.

HSPC　 Wang Hsien-ch'ien 王先謙. *Han-shu pu-chu* 漢書補注. Ch'ang-sha: Wang-shih chiao-k'an ed., 1916.

HSSC　 Shen Ch'in-han 沈欽韓. *Han-shu su-cheng* 漢書疏證. Che-chiang kuan shu-chü, 1900.

HT　　　*Hsün-tzu* 荀子. *SPTK* ed.

HTS　　Ou-yang Hsiu 歐陽修. *Hsin T'ang-shu* 新唐書. Po-na ed.

HWLCMM Li Fu-sun 李富孫. *Han Wei Liu-ch'ao mu-ming tsuan-li* 漢魏六朝墓銘纂例 in *Huai-lu ts'ung-shu* 槐廬叢書. Hsing-su-ts'ao t'ang ts'ang-pan, 1887.

HYKC　 Ch'ang Ch'ü 常璩. *Hua-yang kuo-chih* 華陽國志. *SPTK* ed.

ILCS　 *I-li chu-su* 儀禮注疏. *SPPY* ed.

ILS　　Li Ju-kuei 李如圭. *I-li chi-shih* 儀禮集釋. *WYT*.

JCLCS　 Ku Yen-wu 顧炎武. *Jih-chih-lu* 日知錄; *chi-shih* 集釋 by Huang Ju-ch'eng 黃汝成. *SPPY* ed.

KHTT　 *K'ang-hsi tzu-tien* 康熙字典.

KSY　　*Ku shih yüan* 古詩源, edited by Shen Te-ch'ien 沈德潛. *SPPY* ed.

KTCY　 *K'ung-tzu chia-yü* 孔子家語, commentaries by Wang Su 王肅註. *SPPY* ed.

KYCS　 *Ch'un-ch'iu Kung-yang chuan chu-su* 春秋公羊傳注疏. *SPPY* ed.

LCCS　 *Li-chi chu-su* 禮記注疏. *SPPY* ed.

LH　　　Wang Ch'ung 王充. *Lun-heng* 論衡. *SPTK* ed.

LSCC　 *Lü-shih ch'un-ch'iu* 呂氏春秋. *CHTTS*.

LY　　　*Lun-yü* 論語. *SPPY* ed.

LYCS　 *Lun-yü chu-su* 論語注疏. *SPPY* ed.

Liang　 Yao Ssu-lien *et al.* 姚思廉. *Liang-shu* 梁書. Po-na ed.

Liao　　T'o-t'o 脫脫. *Liao-shih* 遼史. Po-na ed.

MHPT　 Shen K'uo 沈括. *Meng-hsi pi-t'an* 夢溪筆談. *TSCC* ed.

MLL　　*Ming-lü chi-chieh fu-li* 明律集解附例. Peking: Hsiu-ting fa-lü kuan, 1908.

MSCS   *Mao shih chu-su* 毛詩注疏. *SPPY* ed.

MTCS   *Meng-tzu chu-su* 孟子注疏. *SPPY* ed.

NESCC   Chao I 趙翼. *Nien-erh shih cha-chi* 廿二史箚記. *SPPY* ed.

NESKI   Ch'ien Ta-hsin 錢大昕. *Nien-erh shih k'ao-i* 廿二史考異. *TSCC* ed.

PHT   Pan Ku 班固. *Po-hu-t'ung* 白虎通 in *Pao-ching-t'ang ts'ung-shu*
            抱經堂叢書, compiled by Lu Wen-ch'ao 盧文弨.

PTSC   Yü Shih-nan 虞世南. *Pei-t'ang shu-ch'ao* 北堂書鈔. Nan-hai:
            K'ung-shih san-shih-san wan chüan t'ang chiao-chu ch'ung-
            k'an, 1888.

SC   Ssu-ma Ch'ien 司馬遷. *Shi-chi* 史記. Po-na ed.

SCC   Li Tao-yüan 酈道元. *Shui-ching-chu* 水經注. Ssu-hsien chiang-she
            k'an-pen, 1892.

SCSSC   Wang Ming-sheng 王鳴盛. *Shih-ch'i shih shang-ch'üeh* 十七史商榷.
            Tung-ching-ts'ao t'ang, 1787.

SFHT   *San-fu huang-t'u* 三輔黃圖 in *PCKTS*.

SFHT (A) *San-fu huang-t'u*. *SPTK* ed.

SHC   *Shan-hai ching* 山海經 in *CHTTS*.

SHT   Tou I 竇儀. *Sung hsing t'ung* 宋刑統. Liu-shih chia-yeh-t'ang
            劉氏嘉業堂 ed.

SKC   Ch'en Shou 陳壽. *San-kuo-chih* 三國志. Po-na ed.

SKCCP   Chao I-ch'ing 趙一清. *San-kuo-chih chu-pu* 三国志注補. Pei-ching
            Ta-hsüeh reproduction of the Kuang-ya shu-chü edition, 1935.

SKCHW   Yen K'o-chün 嚴可均 (compiler). *Ch'üan shang-ku san-tai Ch'in
            Han san-kuo liu-ch'ao wen* 全上古三代秦漢三國六朝文. Huang-
            kang Wang-shih ed., 1894.

SKK   Takikawa Kametarō 瀧川資言. *Shiki kaichū kōshō* 史記會注考證.
            Tokyo: Tōhō bunka gakuin Tōkyō Kenkyujō, 1932–34.

SMSC   Pi Yüan 畢沅. *Shih-ming su-cheng* 釋名疏證 in *CHTTS*.

SS   Shen Yüeh 沈約. *Sung-shu* 宋書. Po-na ed.

SSCKWS   Sun Hsing-yen 孫星衍. *Shang-shu chin-ku wen chu-su* 尚書今古文
            注疏 in *PCKTS*.

SSCS   *Shang-shu chu-su* 尚書注疏. *SPPY* ed.

SSSI   Ch'ien Ta-hsin 錢大昕. *San shih shih-i* 三史拾遺 in *Ch'ien-yen-
            t'ang ch'üan-shu* 潛研堂全書, 1808.

SWCTC   Tuan Yü-ts'ai 段玉裁. *Shuo-wen chieh-tzu chu* 説文解字注 in the
            series *Kuo-hsüeh chi-pen ts'ung-shu chien-pien*. Shanghai, 1936.

Sui   Wei Cheng 魏徵. *Sui-shu* 隋書. Po-na ed.

TCCS   *Ch'un-ch'iu Tso-chuan chu-su* 春秋左傳注疏. *SPPY* ed.

TCTC   Ssu-ma Kuang 司馬光. *Tzu-chih t'ung-chien* 資治通鑑. *SPPY* ed.

THHY   Hsü T'ien-lin 徐天麟. *Tung-Han hui-yao* 東漢會要. *TSCC* ed.

TKHC   Pan Ku *et al.* 班固等. *Tung-kuan Han-chi* 東觀漢記. *WYT*.

TLSI   Chang-sun Wu-chi 長孫無忌. *T'ang-lü su-i* 唐律疏義. Lan-ling
            Sun-shih ed.

TMTTT   Hsieh Shou-ch'ang *et al.* 謝壽昌. *Chung-kuo ku-chin ti-ming ta
            tz'u-tien* 中國古今地名大辭典. Shanghai: Commercial Press,
            1935.

TPYL   Li Fang *et al.* 李昉. *T'ai-p'ing yü-lan* 太平御覽. *SPTK* ed.

TSTC	Wang Nien-sun 王念孫. *Tu-shu tsa-chih* 讀書雜志. Chin-ling shu-chü, 1870.
TT	Tu Yu 杜祐. *T'ung-tien* 通典. Shanghai: Commercial Press, 1935.
TTL(C)	Tai Te 戴德. *Ta-Tai li-chi* 大戴禮記. *WYT.*
TYMC	T'ao Ch'ien 陶潛. *T'ao Yüan-ming chi* 陶淵明集. *SPTK* ed.
TYTT	Ts'ai Yung 蔡邕. *Tu tuan* 獨斷. *SPTK* ed.
YTL	Huan K'uan 桓寬. *Yen-t'ieh lun* 鹽鐵論 in *Tai-nan ko ts'ung-shu* 岱南閣叢書. Shanghai, 1934.
WH	Hsiao T'ung 蕭統. *Wen-hsüan* in the *Liu-ch'en chu Wen-hsüan* edition 六臣註文選. *SPTK* ed.

MODERN CHINESE AND JAPANESE WORKS

Chang Heng-shou 張恆壽. "Shih-lun liang-Han shih-tai ti she-hui hsing-chih" 試論兩漢時代的社會性質, *LSYC*, No. 9, 1957, 1–31.

Ch'en Chih 陳直. *Liang-Han ching-chi shih-liao lun-ts'ung* 兩漢經濟史料論叢. Sian, 1958.

Ch'en P'an 陳槃. "Chan-kuo Ch'in Han chien fang-shih k'ao-lun" 戰國秦漢間方士考論, *LSYY*, XVII (1948), 7–57.

——. "Ch'an-wei shih ming" 讖緯釋名, *LSYY*, XI (1947), 297–316.

——. "Ch'an-wei so-yüan" 讖緯溯原, *LSYY*, XI (1947), 317–35.

Chien Po-tsan 翦伯贊. "Kuan-yü liang-Han ti kuan-ssu nu-pei wen-ti" 關於兩漢的官私奴婢問題, *LSYC*, No. 4, 1954, 1–24.

Ch'ien Mu 錢穆. *Ch'in Han shih* 秦漢史. Hong Kong, 1957.

——. *Hsien-Ch'in chu-tzu hsi nien k'ao-pien* 先秦諸子繫年考辨. Shanghai: Commercial Press, 1935.

——. *Kuo-shih ta-kang* 國史大綱. 2 vols. Taipei, 1956.

Chin Fa-ken 金發根. "Tung Han tang-ku jen-wu ti fen-hsi" 東漢黨錮人物的分析, *LSYY*, XXXIV (1963), 505–58.

Chü Ch'ing-yüan 鞠清遠. "San kuo shih-tai ti 'k'o'" 三國時代的「客」, *Shih-huo* 食貨, III, No. 4 (1936), 15–19.

Ch'ü Hsüan-ying 瞿宣穎. *Chung-kuo she-hui shih-liao ts'ung-ch'ao* 中國社会史料叢鈔. Ch'ang-sha: Commercial Press, 1937.

Ch'ü T'ung-tsu 瞿同祖. *Chung-kuo fa-lü yü chung-kuo she-hui* 中國法律與中國社會. Shanghai: Commercial Press, 1947.

——. *Chung-kuo feng-chien she-hui* 中國封建社會. Shanghai: Commercial Press, 1937.

Hamaguchi Shigekuni 濱口重國. "Senkō to kakō—Nyojun setsu no hihan" 踐更と過更—如淳説の批判, *Tōyō gakuhō*, XIX, No. 3 (1931), 84–107.

——. "Senkō to kakō—Nyojun setsu no hihan ho i" 踐更と過更—如淳説の批判補遺, *Tōyō gakuhō*, XX, No. 2 (1932), 140–46.

Ho Ch'ang-ch'ün 賀昌羣. "Ch'in Han chien ko-t'i hsiao-nung ti hsing-ch'eng ho fa-chan" 秦漢間個體小農的形成和發展, *LSYC*, No. 12, 1959, 15–41.

——. "Lun Hsi-Han ti t'u-ti chan-yu hsing-t'ai" 論西漢的土地佔有形態, *LSYC*, No. 2, 1955, 77–104.

——. "Tung-Han keng-i shu-i chih-tu ti fei-chih" 東漢更役戌役制度的廢止, *LSYC*, No. 5, 1962, 96–115.

Ho Shih-chi 何士驥. "Pu-ch'ü k'ao" 部曲考, *Kuo-hsüeh lun-ts'ung* 國學論叢, I, No. 1 (1927), 125–49.

Ho Tzu-ch'üan 何茲全. *Ch'in Han shih lüeh* 秦漢史略. Shanghai, 1955.

Hsü Cho-yün 許倬雲. "Hsi-Han cheng-ch'üan yü she-hui shih-li ti chiao-hu tso-yung" 西漢政權與社會勢力的交互作用, *LSYY*, XXXV (1964), 261–81.

Hu Shih 胡適. *Huai-nan-wang shu* 淮南王書. Shanghai: Hsin-yüeh shu-tien, 1931.

Jui I-fu 芮逸夫. "Chiu-tsu chih yü Erh-ya shih ch'in" 九族制與爾雅釋親, *LSYY*, XXII (1950), 209–31.

Kamada Shigeo 鎌田重雄. *Shin Kan seiji seido no kenkyū* 秦漢政治制度の研究. Tokyo, 1963.

Kurihara Tomonobu 栗原朋信. *Shin Kan shi no kenkyū* 秦漢史の研究. Tokyo, 1960.

Lao Kan 勞榦. *Chü-yen Han-chien k'ao-shih, K'ao-cheng chih pu* 居延漢簡考釋, 考證之部. (*Kuo-li chung-yang yen-chiu yüan li-shih yü-yen yen-chiu so chuan-k'an 21* 國立中央研究院歷史語言研究所專刊 21), 1943–44.

——. *Chü-yen Han-chien k'ao-shih* 居延漢簡, 考釋. Taipei, 1960.

——. "Han-ch'ao ti hsien-chih" 漢朝的縣制, *Chung-yang yen-chiu-yüan yüan-k'an* 中央研究院院刊, I (1954), 69–81.

——. "Han-chien chung ti ho-hsi ching-chi sheng-huo" 漢簡中的河西經済生活, *LSYY*, XI (1947), 61–75.

——. "Han-tai ch'a-chü chih-tu k'ao" 漢代察舉制度考, *LSYY*, XVII (1948), 79–129.

——. "Han-tai nu-li chih-tu chi-lüeh" 漢代奴隸制度輯略, *LSYY*, V (1935), 1–11.

——. "Han-tai ping-chih chi Han-chien chung ti ping-chih" 漢代兵制及漢簡中的兵制, *LSYY*, X (1948), 23–55.

——. "Han-tai she-ssu ti yüan-liu" 漢代社祀的源流, *LSYY*, XI (1947), 49–60.

——. "Han-tai ti ku-yung chih-tu" 漢代的雇傭制度, *LSYY*, XXIII (1951), 77–87.

——. "Han-tai ti t'ing-chih" 漢代的亭制, *LSYY*, XXII (1950), 129–38.

——. "Liang-Han tz'u-shih chih-tu k'ao" 兩漢刺史制度考, *LSYY*, XI (1947), 27–48.

——. "Lun Han-tai ti nei-ch'ao yü wai-ch'ao" 論漢代的內朝與外朝, *LSYY*, XIII (1948), 227–67.

——. "Shih Han-tai chih t'ing-chang yü feng-sui" 釋漢代之亭障與烽燧, *LSYY*, XIX (1948), 501–22.

——. "Tsung Han-chien so-chien chih pien-chün chih-tu' 從漢簡所見之邊郡制度, *LSYY*, VIII (1939), 159–80.

Li Chien-nung 李劍農. *Hsien-Ch'in liang-Han ching-chi shih-kao* 先秦兩漢經済史稿. Peking, 1957.

Liang Ch'i-ch'ao 梁啟超. "Chung-kuo nu-li chih-tu" 中國奴隸制度, *THHP*, II, No. 2 (1925), 527–53.

Lü Ssu-mien 呂思勉. *Ch'in Han shih* 秦漢史. 2 vols. Shanghai, 1947.

——. *Hsien-Ch'in shih* 先秦史. Shanghai, 1941.

Ma Ch'eng-feng 馬乘風. *Chung-kuo ching-chi shih* 中國經濟史. 2 vols. 2nd ed. Ch'ang-sha: Commercial Press, 1939.

Ma Fei-pai 馬非百. "Ch'in Han ching-chi shih liao," Part 6: "Nu-li chih-tu" 秦漢經濟史料(六) 奴隷制度, *Shih-huo*, III, No. 8 (1936), 385–400.

Makino Tatsumi 牧野巽. "Kandai no kazoku keitai" 漢代の家族形態, *Tōa gaku* 東亞學 (Part 1), No. 4, 1942, pp. 39–88; (Part 2), No. 5, 1942, 49–138.

———. *Shina kazoku kenkyū* 支那家族研究. Tokyo, 1944.

Masubuchi Tatsuo 增淵龍夫. *Chugoku kodai no shakai to kokka* 中國古代の社會と國家. Tokyo (1940), 1960.

Moriya Mitsuo 守屋美都雄. *Kandai kazoku no keitai ni kansuru kōsatsu* 漢代家族の形態に関する考察. Tokyo, 1956.

———. "Kandai kazoku no keitai ni kansuru sai kōsatsu" 漢代家族の形態に關する再考察, in *Studies in Chinese Ancient History* (1960), 327–52.

Niida Noboru 仁井田陞. *Shina mibumpō shi* 支那身分法史. Tokyo: Tōhō Bunka Gakuin, 1942.

P'ei Hsüeh-hai 裴學海. *Ku-shu hsü-tzu chi-shih* 古書虛字集釋. Shanghai: Commercial Press, 1935.

Shida Fudōmaro 志田不動麿. "Kandai no dorei seido sō tō ni tsuite" 漢代の奴隷制度蒼頭に就いて, *Rekishigaku kenkyū,* II, No. 1 (1934), 20–29.

Ssu T'ieh 馴鐵. "Ch'in Han shih-ch'i tsu-tien kuan-hsi ti fa-sheng yü fa-chan" 秦漢時期租佃關係的發生與發展, *LSYC*, No. 12, 1959, 44–58.

T'ao Hsi-sheng 陶希聖. *Hsi Han ching-chi shih* 西漢經濟史. Shanghai, 1935.

———. "Hsi Han shih-tai ti k'o" 西漢時代的客, *Shih-huo*, V, No. 1 (1937), 1–6.

———. *Pien-shih yü yu-hsia* 辯士與游俠. Shanghai, 1931.

Utsunomiya Seikichi 宇都宮清吉. "Kandai gōzoku ron" 漢代豪族論, *Tōhōgaku,* XXIII (1962), 6–23.

———. *Kandai Shakai keizai shi kenkyū* 漢代社會經濟史研究. Tokyo, 1954.

Wang Shih-chieh 王世杰. "Chung-kuo nu-pei chih-tu" 中國奴婢制度 *She-hui k'e-hsüeh chi-k'an* 社會科學季刊, III, No. 3 (1925), 303–28.

Wang Yü-ch'üan 王毓銓. "Han-tai 't'ing' yü 'hsiang' 'li' pu-t'ung hsing-chih pu-t'ung hsing-cheng hsi-t'ung shuo" 漢代「亭」與「鄉」「里」不同性質不同行政系統説, *LSYC,* No. 2, 1954, 127–35.

Wu Ching-ch'ao 呉景超. "Hsi-Han she-hui chieh-chi chih-tu" 西漢社會階級制度, *THHP*, X, No. 3 (1935), 587–629.

Wu Po-lun 武伯綸. "Hsi Han nu-li k'ao" 西漢奴隷考. *Shih-huo*, I, No. 1 (1935), 275–85.

Yang Chung-i 楊中一. "Pu-ch'ü yen-ko lüeh-k'ao" 部曲沿革畧考, *Shih-huo*, I, No. 3 (1935), 97–107.

Yang Lien-sheng 楊聯陞. "Tung-Han ti hao-tsu" 東漢的豪族, *THHP*, XI, No. 4 (1936), 1007–63.

Yen Keng-wang 嚴耕望. "Ch'in Han lang-li chih-tu k'ao" 秦漢郎吏制度考, *LSYY*, XXIII (1951), 89–143.

———. *Chung-kuo ti-fang hsing-cheng chih-tu shih* 中國地方行政制度史. Shang-pien 上編. 2 vols. Taipei, 1961.

———. "Han-tai ti-fang hsing-cheng chih-tu" 漢代地方行政制度, *LSYY,* XXV (1954), 135–236.

——. "Han-tai ti-fang kuan-li chih chi-kuan hsien-chih" 漢代地方官吏之籍貫限制, *LSYY*, XXII (1950), 233–42.

Yü Ying-shih 余英時. "Tung-Han cheng-ch'üan chih chien-li yü shih-tsu ta-hsing chih kuan-hsi" 東漢政權之建立與士族大姓之關係, *Hsin-ya hsüeh-pao* 新亞學報, I, No. 2 (February, 1956), 207–80.

WORKS IN WESTERN LANGUAGES

Barber, Bernard. *Social Stratification*. New York: Harcourt, Brace and Co., 1957.

Bielenstein, Hans. "The Restoration of the Han Dynasty," *Bulletin of the Museum of Far Eastern Antiquities* (Stockholm), No. 26 (1954) and No. 31 (1959).

Bodde, Derk. *China's First Unifier: A Study of the Ch'in Dynasty as Seen in the Life of Li Ssu*. ("Sinica Leidensia," Vol. III. Leiden: E. J. Brill, 1938.

——. "Feudalism in China," in *Feudalism in History*, edited by Rushton Coulborn. Princeton, N. J: Princeton University Press, 1956.

——. *Statesman, Patriot, and General in Ancient China: Three* Shih Chi *Biographies of the Ch'in Dynasty (255–206 B.C.)*. New Haven: American Oriental Society, 1940.

Chavannes, Édouard. *Les Mémoires historiques de Se-ma Ts'ien*. 5 vols. Paris: Ernest Leroux, 1895–1905.

——. "Les Pays d'Occident d'après le Wei-lio," *T'oung Pao*, VI (1905), 519–63.

——. *Le T'ai chan*. Paris: Ernest Leroux, 1910.

——. "Trois Généraux chinois de la dynastie des Han orientaux," *T'oung Pao*, VII (1906), 210–69.

Ch'ü T'ung-tsu. "Chinese Class Structure and Its Ideology," in *Chinese Thought and Institutions*, edited by John K. Fairbank. Chicago: University of Chicago Press, 1957.

——. *Law and Society in Traditional China*. Paris and The Hague: Mouton and Co., 1961.

Dubs, Homer H. *The History of the Former Han Dynasty*, by Pan Ku. 3 vols. Baltimore: Waverly Press, 1938, 1944, 1955.

Duyvendak, J. J. L. *The Book of Lord Shang: A Classic of the Chinese School of Law*. London: Arthur Probsthain, 1928.

——. "A Scribal Error?," in *Orientalia Neerlandica*. Leiden: Oostersch Genootschap in Nederland, 1948.

Feng Han-yi. "The Chinese Kinship System," *Harvard Journal of Asiatic Studies*, XI (1937), 141–275.

Franke, O. "Feudalism: Chinese," in *Encyclopaedia of the Social Sciences* (New York: Macmillan Co., 1930–34), VI, 213–14.

Gale, Esson M. *Discourses on Salt and Iron: A Debate on State Control of Commerce and Industry in Ancient China*. ("Sinica Leidensia," Vol. II.) Leiden: E. J. Brill, 1931.

Groot, Jan Jacob Maria de. *The Religious System of China*. 6 vols. Leiden: E. J. Brill, 1892–1910.

Ho Ping-ti. "Records of China's Grand Historian: Some Problems of Translation," *Pacific Affairs*, XXXVI, No. 2 (1963), 171–82.

Hoang, Pierre. *Concordance des chronologies néoméniques chinoise et européenne.* *(Variétés Sinologiques*, No. 29.) Shanghai, 1910.

Hulsewé, A. F. P. *Remnants of Han Law*, Vol. I: *Introductory Studies and Annotated Translation of Chapters 22 and 23 of the History of the Former Han Dynasty*. ("Sinica Leidensia," Vol. IX.) Leiden: E. J. Brill, 1955.

Legge, James. *The Chinese Classics*. 5 vols. in 8 vols. Hong Kong and London, 1861–72.

———. *The Sacred Books of China: The Texts of Confucianism*, in *Sacred Books of the East*, edited by F. M. Müller. Vols. III, XVI, XXVII, XXVIII. Oxford: Clarendon Press, 1879–85.

Lowie, Robert H. *Social Organization*. New York: Rinehart and Co., 1948.

Mendelsohn, Isaac. *Slavery in the Ancient Near East*. New York: Oxford University Press, 1949.

Murdock, George P. *Social Structure*. New York: Macmillan Co., 1949.

Parsons, Talcott. *The Social System*. Glencoe: Free Press, 1951.

Schindler, B. "Preliminary Account of the Work of Henri Maspero Concerning the Chinese Documents on Wood and on Paper Discovered by Sir Aurel Stein on His Third Expedition to Central Asia," *Asia Major*, N.S., I, Part 2 (1949), 216–72.

Schumpeter, J. A. *Imperialism and Social Classes*. New York: Meridian Books, 1951.

Steele, John. *The I-li, or Book of Etiquette and Ceremonial*. 2 vols. London: Probsthain and Co., 1917.

Swann, Nancy Lee. *Food and Money in Ancient China*. Princeton, N.J.: Princeton University Press, 1950.

———. *Pan Chao: Foremost Woman Scholar of China*. New York: The Century Co., 1932.

Teggart, Frederick John. *Rome and China: A Study of Correlations in Historical Events*. Berkeley: University of California Press, 1939.

Tjan Tjoe Som. *Po Hu T'ung: The Comprehensive Discussions in the White Tiger Hall*. ("Sinica Leidensia," Vol. VI.) 2 vols. Leiden: E. J. Brill, 1949, 1952.

Wang Yü-ch'üan. "An Outline of the Central Government of the Former Han Dynasty," *Harvard Journal of Asiatic Studies*, XII (1949), 134–87.

Watson, Burton. *Records of the Grand Historian of China: Translated from the Shih chi of Ssu-ma Ch'ien*. 2 vols. New York: Columbia University Press, 1961.

———. *Ssu-ma Ch'ien, Grand Historian of China*. New York: Columbia University Press, 1958.

Weber, Max. *From Max Weber: Essays in Sociology*, translated by H. H. Gerth and C. Wright Mills. New York: Oxford University Press, 1946.

———. *Max Weber: The Theory of Social and Economic Organization*, translated by A. M. Henderson and Talcott Parsons. New York: Oxford University Press, 1947.

Wilbur, Clarence Martin. *Slavery in China During the Former Han Dynasty, 206 B.C.–A.D. 25*. ("Publications of Field Museum of Natural History, Anthropological Series," Vol. XXXIV, Publication 525.) Chicago: Field Museum of Natural History, 1943.

Yang Lien-sheng. "Hostages in Chinese History," *Harvard Journal of Asiatic Studies,* XV (1952), 507–21.

——. "A Note on the So-called TLV Mirrors and the Game *Liu-po,*" *Harvard Journal of Asiatic Studies,* IX (1947), 202–6.

——. "An Additional Note on the Ancient Game *Liu-po,*" *Harvard Journal of Asiatic Studies,* XVI (1952), 124–39.

——. "Schedules of Work and Rest in Imperial China," *Harvard Journal of Asiatic Studies,* XVIII (1955), 301–25.

INDEX

A-p'ang Palace, 399

"Abundantly talented": recommendation of men as, 206, 381n, 388

Account bearer, 276n

Acting officials. *See under name of specific offices*

Administrators. *See* Grand administrators

Adopted sons-in-law, 328 and n

Adoption, 18–20

Adultery, 37, 39

Agriculture, 148, 358n. *See also* Farming

Ai, Emperor: restored gandee secretary, 86n; barred merchants from office, 120; summoned occultists, 124; slave policy of, 156, 158–159, 331n; did not remove powerful families, 199; consort families of, 223, 345n; abolished punishment for slander, 265n; marriage of, 283, 284; and Tung Hsien, 448 and n; mentioned, 60, 71, 78n, 284n, 292n

Amnesty, general, 70, 422

An, Emperor: age at ascension, 215–216; dismissed Teng Chih, 227; teacher of, 312n; did not run government, 464; enthronement of, 465n; legal mother of, 465n; deposed heir apparent, 466n; death of, 466; mentioned, 61

An-Han chiang-chün. See General who pacifies Han

An-kuo Chün, 325

Ancestor temple, 34, 35

Ancestor worship: by sons, 18, 30, 31; importance to marriage, 34; in eunuch families, 98

Animal breeders, 113

Animals, government, 142, 352

Apocryphal texts, 389n

Armies: of powerful families, 454, 455

Artisans: social status of, 101, 111, 113; entrance to officialdom of, 112 and n; legal position of, 112; economic position of, 112; income of, 114, given to a king, 302; mentioned, 358n

Assassions; among *yu-hsia*, 188; work for powerful families, 244; kept by redressers-of-wrongs, 442 and n

Assistant grand provisioner of the Ch'ang-lo Palace, 467

Assistant prefect, 281, 363

Assistant to the grand minister of agriculture, 119

Assistant to the office of the side halls, 297n

Astronomy, 362, 389n

Attendant gentlemen of the Yellow Gate, 214, 460n

Attendant imperial secretary, 347, 368, 377n, 456, 469

Attendant office of the Ch'ang-lo Palace, 488

Attendant secretary, 230, 301n

Attendant within the palace: Cheng Hsüan offered appointment as, 107, 388; members of Teng family as, 217, 306; trans-

Chang Hui, 195n, 442. *See also* Chang Chin

Chang Jang: ennobled, 494; power of, 494; and downfall of Ho Chin, 501–505; death of, 506n

Chang K'ai: career of, 384

Chang K'an, 306

Chang-ku. See Master of precedents

Chang Liang: as *yu-hsia*, 188; career of, 333

Chang Liang (eunuch): and death of Tou Wu, 488, 491; ennobled, 492

Chang Lin, 445n

Chang Ling, 385

Chang Meng: career of, 433 and n; suicide of, 434

Chang Miao, 319n

Chang Pa: career of, 384n

Chang P'eng-tsu, 177

Chang Po, 433n

Chang Shih-chih, 65n, 267

Chang T'ang: as petty official, 86; as grandee secretary, 86, 347; income of, 90; relatives of, in office for generations, 429; as commandant of justice, 347n; career of, 348n; mentioned, 355n, 445n

Chang Ts'an, 457

Chang Ts'ang: concubines of, 267; career of, 267n

Chang Yen-shou, 177, 445n

Chang Yü, 93, 94, 174

Ch'ang-i, King of: dismissed, 74, 280, 427n; enthroned as emperor, 172, 279

Ch'ang-p'ing Granary, 460n

Ch'ang-shui division, one of the five army divisions, 472n

Chao, Duke of, 458n. *See also* Liu Liang

Chao, Emperor: plot to dismiss, 428n; mentioned, 74, 77n

Chao, Empress: originally a dancing girl, 56; killed sons of palace ladies, 221; mentioned, 48, 71, 78

Chao, Empress Dowager, 223

Chao, King of (Liu Ju-i), 259

Chao, King of (Liu Liang): 458; career of, 458n

Chao, King of (old family), 399n

Chao, Prince, mother of, 222

Chao family, of Chao, 164n

Chao family, of Chao Kang, 455

Chao family, of Ch'u, 410

Chao family, of Empress Chao, 77

Chao Ch'eng, 407

Chao Chi, 447

Chao Ch'i, 181, 208

Chao Chou, 424n

Chao Chün-tu, 195n, 442. *See also* Chao Fang

Chao Chung: appointed general of chariots and cavalry, 478n, 494n; influenced official appointments, 494; leaked plot to to Ho Chin, 498; killed, 505

Chao Fang: executed, 195; exploitation by, 440; mentioned, 193. *See also* Chao Chün-ti

Chao Fei-yen. *See* Chao, Empress and Chao, Empress Dowager

Chao Feng, 469

Chao Hsi: as prefect, 458; career of, 458n

Chao Hsiu, 439, 440

Chao Jao, 486, 488

Chao Kang, 456

Chao Kao: rise to power of, 232; executed Li Ssu, 232; and murder of Second Emperor, 233, 407; limited chancellor's access to throne, 239; family background of, 394n; plotted Ch'in succession, 394–396; urged stern laws, 398; became chancellor, 402; planned to make self emperor, 409n

Chao Kuan, 73

Chao Kuang-han: controlled powerful families, 199, 430; career of, 354n, 429; executed, 355

Chao She, 164n

Chao Sheng, Prince, 127

Chao Wang-sun, 423

Chao Yung, 496 and n

Ch'ao Ts'o: learned *Shang-shu*, 56; violated law, 95; on conditions of farmers, 109, 111, 182, 203; on position of merchants, 111, 339–340; advised weakening kings, 166; execution of family of, 251n; on garrison service, 329n; mentioned, 110, 114, 118, 440n

Che. See "Convicted ones"; Convicts

Che Kuo, 93, 379

Che-shu. See Convicts

Chen, term used by emperor, 68

Chen Fu, 364

Chen-nan chiang-chün. See General who subdues the south

Ch'en, Empress (of Emperor Wu): social origins, 77n; cross-cousin marriage of, 272; dismissed, 272n, 277n

Ch'en, the filial woman, 450 and n

Ch'en family, woman of (mother of Emperor Chih), 222

Ch'en Ch'iu: strict with powerful families, 490; career of, 490n

Ch'en Chün, 456n

Ch'en Fan: as grand tutor, 216, 483n; killed by eunuchs, 243, 483n, 491, 492n; as prefect of masters of writing, 389; led Partisans, 482n; planned to wipe out eunuchs, 483n, 485, 486, 487, 491 and n; accused of rebellion, 488; defended by Chang Huan, 489n; mentioned, 485n

defined, 109; landholdings of, 109, 110; entrance to office of, 111–112, 356, 392; illiteracy of, 111; became merchants, 339

Farming: as occupation of scholar, 105; use of slaves in, 149; officially encouraged, 301n. *See also* Agriculture

Father: lineage of, defined 4; authority of, 20, 21, 22, 23, 30, 50, 52; arranged marriage of children, 21, 34; son beaten by, 22, 281–282, 292, 300n, 304, 317–318; urged daughter's divorce, 44, 308; mourning for, 52; in consort family, 59, 61, 78; children's status determined by, 66; and sons live separately, 252–253; mentioned, 25, 311n, 313

Favored beauty, 282n

"Female masters of writing," 486n

Feng family, 165

Feng-chü tu-wei. See Chief commandant custodian of the imperial equipages

Feng-chün. See Baronet

Feng Ch'ün, 434 and n

Feng Fang: career of, 454n; mentioned, 454, 496n

Feng Feng-shih, 434 and n

Feng Hsü, 497n

Feng-shan sacrifices, 71

Feng Shih, 468

Feng Shu, 486, 490

Feng Tzu-tu, 154, 353

Feng Yeh-wang, 435

Feudal lords: of Chou dynasty, 67; as land owners, 108; and officials, 166n, 441; rebelled against Ch'in, 334. *See also* Nobles

Feudalism, 76

Filial Piety, 304, 312, 318

"Filially and brotherly respectful," 280

"Filially pious," 302

"Filially pious and incorrupt": recommendation as, introduced, 65n; farmer recommended as, 112; veterinarian's son recommended as, 123; subordinate officials recommended as, 180; as category for recommendation, 205 and n, 311n, 470; mentioned, 123, 206, 285n, 299 and n, 301, 319, 379n, 380, 382, 386

First Emperor of Ch'in dynasty: honored wealthy men, 54–55, 117, 328; mother of, 56, 326–327; created imperial title, 67–68; convicts employed by, 144; ascension to throne, 327; death of, 394; mentioned, 22, 147, 162

Fish raising, 287

Fishing, 148, 322

Five basic relations, 324n

Five camps. *See* Five divisions

Five degrees of mourning, 313n

Five degrees of relationship, 313 and n

Five divisions, 472n, 489, 490

Five equalizations and the six controls, 361

Five *hsiao. See* Five divisions

"Five marquises," 478

Five offices, 384 and n

Five offices of Ch'ang-lo Palace, 487–488, 491

Five punishments, 402 and n

Five *tsu*, 317 and n

Forest of feathers cavalry, 470n

Forest of feathers guards, 468, 489–490, 491

"Four conducts," 381n

Fu, Empress (of Emperor Ai), 78n, 283

Fu, Empress (of Emperor Hsien), 220, 221

Fu, Empress Dowager (of Emperor Ai), 60, 71, 284n

Fu-cheng ("to assist the emperor in the government"), 79

Fu-ch'u ("to purify"), 55n

Fu family (Early Han consort family), 223, 284, 448n

Fu family (Later Han consort family), 82

Fu Hsi, 60, 170

Fu Huan, 82

Fu-jen, 475

Fu-kuo chiang-chün. See General who supports the state

Fu-pei. See Slaves

Fu-po chiang-chun. See Billow-subduing general

Fu Sheng, 56, 347n

Fu-su, Prince, 22, 394, 397

Fugitives, 328

Functionary. *See* Officials, subordinate

Funeral gifts, 449n

Funerary park town, 268n

Garrison cavalry division, 472n

Garrison service, 329n

General-grandee, 215

General of chariots and cavalry: consort family men as, 79, 80, 82, 216 and n, 301n, 357, 466n, 505; rank of, 83n; defended *yu-hsia*, 421; defeated Hsiung-nu, 460n; eunuchs as, 467n, 478 and n, 492, 494n, 495n; mentioned, 56, 78n, 169, 177, 224, 226, 279, 355n, 376n, 390, 413n, 432n, 445n, 466n, 489

General of the brave cavalry, 289n

General of the flank, 288, 291 and n

General of the flash cavalry, 79, 83n, 374n

General of the gentlemen of the palace, 230, 231, 311n, 416n

General of the guards, 83n, 355n

General of the left, 121n, 428n, 434

General of the palace gentlemen: Ssu-ma

472n

Inheritance, 13, 17

Inner court: definition of, 170; duties of, 170–171; increase in power of, 171, 217; controlled by empress dowager, 216; eunuchs' role in, 234–235; mentioned, 499. *See also* Outer court

Inspectors of regional divisions: supervised kings, 166n, 167; Ho Wu as, 176; and powerful families, 201–202, 453, 470; from Teng family, 217; Chu Mu as, 242; sale of office of, 317, 381; duties of, 365n; from Ma family, 377; eunuch relatives as, 493; mentioned, 107, 127, 178, 308, 377n, 383n, 392n, 441n, 474. *See also* Regional divisions, officials of; Shepherds

Internuncio: supervised kings, 167n; from Teng family, 217; gifts to, 377n; mentioned, 300n

Internuncio of Ch'ang-lo Palace, 491

Internuncios of the palace writers, 431n

Investigators of transgressions: dominated by local family, 232; recalled, 301–302; functions of, 302n; accused eunuch, 481; mentioned, 297n, 311n

Iron collar, 335n

Iron manufacturing: as merchant activity, 113; workers in, 143, 148; Cho Wang-sun in, 88, 344n; mentioned, 115, 270n

Iron monopoly, 119, 348n, 352

Jail officer, 342, 438n

Jealousy: as grounds for divorce, 37, 39, 282 and n; problem of, 46, 47; in family of a king, 47; in imperial family, 47, 48; of Empress Lü, 258–259; mentioned, 273

Jen family, 27, 113, 260

Jen-hsia. See Yu-hsia

Jen-tzu privilege: for officials, 65n, 94; favored official families, 176, 204–205

Jen Wei, 375

Jen Yen: career of, 456n; mentioned, 457

Ju-tzu Ying, 229

Junior tutor of the heir apparent, 292, 357, 432n

Kai Hsün, 206n, 229

Kan Ning: slaves and guests of, 132n, 345n; as *yu-hsia*, 247; became prefect, 345n

Kao, Eastern, 439

Kao, Emperor: and heir apparent, 14; ennoblements by, 16n, 76, 78, 165, 261; marriage of, 34, 254–255; employed sorcerers, 55n; relations with father, 67; and merchants, 118, 337, 338; and slaves, 141, 158, 334, 337; and T'ien family, 163, 427n; removed powerful families, 196,

410–411, 419n; as guest, 256n; abolished punishment of three *tsu*, 265; as King of Han, 333n; mentioned, 11, 83, 126, 155, 168, 190, 291, 399n

Kao, Western, 439

Kao family, 199, 201, 244–245

Kao Feng, 126, 375–376

Kao Kung-tzu, 423

Kao-tsu. *See* Kao, Emperor

Keng family, 208, 287–289

Keng Chi, 289

Keng Chih, 288 and n

Keng Ch'un: organized lineage, 12, 25, 287–288; supported Emperor Kuang-wu, 287–288; career of, 287n

Keng Hsin, 288n

Keng Pao: position of, 216n, 466n; death of, 222; and eunuchs, 465, 466n; accused, 466; demoted, 466n

Keng-shih Emperor: killed Liu Po-sheng, 363n; appointed P'eng Ch'ung, 369n; and Emperor Kuang-wu, 457n; mentioned, 81, 132, 231, 287n, 291n, 362n, 458n, 459n

Keng Su, 288 and n

Kerchief, identifying, 387n

Kindred, 300, 313n

Kingdoms, 15, 165, 166n

Kings: sons of, 20, 76, 166–167, 275n; concubines of, 45, 167; jealousy in family of, 47; political status of daughters of, 57; power of, 76, 165–167, 245; limited to Liu family, 76, 83, 165, 168n; marriage of, 86; guests of, 135, 167, 245 and n; and slaves, 152, 159, 377; government borrowed from, 480; mentioned, 68, 339

Kinship: system of, defined, 3; group, socialization in, 29–30; limits of, 315n

Kinsmen: defined by mourning group, 10; mobilized, 25, 32, 260, 287–288, 289, 290, 455; support for, 29, 30, 287, 292, 294, 296; self-identity of, 31; illegal activities of, 180, 246, 429–430; of Partisans, 313 and n, 317; number of, 319; of powerful families killed, 430, 477, 490, 505n; and eunuchs, 431n, 479, 493; mentioned, 210, 281, 299. *See also Tsung-jen*

Kitchen god, 31

Knights-errant. *See Yu-hsia*

K'o. See Guests

Kou-tun-ling. See Prefect of the palace parks

K'ou family, 290–291

K'ou Hsün: career of, 290n

Ku-shu. See "Merchant-small men"

Ku Yung, 345n

K'u-li. See Officials, harsh

Kuan family, 175, 417–418

DATE DUE

GAYLORD			PRINTED IN U.S.A.